Why Do You Need This New Edition?

Six good reasons why you should buy this new Fourth Edition of *American Destiny*!

1. This edition is tied more closely than ever to the innovative website, MyHistoryLab, which helps you save time and improve results as you study history (www.myhistorylab.com). MyHistoryLab icons now appear throughout the textbook, connecting the main narrative of each chapter to a powerful array of MyHistoryLab resources, including primary source documents, analytical video segments, interactive maps, and more. Also tied to each chapter of the textbook, a powerful and personalized Study Plan is available on MyHistoryLab that will help you build a deeper and more critical understanding of the subject.

2. The new edition strengthens the guiding principle of the textbook—to survey American history in a way that bridges the present and the past, showing the relevance of history to contemporary readers. For example, the essays that open each chapter connect a major topic of the chapter to experiences that pertain to many readers. For the Fourth Edition these essays are either entirely new or have been thoroughly updated; nearly all pertain to events or developments since 2008.

3. Other elements designed to bridge the present and the past, such as the *American Lives* and *Re-Viewing the Past* essays, have also been thoroughly revised. Most of these essays are entirely new to the Fourth Edition.

4. The maps and graphs in this book have been completely reworked to convey new ideas and to enhance comprehension. Many entirely new maps have been created to illuminate important themes, including a stronger global emphasis.

5. Each chapter has been revised to reflect new scholarship, to offer important new perspectives, and to streamline and sharpen the writing. For instance, the Prologue and first few chapters reflect new insights concerning the "pre-historic" period. These chapters also feature a more detailed comparison of the civilizations of the Americas with those of the "Old World"—Europe, Africa, and Asia. An almost entirely new chapter "From Boomers to Millennials" (Chapter 31), draws an explicit comparison between the social and cultural foundations of young modern Americans and their parents; it especially explores the culture of consumption and the impact of the Internet.

6. To facilitate study and review, each chapter now ends with a set of review questions, and a list of key terms that are defined in a new glossary.

PEARSON

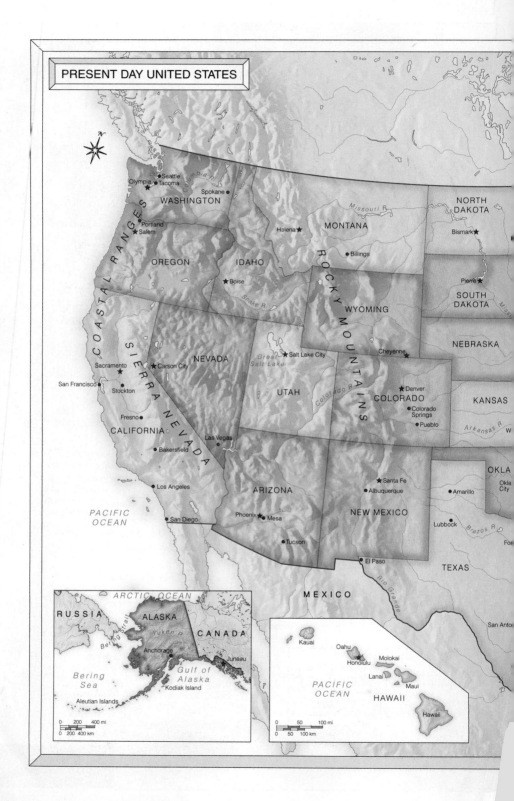

PRESENT DAY UNITED STATES

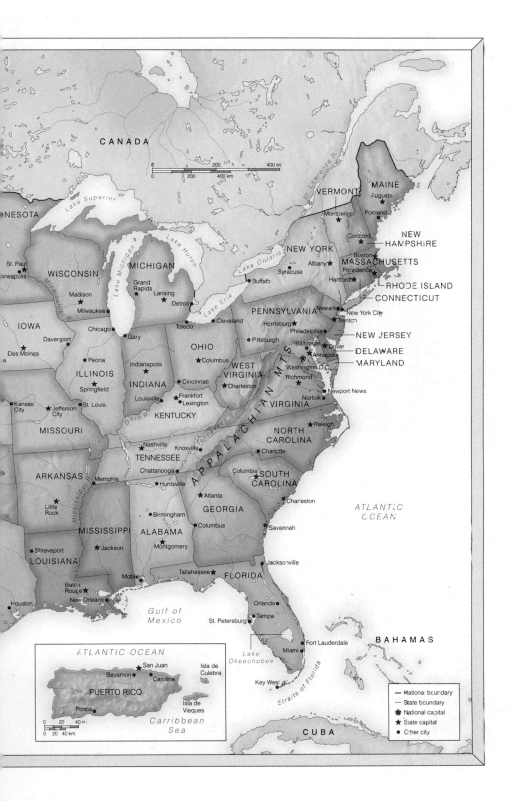

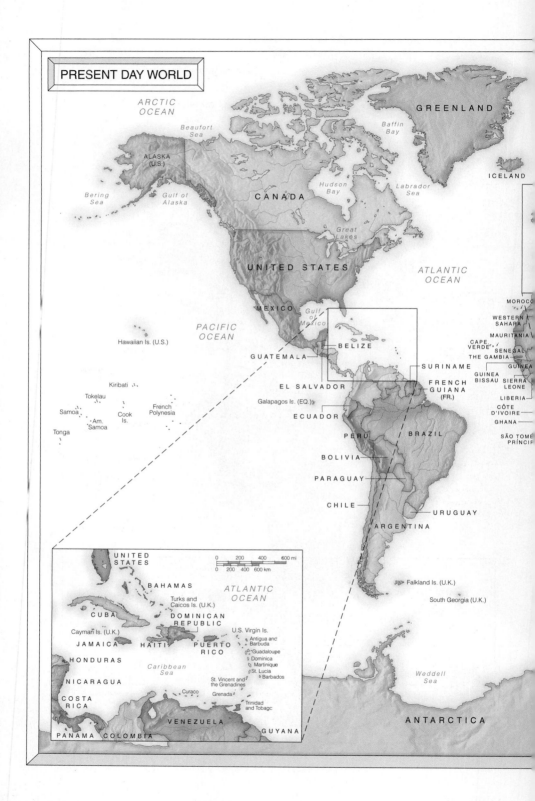

PRESENT DAY WORLD

ARCTIC OCEAN

GREENLAND

Beaufort Sea

Baffin Bay

ALASKA (U.S.)

ICELAND

Bering Sea

Gulf of Alaska

Hudson Bay

Labrador Sea

CANADA

Great Lakes

UNITED STATES

ATLANTIC OCEAN

MOROCCO

WESTERN SAHARA

MEXICO

Gulf of Mexico

MAURITANIA

PACIFIC OCEAN

Hawaiian Is. (U.S.)

BELIZE

CAPE VERDE

SENEGAL

THE GAMBIA

GUATEMALA

SURINAME

GUINEA BISSAU

GUINEA

SIERRA LEONE

Kiribati

EL SALVADOR

FRENCH GUIANA (FR.)

LIBERIA

Tokelau

Galapagos Is. (EQ.)

CÔTE D'IVOIRE

Samoa

Cook Is.

French Polynesia

ECUADOR

GHANA

Am. Samoa

PERÚ

BRAZIL

SÃO TOMÉ PRÍNCIP

Tonga

BOLIVIA

PARAGUAY

CHILE

URUGUAY

ARGENTINA

UNITED STATES

0   200   400   600 mi

0   200   400 600 km

BAHAMAS

ATLANTIC OCEAN

Falkland Is. (U.K.)

Turks and Caicos Is. (U.K.)

South Georgia (U.K.)

CUBA

DOMINICAN REPUBLIC

Cayman Is. (U.K.)

U.S. Virgin Is.

Antigua and Barbuda

JAMAICA

HAITI

PUERTO RICO

Guadaloupe

Dominica

HONDURAS

Caribbean Sea

Martinique

St. Lucia

Weddell Sea

NICARAGUA

Barbados

St. Vincent and the Grenadines

Curaço

Grenada

COSTA RICA

Trinidad and Tobago

PANAMA

COLOMBIA

VENEZUELA

GUYANA

ANTARCTICA

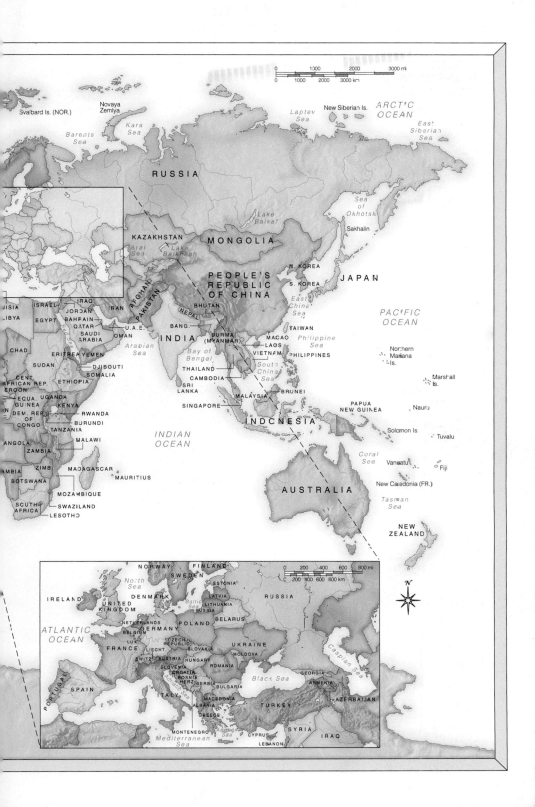

AMERICAN DESTINY
NARRATIVE OF A NATION

VOLUME ONE

FOURTH EDITION

MARK C. CARNES
Ann Whitney Olin Professor of History
Barnard College, Columbia University

JOHN A. GARRATY
Gouverneur Morris Professor of History, Emeritus
Columbia University

PEARSON

Boston   Columbus   Indianapolis   New York   San Francisco   Upper Saddle River
Amsterdam   Cape Town   Dubai   London   Madrid   Milan   Munich   Paris   Montréal   Toronto
Delhi   Mexico City   São Paulo   Sydney   Hong Kong   Seoul   Singapore   Taipei   Tokyo

Editorial Director: Craig Campanella
Editor in Chief: Dickson Musslewhite
Executive Editor: Ed Parsons
Editorial Assistants: Alex Rabinowitz, Emily Tamburri
Director of Marketing: Brandy Dawson
Senior Marketing Manager: Maureen E. Prado Roberts
Marketing Assistant: Samantha Bennett
Senior Managing Editor: Ann Marie McCarthy
Senior Project Manager: Debra A. Wechsler
AV Project Manager: Mirella Signoretto
Operations Specialist: Christina Amato
Senior Art Director: Maria Lange

Text Designer: GEX Publishing Services
Cover Designer: Art-Tronic Design
Cover Art: Cornish-Windsor Covered Bridge, Vermont, USA. © age fotostock / SuperStock
Director of Media and Assessment: Brian Hyland
Media Editor: Andrea Messineo
Media Project Manager: Tina Rudowski
Full-Service Project Management: GEX Publishing Services
Composition: GEX Publishing Services
Printer/Binder: Courier/Kendallville
Cover Printer: Lehigh-Phoenix Color / Hagerstown
Text Font: 10/12 Minion Pro

Credits and acknowledgments borrowed from other sources and reproduced, with permission, in this textbook appear on appropriate page within text (or starting on page C-1).

Library of Congress Cataloging-in-Publication Data
Carnes, Mark C. (Mark Christopher), 1950-
  American destiny : narrative of a nation / Mark C. Carnes, John A. Garraty. — 4th ed.
    p. cm.
  Includes bibliographical references and index.
  ISBN-13: 978-0-205-79041-8
  ISBN-10: 0-205-79041-0
  ISBN-13: 978-0-205-79039-5 (v. 1)
  ISBN-10: 0-205-79039-9 (v. 1)
  [etc.]
  1. United States—History. I. Garraty, John A. (John Arthur), 1920-2007. II. Title.

  E178.6.C33 2012
  973—dc22
                          2011015068
10 9 8 7 6 5 4 3 2 1

Combined Volume
ISBN 10: 0-205-79041-0
ISBN 13: 978-0-205-79041-8
Examination Copy
ISBN 10: 0-205-00149-1
ISBN 13: 978-0-205-00149-1
Volume 1
ISBN 10: 0-205-79039-9
ISBN 13: 978-0-205-79039-5
Volume 2
ISBN 10: 0-205-79040-2
ISBN 13: 978-0-205-79040-1

PEARSON

Brief Contents

PROLOGUE   Beginnings 1

CHAPTER 1   Alien Encounters: Europe in the Americas 14

CHAPTER 2   American Society in the Making 48

CHAPTER 3   America in the British Empire 79

CHAPTER 4   The American Revolution 112

CHAPTER 5   The Federalist Era: Nationalism Triumphant 143

CHAPTER 6   Jeffersonian Democracy 171

CHAPTER 7   National Growing Pains 193

CHAPTER 8   Toward a National Economy 224

CHAPTER 9   Jacksonian Democracy 247

CHAPTER 10   The Making of Middle-Class America 271

CHAPTER 11   Westward Expansion 299

CHAPTER 12   The Sections Go Their Own Ways 323

CHAPTER 13   The Coming of the Civil War 347

CHAPTER 14   The War to Save the Union 375

CHAPTER 15   Reconstruction and the South 409

Contents

Maps, Graphs, and Features xiii
Preface xv
Supplements for Instructors and Students xviii
Acknowledgments xxii
About the Authors xxiv

PROLOGUE Beginnings 1

First Peoples 1 ■ The Demise of the Big Mammals 2 ■ The Archaic Period: Surviving without Big Mammals 2 ■ The Maize Revolution 4 ■ The Diffusion of Corn 5 ■ Population Growth after AD 800 6 ■ Cahokia: The Hub of Mississippian Culture 7 ■ The Collapse of Urban Centers 8 ■ Eurasia and Africa 9 ■ Europe in Ferment 11

CHAPTER 1 Alien Encounters: Europe in the Americas 14

Columbus's Great Triumph—and Error 15 ■ Spain's American Empire 17 ■ Extending Spain's Empire to the North 19 ■ Disease and Population Losses 20 ■ Ecological Imperialism 21 ■ Spain's European Rivals 24 ■ The Protestant Reformation 24 ■ English Beginnings in America 25 ■ The Settlement of Virginia 27 ■ "Purifying" the Church of England 30 ■ Bradford and Plymouth Colony 31 ■ Winthrop and Massachusetts Bay Colony 32 ■ Troublemakers: Roger Williams and Anne Hutchinson 34 ■ Other New England Colonies 35 ■ Pequot War and King Philip's War 36 ■ Maryland and the Carolinas 37 ■ French and Dutch Settlements 38 ■ The Middle Colonies 39 ■ Cultural Collisions 40 ■ Cultural Fusions 44

CHAPTER 2 American Society in the Making 48

Settlement of New France 49 ■ Society in New Mexico, Texas, and California 49 ■ The English Prevail on the Atlantic Seaboard 52 ■ The Chesapeake Colonies 53 ■ The Lure of Land 54 ■ "Solving" the Labor Shortage: Slavery 55 ■ Prosperity in a Pipe: Tobacco 57 ■ Bacon's Rebellion 59 ■ The Carolinas 60 ■ Home and Family in the South 61 ■ Georgia and the Back Country 62 ■ Puritan New England 63 ■ Democracies without Democrats 65 ■ The Dominion of New England 66 ■ Salem Bewitched 66 ■ A Merchant's World 68 ■ The Middle Colonies: Economic Basis 70 ■ The Middle Colonies: An Intermingling of Peoples 71 ■ "The Best Poor Man's Country" 73 ■ The Politics of Diversity 73 ■ Becoming Americans 77

CHAPTER 3 America in the British Empire 79

The British Colonial System 80 ■ Mercantilism 81 ■ The Navigation Acts 82 ■ The Effects of Mercantilism 83 ■ The Great Awakening 85 ■ The Rise and Fall of Jonathan Edwards 87 ■ The Enlightenment in America 88 ■ Colonial Scientific Achievements 89 ■ Repercussions of Distant Wars 90 ■ The Great War for the Empire 91 ■ Britain Victorious: The Peace of Paris 95 ■ Burdens of an Expanded Empire 95 ■ Tightening Imperial Controls 97 ■ The Sugar Act 99 ■ American Colonists Demand Rights 100 ■ The Stamp Act: The Pot Set to Boiling 100 ■ Rioters or Rebels? 102 ■ The

Declaratory Act   103   ■   The Townshend Duties   104   ■   The Boston Massacre   105   ■   The Boiling Pot
Spills Over   106   ■   The Tea Act Crisis   106   ■   From Resistance to Revolution   108

CHAPTER 4   The American Revolution   112

The Shot Heard Round the World   113   ■   The Second Continental Congress   114   ■   The Battle of Bunker
Hill   115   ■   The Great Declaration   116   ■   1776: The Balance of Forces   119   ■   Loyalists   120   ■   The
British Take New York City   120   ■   Saratoga and the French Alliance   123   ■   The War Moves South   125   ■
Victory at Yorktown   126   ■   Negotiating a Favorable Peace   128   ■   National Government under the Articles
of Confederation   130   ■   Financing the War   131   ■   State Republican Governments   131   ■   Social Reform
and Antislavery   132   ■   Women and the Revolution   134   ■   Growth of a National Spirit   135   ■   The Great
Land Ordinances   136   ■   National Heroes   140

CHAPTER 5   The Federalist Era: Nationalism Triumphant   143

Inadequacies of the Articles of Confederation   144   ■   Daniel Shays's "Little Rebellion"   145   ■   To
Philadelphia, and the Constitution   146   ■   The Great Convention   147   ■   The Compromises That
Produced the Constitution   148   ■   Ratifying the Constitution   151   ■   Washington as President   153   ■
Congress under Way   155   ■   Hamilton and Financial Reform   155   ■   The Ohio Country: A Dark and
Bloody Ground   159   ■   Revolution in France   159   ■   Federalists and Republicans: The Rise of
Political Parties   161   ■   1794: Crisis and Resolution   162   ■   Jay's Treaty   163   ■   1795: All's Well
That Ends Well   164   ■   Washington's Farewell   165   ■   The Election of 1796   165   ■   The XYZ Affair
166   ■   The Alien and Sedition Acts   167   ■   The Kentucky and Virginia Resolves   168

CHAPTER 6   Jeffersonian Democracy   171

Jefferson Elected President   172   ■   The Federalist Contribution   173   ■   Thomas Jefferson: Political
Theorist   173   ■   Jefferson as President   174   ■   Jefferson's Attack on the Judiciary   176   ■   The Barbary
Pirates   177   ■   The Louisiana Purchase   177   ■   The Federalists Discredited   181   ■   Lewis and Clark
183   ■   The Burr Conspiracy   184   ■   Napoleon and the British   185   ■   The Impressment Controversy
187   ■   The Embargo Act   187   ■   Jeffersonian Democracy   190

CHAPTER 7   National Growing Pains   193

Madison in Power   194   ■   Tecumseh and Indian Resistance   194   ■   Depression and Land Hunger   196
■   Opponents of War   196   ■   The War of 1812   197   ■   Britain Assumes the Offensive   201   ■   "The Star
Spangled Banner"   202   ■   The Treaty of Ghent   203   ■   The Hartford Convention   203   ■   The Battle of New
Orleans and the End of the War   204   ■   Anglo-American Rapprochement   206   ■   The Transcontinental
Treaty   206   ■   The Monroe Doctrine   207   ■   The Era of Good Feelings   210   ■   New Sectional Issues   211
■   New Leaders   214   ■   The Missouri Compromise   216   ■   The Election of 1824   219   ■   John Quincy
Adams as President   220   ■   Calhoun's *Exposition and Protest*   220   ■   The Meaning of Sectionalism   221

CHAPTER 8   Toward a National Economy   224

Gentility and the Consumer Revolution   225   ■   Birth of the Factory   226   ■   An Industrial Proletariat?
227   ■   Lowell's Waltham System: Women as Factory Workers   229   ■   Irish and German Immigrants   230
■   The Persistence of the Household System   231   ■   Rise of Corporations   231   ■   Cotton Revolutionizes
the South   232   ■   Revival of Slavery   235   ■   Roads to Market   236   ■   Transportation and the
Government   238   ■   Development of Steamboats   239   ■   The Canal Boom   240   ■   New York City:
Emporium of the Western World   241   ■   The Marshall Court   243

CHAPTER 9   Jacksonian Democracy   247

"Democratizing" Politics   248   ■   1828: The New Party System in Embryo   249   ■   The Jacksonian
Appeal   250   ■   The Spoils System   251   ■   President of All the People   252   ■   Sectional Tensions
Revived   253   ■   Jackson: "The Bank . . . I Will Kill It!"   253   ■   Jackson's Bank Veto   255   ■   Jackson
versus Calhoun   256   ■   Indian Removals   257   ■   The Nullification Crisis   260   ■   Boom and Bust   262
■   The Jacksonians   263   ■   Rise of the Whigs   263   ■   Martin Van Buren: Jacksonianism without
Jackson   265   ■   The Log Cabin Campaign   268

CHAPTER 10   The Making of Middle-Class America 271

Tocqueville: Democracy in America   272 ■ The Family Recast   273 ■ The Second Great Awakening   274 ■ The Era of Associations   276 ■ Backwoods Utopias   277 ■ The Age of Reform   279 ■ "Demon Rum"   281 ■ The Abolitionist Crusade   282 ■ Women's Rights   285 ■ The Romantic View of Life   288 ■ Emerson and Thoreau   289 ■ Edgar Allan Poe   290 ■ Nathaniel Hawthorne   291 ■ Herman Melville   292 ■ Walt Whitman   292 ■ Reading and the Dissemination of Culture   294 ■ Education for Democracy   294 ■ The State of the Colleges   296

CHAPTER 11   Westward Expansion 299

Tyler's Troubles   299 ■ The Webster-Ashburton Treaty   300 ■ The Texas Question   301 ■ Manifest Destiny   303 ■ Life on the Trail   303 ■ California and Oregon   304 ■ The Election of 1844   307 ■ Polk as President   307 ■ War with Mexico   308 ■ To the Halls of Montezuma   310 ■ The Treaty of Guadalupe Hidalgo   312 ■ The Fruits of Victory: Further Enlargement of the United States   312 ■ Slavery: Storm Clouds Gather   313 ■ The Election of 1848   314 ■ The Gold Rush   316 ■ The Compromise of 1850   317

CHAPTER 12   The Sections Go Their Own Ways 323

The South   324 ■ The Economics of Slavery   324 ■ Antebellum Plantation Life   327 ■ The Sociology of Slavery   328 ■ Psychological Effects of Slavery   330 ■ Manufacturing in the South   333 ■ The Northern Industrial Juggernaut   334 ■ A Nation of Immigrants   335 ■ How Wage Earners Lived   335 ■ Progress and Poverty   337 ■ Foreign Commerce   338 ■ Steam Conquers the Atlantic   339 ■ Canals and Railroads   339 ■ Financing the Railroads   340 ■ Railroads and the Economy   341 ■ Railroads and the Sectional Conflict   344 ■ The Economy on the Eve of Civil War   345

CHAPTER 13   The Coming of the Civil War 347

Slave-Catchers Come North   348 ■ *Uncle Tom's Cabin*   350 ■ Diversions Abroad: The "Young America" Movement   351 ■ Stephen Douglas: "The Little Giant"   352 ■ The Kansas-Nebraska Act   353 ■ Know-Nothings, Republicans, and the Demise of the Two-Party System   355 ■ "Bleeding Kansas"   356 ■ Senator Sumner Becomes a Martyr for Abolitionism   358 ■ Buchanan Tries His Hand   359 ■ The Dred Scott Decision   360 ■ The Proslavery Lecompton Constitution   362 ■ The Emergence of Lincoln   363 ■ The Lincoln-Douglas Debates   364 ■ John Brown's Raid   366 ■ The Election of 1860   367 ■ The Secession Crisis   371

CHAPTER 14   The War to Save the Union 375

Lincoln's Cabinet   375 ■ Fort Sumter: The First Shot   376 ■ The Blue and the Gray   378 ■ The Test of Battle: Bull Run   380 ■ Paying for the War   381 ■ Politics as Usual   382 ■ Behind Confederate Lines   383 ■ War in the West: Shiloh   384 ■ McClellan: The Reluctant Warrior   385 ■ Lee Counterattacks: Antietam   387 ■ The Emancipation Proclamation   388 ■ The Draft Riots   391 ■ The Emancipated People   392 ■ African American Soldiers   392 ■ Antietam to Gettysburg   393 ■ Lincoln Finds His General: Grant at Vicksburg   395 ■ Economic and Social Effects, North and South   396 ■ Women in Wartime   397 ■ Grant in the Wilderness   398 ■ Sherman in Georgia   400 ■ To Appomattox Court House   403 ■ Winners, Losers, and the Future   403

CHAPTER 15   Reconstruction and the South 409

The Assassination of Lincoln   410 ■ Presidential Reconstruction   411 ■ Republican Radicals   413 ■ Congress Rejects Johnsonian Reconstruction   413 ■ The Fourteenth Amendment   415 ■ The Reconstruction Acts   416 ■ Congress Supreme   416 ■ The Fifteenth Amendment   417 ■ "Black Republican" Reconstruction: Scalawags and Carpetbaggers   419 ■ The Ravaged Land   421 ■ Sharecropping and the Crop-Lien System   422 ■ The White Backlash   424 ■ Grant as President   426 ■ The Disputed Election of 1876   427 ■ The Compromise of 1877   429

Appendix A-1
Credits C-1
Glossary G-1
Index I-1

Maps, Graphs, and Features

MAPS

	PAGE
Major Indian Cultures, AD 1–1500	6
Population of Major Civilizations of Europe, Asia, and Africa, AD 1500	10
European Voyages of Discovery	15
Columbian Exchange	22
Spain's North American Frontier, c. 1750	51
English Colonies on the Atlantic Seaboard	53
Atlantic Slave Trade, 1451–1870	57
Ethnic Groups of Eastern North America, 1750	72
British Successes, 1758–1763	94
European Claims in North America after British Victory, 1763	96
Proclamation of 1763	98
New York and New Jersey Campaigns, 1776–1777	121
Saratoga Campaign, September 19 to October 17, 1777	124
Campaign in the South, 1779–1781	126
The Yorktown Campaign, April to September 1781	127
The United States under the Articles of Confederation, 1787	130
Ratification of the Federal Constitution, 1787–1790	151
The United States and Its Territories, 1787–1802	163
The Wild Election of 1800	172
Louisiana Purchase	181
The War of 1812	200
The United States, 1819	209
The Missouri Compromise, 1820	218
Population Density, 1790	230
Population Density, 1820	230
The Rise of the Second American Party System, 1828	251
Osceola's Rebellion	259
New England Roots of Utopian Communities	279
Trails West	306
The War with Mexico, 1846–1848	309
Missouri Compromise 1820 and Compromise of 1850	319
Cotton and Slaves in the South, 1860	326
Railroads, 1860	342
Agriculture, 1860	343
Free Blacks in 1850	349
"Bleeding Kansas"	357
Presidential Election, 1860	369
Secession of the South, 1860–1861	372
Battles in the West	385
War in the East, 1861–1862	387
Gettysburg Campaign, 1863	394
Vicksburg Campaign	395
Toward Lee's Surrender in Virginia, 1864–1865	399

Sherman Pierces the Heart of the South, 1864–1865   *400*
Republicans Win in Deep South   *420*
Sharecroppings, 1880   *423*
The Republicans Gain the Presidency, the White South Loses the Union Army, 1877   *428*

GRAPHS   PAGE

Colonial Trade with England, 1700–1774   *84*
American Foreign Trade, 1790–1812   *189*
Cotton Production and Slave Population, 1800–1860   *234*
Prices for Cotton and for Slaves, 1802–1860   *234*
Rural versus Urban Population, 1820–1860   *272*
Men Present for Service during the Civil War   *379*
Casualities of the Civil War   *406*

AMERICAN LIVES   PAGE

Davy Crockett   *266*
Sojourner Truth   *332*

RE-VIEWING THE PAST   PAGE

Black Robe   *42*
The Crucible   *74*
The Patriot   *138*
The Alamo   *320*
Glory   *404*

Preface

"A New American Destiny begins"—so trumpeted a liberal newspaper after the election of Barack Obama as president in 2008. Shortly after his inauguration a conservative newsletter asked, "What is Barack Obama making of our American destiny?" Its reply was brusque: "a hash."

Despite their divergent views on the merits of the new president, both publications assumed that the United States **had** a "destiny." The term "destiny" refers to an inevitable course of events. The liberal newspaper believed that the United States was predestined to embrace diversity while the conservative paper regarded the nation as foreordained to promote traditional religious values. Some contend, by contrast, that history moves in no preset direction.

This book takes no stand on these issues. But it does agree that Americans have long **assumed** a national destiny, such as John Louis O'Sullivan's 1845 editorial proclaiming it "our manifest destiny" for Americans to spread throughout North America; or Daniel Webster's terse repudiation of the looming sectional crisis: "One country, one constitution, one destiny"; or Walt Whitman's celebration, after that crisis had erupted in civil war, of "one common indivisible destiny for ALL"; or Franklin D. Roosevelt's reference during the Great Depression to his generation's "rendezvous with destiny"; or the letter from a Birmingham jail by African American leader Martin Luther King, Jr. in which he declared that "our destiny is tied up with America's destiny."

But if Americans have commonly accepted the concept of a national purpose, they have endlessly debated where the nation was headed and the nature of the force impelling it there. Some have discerned the hand of God lifting the nation up—or perhaps hurling it down. Others have claimed that the nation's destiny was dictated by accident of geography or economics, by the "laws" of social evolution or the "spirit" of democratic liberalism, by the "patterns" of demography or "processes" of modernity, and so on.

This book maintains that no single model explains the complexity of American history. Because historians are poor prophets, we make no attempt to peer into the future. For us, the concept of an American destiny refers to a vague notion that has long exerted a hold on the American imagination.

The subtitle—"Narrative of a Nation"—may also strike readers as provocative. Some contend that the diverse peoples of the United States cannot be encompassed within the analytical boundaries of a single nation. Thus we have not attempted to write a history of "the American people": No book can possibly do justice to all its infinite variations of identity—racial, gender-related, and cultural. Rather, we describe how the voices and actions of its many peoples have produced a particular political structure—the United States—and how that nation has influenced the lives of everyone.

"Relevant History"

This narrative seeks to speak directly to students. Each of the features serves to connect past and present, a bridge to help students relate the people and events of history to their own lives.

Chapter Openers

To that end, every chapter opens with questions that pertain to many readers: Chapter 6—on Jeffersonian Democracy—begins: "Do you have too much debt?" The essay that follows examines the problem of credit card debt among college students today and shows how similar concerns occupied Jefferson and his followers. Chapter 18, on society and culture during the late nineteenth century, opens with: "Have you ever been kicked out of a mall?" The succeeding paragraphs show how much more of our lives are played out in public spaces compared to a century ago. Such questions bridge present and past; they connect our lives to those of our forebears.

Re-Viewing the Past

Because movies on historical themes often figure prominently in how we think about the past, ten of the chapters include *Re-Viewing the Past* essays, which contrast Hollywood's rendering of history with what really happened. The selected movies range from those with obvious "historical" themes, such as *The Alamo* and *Saving Private Ryan*, to popular movies whose historical themes are less well known, such as *Chicago*, a musical based on the actual story of women who murdered their lovers.

American Lives

Ten of the chapters include *American Lives* essays, ranging from Sojourner Truth, a slave who became a preacher and reformer, to contemporary figures such as Bill Gates and Barack Obama. These essays focus on the young adulthood of such figures; we hope that readers of the same age will in this way find it easier to relate to them.

New to This Edition

- Each chapter has been revised to reflect new scholarship, offer new perspectives, and streamline and sharpen the prose. An almost entirely new chapter, "From Boomers to Millennials" (Chapter 31), draws an explicit comparison between the social and cultural foundations of young modern Americans and their parents; it especially explores the culture of consumption and the impact of the Internet.
- The essays that introduce each chapter are either entirely new or have been updated; nearly all pertain to events or developments since 2008.
- The Prologue and first few chapters reflect new insights unearthed (literally) by archaeologists and anthropologists concerning the "pre-historic" period. These chapters also feature a more detailed comparison of the civilizations of the Americas with those of the "Old World"—Europe, Africa, and Asia.
- This edition includes several new *American Lives*: Davy Crockett—perhaps the first person who became famous for being famous; Charlotte Perkins Gilman, a visionary who perceived that women's legal and political emancipation was largely dependent on their gaining paid work; civil rights leader Martin Luther King, Jr.; Barack Obama, the first African American to be elected president; and three randomly selected heroes who were killed in the recent wars in Afghanistan and Iraq.

- This edition also includes three new *Re-Viewing the Past* essays. *Black Robe* thoughtfully explores the interaction of Indians and colonists in the seventeenth century. Two versions of *The Alamo*: The first, released in 1960, stars John Wayne; the second (2004) tells a different story with Billy Bob Thornton as Davy Crockett. The widely acclaimed *There Will Be Blood* presents Daniel Day Lewis's searing performance as an unscrupulous wildcatting oilman loosely based on the life of Edward Doheny, who opened up the major oil fields of California and Mexico early in the twentieth century.
- The maps in this book have been completely reworked to convey new ideas and to enhance comprehension.
- Nearly every chapter now includes at least one "conceptual" table illuminating key themes and topics.
- To encourage and facilitate study and review, each chapter now ends with a set of review questions, and a list of key terms that are defined in a new glossary.

Supplements for
Instructors and Students

Supplements for Qualified College Adopters	Supplements for Students
MyHistoryLab **MyHistoryLab** (www.myhistorylab.com) **Save Time. Improve Results.** MyHistoryLab is a dynamic website that provides a wealth of resources geared to meet the diverse teaching and learning needs of today's instructors and students. MyHistoryLab's many accessible tools will encourage students to read their text and help them improve their grade in their course.	MyHistoryLab **MyHistoryLab** (www.myhistorylab.com) **Save Time. Improve Results.** MyHistoryLab is a dynamic website that provides a wealth of resources geared to meet the diverse teaching and learning needs of today's instructors and students. MyHistoryLab's many accessible tools will encourage you to read your text and help you improve your grade in your course.
Instructor's Resource Manual with Test Bank Available at the Instructor's Resource Center, at **www.pearsonhighered.com/irc**, the Instructor's Resource Manual with Test Bank contains chapter outlines, summaries, key points and vital concepts, and information on audio-visual resources that can be used in developing and preparing lecture presentations. The Test Bank includes multiple-choice questions and essay questions and is text-specific.	**CourseSmart www.coursesmart.com** CourseSmart eTextbooks offer the same content as the printed text in a convenient online format— with highlighting, online search, and printing capabilities. You **save 60% over the list price** of the traditional book.
PowerPoint Presentation Available at the Instructor's Resource Center, at **www.pearsonhighered.com/irc**, the PowerPoints contain chapter outlines and full-color images of maps and art. They are text-specific and available for download.	**Library of American Biography Series** www.pearsonhighered.com/educator/series/Library-of-American-Biography/10493.page Pearson's renowned series of biographies spotlighting figures who had a significant impact on American history. Included in the series are Edmund Morgan's *The Puritan Dilemma: The Story of John Winthrop*, B. Davis Edmund's *Tecumseh and the Quest for Indian Leadership*, J. William T. Young's, *Eleanor Roosevelt: A Personal and Public Life*, John R. M. Wilson's *Jackie Robinson and the American Dilemma*, and Sandra Opdycke's *Jane Addams and Her Vision For America*.
MyTest Available at **www.pearsonmytest.com**, MyTest is a powerful assessment generation program that helps instructors easily create and print quizzes and exams. Questions and tests can be authored online, allowing instructors ultimate flexibility and the ability to efficiently manage assessments anytime, anywhere! Instructors can easily access existing questions and edit, create, and store using simple drag-and-drop and Word-like controls.	**Penguin Valuepacks** www.pearsonhighered.com/penguin A variety of Penguin-Putnam texts is available at discounted prices when bundled with *The American Nation, 14/e*. Texts include Benjamin Franklin's *Autobiography and Other Writings*, Nathaniel Hawthorne's *The Scarlet Letter*, Thomas Jefferson's *Notes on the State of Virginia*, and George Orwell's *1984*.

Supplements for Qualified College Adopters	Supplements for Students
Retreiving the American Past Available through the Pearson Custom Library (**www.pearsoncustom.com, keyword search | rtap**), the *Retrieving the American Past* (RTAP) program lets you create a textbook or reader that meets your needs and the needs of your course. RTAP gives you the freedom and flexibility to add chapters from several best-selling Pearson textbooks, in addition to *The American Nation, 14/e,* and/or 100 topical reading units written by the History Department of The Ohio State University, all under one cover. Choose the content you want to teach in depth, in the sequence you want, at the price you want your students to pay.	**A Short Guide to Writing About History, 7/e** Written by Richard Marius, late of Harvard University, and Melvin E. Page, East Tennessee State University, this engaging and practical text helps students get beyond merely compiling dates and facts. Covering both brief essays and the documented resource paper, the text explores the writing and researching processes, identifies different modes of historical writing, including argument, and concludes with guidelines for improving style. **ISBN-10: 0205673708; ISBN-13: 9780205673704**
	Longman American History Atlas This full-color historical atlas designed especially for college students is a valuable reference tool and visual guide to American history. This atlas includes maps covering the scope of American history from the lives of the Native Americans to the 1990s. Produced by a renowned cartographic firm and a team of respected historians, the *Longman American History Atlas* will enhance any American history survey course. **ISBN: 0321004868; ISBN-13: 9780321004864**
	Study Card for American History This timeline of major events in American social, political, and cultural history distills course information to the basics, helping you quickly master the fundamentals and prepare for exams. **ISBN: 0321292324; ISBN-13: 9780321292322**

MyHistoryLab

The Moment You Know

Educators know it. Students know it. It's that inspired moment when something that was difficult to understand suddenly makes perfect sense. MyHistoryLab has been designed and refined with a single purpose in mind: to help history teachers create that moment of understanding with their students.

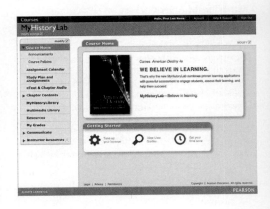

Features of MyHistoryLab

MyHistoryLab provides **engaging experiences** that personalize, stimulate, and measure learning for each student.

- *Closer Look tours*—walk students through a variety of images, maps, and primary sources in detail, helping them to uncover their meaning and understand their context.
- **A History Bookshelf**—enables students to read, download, or print up to 100 of the most commonly assigned history works, like Thomas Paine's, *Common Sense*, Booker T. Washington's, *Up From Slavery*, and Andrew Carnegie's *Autobiography*.
- The **Pearson eText**—lets students access their textbook anytime, anywhere, and any way they want—including listening online or downloading to their iPad.
- A **personalized study plan** for each student, based on a chapter Pre-Test, arranges content from less complex thinking—like remembering basic facts—to more complex critical thinking—like understanding connections and analyzing the past. This layered approach promotes better critical-thinking skills, and helps students succeed in the course and beyond.
- **Assessment** tied to every chapter enables both instructors and students to track progress and get immediate feedback. With results flowing into a powerful

gradebook, the assessment program helps instructors identify student challenges early—and find the best resources with which to help students.

- An **assignment calendar** allows instructors to assign graded activities, with specific deadlines, and measure student progress.
- *ClassPrep* collects the very best class presentation resources in one convenient online destination, so instructors can keep students engaged throughout every class.
- **Audio Files**—Full audio of the entire text is included to suit the varied learning styles of today's students. In addition there are audio clips of speeches, readings, and music that provide another engaging way to experience history.
- **Text and Visual Documents**—Over 1,500 primary source documents, images, and maps are available organized by chapter in the text. Primary source documents are also available in the MyHistoryLibrary and can be searched by author, title, theme, and topic. Many of these documents include critical thinking questions.
- **Lecture and Archival Videos**—Lectures by leading scholars on provocative topics give students a critical look at key points in history. Videos of speeches, news footage,

key historical events, and other archival video take students back to the moment in history.

- **MySearchLab**—This website provides students access to a number of reliable sources for online research, as well as clear guidance on the research and writing process.
- **Gradebook**—Students can follow their own progress and instructors can monitor the work of the entire class. Automated grading of quizzes and assignments helps both instructors and students save time and monitor their results throughout the course.

NEW In-text References to MyHistoryLab Resources

Read, View, See, Watch, Hear, Study, and Review Icons integrated in the text connect resources on MyHistoryLab to specific topics within the chapters. The icons are not exhaustive; many more resources are available than those highlighted in the book, but the icons draw attention to some of the most high-interest resources available on MyHistoryLab.

Read the **Document**

Points students to primary and secondary source documents related to the chapter.

View the **Image**

Identifies primary and secondary source images, including photographs, fine art, and artifacts to provide students with a visual perspective on history.

See the **Map**

Directs students to atlas and interactive maps; these present both broad overviews and detailed examinations of historical developments.

Watch the **Video**

Notes pertinent archival videos and videos of Pearson History authors that probe various topics.

Hear the **Audio**

Marks audio clips from historically significant songs and speeches that enrich students' engagement with history.

Study and **Review**

Alerts students to study resources for each chapter of the textbook available online through www.myhistorylab.com. These resources include practice tests and flashcards.

Acknowledgments

I THANK THE MANY FRIENDS, colleagues, and students who have helped me in writing this edition of *American Destiny*. My debt to John A. Garraty—teacher, colleague, co-author—warrants many paragraphs of acknowledgment. But his scorn for wordiness obliges me to acknowledge that he taught me the art of writing.

Mary Elin Korchinsky has lived this book (and nearly everything else) with me. My journey with her is a joy. For this edition, our particular challenge has been to relate the American nation's past to college students today. Much of the creativity in the chapters that follow—"Do you vote for *American Idol*?" "Do you illegally download?" "Do you space out during political debates?"—was a product of her special genius.

I especially thank E. Ward Smith for guidance through the murky depths of modern banking and finance. And I thank Prakhar Sharma for similarly leading me through the shrouded landscape of contemporary Iraq and Afghanistan.

Modern publishing, too, is a world of labyrinthine complexity. I thank the expert team at Pearson for sharing their mastery of its many arcane and demanding arts: Yolanda de Rooy, Roberta Meyer, Craig Campanella, Ed Parsons, Debra Wechsler, Mirella Signoretto, Maria Lange, Marisa Taylor, Brandy Dawson, Maureen Prado Roberts, and Alex Rabinowitz. Although they left me plenty of thread to find my way out, they also showed good sense in sometimes getting behind me and pushing. For that, and everything else, I am grateful.

I also thank:

Armando C. Alonzo, Texas A & M University
Andrew Bagley, Phillips Community College
Mary E. Barnes, Blinn College
Mack Bean, Blinn College
Thomas Born, Blinn College
Robert Brooks, Tyler Junior College
Dale Carnagey, Blinn College
Carrie Coston, Blinn College
Shannon Cross, Tyler Junior College
Alan Harazin, Holyoke Community College
Billy Hathorn, Laredo Community College
Peter Jones, Tyler Junior College
Gene Kirkpatrick, Tyler Junior College
Martha Kline, Blinn College
Alan Lehman, Blinn College
Jan McCauley, Tyler Junior College

Nora McMillan, San Antonio College
Horacio Salinas, Jr., Laredo Community College
Malcolum Saunders, University of the South Pacific
Kenneth McCullough, Blinn College
Dennis M. Nilsen, Molloy College
Jeff Owens, Tyler Junior College
Kahne Parsons, Tyler Junior College
Madeleine Ross, Tyler Junior College
James R. Sisson, Central Texas College
Herbert Sloan, Barnard College
Isaac Solis, Navarro College
Brian Steele, University of Alabama at Birmingham
Tracy Teslow, University of Cincinnati
Hubert P. van Tuyll, Augusta State University
Larry Watson, Blinn College
Stan Watson, Tyler Junior College
Don Whatley, Blinn College
Geoffrey Willbanks, Tyler Junior College

I thank the families of the American heroes, featured in Chapter 32, for sharing the stories of their children who served and died in the wars in Afghanistan and Iraq.

My daughter, Stephanie, read the book carefully and critically, and her comments have proven invaluable. My goal of connecting with younger readers was surely influenced by her own immense capacity for sharing love with her parents. This book is dedicated to her—in acknowledgment of that special gift and so many others.

Mark C. Carnes

Barnard College, Columbia University

About the Authors

MARK C. CARNES received his undergraduate degree from Harvard and his PhD in history from Columbia University. He has chaired both the history and American studies departments at Barnard College, Columbia University, where he serves as the Ann Whitney Olin Professor of History. Carnes and Garraty were General Editors of the 26-volume *American National Biography*, for which they were awarded the Waldo Leland Prize of the American Historical Association. Carnes has published numerous books on American social and cultural history, including *Secret Ritual and Manhood in Victorian America* (1989), *Past Imperfect: History According to the Movies* (1995), *Novel History: Historians and Novelists Confront America's Past* (2001), and *Invisible Giants: 50 Americans That Shaped the Nation but Missed the History Books* (2002). Carnes also pioneered the *Reacting to the Past* pedagogy, winner of the Theodore Hesburgh Award, sponsored by TIAA-CREF, as the outstanding pedagogical innovation in the nation (2004). In *Reacting to the Past*, college students play elaborate games, set in the past, their roles informed by classic texts. (For more on *Reacting*, see: www.barnard.edu/reacting.) In 2005 the American Historical Association named Carnes the recipient of the William Gilbert Prize for the best article on teaching history.

The late John A. Garraty, formerly Gouverneur Morris Professor Emeritus of History at Columbia University, received his PhD from Columbia University and an LHD from Michigan State University. He authored and edited scores of books, among them biographies of Silas Wright, Henry Cabot Lodge, Woodrow Wilson, George W. Perkins, and Theodore Roosevelt. Garraty's *The New Commonwealth*, included in the new *American Nation* series, challenged earlier dismissals of what was commonly known as "the Gilded Age." His *The Great Depression* argued that political leaders throughout the world happened upon "solutions" much like those proposed by Franklin D. Roosevelt. Garraty was co-General Editor with Mark Carnes of the *American National Biography*.

PROLOGUE: Beginnings

((•—[Hear the Audio Prologue at myhistorylab.com

Were ancient peoples different from you?

SOME 400 YEARS BEFORE COLUMBUS WAS BORN, INDIANS LIVING NEAR what is now Peebles, Ohio, built the Great Serpent Mound. The mound is shaped like a snake, tail coiled and mouth open—perhaps in the act of devouring an egg or spitting it out. Why the Indians built the mound remains a mystery, especially since the effigy is so huge—a quarter of a mile long—that it can only be identified as a snake from high in the sky.

Perhaps the snake functioned as a territorial marker, rather like the graffiti urban gangs use to scare rivals. Perhaps it was a religious symbol; snakes figured prominently in the beliefs of later Indians. Perhaps the serpent conveyed astronomical meanings: Its shape mirrors the constellation *Draco*; and on June 21st, the longest day of the year in the Northern Hemisphere, the snake's head points exactly at the spot where the sun sets. (Was the serpent gobbling up the sun?) Perhaps the mound is some type of memorial to the dead; skeletons dating from the period are found in nearby mounds.

Why begin a book on the American nation with a discussion of peoples who lived many generations before George Washington, especially when the historical record of their lives is so incomplete? The simplest answer is that the early peoples of the Americas proved peculiarly susceptible to a calamity none of them could have foreseen: the sudden appearance of strange, bellicose peoples. Possessing formidable weapons, riding terrifying animals, and endowed with an unfathomable power to wreak sickness and death on entire villages, these invaders swiftly seized much of the Western Hemisphere. The American nation was one product of these developments.

But first things first.

First Peoples

The first human beings emerged over 3 million years ago, probably in Africa. Some eventually devised stone tools, thus inaugurating the **Paleolithic revolution**, a life based on hunting and gathering nuts, berries, and edible plants. About 40,000 years ago human beings of a different sort—people similar to us in their aptitude for tools and language—appeared in Africa, Europe, and Asia displacing those humans who had preceded them.

The earth was colder than it is now, and the northward advance of these Eurasian hunters was halted by immense sheets of ice, some as broad as Australia and over 10,000-feet thick—the height of ten Empire State buildings. These ice slabs, which had been expanding for tens of thousands of years, gouged deep holes in the earth's crust.

Paleolitic hunters in Asia pushed deeper into the arctic tundra, pursuing big game—especially woolly mammoths. Weighing nearly 16,000 pounds, about as much as a large elephant, a single mammoth provided enough meat to feed two dozen hunters nearly all winter. Its fur could be worn as clothing and its fat could be burned for heat. Its bones, when stretched with fur, functioned as simple tents. A woolly mammoth was a kind of movable mall, and Paleolithic hunters regarded it with the avidity of shoppers at a clearance sale.

Some Paleolithic hunters eventually crossed into what is now Alaska. What occurred next is a matter of conjecture. Eventually these Paleo-Indians, moving south, happened upon lush grasslands, on which grazed vast herds of large mammals: mammoths and equally enormous mastodons, with massive legs and stout feet; giant beavers the size of bears; 20-foot-long ground sloths weighing over 6,000 pounds; strange monsters such as glyptodonts, which resembled armadillos but weighed over a ton; and also countless camels, horses, cheetahs, caribou, and deer.

The Demise of the Big Mammals

Loosed upon herds of unwary animals, Paleo-Indians (hereafter, simply Indians) slaughtered them or stampeded them over cliffs. They chiseled long stone blades especially designed to penetrate thick hides. Archaeologists have named these hunters after their ingenious blades, first found at Clovis, New Mexico. Archaeologists have found Clovis blades in nearly every state of the United States and even at the southern tip of South America.

View the Image

Clovis Points at **myhistorylab.com**

But around 12,000 years ago, the big mammals were disappearing from the Western Hemisphere. Thirty-three species became extinct, including mammoths, mastodons, saber-toothed cats, giant beavers, horses, and camels. Perhaps the hunters killed off the big mammals; or perhaps the heavily furred animals were ill-suited to a warming trend.

The disappearance of these mammals nearly coincided with the closing of the route from Beringia to the Americas, as melting ice worldwide raised ocean levels hundreds of feet, flooding the low-lying land that had joined Asia and Alaska. No more big mammals could make their way into the Americas.

These two factors profoundly influenced the course of human development in the Americas: The absence of big mammals deprived Indian peoples of ready sources of food and draft animals, and the geographical isolation of the Americas meant that the Indians would not be exposed to the waves of biological diversity—plants, animals, bacteria, and viruses—that repeatedly washed over Europe, Asia, and Africa.

The Archaic Period: Surviving without Big Mammals

With the big mammals gone, Indians struggled to find alternative sources of food. Prolonged droughts or severe winters resulted in starvation. North of Mexico, in what is now the United States, population likely remained stagnant: The garbage pits

A woolly mammoth consumed about 400 pounds of grass a day. This mammoth skeleton is thirteen feet high.

from archaeological sites show that diets lacked sufficient fats and proteins to promote fertility.

But over time, these Indians—termed Archaic—adapted to conditions of scarcity. They migrated according to a seasonal schedule, often returning to the same campsites year after year. In woodland areas east of the Mississippi River, they learned to hunt small animals, like rabbits and beaver, that had previously not been worth the bother; or they learned to find stealthy animals like bear and caribou or to sneak up on skittish ones like elk and deer. On the Great Plains, Indians thrived on bison, among the few large mammals that had not become extinct.

Some Archaic peoples discovered rich habitats that could sustain them throughout the year. Indians living along the coast and rivers of the Pacific Northwest and Alaska found fish to be so plentiful that they could be scooped up in baskets. These people made nets and fishhooks. Eventually they built boats out of bark and animal skins. Those living along the New England coast discovered a seemingly inexhaustible supply of shellfish. But for even these people, survival was a full-time job: it takes 83,000 clams to provide as much fat as a single deer.

As tribes remained longer in one area, they began to regard it as their own. They built more substantial habitations, developed pottery to carry water and cook food, and buried the dead with distinctive rituals in special places, often marked with mounds.

One of the earliest sedentary communities was located at what is now Poverty Point, on the Mississippi River floodplains north of Delhi, Louisiana. It was founded 3,500 years ago. Poverty Point peoples filled countless grass baskets with earth and dumped them onto enormous mounds. One mound, shaped like an octagon, had six terraced levels on which were built some 400 to 600 houses. Another was more than 700 feet long and 70 feet high. Viewed from above, it resembled a hawk. In all, the mounds consisted of over a million cubic yards of dirt.

The enormity of their construction projects reveals much about Poverty Point peoples. They could not have diverted so much time and energy to construction if they were not proficient at acquiring food. Moreover, while most Archaic bands were egalitarian, with little differentiation in status, the social structure of Poverty Point was hierarchical. Leaders conceived the plans and directed the labor to build the earthworks.

After about a thousand years, Poverty Point was abandoned. No one knows why. Several hundred years later, scores of smaller mound communities, known as Adena, sprouted in the Ohio and Mississippi River valleys. The inhabitants of these communities were also hunters and foragers who cultivated plants in their spare time. The Adena communities lasted several hundred years.

Around 2200 BP, another cluster of mound builders, known as Hopewell, flourished in Ohio and Illinois. Hopewell mounds were often shaped into squares, circles, and cones; some, viewed from above, resembled birds or serpents. Around AD 400, the Hopewell sites were abandoned.

The impermanence of these communities serves as a reminder that the transition from a nomadic existence of hunting and foraging to a settled life based on agriculture was slow and uneven. For the Indians living north of the Rio Grande, this was about to change. For people living in what is now Central America, it already had.

The Maize Revolution

Maize did not exist 7,000 years ago. But around that time, perhaps far earlier, Indians in southern Mexico interbred various species of grasses, exploiting subtle changes and perhaps significant mutations. Eventually they created maize. A geneticist writing in *Science* in 2003 declared this to be "arguably man's first, and perhaps his greatest, feat of genetic engineering." The original ears were too small to provide much food, but within several thousand years farmers in Central America had developed maize that resembled modern corn.

The **Neolithic revolution**—the transition from hunting and gathering to farming—had come to Central America. Soon most valleys in central Mexico bristled with cornstalks. Population grew and cities emerged. By AD 100 Teotihuacan, forty miles north of what is now Mexico City, had a population approaching 100,000 and featured miles of paved streets and a pyramid as large as those of Egypt. Mesoamerica was approaching its classical period, which would culminate in the great corn-growing civilizations of the Mayans and Aztecs.[1]

Eventually corn cultivation leapfrogged the deserts of northern Mexico and was adopted by the Indians of the Southwest: the Hohokam and Mogollon of Arizona and New Mexico, and the Anasazi of the Colorado Plateau. Abandoning their nomadic life, these Indians settled near rivers, built trenches and canals to channel water to the crops, dammed gullies to capture runoff from flash floods, and constructed homes near the cornfields.

Their culture revolved around corn. Sun and water became the focus of their religious beliefs, symbols of life and rebirth. Priest-astronomers carefully observed changes of the seasons. If corn was planted too early, it might shrivel before the late summer

---

[1]Less relevant to the development of the peoples of North America was the remarkable potato-cultivating Incan civilization that took root in Peru and other highland regions of South America.

Some scientists believe that thousands of years ago Indian farmers genetically engineered the transformation of teosinte, a wild grass with tiny seeds (left), to evolve into maize.

A statue of a corn goddess of the Moche peoples of coastal Peru, around 400 BP. Within several centuries, corn would spread into North America.

rains; if planted too late, it might be destroyed by frost. Corn Mother symbolism, suggesting a relationship between the fertility of the earth and of women, dominated religious practices. Control of the corn surplus was a key to political power.

Despite the arid heat of the Southwest, the corn-cultivating peoples increased in number after AD 800. The Chaco Canyon, a twenty-two-mile-long gorge in western New Mexico, witnessed the development of a most improbable human habitat. The Anasazi carved entire villages into the sandstone and shale cliffs. As population increased, they built dozens of towns and villages that were linked by an elaborate system of roads. The largest of these cliff towns, Pueblo Bonito, had buildings more than five stories tall. The Hohokam constructed an irrigation canal system that spanned hundreds of miles and contained an intricate network of dams, sluices, and headgates. Snaketown, a Hohokam village near modern Phoenix, had a population of several thousand.

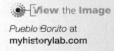

View the Image
Pueblo Bonito at
myhistorylab.com

These communities were far less populous than those of their mightier neighbors to the south. But the triumph of the corn-growing Anasazi, Hohokam, and Mogollon is measured not by wealth and population figures, but by the magnitude of the environmental challenges they overcame.

The Diffusion of Corn

Corn cultivation spread east and north. By AD 200, cornfields dotted the southern Mississippi River valley. Thereafter, the advance of corn slowed. Farther north, early cold snaps killed existing varieties of the plant. Corn cultivation in forested regions required unremitting labor, and few Indians were eager to subject themselves to its incessant demands. Fields had to be cleared, usually by burning away the undergrowth. Then the soil was hoed using flat stones, clamshells, or the shoulder blades of large animals. After planting, the fields required constant weeding. Compared to the thrill of the hunt, the taste of game, and the varied tasks associated with hunting and gathering, farming held little appeal. Males regarded it as a subsidiary activity, a task best relegated to women.

But over time many Indians learned that the alternative to agricultural labor was starvation. Fields farther north and east were cleared and planted with corn, beans, and squash. Old skeletons provide a precise means of tracking corn's advance. When corn is chewed, enzymes in the mouth convert its carbohydrates to sugar, a major cause of dental cavities. Radiocarbon dating of skeletons from the vicinity of what is now St. Louis first shows dental cavities around AD 700 and those from southern Wisconsin, around AD 900. By AD 1000 dental cavities can be found in skeletons throughout the Midwest and the East. Corn had become king.

Population Growth after AD 800

Corn stimulated population growth. An acre of woodlands fed two or three hunters or foragers; that same acre, planted in corn, provided for as many as 200 people. Hunting and foraging Indians usually found enough to eat in summer and fall, but in winter, food sources might disappear. But dried corn, stored in glazed pots or sealed in underground pits, could sustain many people over a period. Corn cultivators may not have had a particularly nutritious diet, but they were more likely to survive a long, hard winter.

◉ See the Map

Pre-Columbian Societies of the Americas at **myhistorylab.com**

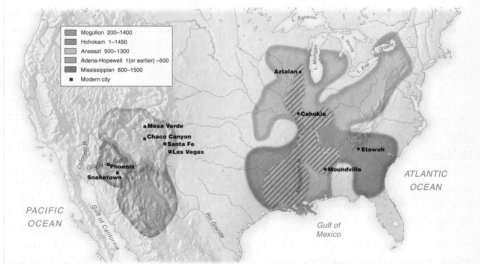

Major Indian Cultures, AD 1–1500 Thousands of Indian tribes existed in North America before 1500. Little is known about most of them, but five farming civilizations left a deep imprint on the historical record: the Mogollon and Hohokam of the desert Southwest; the Anasazi of the cliff regions and high plateaus farther north; the Adena–Hopewell mound builders of the Mississippi and Ohio valleys; and the Mississippian civilization, the successor of the Adena–Hopewell peoples, who inhabited much of what would eventually be the eastern United States. Each civilization mastered agriculture, ceramics, textiles, and metalworking, although each did so in different ways. Their surviving artifacts provide the clues to their distinctive cultures.

A sedentary lifestyle promoted population growth in other ways. Infants and toddlers were a nuisance on the trail; some hunting and foraging Indians practiced abortion or even infanticide to ensure mobility and reduce the number of mouths to feed. But farming Indians nearly always could make use of additional hands, even young ones, to help with plowing, hoeing, weeding, and harvesting. Because farmers rarely moved, they built more permanent homes and more successfully sheltered infants from inclement weather and physical dangers.

As in the Southwest, the corn-cultivating peoples of the Mississippi Valley responded to increasing population by clearing more woodland and planting more corn. At first, corn cultivators and hunting-foraging peoples successfully cohabited within the same ecosystem: Hunters traded for corn, essential for survival during winter, and corn cultivators traded for game, a source of complex protein. But over time the two groups often came into conflict, and when they did, the more numerous corn cultivators prevailed.

The corn-cultivating societies expanded west into Dakota, east through the Carolinas, south into Florida, and north into Wisconsin. Their villages consisted of clusters of homes, surrounded by cornfields. They shared a constellation of beliefs and ritual practices known as the Mississippian cultural complex. Like the Hopewell, they built burial mounds, but those of the corn cultivators were much larger. Some villages became towns and even small cities. Large temples and granaries and the homes of the governing elite were located on top of the mounds.

The most important and populous of these communities was located in the vicinity of St. Louis. Archaeologists call it Cahokia.

Cahokia: The Hub of Mississippian Culture

By AD 1000, Cahokia was a major center of trade, shops and crafts, and religious and political activities. It was the first true urban center in what is now the United States. By 1150, at the height of its development, it covered six square miles and had more than 15,000 inhabitants.

⚫ View the Image
Reconstructed View of Cahokia at
myhistorylab.com

The earthworks at Cahokia included some twenty huge mounds around a downtown plaza, with another 100 large mounds in the outlying areas. The largest mound was 110 feet high, covered fourteen acres, and contained 20 million cubic yards of earth. It was probably the largest earthen structure in the Americas. Atop the mound was a fifty-foot-high wood-framed temple.

Cahokian society was characterized by sharp class divisions. The elite lived in larger homes and consumed a better and more varied diet (their garbage pits included bones from the best cuts of meat). The corpse of one chieftain was buried upon a bed of 20,000 beaded shells; nearby was a long piece of shaped copper from Lake Superior, several bushels of bird and animal sculptures made of mica, and over 1,000 arrows, many with beautiful quartz or obsidian points. Near the chieftain's bones were the skeletons of fifty women ranging from eighteen to twenty-three years old, likely sacrifices to the gods. Their bones were genetically different from the Cahokian skeletons, suggesting that the young women were captives in war or tribute sent by vassal states.

That the Cahokia had enemies is confirmed by the existence of a three-mile-long wooden palisade surrounding the central core of the city. It consisted of 20,000 enormous

An artist's rendering shows downtown Cahokia, around 1150 CE. Cahokia was surrounded by a palisade, made of enormous tree trunks (far left). On the great mounds within, the elite built homes and performed the ceremonial tasks of Mississippian culture. The open space in the center was probably filled with the stalls of craftspeople.

tree trunks, pounded deep into the ground, interspersed with several dozen watchtowers from which defenders could unloose arrows upon besiegers.

Cahokia dominated a region of several hundred miles. Smaller mound-building communities emerged throughout the eastern woodlands and the Southeast. Two of the largest were Moundville, Alabama, and Etowah, Georgia. Cahokia also established (or perhaps inspired) distant satellite communities. Around AD 800, Mississippian Indians moved into southern Wisconsin and built Aztalan (in what is now Jefferson County), with similar corn storage depots and large ceremonial mounds surrounding a central plaza.

Like Cahokia, Aztalan erected a massive tree-trunk palisade with watchtowers. Archaeologists have found burned and butchered body parts throughout the ruins, evidence of warfare. Some speculate that the corn-growing Mississippians encroached on the Oneota, a hunting and gathering people, and that the communities long remained hostile.

The Mississippian elites did more than supervise construction of their own massive earthen tombs. They also solved complicated problems of political and social organization.

The Collapse of Urban Centers

Yet Cahokia and Aztalan soon declined. By AD 1200, Cahokia's population had been reduced to several thousand people; by AD 1350, it was deserted. Etowah and Moundville went into decline somewhat later.

The major towns and villages of the Southwest civilizations faded as well. By AD 1200, the inhabitants of Chaco Canyon had vanished and nearly all of the pueblos of the Anasazi had been abandoned. Snaketown and dozens of towns of the Hohokam had become empty ruins, their canals choked with weeds.

What caused the collapse of these communities has long been a source of debate. Some scholars cite protracted droughts during the 1200s and 1300s. Others note that population growth harmed the environment. Slash-and-burn wood clearance thinned the eastern forests, and corn cultivation exhausted the soil. The palisade at Cahokia consisted of thousands of the trunks of fully grown trees, and it was repeatedly rebuilt. Denuded of big trees, the watershed around Cahokia became susceptible to erosion and flooding, further depleting exhausted topsoils.

Crop yields declined as the demand for food in towns and villages increased. Studies of human skeletons in Mississippian burial mounds show higher incidences of disease and malnutrition after AD 1250. What happened next is unclear. Some archaeologists believe that many Mississippian Indians abandoned the cities and villages and quietly reverted to the hunting and foraging life of their Archaic forebears. Others argue that the end was calamitous. Late Mississippian skeletons were smaller and more likely to show signs of disease; they also had more broken bones; often arms, feet, and hands were dismembered. Recurrent famines and disease may have undermined the credibility of elites and the cultural system they supervised, weakening their control of poor urban people as well as chieftains in the hinterlands. The towering log palisades of the Mississippians and the impenetrable cliff dwellings of the Anasazi were manifestations of this collective insecurity.

Warfare became endemic among the corn-growing tribes of the Northeast. By AD 1300, the Iroquoian peoples of New York and Pennsylvania were building forts with defensive earthworks and palisades. Some tribes joined together to form military alliances. Soil exhaustion, perhaps aggravated by the droughts that had parched the cornfields of the Southwest, may have forced tribes to compete for land and resources. Some scholars propose that gender tensions may have exacerbated these conflicts. Men performed most of the hunting and foraging tasks, while women did most of the work in the cornfields. As corn supplanted game and fish as staples of the diet, women acquired more status and power. To reassert male dominance, men embarked on raids and warfare.

By AD 1500, nearly all of the large towns had been abandoned. New generations of Indians puzzled over who had inhabited the ruins, or who had erected the massive earthen mounds. The Navajo Indian word for their predecessors—"Anasazi"—means the "Ancient Ones."

The collapse of the cities disrupted trade networks. Some goods continued to move many, many miles, being passed from one tribe to another; but the flow of trade goods slowed to a trickle. Moreover, if the rise of powerful urban communities had forced earlier groups to band together, the demise of the urban communities precipitated the breakup of large groups and tribes. Hundreds, perhaps thousands of small bands lived in relative isolation.

To them, the great Aztec city of Tenochtitlán, beyond the Mexican desert, was only a rumor. Of Europe, Africa, and Asia, they knew nothing. That was about to change.

⊙ See the **Map**

Location of Major Indian Groups and Cultural Areas in the 1500s at **myhistorylab.com**

Eurasia and Africa

If the Neolithic revolution had made but fitful progress north of Mexico by 1500, its advance through Eurasia and Africa was nearly complete. Wheat, first domesticated in Southwest Asia well over 10,000 years ago, spread through the Nile Valley and the Mediterranean and eastward to India and China. Rice, domesticated in China much later, diffused throughout Eurasia. These lead crops were followed by others—oats, peas, olives, grapes, almonds, barley, oranges, lentils, and millet. Several thousand years later, farmers in Africa domesticated sorghum, palm oil, and yams.

The animals of Eurasia were as diverse as its crops. While few large mammals in the Americas survived the Clovis era, the ancient peoples of Eurasia learned how to

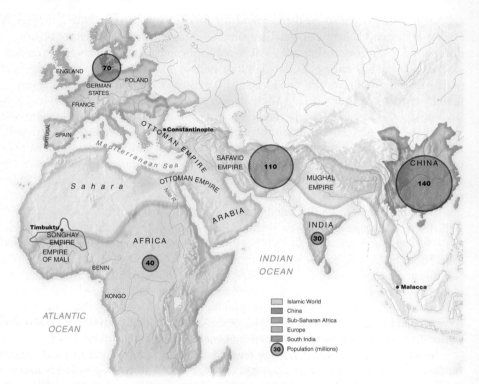

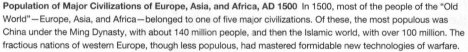

Population of Major Civilizations of Europe, Asia, and Africa, AD 1500 In 1500, most of the people of the "Old World"—Europe, Asia, and Africa—belonged to one of five major civilizations. Of these, the most populous was China under the Ming Dynasty, with about 140 million people, and then the Islamic world, with over 100 million. The fractious nations of western Europe, though less populous, had mastered formidable new technologies of warfare.

domesticate horses, pigs, cows, goats, sheep, and oxen. In addition to protein-rich meat, cows and goats provided milk and dairy products such as cheese that could be stored for winter; horses and oxen dragged trees and boulders from fields, pulled ploughs through tough sod, and contributed manure for fertilizer. Because of the diversity and nutritional value of its food sources, the Eurasian population increased rapidly.

To accommodate the growing demand for food, Eurasian farmers cut down forests, filled in marshlands, and terraced hillsides. Monarchs joined with merchants and bankers to build port facilities, canals, and fleets of ships to ensure the food supply to urban centers.

Cereal crops and animals dispersed throughout the vast Eurasian landmass, but so did new diseases. New strains of viruses and bacteria appeared in cows, pigs, goats, and sheep and readily spread to the humans who kept them. Diseases also proliferated in cities, whose sanitation facilities were poor. Recurrent plagues swept across Eurasia. But those who survived acquired biological resistance.

West Africa evolved differently. The grassy savannah just south of the Sahara became the home for mostly herding peoples. Cities emerged in response to the growth of trans-Sahara trade: Finished goods, including cloth from North Africa, were traded for gold, salt, kola (a caffeine rich nut), and slaves. Warlords command-ing horse-mounted troops vied for the control of the trade routes, and eventually

This depicts a scene of a city on the Yellow River in northern China around 1500. Chinese cities were generally cleaner, with better water supplies and sewage disposal, than their European counterparts.

founded the great kingdoms of Mali and Songhay. By AD 1500, Timbuktu had become a major city, home to an important Islamic university and library.

Seldom did pastoral and trading empires penetrate far into the tropical regions farther south. The religion of Islam, which had spread through the grasslands south of the Sahara, also made less progress among Africans on the tropical coast. There the tsetse fly, carrier of sleeping sickness, decimated horse and cattle herds. Malaria, too, discouraged potential invaders.

The village was the main unit of social organization of sub-Saharan Africa. Some villages merged into far-flung kinship networks and even small kingdoms, such as Benin and Congo. Relatively insulated from the imperial struggles farther north, these Africans mostly kept to themselves, growing crops and harvesting the lush vegetation of the forest. By 1500, the lives of these people, too, were about to change.

By 1500 China, with a population of 100–150 million people, had literally walled itself away from "barbarians" elsewhere in Asia; its own kingdom was effectively ruled by a highly-educated class of bureaucrats steeped in the principles of Confucianism. The Islamic world was nearly as populous, but stretched across three continents, ranging from the North Africa and eastern Europe through Arabia, Persia, and northern India with outposts in Southeast Asia. Unlike China, it was divided into many different empires.

Europe in Ferment

Christendom, the predominant civilization of Europe, was less consequential; its total population—perhaps 70 million—was far less than China or the Islamic World; its main cities and institutions of learning were less well-developed. But in 1500, Europe was in dynamic ferment. During the 1400s, after a period of severe plagues, Europe's population had increased by nearly a third; by 1500, population pressure was acute.

When harvests were poor or grain shipments failed to arrive in towns, hunger riots destabilized the political order. Genoa, Italy, for example, was convulsed by fourteen revolutions from 1413 to 1453. Overpopulation was one reason why Jews, a vulnerable minority, were expelled from Spain and Portugal in 1492, and from Sicily in 1493.

Scarcity shook many peasants from the land and drove the urban poor from one city to another. Christoforo Colombo—or Columbus, as we call him—was among the restless youths who left home and took to the sea in search of a better life.

New ideas also unsettled European society. Movable type, which made the printing of books profitable, was perfected during the 1440s. By 1500, over 100 cities in Europe had at least one printing press and as many as 20 million volumes had been published. Books advanced new ideas and weakened the hold of traditional ones. Within a few decades, the treatises of Martin Luther and John Calvin initiated the Protestant Reformation. Books also excited the imagination and gave tangible expression to all manner of dreams and longings. (Columbus's restless curiosity had been stimulated by books on geography and navigation, especially Marco Polo's account of his journey to China.)

Incessant squabbles over land resulted in nearly constant warfare. The military arts advanced accordingly. Improvements in metallurgy made it possible to cast bronze and iron cannon capable of containing charges of gunpowder sufficient to hurl heavy balls great distances. Mighty stone fortresses that had stood for centuries were reduced to rubble by these cannon in a few hours. By the early 1500s cannons weighing a ton or more were mounted in sailing ships or upon carriages pulled by teams of horses. Warfare of this nature was expensive; constructing fleets, equipping armies, and building massive fortifications required the resources of entire nations.

A restless hunger for land, a population made resistant to biological pathogens, an explosion in communication and knowledge, a new technology and organization of warfare, and the emergence of powerful and contentious nation-states all imparted a fateful dynamism to late fifteenth-century European society. Plainly, these Europeans had not solved pressing social problems: Population growth exceeded available food sources, poverty undermined political stability, and war loomed larger and more ominous.

Equally plainly, the people of North America had failed to solve basic social problems: Nomadic Indians who practiced a hunting-gathering lifestyle were vulnerable to starvation as well as to encroachments by the more numerous peoples of the corn-farming tribes. Farming Indians, on the other hand, found it difficult to sustain even small urban communities over a long period. The absence of writing systems made it more difficult to undertake complex administrative tasks over large distances. None of the Indians possessed military technologies comparable to the Europeans. And, more fatal still, the peoples of the Americas lacked the immunity from infectious diseases that so many Europeans had acquired.

Separating these worlds was the impenetrable void of the Atlantic Ocean. Five hundred years earlier a Norseman, Leif Eriksson, had sailed along the coast of Greenland to the shores of Labrador, but little came of his expeditions. But toward the close of the fifteenth century, European sailors of a different type, adept at navigating through the open sea and willing to sail far from land, were about to venture across the expanses of the Atlantic. In so doing they would transform it into a bridge that would join these worlds, and the West African coast as well, bringing all three into fateful collision.

Milestones

c. 14,000 BP (perhaps earlier)	Humans from Asia cross Beringia to Alaska	**c. 3700 BP**	First sedentary North American community is founded at today's Poverty Point, Louisiana
c. 14,000– 10,000 BP	Humans diffuse throughout Americas		
	Many species of large mammals become extinct in Western Hemisphere	**c. 300 BP**	Corn cultivation begins in the Southwest
		c. AD 200	Corn cultivation begins in the lower Mississippi Valley
	Clovis era ends	**c. AD 900**	Corn cultivation begins in Wisconsin
	Eurasians domesticate wheat	**c. AD 1150**	Cahokia is at its peak
c. 6300 BP	Mesoamerican peoples cultivate corn and initiate Neolithic revolution	**c. 1200s– 1300s**	Protracted droughts in North America disrupt food supply; urban areas are abandoned
c. 4500 BP	Peoples of midwestern North America domesticate sunflowers and sumpweed		

✔•—[**Study** and **Review** at www.myhistorylab.com

Review Questions

1. How and when did the first peoples come to the Americas from Asia?
2. Why had most of the large mammals of the Americas become extinct by 8000 BP? Why *didn't* horses, cattle, camel, and other large mammals become extinct in Europe, Asia, and Africa?
3. Why does the onset of the Neolithic revolution—especially corn cultivation—result in the rapid increase of population in the Americas?

4. What explanations have been proposed to explain the pre-1500 collapse of the urban centers of the major Indian civilizations in what is now the United States?
5. In what ways did the major civilizations of the "Old World"—Europe, Asia, and Africa—differ from those of North America in AD 1500?

Key Terms

Neolithic
  revolution   *4*

Paleolithic
  revolution   *1*

1 Alien Encounters: Europe in the Americas

(•—⎡Hear the Audio Chapter 1 at myhistorylab.com

How do you rate your college's food?

SOME STUDENTS CHOOSE A COLLEGE FOR ITS FOOD, A REASON WHY the Princeton Review now publishes a "Best Campus Food" list. In 2008 Wheaton College topped the list after its food manager, who previously worked at the Ritz-Carlton in Boston, created menus with lavender-infused pork chops and cumin-lime chicken with avocado cream sauce. The next year Virginia Tech climbed over Wheaton, chiefly because of the freshness of its herbs and spices, grown by the school's horticulture department. In 2009 Sodexo, a food management company that tracks trends in student tastes, noted that college students craved spicy foods such as garlic-ginger chicken wings, Vietnamese pho (a peppery soup), green tea, pomegranate smoothies, crab cakes, and samosas. The lesson for college food services was simple: Make it spicy!

If students choose a college because of the tastiness of its fare, imagine how early modern Europeans (whose diet chiefly consisted of bread, porridge, boiled meats, and salted fish) reacted when they first tasted pepper, cinnamon, ginger, nutmeg, cloves, and other spicy foods from South Asia and the Pacific. Beyond titillating the palate, spices disguised the taste of spoiled meats in regions that had little ice. Europeans also prized such tropical foods as rice, figs, and oranges, as well as perfumes (often used as a substitute for soap), silk and cotton, rugs, textiles such as muslin and damask, dyestuffs, fine steel products, precious stones, and various drugs.

But the cost of transporting such goods from East Asia and the Pacific was exorbitant. The combined routes through central Asia were long and complicated—across strange seas, through deserts, over high mountain passes—with pirates or highwaymen as a constant threat. If the produce of eastern Asia could be carried to Europe by sea, the trip would be both cheaper and more comfortable. Christopher Columbus imagined that by sailing west, he would find an all-water route to the spicy riches of India and East Asia. By providing a cheap means of satisfying the European craving for spices, he would find a path to fame and fortune. He was half right.

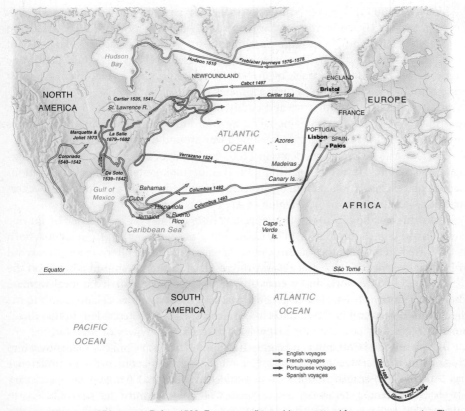

European Voyages of Discovery Before 1500, European sailors seldom ventured far across open water. They preferred to hug the coastline, like Vasco da Gama's journey around Africa in 1497–1499. Columbus's 1492 voyage across the Atlantic was extraordinarily daring. But his successful example inspired others to try alternative routes westward: Cabot, in 1497, sailed across the North Atlantic to Newfoundland; Verrazano, in 1524, sailed due west from the Azores to the Carolinas and the east coast of what is now the United States; Hudson, in 1610, took a far northern route, skirting the ice floes of the Arctic, and "discovered" Hudson Bay. Such men were the superstars of their age; and like superstars of all ages, they became free agents, selling their services to the highest bidder. Thus Columbus, an Italian, claimed Hispaniola for his employer, the Spanish monarchs; and Hudson, an Englishman, claimed the Hudson River for the Dutch East India Company.

Columbus's Great Triumph—and Error

Columbus was an intelligent and skillful mariner. Having read carefully Marco Polo's account of his adventures in the service of Kublai Khan, Columbus had decided that these rich lands could be reached by sailing directly west from Europe. The idea was not original, but while others merely talked about it, Columbus pursued it with dogged persistence.

For much of the fifteenth century, European sailors had been venturing far beyond familiar shores. The great figure in the transformation was Prince Henry the Navigator, third son of John I, king of Portugal. After distinguishing himself in 1415 in the capture of Ceuta, on the African side of the Strait of Gibraltar, he became interested

Watch the Video

So Why Did Columbus Sail Across the Atlantic Anyway? at **myhistorylab.com**

in navigation and exploration. Sailing a vessel out of sight of land was still, in Henry's day, more an art than a science and was extremely hazardous. Ships were small and clumsy. Primitive compasses and instruments for reckoning latitude existed, but under shipboard conditions they were very inaccurate. Navigators could determine longitude only by keeping track of direction and estimating speed; even the most skilled could place little faith in their estimates.

Henry attempted to improve and codify navigational knowledge. Searching for a new route to Asia, Henry's captains sailed westward to the Madeiras and the Canaries and south along the coast of Africa, seeking a way around that continent.

For 20 years after Henry's death in 1460, the Portuguese concentrated on exploiting his discoveries. In the 1480s King John II undertook systematic new explorations focused on reaching India. Gradually his caravels probed southward along the sweltering coast—to the equator, to the region of Angola, and beyond.

Into this bustling, prosperous, expectant little country in the corner of Europe came Christopher Columbus in 1476. Columbus was a weaver's son from Genoa, born in 1451. He had taken to the sea early, ranging widely in the Mediterranean. His arrival in Portugal was unplanned, since it was the result of losing his ship in a battle off the coast. For a time he worked as a chart maker in Lisbon. He married a local woman. Then he was again at sea. He cruised northward, perhaps as far as Iceland, south to the equator, and westward in the Atlantic to the Azores. Had his interest lain in that direction, he might well have been the first person to reach Asia by way of Africa.

But by this time Columbus had committed himself to reach China by sailing west into the Atlantic. How far west no one knew. Columbus believed that the earth's circumference was 18,000 miles. Because the known world stretched about 14,000 miles from the Canary Islands in the Atlantic Ocean eastward to Japan, Columbus assumed that he would have to sail west 4,000 miles across the Atlantic to reach Japan and the East Indies. A voyage of this length across open sea would be challenging but not impossible. There were doubters. Ancient Greek astronomers had estimated the earth's circumference at 24,000 miles. If they were right, a ship sailing from the Canary Islands westward across the Atlantic would have to travel 10,000 miles before reaching Asia, an impossibility because no ship of that time was large enough to carry sufficient provisions for such a voyage.

When King John II refused to finance him, Columbus turned to the Spanish court, where, after many disappointments, he persuaded Queen Isabella to equip his expedition. He also persuaded Isabella to grant him the title Admiral of the Ocean Sea, political control over all the lands he might discover, and 10 percent of the profits of the trade that would follow in the wake of his expedition. In August 1492 he set out from the port of Palos with his tiny fleet: the *Santa Maria*, the *Pinta*, and the *Niña*.

●◆●⌐Read the Document

The Journal of Christopher Columbus at myhistorylab.com

At about two o'clock on the morning of October 12, 1492, a sailor named Roderigo de Triana saw a gleam of white on the moonlit horizon and shouted *"Tierra! Tierra!"* The land he had spied was an island in the West Indies called Guanahani by its inhabitants, a place distinguished neither for beauty nor size. Nevertheless, when Columbus went ashore bearing the flag of Spain, he named it San Salvador, or Holy Savior. Columbus selected this imposing name for the island out of gratitude and wonder at having found it: He had sailed with three frail vessels for thirty-three days without sighting land. According to his estimates, he was nearly on course, having traveled nearly 4,000 miles. But he was nowhere near Japan or China.

The ancient Greek astronomers were right and Columbus was wrong. He had greatly underestimated the size of the earth.

Now the combination of zeal and tenacity that had gotten Columbus across the Atlantic cost him dearly. He refused to accept the plain evidence, which everywhere confronted him, that this was an entirely new world. The copper-colored people who paddled out to inspect his fleet could no more follow the Arabic widely understood in Asia than they could Spanish. Yet Columbus, consulting his charts, convinced himself that he had reached the Indies. That is why he called the natives Indians, a misnomer that became nearly universal, and was increasingly used even by the native peoples themselves.

Searching for treasure, Columbus pushed on to Cuba. When he heard the native word *Cubanocan,* meaning "middle of Cuba," he mistook it for *El Gran Can* (Marco Polo's "Grand Khan") and sent emissaries on a fruitless search through the tropical jungle for the khan's palace. He finally returned to Spain relatively empty-handed, but certain that he had explored the edge of Asia. Three later voyages failed to shake his conviction.

Spain's American Empire

Columbus died in 1506. By that time other captains had taken up the work, most of them more willing than he to accept what Europeans called the New World on its own terms. As early as 1493, Pope Alexander VI had divided the non-Christian world between Spain and Portugal. The next year, in the **Treaty of Tordesillas**, these powers negotiated an agreement about exploiting the new discoveries. In effect, Portugal continued to concentrate on Africa, leaving the New World, except for what eventually became Brazil, to the Spanish. Thereafter, from their base on Hispaniola (Santo Domingo), founded by Columbus, the Spaniards quickly fanned out through the Caribbean and then over large parts of the two continents that bordered it.

Watch the Video
Achievement of Columbus at
myhistorylab.com

In 1513 Vasco Nuñez de Balboa crossed the Isthmus of Panama and "discovered" the Pacific Ocean. In 1519 Hernán Cortés landed an army in Mexico and overran the empire of the Aztecs, rich in gold and silver. That same year Ferdinand Magellan set out on his epic three-year voyage around the world. By discovering the strait at the southern tip of South America that bears his name, he gave the Spanish a clear idea of the size of the continent. In the 1530s Francisco Pizarro subdued the Inca empire in Peru, providing the Spaniards with still more treasure, drawn chiefly from the silver mines of Potosí.

The *conquistadores* were brave and imaginative men. But they wrenched their empire from innocent hands; in an important sense, the settlement of the New World ranks among the most flagrant examples of unprovoked aggression in human history. When Columbus landed on San Salvador he planted a cross, "as a sign," he explained to Ferdinand and Isabella, "that your Highnesses held this land as your own." Of the Lucayans, the native inhabitants of San Salvador, Columbus wrote, "The people of this island . . . are

View the Image
Cabeza de Vaca, "Indians of the Rio Grande" at
myhistorylab.com

artless and generous with what they have, to such a degree as no one would believe. . . . If it be asked for, they never say no, but rather invite the person to accept it, and show as much lovingness as though they would give their hearts."

Columbus and his compatriots tricked and cheated the Indians at every turn. Before entering a new area, Spanish generals customarily read a *Requerimiento* (requirement) to the inhabitants. This long-winded document recited a Spanish version of the history of the human race from the Creation to the division of the non-Christian world by Pope Alexander VI, and then called on the Indians to recognize the sovereignty of the reigning Spanish monarch: "If you do so . . . we shall receive you in all love and charity." If this demand was rejected, the Spanish promised, "We shall powerfully enter into your country, and . . . shall take you, your wives, and your children, and shall make slaves of them. . . . The death and losses which shall accrue from this are your fault." This arrogant harangue was read in Spanish and often out of earshot of the Indians. When they responded by fighting, the Spaniards decimated them, drove them from their lands, and held the broken survivors in contempt.

●●●▶Read the Document

Conquistadores Torturing Native Amerindians at **myhistorylab.com**

From the outset of the Europeans' invasion of the New World, sensitive observers had been appalled by their barbarity. Bartolomé de Las Casas, a Dominican missionary who arrived in Hispaniola nearly a decade after Columbus, compiled a passionate and grisly indictment:

It was the general rule among Spaniards to be cruel; not just cruel, but extraordinarily cruel so that harsh and bitter treatment would prevent Indians from daring to think of themselves as human beings or having a minute to think at all. So they would cut an Indian's hands and leave them dangling by a shred of skin and they would send him on saying "Go now, spread the news to your chiefs." They would test their swords and their manly strength on captured Indians and place bets on the slicing off of heads or the cutting of bodies in half with one blow.

After stealing all the gold and silver they could find, the *conquistadores* sought alternatives sources of wealth. They soon learned that land was worthless without labor to cultivate crops or extract precious metals. They therefore imposed the **encomienda system**, a kind of feudalism granting the first Spanish colonists control of conquered lands and obliging the Indians to provide forced labor and a fixed portion of their harvests. Because the conquerors' income was proportionate to the number of villagers under their authority, *conquistadores* subjugated the heavily populated regions of Mexico—that is, those with the most extensive fields of maize. Cortés, for example, received payments from 23,000 families in the fertile Oaxaca valley; their labor made him the wealthiest man in Spain.

Much of the work of implanting Spanish civilization was undertaken by Catholic missionaries. Like the *conquistadores*, Spanish friars built their first missions in the largest Indian villages and towns. In an effort to "love their neighbor," as Christ enjoined, they sought to save as many Indian souls as possible. But when some Indians held tight to their own gods and beliefs, missionaries destroyed *kivas* and temples, banned Indian dances and games, and outlawed polygamy. When Indians resisted, the friars called on Spanish soldiers to arrest the rebels.

By the 1570s the Spanish had founded some 200 cities and towns, each with a central plaza that included a town hall and church and precisely rectilinear street plans. They had also set up printing presses and published pamphlets and books, and

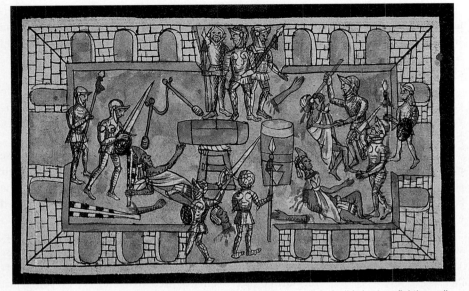

European soldiers, clad in armor and wielding iron weapons, were nearly invincible in close fighting—all the more so when their foes were unarmed, as in this drawing. Here Cortés and his men slash through Montezuma's Aztec court.

established universities in Mexico City and Lima. With the help of Indian artisans, they constructed and decorated lavishly a large number of impressive cathedrals.

Extending Spain's Empire to the North

By the early 1600s, Spanish explorers had reached Virginia, and in Florida a single Spanish military garrison remained at San Augustin—today's Saint Augustine. Years later the governor of Cuba, having failed to promote Spanish settlement of San Augustin, explained that "only hoodlums and the mischievous go there."

More consequential was the attempt to extend the Spanish empire beyond the Rio Grande into New Mexico. By the close of the sixteenth century, the Spaniards had learned that it was more profitable to acquire the crops and labor of Indian farmers than to search for rumored cities of gold. In 1598, the viceroy of New Spain charged Don Juan de Oñate with the task of conquering the Indians of New Mexico and founding a colony in their midst. Oñate led an expedition of 500 Spanish colorists and soldiers and a handful of Catholic missionaries across the Rio Grande into the territory of the Pueblo Indians, a farming people.

But the Pueblo were poor and their settlements meager; a Spanish soldier described New Mexico as "at the ends of the earth—remote beyond compare." When Oñate extorted maize, seized farmlands, and allowed cattle and pigs to plunder the fields, the Indians seethed. Eventually they ambushed and killed a Spanish patrol. Oñate retaliated by butchering 800 Pueblo, including women and children, and arresting another 500. The captured males over twenty-five years of age were sold into slavery; to prevent them from running away, one of each of their feet was chopped off. Oñate's brutality generated no profits; in 1614 he was dismissed.

Franciscan missionaries were given the task of Christianizing the Pueblo. The friars were, for the most part, dedicated men. They baptized thousands of mission Indians and instructed them in the rudiments of the Catholic faith. They also taught Indians to use European tools; to grow wheat and other European crops; and to raise chickens, pigs, and other barnyard animals.

The friars exacted a heavy price in labor from the people they presumed to enlighten and civilize. The Indians built and maintained the missions, tilled the surrounding fields, and served the every need of the friars and other Spanish colonists. For this they were paid little or nothing.

By the 1670s, after years of drought, the Pueblo became restive with these arrangements. They especially resented being coerced to take part in slave raids. Their shamans, too, increasingly called for a revival of the traditional religion. In 1675 the Spanish arrested forty-seven shamans; three were hanged and the remainder whipped as witches.

One of the latter, named Popé, secretly organized a rebellion. Without warning, some 17,000 Pueblo rose against the Spaniards, driving them out of towns and missions, destroying churches and killing priests, and plundering farms. The Spaniards fled to Santa Fe, escaping just before the Indians razed the town. The Pueblo drove the survivors all the way back to El Paso. Of the 1,000 Spanish in New Mexico, over 200 were killed.

•‡•⌐Read the **Document**

Legal Statement by Pedro
Hidalgo, soldier, Santa Fe
1680 at **myhistorylab.com**

In the mid-1690s the Spaniards regained control of most of the upper Rio Grande. Thereafter they maintained power with little difficulty. This was partly because they had learned to deal less harshly with the Pueblo people. The Spanish also recruited the nomadic Indians of the region to capture more distant Indians and sell them to the Spaniards as slaves.

By the early 1700s Spain had become master of a huge American empire covering all of South America except Brazil, and also all of Central America as well as a region extending from California east to Florida. New Spain was ten times larger than Spain itself. The Spanish monarch ruled three times more Indian subjects than Spaniards.

But while Spain had founded a vast empire, one major and literally fatal problem remained: The Indian population was declining rapidly, and had done so from the start. Almost as soon as Europeans set foot on American soil, Indians began to die.

Disease and Population Losses

Of all the weapons the Europeans brought to the Americas, the most potent was one they could not see and of which they were mostly unaware: microorganisms that carried diseases such as smallpox, measles, bubonic plague, diphtheria, influenza, malaria, yellow fever, and typhoid. For centuries, these diseases had ravaged Asia, Europe, and Africa. By the 1500s Eurasian and African populations had acquired some resistance to such diseases. An outbreak of smallpox or diphtheria might take a severe toll on infants and the elderly, but no longer would it decimate entire populations.

But American Indians had evolved over hundreds of generations without contact with these diseases. They lacked the requisite biological defenses. When these diseases first struck, many Indian villages were nearly wiped out. In 1585, for example, Sir Francis Drake, preparing for a raid against the Spanish, stopped at the Cape Verde

Islands. While there some of his men contracted a fever—probably typhus—but sailed for Florida undaunted by their discomfort. When they landed at St. Augustine, the disease spread to the Indians who, according to Drake, "died verie fast and said amongst themselves, it was the Englisshe God that made them die so faste."

Indian losses from diseases were incalculable, although the lowest estimates begin in the millions. Scholars agree on only one fact concerning the population history of the North American Indians following the arrival of Columbus: The number of Indians declined precipitously.

⊙ See the **Map**

Native American Population Loss, 1500–1700 at **myhistory lab.com**

Ecological Imperialism

Another reason why so many Indians succumbed to disease was that they suffered from malnutrition. This was because European plants and animals had disrupted the Indian ecosystem. Pigs and cattle, brought in the first Spanish ships, were commonly set loose in the Americas. Unchallenged by the predators and microbes that had thinned their populations in Europe and Asia, pigs reproduced rapidly and ate their way through fields of maize, beans, and squash. Rats, stowaways on most European ships, also proliferated in the Americas, infesting Indian crops. Europeans also brought plants to the New World, and in the process unknowingly introduced the seeds of hardy European weeds. Like the kudzu vines from Japan that have overrun much of the southeastern United States during the twentieth century, dandelions and other weeds from Europe choked Indian crops in the sixteenth century.

The ships that brought Europeans to the Americas

Horses (blindfolded) were loaded onto Spanish warships for shipment to the Americas. Native peoples had never seen horses (which had been extinct in the Americas for over 10,000 years). Nor had they seen enormous wooden warships, powered by sails and carrying heavy cannons, or warriors, seated on horses and encased in armor.

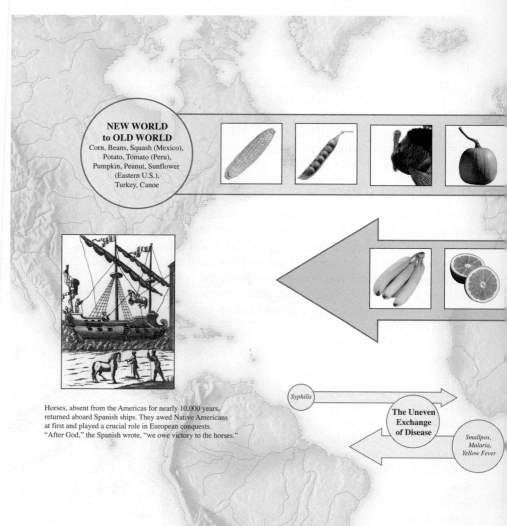

NEW WORLD to OLD WORLD
Corn, Beans, Squash (Mexico), Potato, Tomato (Peru), Pumpkin, Peanut, Sunflower (Eastern U.S.), Turkey, Canoe

Horses, absent from the Americas for nearly 10,000 years, returned aboard Spanish ships. They awed Native Americans at first and played a crucial role in European conquests. "After God," the Spanish wrote, "we owe victory to the horses."

Syphilis

The Uneven Exchange of Disease

Smallpox, Malaria, Yellow Fever

Columbian Exchange   The Western Hemisphere—the Americas—has for many thousands of years been separated from the rest of the world by two great oceans. This has meant that its plants, animals, and even bacteria and viruses evolved differently. Columbus's voyage thus inaugurated an exchange, as plants and animals native to the Americas (such as corn and turkeys) were transmitted to the "Old World," and those from Europe, Africa, or Asia (bananas and horses) found their way to the Americas. The intersection of two worlds also resulted in an exchange of technologies and diseases.

returned carrying more than gold and silver. European ships also brought back maize and potato plants. These American crops yielded 50 percent more calories per acre than wheat, barley, and oats, the major European grains. Hungry European peasants swiftly shifted to maize and potato cultivation; the population of Europe rose sharply. Manioc (cassava), another Indian plant with a high caloric yield, did not grow in the colder climate of Europe, but it transformed tropical Africa. Population levels soared. As declining Indian populations proved insufficient to exploit the seemingly inexhaustible lands

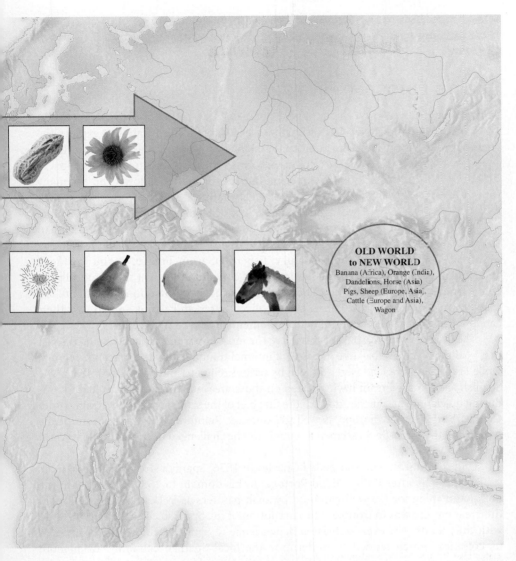

OLD WORLD
to NEW WORLD
Banana (Africa), Orange (India),
Dandelions, Horse (Asia)
Pigs, Sheep (Europe, Asia),
Cattle (Europe and Asia),
Wagon

of the Western Hemisphere, European conquerors imported African slaves to do more of the work.

Indians nevertheless benefited from some aspects of the ecological transformation of the Western Hemisphere. Horses were among the many big mammals that became extinct in the Americas over 10,000 years ago. When Spanish *conquistadors* brought horses back to the Americas, the Indians were terrified by the strange beasts. The horses, however, thrived in the vast grasslands of North America. Plains Indians used horses to hunt buffalo and harass Europeans. Farming Indians such as the Navajo profited from sheep cultivation by learning to weave fine woolen cloth.

The **Columbian Exchange** of plants and animals went both ways, yet it remained unequal. American Indians usually fared far worse than Europeans. The best indicator is the shift in population: During the 300 years after Columbus, Europe's share of the world's population nearly doubled, increasing from about 11 percent to 20 percent. During the same period, the American Indian's share declined from about 7 percent to 1 percent.

Spain's European Rivals

At first, Spain's rivals did little to oppose Spanish colonization of the New World. In 1497 and 1498 King Henry VII of England sent Captain John Cabot to explore the New World. Cabot visited Newfoundland and the northeastern coast of the continent.

•◆•─Read the Document

Letters of Patent Granted to John Cabot at
myhistorylab.com

His explorations formed the basis for later British claims in North America, but they were not followed up for many decades. In 1524 Giovanni da Verrazano made a similar voyage for France, coasting the continent from Carolina to Nova Scotia. Some ten years later the Frenchman Jacques Cartier explored the St. Lawrence River as far inland as present-day Montréal. During the sixteenth century, fishermen from France, Spain, Portugal, and England exploited the limitless supplies of cod and other fish they found in the cold waters off Newfoundland. They landed at many points along the mainland coast from Nova Scotia to Labrador to collect water and wood and to dry their catches, but they made no permanent settlements until the next century.

There were many reasons for this delay, the most important probably being the fact that Spain had achieved a large measure of internal tranquility by the sixteenth century, while France and England were still torn by serious religious and political conflicts. The Spanish also profited from having seized on those areas in America best suited to producing quick returns. Furthermore, in the first half of the sixteenth century, Spain, under Charles V, dominated Europe as well as America. Reinforced by the treasure of the Aztecs and the Incas, Spain seemed too mighty to be challenged in either the New World or the Old World.

Under Philip II, who succeeded Charles in 1556, Spanish strength seemed at its peak, especially after Philip added Portugal to his domain in 1580. But beneath the pomp and splendor (so well-captured by such painters as Velázquez and El Greco) the great empire was in trouble. The corruption of the Spanish court had much to do with this. So did the ever-increasing dependence of Spain on the gold and silver of its colonies, which tended to undermine the local Spanish economy. Even more important was the disruption of the Catholic Church throughout Europe by the Protestant Reformation.

The Protestant Reformation

Many factors contributed to the **Protestant Reformation**. The spiritual lethargy and bureaucratic corruption besetting the Roman Catholic Church in the early sixteenth century made it a fit target for reform. The thriving business in the sale of indulgences, payments to the church to help release dead relatives from purgatory, was a public scandal; while the luxurious lifestyle of the popes and the papal court in Rome was another. Yet countless earlier religious reform movements had generated little or no change. The fact that the movement launched by Martin Luther in 1517 and carried forward by men like John Calvin addressed genuine shortcomings in the Roman Catholic Church does not entirely explain why it led so directly to the rupture of Christendom.

The charismatic leadership of Luther and the compelling brilliance of Calvin made their protests more effective than earlier efforts at reform. Probably more important, so did the political possibilities let loose by their challenge to Rome's spiritual authority. German princes seized on Luther's campaign against the sale of indulgences to stop all payments to Rome and to confiscate church property within their domains. Swiss cities like Geneva, where Calvin took up residence in 1536, and Zurich joined the Protestant revolt for spiritual reasons, but also to establish their political independence from Catholic kings.

The decision of Henry VIII of England in 1534 to break with Rome was at bottom a political one. The refusal of Pope Clement VII to agree to an annulment of Henry's marriage of twenty years to Catherine of Aragon, the daughter of Ferdinand and Isabella, provided the occasion. Catherine had given birth to six children, but only a daughter, Mary, survived childhood; Henry was without a male heir. By repudiating the pope's spiritual authority and declaring himself head of the English (Anglican) church, Henry freed himself to divorce Catherine and to marry whomever—and however often—he saw fit. By the time of his death, five wives and thirteen years later, England had become a Protestant nation. More important for our story, the English colonies in America were mostly Protestant.

As the commercial classes rose to positions of influence, England, France, and the United Provinces of the Netherlands experienced a flowering of trade and industry. The Dutch built the largest merchant fleet in the world. Dutch traders captured most of the Far Eastern business once monopolized by the Portuguese, and they infiltrated Spain's Caribbean stronghold. A number of English merchant companies, soon to play a vital role as colonizers, sprang up in the last half of the sixteenth century. These **joint-stock companies**, ancestors of the modern corporation, enabled groups of investors to pool their capital and limit their individual responsibilities to the sums actually invested—a very important protection in such risky enterprises. The Muscovy Company, the Levant Company, and the East India Company were the most important of these ventures.

English Beginnings in America

English merchants took part in many kinds of international activity. The Muscovy Company spent large sums searching for a passage to China around Scandinavia and dispatched six overland expeditions in an effort to reach East Asia by way of Russia and Persia. In the 1570s Martin Frobisher made three voyages across the Atlantic, hoping to discover a northwest passage to East Asia or new gold-bearing lands.

Such projects, particularly in the area of North America, received strong but concealed support from the Crown. Queen Elizabeth I (1558–1603) invested heavily in Frobisher's expeditions. England was still too weak to challenge Spain openly, but Elizabeth hoped to break the Spanish overseas monopoly just the same. When Captain Francis Drake was about to set sail on his fabulous round-the-world voyage in 1577, the queen said to him, "Drake . . . I would gladly be revenged on the King of

Spain for divers injuries that I have received." Drake took her at her word. He sailed through the Strait of Magellan and terrorized the west coast of South America. After exploring the coast of California, which he claimed for England, Drake crossed the Pacific and went on to circumnavigate the globe, returning home in triumph in 1580. Although Elizabeth took pains to deny it to the Spanish ambassador, Drake's voyage was officially sponsored.

When schemes to place settlers in the New World began to mature at about this time, the queen again became involved. The first English effort was led by Sir Humphrey Gilbert, an Oxford-educated soldier and courtier. Elizabeth authorized him to explore and colonize "heathen lands not actually possessed by any Christian prince."

We know almost nothing about Gilbert's first attempt except that it occurred in 1578 and 1579; in 1583 he set sail again with five ships and over 200 settlers. He landed them on Newfoundland, then evidently decided to seek a more congenial site farther south. However, no colony was established, and on his way back to England his ship went down in a storm off the Azores.

Gilbert's half brother, Sir Walter Raleigh, took up the work. Handsome, ambitious, and impulsive, Raleigh was a great favorite of Elizabeth. He sent a number of expeditions to explore the east coast of North America, a land he named Virginia in honor of his unmarried sovereign. In 1585 he settled about a hundred men on Roanoke Island, off the North Carolina coast, but these settlers returned home the next year. In 1587 Raleigh sent another group to Roanoke, including a number of women and children. Unfortunately, the supply ships sent to the colony in 1588 failed to arrive; when help did get there in 1590, not a soul could be found. The fate of the settlers has never been determined.

One reason for the delay in getting aid to the Roanoke colonists was the attack of the Spanish Armada on England in 1588. Angered by English raids on his shipping and by the assistance Elizabeth was giving to the rebels in the Netherlands, King Philip II decided to invade England. His motives were religious as well as political and economic, for England now seemed committed to Protestantism. His great fleet of some 130 ships bore huge crosses on the sails as if on another crusade. The Armada carried 30,000 men and 2,400 guns, the largest naval force ever assembled up to that time. However, the English fleet of 197 ships shattered this armada, and a series of storms completed its destruction. Thereafter, although the war continued and Spanish sea power remained formidable, Spain could no longer block English penetration of the New World.

Experience had shown that the cost of planting settlements in a wilderness 3,000 miles from England was more than any individual purse could bear. (Raleigh lost about £40,000 in his overseas ventures; early in the game he began to advocate government support of colonization.) As early as 1584 Richard Hakluyt, England's foremost authority on the Americas and a talented propagandist for colonization, made a convincing case for royal aid. In his *Discourse on Western Planting*, Hakluyt stressed the military advantages of building "two or three strong fortes" along the Atlantic coast of North America. Ships operating from such bases would make life uncomfortable for "King Phillipe" by intercepting his treasure fleets—a matter, Hakluyt added coolly, "that toucheth him indeede to the quicke." Colonies in America would also spread the Protestant religion and enrich the parent country by expanding the market for English woolens, bringing in valuable tax revenues, and

Queen Elizabeth's right hand rests comfortably upon the globe, while in the distance the British navy destroys the Spanish Armada. This 1588 painting said it all: Elizabeth ruled the world. Such presumption helped build an empire—and eventually lose it.

Source: George Gower (1540–96), *Elizabeth I, Armada Portrait*, c.1588 (oil on panel), Gower, George (1540–96) (attr. to), Woburn Abbey, Bedfordshire, UK/The Bridgeman Art Library.

providing employment for the swarms of "lustie youthes that be turned to no provitable use" at home. From the great American forests would come the timber and naval stores needed to build a bigger navy and merchant marine.

Queen Elizabeth read Hakluyt's essay, but she was too cautious to act on his suggestions. Only after her death in 1603 did full-scale efforts to found English colonies in America begin, and even then the organizing force came from merchant capitalists, not from the Crown.

The Settlement of Virginia

In September 1605 two groups of English merchants petitioned the new king, James I, for a license to colonize Virginia, as the whole area claimed by England was then named. This was granted the following April, and two joint-stock companies were organized: one controlled by London merchants, the other by a group from the area around Plymouth and Bristol.[1] Both were under the control of a royal council for Virginia, but James appointed prominent stockholders to the council, which meant that the companies had considerable independence.

This first charter revealed the commercial motivation of both king and company in the plainest terms. Although it spoke of spreading Christianity and bringing "the Infidels and Savages, living in those Parts, to human Civility," it stressed the right "to dig, mine, and search for all Manner of Mines of Gold, Silver, and Copper." On December 20, 1606, the London Company dispatched about 100 settlers aboard the *Susan Constant*, *Discovery*, and *Godspeed*. This little band reached the Chesapeake Bay area in May 1607 and founded Jamestown, the first permanent English colony in the New World.

From the start everything went wrong. The immigrants established themselves in what was a mosquito-infested swamp simply because it appeared easily defensible against Indian attack. They failed to get a crop in the ground because of the lateness of the season and were soon almost without food. The settlers lacked the skills of pioneers. More than a third of them were "gentlemen" unused to manual labor, and

---

[1]The London Company was to colonize southern Virginia, while the Plymouth Company (the Plymouth–Bristol group of merchants) was granted northern Virginia.

many of the rest were the gentlemen's servants, almost equally unequipped for the task of colony building. During the first winter more than half of the settlers died.

The situation demanded people skilled in agriculture. But all the land belonged to the company, and aside from the gentlemen and their retainers, most of the settlers were only hired laborers who had contracted to work for it for seven years. They had little stake in establishing permanent farms. The merchant directors of the London Company, knowing little or nothing about Virginia, made matters worse. Instead of stressing farming and public improvements, they directed the energies of the colonists into such futile labors as searching for gold, glassblowing, silk raising, winemaking, and exploring the local rivers in hopes of finding a water route to the Pacific. Although the directors set up a council of settlers, they kept all real power in their own hands.

One colonist, Captain John Smith, tried to stop some of this foolishness. Smith had come to Virginia after a fantastic career as a soldier of fortune in eastern Europe, where he had fought many battles, been enslaved by a Turkish pasha, and triumphed in a variety of adventures (military and amorous). He quickly realized that building houses and raising food were essential to survival, and he soon became an expert forager and Indian trader. Smith was as eager as any seventeenth-century European to take advantage of the Indians, and he had few compunctions about the methods employed in doing so. But he recognized both the limits of the colonists' power and the vast differences between Indian customs and values and his own. It was necessary, he insisted, to dominate the "proud Savages" yet to avoid bloodshed.

●●●▢**Read the Document**

John Smith, *The Starving Time*
at **myhistorylab.com**

Smith pleaded with company officials in London to send over more people accustomed to working with their hands, such as farmers, fishermen, carpenters, masons, "diggers up of trees," and fewer gentlemen and "Tuftaffety humorists."[2] His request was for "a plaine soldier who can use a pickaxe and a spade is better than five knights."

Lacking intelligent leaders and faced with appalling hardships, the Jamestown colonists failed to develop a sufficient sense of common purpose. Each year they died in wholesale lots from disease, starvation (there were even some cases of cannibalism among the desperate survivors), Indian attack, and, above all, ignorance and folly.

What saved the colonists was the gradual realization that they must produce their own food—cattle raising was especially important—and the cultivation of tobacco, which flourished there and could be sold profitably in England. Once the settlers discovered tobacco, no amount of company pressure could keep them at wasteful tasks like looking for gold. The "restraint of plantinge Tobacco," one company official commented, "is a thinge so distastefull to them that they will with no patience indure to heare of it."

John Rolfe introduced West Indian tobacco—much milder than the local "weed" and thus more valuable—in 1612. With money earned from the sale of tobacco, the colonists could buy the manufactured articles they could not produce in a raw new country; this freed them from dependence on outside subsidies. It did not mean profit for the London Company, however, for by the time tobacco caught on, the surviving original colonists had served their seven years and were no longer hired hands. To attract more settlers, the company had permitted first tenancy and then outright ownership of farms. Thus the profits of tobacco went largely to the planters, not to the "adventurers" who had organized the colony.

---

[2]Smith was referring to the gold tassels worn by titled students at Oxford and Cambridge at that time.

This 1616 portrait depicts Pocahontas, daughter of Powhatan, the foremost chief of coastal Virginia. The colonists, in a dispute with Powhatan, took her hostage in 1613 and kept her in Jamestown. The next year she converted to Anglicanism, took the name "Lady Rebecca," and married John Rolfe, an alliance that helped defuse tensions between colonists and Indians. In 1616 the couple came to England with their infant son, where "Lady Rebecca" was received by King James I. She became celebrated as the "belle sauvage." She was the most prominent exemplar of those "intermediaries" who readily crossed the porous boundaries between colonist and Indian cultures.

Ætatis suæ 21. A°. 1616.

The colonists erred grievously in mistreating the Powhatan Indians. It is quite likely that the settlement would not have survived if the Powhatan Indians had not given the colonists food in the first hard winters, taught them the ways of the forest, introduced them to valuable new crops such as corn and yams, and showed them how to clear dense timber by girdling the trees and burning them down after they were dead. The settlers accepted Indian aid, then took whatever else they wanted by force. English barbarities rivaled those of the Spaniards.

In 1610, for example, George Percy (an English officer), when ordered to punish a Powhatan chief for insolence, proudly described how his men marched into an Indian town, seized some of the natives, "putt some fiftene or sixtene to the Sworde" and cut off their heads. Then he ordered his men to burn the houses and crops. When the expedition returned to its boats, his men complained that Percy had spared an Indian "quene and her Children." Percy relented, and threw the children overboard "shoteinge owtt their Braynes in the water." His men insisted that he burn the queen alive, but Percy, less cruel, stabbed her to death.

The Indians did not submit meekly to such treatment. They proved brave, skillful, and ferocious fighters once they understood that their very existence was at stake. When Powhatan Chief Openchancanough concluded that the English lust for land was inexhaustible, he made plans to wipe them out. To put the Virginians at ease, he sent presents of food to Jamestown. The next day his warriors attacked, killing 347 colonists. Most of the survivors fled to the fort. They remained there for months, neglecting the crops. When winter struck, hundreds more died of hunger.

Between 1606 and 1622 the London Company invested more than £160,000 in Virginia and sent over about 6,000 settlers. Yet no dividends were ever earned, and of this group, fewer than 1,500 were still alive in 1624.

That year King James revoked the company's charter. Now a royal colony, Virginia was subject to direct control by the royal bureaucracy in London.

The story of the first thirty years of pilgrim life in Plymouth, Massachusetts, is preserved in Governor William Bradford's *Of Plymouth Plantation*. A glimpse of the first colony is shown in this reconstruction.

readily because so many had died of smallpox, likely brought by settlers. And the Pilgrims, after hearing of the Powhatan attack on Jamestown in 1622, ambushed a band of Massachusetts Indians, killing seven, and put the leader's head atop a post at the Plymouth fort.

Yet by 1650 there were still fewer than 1,000 settlers, most of them living beyond the reach of the original church.

Winthrop and Massachusetts Bay Colony

The Pilgrims were not the first English colonists to inhabit the northern regions. The Plymouth Company had settled a group on the Kennebec River in 1607. These colonists gave up after a few months, but fishermen and traders continued to visit the area, which was christened New England by Captain John Smith after an expedition there in 1614.

In 1620 the Plymouth Company was reorganized as the Council for New England, which had among its principal stockholders Sir Ferdinando Gorges and his friend John Mason, former governor of an English settlement on Newfoundland. Their particular domain included a considerable part of what is now Maine and New Hampshire. More interested in real estate deals than in colonizing, the council disposed of a number of tracts in the area north of Cape Cod. The most significant of these grants was a small one made to a group of puritans from Dorchester, who established a settlement at Salem in 1629.

Later that year these Dorchester puritans organized the Massachusetts Bay Company and obtained a royal grant to the area between the Charles and Merrimack rivers. The

Massachusetts Bay Company was organized like any other commercial venture, but the puritans, acting with single-minded determination, made it a way of obtaining religious refuge in America.

Unlike the Separatists in Plymouth, most puritans had managed to satisfy both Crown and conscience while James I was king. The England of his son Charles I, who succeeded to the throne in 1625, posed a more serious challenge. Whereas James had been content to keep puritans at bay, Charles and his favorite Anglican cleric, William Laud, intended to bring them to heel. With the king's support, Laud proceeded to embellish the already elaborate Anglican ritual and to tighten the central control that the puritans found so distasteful. He removed ministers with puritan leanings from their pulpits and threatened church elders who harbored such ministers with imprisonment.

No longer able to remain within the Anglican fold in good conscience and now facing prison if they tried to worship in the way they believed right, many puritans decided to migrate to America. In the summer of 1630 nearly a thousand of them set out from England, carrying the charter of the Massachusetts Bay Company with them. By fall, they had founded Boston and several other towns.

The early settlements struggled. The tasks of founding a new society in a strange land were more difficult than anyone had anticipated. Of the 1,000 English settlers who arrived in Massachusetts in the summer of 1630, 200 died during their first New England winter. Governor Winthrop himself lost eleven family servants. When ships arrived the following spring, they returned to England nearly filled with immigrants who had given up.

But they were replaced many times over. Continuing bad times in England and the persecution of puritans there led to the Great Migration of the 1630s. Within a decade, over 10,000 puritans had arrived in Massachusetts. This infusion of industrious, well-educated, and often prosperous colonists swiftly created a complex and distinct culture on the edge of what one of the pessimists among them called "a hideous and desolate wilderness, full of wild beasts and wild men."

The directors of the Massachusetts Bay Company believed their enterprise to be divinely inspired. Before leaving England, they elected John Winthrop, a twenty-nine-year-old Oxford-trained attorney, as governor of the colony. Throughout his twenty years of almost continuous service as governor, Winthrop spoke for the solid and sensible core of the puritans and their high-minded experiment. His lay sermon, "A Modelle of Christian Charity," delivered mid-Atlantic on the deck of the *Arbella* in 1630, made clear his sense of the momentousness of that experiment:

●●●─ Read the **Document**

Winthrop, *A Model of Christian Charity* at **myhistorylab.com**

Wee must Consider that wee shall be as a Citty upon a Hill, the eies of all people are upon us; soe that if wee shall deale falsely with our god in this worke wee have undertaken and soe cause him to withdrawe his present help from us, wee shall be made a story and a by-word through the world, wee shall open the mouthes of enemies to speake evill of the wayes of god and all professours for Gods sake.

The colonists created an elected legislature, the General Court. Their system was not democratic in the modern sense because the right to vote and hold office was limited to male church members, but this did not mean that the government was run by the Fundamental Orders, a sort of constitution creating a government for the valley towns, in 1639. The Fundamental Orders resembled the Massachusetts system, except that they did not limit voting to church members. Other groups of puritans came directly from England to settle towns in and around New Haven in the 1630s. These were incorporated into Connecticut shortly after the Hooker colony obtained a royal charter in 1662.

Pequot War and King Philip's War

New England colonists repeatedly exploited disunity among Indians, who identified more with their hunting group, headed by a sachem, than with a particular tribe. Savvy English settlers could often turn one group against another. In both of the major Indian uprisings in New England during the seventeenth century, the colonists prevailed in part because they were assisted by Indian allies.

In the 1630s the Pequot Indians grew alarmed at the steady stream of English settlers to southeastern Connecticut. After several clashes in 1636, the colonists demanded that the Pequots surrender tribe members responsible for the attacks and pay tribute in wampum. When the Pequots refused, the governments of Massachusetts, Connecticut, and Plymouth declared war. In 1637 the New England armies, bolstered by warriors of the Narragansett and Mohegan tribes, traditional foes of the Pequots, attacked a Pequot village enclosed by a wooden palisade. When Pequots attempted to flee, the English set fire to the village, trapping the Indians and killing nearly all 400 inhabitants.

The Narragansett and Mohegan Indians were aghast. They had intended to replace their own deceased relatives by adopting captured foes, especially women and children. The English way of fighting, they complained, was "too furious and slays too many people." Bradford, too, commented on the "fearful sight" of the trapped Pequots "thus frying in the fire," but he remembered to praise God for "so speedy a victory." The Pequots were crushed.

In the 1670s Metacom, a Wampanoag sachem, concluded that the only way to resist the English incursion was to drive them out by force of arms. By then, many Wampanoags had acquired flintlock muskets and learned to use them; warfare had become far more lethal. In 1675, after Plymouth colony had convicted and executed three Wampanoags, Metacom ignited an uprising that ravaged much of New England. Scores of sachems led attacks on more than half of the ninety puritan towns in New England, destroying twelve. About 1,000 puritans were massacred; many more abandoned their farms.

The next year the colonists went on the offensive, bolstered by Mohawk allies. The New England militias destroyed Wampanoag villages and exhausted the Wampanoag's gunpowder. The Mohawks ambushed and killed Metacom, presenting his severed head to puritan authorities in Boston. The Wampanoag retreated into the Great Swamp in Rhode Island and built a large fort. The colonists surrounded and burned the fort, massacred 300 Indians, and destroyed the winter stores. In all, about 4,000 Wampanoags and their allies died in what was called "King Philip's" war—King Philip being the colonist's derisive name for Metacom.

Maryland and the Carolinas

The Virginia and New England colonies were essentially corporate ventures. Most of the other English colonies in America were founded by individuals or by a handful of partners who obtained charters from the ruling sovereign. It was becoming easier to establish settlements in America, for experience had taught the English a great deal about the colonization process. Settlers knew better what to bring with them and what to do after they arrived.

Many influential Englishmen were eager to try their luck as colonizers. The grants they received made them "proprietors" of great estates, which were, at least in theory, their personal property. By granting land to settlers in return for a small annual rent, they hoped to obtain a steadily increasing income while holding a valuable speculative interest in all undeveloped land. At the same time, their political power, guaranteed by charter, would become increasingly important as their colonies expanded. In practice, however, the realities of life in America limited their freedom of action and their profits.

One of the first proprietary colonies was Maryland, granted by Charles I to George Calvert, Lord Baltimore. Calvert had a deep interest in America, being a member both of the London Company and of the Council for New England. He hoped to profit financially from Maryland, but, since he was a Catholic, he also intended the colony to be a haven for his co-religionists.

Calvert died shortly before Charles approved his charter, so the grant went to his son Cecilius. The first settlers arrived in 1634, founding St. Mary's, just north of the Potomac. The presence of the now well-established Virginia colony nearby greatly aided the Marylanders; they had little difficulty in getting started and in developing an economy based, like Virginia's, on tobacco. According to the Maryland charter, Lord Baltimore had the right to establish feudal manors, hold people in serfdom, make laws, and set up his own courts. He soon discovered, however, that to attract settlers he had to allow them to own their farms, and that to maintain any political influence at all he had to give the settlers considerable say in local affairs. Other wise concessions marked his handling of the religious question. He would have preferred an exclusively Catholic colony, but while Catholics did go to Maryland, Protestants greatly outnumbered them. Baltimore dealt with this problem by agreeing to a Toleration Act (1649) that guaranteed freedom of religion to anyone "professing to believe in Jesus Christ." Though religious disputes persisted, Calvert's compromise enabled them to make a fortune and maintain an influence in Maryland until the Revolution.

The Carolina charter, like that of Maryland, accorded the proprietors wide authority. With the help of the political philosopher John Locke, they drafted a grandiose plan of government called the Fundamental Constitutions, which created a hereditary nobility and provided for huge paper land grants to a hierarchy headed by the proprietors and lesser "landgraves" and "caciques." The human effort to support the feudal society was to be supplied by peasants.

This complicated system proved unworkable. The landgraves and caciques got grants, but they could not find peasants willing to toil on their domains. Probably the purpose of all this elaborate feudal nonsense was promotional: the proprietor hoped to convince investors that they could make fortunes in Carolina rivaling those of English lords. Life followed a more mundane pattern similar to what was going on in Virginia and Maryland, with property relatively easy to obtain.

The first settlers arrived in 1670, most of them from the sugar plantations of Barbados, where slave labor was driving out small independent farmers. Charles Town (now Charleston) was founded in 1680. Another center of population sprang up in the Albemarle district, just south of Virginia, settled largely by individuals from that colony. Two quite different societies grew up in these areas. The Charleston colony, with an economy based on a thriving trade in furs and on the export of foodstuffs to the West Indies, was prosperous and cosmopolitan. The Albemarle settlement, where the soil was less fertile, was poorer and more primitive. Eventually, in 1712, the two were formally separated, becoming North and South Carolina.

French and Dutch Settlements

While the English were settling Virginia and New England, other Europeans were challenging Spain's monopoly elsewhere in the New World. Jacques Cartier attempted to found a French colony at Québec in the 1530s. Spain, initially alarmed by the French incursion, considered intervening; but the Spanish emperor thought the northern region too cold and not worth the bother. Cartier soon concurred, as his settlement quickly succumbed to brutal winters, scurvy, and Indian attacks.

Not until the end of the century was another attempt made to colonize the region. Then some intrepid French traders traded with Indians for fur, which had become valuable in Europe.

Unlike the English, who occupied the Indian's land, or the Spanish, who subjugated Indians and exploited their labor, French traders viewed the Indians as essential trading partners. A handful of French traders, carrying their goods in canoes and small boats, made their way to Indian settlements along the St. Lawrence River and the shores of Lake Ontario and Lake Erie. But by 1650, there were only 700 French colonists in New France.

By then, France had perceived both the economic and military potential of North America and the vulnerability of France's thinly populated string of settlements. To protect its toehold in North America, the French government built forts on key northern waterways and sent soldiers to protect the traders. French military expenditures helped sustain the fledgling colony. By 1700, about 15,000 French colonists lived in scattered settlements along an arc ranging from the mouth of the St. Lawrence in the northeast, through the Great Lakes, and down the Mississippi to the Gulf of Mexico.

By contrast, nearly a quarter of a million English settlers (and 34,000 Africans, most brought as slaves) had occupied the English colonies. As the English filled up the Atlantic seaboard and pushed steadily westward, the French recruited the Algonquian Indians as military allies. The Algonquians were linguistically similar tribes who had been driven from the Atlantic seaboard into territory occupied by the Iroquois, a confederation of powerful tribes. English settlers commonly entered into treaties with the Iroquois.

Warfare ensued, usually French–Algonquian against English–Iroquois. But now that the Indians had guns and ammunition, warfare became bloodier, and all frontier settlements—Indian and colonist alike—became more vulnerable.

Complicating matters further was the Dutch settlement of New Netherland in the Hudson Valley. The settlers based their claim to the region on the explorations of Henry

Hudson in 1609. As early as 1624 they established an outpost, Fort Orange, on the site of present-day Albany. Two years later they founded New Amsterdam at the mouth of the Hudson River, and Peter Minuit, the director general of the West India Company, purchased Manhattan Island from the Indians for trading goods worth about sixty guilders.

The Dutch traded with the Indians for furs and plundered Spanish colonial commerce enthusiastically. Through the Charter of Privileges of Patroons, which authorized large grants of land to individuals who would bring over fifty settlers, they tried to encourage large-scale agriculture. Only one such estate—Rensselaerswyck, on the Hudson south of Fort Orange, owned by the rich Amsterdam merchant Kiliaen Van Rensselaer—was successful. Peter Minuit was removed from his post in New Amsterdam in 1631, but he organized a group of Swedish settlers several years later and founded the colony of New Sweden on the lower reaches of the Delaware River. New Sweden was in constant conflict with the Dutch, who finally overran it in 1655.

The Middle Colonies

Gradually it became clear that the English would dominate the entire coast between the St. Lawrence Valley and Florida. After 1660 only the Dutch challenged their monopoly. The two nations, once allies against Spain, had fallen out because of the fierce competition of their textile manufacturers and merchants. England's efforts to bar Dutch merchant vessels from its colonial trade also brought the two countries into conflict in America. Charles II precipitated a showdown by granting his brother James, Duke of York, the entire area between Connecticut and Maryland. This was tantamount to declaring war. In 1664 English forces captured New Amsterdam without a fight—there were only 1,500 people in the town—and soon the rest of the Dutch settlements capitulated. New Amsterdam became New York. The duke did not interfere much with the way of life of the Dutch settlers, and they were quickly reconciled to English rule.

In 1664, even before the capture of New Amsterdam, the Duke of York gave New Jersey, the region between the Hudson and the Delaware, to John, Lord Berkeley, and Sir George Carteret. To attract settlers, these proprietors offered land on easy terms and established freedom of religion and a democratic system of local government. A considerable number of puritans from New England and Long Island moved to the new province.

In 1674 Berkeley sold his interest in New Jersey to two **Quakers**. Quakers believed that they could communicate directly with their Maker; their religion required neither ritual nor ministers. Originally a sect emotional to the point of fanaticism, by the 1670s the Quakers had come to stress the doctrine of the Inner Light—the direct, mystical experience of religious truth—which they believed possible for all persons. They distrusted the intellect in religious matters and, while ardent proselytizers of their own beliefs, they tolerated those of others cheerfully. When faced with opposition, they resorted to passive resistance, a tactic that embroiled them in grave difficulties in England and in most of the American colonies. In Massachusetts Bay, for example, four Quakers were executed when they refused either to conform to puritan ideas or to leave the colony.

The acquisition of New Jersey gave the Quakers a place where they could practice their religion in peace. The proprietors, in keeping with their principles, drafted an extremely liberal constitution for the colony, the Concessions and Agreements of 1677, which created an autonomous legislature and guaranteed settlers freedom of conscience, the right of trial by jury, and other civil rights.

The main Quaker effort at colonization came in the region immediately west of New Jersey, a fertile area belonging to William Penn, the son of a wealthy English admiral. Penn had early rejected a life of ease and had become a Quaker missionary. As a result, he was twice jailed. Yet he possessed qualities that enabled him to hold the respect and friendship of people who found his religious ideas abhorrent. From his father, Penn had inherited a claim to £16,000 that the admiral had lent Charles II. The king, reluctant to part with that much cash, paid off the debt in 1681 by giving Penn the region north of Maryland and west of the Delaware River, insisting only that it be named Pennsylvania, in honor of the admiral. In 1682 Penn founded Philadelphia. The Duke of York then added Delaware, the region between Maryland and the Delaware Bay, to Penn's holdings.

William Penn considered his colony a "Holy Experiment." He treated the Indians fairly, buying title to their lands and trying to protect them in their dealings with settlers and traders. Anyone who believed in "one Almighty and Eternal God" was entitled to freedom of worship. Penn's political ideas were paternalistic rather than democratic; the assembly he established could only approve or reject laws proposed by the governor and council. But individual rights were as well protected in Pennsylvania as in New Jersey.

Penn's altruism, however, did not prevent him from taking excellent care of his own interests. He sold both large and small tracts of land to settlers on easy terms but reserved huge tracts for himself. He promoted Pennsylvania tirelessly, writing glowing, although perfectly honest, descriptions of the colony, which were circulated widely in England and, in translation, in Europe. These attracted many settlers, including large numbers of Germans—the Pennsylvania "Dutch" (a corruption of *Deutsch*, meaning "German").

William Penn was neither a doctrinaire nor an ivory tower philosopher. He came to Pennsylvania himself when trouble developed between settlers and his representatives and agreed to adjustments in his first Frame of Government when he realized that local conditions demonstrated the need for change. His combination of toughness, liberality, and good salesmanship helped the colony to prosper and grow rapidly. By 1685 there were almost 9,000 settlers in Pennsylvania, and by 1700 twice that number, a heartening contrast to the early history of Virginia and Plymouth. Pennsylvania produced wheat, corn, rye, and other crops in abundance and found a ready market for its surpluses on the sugar plantations of the West Indies.

Cultural Collisions

Since the Indians did not worship the Christian God, the Europeans dismissed them as contemptible heathens. Some insisted that the Indians were servants of Satan. Other Europeans, such as the Spanish friars, did try to convert the Indians, and with considerable success; but as late as 1569, when Spain introduced the Inquisition into its colonies, the natives were exempted from its control on the ground that they were incapable of rational judgment and thus not responsible for their "heretical" religious beliefs.

Indians who depended on hunting and fishing had little use for personal property that was not easily portable. They saw no reason to amass possessions as individuals or as tribes. Even the Aztecs, with their treasures of gold and silver, valued the metals for

Historian James Merrell notes several errors in Benjamin West's famous 1771 painting, *William Penn's Treaty with the Indians*. In 1682, when the treaty was negotiated, Penn (in brown coat) was not yet so fat; the colonists' clothing and brick buildings resemble a scene in Philadelphia in the 1750s, not the 1680s; and the Indians are implausibly posed like Greek and Roman statues. Most important, the painting includes no translator, the one indispensable figure in the proceedings. All Indian and settler exchanges required "go-betweens" or "negotiators" to help each group explain itself to the other.

their durability and the beautiful things that could be made with them rather than as objects of commerce.

Indians were puzzled that European men worked so hard in the fields. In many Indian societies, crop cultivation was women's work. Moreover, the bounty of the earth was such that no one needed to work all the time. The Europeans' ceaseless drudgery and relentless pursuit of material goods struck the Indians as perverse. In many Indian societies, sachems acquired power by giving away their goods. The Narragansett Indians even had a ritual in which they collected "almost all the riches they have to their gods"— kettles, hatchets, beads, knives—and burned them in a great fire.

This lack of concern for material things led Europeans to conclude that the native people of America were lazy and childlike. "[Indians] do but run over the grass, as do also foxes and wild beasts," an English settler wrote in 1622, "so it is lawful now to take a land, which none useth, and make use of it." In the sense that the Indians continuously interacted with nature, the first part of this statement contained a grain of truth, although of course the second did not follow from it logically.

That the Indians allowed their environment to remain pristine is a myth. Long before contact with the Europeans, Indians cleared fields, burned the underbrush of forests, diverted rivers and streams, built roads and settlements, and deposited immense quantities of earth upon mounds.

But Europeans left a deeper imprint on the land. Their iron-tipped ploughs dug into the earth and made more of it accessible to cultivation, and their iron axes and saws enabled them to clear vast forests with relative ease. Pigs and cattle, too, ate their way through fields. Indians resented the intensity of English cultivation. After capturing several

Black Robe

In 1493 Pope Alexander VI praised Christopher Columbus, "our beloved son," for having discovered "certain very remote islands and even mainlands" whose inhabitants "seem sufficiently disposed to embrace the Catholic faith." In order to save their souls, Alexander continued, such "barbaric" peoples must be "humbled." In 1629 the church dispatched to New France its most effective missionaries, the Jesuits, a militant evangelical order founded by Ignatius Loyola in 1540. The Indians, fascinated by the Jesuits' austere cassocks, called them Black Robes.

Black Robe, directed by Bruce Beresford, tells the story of Father Laforgue: a young French Jesuit who arrives in Québec in 1634. Laforgue's superiors charge him with reviving a faltering mission to the Huron Indians in the upper Great Lakes. Samuel Champlain, Governor of New France, persuades a band of Algonquin Indians to escort Laforgue on this 1,500-mile journey.

The movie is partly an adventure story that chronicles the group's voyage to the interior of the continent: paddling through ice-choked rivers, hauling canoes along snowy portages, and enduring capture and torture by Iroquois. But the movie also explores the deep cultural chasm between Indians and Europeans. When the Algonquin chief tells a story, Laforgue writes it down and takes the chief to another European, not present for the conversation, shows him the paper, and asks him to read it aloud. As he does, the chief's face falls in horror: What manner of sorcery resides in those squiggly lines? The Europeans, by contrast, were plagued with illiteracy of the arboreal kind. After losing his way in a forest, Laforgue embraces his Indian rescuers. "I was lost," he tells them, tears streaming down his face. "How was that?" the Indians ask. "Did you forget to look at the trees, Black Robe?"

When Laforgue finally arrives at the mission, he finds all but one of the missionaries have been butchered; the last, just before dying, explains that the Huron had been decimated by

disease and blamed the Jesuits. As Laforgue buries him, a shattered remnant of the Huron watch in silence, their blank faces symbolizing the mutual incomprehension of Indians and Jesuits. Laforgue raises his head to the heavens, sunshine framing the church's cross. "Spare them," he intones. "Spare them, Oh Lord." The movie ends with a notice that, by 1650, the Iroquois had crushed the Hurons and the Jesuits had abandoned the mission.

Is *Black Robe* a plausible account of the relationship between Indians and Jesuit missionaries? No definitive answer is possible because our knowledge is almost entirely based on the missionaries' letters to their superiors. Sometimes the movie departs from these accounts. For example, no Indian of New France would have agreed to a 1,500-mile expedition in the middle of winter. As one missionary explained, his Indians seldom strayed from their camp during the winter "on account of the great masses of ice which are continually floating about, and which would crush not only a small boat but even a great ship."

On the other hand, the movie scrupulously depicts the physical world described by the missionaries. Viewers may complain that the interior scenes are obscured by smoke, but this reflects the historical reality. Laforgue was based in part on Paul Le Jeune, a Jesuit missionary who wrote in 1634 that the bitter cold required the Indians to build large fires indoors. The smoke from the fires was a form of "martyrdom" that

> made me weep continually. . . it caused us to place our mouths against the earth in order to breathe.

The director painstakingly reconstructed Indian villages, used Indians (who spoke Cree) as actors, and clothed them in seemingly random layers of textiles and animal skills. This, too, accorded with the accounts of missionaries, one of whom was surprised that the Indians used the same

Father Laforgue, played by Lothaire Bluteau, walks along the shores of Lake Huron, a grim and solitary figure.

Father Paul Le Jeune, the Jesuit missionary on which "Father Laforgue" was largely based, doubtless visited St. Eustache Cathedral in Paris (above), completed in the 1630s. His letters to his superiors explain his difficult adjustment to worship in the wilds of North America.

clothing for men and women. "They care only to stay warm," he sniffed. Doubtless the northern Indians were puzzled that anyone would dress for any other purpose.

The sharpest criticism of the movie has come from controversialist Ward Churchill. Churchill, who claims to be part-Indian, asserted that the movie vilified the Indians and justified their extermination.

It is tempting to dismiss Churchill's argument because of the reputation of its author, who made provocative remarks after the 9/11 attack on the World Trade Center in New York City. Whether the Jesuits undermined Indian belief systems cannot be determined from the letters of the missionaries. But there can be little doubt that many Jesuits were motivated by a desire to do what they regarded as God's work. Nothing else explains their willingness to endure the sufferings chronicled in their letters.

What the Indians thought of the Jesuits is much harder to determine. Neither side—as the movie shows—understood the other. But the movie advances a secondary hypothesis, conveyed by the haunting musical score and panoramic shots of endless forests, clad in snow and shadowed in a fading winter light. This all suggested that the Indians, consigned to live in a solitary and harsh environment, were a grim and stoical people, "noble savages," who endured unimaginable privations. This stereotype remains a staple of popular culture to this day.

But it may be wrong. Consider the account of Le Jeune, the actual missionary who was tormented by an Indian shaman named Mestigoit. Le Jeune described his relationship with the "Sorcerer" as one of "open warfare"; he expected Mestigoit to murder him at any time. But a closer reading of Le Jeune's

account suggests that Mestigoit's purposes were more comedic than homicidal.

Le Jeune wrote that Mestigoit

> tried to make me the laughingstock. . . [His followers] continually heaped upon me a thousand taunts and insults. They were saying to me at every turn *sasegau,* "He looks like a Dog;" *attimonai oukhimau,* "He is Captain of the Dogs;" *cou oucousimas ouchtigonan,* "He has a head like a pumpkin;" *matchiriniou,* "He is deformed, he is ugly;" *khichcouebeon,* "He is drunk."

Le Jeune, alone and alienated, likely projected his own sentiments onto the Indians. An alternative reading of this and similar missionary accounts suggests that the Indians did not regard their world as harsh and difficult, nor their lives as grim and solitary. While preparing to leave for a difficult winter hunt, Le Jeune's Indians offered him encouragement: "Let thy soul be strong to endure suffering and hardship; keep thyself from being sad, otherwise thou wilt be sick; see how we do not cease to laugh, although we have little to eat?" Indeed, nothing surprised the Indians more than the joylessness of the Jesuits. How, the Indians asked, could the Black Robes speak of heaven if they had never slept with a woman?

Questions for Discussion
- Whose religious beliefs were more difficult to understand, those of the Algonquins or the Jesuit missionaries?
- Do all human beings share a similar sense of humor?

English farmers, some Algonquians buried them alive, all the while taunting: "You English have grown exceedingly above the Ground. Let us now see how you will grow when planted into the ground."

The Europeans' inability to grasp the communal nature of land tenure among Indians also led to innumerable quarrels. Traditional tribal boundaries were neither spelled out in deeds or treaties nor marked by fences or any other sign of occupation. Often corn grown by a number of families was stored in a common bin and drawn on by all as needed. Such practices were utterly alien to the European mind.

Nowhere was the cultural chasm between Indians and Europeans more evident than in warfare. Indians did not seek to possess land, so they sought not to destroy an enemy but to display their valor, avenge an insult or perceived wrong, or acquire captives who could take the place of deceased family members. The Indians preferred to ambush an opponent and seize the stragglers; when confronted by a superior force, they usually melted into the woods. The Europeans preferred to fight in heavily armed masses in order to obliterate the enemy.

Colonists denounced Indian perfidy for burning houses and towns; but they saw no inconsistency in burning Indian "nests," "wigwams," and "camps." Conversely, the Indians thought it within their rights to slaughter the cattle that devoured their crops and spoiled their hunting grounds. But when the Indians tortured the beasts in fury, the colonists regarded them as savages.

Cultural Fusions

Increase Mather, a puritan leader, worried that "Christians in this Land have become too like unto the Indians." Little wonder, he observed, that God had "afflicted us by them" through disease and other trials. Yet Mather's comments suggested that interaction between European settlers and the native peoples was characteristic of life in all the colonies. *Interaction* is the key word in this sentence. The so-called Columbian Exchange between Indian and European was a two-way street. The colonists learned a great deal about how to live in the American forest from the Indians: the names of plants and animals (hickory, pecan, raccoon, skunk, moose); what to eat in their new home and how to catch or grow it; what to wear (leather leggings and especially moccasins); how best to get from one place to another; how to fight; and in some respects how to think.

The colonists learned from the Indians how best to use many plants and animals for food and clothing, but they would probably have discovered most of these if the continent had been devoid of human life when they arrived. Corn, however, the staple of the diet of agricultural tribes, was something the Indians had domesticated. Its contribution to the success of English colonization was enormous.

The fur trade illustrates the pervasiveness of Indian–European interaction. It was in some ways a perfect business arrangement. Both groups profited. The colonists got "valuable" furs for "cheap" European products, while the Indians got "priceless" tools, knives, and other trade goods in exchange for "cheap" beaver pelts and deerskins. The demand for furs caused the Indians to become more efficient hunters and trappers and even to absorb some of the settlers' ideas about private property and capitalist accumulation. Hunting parties became larger. Farming tribes shifted their villages in order to be nearer trade routes and waterways. In some cases tribal organization was altered: Small groups combined into confederations in order to control more territory when their hunting reduced the supplies

Indians were befuddled by the Europeans' craving for gold, such as these Spanish coins (left). Europeans were similarly baffled by the Indians' attraction to wampum, seashells that were drilled, placed on a string, and formed into belts, such as this eighteenth-century Oneida belt (right). No negotiations or trade with many Indian tribes could commence without gifts of wampum. The gold coins are imprinted with the Christian cross; purple beads, the most valuable, were also suffused with spiritual import among Indians.

of furs nearer home. Early in the seventeenth century, Huron Indians in the Great Lakes region, who had probably never seen a Frenchman, owned French products obtained from eastern tribes in exchange for Huron corn.

Europeans and Indians became interdependent. The colonists relied on Indian labor and products. Indians relied on European guns and metal tools. Some Indians became so enamored of European knives and metal tools that they forgot the stone-working skills of their Paleo-Indian ancestors. They now depended on Europeans for those products, much as the colonists themselves depended on Indian corn, potatoes, and other crops.

Although the colonists learned much from the Indians and adopted certain elements of Indian culture and technology eagerly, their objective was not to be like the Indians, whom they considered the epitome of savagery and barbarism. The constant conflicts with Indians forced the colonists to band together and in time gave them a sense of having shared a common history. Later, when colonists broke away from Great Britain, they used the image of the Indian to symbolize the freedom and independence they sought for themselves.

In sum, during the first 200-odd years that followed Columbus's first landfall in the Caribbean, a complex development had taken place in the Americas. Sometimes these alien encounters were amiable, as Indians and colonists exchanged ideas, skills, and goods; while sometimes the encounters were hostile and bloody, with unimaginable cruelties inflicted by and on both sides. But the coming together of Indians and European settlers was mostly characterized by ambiguity and confusion, as markedly different peoples drew from their own traditions to make sense of a new world that little resembled what they knew. In time, their world would become our own.

Christopher Columbus's fateful voyage brought alien worlds together, an encounter characterized by mutual incomprehension. In consequence, millions of American Indians perished, millions of Europeans immigrated to the Americas, and millions of Africans were sent there as slaves. The cultures of all peoples—food and diet, religious beliefs and practices, and modes of sustenance and social organization—changed in fundamental ways. During that fateful first century, American Indians, Europeans, and Africans interacted continuously—negotiating, fighting, trading, and intermarrying—without really understanding one another.

Milestones

EXPLORATION

c. 1000	Leif Eriksson reaches Newfoundland
1445–1488	Portuguese sailors explore west coast of Africa
1492	First voyage of Christopher Columbus
1497	John Cabot explores east coast of North America
1498	Vasco da Gama sails around Africa to India
1513	Ponce de Leon explores Florida
1519–1521	Hernán Cortés conquers Mexico
1519–1522	Ferdinand Magellan's crew circumnavigates globe
1539–1542	Hernando de Soto explores lower Mississippi River Valley
1540–1542	Francisco Vasquez de Coronado explores Southwest
1579	Francis Drake explores coast of California
1609	Henry Hudson discovers Hudson River

SETTLEMENT

1493	Columbus founds La Navidad, Hispaniola
1494	Treaty of Tordesillas divides New World between Spain and Portugal
1576	Spanish settle St. Augustine
1587	English found "Lost Colony" of Roanoke Island
1607	English settle Jamestown
1608	French found Québec
1612	John Rolfe introduces tobacco cultivation in Virginia
1620	Pilgrims settle Plymouth, sign Mayflower Compact
1624	Dutch settle New Amsterdam
1630	English puritans settle Massachusetts Bay
1630–1640	Waves of English come to America during the Great Migratio
1634	George Calvert, Lord Baltimore, founds Maryland as Catholic haven
1636	Roger Williams founds Rhode Island
	General Court of Massachusetts Bay Colony banishes Anne Hutchinson
1639	Thomas Hooker founds Connecticut
1642	French found Montréal
1664	English conquer Dutch New Amsterdam
1670	First settlers arrive in Carolina
1680	Charles Town (now Charleston, South Carolina) is settled
1682	William Penn founds Philadelphia

✓●─Study and Review at www.myhistorylab.com

Review Questions

1. Why did Columbus choose to embark on his 1492 voyage and what was his "great error"?

2. What factors accounted for the ease with which Spain imposed its will upon the Indians of south and central America?

3. What accounted for the Indian susceptibility to European diseases? Why do scholarly estimates of Indian population losses vary so greatly?

4. What reasons prompted English peoples to come to the Americas? How did they choose different settlements on the Atlantic coast?

5. Why did Europeans so often treat Indians with such brutality? In what ways did Europeans and Indians interact positively?

Key Terms

antinomianism *35*
Arminianism *30*
Columbian
    Exchange *23*
conquistadores *17*
encomienda
    system *18*

joint-stock
    companies *25*
Mayflower
    Compact *31*
predestination *30*
Protestant
    Reformation *24*

puritans *30*
Quakers *39*
Treaty of
    Tordesillas *17*

2 American Society in the Making

((•—Hear the Audio Chapter 2 at myhistorylab.com

Do you take risks?

THE UNITED STATES IS A NATION OF MIGRATORY PEOPLES: PALEO-INDIANS who ventured from Siberia tens of thousands of years ago, Europeans who explored and settled the "new" world in the sixteenth and seventeenth centuries, millions of immigrants who have arrived from other parts of the world ever since.

Alexis de Tocqueville, a French writer who visited the United States in 1831, was struck by the "restless curiosity" of Americans as they "travel up and down the vast territories" of their nation. A "feverish ardor" similarly characterized their pursuit of wealth: "They have been told that fortune is to be found somewhere toward the west, and they hasten to find it." Americans approached life "like a game of chance."

Does a uniquely American character exist and is it inspired by a migratory impulse? Some scientists think so, and their explanation is rooted in a gene that influences the release of chemicals in the brain that promote risk-taking.[1] A 2009 psychology study at Harvard found that college students with this gene bet larger sums when gambling than those without it.

Scientists speculate that people with the "risk-taking" gene are more likely to migrate to distant lands. Support for this hypothesis rests in the fact that the gene is far more common among nomadic tribes in Africa than sedentary ones, and is more common among South American Indians who migrated from East Asia tens of thousands of years ago than East Asians.

But even if this speculation is true, other factors have influenced the development of a distinctively American character. Sometimes migrants came to the Americas because staying put was riskier than moving. Land in the Americas seemed limitless and, by European standards, nearly uninhabited. Because the labor to farm it and extract its wealth was scarce, immigrants could reasonably bet that wages would be higher. Immigrants quickly discovered that the social and cultural institutions of their home country were often ill-adapted to American conditions, necessitating innovation and further risk taking: The widely spaced pattern of large American farms, for example, discouraged the residential clumping of European villages. Religious enthusiasts and educational reformers also learned that they had a broader canvas on which to realize ambitious visions.

---

[1]The "risk-taking" gene is a variant of the D4 gene that influences the release of dopamine, a neurotransmitter. It is also associated with hyperactivity and ADD.

Factors as material as the landscape, as quantifiable as population patterns, and as elusive as chance and calculation, all shaped colonial social developments. Their cumulative impact did not at first produce anything like a uniform society. The "Americans" who evolved in what is now the United States were in many ways as different from each other as they were from their foreign cousins. The process by which these identities merged into an American nation remained incomplete. It was—and is—ongoing.

Settlement of New France

After 1700 France's colonial enterprise in North America stagnated. The main problem, as before, was the difficulty in persuading French people to occupy isolated settlements in remote American frontiers. But some did come. The French government built and occupied forts along the shores of the Great Lakes and at strategic positions overlooking the Mississippi, Illinois, and other rivers. Solitary French traders ventured deep into the wilderness in search of increasingly scarce animal pelts. Jesuit missionaries endeavored to plant Christianity among the Indians. Missionaries founded Detroit in 1701, Kaskaskia (south of Cahokia) in 1703, and Fort de Chartres in 1720.

Attempts to anchor New France with a colony at the mouth of the Mississippi were frustrated by the region's maze of swamps, marshes, and meandering waterways which, though ideal for pirates, discouraged settlement. One French missionary, unable to locate the mouth of the Mississippi, complained that the "coast changes shape at every moment." In 1712 France chartered a private company to build a colony in the region. It laid out a town called New Orleans at the site of a short portage between the Mississippi River and Lake Pontchartrain. The company granted tracts of land to settlers and transported several thousand of them to Louisiana. Some established farms, planting indigo, tobacco, rice, and cotton; others acquired forest products, such as lumber, tar, and resin; and still others traded for furs. The company established more settlements in the region, including one at Natchez, on a bluff above the Mississippi. But in 1729 the Natchez Indians wiped out the settlement. The company went bankrupt.

In 1731 the French government took control of Louisiana, with New Orleans as its administrative capital. Settlement lagged. The region was unsuited for farming, bemoaned one French official: "Now there is too much drought, now too much rain." By 1750 no more than 10,000 Europeans had colonized the region.

As beaver and other game became scarce, traders ventured farther west. Eventually they came upon tribes that had been driven from Pennsylvania and New York by the mighty Iroquois confederation. These Indians, fearful of the Iroquois, sought guns and ammunition. The traders complied, though not without misgivings. This escalation in armaments ensured that warfare would be more deadly, and that the isolated outposts of New France would be more vulnerable.

Society in New Mexico, Texas, and California

Once the Indians of the upper Mississippi acquired guns from French traders, the new weaponry quickly spread to the Indians of the Great Plains. Far earlier, the Apache and Comanche had become experts at riding European horses, which proliferated on the

Architectural historians regard the Mission of San José de Laguna, completed between 1699 and 1701, as illustrative of an "architecture of permanence." This was hopeful: The previous mission church had been destroyed during the revolt of the Pueblo Indians ten years earlier.

vast grasslands in the heart of the continent. Now armed with light muskets, the Plains Indians became formidable foes; the Comanche were nearly invincible. Spanish raiders who had formerly seized Plains Indians for the slave trade now preyed upon less fearsome nomadic tribes, such as the Ute, who lived in the foothills of the Rockies.

The Comanche, always adept buffalo hunters, were even better with guns. As the number and size of their hunting bands increased, the Comanche encroached on Apache territory. Soon Comanche warriors, occasionally assisted by French traders and soldiers, raided remote Spanish and Pueblo settlements in New Mexico and Texas. "We do not have a single gun," declared one Spanish missionary in 1719, "while we see the French giving hundreds of arms to Indians."

This new threat prompted the Spanish to strengthen the *presidio*—fortified bases—at Santa Fe and San Antonio and to build new missions in east Texas. In an effort to preempt future attacks, the Spanish also dispatched a military expedition into Nebraska. But Pawnee Indians and the French ambushed and routed the invaders; from now on, Spanish garrisons and their Pueblo allies rarely ventured beyond their towns and missions.

The ascendancy of the Plains Indians endangered all of the new frontier missions and discouraged further settlement. In 1759 a Spanish commander of a

Spain's North American Frontier, c. 1750 This map of Spanish settlement is somewhat deceptive: It shows a broad swath of land "under Spanish control" extending far north of New Spain, to Santa Fe, and to San Antonio. In fact, Spanish colonization in the northern regions was patchy, consisting of scattered religious missions and military garrisons. By 1750, Spanish colonists, Indian natives, and slaves had intermarried, changing the cultures of all.

presidio complained that the Comanche were "so superior in firearms as well as in numbers that our destruction seems probable." San Antonio, the largest town, had only 600 Hispanic settlers.

The Indian slave trade remained an enduring aspect of life along the sparsely populated northern rim of New Spain. Catholic missionaries usually prevented Spanish traders from enslaving Pueblo Indians, many of whom lived in mission towns and knew the rudiments of Catholicism. But no such arguments could protect the "wild" Indians such as the Ute of the foothills of the Rockies.

Because adult males resisted capture and incorporation into colonial society, most Indian slaves were women and children. In 1761 Father Pedro Serrano reported that at one New Mexican trade fair Indian women over the age of ten were raped "in the sight of innumerable assemblies of barbarians and Catholics" before they were sold.

Indian slaves often had children by Hispanic fathers, who rarely acknowledged these offspring. Known as *genizaros*, these children occupied the bottom rung of a social system largely based on the status of fathers. *Genizaros* learned Spanish and received training in Catholicism. In some towns, they comprised a third of the population. Females usually worked as household servants, and males, as indentured servants on ranches. Spanish officials, eager to increase the numbers of Spanish colonists, granted *genizaros* the right to own property. Many became ranchers and herders.

While the Comanche terrorized the frontier of New Mexico and Texas, Spanish officials learned of a new threat in the 1760s: Britain and Russia were attempting to colonize the Northwest, the region that now comprises Oregon and Washington. This threatened Spain's claims to California, a remote wilderness inhabited by some 300,000 Indians. As in New Mexico, Spain failed to attract Hispanic settlers; so it invited Franciscan missionaries to *create* "Spanish" settlers by converting the Indians to Catholicism and Hispanicizing their language and culture. This did not prove easy. The Indians of California belonged to over 300 tribes that spoke nearly 100 different languages.

In 1769 several score Franciscans and a detachment of Spanish soldiers established a *presidio* and mission in San Diego. Other missions followed at Monterey, Santa Barbara, and San Francisco; within several decades some twenty missions had been established in California.

The Franciscans monitored Indian life closely. They segregated all unmarried girls over the age of seven so as to prevent them from indulging in freer Indian sexual mores and to protect them from lustful European men. The friars also inculcated the discipline of work; the digging of irrigation ditches; the cultivation of crops; the tending of livestock; the manufacture of handicrafts; and the construction of churches, forts, and homes. The Indians received no wages, but instead were fed and cared for by the priests, whose first obligation was to God and the church. Because the California settlements were distant from New Spain, the missions survived chiefly by provisioning Spanish military garrisons.

Whatever success the Franciscans had in establishing the missions, however, was undone by disease. As had happened throughout the Western Hemisphere, the introduction of European pathogens among formerly isolated Indian populations resulted in catastrophic losses. European diseases hit all California Indians, not just those in the missions. By the close of the eighteenth century, Spain had failed in its effort to establish a strong Hispanic colony in California.

The English Prevail on the Atlantic Seaboard

By the mid-eighteenth century, England had successfully addressed the chief problem that bedeviled the French and Spanish colonial efforts: a dearth of colonists. By then, European settlers, most of them English, had taken possession of much of the Atlantic seaboard. But this basic fact overlooks the important differences among the colonies. Each of the Middle Colonies had distinctive histories and settlement patterns. Even the New England colonies, though originally founded for similar religious purposes, soon diverged.

The southern parts of English North America comprised three regions: the Chesapeake Bay, consisting of "tidewater" Virginia and Maryland; the "low country" of the Carolinas (and eventually Georgia); and the "back country," a vast territory that extended from the "fall line" in the foothills of the Appalachians (where falls and rapids put an end to navigation on the tidal rivers) to the farthest point of western settlement. Not until well into the eighteenth century would the emergence of common features—export-oriented agricultural economies, a labor force in which black slaves figured prominently, and the absence of towns of any size—prompt people to think of the "South" as a single region.

The Chesapeake Colonies

When the English philosopher Thomas Hobbes wrote in 1651 that human life tended to be "nasty, brutish, and short," he might well have had in mind the royal colony of Virginia. Although the colony grew from about 1,300 to nearly 5,000 in the decade after the Crown took it over in 1624, the death rate remained appalling. Since more than 9,000 immigrants had entered the colony, nearly half the population died during that decade.

English Colonies on the Atlantic Seaboard The boundaries of English colonies were partially determined by geographical factors—usually the Atlantic Ocean to the east and the Appalachian mountains in the west, beyond which few colonists settled prior to 1750. Most colonial charters set the north/south borders of a colony according to a particular line of latitude—that is to say, the distance a place is located in relation to the equator.

The climate was largely to blame. Almost without exception newcomers underwent "seasoning," a period of illness that in its mildest form consisted of "two or three fits of a feaver and ague." The relatively dry summers were the chief cause of the high death rate. During the summer the slower flow of the James River allowed relatively dense salt water to penetrate inland. This blocked the flow of polluted river water, which the colonists drank. The result was dysentery, the "bloody flux." If they survived the flux, and a great many did not, settlers still ran the seasonal risk of contracting a particularly virulent strain of malaria, which, though seldom fatal in itself, could so debilitate its victims that they often died of typhoid fever and other ailments.

Long after food shortages and Indian warfare had ceased to be serious problems, life in the Chesapeake colonies remained precarious. Well into the 1700s a white male of twenty in Middlesex County, Virginia, could look forward only to about twenty-five more years of life. Across Chesapeake Bay, in Charles County, Maryland, life expectancy was even lower. The high death rate had important effects on family structure. Because relatively few people lived beyond their forties, more often than not children lost at least one of their parents—and in many instances both—before they reached maturity.

All Chesapeake settlers felt the psychological effects of their precarious and frustrating existence. Random mayhem and calculated violence posed a continuous threat. Life was coarse at best and often as "brutish" as Hobbes had claimed, even allowing for the difficulties involved in carving out a community in the wilderness.

The Lure of Land

Agriculture was the bulwark of life for the Chesapeake settlers and the rest of the colonial South; the tragic experiences of the Jamestown settlement revealed this quickly enough. Jamestown also suggested that a colony could not succeed unless its inhabitants were allowed to own their own land. The first colonists had agreed to work for seven years in return for a share of the profits. When their contracts expired there were few profits. To satisfy these settlers and to attract new capital, the London Company declared a "dividend" of land, its only asset. The surviving colonists each received 100 acres. Thereafter, as prospects continued to be poor, the company relied more and more on grants of land to attract both capital and labor. A number of wealthy Englishmen were given immense tracts, some running to several hundred thousand acres. Lesser persons willing to settle in Virginia received more modest grants. Whether dangled before a great tycoon, a country squire, or a poor farmer, the offer of land had the effect of encouraging immigration to the colony. This was a much-desired end, for without the labor to develop it the land was worthless.

Soon what was known as the **headright** system became entrenched in both Virginia and Maryland. Behind the system lay the principle that land should be parceled out according to the availability of labor to cultivate it. For each "head" entering the colony authorities issued a "right" to take any fifty acres of unoccupied land. To "seat" a claim and receive title to the property, the holder of the headright had to mark out its boundaries, plant a crop, and construct some sort of habitation. This system was adopted in all the southern colonies and in Pennsylvania and New Jersey.

The headright system encouraged landless Europeans to migrate to English America. More often than not, however, those most eager to come could not afford passage across the Atlantic. To bring such people to America, the **indentured servant** system was developed. Indenture resembled apprenticeship. In return for transportation indentured servants agreed to work for a stated period, usually about five years.

During that time they were subject to strict control by the master and received no compensation beyond their keep. Servants lacked any incentive to work hard, whereas masters tended to "abuse their servantes . . . with intollerable oppression." In this clash of wills the advantage lay with the master; servants lacked full political and civil rights, and masters could administer physical punishment and otherwise abuse them. An indenture, however, was a contract; servants could and did sue when planters failed to fulfill their parts of the bargain, and surviving court records suggest that they fared reasonably well when they did so.

Servants who completed their years of labor became free. Usually the former servant was entitled to an "outfit" (a suit of clothes, some farm tools, seed, and perhaps a gun), and occasionally to a small grant of land.

Most servants eventually became landowners, but with the passage of time their lot became harder. The best land belonged to the large planters, and as more land went into cultivation, crop prices fell. Many owners of small farms, former servants especially, slipped into dire poverty. Some were forced to become "squatters" on land along the fringes of settlement that no one had yet claimed. Squatting often led to trouble; eventually, when someone turned up with a legal title to the land, the squatters demanded "squatters' rights," the privilege of buying the land from the legal owner without paying for the improvements the squatters had made upon it. This led to lawsuits and sometimes to violence.

In the 1670s conflicts between Virginians who owned choice land and former servants on the outer edge of settlement brought the colony to the brink of class warfare. The costs of meeting the region's ever-growing need for labor with indentured servants were becoming prohibitive. Some other solution was needed.

"Solving" the Labor Shortage: Slavery

Probably the first African blacks brought to English North America arrived on a Dutch ship and were sold at Jamestown in 1619. Early records are vague and incomplete, so it is not possible to say whether these Africans were treated as slaves or freed after a period of years as were indentured servants. What is certain is that by about 1640 *some* blacks were slaves (a few, with equal certainty, were free) and that by the 1660s local statutes had firmly established the institution of slavery in Virginia and Maryland.

Slavery soon spread throughout the colonies. As early as 1626 there were only a handful of slaves in New Netherland, and when the English conquered that colony in 1664 there were 700 slaves in a population of about 8,000. The Massachusetts Body of Liberties of 1641—strange title—provided that "there shall never be any bond-slavery . . . amongst us; unlesse it be lawful captives taken in just warrs [i.e., Indians] and such strangers as willingly sell themselves, or *are solde* to us." However, relatively few blacks were imported until late in the seventeenth century, even in the southern colonies. In 1650 there were only 300 blacks in Virginia and as late as 1670 no more than 2,000.

In 2009, President Barack Obama visited the Cape Coast Castle in Ghana, a fortress that held Africans before they were shipped to the Americas. "It is here," Obama declared, "where the journey of much of the African American experience began."

White servants were much more highly prized. The African, after all, was almost entirely unaccustomed to both the European and the American ways of life. In a country starved for capital, the cost of slaves—roughly five times that of indentured servants—was another disadvantage. In 1664 the governor of Maryland informed Lord Baltimore that local planters would use more "neigros" "if our purses would endure it." As long as white servants were available, few planters acquired slaves.

In the 1670s the flow of indentured servants slackened as the result of improving economic conditions in England and the competition of other colonies for servants. At the same time, the formation of the Royal African Company (1672) made slaves more readily available. By 1700, nearly 30,000 slaves lived in the English colonies.

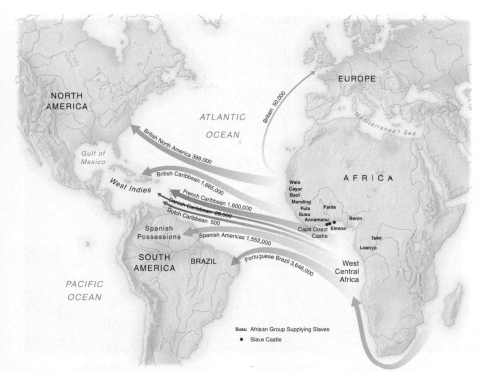

Atlantic Slave Trade, 1451–1870 From 1619, when a Dutch frigate sold several dozen slaves to English colonists at Jamestown, until 1808, when Congress abolished the African slave trade, nearly 400,000 Africans were brought against their will to what is now the United States. Approximately 8 million more were taken to the sugar or coffee plantations in Brazil and the Caribbean and to the mines and farms of Spanish America. Although most of the slaves came from western Africa and central Africa, some (not shown on this map) came from Africa's eastern coast as well.

Prosperity in a Pipe: Tobacco

Labor and land made agriculture possible, but it was necessary to find a market for American crops in the Old World if the colonists were to enjoy anything but the crudest existence. They could not begin to manufacture all the articles they required; to obtain from England such items as plows, muskets, books, and china-ware, they had to have cash crops—what their English creditors called "merchantable commodities." Here, at least, fortune favored the Chesapeake.

The founders of Virginia tried to produce all sorts of things that were needed in the old country: grapes and silk in particular, indigo, cotton, oranges, olives, sugar, and many other plants. But it was tobacco, unwanted, even strongly opposed at first, that became for farmers on both sides of Chesapeake Bay "their darling."

Tobacco was unknown in Europe until Spanish explorers brought it back from the West Indies. Since it clearly contained some habit-forming drug, many people opposed its use. King James I wrote a pamphlet attacking the weed, in which, among other things, he anticipated the findings of

Read the Document

James I, *A Counterblaste to Tobacco* at **myhistorylab.com**

A denunciation of the tobacco craze that swept Europe in the mid-1600s, by Abraham Teniers.
Source: Erich Lessing/Art Resource, NY.

modern cancer researchers by saying that smoking was a "vile and stinking" habit "dangerous to the Lungs." The London Company initially discouraged its colonists from growing tobacco. But English smokers and partakers of snuff ignored their king, and the Virginians ignored their company. By 1617 a pound of tobacco was worth more than 5 shillings in London. Company and Crown then changed their tune, granting the colonists a monopoly and encouraging them in every way.

Unlike wheat, which required expensive plows and oxen to clear the land and prepare the soil, tobacco plants could be set on semicleared land and cultivated with a simple hoe. Although tobacco required lots of human labor, a single laborer working two or three acres could produce as much as 1,200 pounds of cured tobacco, which, in a good year, yielded a profit of more than 200 percent. This being the case, production in America leaped from 2,500 pounds in 1616 to nearly 30 million pounds in the late seventeenth century, or roughly 400 pounds of tobacco for every man, woman, and child in the Chesapeake colonies.

The tidewater region was blessed with many navigable rivers, and the planters spread along their banks giving the Chesapeake a shabby, helter-skelter character of rough habitations and growing tobacco that was mostly planted in stump-littered fields, surrounded by fallow land and thickets interspersed with dense forest. There were no towns and almost no roads. English ships made their way up the rivers from farm to farm, gathering the tobacco at each planter's wharf. The vessels also served as general stores of a sort where planters could exchange tobacco for everything from cloth, shoes, tools, salt, and nails to such exotic items as tea, coffee, chocolate, and spices.

However, the tremendous increase in the production of tobacco caused the price to plummet in the late seventeenth century. This did not stop the expansion of the colonies, but it did alter the structure of their society. Small tobacco farmers found it more difficult to make a decent living. At the same time men with capital and individuals with political influence were amassing large tracts of land. If well-managed, a big plantation gave its owner important competitive advantages over the small farmer. Tobacco was notorious for the speed with which it exhausted the fertility of the soil. Growers with a lot of land could shift frequently to new fields within their holdings, allowing the old fields to lie fallow and thus maintain high yields; but the only option that small farmers had when their land gave out was to move to unsettled land on the frontier. To do that in the 1670s was to risk trouble with Indians. It might also violate colonial laws designed to slow westward migration and limit tobacco production. Neither was about to stop settlement.

Bacon's Rebellion

Chesapeake settlers showed little respect for constituted authority, partly because most people lived on isolated plantations and partly because the London authorities were usually ignorant of their needs. The first Virginians often disregarded directives of the London Company. The most serious challenge took place in Virginia in 1676. Planters in the outlying counties disliked the officials in Jamestown who ran the colony. The royal governor, Sir William Berkeley, and his "Green Spring" faction (the organization took its name from the governor's plantation) had ruled Virginia for more than thirty years. Outsiders resented the way Berkeley and his henchmen used their offices to line their pockets. They also resented their social pretensions, for Green Springers made no effort to conceal their opinion (which had considerable basis in fact) that western planters were a crude and vulgar lot.

Early in 1676 planters on the western edge of settlement asked Berkeley to authorize an expedition against Indians who had been attacking nearby plantations. Berkeley refused. The planters then took matters into their own hands. Their leader, Nathaniel Bacon, was (and remains today) a controversial figure. His foes described him as extremely ambitious and possessed "of a most imperious and dangerous hidden Pride of heart." But even his sharpest critics conceded that he was "of an inviting aspect and powerful elocution" and well qualified "to lead a giddy and unthinking multitude."

When Berkeley refused to authorize him to attack the Indians, Bacon promptly showed himself only too willing to lead that multitude not only against Indians but against the governor. Without permission he raised an army of 500 men, described by the Berkeley faction as a "rabble of the basest sort." Berkeley then declared him a traitor.

Several months of confusion followed during what is known as **Bacon's Rebellion**. Bacon murdered some peaceful Indians, marched on Jamestown and forced Berkeley to legitimize Bacon's command, then headed west again to kill more Indians. In September he returned to Jamestown and burned it to the ground. Berkeley fled across Chesapeake Bay to the Eastern Shore. A few weeks later, Bacon came down with a "violent flux"—probably it was a bad case of dysentery—and he died. Soon thereafter an English naval squadron arrived with enough soldiers to restore order. Bacon's Rebellion came to an end.

On the surface, the uprising changed nothing. No sudden shift in political power occurred. Indeed, Bacon had not sought to change either the political system or the social and economic structure of the colony. But if the *rebellion* did not change anything, nothing was ever again quite the same. With seeming impartiality, the Baconites had warred against Indians and against wealthy planters. But which was their real enemy? Would some future Baconite overthrow the wealthy planters? Leaders in the Chesapeake colonies increasingly looked for cheap labor that would not acquire political power.

In the quarter-century following Bacon's Rebellion, the wealthier planters increasingly bought African slaves. This intensified the differences between rich and poor tobacco growers. The few who succeeded in accumulating twenty or more slaves and enough land to keep them occupied grew richer. The majority of people either grew poorer or at best had to struggle to hold their own.

More important, however, Bacon's Rebellion sealed an implicit contract between the inhabitants of the "great houses" and those who lived in more modest lodgings: Southern whites might have differed greatly in wealth and influence, but they stood as one behind the principle that Africans must have neither. This was the basis—the price—of the harmony and prosperity achieved by those who survived "seasoning" in the Chesapeake colonies.

The Carolinas

The English and, after 1700, the Scots-Irish settlers of the tidewater parts of the Carolinas turned to agriculture as enthusiastically as had their Chesapeake neighbors. In substantial sections of what became North Carolina, tobacco flourished. In South Carolina, after two decades in which furs and cereals were the chief products, Madagascar rice was introduced in the low-lying coastal areas in 1696. It quickly proved its worth as a cash crop. By 1700 almost 100,000 pounds were being exported annually; by the eve of the Revolution rice exports from South Carolina and Georgia exceeded 65 million pounds a year.

In the 1740s another cash crop, indigo, was introduced in South Carolina by Eliza Lucas, a plantation owner. Indigo did not compete with rice either for land or labor. It prospered on high ground and needed care in seasons when the slaves were not busy in the rice paddies. The British were delighted to have a new source of indigo because the blue dye was important in their woolens industry. Parliament quickly placed a bounty— a bonus—on it to stimulate production.

Their tobacco, rice, and indigo, along with furs and forest products, meant that the southern colonies had no difficulty in obtaining manufactured articles from abroad. Planters dealt with agents in England and Scotland who managed the sale of their crops, filled their orders for manufactures, and supplied them with credit. This was a great convenience but not necessarily an advantage, for it prevented the development of a diversified economy. Throughout the colonial era, while small-scale manufacturing developed rapidly in the North, it stagnated in the South.

Slave labor predominated from the beginning on the South Carolina rice planta-tions, for free workers would not submit to the backbreaking and unhealthy regimen of cultivation. The first quarter of the eighteenth century saw an enormous influx of Africans into all the southern colonies. By 1730 roughly three out of every ten people south of Pennsylvania were black, and in South Carolina the blacks outnumbered the whites by two to one. "Carolina," remarked a newcomer in 1737, "looks more like a negro country than like a country settled by white people."

Given the existing race prejudice and the degrading impact of slavery, this demo-graphic change had an enormous impact on life wherever African Americans were concen-trated. In each colony regulations governing the behavior of blacks, both free and enslaved, increased in severity. The South Carolina Negro Act of 1740 denied slaves "freedom of movement, freedom of assembly, freedom to raise [their own] food, to earn money, to learn to read English." The blacks had no civil rights under any of these codes, and punishments were severe. For minor offenses whipping was common, and for serious crimes death by hanging or by being burned alive was practiced. Slaves were sometimes castrated for sexual offenses—even for lewd talk about white women—or for repeated attempts to escape.

Although organized slave rebellions were infrequent, individual assaults by blacks on whites were common enough. (Personal violence was also common among whites, then and throughout American history.) But the masters had sound reasons for fearing their slaves; the particular viciousness of the system lay in the fact that oppression bred resentment, which in turn produced still greater oppression.

Thus the "peculiar institution" was fastened on America with economic, social, and psychic barbs. Ignorance and self-interest, lust for gold and for the flesh, primitive prejudices, and complex social and legal ties all combined to convince the whites that black slavery was not so much good as a fact of life.

Home and Family in the South

Life for all but the most affluent planters was by modern standards uncomfortable. Houses were mostly one- and two-room affairs that were small, dark, and crowded. Furniture and utensils were sparse and crudely made. Chairs were rare; if a family pos-sessed one it was reserved for the head of the house. People sat, slept, and ate on benches and planks. Toilets and plumbing of any kind were unknown; even chamber pots, which eliminated the nighttime trek to the outhouse, were beyond the reach of poorer families.

((•—[Hear the **Audio**
Lookie There! at
myhistorylab.com

White women (even indentured ones) rarely worked in the fields. Their responsibili-ties included tending to farm animals, making butter and cheese, pickling and preserving, spinning and sewing, and, of course, caring for children, which often involved orphans and stepchildren because of the fragility of life in the region. For exceptional women, the labor shortage created opportunities. Some managed large plantations; Eliza Lucas ran three in South Carolina for her absent father while still in her teens, and after the death of her hus-band, Charles Pinckney, she managed his extensive property holdings.

Southern children were not usually subjected to as strict discipline as were children in New England, but the difference was relative. Formal schooling for all but the rich

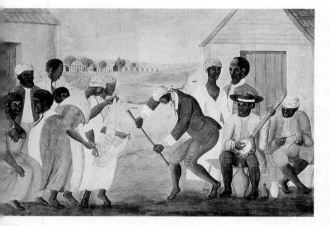

This depicts slaves on a South Carolina plantation, around 1790. Likely of Yoruba descent, they play West African instruments, such as the banjo, and also wear elaborate headgear, another Yoruba trait. But unlike their Yoruban contemporaries, who adorned faces and limbs with elaborate tattoos or scars, these slaves bear no evident body decorations. They are African, indisputably, but also American.

was nonexistent; the rural character of society made the maintenance of schools prohibitively expensive. Whatever most children learned, they got from their parents or other relatives. A large percentage of Southerners were illiterate. As in other regions, children were put to some kind of useful work at an early age.

Until the early eighteenth century only a handful of planters achieved real affluence. (The richest by far was Robert "King" Carter of Lancaster County, Virginia, who at the time of his death in 1732 owned 1,000 slaves and 300,000 acres.) Those fortunate few (masters of several plantations and many slaves) lived in solid, two-story houses of six or more rooms, furnished with English and other imported carpets, chairs, tables, wardrobes, chests, china, and silver. When the occasion warranted, the men wore fine broadcloth, the women the latest (or more likely the next-to-latest) fashions. Some even sent their children abroad for schooling. The founding of the College of William and Mary in Williamsburg, Virginia, in 1693 was an effort to provide the region with its own institution of higher learning, mainly in order to train clergymen. For decades, however, the College of William and Mary was not much more than a grammar school. Lawyers were relatively numerous, though rarely learned in the law. Doctors were so scarce that one sick planter wrote a letter to his brother in England describing his symptoms and asking him to consult a physician and let him know the diagnosis.

No matter what their station, southern families led relatively isolated lives. Churches, which might be expected to serve as centers of community life, were few and far between. By the middle of the eighteenth century the Anglican Church was the "established" religion, its ministers supported by public funds. The Virginia assembly had made attendance at Anglican services compulsory in 1619. In Maryland, Lord Baltimore's Toleration Act did not survive the settlement in the colony of large numbers of militant puritans. It was repealed in 1654, reenacted in 1657, then repealed again in 1692 when the Anglican Church was established.

Georgia and the Back Country

West of the fall line of the many rivers that irrigated tidewater Chesapeake and Carolina lay the back country. This region included the Great Valley of Virginia, the Piedmont, and what became the final English colony, Georgia, founded by a group of London philanthropists in 1733. These men were concerned over the plight of honest persons imprisoned for debt, whom they intended to settle in the New

World. (Many Europeans were still beguiled by the prospect of regenerating their society in the colonies. All told, about 50,000 British convicts were "transported" to America in the colonial period, partly to get rid of "undesirables," but partly for humane reasons.) The government, eager to create a buffer between South Carolina and the hostile Spanish in Florida, readily granted a charter (1732) to the group, whose members agreed to manage the colony without profit to themselves for a period of twenty-one years.

In 1733 their leader, James Oglethorpe, founded Savannah. Oglethorpe was a complicated person—vain and high-handed, yet idealistic. He hoped to people the colony with sober and industrious yeoman farmers. Land grants were limited to fifty acres and made nontransferable. To ensure sobriety, rum and other "Spirits and Strong Waters" were banned. To guarantee that the colonists would have to work hard, the entry of "any Black . . . Negroe" was prohibited. Trade with Indians was to be strictly regulated in the interest of fair dealing.

Oglethorpe intended that silk, wine, and olive oil would be the main products— none of which, unfortunately, could be profitably produced in Georgia. His noble inten- tions were in vain. The settlers swiftly found ways to circumvent all restrictions: Rum flowed, slaves were imported, large land holdings amassed. Georgia developed an econ- omy much like South Carolina's. In 1752 the founders, disillusioned, abandoned their responsibilities. Georgia then became a royal colony.

Now settlers penetrated the rest of the southern back country. So long as cheap land remained available closer to the coast and Indians along the frontier remained a threat, only the most daring and footloose hunters or fur traders lived far inland. But once settlement began, it came with a rush. Chief among those making the trek were Scots-Irish and German immigrants. By 1770 the back country contained about 250,000 settlers, 10 percent of the population of the colonies.

This internal migration did not proceed altogether peacefully. In 1771 frontiers- men in North Carolina calling themselves "Regulators" fought a pitched battle with 1,200 troops dispatched by the Carolina assembly, which was dominated by low- country interests. The Regulators were protesting their lack of representation in the assembly. They were crushed and their leaders executed. This was neither the last nor the bloodiest sectional conflict in American history.

Puritan New England

If survival in the Chesapeake colonies required junking many European notions about social arrangements and submitting to the dictates of the wilderness, was this also true in Massachusetts and Connecticut? Ultimately it probably was, but at first puritan ideas certainly fought the New England reality to a draw.

Boston, like other early New England towns and unlike these southern ones, had a dependable water supply. The surrounding patchwork of forest, pond, dunes, and tide marsh was much more open than the malaria-infected terrain of the tidewater and low- country South. As a consequence New Englanders escaped "the agues and fevers" that beset settlers to the south, leaving them free to attend to their spiritual, economic, and social well-being. These differences alone made New England a much healthier habitat for settlers.

New England children like David, Joanna, and Abigail Mason (painted by an unknown artist around 1670) were expected to emulate adults in their chores and their appearance. Nevertheless, diaries and letters indicate that children were cherished by their parents in a way closer to modern family love than what their European contemporaries experienced.

When it came to religion, puritans believed that church membership ought to be the joint decision of a would-be member and those already in the church. Those seeking admission would tell the congregation why they believed that they had received God's grace. Obvious sinners and those ignorant of Christian doctrine were rejected out of hand. But what of pious and God-fearing applicants who lacked compelling evidence of salvation? In the late 1630s, with the Great Migration in full swing and new arrivals clamoring for admission to the churches, such "merit-mongers" were excluded, thereby limiting church membership to the community's "visible saints." A decade later, the Great Migration over and applications down, some of the saints began to have second thoughts.

View the Image
Colonial Families: Adult and Child Reading at
myhistorylab.com

By the early 1650s fewer than half of all New England adults were church members. The examination for membership had become so exacting that most young people refused to submit themselves to it. How these growing numbers of nonmembers could be compelled to attend church services was a problem ministers could not ignore. Meanwhile, the magistrates found it harder to defend the policy of not letting taxpayers vote because they were not church members. But what really forced reconsideration of the membership policy were the concerns of nonmember parents about the souls of their children, who could not be baptized.

At first the churches permitted baptism of the children of church members. Later, some biblical purists came out against infant baptism altogether, but most puritans approved this practice, which allowed them the hope that a child who died after receiving baptism might at least be spared Hell's hottest precincts. Since most of the first generation were church members, nearly all the second-generation New Englanders were baptized, whether they became church members or not. The problem began with the third generation, the offspring of parents who had been baptized but who did not become church members. By the mid-1650s it was clear that if nothing were done, a majority of the people would soon be living in a state of original sin. If that happened, how could the churches remain the dominant force in New England life?

Fortunately, a way out was at hand. In 1657 an assembly of Massachusetts and Connecticut ministers recommended a form of intermediate church membership that would permit the baptism of people who were not visible saints. Five years later, some eighty ministers and laymen met at Boston's First Church to hammer out what came to be called the **Half-Way Covenant**. It provided limited (halfway) membership for any applicant not known to be a sinner who was willing to accept the provisions of the church covenant. They and their children could be baptized, but the sacrament of communion and a voice in church decision making were reserved for full members.

The General Court of Massachusetts endorsed the recommendations of the Half-Way Synod and urged all the churches of the Commonwealth to adopt them. Two years later it quietly extended the right to vote to halfway church members.

Opponents of the Half-Way Covenant argued that it reflected a slackening of religious fervor. Michael Wigglesworth gave poetic voice to these views in "God's Controversy with New England" and "The Day of Doom," both written in 1662. New Englanders may have lost some religious intensity, but the rise in church memberships, the continuing prestige accorded ministers, and the lessening of the intrachurch squabbling after the 1660s suggest that the secularization of New England society had a long way to go.

Democracies without Democrats

Like the southern colonies, the New England colonies derived their authority from charters granted by the Crown or Parliament. Except for rare fits of meddling by London bureaucrats, they were largely left to their own devices where matters of purely local interest were concerned. This typically involved maintaining order by regulating how people behaved.

According to puritan theory, government was both a civil covenant, entered into by all who came within its jurisdiction, and the principal mechanism for policing the institutions on which the maintenance of the social order depended. When Massachusetts and Connecticut passed laws requiring church attendance, levying taxes for the support of the clergy, and banning Quakers from practicing their faith, they were acting as "shield of the churches." When they provided the death penalty both for adultery and for blaspheming a parent, they were defending the integrity of families. When they set the price a laborer might charge for his services or even the amount of gold braid that servants might wear on their jackets, they believed they were enforcing the puritan principle that people must accept their assigned stations in life. Puritan communities were, for a time, close-knit: murder, assault, and theft were rare. Disputes were adjudicated through an active court system.

But puritan civil authorities and ministers of the puritan (Congregational) church came under sharp attack from English Anglicans, Presbyterians, and Quakers. When the Massachusetts General Court hanged four Quakers who returned after being expelled from the colony, a royal order of 1662 forbade further executions.

Laws like these have prompted historians and Americans generally to characterize New England colonial legislation as socially repressive and personally invasive. Yet many of the laws remained in force through the colonial period without rousing much local opposition. Others, particularly those upholding religious discrimination or restricting economic activity, were repealed at the insistence of Parliament.

A healthy respect for the backsliding ways of humanity obliged New Englanders not to depend too much on provincial governments, whose jurisdiction extended over several thousand square miles. Almost of necessity, the primary responsibility for maintaining "Good Order and Peace" fell to the more than 500 towns of the region. These differed greatly in size and development. By the early eighteenth century, the largest—Boston, Newport, and Portsmouth—were on their way toward becoming urban centers. This was before "frontier" towns like Amherst, Kent, and Hanover had even been founded. Nonetheless, town life gave New England the distinctiveness it has still not wholly lost.

The Dominion of New England

The most serious threat to these arrangements occurred in the 1680s. Following the execution of Charles I in 1649, England was ruled by one man, the Lord Protector, Oliver Cromwell, a puritan. Cromwell's death in 1658 led to the restoration of the Stuart monarchy in the person of Charles II (1660–1685). During his reign and the abbreviated one of his brother, James II (1685–1688), the government sought to bring the colonies under effective royal control.

Massachusetts seemed in particular need of supervision. Accordingly, in 1684 its charter was annulled and the colony, along with all those north of Pennsylvania, became part of the Dominion of New England, governed by Edmund Andros.

Andros arrived in Boston in late 1686 with orders to make the northern colonies behave like colonies, not like sovereign powers. He set out to abolish popular assemblies and to enforce religious toleration, particularly of Anglicans. Andros, being a professional soldier and administrator, scoffed at those who resisted his authority. "Knoweing no other government than their owne," he said, they "think it best, and are wedded to . . . it."

Fortunately for New Englanders so wedded, the Dominion fell victim two years later to yet another political turnabout in England, the **Glorious Revolution**. In 1688 Parliament decided it had had enough of the Catholic-leaning Stuarts and sent James II packing. In his place it installed James's daughter Mary and her resolutely Protestant Dutch husband, William of Orange. When news of these events reached Boston in the spring of 1689, a force of more than a thousand colonists led by a contingent of ministers seized Andros and lodged him in jail. Two years later Massachusetts was made a royal colony that also included Plymouth and Maine. As in all such colonies the governor was appointed by the king. The new General Court was elected by property owners; church membership was no longer a requirement for voting.

Salem Bewitched

In 1666, families living in the rural outback of the thriving town of Salem petitioned the General Court for the right to establish their own church. For political and economic reasons this was a questionable move, but in 1672 the General Court authorized the establishment of a separate parish. In so doing the Court put the 600-odd inhabitants of the village on their own politically as well.

Over the next fifteen years three preachers came and went before. in 1689, one Samuel Parris became minister. Parris had spent twenty years in the Caribbean as a merchant and had taken up preaching only three years before coming to Salem. Accompanying him were his wife; a daughter, Betty; a niece, Abigail; and the family's West Indian slave, Tituba, who told fortunes and practiced magic on the side.

Parris proved as incapable of bringing peace to the feuding factions of the Salem Village as had his predecessors. In January 1692 the church voted to dismiss him. At this point Betty and Abigail, now nine and eleven, along with Ann Putnam, a twelve-year-old, started "uttering foolish, ridiculous speeches which neither they themselves nor any others could make sense of." A doctor diagnosed the girls' ravings as the work of the "Evil Hand" and declared them bewitched.

●●●—|Read the **Document**

Ann Putnam's Deposition (1692) at **myhistorylab.com**

But who had done the bewitching? The first persons accused were three women whose unsavory reputations and frightening appearances made them likely candidates. Sarah Good, a pauper with a nasty tongue; Sarah Osborne, a bedridden widow; and the slave Tituba, who had brought suspicion on herself by volunteering to bake a "witch cake," made of rye meal and the girls' urine. The cake should be fed to a dog, Tituba said. If the girls were truly afflicted, the dog would show signs of bewitchment.

The three women were brought before the local deputies to the General Court. As each was questioned, the girls went into contortions: "their arms, necks and backs

Examination of a Witch. A stern puritan patriarch adjusts his glasses to better examine a beautiful—and partially disrobed—young woman. Ostensibly, he is looking for the "witch's teats" with which she suckled 'black dogs" and other creatures of the Devil. Completed in 1853 by T. H. Matteson, this painting subtly indicts puritan men as lecherous hypocrites. In fact, most accused witches were in their forties or fifties. The painting thus reveals more about the nineteenth-century reaction against puritanism than about the puritans themselves.
Source: Museum Purchase, 1978. Peabody Essex Museum, Salem, Massachussetts.

turned this way and that way . . . their mouths stopped, their throats choaked, their limbs wracked and tormented." Tituba, likely impressed by the powers ascribed to her, promptly confessed to being a witch. Sarah Good and Sarah Osborne each claimed to be innocent, although Sarah Good expressed doubts about Sarah Osborne. All three were sent to jail on suspicion of practicing witchcraft.

These proceedings triggered new accusations. By the end of April 1692, twenty-four more people had been charged with practicing witchcraft. Officials in neighboring Andover, lacking their own "bewitched," called in the girls to help with their investigations. By May the hunt had extended to Maine and Boston and up the social ladder to some of the colony's most prominent citizens, including Lady Mary Phips, whose husband, William, had just been appointed governor.

By June, when Governor Phips convened a special court consisting of members of his council, more than 150 persons (Lady Phips no longer among them) stood formally charged with practicing witchcraft. In the next four months the court convicted twenty-eight of them, most of them women. Five "confessed" and were spared; the rest were condemned to death. Several others escaped. But nineteen persons were hanged. The husband of a convicted witch refused to enter a plea when charged with being a "wizard." He was executed by having stones piled on him until he suffocated.

Anyone who spoke in defense of the accused was in danger of being charged with witchcraft, but some brave souls challenged both the procedures and the findings of the court. Finally, at the urging of the leading ministers of the Commonwealth, Governor Phips adjourned the court and forbade any further executions.

No one involved in these gruesome proceedings escaped with a reputation intact, but those whose reputations suffered most were the ministers. Among the clergy only Increase Mather deserves any credit. He persuaded Phips to halt the executions, arguing that "it were better that ten witches should escape, than that one innocent person should be condemned." The behavior of his son Cotton defies apology. It was not that Cotton Mather accepted the existence of witches—at the time everyone did, which incidentally suggests that Tituba was not the only person in Salem who practiced witchcraft—or even that Mather took such pride in being the resident expert on demonology. It was rather his vindictiveness. He even stood at the foot of the gallows bullying hesitant hangmen into doing "their duty."

The episode also highlights the anxieties puritan men felt toward women. Many puritans believed that Satan worked his will especially through the allure of female sexuality. Moreover, many of the accused witches were widows of high status or older women who owned property; some of the women, like Tituba, had mastered herbal medicine and other suspiciously potent healing arts. Such women, especially those who lived apart from the daily guidance of men, potentially subverted the patriarchal authorities of church and state. (For more on this topic, see Re-Viewing the Past, *The Crucible*, pp. 74–75.)

A Merchant's World

Prior experience (and the need to eat) turned the first New Englanders to farming. They grew barley (used to make beer), rye, oats, green vegetables, and also native crops such as potatoes, pumpkins, and (most important) Indian corn, or maize. Corn was easily cultivated. In the form of corn liquor it was easy to store, to transport, and (in a pinch) to imbibe.

The colonists also had plenty of meat. They grazed cattle, sheep, and hogs on the common pastures or in the surrounding woodlands. Deer, along with turkey and other game birds, abounded. The Atlantic provided fish, especially cod, which was preserved by salting. In short, New Englanders ate an extremely nutritious diet. Abundant surpluses of firewood kept the winter cold from their doors. The combination contributed significantly to their good health and longevity.

But the shortness of the growing season, the rocky and often hilly terrain, and careless methods of cultivation, which exhausted the soil, meant that farmers did not produce large surpluses. Thus, while New Englanders could feed themselves without difficulty, they had relatively little to spare.

John Winthrop's generation of puritans accepted this economic marginality. They were to fasten their attention upon the next world rather than the one they occupied on Earth.

But later generations did not share the anticommercial bias of the early puritans. At the beginning of the eighteenth century a Boston minister told his congregation of another minister who reminded his flock that "the main end of planting this wilderness" was religion. A prominent member of the congregation could not contain his disagreement. "Sir," he cried out, "you are mistaken. You think you are preaching to the people of the Bay; our main end was to catch fish."

Fish, caught offshore from Cape Cod to Newfoundland, provided merchants with their opening into the world of transatlantic commerce. In 1643 five New England vessels set out with their holds packed with fish that they sold in Spain and the Canary Islands; they took payment in sherry and Madeira, for which a market existed in England. One of these ships also had the dubious distinction of initiating New England into the business of trafficking in human beings when its captain took payment in African slaves, whom he subsequently sold in the West Indies. This was the start of the famous **triangular trade**. Only occasionally was the pattern truly triangular; more often, intermediate legs gave it a polygonal character. So long as their ships ended up with something that could be exchanged for English goods needed at home, it did not matter what they started out with or how many things they bought and sold along the way.

So maritime trade and those who engaged in it became the driving force of the New England economy, important all out of proportion to the number of persons directly involved. Because mariners congregated in Portsmouth, Salem, Boston, Newport, and New Haven, these towns soon differed greatly from towns in the interior. They were larger and faster growing, and a smaller percentage of their inhabitants were farmers.

The largest and most thriving town was Boston, which by 1720 had become the commercial hub of the region. It had a population of more than 10,000; in the entire British Empire, only London and Bristol were larger. More than one-quarter of Boston's male adults had either invested in shipbuilding or were directly employed in maritime commerce. Ship captains and merchants held most of the public offices.

Beneath this emergent mercantile elite lived a stratum of artisans and small shopkeepers, and beneath these a substantial population of mariners, laborers, and "unattached" people with little or no property and still less political voice. By 1720 crime and

The Crucible

Winona Ryder stars in the 1996 movie based on Arthur Miller's 1953 play, *The Crucible*, an interpretation of the Salem witch trials of 1692. Ryder plays Abigail Williams, consumed with desire for John Proctor (Daniel Day-Lewis), a married man. Proctor has broken off their affair and reconciled with his wife, Elizabeth (Joan Allen). As the movie begins, Abigail and some other girls have sneaked into the woods with Tituba, a slave who practices black magic. They ask about their future husbands, and some beg her to cast a spell on their favorites. Abigail whispers something to Tituba, who recoils in horror. Abigail's dark eyes glow with fury: She wants Elizabeth Proctor dead. Tituba slips into a trance and begins conjuring. Exhilarated by this illicit flouting of convention the girls throw off their clothes and dance wildly around a fire.

Then the minister happens onto the scene. The girls flee in terror. Some become hysterical. Later, when confronted by church elders, Abigail blurts out that Tituba was a witch who was trying to steal their souls. Tituba initially denies the charges, but after being whipped she confesses. Pressed further, she names two other women as accomplices. At the mention of their names, Abigail's face contorts with pain and she moans; taking the cue, the other girls scream and writhe upon the floor. They supply the names of more witches. Alarmed by the enormity of Satan's plot, Massachusetts authorities initiate an investigation.

After one court session, Abigail saunters over to John, standing by the side of the church. When he asks what "mischief" she has been up to, Abigail averts her eyes demurely and then gives him a wicked grin. John smiles at this prodigy in the seductive arts. She responds with a kiss. He hesitates, but then roughly pushes her away. He has reconciled with Elizabeth; he wants nothing more of Abigail. Her eyes blaze with hatred.

The girls' hysterics intensify. Eventually over 100 suspected witches, most of them women, are arrested. The Proctors themselves come under suspicion. When Abigail accuses Elizabeth of being a witch, John lashes out at the girl.

"She is a whore," he declares in court. "I have known her, sir."

"He is lying," Abigail hisses. Suddenly her eyes widen, horror-stricken, and she screams that he, too, is in league with Satan. Her flawless histrionics again prevail: He is arrested.

During the trials, the magistrates look for physical evidence of satanic possession: unnatural flaps of skin or unusual warts—witch's teats—with which Satan's minions sap human souls. Family and neighbors, too, furnish evidence. Some cite occasions when the accused lost their tempers or stole livestock. But the main evidence is the behavior of the girls, who squirm and howl, claiming that the spirits of the accused torment them. This "spectral" evidence unsettles the magistrates. Seeking stronger proof, they urge prisoners to confess. Those who do will be spared, for the act of confession signifies their break with Satan. Those who refuse must be hanged.

The Proctors are among those convicted and sentenced to death. (Because Elizabeth is pregnant, her execution is postponed.) When given the opportunity to save himself, John signs a confession. But inspired by his wife's quiet courage, he repudiates it, choosing to die with honor rather than live in shame. His noble death at the scaffold, and the deaths of others like him, cause the people of Massachusetts to end the witch hunt.

The Crucible warrants consideration apart from Ryder's remarkable performance. For one, the movie vividly recreates a puritan world inhabited by palpable spirits. Contemporary viewers may snicker at scenes of adults scanning the night sky for flying witches and evil birds, but the puritans believed in such things. They regarded comets, meteors, and lightning as signals from God. For example, when Cotton Mather lost the pages of a lecture, he concluded that "Spectres, or Agents in the invisible World, were the Robbers."

The movie's rendering of the girls' hysteria mostly corresponds with what we know from the historical record. A bewildered John Hale, a minister from Beverly, recorded that Abigail and her cousin were

> bitten and pinched by invisible agents. Their arms, necks and backs turned this way and that way, and returned back again, so as it was impossible for them to do of themselves. . . . Sometimes they were taken dumb, their mouths stopped, their throats choked, their limbs wracked and tormented so as might move an heart of stone.

The movie mostly attributes the girls' hysteria to sexual frustration, a consequence of puritan repression.

Ryder's Abigail symbolizes adolescent sexuality: Her lust for John (and hatred of Elizabeth) precipitates the witch hunt. A few historical details provide some basis for Abigail's conjectured affair with Elizabeth's husband, but others call it into question, the most telling being the gap in their ages: The real Abigail was eleven and Proctor, sixty.

Whatever the merits of playwright Arthur Miller's speculation about Abigail and John, his larger questions have long intrigued historians: Were the puritans sexually repressive? If so, did young people assent to puritan strictures or rebel against them?

Such questions cannot be answered with certainty. Few puritans left written accounts of their illicit thoughts and sexual behavior. Social historians have approached the matter from a different angle. Nearly all marriages and births in colonial New England (and most other places) were recorded. Scholars have scoured such records to determine how many brides gave birth to babies within six months of marriage; such women almost certainly had engaged in premarital intercourse.

This data for about a dozen communities in puritan New England indicate an extraordinarily low rate of premarital intercourse, far below

This image shows actress Winona Ryder as a young puritan who accuses others of witchcraft.

England's at the same time or New England's a century later. This suggests that young puritan couples were watched closely. Governor William Bradford of Plymouth Colony, commenting on the relative absence of premarital pregnancy, concluded that sinners there were "more discovered and seen and made public by due search, inquisition and due punishment; for the churches look narrowly to their members, and the magistrates over all, more strictly than in other places." On the other hand, the low rate of premarital pregnancy might not signify puritan repression so much as young people's acceptance of puritan values.

When critics confronted Arthur Miller on his deviations from the historical record, and especially when they expressed skepticism over whether young Abigail Williams and the elderly John Proctor had an affair, Miller was unrepentant. "What's real?" he retorted. "We don't know what these people were like." Perhaps so, but one suspects that Winona Ryder's Abigail would have had a hard time in Salem in 1692. Could a bloom of such poisonous precocity have emerged through the stony soil of New England puritanism, and if so, could it have survived the attentive weeding of the puritans themselves?

Questions for Discussion

- What factors, apart from those mentioned in this essay, explain why puritan brides rarely had babies within six months of their marriage? Is this a good measure of premarital chastity?

- How did puritan courtship differ from modern courtship?

New York politics continued to be a struggle between the Leislerians and other self-conscious "outs" who shared Leisler's dislike of English rule, and anti-Leislerians. Each group sought the support of a succession of ineffective governors, and the group that failed to get it invariably proceeded to make that governor's tenure as miserable as possible.

New York enjoyed political tranquility during the governorship of Robert Hunter (1710–1719), but in the early 1730s conflict broke out over a claim for back salary by Governor William Cosby. When Lewis Morris, the chief justice of the supreme court, opposed Cosby's claim, the governor replaced him. Morris and his assembly allies responded by establishing the *New York Weekly Journal*. To edit the paper they hired German printer, John Peter Zenger.

Governor Cosby might have tolerated the *Weekly Journal*'s front-page lectures on the right of the people to criticize their rulers had the back pages not contained advertisements referring to his supporters as spaniels and to him as a monkey. After submitting to two months of "open and implacable malice against me," he shut down the paper, arrested Zenger, and charged him with seditious libel.

What began as a salary dispute became one of the most celebrated tests of freedom of the press in the history of journalism. At the trial Zenger's attorney, Andrew Hamilton, argued that the truth of his client's criticisms of Cosby constituted a proper defense against seditious libel. This reasoning (though contrary to English law at the time) persuaded the jury to acquit Zenger.

Politics in Pennsylvania spurred conflict between two interest groups, one clustered around the proprietor, the other around the assembly, which was controlled by a coalition of Quaker representatives from Philadelphia and the German-speaking Pennsylvania Dutch.

Neither the proprietary party nor the Quaker party qualifies as a political party in the modern sense of being organized and maintained for the purpose of winning elections. Nor can they be categorized as standing for "democratic" or "aristocratic" interests. But their existence guaranteed that the political leaders had to take popular opinion into account. Moreover, having once appealed to public opinion, they had to be prepared to defer to it. Success turned as much on knowing how to follow as on knowing how to lead.

The 1763 uprising of the "Paxton Boys" of western Pennsylvania put this policy to a full test. The uprising was triggered by eastern indifference to Indian attacks on the frontier—an indifference made possible by the fact that the east outnumbered the west in the assembly, twenty-six to ten. Fuming because it could obtain no help from Philadelphia against the Indians, a group of Scots-Irish from Lancaster county fell on a village of peaceful Conestoga Indians and murdered them. Then these Paxton Boys marched on Philadelphia, several hundred strong.

Fortunately a delegation of burghers, headed by Benjamin Franklin, talked the Paxton Boys out of attacking the town by acknowledging the legitimacy of their grievances about representation and by promising to vote a bounty on Indian scalps. It was just such fancy footwork that established Franklin, the leader of the assembly party, as Pennsylvania's consummate politician. Soon thereafter, the assembly sent Franklin to London to defend local interests against the British authorities, a situation in which he would definitely not be "with the majority."

Becoming Americans

In 1650, nearly 50,000 English settlers lived in what is now the United States. Most clung to the Atlantic coast, within easy reach of ships that could bring essential supplies, protection, and means of escape. Indians outnumbered them by about ten to one; African slaves were rare. French and Spanish colonization in what is now the United States was numerically even more inconsequential, with only about 1,000 Hispanics and even fewer Frenchmen. From the Appalachian Mountains to the Pacific, most Indians had probably never seen a European.

By 1750 the demographic situation had been transformed. Nearly a million Europeans, the great majority of English background, and perhaps a quarter of a million African slaves occupied the Atlantic seaboard. The Indians had not been entirely removed: Scores of Indian villages had been enveloped by English settlement. Tens of thousands more Indians had retreated into coastal swamplands or the foothills of the Appalachians. But English-speaking peoples had become masters of the land east of the Appalachians.

◉ See the **Map**

The Colonies to 1740 at **myhistorylab.com**

After 1750, the immense sea of risk-taking English-speaking peoples and African slaves that had flooded into the eastern portion of the continent would spill beyond the Appalachians. By sheer force of their numbers, the English would decisively influence American identity, if only by making English the dominant language. Most of the immigrants, too, were farmers, united by a seemingly inexhaustible craving for land. But these enterprising immigrants also differed in fundamental ways. The cultures the immigrants brought with them varied according to the nationality, social status, and taste of the individual. The newcomers never lost their foreign heritage entirely, but they—and certainly their descendants—became something quite different from their relatives who remained in the Old World. They became what we call Americans.

But not right away.

Milestones

1619	First Africans are sold in Virginia	**1692**	Salem Village holds witchcraft trials
1636	Puritans found Boston Latin School and Harvard College	**1696**	Virginia colonists found College of William and Mary
1657	Half-Way Covenant leads to rise in Puritan church memberships		Rice cultivation is introduced in South Carolina
1676	Western planters launch Bacon's Rebellion in Virginia	**1701**	Connecticut ministers found Yale College
1684–1688	Edmund Andros rules Dominion of New England	**1733**	George Oglethorpe leads settlement of Georgia
1689	Leisler's Rebellion in New York seizes control of government		

✓•Study and **Review** at www.myhistorylab.com

Review Questions

1. How did the strategies used by Spain, France, and England differ in peopling their colonies in North America? Why did the English prevail?

2. How did the English colonies along the Atlantic coastline differ from each other? What were the strengths and long-term weaknesses of each pattern of settlement and development?

3. Why did slavery supplant indentured servitude in the South? Why didn't slavery take hold in the northern colonies?

4. This chapter outlines the ways in which the area that now constitutes the United States was settled by people who differed in terms of nationality and religion, race and ethnic group, and even by contending classes. What did they share in common?

Key Terms

Bacon's
Rebellion   *59*
Glorious
Revolution   *66*

Half-Way
Covenant   *65*
headright   *54*

indentured servants   *55*
Leisler's Rebellion   *73*
triangular trade   *69*

America in the
British Empire

3

((•—Hear the Audio Chapter 3 at myhistorylab.com

Do you pay too much in taxes?

IN 2009 THE AVERAGE AMERICAN PAID ABOUT ONE-THIRD OF HIS OR HER income to the federal government. Polls show that most Americans believe their taxes are too high. According to the Internal Revenue Service, about 17 percent of American taxpayers in 2008 failed to comply with the tax laws. Many say that they pay taxes only because they are forced to do so.

Yet most Americans pay, and do so voluntarily. Of the 170 million Americans who owed federal taxes in 2008, 155 million filed returns. And while the tax code includes stern punishments for cheaters, criminal prosecutions are rare. In 2008 fewer than 2,500 Americans were convicted of tax crimes, a number that has steadily declined over the past decade.

In the mid-1700s, by contrast, American colonists paid no more than one-twentieth of their income in taxes, far less than their relatives in England. Yet taxation provoked the colonists more than any other issue. John Adams, a Massachusetts lawyer whose opposition to taxes catapulted him to fame, blamed the American Revolution on England's "enormous taxes, burdensome taxes, oppressive, ruinous, intolerable taxes."

Colonial fury was partly due to a change in how London assessed and collected taxes. During the first half of the eighteenth century, most taxes were set by colonial assemblies and based on landholdings. But after 1763 the British government in London imposed new taxes on trade. When ships entered American ports, captains were required to pay taxes before the "enumerated" (taxable) cargos could be moved from the docks. Whenever Americans bought a bag of nails or a tin of tea, they were making indirect tax payments to London. Tax cheats avoided customs officials by smuggling goods. But rather than evade the "intolerable" tax burden, colonists increasingly decided to eliminate it altogether.

Resistance to taxation was only one of the sources of tumult in mid-eighteenth-century America. The taxes themselves had been necessitated by war, always a destabilizing force in human affairs. Some people, too, experienced a "great awakening" in religious faith; others looked to the European Enlightenment and its enshrinement of reason and science. Traditional ideas and institutions were being scrutinized more closely. By the 1760s and 1770s, irritation over taxes was symptomatic of a more profound societal unease.

The British Colonial System

In the earliest days of any settlement, the need to rely on home authorities was so strong that few questioned England's sovereignty. Thereafter, distance and British political inefficiency combined to allow those living in the colonies a great deal of freedom. External affairs were controlled entirely by London, and royal representatives in America tried to direct colonial policy. But in practice the Crown generally ceded control in local matters to the colonies while reserving the right to veto actions it deemed to be against national interest.

Each colony had a governor chosen by the king in the case of the royal colonies and by the proprietors of Maryland, Delaware, and Pennsylvania. The governors' powers were much like those of the king in Great Britain. They executed the local laws, appointed many minor officials, summoned and dismissed the colonial assemblies, and proposed legislation to them. They possessed the right to veto colonial laws, but in most colonies they were financially dependent on their "subjects."

Each colony also had a legislature. Except in Pennsylvania, these assemblies consisted of two houses. The lower house, chosen by qualified voters, had general legislative powers, including some control of finances. In all the royal colonies members of the upper house, or council, were appointed by the king, except in Massachusetts, where they were elected by the General Court. The councils served primarily as advisors to the governors, but they also had some judicial and legislative powers. Judges were appointed by the king and served at his pleasure. Yet both councilors and judges were normally selected from among the leaders of the local communities; London had neither the time nor the will to investigate their political beliefs. The system therefore tended to strengthen the influence of the entrenched colonials.

Most colonial legislators were practical men. Knowing their own interests, they pursued them steadily, without much regard for political theories or the desires of the royal authorities. They saw themselves as miniature Houses of Commons, steadily "nibbling" at the authority of the Crown. The king appointed governors, but governors came and went. The lawmakers remained, accumulating experience, building on precedent, and widening decade by decade their control over colonial affairs.

The official representatives of the Crown, whatever their powers or intentions, were prisoners of their surroundings. In their dealings with the assemblies they were often bound by rigid and impractical royal instructions. They had few jobs and favors to offer in their efforts to influence the legislators. Judges might interpret the law according to English precedents, but in local matters colonial juries had the final say.

Within the British government the king's Privy Council had the responsibility for formulating colonial policy. It could and did disallow (annul) specific colonial laws, but it did not proclaim constitutional principles to which all colonial legislatures must conform. It acted as a court of last appeal in colonial disputes and handled each case individually. One day the council might issue a set of instructions to the governor of Virginia, and the next day distribute a different set to the governor of South Carolina. No one person or committee thought broadly about the administration of the overseas empire.

In 1696 colonial policy was effectively determined by a new Board of Trade, which nominated colonial governors and other high officials. It reviewed all the laws passed by the colonial legislatures, recommending the disallowance of those that seemed to conflict with imperial policy. The efficiency and wisdom of the Board of Trade fluctuated over the years, but the Privy Council and the Crown nearly always accepted its recommendations.

Colonists naturally disliked having their laws disallowed, but London exercised this power with considerable restraint; only about 5 percent of the laws reviewed were rejected. Furthermore, the board served as an important intermediary for colonists seeking to influence the king and Parliament. All the colonies in the eighteenth century maintained agents in London to present the colonial point of view before board members. The most famous colonial agent was Benjamin Franklin, who represented Pennsylvania, Georgia, New Jersey, and Massachusetts at various times during his long career. In general, however, colonial agents were seldom able to exert much influence on British policy.

The British never developed an effective, centralized government for the American colonies. By and large, their American "subjects" ran their own affairs. This fact more than any other explains our present federal system and the wide areas in which the state governments are sovereign and independent.

Mercantilism

The Board of Trade was concerned with commerce as well as colonial administration. According to prevailing European opinion, colonies were important for economic reasons, chiefly as a source of raw materials. To obtain these materials, British officials developed a number of loosely related policies that later economists called **mercantilism.** The most important raw materials in the eyes of mercantilists were gold and silver, which, being universally valued and relatively rare, could be exchanged at any time or, being durable and compact, stored for future use. For these reasons, how much gold and silver a nation possessed was considered the best barometer of its prosperity and power.

Since gold and silver could not be mined in significant amounts in western Europe, every early colonist dreamed of finding "El Dorado." The Spanish were the winners in this search; from the mines of Mexico and South America gold and silver poured into the Iberian peninsula. Failing to control the precious metals at the source, the other powers tried to obtain them by guile and warfare (witness the state-supported piracy of Francis Drake).

In the mid-seventeenth century the statesman of western Europe shifted to a less hazardous and in the long run far more profitable approach. If a country could make itself as self-sufficient as possible and also keep its citizens busy producing items sought in other lands, it could sell more goods abroad than it imported. This was known as having "a favorable balance of trade." Mercantilists regarded colonies as a means of acquiring precious metals by helping the mother country generate a favorable trade balance. Colonists thus were to supply raw materials that would otherwise have to be purchased from foreign sources or colonists were to buy substantial amounts of manufactured goods produced in the mother country.

If the possession of gold and silver signified wealth, trade was the route that led to riches, and merchants were the captains who would pilot the state to prosperity. One

Carousing in Surinam by John Greenwood, a late eighteenth-century oil painting, describes the effects of alcohol—one man guzzles his rum punch straight from the bowl, another vomits onto the floor, while a third pours his punch onto an insensate colleague. Greenwood implicitly denounces as well the trade in sugar (rum) and slaves in which these captains were engaged.
Source: John Greenwood, American, 1727–1792; *Sea Captians Carousing in Surinam*, c. 1752–58; oil on bed ticking; 37 3/4 × 75 in. (95.9 × 190.5 cm); St. Louis Art Museum, Museum Purchase 256: 1948.

must, of course, have something to sell, so internal production must be stimulated. Parliament encouraged the British people to concentrate on manufacturing by placing tariffs—taxes on trade—on foreign manufactured goods and by subsidizing British-made textiles, iron, and other products.

The Navigation Acts

The promotion of commerce was fundamental. Toward this end Parliament enacted the **Navigation Acts**. These laws, put into effect over a period of half a century and more, were designed to bring gold and silver into the Royal Treasury, to develop the imperial merchant fleet, to channel the flow of colonial raw materials into England, and to keep foreign goods and vessels out of colonial ports.

The system originated in the 1650s in response to stiff commercial competition by the Dutch. Before 1650 a large share of the produce of the English colonies in America reached Europe in Dutch vessels; the first slaves in Virginia arrived on a Dutch ship and were doubtless paid for in tobacco that was later enjoyed in the Dutch cities of Amsterdam and Rotterdam.

The Navigation Act of 1660 reserved the entire trade of the colonies to English ships and required that the captain and three-quarters of his crew be English. (Colonists, of course, were English, and their ships were treated on the same terms as those sailing out of London or Liverpool.) The act also provided that certain colonial "enumerated articles"—sugar, tobacco, cotton, ginger, and dyes like indigo (purple) and fustic (yellow)—could not be "shipped, carried, conveyed or transported" outside the empire. Three years later Parliament required that with trifling exceptions all European products destined for the colonies be brought to England before being shipped across the Atlantic. Since trade between England and the colonies was reserved to English vessels, this meant that the goods would have to be unloaded and reloaded in England.

The English looked on the empire broadly; they envisioned the colonies as part of an economic unit, not as servile dependencies to be exploited for England's selfish benefit. Growing tobacco in England was prohibited, and valuable bounties were paid to colonial producers of indigo and naval stores. The carefully planned British economic system suited the realities of life in an underdeveloped country rich in raw materials and suffering from a chronic labor shortage.

Some historians stress the significance of the restrictions that the British placed on colonial manufacturing. The Wool Act of 1699 prohibited the export (but not the manufacture for local sale) of colonial woolen cloth. A similar law regarding hats was passed in 1732, and in 1750 an Iron Act outlawed the construction of new rolling and slitting mills in America. No other restrictions on manufacturing were imposed.

At most the Wool Act stifled a potential American industry; the law was directed chiefly at Irish woolens rather than American ones. The hat industry cannot be considered a major one. Iron, however, was important; by 1775 the industry was thriving in Virginia, Maryland, New Jersey, and Pennsylvania, and America was turning out one-seventh of the world supply. Yet the Iron Act was designed to steer the American iron industry in a particular direction, not to destroy it. Eager for iron to feed English mills, Parliament eliminated all duties on colonial pig and bar iron entering England, a great stimulus to the basic industry.

The Effects of Mercantilism

Colonists increasingly complained about mercantilism, but did it harm them? The chronic colonial shortage of hard money was superficially caused by the flow of specie—gold and silver—to England to meet the "unfavorable" balance of trade. The rapidly growing colonial economy consumed far more manufactured products than it could pay for out of current production. To be "in debt" to England really meant that the English were investing capital in America, a relationship that benefited lender and borrower alike.

Important colonial products for which no market existed in England (such as fish, wheat, and corn) were never enumerated and moved freely and directly to foreign ports. Most colonial manufacturing was untouched by English law. Shipbuilding benefited from the Navigation Acts, since many English merchants bought vessels built in the colonies. Between 1769 and 1771, Massachusetts, New Hampshire, and Rhode Island yards constructed perhaps 250 ships of 100 to 400 tons for transatlantic commerce and twice that many sloops and schooners for fishermen and coastal traders.

Two forces that worked in opposite directions must be considered before arriving at any judgment about English mercantilism. While the theory presupposed a general imperial interest above that of both colony and mother country, when conflicts of interest arose the latter nearly always predominated. Whenever Parliament or the Board of Trade resolved an Anglo-American disagreement, the colonists tended to lose.

Complementary interests conspired to keep conflicts at a minimum, but in the long run, as the American economy became more complex, the colonies would have been seriously hampered and much more trouble would have occurred had the system continued to operate.

5-Year Averages (1774: 4-Year Average)

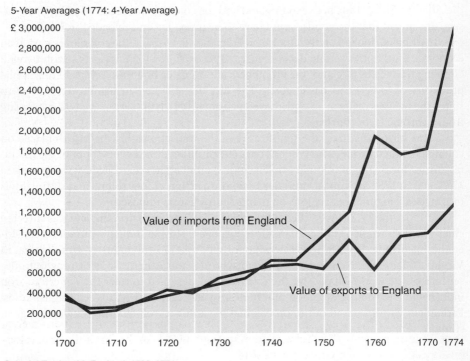

Colonial Trade with England, 1700–1774

On the other hand, the restrictions of English mercantilism were greatly lessened by inefficiency. The king and his ministers handed out government posts to win political favor or to repay political debts, regardless of the recipient's ability to perform the duties of the office.

Transported to remote America, this system scarcely functioned at all when local opinion resisted it. Smuggling became a respected profession and bribery of English officials was a standard practice. Despite a supposedly prohibitive duty of sixpence a gallon imposed by the Molasses Act of 1733, molasses from the French West Indies continued to be imported. The duty was seldom collected.

Mercantilist policies hurt some colonists such as the tobacco planters, who grew far more tobacco than British consumers could smoke. But the policies helped others, and most people proved adept at getting around those aspects of the system that threatened them.

By the same token, England profited greatly from its overseas possessions. With all its inefficiencies, mercantilism worked. Prime Minister Sir Robert Walpole's famous policy of "salutary neglect," which involved looking the other way when Americans violated the Navigation Acts, was partly a bowing to the inevitable, and partly the result of complacency. English manufactures were better and cheaper than those of other nations. This fact, together with ties of language and a common heritage, predisposed Americans toward doing business in England. All else followed naturally; the mercantilist laws merely steered the American economy in a direction it had already taken.

In this painting evangelist George Whitefield appears to be cross-eyed. This is no fault of John Wollaston, the painter. Whitefield had eye problems; his detractors called him "Dr. Squintum." The woman's rapturous gaze is unaffected by Whitefield's own curious visage.

The Great Awakening

Although a majority of the settlers were of English, Scotch, or Scots-Irish descent, and their interests generally coincided with those of their cousins in the mother country, people in the colonies were beginning to recognize their common interests and character. Their loyalties were still predominantly local, but by 1750 the word American, used to describe something characteristic of all the British possessions in North America, had entered the language. Events in one part of America were beginning to have direct effects on other regions. One of the first of these developments was the so-called **Great Awakening**.

By the early eighteenth century, religious fervor had slackened in all the colonies. Prosperity turned many colonists away from their ancestors' preoccupation with the rewards of the next world to the more tangible ones of this one. John Winthrop invested his faith in God and his own efforts in the task of creating a spiritual community; his grandsons invested in Connecticut real estate.

The proliferation of religious denominations made it impracticable to enforce laws requiring regular religious observances. Even in South Carolina, the colony that came closest to having an "Anglican Establishment," only a minority were churchgoers. Settlers in frontier districts lived beyond the reach of church or clergy. The result was a large and growing number of "persons careless of all religion."

This state of affairs came to an abrupt end with the Great Awakening of the 1740s. The Awakening began in the Middle Colonies as the result of religious developments that originated in Europe. In the late 1720s two newly arrived ministers, Theodore Frelinghuysen, a Calvinist from Westphalia, and William Tennent, an Irish-born Presbyterian, sought to instill in their sleepy Pennsylvania and New Jersey congregations the evangelical zeal and spiritual enthusiasm they had witnessed among the Pietists in Germany and the Methodist followers of John Wesley in England. Their example inspired other clergymen, including Tennent's two sons.

A more significant surge of religious enthusiasm followed the arrival in 1738 in Georgia of the Reverend George Whitefield, a young Oxford-trained Anglican minister. Whitefield was a rousing pulpit orator who played on the feelings of his audience the way a conductor directs a symphony. Whitefield undertook a series of fund-raising tours throughout the colonies. The most successful began

Read the Document

Franklin on George Whitefield (1771) at myhistorylab.com

in Philadelphia in 1739. Benjamin Franklin, not a very religious person and not easily moved by emotional appeals, heard one of these sermons. "I silently resolved he should get nothing from me," he later recalled.

> I had in my Pocket a Handful of Copper Money, three or four silver Dollars, and five Pistoles in Gold. As he proceeded I began to soften and concluded to give the Coppers. Another Stroke of his Oratory . . . determin'd me to give the Silver; and he finish'd so admirably that I empty'd my Pocket wholly into the Collector's Dish.

Whitefield's visit changed the "manners of our inhabitants," Franklin added.

Wherever Whitefield went he filled the churches. If no local clergyman offered his pulpit, Whitefield attracted thousands to outdoor meetings. During a three-day visit to Boston, 19,000 people (more than the population of the town) thronged to hear him. His oratorical brilliance aside, Whitefield succeeded in releasing an epidemic of religious emotionalism because his message was so well-suited to American ears. By preaching a theology that one critic said was "scaled down to the comprehension of twelve-year-olds," he spared his audiences the rigors of hard thought. Though he usually began by chastising his listeners as sinners, "half animals and half devils," he invariably took care to leave them with the hope that eternal salvation could be theirs. While not denying the doctrine of predestination, he preached a God responsive to good intentions. He disregarded sectarian differences and encouraged his listeners to do the same. "God help us to forget party names and become Christians in deed and truth," he prayed.

Of course not everyone found the Whitefield style enlightening. Some churches split into factions. Those who supported the incumbent minister were called among Congregationalists, "Old Lights," and among Presbyterians, "Old Sides," while those who favored revivalism were known as "New Lights" and "New Sides." These splits often ran along class lines. The richer, better-educated members of the church tended to support the traditional arrangements.

But many were deeply moved by the new ideas. Those chafing under the restraints of puritan authoritarianism, or feeling guilty over their preoccupation with material goods, now found release. For some the release was more than spiritual; Timothy Cutler, a conservative Anglican clergyman, complained that as a result of the Awakening "our presses are forever teeming with books and our women with bastards." Whether or not Cutler was correct, the Great Awakening helped some people to rid themselves of the idea that disobedience to authority entailed damnation. Anything that God justified, human law could not condemn. The Great Awakening did not entail opposition to British tax policies, but it did undermine traditional conceptions of authority.

Other institutions besides the churches were affected by the Great Awakening. In 1741 the president of Yale College criticized the theology of itinerant ministers who imitated Whitefield. Other revivalists called on the New Light churches of Connecticut to withdraw their support from Yale and endow a college of their own. The result was the College of New Jersey (now Princeton), founded in 1746 by New Side Presbyterians. Three other educational by-products of the Great Awakening followed: the College of Rhode Island (Brown), founded by Baptists in 1765; Queen's College (Rutgers), founded by Dutch Reformers in 1766; and Dartmouth, founded by New Light Congregationalists in 1769.

The Rise and Fall of Jonathan Edwards

Jonathan Edwards, the most famous native-born revivalist of the Great Awakening, was living proof that the evangelical temperament need not be hostile to learning. Edwards, though deeply pious, was passionately devoted to intellectual pursuits. But in 1725, four years after graduating from Yale, he was offered the position of assistant at his grandfather Solomon Stoddard's church in Northampton, Massachusetts. He accepted, and when Stoddard died two years later, Edwards became pastor.

During his six decades in Northampton, Stoddard had so dominated the ministers of the Connecticut Valley that some referred to him as "pope." His prominence came in part from the "open enrollment" admission policy he adopted for his own church. Evidence of saving grace was neither required nor expected of members: mere good behavior sufficed. As a result, the grandson inherited a congregation whose members were possessed of an "inordinate engagedness after this world." How ready they were to meet their Maker in the next world was another question.

Edwards had a talent for dramatizing what was in store for unconverted listeners. The heat of Hell's consuming fires and the stench of brimstone became palpable at his rendering. In his most famous sermon, "Sinners in the Hands of an Angry God," delivered at Enfield, Connecticut, in 1741, he pulled out all the stops, depicting a "dreadfully provoked" God holding the unconverted over the pit of Hell, "much as one holds a spider, or some loathsome insect." Later, on the off-chance that his listeners did not recognize themselves among the "insects" in God's hand, he declared that "this is the dismal case of every soul in this congregation that has not been born again, however moral and strict, sober and religious, they may otherwise be."

> •••—[**Read** the **Document**
> Edwards, *Sinners in the Hands of an Angry God* at **myhistorylab.com**

Unfortunately for some church members, Edwards's warnings about the state of their souls caused much anxiety. One disconsolate member, Joseph Hawley, slit his throat. Edwards took the suicide calmly. "Satan seems to be in a great rage," he declared. But for some of Edwards's most prominent parishioners, Hawley's death roused doubts.

Rather than soften his message, Edwards persisted, and in 1749 his parishioners voted unanimously to dismiss him. He became a missionary to Indians in Stockbridge, Massachusetts. In 1759 he was appointed president of Princeton, but he died of smallpox before he could take office.

By the early 1750s a reaction had set in against religious "enthusiasm" in all its forms. Except in the religion-starved South, where traveling New Side Presbyterians and Baptists continued their evangelizing efforts; the Great Awakening had run its course. Whitefield's tour of the colonies in 1754 attracted little notice.

Although it caused divisions, the Great Awakening also fostered religious tolerance. If one group claimed the right to worship in its own way, how could it deny to other Protestant churches equal freedom?

The Awakening was the first truly national event in American history. It marks the time when the previously distinct histories of New England, the Middle Colonies, and the South began to intersect. Powerful links were being forged. In 1754, not long after the Awakening, the farsighted Benjamin Franklin advanced his **Albany Plan** for a colonial union to deal with common problems, such as defense against Indian attacks on the frontier. Thirteen once-isolated colonies, expanding to the north and south as well as westward, were merging.

The Enlightenment in America

The Great Awakening pointed ahead to an America marked by religious pluralism; by the 1740s many colonists were rejecting not only the stern Calvinism of Edwards but even the easy Arminianism of Solomon Stoddard in favor of a far less forbidding theology, one more in keeping with the ideas of the European **Enlightenment**.

The Enlightenment, whose proponents enshrined reason and scientific inquiry, had an enormous impact in America. The founders of the colonies were contemporaries of the astronomer Galileo Galilei (1564–1642), the philosopher-mathematician René Descartes (1596–1650), and Sir Isaac Newton (1642–1727), who revealed to the world the workings of gravity and other laws of motion. American society developed amid the excitement generated by these great discoverers, who provided both a new understanding of the natural world and a mode of thought that implied that impersonal, scientific laws governed the behavior of all matter. Earth and the heavens, and human beings and the lower animals all seemed parts of an immense, intricate machine. God had set it all in motion and remained the master technician (the divine watchmaker) overseeing it, but he took fewer and fewer occasions to interfere with its immutable operation. If human reasoning powers and direct observation of natural phenomena rather than God's revelations provided the key to knowledge, it followed that knowledge of the laws of nature, by enabling people to understand the workings of the universe, would enable them to control their earthly destinies and to have at least a voice in their eternal destinies.

Most creative thinkers of the European Enlightenment realized that human beings were not entirely rational and that a complete understanding of the physical world was beyond their grasp. They did, however, believe that human beings were becoming more rational and would be able, by using their rational powers, to discover the laws governing the physical world. Their faith in these ideas produced the so-called Age of Reason. And while their confidence in human rationality now seems naive and the "laws" they formulated no longer appear so mechanically perfect (the universe is far less orderly than they imagined) they added immensely to knowledge.

Many churchgoing colonists, especially better educated ones, accepted the assumptions of the Age of Reason wholeheartedly. Some repudiated the doctrine of original sin and asserted the benevolence of God. Others came to doubt the divinity of Christ and

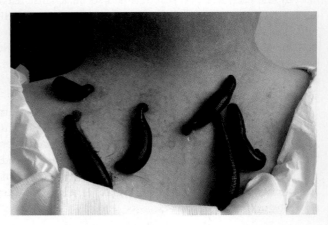

Medicinal leeches on a patient's neck. Today leeches are sometimes used in microsurgery to prevent blood from pooling or coagulating. Leeches fasten onto the skin and tap into blood vessels. Prior to the 19th century, leeches were used to draw off "excess blood," a concept that makes little medical sense.

eventually declared themselves Unitarians. Still others, among them Benjamin Franklin, embraced Deism, a faith that revered God for the marvels of his universe rather than for his power over humankind.

The impact of Enlightenment ideas went far beyond religion. The writings of John Locke and other political theorists found a receptive audience. Of special relevance to American political thinking was Locke's insistence that a person's property was a bulwark of his freedom; if a government could deprive a person of his property, it could enslave him. Also important was the work of the Scottish philosophers Francis Hutcheson and David Hume, and the French *philosophes* Montesquieu and Voltaire. Ideas generated in Europe often reached America with startling speed. No colonial political controversy really heated up in America until all involved had published pamphlets citing half a dozen European authorities. Radical ideas that in Europe were discussed only by an intellectual elite became almost commonplace in the colonies.

As the topics of learned discourse expanded, ministers lost their monopoly on intellectual life. By the 1750s, only a minority of Harvard and Yale graduates were becoming ministers. The College of Philadelphia (later the University of Pennsylvania), founded in 1751, and King's College (later Columbia), founded in New York in 1754, added two institutions to the growing ranks of American colleges, which were never primarily training grounds for clergymen.

Lawyers, who first appeared in any number in colonial towns in the 1740s, swiftly asserted their intellectual authority in public affairs. Physicians and the handful of professors of natural history declared themselves better able to make sense of the new scientific discoveries than clergymen. Yet because fields of knowledge were far less specialized than in modern times, self-educated amateurs could also make useful contributions.

Colonial Scientific Achievements

America produced no Galileo or Newton, but colonists contributed significantly to the collection of scientific knowledge. The unexplored continent provided a laboratory for the study of natural phenomena. The Philadelphia Quaker John Bartram, a "down right plain Country Man," traversed the colonies from Florida to the Great Lakes during the middle years of the eighteenth century, gathering and classifying hundreds of plants. Bartram also studied Indians closely, speculating about their origins and collecting information about their culture.

Franklin's curiosity extended to science. "No one of the present age has made more important discoveries," Thomas Jefferson declared. Franklin's studies of electricity, which he capped in 1752 with his famous kite experiment, established him as a scientist of international stature. He also invented the lightning rod, the iron Franklin stove (a far more efficient way to heat a room than an open fireplace), bifocal spectacles, and several other ingenious devices. In addition he served fourteen years (1751–1764) in the Pennsylvania assembly. He founded a circulating library and helped to get the first hospital in Philadelphia built. He came up with the idea of a lottery to raise money for public purposes. In his spare time he taught himself Latin, French, Spanish, and Italian.

Involvement at even the most marginal level in the intellectual affairs of Europe gave New Englanders, Middle Colonists, and Southerners a chance to get to know one another. Like the spread of evangelical religion, Enlightenment values created new forms of community in English America. Men who in 1750 were discussing botany, physics, and natural phenomena would soon be exchanging ideas about governance.

Repercussions of Distant Wars

The British colonies were part of a great empire that was part of a still larger world. Although Americans were seemingly isolated in their remote communities, scattered between the wide Atlantic and the trackless Appalachian forests, they were constantly affected by outside events both in the Old World and in the New. Under the spell of mercantilism, the western European nations competed fiercely for markets and colonial raw materials. War—hot and cold, declared and undeclared—was almost a permanent condition of seventeenth- and eighteenth-century life, and when the powers clashed they fought wherever they could get at one another, in America, in Europe, and elsewhere.

Although the American colonies were minor pieces in the game and were sometimes casually exchanged or sacrificed by the masterminds in London, Paris, and Madrid, the colonists quickly generated their own international animosities. Frenchmen and Spaniards clashed savagely in Florida as early as the sixteenth century. Before the Pilgrims landed, Samuel Argall of Virginia was sacking French settlements in Maine and carrying off Jesuit priests into captivity at Jamestown. Instead of fostering tranquility and generosity, the abundance of America seemed to make the settlers belligerent and greedy.

The North American fur trade became a source of trouble. The yield of the forest was easily exhausted and traders clashed while trying to control valuable hunting grounds. The French in Canada conducted their fur trading through tribes such as the Algonquin and the Huron. This brought them into conflict with the Five Nations, the powerful Iroquois confederation of central New York. As early as 1609 the Five Nations were at war with the French and their Indian allies. For decades this struggle flared sporadically, the Iroquois more than holding their own both as fighters and as traders. The Iroquois brought quantities of beaver pelts to the Dutch at Albany, some obtained by their own trappers, others taken by ambushing the fur-laden canoes of their enemies. They preyed on and ultimately destroyed the Huron in the land north of Lake Ontario and dickered with Indian trappers in far-off Michigan. When the English took over the New Amsterdam colony, they eagerly adopted the Iroquois as allies, buying their furs and supplying them with trading goods and guns.

By the last decade of the seventeenth century it had become clear that the Dutch lacked the strength to maintain a big empire and that Spain was fast declining. The future, especially in North America, belonged to England and France. In the wars of the next 125 years European alliances shifted dramatically, yet the English and what the Boston lawyer John Adams called "the turbulent Gallicks" were always on opposite sides.

Colonists played only minor parts in the first three of these conflicts. The fighting in America consisted chiefly of sneak attacks on isolated outposts. In King William's War (1689–1697), the American phase of the War of the League of Augsburg, French forces raided Schenectady in New York and frontier settlements in New England. English colonists retaliated by capturing Port Royal, Nova Scotia, only to lose that outpost in a counterattack in 1691. The Peace of Ryswick in 1697 restored all captured territory in America to the original owners.

The next struggle was the War of the Spanish Succession (1702–1713), fought to prevent the union of Spain and France under the Bourbons. The Americans named this conflict Queen Anne's War. Incited by the French, Indians razed Deerfield, Massachusetts. A party of Carolinians burned St. Augustine in Spanish Florida. The New Englanders retook Port Royal. In the Treaty of Utrecht in 1713, France yielded Nova Scotia, Newfoundland, and the Hudson Bay region to Great Britain.

If the colonies were mere pawns in these wars, battle casualties were proportionately high and the civilian population of New England (and of Canada) paid heavily because of the fighting. Many frontier settlers were killed in the raids. Hundreds of townspeople died during the campaigns in Nova Scotia. Massachusetts taxes went up sharply and the colony issued large amounts of paper currency to pay its bills, causing an inflation that ate into the living standards of wage earners.

The American phase of the third Anglo-French conflict, the War of the Austrian Succession (1740–1748), was called King George's War. The usual Indian raids were launched in both directions across the forests that separated the St. Lawrence settlements from the New York and New England frontier. A New England force captured the strategic fortress of Louisbourg on Cape Breton Island, guarding the entrance to the Gulf of St. Lawrence. The Treaty of Aix-la-Chapelle in 1748, however, required the return of Louisbourg, much to the chagrin of the New Englanders.

As this incident suggests, the colonial wars generated a certain amount of trouble between England and the colonies; matters that seemed unimportant in London might loom large in American eyes, and vice versa. But the conflicts were seldom serious. The wars did, however, increase the bad feelings between settlers north and south of the St. Lawrence. Every Indian raid was attributed to French provocateurs, although more often than not the English colonists themselves were responsible for the Indian troubles. Conflicting land claims further aggravated the situation. Massachusetts, Connecticut, and Virginia possessed overlapping claims to the Ohio Valley, and Pennsylvania and New York also had pretensions in the region. Yet the French, ranging broadly across the mid-continent, insisted that the Ohio country was exclusively theirs.

The Great War for the Empire

In this beautiful, almost untouched land, a handful of individuals determined the future of the continent. Over the years the French had established a chain of forts and trading posts running from Mackinac Island in northern Michigan to Kaskaskia on the Mississippi and Vincennes on the Wabash, and from Niagara in the east to the Bourbon River, near Lake Winnipeg, in the west. By the 1740s, however, Pennsylvania fur traders, led by George Croghan, were setting up posts north of the Ohio River and bargaining with Miami and Huron Indians, who ordinarily sold their furs to the French. In 1748 Croghan built a fort at Pickawillany, deep in the Miami country, in what is now western Ohio. That same year agents of a group of Virginia land speculators who had recently organized what they called the Ohio Company reached this area.

With trifling exceptions, an insulating band of wilderness had always separated the French and English in America. Now the two powers came into contact. The immediate result was a battle for control of North America, the "great war for the empire." Thoroughly alarmed by the presence of the English on land they had long considered

This is the first portrait of George Washington, painted by John Gadsby Chapman. Washington's right hand is inside his vest, a convention later associated with Napoleon; his left hand is behind his back. Perhaps this was to spare the painter of the trouble of rendering hands and fingers, which were always a challenge.

their own, the French struck hard. Attacking suddenly in 1752, they wiped out Croghan's post at Pickawillany and drove his traders back into Pennsylvania. Then they built a string of barrier forts south from Lake Erie along the Pennsylvania line: Fort Presque Isle, Fort Le Boeuf, and Fort Venango.

The Pennsylvania authorities chose to ignore this action, but Lieutenant Governor Robert Dinwiddie of Virginia (who was an investor in the Ohio Company) dispatched a twenty-one-year-old surveyor named George Washington to warn the French that they were trespassing on Virginia territory.

Washington, a gangling, inarticulate, and intensely ambitious young planter, made his way northwest in the fall of 1753 and delivered Dinwiddie's message to the commandant at Fort Le Boeuf. It made no impression. "[The French] told me," Washington reported, "that it was their absolute Design to take Possession of the Ohio, and by G— they would do it." Governor Dinwiddie thereupon promoted Washington to lieutenant colonel and sent him back in the spring of 1754 with 150 men to seize a strategic junction south of the new French forts, where the Allegheny and Monongahela Rivers join to form the Ohio River.

Eager but inexperienced in battle, Washington botched his assignment. As his force labored painfully through the tangled mountain country southeast of the fork of the Ohio, he received word that the French had already occupied the position and were constructing a powerful post, Fort Duquesne. Outnumbered by perhaps four to one, Washington pushed on. He surprised and routed a French reconnaissance party, and then blundered into the main body of enemy troops.

Hastily he threw up a defensive position, aptly named Fort Necessity, but the ground was ill chosen; the French easily surrounded the fort and Washington had to surrender. After tricking the young officer, who could not read French, into signing an admission that he had "assassinated" the leader of the reconnaissance party, his captors, with the gateway to the Ohio country firmly in their hands, permitted him and his men to march off. Nevertheless, Washington returned to Virginia a hero, for although still undeclared, this was war, and he had struck the first blow against the French.

In the resulting conflict, which historians call the **French and Indian War** (to the colonists it was simply "the French War"), the English outnumbered the French by about 1.5 million to 90,000. But the English were divided and disorganized, while the

Table 3.1   English Wars, 1689–1763

War	Date	Purpose in North America	Outcome
King William's War	1689–1697	Control of New England and New York frontier, St. Lawrence Valley	No change
Queen Anne's War	1702–1713	Control of northern frontier, also much of Canada	France surrenders Nova Scotia, Newfoundland, and Hudson Bay to Great Britain
King George's War	1744–1748	Control of St. Lawrence River and its Approaches	Louisbourg fortress captured by British but returned to France by treaty
Great War for the Empire	1754–1763	Control of New France	France cedes nearly all of New France to Great Britain

French were disciplined and united. The French controlled the disputed territory, and most of the Indians took their side. As a colonial official wrote, together they made formidable forest fighters, "sometimes in our Front, sometimes in our Rear, and often on all sides of us, Hussar Fashion, taking the Advantage of every Tree and Bush." With an ignorance and arrogance typical of eighteenth-century colonial administration, the British mismanaged the war and failed to make effective use of local resources. For several years they stumbled from one defeat to another.

●─ See the **Map**

The Seven Years' War at **myhistorylab.com**

General Edward Braddock was dispatched to Virginia to take command. In June 1755 he marched against Fort Duquesne with 1,400 Redcoats and a smaller number of colonials, only to be decisively defeated by a much smaller force of French and Indians. Braddock died in battle, and only 500 of his men, led by Colonel Washington, who was serving as his aide-de-camp, made their way back to Virginia.

Elsewhere Anglo-American arms fared little better in the early years of the war. Expeditions against Fort Niagara, key to all French defenses in the West, and Crown Point, gateway to Montréal, bogged down. Meanwhile Indians, armed by the French, bathed the frontier in blood. Venting the frustration caused by 150 years of white advance, they attacked defenseless outposts with unrestrained brutality.

The most feared of the "French" Indians were the Delaware, a once-peaceful Pennsylvania tribe that had been driven from their homelands by English and Iroquois. General Braddock paid his Indian allies only £5 each for French scalps but offered £200 for the hair of Shinngass, the Delaware chieftain.

In 1756 the conflict spread to Europe to become the **Seven Years' War**. Prussia sided with Great Britain, and Austria with the French. On the world stage, too, things went badly for the British. Finally, in 1758, as defeat succeeded defeat, King George II was forced to allow William Pitt, whom he detested, to take over leadership of the war effort. Pitt, grandson of "Diamond" Pitt, a nouveau riche East India merchant, was an unstable man who spent much of his life on the verge of madness, but he was a brilliant strategist and capable of inspiring the nation in its hour of trial.

Pitt recognized, as few contemporaries did, the potential value of North America. Instead of relying on the tightfisted and shortsighted colonial assemblies for men and money, he poured regiment after regiment of British regulars and the full resources of the British treasury into the contest, mortgaging the future recklessly to ensure victory over the French. Grasping the importance of sea power in fighting a war on the other side of the Atlantic, he used the British navy to bottle up the enemy fleet and hamper French communications with Canada. He possessed a keen eye for military genius, and when he discovered it, he ignored seniority and the outraged feelings of mediocre generals and promoted talented young officers to top commands.

In the winter of 1758, as Pitt's grand strategy matured, Fort Duquesne fell. It was appropriately renamed Fort Pitt, the present Pittsburgh. The following summer Fort Niagara was overrun. General Jeffrey Amherst took Crown Point, and Wolfe sailed up the St. Lawrence to Québec. There General Louis Joseph de Montcalm had prepared formidable defenses, but after months of probing and planning, Wolfe found and exploited a chink in the city's armor and captured it. Both he and Montcalm died in the battle. In 1760 Montréal fell and the French abandoned all Canada to the British. The British also won major victories against Spanish forces in Cuba and Manila, and against the French in the West Indies and India.

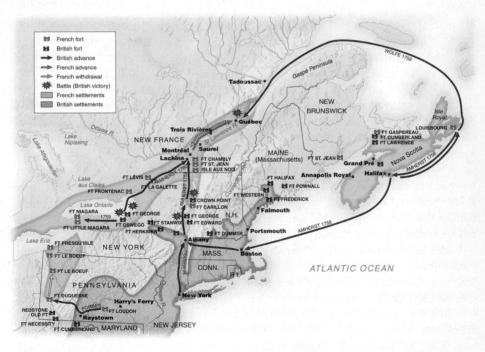

British Successes, 1758–1763 In 1758, in western Pennsylvania, British General John Forbes seized Ft. Duquesne and renamed it Ft. Pitt, in honor of William Pitt, who had orchestrated the military campaign in London. (In 1909 Forbes was posthumously honored when the Pittsburgh Pirates named their new stadium after him.) In 1759 a multipronged British expedition seized northern and western New York while another British army, commanded by James Wolfe, sailed down the St. Lawrence and captured Montréal in 1760.

Britain Victorious: The Peace of Paris

Peace was restored in 1763 by the Treaty of Paris. Its terms were moderate considering the extent of the British triumph. France abandoned all claim to North America except for two small islands near Newfoundland; Great Britain took over Canada and the eastern half of the Mississippi Valley. Spain got back both the Philippine Islands and Cuba, but in exchange ceded East and West Florida to Great Britain. In a separate treaty, Spain also got New Orleans and the huge area of North America west of the Mississippi River.

No honest American could deny that the victory had been won chiefly by British troops and with British gold. Colonial militiamen fought well in defense of their homes or when some highly prized objective seemed ripe for the plucking; they lacked discipline and determination when required to fight far from home and under commanders they did not know. As one American official admitted, it was difficult to get New Englanders to enlist "unless assurances can be given that they shall not march to the southward of certain limits."

Colonials were delighted that scarlet-clad British regulars had borne the brunt of the fighting and happier still that the Crown had shouldered most of the financial burden of the long struggle. The local assemblies contributed to the cost, but except for Massachusetts and Virginia their outlays were trivial compared with the £82 million poured into the worldwide conflict by the British.

Little wonder that great victory produced a burst of praise for king and mother country throughout America. Parades, cannonading, fireworks, banquets, the pealing of church bells were the order of the day in every colonial town. "Nothing," said Thomas Pownall, wartime governor of Massachusetts and a student of colonial administration, "can eradicate from [the colonists'] hearts their natural, almost mechanical affection to Great Britain." A young South Carolinian who had been educated in England claimed that the colonists were "more wrapped up in a king" than any people he had ever known.

Burdens of an Expanded Empire

In London peace proved a time for reassessment; it was obvious that the empire of 1763 was not the same as the empire of 1754. The new, far larger dominion would be much more expensive to maintain. Pitt had spent a huge sum winning and securing it, much of it borrowed money. Great Britain's national debt had doubled between 1754 and 1763. Now this debt must be repaid, and the strain that this would place on the economy was clear to all. Furthermore, the day-to-day cost of administering an empire that extended from the Hudson Bay to India was far larger than that which the already burdened British taxpayer could be expected to bear. Before the great war for the empire, Britain's North American possessions were administered for about £70,000 a year; after 1763 the cost was five times as much.

The American empire had also become far more complex. A system of administration that treated the colonies as a string of separate plantations struggling to exist on the edge of the forest would no longer suffice. The war had been fought for control of the Ohio Valley. Now that the prize had been secured, 10,000 hands were eager to make off

PACIFIC
OCEAN

ATLANTIC
OCEAN

Gulf of
Mexico

Caribbean Sea

- British
- French
- Spanish
- Russian

European Claims in North America after British Victory, 1763 The British victory in the French and Indian War caused nearly all of New France to be transferred to Great Britain. The Mississippi and Ohio Valleys, the Great Lakes region, and most of what is now eastern Canada were now under British rule. Only Spain now vied with Britain for control of what is now the continental United States. Russia claimed the coastline of what is now Alaska.

with it. The urge to expand was, despite the continent's enormous empty spaces, an old American drive. As early as the 1670s eastern stay-at-homes were lamenting the "insatiable desire after Land" that made people willing to "live like Heathen, only that so they might have Elbow-room enough in the world." Frontier warfare had frustrated this urge for seven long years. How best could it be satisfied now that peace had come?

Conflicting colonial claims, based on charters drafted by men who thought the Pacific lay over the next hill, threatened to make the Ohio valley a battleground once more. The Indians remained "unpacified." Rival land companies contested for charters, while fur traders strove to hold back the wave of settlement that would inevitably destroy the world of the beaver and the deer.

Apparently only Great Britain could deal with these problems and rivalries, for when Franklin had proposed a rudimentary form of colonial union—the Albany Plan of 1754—it was rejected by almost everyone. Unfortunately, the British government did not rise to the challenge. Perhaps this was to be expected. A handful of aristocrats (fewer than 150 peers were active in government affairs) dominated British politics, and they were more concerned with local offices and personal advantage than with large questions of policy. An American who spent some time in London in 1764 trying to obtain approval for a plan for the development of the West reported, "The people hear Spend thire time in Nothing but abuseing one Another and Striveing who shall be in power with a view to Serve themselves and Thire friends." King George III was not a tyrant, as once was commonly believed, but he was an inept politician and the victim of frequent bouts of illness.

This engraving depicts Pontiac confronting Colonel Henry Bouquet. Pontiac had good reason to be angry. In a letter dated July 16, 1763, Sir Jeffrey Amherst, commander of British forces in North America, advised Bouquet to infect Pontiac's Indians with smallpox: "You will do well to try to Innoculate the Indians by means of Blanketts, as well as to try Every other method that can serve to Extirpate this Execrable Race." Bouquet responded a week later: "All your directions will be observed."

Most English leaders insisted that colonials were uncouth and generally inferior beings. During the French and Indian War, British commanders repeatedly expressed contempt for colonial militiamen, whom they considered fit only for "fatigue" duties such as digging trenches, chopping wood, and other noncombat tasks. General Wolfe characterized colonial troops as the "most contemptible cowardly dogs you can conceive," and another English officer, annoyed by their unsanitary habits, complained that they "infect the air with a disagreeable stink." The British officers failed to understand that colonial soldiers were volunteers who had agreed to serve under specific conditions. Lord Loudoun, the British commander-in-chief during the French and Indian War, was flabbergasted to discover that New England troops refused to obey one of his direct orders on the ground that it violated their contracts.

Many English people resented Americans simply because the colonies were rapidly becoming rich and powerful. As Franklin predicted, the population growth rate in British America was extraordinary, increasing from 1 million to more than 2 million from 1750 to 1770. (His long-term predictions were nearly on the mark: In 1850 the population of Great Britain was 20.8 million, that of the United States 23.1 million, including some 4 million slaves and others who were not of British descent.) If the English did not say much about this possibility, they too considered it from time to time—without Franklin's complacency.

Tightening Imperial Controls

The attempt of the inefficient British government to deal with the intricate colonial problems that resulted from the great war for the empire led to the American Revolution. Trouble began when the British decided after the French and Indian War to intervene more actively in American affairs. Theoretically the colonies were entirely subordinate to Crown and Parliament; yet except for the disastrous attempt to centralize control of the

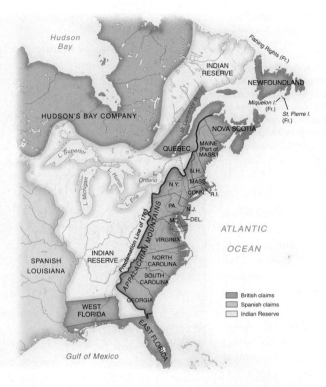

Proclamation of 1763 Although France ceded nearly all of New France to Great Britain in 1763, that same year King George III proclaimed that colonists would not be allowed to move into "British territory" west of the Appalachians. These lands were to be reserved for Indians.

colonies in the 1680s, they had been allowed a remarkable degree of freedom to manage their own affairs. They had come to expect this as their right.

Parliament had never attempted to tax American colonists. "Compelling the colonies to pay money without their consent would be rather like raising contributions in an enemy's country than taxing Englishmen for their own benefit," Benjamin Franklin wrote. Sir Robert Walpole, initiator of the policy of salutary neglect, recognized the colonial viewpoint. He responded to a suggestion that Parliament tax the colonies by saying, "I will leave that for some of my successors, who may have more courage than I have." Nevertheless, the *legality* of parliamentary taxation, or of other parliamentary intervention in colonial affairs, had not been seriously contested. During King George's War and again during the French and Indian War many British officials in America suggested that Parliament tax the colonies.

Despite the peace treaty of 1763, the American colonies continued to be a drain on the British treasury. Mostly this was due to the cost of fighting Indians. Freed of the restraint posed by French competition, Englishmen and colonists increased their pressure on the Indians. Fur traders cheated them outrageously, while callous military men hoped to exterminate them like vermin. One British officer expressed the wish that they could be hunted down with dogs.

Led by an Ottawa chief named Pontiac, the Indian tribes made one last effort to drive the whites back across the mountains. What the whites called Pontiac's "Rebellion" caused much havoc, but it failed. By 1764 most of the western tribes had accepted the peace terms offered by a royal commissioner, Sir William Johnson, one of the few whites who understood and sympathized with them. The British government then placed 15 regiments, some 6,000 soldiers, in posts along the entire arc of the frontier, as much to protect the Indians from the settlers as the settlers from the Indians. It proclaimed a new western policy: No settlers were to cross the Appalachian divide.

Originally the British had intended the Proclamation of 1763 to be temporary. With the passage of time, however, checking westward expansion seemed a good way to save money, prevent trouble with the Indians, and keep the colonies tied closely to the mother country. The proclamation line, the Board of Trade declared, was "necessary for the preservation of the colonies in due subordination."[1] Naturally this attitude caused resentment in America. To close off the West temporarily in order to pacify the Indians made some sense; to keep it closed was like trying to contain a tidal wave.

The Sugar Act

Americans disliked the new western policy but realized that the problems were complex and that no simple solution existed. Great Britain's effort to raise money in America to help support the increased cost of colonial administration caused far more vehement complaints. George Grenville, who became prime minister in 1763, was a fairly able man, although narrow in outlook. His reputation as a financial expert was based chiefly on his eagerness to reduce government spending. Under his leadership Parliament passed, in April 1764, the so-called Sugar Act. This law placed tariffs on sugar, coffee, wines, and other things imported into America in substantial amounts. At the same time, measures aimed at enforcing all the trade laws were put into effect. Those accused of violating the Sugar Act were to be tried before British naval officers in vice admiralty courts. Grenville was determined to end smuggling, corruption, and inefficiency. Soon the customs service was collecting each year 15 times as much in duties as it had before the war.

More alarming was the nature of the Sugar Act and the manner of its passage. The Navigation Act duties had been intended to regulate commerce, and the sums collected had not cut deeply into profits. Yet few Americans were willing to concede that Parliament had the right to tax them. As Englishmen they believed that no one should be deprived arbitrarily of property and that, as James Otis put it in his stirring pamphlet *The Rights of the British Colonies Asserted and Proved* (1764), everyone should be "free from all taxes but what he consents to in person, or by his representative." John Locke had made clear in his *Second Treatise on Government* (1690) that property ought never be taken from people without their consent, not because material values transcend all others, but because human liberty can never be secure when arbitrary power of any kind exists. "If our Trade may be

•••—Read the Document

Otis, *The Rights of the British Colonies Asserted and Proved* at myhistorylab.com

---

[1] The British were particularly concerned about preserving the colonies as markets for their manufactures. They feared that the spread of population beyond the mountains would stimulate local manufacturing because the high cost of land transportation would make British goods prohibitively expensive.

taxed why not our Lands?" the Boston town meeting asked when news of the Sugar Act reached America. "Why not the produce of our Lands and every Thing we possess or make use of?"

American Colonists Demand Rights

To most people in Great Britain the colonial protest against taxation without representation seemed a hypocritical quibble, and it is probably true that in 1764 many of the protesters had not thought the argument through. The distinction between tax laws and other types of legislation was artificial, the British reasoned. Either Parliament was sovereign in America or it was not, and only a fool or a traitor would argue that it was not. If the colonists were loyal subjects of George III, as they claimed, they should bear their fair share of the cost of governing his widespread dominions. As to representation, the colonies *were* represented in Parliament; every member of that body stood for the interests of the entire empire. If Americans had no say in the election of members of Commons, neither did most English subjects.

This concept of "virtual" representation accurately described the British system. But it made no sense in America, where from the time of the first settlements members of the colonial assemblies had represented the people of the districts in which they stood for office. The confusion between virtual and actual (geographically based) representation revealed the extent to which colonial and British political practices had diverged over the years.

The British were correct in concluding that selfish motives influenced colonial objections to the Sugar Act. The colonists denounced taxation without representation, but an offer of a reasonable number of seats in Parliament would not have satisfied them. American abundance and the simplicity of colonial life had enabled them to prosper without assuming any considerable tax burden. Now their maturing society was beginning to require communal rather than individual solutions to the problems of existence. Not many of them were prepared to face this hard truth.

Over the course of colonial history Americans had taken a narrow view of imperial concerns. They had avoided complying with the Navigation Acts whenever they could profit by doing so. Colonial militiamen had compiled a sorry record when asked to fight for Britain or even for the inhabitants of colonies other than their own. True, most Americans professed loyalty to the Crown, but not many would voluntarily open their purses except to benefit themselves.

Although the colonists were opposed in principle to taxation without representation, they failed to agree on a common plan of resistance. Many of the assemblies drafted protests, but these varied in force as well as in form. Merchant groups that tried to organize boycotts of products subject to the new taxes met with indifferent success. Then in 1765 Parliament galvanized colonial opinion by passing the Stamp Act.

The Stamp Act: The Pot Set to Boiling

◆ View the Image

Stamp Act Stamps at
myhistorylab.com

The Stamp Act placed stiff excise taxes on all kinds of printed matter. No one could sell newspapers or pamphlets, or convey licenses, diplomas, or legal papers without first buying special stamps and affixing them to the printed matter. Stamp duties

Outraged at the Stamp Act of 1765, which implemented a direct tax on printed matter, an angry mob burned the stamps in protest. Note the enthusiastic participation of women and a young black man; that they are not wearing shoes indicates that they were of working-class background.

were intended to be relatively painless to pay and cheap to collect; in England similar taxes brought in about £100,000 annually. Grenville hoped the Stamp Act would produce £60,000 a year in America, and the law provided that all revenue should be applied to "defraying the necessary expenses of defending, protecting, and securing, the ... colonies."

Hardly a penny was collected. As the Boston clergyman Jonathan Mayhew explained, "Almost every British American ... considered it as an infraction of their rights, or their dearly purchased privileges." The Sugar Act had been related to Parliament's uncontested power to control colonial trade, but the Stamp Act was a direct tax. When Parliament ignored the politely phrased petitions of the colonial assemblies, more vigorous protests swiftly followed.

Virginia took the lead. In late May 1765 Patrick Henry introduced resolutions asserting that the Burgesses possessed "the only and sole and exclusive right and power to lay taxes" on Virginians and suggesting that Parliament had no legal authority to tax the colonies at all. Henry spoke for what the royal governor called the "Young, hot and Giddy Members" of the legislature (most of whom, incidentally, had absented themselves from the meeting). The more extreme of Henry's resolutions were defeated, but the debate they occasioned attracted wide and favorable attention. On June 6 the Massachusetts assembly proposed an intercolonial **Stamp Act Congress**, which, when it met in New York City in October, passed another series of resolutions of protest. The Stamp Act and other recent acts of Parliament were "burthensome and grievous," the delegates declared. "It is unquestionably essential to the freedom of a people ... that no taxes be imposed on them but with their own consent."

During the summer irregular organizations known as Sons of Liberty began to agitate against the act. Far more than anyone realized, this marked the start of the revolution. For the first time extralegal organized resistance was taking place, distinct from protest and argument conducted by constituted organs of government like the House of Burgesses and the Massachusetts General Court.

Although led by men of character and position, the "Liberty Boys" frequently resorted to violence to achieve their aims. In Boston they staged riots, looting and vandalizing the houses of the stamp master and his brother-in-law, Lieutenant Governor Thomas Hutchinson. In Connecticut, stamp master Jared Ingersoll, a man of great courage and dignity, faced an angry mob demanding his resignation.

The stamps were printed in England and shipped to stamp masters (all Americans) in the colonies well in advance of November 1, 1765, the date the law was to go into effect. The New York stamp master had resigned, but the stamps were stored in the city under military guard. Radicals distributed placards reading, "The first Man that either distributes or makes use of Stampt Paper let him take care of his House, Person, and Effects. We dare." When Major Thomas James, the British officer who had charge of the stamps, promised that "the stamps would be crammed down New Yorkers' throats," a mob responded by breaking into his house, drinking all his wine, and smashing his furniture and china.

●●●─Read the **Document**

Franklin, *Testimony Against the Stamp Act* at **myhistorylab.com**

In some colonies the stamps were snatched by mobs and put to the torch amid rejoicing. Elsewhere they were locked up in secret by British officials or held on shipboard. For a time no business requiring stamped paper was transacted; then, gradually, people began to defy the law by issuing and accepting unstamped documents. Threatened by mob action should they resist, British officials stood by helplessly. The law was a dead letter.

The looting associated with this crisis alarmed many colonists, including some prominent opponents of the Stamp Act. "When the pot is set to boil," the lawyer John Adams remarked sadly, "the scum rises to the top." Another Bostonian called the vandalizing of Thomas Hutchinson's house a "flagrant instance of to what a pitch of infatuation an incensed populace can rise." Such people worried that the protests might be aimed at the wealthy and powerful in America as well as at British tyranny. This does not mean that they disapproved of crowd protests, or even the destruction of property during such protests, as distinct from stealing. Many such people took part in the rioting. "State-quakes," John Adams also said, this time complacently, were comparable to "earth-quakes" and other kinds of natural violence.

Rioters or Rebels?

That many of the poor resented the colonial elite goes without saying, as does the fact that in many instances the rioting got out of hand and took on a social as well as a political character. Times were hard, and the colonial elite, including most of the leading critics of British policy, had little compassion for the poor, whom they feared could be corrupted by anyone who offered them a square meal or a glass of rum. Once roused, laborers and artisans may well have directed their energies toward righting what they considered local wrongs. Yet the mass of the people, being owners of property and capable of influencing political decisions, were not social revolutionaries.

The British were not surprised that Americans disliked the Stamp Act. They had not anticipated, however, that Americans would react so violently and so unanimously. Americans did so for many reasons. Business continued to be poor in 1765, and at a time when 3 shillings was a day's wage for an urban laborer, the stamp tax was 2 shillings for an advertisement in a newspaper, 5 shillings for a will, and 20 shillings for a license to sell liquor. The taxes would hurt the business of lawyers, merchants, newspaper editors, and tavern keepers. The protests of such influential and articulate people had a powerful impact on public opinion.

The greatest cause of concern to the colonists was Great Britain's flat rejection of the principle of no taxation without representation. This alarmed them for two closely related reasons. First of all, *as Americans* they objected to being taxed by a legislative body they had not been involved in choosing. To buy a stamp was to surrender all claim to self-government. Secondly, as *British subjects* they valued what they called "the rights of Englishmen." They saw the Stamp Act as only the worst in a series of arbitrary invasions of these rights.

Already Parliament had passed still another measure, the Quartering Act, requiring local legislatures to house and feed new British troops sent to the colonies. Besides being a form of indirect taxation, a standing army was universally deemed to be a threat to liberty. Why were Redcoats necessary in Boston and New York where there was no foreign enemy for thousands of miles in any direction? In hard times, soldiers were particularly unwelcome because, being miserably underpaid, they took any odd jobs they could get in their off hours, thus competing with unemployed colonists. Reluctantly, many Americans were beginning to fear that the London authorities had organized a conspiracy to subvert the liberties of all British subjects.

Americans also responded to the Stamp Act by boycotting British goods. Nearly a thousand merchants signed nonimportation agreements. These struck British merchants hard in their pocketbooks, and they began to pressure Parliament for repeal. After a hot debate the hated law was repealed in March 1766. The ban on British goods was lifted and the colonists congratulated themselves on having stood fast in defense of principle.

The Declaratory Act

The great controversy over the constitutional relationship of colony to mother country was only beginning. The same day that it repealed the Stamp Act, Parliament passed a Declaratory Act stating that the colonies were "subordinate" and that Parliament could enact any law it wished "to bind the colonies and people of America."

To most Americans this bald statement of parliamentary authority seemed unconstitutional—a flagrant violation of their understanding of how the British imperial system was supposed to work. Actually the Declaratory Act highlighted the degree to which British and American views of the system had drifted apart. The English and the colonials were using the same words but giving them different meanings. Their conflicting definitions of the word *representation* was a case in point. Another involved the word *constitution*. To the British the Constitution meant the totality of laws, customs, and institutions that had developed over time and under which the nation functioned. If Parliament passed an "unconstitutional" law, the result might be rebellion, but that the law existed none would deny. In America, partly because governments were based on specific charters, the word meant a written document or contract spelling out, and thus limiting, the powers of government. If a law were unconstitutional, it simply had no force.

Even more basic were the differing meanings that English and Americans were giving to the word *sovereignty*. Eighteenth-century English political thinkers believed that sovereignty (ultimate political power) could not be divided. Government and law being based ultimately on force, some "final, unqualified, indivisible" authority had to exist if social order was to be preserved. The Glorious Revolution in England had settled the question of where sovereignty resided—in Parliament.

Given these ideas and the long tradition out of which they had sprung, one can sympathize with the British failure to follow the colonists' reasoning (which had not yet evolved into a specific proposal for constitutional reform). But most responsible British officials refused even to listen to the American argument.

The Townshend Duties

Despite the repeal of the Stamp Act, the British did not abandon the policy of taxing the colonies. If direct taxes were challenging to collect, indirect ones like the Sugar Act were not. To persuade Parliament to repeal the Stamp Act, some Americans (most notably Benjamin Franklin) had claimed that the colonists objected only to direct taxes. Therefore, in June 1767, the chancellor of the exchequer, Charles Townshend, introduced a new series of indirect taxes, this time on glass, lead, paints, paper, and tea imported into the colonies.

By this time the colonists were thoroughly on guard, and they responded quickly to the Townshend levies with a new boycott of British goods. In addition they made elaborate efforts to stimulate colonial manufacturing. By the end of 1769 imports from the mother country had been almost halved. Meanwhile, administrative measures enacted along with the Townshend duties were creating more ill will. A Board of Customs Commissioners, with headquarters in Boston, took charge of enforcing the trade laws, and new vice admiralty courts were set up at Halifax, Boston, Philadelphia, and Charleston to handle violations. These courts operated without juries, and many colonists considered the new commissioners racketeers who systematically attempted to obtain judgments against honest merchants in order to collect their share of all seizures.

The struggle forced Americans to do some deep thinking about both American and imperial political affairs. The colonies' common interests and growing economic and social interrelationships probably made some kind of union inevitable. Trouble with England speeded the process. In 1765 the Stamp Act Congress (another extralegal organization and thus a further step in the direction of revolution) had brought the delegates of nine colonies to New York. Now, in 1768, the Massachusetts General Court took the next step. It sent the legislatures of the other colonies a "Circular Letter" expressing the "humble opinion" that the Townshend Acts were "Infringements of their natural & constitutional Rights."

After the passage of the Townshend Acts, John Dickinson, a Philadelphia lawyer, published "Letters from a Farmer in Pennsylvania to the Inhabitants of the British Colonies." Dickinson considered himself a loyal British subject trying to find a solution to colonial troubles. "Let us behave like dutiful children, who have received unmerited blows from a beloved parent," he wrote. Nevertheless, he stated plainly that Parliament had no right to tax the colonies. Another moderate Philadelphian, John Raynell, put it this way: "If the Americans are to be taxed by a Parliament where they are not . . . Represented, they are no longer Englishmen but Slaves."

Some Americans were much more radical than Dickinson. Samuel Adams of Boston, a genuine revolutionary agitator, believed by 1768 that Parliament had no right at all to legislate for the colonies. If few were ready to go that far, fewer still accepted the reasoning behind the Declaratory Act.

The British ignored American thinking. The Massachusetts Circular Letter had been framed in moderate language and clearly reflected the convictions of most of the people in the Bay Colony, yet when news of it reached England, the secretary of state for the colonies, Lord Hillsborough, ordered the governor to dissolve the legislature. Two regiments of British troops were transferred from the frontier to Boston, part of the aforementioned policy of bringing the army closer to the centers of colonial unrest.

The Boston Massacre

These acts convinced more Americans that the British were conspiring to destroy their liberties. Resentment was particularly strong in Boston, where the postwar depression had come on top of two decades of economic stagnation. Crowding 4,000 tough British

This engraving of the Boston Massacre (1770) became the most reprinted depiction of the event, and probably the most inaccurate. It was done by Paul Revere, engraver, silversmith, and eventual patriot. The British soldiers did not form ranks and fire on command at the crowd. The judge at the subsequent trial of the British soldiers warned jurors not to be influenced by "the prints exhibited in our houses" that added "wings to fancy"—prints, specifically, such as this one. The jury of colonists acquitted all the British soldiers but two, who received mild punishments.

soldiers into a town of 16,000 people, many of them as capable of taking care of themselves when challenged as any Redcoat, was a formula for disorder.

How many brawls and minor riots took place in the waterfront taverns and darkened alleys of the colonial ports that winter is lost to history. In January 1770 scuffles between Liberty Boys and Redcoats in the Golden Hill section of New York City resulted in a number of injuries. Then, in Boston on March 5, 1770, real trouble erupted. Late that afternoon a crowd of idlers began tossing snowballs at a company of Redcoats guarding the Custom House. Some of the snowballs had been carefully wrapped around rocks. Gradually the crowd grew larger and angrier. The soldiers panicked and began firing their muskets. When the smoke cleared, five Bostonians lay dead or dying on the bloody ground.

This so-called **Boston Massacre** infuriated the populace. The violence played into the hands of radicals like Samuel Adams. But just as at the time of the Stamp Act riots, cooler heads prevailed. Announcing that he was "defending the rights of man and unconquerable truth," John Adams volunteered his services to make sure the soldiers got a fair trial. Most were acquitted; the rest were treated leniently by the standards of the day. In Great Britain, confrontation also gave way to adjustment. In April 1770 all the Townshend duties except a threepenny tax on tea were repealed. The tea tax was maintained as a matter of principle.

A kind of postmassacre truce settled over Boston and the rest of British America. During the next two years no crisis erupted. Imports of British goods were nearly 50 percent higher than before the nonimportation agreement. So long as the British continued to be conciliatory, the colonists seemed satisfied with their place in the empire.

The Boiling Pot Spills Over

In 1772 this informal truce ended and new troubles broke out. The first was plainly the fault of the colonists involved. Early in June the British patrol boat *Gaspee* ran aground in Narragansett Bay, south of Providence, while pursuing a suspected smuggler. The *Gaspee*'s commander, Lieutenant Dudingston, had antagonized everyone in the area with his officiousness and zeal; that night a gang of local people boarded the *Gaspee* and put it to the torch. This action was clearly criminal, but when the British attempted to bring the culprits to justice no one would testify against them. The British, frustrated and angry, were strengthened in their conviction that the colonists were utterly lawless.

Then Thomas Hutchinson, governor of Massachusetts, announced that henceforth the Crown rather than the local legislature would pay his salary. Since control over the salaries of royal officials gave the legislature a powerful hold on them, this development was disturbing. Groups of radicals formed "committees of correspondence" and stepped up communications with one another, planning joint action in case of trouble. This was another monumental step along the road to revolution; an organized colonywide resistance movement, lacking in any "legitimate" authority but ready to consult and act in the name of the public interest, was taking shape.

The Tea Act Crisis

In the spring of 1773 an entirely unrelated event precipitated the final crisis. The British East India Company held a monopoly of all trade between India and the rest of the empire. This monopoly had yielded fabulous returns, but decades of corruption and

A noose hanging from a "Liberty Tree" reveals this artist's bias: The "tar-and-feathering" of a British official would doubtlessly culminate in greater violence. As historian Gordon Wood points out, however, the mob actions of the colonists often "grew out of folk festivals and traditional popular rites." Tarring and feathering, though painful and occasionally dangerous, was mostly a humiliation. By the early 1770s, though, the mockery was becoming tinged with violence.

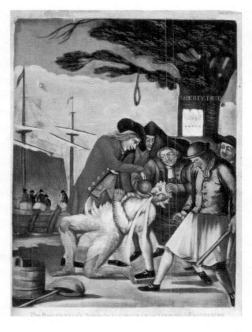

inefficiency together with heavy military expenses in recent years had weakened the company until it was almost bankrupt.

Among the assets of this venerable institution were some 17 million pounds of tea stored in English warehouses. The decline of the American market, a result first of the boycott and then of the smuggling of cheaper Dutch tea, partly accounted for the glut. Normally, East India Company tea was sold to English wholesalers. They in turn sold it to American wholesalers, who distributed it to local merchants for sale to the consumer. A substantial British tax was levied on the tea as well as the threepenny Townshend duty. Now Lord North, the new prime minister, decided to remit the British tax and to allow the company to sell directly in America through its own agents. The savings would permit a sharp reduction of the retail price and at the same time yield a nice profit to the company. The Townshend tax was retained, however, to preserve (as Lord North said when the East India Company directors suggested its repeal) the principle of Parliament's right to tax the colonies.

The company then shipped 1,700 chests of tea to colonial ports. Though the idea of high-quality tea offered at bargain prices was tempting, after a little thought nearly everyone in America appreciated the dangers involved in buying it. If Parliament could grant the East India Company a monopoly of the tea trade, it could parcel out all or any part of American commerce to whomever it pleased. More important, the act appeared utterly diabolical, a dastardly trick to trap them into paying the tea tax. The plot seemed obvious: The real price of Lord North's tea was American submission to parliamentary taxation.

Public indignation was so great in New York and Philadelphia that when the tea ships arrived, the authorities ordered them back to England without attempting to unload. The tea could be landed only "under the Protection of the Point of the Bayonet and Muzzle of the Cannon," the governor of New York reported. "Even then," he added, "I do not see how the Sales or Consumption could be effected."

The situation in Boston was different. The tea ship *Dartmouth* arrived on November 27. The radicals, marshaled by Sam Adams, were determined to prevent it from landing its cargo. Governor Hutchinson (who had managed to have two of his sons appointed to receive and sell the tea) was equally determined to collect the tax and enforce the law. For days the town seethed. Crowds milled in the streets, harangued by Adams and his friends, while the *Dartmouth* and two later arrivals swung with the tides on their moorings. Then, on the night of December 16, as Hutchinson was preparing to seize the tea for nonpayment of the duty, a band of colonists disguised as Indians rowed out to the ships and dumped the tea chests into the harbor.

The destruction of the tea was a serious crime and it was obvious that a solid majority of the people of Boston approved of it. The painted "Patriots" who jettisoned the chests were a cross-section of society, and a huge crowd gathered at wharfside and cheered them on. The British burned with indignation when news of the "Tea Party" reached London. People talked (fortunately it was only talk) of flattening Boston with heavy artillery. Nearly everyone, even such a self-described British friend of the colonists as Edmund Burke, agreed that the colonists must be taught a lesson. George III himself said, "We must master them or totally leave them to themselves."

What particularly infuriated the British was the certain knowledge that no American jury would render a judgment against the criminals. The memory of the *Gaspee* affair was fresh in everyone's mind in England, as undoubtedly it was in the minds of those Bostonians who, wearing the thinnest of disguises, brazenly destroyed the tea.

From Resistance to Revolution

Parliament responded in the spring of 1774 by passing the **Coercive Acts**. The Boston Port Act closed the harbor of Boston to all commerce until its citizens paid for the tea. The Administration of Justice Act provided for the transfer of cases to courts outside Massachusetts when the governor felt that an impartial trial could not be had within the colony. The Massachusetts Government Act revised the colony's charter drastically, strengthening the power of the governor, weakening that of the local town meetings, making the council appointive rather than elective, and changing the method by which juries were selected. These were unwise laws—they cost Great Britain an empire. All of them, and especially the Port Act, were unjust laws as well. Parliament was punishing the entire community for the crimes of individuals. Even more significant, they marked a drastic change in British policy—from legislation and strict administration to treating colonial protesters as criminals, and from attempts to persuade and conciliate to coercion and punishment.

The Americans named the Coercive Acts the Intolerable Acts. Although neither the British nor the colonists yet realized it, the American Revolution had begun.

Step by step, in the course of a single decade, a group of separate political bodies, inhabited by people who (if we put aside the slaves who were outside the political system) were loyal subjects of Great Britain, had been forced to take political power into their own hands and to unite with one another to exercise that power effectively. Ordinary working people, not just merchants, lawyers, and other well-to-do people, played increasingly more prominent roles in public life as crisis after crisis roused their indignation. This did not yet mean that most Americans wanted to be free from British rule. Nearly every colonist was willing to see Great Britain continue to control, or at least regulate, such things as foreign relations, commercial policy, and other matters of general American interest. Parliament, however—and in the last analysis George III and most supporters of the British—insisted that their authority over the colonies was unlimited.

Lord North directed the Coercive Acts at Massachusetts alone because he assumed that the other colonies, profiting from the discomfiture of Massachusetts, would not intervene, and because of the British tendency to think of the colonies as separate units connected only through London. His strategy failed because his assumption was incorrect: The colonies began at once to act in concert.

Extralegal political acts now became a matter of course. In June 1774 Massachusetts called for a meeting of delegates from all the colonies to consider common action. This **First Continental Congress** met at Philadelphia in September; only Georgia failed to send delegates. Many points of view were represented, but even the so-called conservative proposal, introduced by Joseph Galloway of Pennsylvania, called for a thorough overhaul of the empire. Galloway suggested an *American* government, consisting of a president general appointed by the king and a grand council chosen by the colonial assemblies, that would manage intercolonial affairs and possess a veto over parliamentary acts affecting the colonies.

This was not what the majority wanted. If taxation without representation was tyranny, so was all legislation. Therefore Parliament had no right to legislate in any way for the colonies. John Adams, while prepared to *allow* Parliament to regulate colonial trade, now believed that Parliament had no inherent right to control it. "The foundation . . . of all free government," he declared, "is a right in the people to participate in their legislative council." Americans "are entitled to a free and exclusive power of legislation in their several provincial legislatures."

Propelled by the reasoning of Adams and others, the Congress passed a declaration of grievances and resolves that amounted to a complete condemnation of Britain's actions since 1763. A Massachusetts proposal that the people take up arms to defend their rights was endorsed. The delegates also organized a "Continental Association" to boycott British goods and to stop all exports to the empire. To enforce this boycott, committees were appointed locally "to observe the conduct of all persons touching this association" and to expose violators to public scorn.

If the Continental Congress reflected the views of the majority—there is no reason to suspect that it did not—it is clear that the Americans had decided that drastic changes must be made. It was not merely a question of mutual defense against the threat of British power, nor was it (in Franklin's aphorism) a matter of hanging together lest they hang separately. A nation was being born.

Table 3.2   Major British Tax Policies and American Resistance, 1763–1776

Year	British Policy	Colonist Response
1763	Proclamation of 1763	Wealthy speculators, coveting Indian lands west of Appalachians, protest
1764	Sugar Act	Massachusetts legislature denounces "taxation without representation"
1765	Stamp Act	Sons of Liberty emerge and call for radical measures; boycott of British goods
1767	Townshend Duties	Widespread protests, riots in port cities, culminating in "Boston Massacre"
1773	Tea Act	Boston Tea Party
1774	Coercive Acts	First Continental Congress

Looking back many years later, one of the delegates to the First Continental Congress made just these points. He was John Adams of Massachusetts, and he said, "The revolution was complete, in the minds of the people, and the Union of the colonies, before the war commenced."

American resistance to the new taxes baffled British officials. In 1774 Lord North declared that colonial opposition betrayed a "distempered state of turbulence." Some members of Parliament declared that the Americans had gone "stark staring mad" over taxes any reasonable person would pay willingly.

But what had begun as a dispute over taxes had shifted to a struggle over sovereignty. Colonists were not against taxes in principle—and their descendants would willingly (if not happily) pay taxes that most colonists would have regarded as enslavement. The colonists insisted, however, that they also have a say in their governance. Their "madness," originally manifested in bitter opposition to trade taxes, would become a feverish commitment to war.

⊙–Watch the Video

The American Revolution as Different Americans Saw It at **myhistorylab.com**

Milestones

1650–1696	Parliament enacts Navigation Acts	1754–1763	British and American Colonists fight French and Indians in French and Indian War (Seven Years' War)
1689–1697	King William's War (War of the League of Augsburg)	1760	George III becomes king of England
1699–1750	Parliament enacts laws regulating colonial manufacturing	1763	George III's Proclamation forbids settlement beyond Appalachians
1702–1713	Queen Anne's War (War of the Spanish Succession): France loses Nova Scotia, Newfoundland, and Hudson Bay to Britain	1764	Sugar Act places tariffs on sugar, coffee, wines, and other imports
		1765	Stamp Act places excise taxes on all printed matter; leads to Stamp Tax Congress
1733	Molasses Act's duty leads to smuggling		
1738–1742	Religious enthusiasm surges during Great Awakening	1766	Stamp Act is repealed; Declaratory Act asserts parliamentary authority over colonies
1740–1748	King George's War (War of the Austrian Succession)	1767	Townshend Duties lead to Massachusetts Circular Letter
1743	Benjamin Franklin founds American Philosophical Society	1770	Five American colonists die in Boston Massacre
1752	Franklin discovers nature of lightning	1772	Colonists burn *Gaspee*
		1773	Tea Act leads to Boston Tea Party
1754	Albany Congress paves way for Stamp Act Congress and Continental Congress	1774	Coercive Acts lead to First Continental Congress

✓●—Study and Review at www.myhistorylab.com

Review Questions

1. Nowadays American manufacturers seek protection—high import taxes—on imported manufactured goods. Why did American colonists oppose such taxes in the eighteenth century?

2. The 1700s witnessed an explosion of interest in evangelical religion, and also the broader diffusion of Enlightenment ideas. What did these phenomena have in common?

3. Why did the British finally prevail in the French and Indian War in 1763 and what were the repercussions of their victory?

4. The colonists believed that the British government was depriving them of the customary liberties accorded all Englishmen; and yet many of the same colonists owned slaves. Can such opinions be reconciled, or were the slave-owning Patriots hypocrites?

5. From 1763 to 1775, the British government made many mistakes: Would different policies have long kept the American colonies within the British empire?

Key Terms

Albany Plan   *87*
Boston Massacre   *106*
Coercive Acts   *108*
Enlightenment   *88*
First Continental
   Congress   *109*

French and Indian
   War   *92*
Great Awakening   *85*
mercantilism   *81*

Navigation Acts   *82*
Seven Years' War   *93*
Stamp Act
   Congress   *101*

4 The American Revolution

Do you rebel against authority?

IN 2010 THE SAMUEL ADAMS BEER COMPANY TRUMPETED BEER'S ROLE IN founding the nation. It claimed that William Bradford's Pilgrims came ashore in Plymouth, Massachusetts, only because they were "out of beer." The Boston beer company further claimed that the American Revolution originated in the taverns of New England. "The revolutionaries gathered over beer to plot their rebellion," it added, noting that George Washington and Thomas Jefferson were home brewers. Samuel Adams inherited his father's beer company, although he "clearly preferred fomenting rebellion to fermenting beer." This was true: Adams's chief claim to posterity is related to tea.

Yet the founders are so deeply embedded in our culture that their names, in addition to appearing on beer bottles, can be spotted almost everywhere. "Washington" is the name of thirty-one counties and forty-two cities. Iowa and Indiana together have nearly 100 "Washington" townships; California has twenty-eight "Washington Elementary Schools." After "Main Street," Washington is the most common street name in the United States. School children also relish his name: Since Washington's birthday was declared a national holiday in 1968, most states have chosen to honor him by closing schools.

Indeed, the founders now loom so large that it may seem that they could not have lost to the British. But their triumph was not inevitable. To understand the American Revolution, we must examine it from the perspective of the past, before the names of the founders adorned beer bottles and elementary schools, and before the United States had become a mighty nation. The simple truth is that the American Revolution was accomplished by men and women who did not know if they would succeed. At the outset, they did not even know whether they sought British concessions or independence, whether most colonists would side with them or remain loyal to His Majesty's government, whether foreign powers such as France could be enlisted to provide support, whether rebellion against political authority in London would undermine social order in America, or whether the many different peoples of the colonies could be knitted into a single nation. The revolutionaries did know, however, that if they failed they would likely face arrest, imprisonment, and even death.

As the rebellion escalated into a full-scale war for independence, the colonists confronted the challenge of creating and financing an army that could defeat the mightiest empire in the world. In the midst of fighting, and in the wake of freedom from British rule, they faced an even greater challenge—the founding of a new nation, with a new government and a new national spirit.

The Shot Heard Round the World

The actions of the First Continental Congress led the British authorities to force a showdown with their colonial offspring. "The New England governments are in a state of rebellion," George III announced. "Blows must decide whether they are to be subject to this country or independent." General Thomas Gage, veteran of Braddock's ill-fated expedition against Fort Duquesne and now commander-in-chief of all British forces in North America, had already been appointed governor of Massachusetts. Some 4,000 Redcoats were concentrated in Boston, camped on the town common—a place once peacefully reserved for the citizens' cows.

Parliament echoed with demands for a show of strength in America. After the Tea Party the general impression was that resistance to British rule was concentrated in Massachusetts. Based on the behavior of colonial militia in the French and Indian War, most British subjects did not think people in the other colonies would be inclined to fight outside their own region. General James Grant announced that with 1,000 men he "would undertake to go from one end of America to the other, and geld all the males, partly by force and partly by a little coaxing." Some opposed the idea of crushing the colonists, and others believed that it could not be easily managed, but they were a small minority. The House of Commons listened to Edmund Burke's magnificent speech on conciliating the colonies and then voted 270 to 78 against him.

The London government decided to use troops against Massachusetts in January 1775, but the order did not reach General Gage until April. In the interim both sides were active. Parliament voted new troop levies and declared Massachusetts to be in a state of rebellion. The Massachusetts Patriots, as they were now calling themselves, formed an extralegal provincial assembly, reorganized the militia, and began training "Minute Men" and other fighters. Soon companies armed with anything that would shoot were drilling on town commons throughout Massachusetts and in other colonies too.

When Gage received his orders on April 14, he acted swiftly. The Patriots had been accumulating arms at Concord, some twenty miles west of Boston. On the night of April 18, Gage dispatched 700 crack troops to seize these supplies. The Patriots were prepared. Paul Revere and other horsemen rode off to alert the countryside and warn John Hancock and Sam Adams, leaders of the provincial assembly, whose arrests had been ordered.

When the Redcoats reached Lexington early the next morning, they found the common occupied by about seventy Minute Men. After an argument, the Americans began to withdraw. Then someone fired a shot. There was a flurry of gunfire and the Minute Men fled, leaving eight of their number dead. The British then marched on to Concord, where they destroyed whatever supplies the Patriots had been unable to carry off.

But militiamen were pouring into the area from all sides. A hot skirmish at Concord's North Bridge forced the Redcoats to yield that position. Becoming alarmed, they began to march back to Boston. Soon they were being subjected to a withering fire from American irregulars along their line of march. A strange battle developed on a "field" sixteen miles

Two weeks after the battle of Lexington and Concord, Ralph Earl, a colonial militiaman from Connecticut, was ordered to make sketches and paintings of what had transpired. Earl revisited the battlefield and interviewed those who had fought. He was an accurate painter, but not a very good one. Each of the British formations, facing the officers, contains exactly twenty-five men.

long and only a few hundred yards wide. Gage was obliged to send out an additional 1,500 soldiers, and total disaster was avoided only by deploying skirmishers to root out snipers hiding in barns and farmhouses along the road to Boston. When the first day of the Revolutionary War ended, the British had sustained 273 casualties, the Americans fewer than 100. "The Rebels are not the despicable rabble too many have supposed them to be," General Gage admitted.

For a brief moment of history, tiny Massachusetts stood alone at arms against an empire that had humbled France and Spain. Yet Massachusetts assumed the offensive! The provincial government organized an expedition that captured Fort Ticonderoga and Crown Point, on Lake Champlain. The other colonies rallied quickly to the cause, sending reinforcements to Cambridge. When news of the battle reached Virginia, George Washington wrote sadly, "A brother's sword has been sheathed in a brother's breast and the once happy and peaceful plains of America are either to be drenched in blood or inhabited by a race of slaves." And then he added, "Can a virtuous man hesitate in his choice?"

●●●─[Read the **Document**

Warren, *Account of the Battle of Lexington* at
myhistorylab.com

The Second Continental Congress

On May 10, 1775, the day Ticonderoga fell, the **Second Continental Congress** met in Philadelphia. It was a distinguished group, more radical than the First Congress. Besides John and Sam Adams, Patrick Henry and Richard Henry Lee of Virginia, and Christopher Gadsden of South Carolina (all holdovers from the First Congress), there was Thomas Jefferson, a young planter from Virginia. Jefferson had recently published "A Summary View of the Rights of British America," an essay criticizing the institution of monarchy and warning George III that "kings are the servants, not the proprietors of the people." The Virginia convention had also sent George Washington, who knew more than any other colonist about commanding men and who wore his buff-and-blue colonel's uniform, a not-too-subtle indication of his willingness to place this knowledge at the disposal of the Congress. The renowned Benjamin Franklin was a delegate, moving rapidly to the radical position.

The Boston merchant John Hancock was chosen president of the Congress, which, like the first, had no legal authority. Yet the delegates had to make agonizing decisions under the pressure of rapidly unfolding military events, with the future of every American depending on their actions. Delicate negotiations and honeyed words might yet persuade king and Parliament to change their ways, but precipitate, bold effort was essential to save Massachusetts.

In this predicament the Congress naturally dealt first with the military crisis. It organized the forces gathering around Boston into the so-called **Continental army** and appointed George Washington commander-in-chief. After Washington and his staff left for Massachusetts on June 23, the Congress turned to the task of requisitioning men and supplies.

The Battle of Bunker Hill

Meanwhile, in Massachusetts, the first major battle of the war had been fought. The British position on the peninsula of Boston was impregnable to direct assault, but high ground north and south, at Charlestown and Dorchester Heights, could be used to

On June 17, the British tried to dislodge Continentals from fortified (and concealed) positions atop Breed's Hill in Charlestown. Note the British cannon batteries on the shore in Boston, lobbing shells into Charlestown. When colonists brought a cannon from Ticonderoga and placed it on hills commanding Boston, the British had no choice but to leave the city.

Source: Winthrop Chandler, American, *The Battle of Bunker Hill* (detail), c. 1776–1777. Oil on panel, 88.58 x 136.21 cm (34-7/8 x 53-5/8"). Museum of Fine Arts, Boston. Gift of Mr. and Mrs. Gardner Richardson, 1982.281. Photograph © 2002 Museum of Fine Arts, Boston.

pound the British positions in the city. When the Continentals seized Bunker Hill and Breed's Hill at Charlestown and set up defenses on the latter, Gage determined at once to drive them off. This was accomplished on June 17. Twice the Redcoats marched in close ranks, bayonets fixed, up Breed's Hill, and each time were driven back after suffering heavy losses. Stubbornly they came again, and this time they carried the redoubt, for the defenders had run out of ammunition.

The British then cleared the Charlestown peninsula, but the victory was really the Americans', for they had proved themselves against professional soldiers and had exacted a terrible toll. More than 1,000 Redcoats had fallen in a couple of hours, out of a force of some 2,500, while the Continentals lost only 400 men, most of them cut down by British bayonets after the hill was taken. "The day ended in glory," a British officer wrote, "but the loss was uncommon in officers for the number engaged."

The Battle of Bunker Hill greatly reduced whatever hope remained for a negotiated settlement. The British recalled General Gage, replacing him with General William Howe, a respected veteran of the French and Indian War, and George III formally proclaimed the colonies to be "in open rebellion." The Continental Congress dispatched one last plea to the king, but this was a sop to the moderates. Immediately thereafter it adopted the Declaration of the Causes and Necessity of Taking Up Arms, which condemned everything the British had done since 1763. Americans were "a people attacked by unprovoked enemies"; the time had come to choose between "submission" to "tyranny" and "resistance by force." The Congress then ordered an attack on Canada and created committees to seek foreign aid and to buy munitions abroad.

The Great Declaration

The Congress (and the bulk of the people) still hung back from a break with the Crown. To declare for independence would be to burn the last bridge, to become traitors in the eyes of the mother country. It was sobering to think of casting off everything that being English meant: love of the king, the traditions of a great nation, pride in the power of a mighty empire.

Then, too, rebellion might end in horrors worse than submission to British tyranny. The disturbances following the Stamp Act and the Tea Act had revealed an alarming fact about American society. The organizers of those protests, mostly persons of wealth and status, had thought in terms of "ordered resistance." They countenanced violence only as a means of forcing the British authorities to pay attention to their complaints. But protest meetings and mob actions had brought thousands of ordinary citizens into the struggle for local self-government. Some of the upper-class leaders among the Patriots, while eager to have the support of the lower classes, were concerned about what they would make of actual independence. Too much exalted talk about "rights" and "liberties" might well give the poor (to say nothing of the slaves) an exaggerated impression of their importance.

Finally, in a world where every country had some kind of monarch, could common people *really* govern themselves? The most ardent defender of American rights might well hesitate after considering all the implications of independence.

Yet independence was probably inevitable by the end of 1775. The belief that George III had been misled by evil or stupid advisers on both sides of the Atlantic became progressively more difficult to sustain. Mistrust of Parliament—indeed, of the whole of British society—grew apace.

Two events in January 1776 pushed the colonies a long step toward a final break. First came the news that the British were sending hired Hessian soldiers to fight against them. Colonists associated mercenaries with looting and rape and feared that the German-speaking Hessians would run amok among them. Such callousness on the part of Britain made reconciliation seem out of the question.

The second decisive event was the publication of **Common Sense**. This tract was written by Thomas Paine, a one-time English corset-maker and civil servant turned pamphleteer, who had been in America scarcely a year. *Common Sense* called for complete independence. It attacked not only George III but the idea of monarchy itself. Paine applied the uncomplicated logic of the zealot to the recent history of America and called George a "Royal Brute" and "the hardened sullen-tempered Pharaoh of England." Many Americans had wanted to control their own affairs but feared the instability of untried republican government. To them Paine said, "We have it in our power to begin the world again." "A government of our own is our natural right," he insisted. "O! ye that love mankind! Ye that dare oppose not only tyranny but the tyrant, stand forth!"

The tone of the debate changed sharply as Paine's slashing attack took effect. In March 1776 the Congress unleashed privateers against British commerce; in April it opened American ports to foreign shipping; in May it urged the Patriots who had set up extralegal provincial conventions to frame constitutions and establish state governments.

On June 7 Richard Henry Lee of Virginia introduced a resolution of the Virginia Convention:

> RESOLVED: That these United Colonies are, and of right ought to be, free and independent States, that they are absolved from all allegiance to the British Crown, and that all political connection between them and the State of Great Britain is, and ought to be, totally dissolved.

This momentous resolution was not passed until July 2; the Congress first appointed a committee consisting of Thomas Jefferson, Benjamin Franklin, John Adams, Roger Sherman, and Robert Livingston to frame a suitable justification of independence. Livingston, a member of one of the great New York landowning families, was put on the committee in an effort to push New York toward independence. Sherman, a self-educated Connecticut lawyer and merchant, was a conservative who opposed parliamentary control over colonial affairs. Franklin, the best known of all Americans and an experienced writer, was a natural choice; so was John Adams, whose devotion to the cause of independence combined with his solid conservative qualities made him perhaps the typical man of the Revolution.

Thomas Jefferson was probably placed on the committee because politics required that a Virginian be included and because of his literary skill and general intelligence. Aside from writing *A Summary View of the Rights of British America*, he had done little to attract notice. At age 33 he was the youngest member of the Continental Congress and was only marginally interested in its deliberations. He had been slow to take his seat in the fall of 1775, and arrived in Philadelphia only on May 14. Had he delayed another month, someone else would have written the Declaration of Independence.

●●●─[Read the Document

Jefferson, *"Rough Draft"* of the
Declaration of Independence at
myhistorylab.com

The committee asked Jefferson to prepare a draft. The result, with a few amendments made by Franklin and Adams and somewhat toned down by the whole Congress, was officially adopted by the delegates on July 4, 1776, two days after the delegates had voted for the decisive break with Great Britain.

Jefferson's Declaration of Independence consisted of two parts. The introductory section justified the abstract right of any people to revolt and described the theory on which the Americans based their creation of a new, republican government. The second section was a list of the "injuries and usurpations" of George III, a bill of indictment explaining why the colonists felt driven to exercise the rights outlined in the first part of the document. Here Jefferson stressed the monarch's interference with the functioning of representative government in America, his harsh administration of colonial affairs, his restrictions on civil rights, and his maintenance of troops in the colonies without their consent.

Jefferson sought to marshal every possible evidence of British perfidy, and he made George III, rather than Parliament, the villain because the king was the personification of the nation against which America was rebelling. He held the monarch responsible for Parliament's efforts to tax the colonies and restrict their trade, for many actions by subordinates that George III had never deliberately authorized, and for some things that never happened. He even blamed the king for the existence of slavery in the colonies, a charge the Congress cut from the document not entirely because of its concern for accuracy. The long bill of particulars was intended to convince the world that the Americans had good reasons for exercising their right to form a government of their own.

Jefferson's general statement of the right of revolution has inspired oppressed peoples all over the world for more than 200 years:

> We hold these truths to be self-evident, that all men are created equal, that they are endowed by their Creator with certain unalienable Rights, that among these are Life, Liberty and the pursuit of Happiness.—That to secure these rights, Governments are instituted among Men, deriving their just powers from the consent of the governed,—That whenever any Form of Government becomes destructive of these ends, it is the Right of the People to alter or to abolish it, and to institute new Government. . . .

The Declaration was intended to influence foreign opinion, but its proclamation had little immediate effect outside Great Britain, and there it only made people angry and determined to subdue the rebels. Why, then, has the Declaration had so much influence on modern history? Not because the thought was original with Jefferson. As John Adams later pointed out, the basic idea was commonplace among eighteenth-century liberals. "I did not consider it any part of my charge to invent new ideas," Jefferson explained, "but to place before mankind the common sense of the subject, in terms so plain and firm as to command their assent. . . . It was intended to be an expression of the American mind."

Revolution was not new, but the spectacle of a people solemnly explaining and justifying their right, in an orderly manner, to throw off their oppressors and establish a new system on their own authority was almost without precedent. Soon the French would be drawing on this example in their revolution, and rebels everywhere have since done likewise. And if Jefferson did not create the concept, he gave it a nearly perfect form.

1776: The Balance of Forces

A formal declaration of independence merely cleared the way for tackling the problems of founding a new nation. Lacking both traditions and authority based in law, the Congress had to create political institutions and a new national spirit, all in the midst of war.

Always the military situation took precedence, for a single disastrous setback might make everything else meaningless. At the start the Americans already possessed their lands (except for the few square miles occupied by British troops). Although thousands of colonists fought for George III, the British soon learned that to put down the American rebellion they would have to bring in men and supplies from bases on the other side of the Atlantic.

Certain long-run factors operated in America's favor. Although His Majesty's soldiers were brave and well disciplined, the army was as inefficient as the rest of the British government. Whereas nearly everyone in Great Britain wanted to crack down on Boston after the Tea Party, many boggled at engaging in a full-scale war against all the colonies. Aside from a reluctance to spill so much blood, there was the question of expense. Finally, the idea of dispatching the cream of the British army to America while powerful enemies on the continent still smarted from past defeats seemed risky. For all these reasons the British approached gingerly the task of subduing the rebellion. When Washington fortified Dorchester Heights overlooking Boston, General Howe withdrew his troops to Halifax rather than risk another Bunker Hill.

Awareness of Britain's problems undoubtedly spurred the Continental Congress to the bold actions of the spring of 1776. However, on July 2, 1776, the same day that Congress voted for independence, General Howe was back on American soil, landing in force on Staten Island in New York harbor in preparation for an assault on the city. Soon Howe had at hand 32,000 well-equipped troops and a powerful fleet commanded by his brother, Richard, Lord Howe. If the British controlled New York City and the Hudson River, they could, as Washington realized, "stop intercourse between the northern and southern Colonies, upon which depends the Safety of America."

Suddenly the full strength of the empire seemed to have descended on the Americans. Superior British resources (a population of 9 million to the colonies' 2.5 million, large stocks of war materials and the industrial capacity to boost them further, mastery of the seas, a well-trained and experienced army, a highly centralized and, when necessary, ruthless government) were now all too evident.

The demonstration of British might in New York harbor accentuated American military and economic weaknesses: Both money and the tools of war were continually in short supply in a predominantly agricultural country. Many of Washington's soldiers were armed with weapons no more lethal than spears and tomahawks. Few had proper uniforms. Even the most patriotic resisted conforming to the conventions of military discipline; the men hated drilling and all parade-ground formality. And all these problems were complicated by the fact that Washington had to create an army organization out of whole cloth at the same time that he was fighting a war.

See the **Map**

The American Revolution at
myhistorylab.com

Loyalists

Behind the lines, the country was far from united. Whereas nearly all colonists had objected to British policies, many still hesitated to take up arms against the mother country. Even Massachusetts harbored many **Loyalists**, or Tories, as they were called; about a thousand Americans left Boston with General Howe, abandoning their homes rather than submit to the rebel army.

No one knows exactly how the colonists divided on the question of independence. John Adams's off-the-cuff estimate was that a third of the people were ardent Patriots, another third loyal to Great Britain, and the rest neutral or tending to favor whichever side seemed to be winning. Most historians think that about a fifth of the people were Loyalists and about two-fifths Patriots, but there are few hard figures to go by. What is certain is that large elements, perhaps a majority of the people, were more or less indifferent to the conflict or, in Tom Paine's famous phrase, were summer soldiers and sunshine patriots—they supported the Revolution when all was going well and lost their enthusiasm in difficult hours.

The divisions cut across geographical, social, and economic lines. A high proportion of those holding royal appointments and many Anglican clergymen remained loyal to King George, as did numbers of merchants with close connections in Britain. There were important pockets of Tory strength in rural sections of New York, in the North Carolina backcountry, and among persons of non-English origin and other minority groups who tended to count on London for protection against the local majority (see the map "Campaign in the South, 1779–1781," p. 126).

Although the differences separating Patriots and Loyalists were sometimes unclear, feelings were nonetheless bitter. Individual Loyalists were often set upon by mobs, tarred and feathered, and otherwise abused. Some were thrown into jail for no legitimate reason; others were exiled and their property confiscated. Battles between Tory units and the Continental army were often exceptionally bloody. "Neighbor was against neighbor, father against son and son against father," one Connecticut Tory reported. "He that would not thrust his own blade through his brother's heart was called an infamous villain."

The British Take New York City

General Howe's campaign against New York brought to light another American weakness—the lack of military experience. Washington, expecting Howe to attack New York, had moved south to meet the threat immediately after Howe had abandoned Boston. But both he and his men failed badly in this first major test. Late in August Howe crossed from Staten Island to Brooklyn. In the Battle of Long Island he easily outflanked and defeated Washington's army. Had he acted decisively, he probably could have ended the war on the spot, but Howe could not make up his mind whether to be a peacemaker or a conqueror. This hesitation in consolidating his gains permitted Washington to withdraw his troops to Manhattan Island.

Howe could still have trapped Washington simply by using his fleet to land troops on the northern end of Manhattan; instead he attacked New York City directly, leaving the Americans an escape route to the North. Again Patriot troops proved no match for

British regulars. Although Washington threatened to shoot cowardly Connecticut soldiers as they fled the battlefield, he could not stop the rout and had to fall back on Harlem Heights in upper Manhattan. Yet once more Howe failed to pursue his advantage promptly.

Still, Washington refused to see the peril in remaining on an island while the enemy commanded the surrounding waters. Only when Howe shifted a powerful force to Westchester, directly threatening his rear, did Washington move north to the mainland. Finally, after several narrow escapes, he crossed the Hudson River and marched south to New Jersey, where the British could not use their naval superiority against him.

The battles in and around New York City suggested that the British would win easily. Yet somehow Washington salvaged a moral victory from these ignominious defeats. He learned rapidly; seldom thereafter did he place his troops in such vulnerable positions. And his men, in spite of repeated failure, had become an army. In November and December 1776

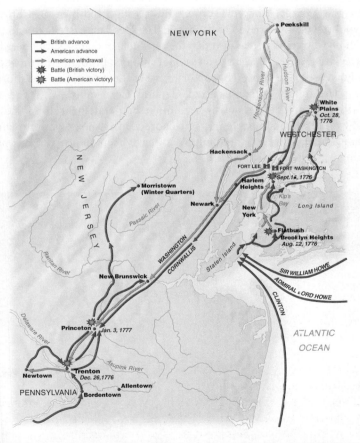

New York and New Jersey Campaigns, 1776–1777 In the summer of 1776, after abandoning Boston, several British fleets converged on New York City. After taking Staten Island, the British crossed to Brooklyn, and won a string of decisive battles in the New York region. Washington's troops retreated through New Jersey nearly to Newtown, Pennsylvania. But in the final week of 1776, Washington recrossed the Delaware River and won morale-boosting battles at Trenton and Princeton.

Emanuel Leutze's *Washington Crossing the Delaware* (1851) is riddled with historical inaccuracies, most obviously, the time of day: Washington's face shines and the ice gleams white, but the December 1776 crossing was actually made at night during a snowstorm.

they retreated across New Jersey and into Pennsylvania. General Howe then abandoned the campaign, going into winter quarters in New York but posting garrisons at Trenton, Princeton, and other strategic points.

The troops at Trenton were Hessian mercenaries, and Washington decided to attack them. He crossed the ice-clogged Delaware River with 2,400 men on Christmas night during a wild storm, and arrived at daybreak. The Hessians were taken completely by surprise. Those who could fled in disorder; the rest—900 of them—surrendered.

The Hessians were first-class professional soldiers, probably the most competent troops in Europe at that time. The victory gave a boost to American morale. A few days later Washington outmaneuvered General Cornwallis, who had rushed to Trenton with reinforcements, and won another battle at Princeton. These engagements had little strategic importance, since both armies then went into winter quarters. Without them, however, there might not have been an army to resume the war in the spring.

William Mercer, painter of *The Battle of Princeton* (1786–1790), was deaf and mute. Charles Wilson Peale, perhaps the foremost painter of the day, took Mercer on as a student in part to see if Mercer could learn the craft.

Saratoga and the French Alliance

When spring reached New Jersey in April 1777, Washington had fewer than 5,000 men under arms. Great plans—far too many and too complicated, as it turned out—were afoot in the British camp. The strategy called for General John Burgoyne to lead a large army from Canada down Lake Champlain toward Albany while a smaller force under Lieutenant Colonel Barry St. Leger pushed eastward toward Albany from Fort Oswego on Lake Ontario. General Howe was to lead a third force north up the Hudson. The Patriots would be trapped and the New England states isolated from the rest.

As a venture in coordinated military tactics, the British campaign of 1777 was a fiasco. General Howe had spent the winter in New York wining and dining his officers and prominent local Loyalists. He was less attentive to his responsibilities for the British army advancing south from Canada.

General "Gentleman Johnny" Burgoyne, a charming if somewhat bombastic character (part politician, part poet, part gambler, part ladies' man) yet also a brave soldier, had begun his march from Canada in mid-June. By early July his army, which consisted of 500 Indians, 650 Loyalists, and 6,000 regulars, had captured Fort Ticonderoga at the southern end of Lake Champlain. He quickly pushed beyond Lake George but then got bogged down. Burdened by a huge baggage train he could advance at but a snail's pace through the woods north of Saratoga. Patriot militia impeded his way by felling trees across the forest trails.

St. Leger was also slow in carrying out his part of the grand design. He did not leave Fort Oswego until July 26, and when he stopped to besiege a Patriot force at Fort Stanwix, General Benedict Arnold had time to march west with 1,000 men from the army resisting Burgoyne and drive him back to Oswego.

Meanwhile, with magnificent disregard for the agreed-on plan, Howe wasted time trying to trap Washington into exposing his army in New Jersey. This enabled Washington to send some of his best troops to buttress the militia units opposing Burgoyne. Then, just when St. Leger was setting out for Albany, Howe took the bulk of his army off by sea to attack Philadelphia, leaving only a small force commanded by General Sir Henry Clinton to aid Burgoyne.

When Washington moved south to oppose Howe, the British commander taught him a series of lessons in tactics, defeating him at the Battle of Brandywine, then feinting him out of position and moving unopposed into Philadelphia. But by that time it was late September, and disaster was about to befall General Burgoyne.

The American forces under Philip Schuyler and later under Horatio Gates and Benedict Arnold had erected formidable defenses immediately south of Saratoga. Burgoyne struck at this position twice and was thrown back both times with heavy losses. Each day more local militia swelled the American forces. Soon Burgoyne was under siege, his troops pinned down by withering fire from every direction, unable even to bury their dead. The only hope was General Clinton, who had finally started up the Hudson from New York. Clinton got as far as Kingston, about 80 miles south of Saratoga, but on October 16 he decided to return to New York for reinforcements. The next day, at Saratoga, Burgoyne surrendered. Some 5,700 British prisoners were marched off to Virginia.

This overwhelming triumph changed the course and character of the war. France would probably have entered the war in any case; the country had never reconciled itself to its losses in the Seven Years' War and for years had been building a navy capable of taking on the British. Helping the Americans was simply another way of weakening their British enemy. Spain also contributed, not out of sympathy for the Revolution, but because of its desire to injure Great Britain. When news of the victory at Saratoga reached Paris, the time seemed ripe and Louis XVI recognized the United States. Then Comte de Vergennes, France's foreign minister, and three American commissioners in Paris (Benjamin Franklin, Arthur Lee, and Silas Deane) drafted a commercial treaty and a formal treaty of alliance. The two nations agreed to make "common cause and aid each other mutually" should war "break out" between France and Great Britain. Meanwhile, France guaranteed "the sovereignty and independence absolute and unlimited" of the United States. The help of Spain and France, Washington declared, "will not fail of establishing the Independence of America in a short time."

When the news of Saratoga reached England, Lord North realized that a Franco-American alliance was almost inevitable. To forestall it, he was ready to give in on all the issues that had agitated the colonies before 1775. Both the Coercive Acts and the Tea Act would be repealed; Parliament would pledge never to tax the colonies.

Instead of implementing this proposal promptly, Parliament delayed until March 1778. Royal peace commissioners did not reach Philadelphia until June, a month after Congress had ratified the French treaty. The British proposals were rejected, and while the peace commissioners were still in Philadelphia, war broke out between France and Great Britain.

Saratoga Campaign, September 19 to October 17, 1777 In 1777 the British, who controlled New York City, decided to drive the Patriots from the rest of the colony through a three-pronged attack on Albany. All three British generals failed to achieve their objectives: St. Leger, coming from the west, failed to advance beyond Ft. Stanwix; Burgoyne, from the north, bogged down and found himself surrounded; and Clinton, from New York City, made it to Kingston, but failed to relieve Burgoyne, whose army surrendered.

The American Revolution, however, had yet to be won. After the loss of Philadelphia, Washington had settled his army for the winter at Valley Forge, 20 miles to the northwest. The army's supply system collapsed. According to the Marquis de Lafayette, one of many Europeans who volunteered to fight on the American side, "the unfortunate soldiers . . . had neither coats, nor hats, nor shirts, nor shoes; their feet and legs froze till they grew black, and it was often necessary to amputate them."

As the winter dragged on, the Continental army melted away. So many officers resigned that Washington was heard to say that he was afraid of "being left Alone with the Soldiers only." Since enlisted men could not legally resign, they deserted by the hundreds. Yet the army survived. Gradually the soldiers who remained became a tough, professional fighting force.

The War Moves South

Spring brought a revival of American hopes in the form of more supplies, new recruits, and, above all, word of the French alliance. In May 1778 the British replaced General Howe as commander with General Clinton, who decided to transfer his base back to New York. While Clinton was moving across New Jersey, Washington attacked him at Monmouth Court House. The fight was inconclusive, but the Americans held the field when the day ended and were able to claim a victory.

Thereafter British strategy changed. Fighting in the northern states degenerated into skirmishes and other small-unit clashes. Instead, relying on sea power, the supposed presence of many Tories in the South, and the possibility of obtaining the help of slaves, the British concentrated their efforts in South Carolina and Georgia. Savannah fell to them late in 1778, and most of the settled parts of Georgia were overrun during 1779. In 1780 Clinton led a massive expedition against Charleston. When the city surrendered in May, more than 3,000 soldiers were captured, the most overwhelming American defeat of the war. Leaving General Cornwallis and some 8,000 men to carry on the campaign, Clinton then sailed back to New York.

The Tories in South Carolina and Georgia came closer to meeting British expectations than in any other region, but the callous behavior of the British troops persuaded large numbers of hesitating citizens to join the Patriot cause. Guerrilla bands led by Francis Marion, the "Swamp Fox," Thomas Sumter (after whom Fort Sumter, famous in the Civil War, was named), and others like them provided a nucleus of resistance in areas that had supposedly been subdued. (For an additional perspective on this campaign, see Re-Viewing the Past at the end of this chapter about the movie, *The Patriot.*)

But the tide soon turned. In 1779 the Spanish governor of Louisiana, José de Gálvez, administered a stinging defeat to British troops in Florida, and in 1780 and 1781 he captured the British-held Gulf ports of Pensacola and Mobile. More important, in June 1780 Congress placed Horatio Gates in charge of a southern army consisting of the irregular militia units and a hard core of Continentals transferred from Washington's command. Gates encountered Cornwallis at Camden, South Carolina. Foolishly, he entrusted a key sector of his line to untrained militiamen, who panicked when the British charged with fixed bayonets. Gates suffered heavy losses and had to fall back. Congress then recalled him, permitting Washington to replace him with General Nathanael Greene, a first-rate officer.

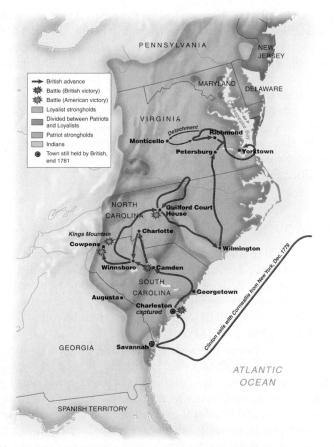

Campaign in the South, 1779–1781 In 1779 the British moved south, seeking support from Loyalist strongholds in the port cities of Savannah, Charleston, and Wilmington, as well as some interior regions. After taking Charleston, the British were harried throughout South Carolina and North Carolina, prompting their retreat northward to Virginia.

A band of militiamen had trapped a contingent of Tories at King's Mountain and forced its surrender. Greene, avoiding a major engagement with Cornwallis's superior numbers, divided his troops and staged a series of raids on scattered points. In January 1781, at the Battle of Cowpens in northwestern South Carolina, General Daniel Morgan inflicted a costly defeat on Colonel Banastre Tarleton, one of Cornwallis's most effective officers. Cornwallis pursued Morgan hotly, but the American rejoined Greene, and at Guilford Court House they again inflicted heavy losses on the British. Then Cornwallis withdrew to Wilmington, North Carolina, where he could rely on the fleet for support and reinforcements. Greene's Patriots quickly regained control of the Carolina backcountry.

Victory at Yorktown

Seeing no future in the Carolinas and unwilling to vegetate at Wilmington, Cornwallis marched north into Virginia, where he joined forces with troops under Benedict Arnold. (Disaffected by what he considered unjust criticism of his generalship, Arnold

The Yorktown Campaign, April to September 1781 Cornwallis assumed that his army at Yorktown could be provisioned and, if necessary, evacuated by the mighty British navy. But when several French admirals converged on the Chesapeake Bay in August and defeated the British fleet commanded by Admiral Graves. Cornwallis was trapped. He surrendered in October.

had sold out to the British in 1780. He intended to betray the bastion of West Point on the Hudson River. The scheme was foiled when incriminating papers were found on the person of a British spy, Major John André. Arnold fled to the British and André was hanged.) As in the Carolina campaign, the British had numerical superiority at first but lost it rapidly when local militia and Continental forces concentrated against them. Cornwallis soon discovered that Virginia Tories were of little help in such a situation. "When a Storm threatens, our friends disappear," he grumbled.

General Clinton ordered Cornwallis to establish a base at Yorktown where he could be supplied by sea. It was a terrible mistake. The British navy in American waters far outnumbered American and French vessels, but the Atlantic is wide, and in those days communication was slow. The French had a fleet in the West Indies under Admiral François de Grasse and another squadron at Newport, Rhode Island, where a French army was stationed. In the summer of 1781 Washington, de Grasse, and the Comte de Rochambeau, commander of French land forces, designed and carried out with an efficiency unparalleled in eighteenth-century warfare a complex plan to bottle up Cornwallis.

The British navy in the West Indies and at New York might have forestalled this scheme had it moved promptly and in force. But Admiral Sir George Rodney sent only part of his Indies fleet. As a result, de Grasse, after a battle with a British fleet commanded by Admiral Thomas Graves, won control of the Chesapeake and cut Cornwallis off from the sea.

The next move was up to Washington, and this was his finest hour as a commander. He desperately wanted to attack the British base at New York, but at the urging of

This painting of the surrender of Cornwallis at Yorktown on October 19, 1781 was done by John Trumbull in 1820. Trumbull's original version of the painting depicted Cornwallis in the act of surrender. But this was a serious mistake: Cornwallis, unwilling to admit defeat in person, had sent a subordinate to surrender on his behalf. Trumbull repainted the scene, changing the uniform color of the central figure from red to blue: An American officer reaches for a sword presented by Cornwallis's second-in-command.

Rochambeau he agreed instead to strike at Yorktown. After tricking Clinton into thinking he was heading for New York, he pushed boldly south. In early September he reached Yorktown and joined up with an army commanded by Lafayette and troops from de Grasse's fleet. He soon had nearly 17,000 French and American veterans in position.

Cornwallis was helpless. He held out until October 17 and then asked for terms. Two days later more than 7,000 British soldiers marched out of their lines and laid down their arms. Then the jubilant Lafayette ordered his military band to play "Yankee Doodle."

Negotiating a Favorable Peace

((•─|Hear the **Audio**

The Liberty Song at
myhistorylab.com

The British gave up trying to suppress the rebellion after Yorktown, but the event that confirmed the existence of the United States as an independent nation was the signing of a peace treaty with Great Britain. But the problem of peacemaking was complicated. The United States and France had pledged not to make a separate peace.

The Continental Congress appointed John Adams, Benjamin Franklin, John Jay, Thomas Jefferson, and Henry Laurens as a commission to conduct peace talks in Paris, France. Franklin and Jay did most of the actual negotiating. Congress, grateful for French aid during the Revolution, had instructed the commissioners to rely on the advice of the Comte de Vergennes. In Paris, however, the commissioners soon discovered that Vergennes was not the perfect friend of America that Congress believed him to be. He was, after all, a French official, and France had other interests far more important than concern for its American ally. Vergennes "means to keep his hand under our chin to prevent us from drowning," Adams complained, "but not to lift our head out of the water."

Franklin, whose fame as a scientist and sage had spread to Europe, was wined and dined by the cream of Paris. He did not press the American point of view as forcefully as he might have. But this was because he took the long view, which was to achieve a true reconciliation with the British, not simply to drive the hardest bargain possible. John Jay was somewhat more tough-minded. But on basic issues all the Americans were in agreement. They hinted to the British representative, Richard Oswald, that they would consider a separate peace if it were a generous one and suggested that Great Britain would be far better off with America, a nation that favored free trade, in control of the trans-Appalachian region than with a mercantilist power like Spain.

The British government reacted favorably, authorizing Oswald "to treat with the Commissioners appointed by the Colonys, under the title of Thirteen United States." Soon the Americans were deep in negotiations with Oswald. They told Vergennes what they were doing but did not discuss details.

By the end of November 1782 a preliminary treaty had been signed. "His Britannic Majesty," Article 1 began, "acknowledges the said United States . . . to be free, sovereign and independent States." Other terms were equally in line with American hopes and objectives. The boundaries of the nation were set at the Great Lakes, the Mississippi River, and 31° north latitude (roughly the northern boundary of Florida, which the British turned over to Spain).[1] Britain recognized the right of Americans to take fish on the Grand Banks off Newfoundland and, far more important, to dry and cure their catch on unsettled beaches in Labrador and Nova Scotia. The British agreed to withdraw their troops from American soil "with all convenient speed." On the touchy problem of Tory property seized during the Revolution, the Americans agreed only that Congress would "earnestly recommend" that the states "provide for the restitution of all estates, rights and properties which have been confiscated." They promised to prevent further property confiscation and prosecutions of Tories—certainly a wise as well as a humane policy—and they agreed not to impede the collection of debts owed British subjects. Vergennes was flabbergasted by the success of the Americans. "The English buy the peace more than they make it," he wrote. "Their concessions . . . exceed all that I should have thought possible."

The American commissioners obtained these favorable terms because they were shrewd diplomats and because of the rivalries that existed among the great European powers. In the last analysis, Britain preferred to have a weak nation of English-speaking people in command of the Mississippi Valley rather than France or Spain.

From their experience at the peace talks, the American leaders learned the importance of playing one power against another without committing themselves completely to any. This policy demanded constant contact with European affairs and skill at adjusting policies to changes in the European balance of power. It enabled the United States, a young and relatively feeble country, to grow and prosper.

---

[1]Much of this vast region, of course, was controlled not by the British but by various Indian tribes.

The United States under the Articles of Confederation, 1787 New York and Virginia gave up their claims to the vast area that became the Northwest Territory and thus set a precedent for trans-Appalachian land policy. By 1802 the various state claims had been ceded to the national government. The original Northwest Territory (the Old Northwest) was bounded by the Ohio and Mississippi rivers and the Great Lakes.

National Government under the Articles of Confederation

Independence was won on the battlefield and at the Paris Peace Conference, but it could not have been achieved without the work of the Continental Congress and the new state governments. The delegates recognized that the Congress was essentially a legislative body rather than a complete government and from the start they struggled to create a workable central authority. In July 1776 John Dickinson prepared a draft national constitution, but it could not command much support. The larger states objected to equal representation of all the states, and the states with large western land claims refused to cede them to the central government. It was not until November 1777 that the **Articles of Confederation** were submitted to the states for ratification. The approval of all states was required before the Articles could go into effect. All acted fairly promptly but Maryland, which did not ratify the document until 1781.

●●●─Read the Document

The Articles of Confederation
at **myhistorylab.com**

The Articles merely provided a legal basis for authority that the Continental Congress had already been exercising. Each state, regardless of size, was to have but one vote; the union it created was only a "league of friendship." Article 2 defined the limit of national power: "Each state retains its sovereignty, freedom, and independence, and every Power, jurisdiction, and right, which is not by this confederation expressly delegated to the United States, in Congress assembled." Time proved this an inadequate arrangement, chiefly because the central government lacked the authority to impose taxes and had no way of enforcing the powers it did have.

● See the **Map**

Western Land Claims Ceded by the States at **myhistorylab.com**

Financing the War

In practice, Congress and the states carried on the war cooperatively. General officers were appointed by Congress, lesser ones locally. The Continental army, the backbone of Washington's force, was supported by Congress. The states raised militia chiefly for short-term service. Militiamen fought well at times but often proved unreliable, especially when asked to fight at any great distance from their homes. Washington continually fretted about their "dirty mercenary spirit" and their "intractable" nature, yet he could not have won the war without them.

The fact that Congress's requisitions of money often went unhonored by the states does not mean that the states failed to contribute heavily to the war effort. Altogether they spent about $5.8 million in hard money, and they met Congress's demands for beef, corn, rum, fodder, and other military supplies. In addition, Congress raised large sums by borrowing. Americans bought bonds worth between $7 and $8 million during the war. Foreign governments lent another $8 million, most of this furnished by France. Congress also issued more than $240 million in paper money, and the states issued over $200 million more. This currency fell rapidly in value, resulting in an inflation that caused hardship and grumbling. The people, in effect, paid much of the cost of the war through the depreciation of their savings, but it is hard to see how else the war could have been financed, given the prejudice of the populace against paying taxes to fight a war against British taxation.

State Republican Governments

However crucial the role of Congress, in an important sense the real revolution occurred when the individual colonies broke their ties with Great Britain. Using their colonial charters as a basis, the states began framing new constitutions even before the Declaration of Independence. By early 1777 all but Connecticut and Rhode Island, which continued under their colonial charters well into the nineteenth century, had taken this decisive step.

On the surface the new governments were not drastically different from those they replaced. The most significant change was the removal of outside control, which had the effect of making the governments more responsive to public opinion. Gone were the times when a governor could be appointed and maintained in office by orders from

London. The new constitutions varied in detail, but all provided for an elected legislature, an executive, and a system of courts. In general the powers of the governor and of judges were limited, the theory being that elected rulers no less than those appointed by kings were subject to the temptations of authority, that, as one Patriot put it, all men are "tyrants enough at heart." The typical governor had no voice in legislation and little in appointments. Pennsylvania went so far as to eliminate the office of governor, replacing it with an elected council of twelve.

Power was concentrated in the legislature, which the people had come to count on to defend their interests. In addition to the lawmaking authority exercised by the colonial assemblies, the state constitutions gave the legislatures the power to declare war, conduct foreign relations, control the courts, and perform many other essentially executive functions. While continuing to require that voters be property owners or tax-payers, the constitution makers remained suspicious even of the legislature.

They rejected the British concept of virtual representation. They saw legislators as representatives—that is, as agents reflecting the interests of the voters of a particular district rather than superior persons chosen to decide public issues according to their own best judgment. Where political power was involved, the common American principle was every man for himself, but also everyone for the nation, the republic. People were no longer subjects, but citizens, *parts* of government, obedient to its laws, but not blindly subordinate to governmental authority epitomized in the monarch.

A majority of the constitutions contained bills of rights (such as the one George Mason wrote for Virginia) protecting the people's civil liberties against all branches of the government. In Britain such guarantees checked only the Crown; the Americans invoked them against their elected representatives as well.

The state governments combined the best of the British system, including its respect for status, fairness, and due process with the uniquely American stress on individualism and a healthy dislike of excessive authority. The idea of drafting written frames of government—contracts between the people and their representatives that carefully spelled out the powers and duties of the latter—grew out of the experience of the colonists after 1763, when the vagueness of the unwritten British constitution had caused so much controversy, and from the compact principle, the heart of republican government as described so eloquently in the Declaration of Independence. This constitutionalism represented one of the most important innovations of the Revolutionary era: a peaceful method for altering the political system. In the midst of violence, the states changed their frames of government in an orderly, legal manner—a truly remarkable achievement that became a beacon of hope to reformers all over the world. The states' example, the Reverend Simeon Howard of Massachusetts predicted, "will encourage the friends and rouse a spirit of liberty through other nations."

Social Reform and Antislavery

Many states seized the occasion of constitution making to introduce important political and social reforms. In Pennsylvania, Virginia, North Carolina, and other states the seats in the legislature were reapportioned in order to give the western districts their fair share. Primogeniture, entail (the right of an owner of property to prevent heirs from ever selling it), and quitrents were abolished wherever they had existed. Steps toward greater freedom of religion were taken, especially in states where the Anglican Church had enjoyed a privileged position. In Virginia the movement to separate church and state was given the force of law by Jefferson's Statute of Religious Liberty, enacted in 1786. "Our civil rights have no dependence on our religious opinions, any more than our opinions in physics or geometry," the statute declared. "Truth is great and will prevail if left to herself."

A number of states moved tentatively against slavery. In attacking British policy after 1763, colonists had frequently claimed that Parliament was trying to make slaves of them. No less a personage than George Washington wrote in 1774: "We must assert our rights, or submit to every imposition, that can be heaped upon us, till custom and use shall make us tame and abject slaves." However exaggerated the language, such reasoning led to denunciations of slavery, often vague but significant in their effects on public opinion. The fact that practically every important thinker of the European Enlightenment (Montesquieu, Voltaire, Diderot, and Rousseau in France; David Hume, Samuel Johnson, and Adam Smith in England, to name the most important) had criticized slavery on moral and economic grounds also had an impact on educated opinion. Then, too, the forthright statements in the Declaration of Independence about liberty and equality seemed impossible to reconcile with slaveholding. "How is it," asked Dr. Samuel Johnson, the celebrated English writer who opposed independence, "that we hear the loudest yelps for liberty among the drivers of negroes?"

The war opened direct paths to freedom for some slaves. In November 1775 Lord Dunmore, the royal governor of Virginia, proclaimed that all slaves "able and willing to bear arms" for the British would be liberated. In fact, the British treated slaves as captured property, seizing them by the thousands in their campaigns in the South. The fate of these blacks is obscure. Some ended up in the West Indies, still slaves. Others were evacuated to Canada and liberated, and some of them settled the British colony of Sierra Leone in West Africa, founded in 1787. Probably many more escaped from bondage by running away during the confusion accompanying the British campaigns in the South.

About 5,000 blacks served in the Patriot army and navy. Most black soldiers were assigned noncombat duties, but there were some African American soldiers in every major battle from Lexington to Yorktown.

Beginning with Pennsylvania in 1780, the northern states all did away with slavery. In most cases slaves born after a certain date were to become free on reaching maturity. Since New York did not pass a gradual emancipation law until 1799 and New Jersey not until 1804, there were numbers of slaves in the so-called free states well into the nineteenth century—more than 3,500 as late as 1830. But the institution was on its way toward extinction. All the states prohibited the importation of slaves from abroad, and except for Georgia and South Carolina, the southern states passed laws removing restrictions on the right of individual owners to free their slaves. The greatest success of voluntary emancipation came in Virginia, where, between 1782 and 1790, as many as 10,000 blacks were freed.

These advances encouraged foes of slavery to hope that the institution would soon disappear. But slavery died only where it was not economically important. Except for owners whose slaves were "carried off" by the British, only in Massachusetts (where the state supreme court ruled slavery unconstitutional in 1783) were slaves taken away from their owners.

Despite the continuing subordination of blacks, the Revolution permanently changed the tone of American society. In the way they dressed, in their manner of speech, and in the way they dealt with one another in public places, Americans paid at least lip service to the idea of equality.

Little of the social and economic upheaval usually associated with revolutions occurred, before, during, or after 1776. At least part of the urban violence of the period (just how large a part is difficult to determine at this distance) had no social objective. America had its share of criminals, mischievous youths eager to flex their muscles, and other people unable to resist the temptation to break the law when it could be done without much risk of punishment.

The property of Tories was frequently seized by the state governments, but almost never with the idea of redistributing wealth or providing the poor with land. While some large Tory estates were broken up and sold to small farmers, others passed intact to wealthy individuals or to groups of speculators. The war disrupted many traditional business relationships. Some merchants were unable to cope with the changes; others adapted well and grew rich. But the changes occurred without regard for the political beliefs or social values of either those who profited or those who lost.

Finally, the new governments became more responsive to public opinion, no matter what the particular shape of their political institutions. This was true principally because *Common Sense*, the Declaration of Independence, and the experience of participating in a revolution had made people conscious of their rights in a republic and of their power to enforce those rights. Conservatives swiftly discovered that state constitutions designed to insulate legislators and officials from popular pressures were ineffective when the populace felt strongly about any issue.

Women and the Revolution

In the late eighteenth century women in the Western world were acquiring more legal rights, although the change was barely perceptible at the time. This movement was strengthened in America by the events leading up to the break with Great Britain and still more by the Declaration of Independence. When Americans began to think and talk about the rights of the individual and the evils of arbitrary rule, subtle effects on relations between the sexes followed. For example, it became somewhat easier for women to obtain divorces. In colonial times divorces were relatively rare, but easier for men to obtain than for women. After the Revolution the difference did not disappear, but it became considerably smaller. In 1791 a South Carolina judge went so far as to say that the law protecting "the absolute dominion" of husbands was "the offspring of a rude and barbarous age." The "progress of civilization," he continued, "has tended to ameliorate the condition of women, and to allow even to wives, something like personal identity."

As the tone of this "liberal" opinion indicates, the change in male attitudes that took place in America because of the Revolution was small. Courts in New York and Massachusetts refused to take action against Tory women whose husbands were Tories on the grounds that it was the duty of women to obey their husbands; and when John Adams's wife Abigail warned him in 1776 that if he and his fellow rebels did not "remember the ladies" when reforming society, the women would "foment a

In 2009, historian Woody Holton described how Abigail Adams shrewdly invested in the Continental Congress's war debts; when the new government decided to pay those debts in full, those who had invested in the debt made a killing. Because John Adams himself supported this policy, Holton suggests that she had engaged in unsavory (but not uncommon) investment practices.

Rebellion" of their own, he treated her remarks as a joke. Adams believed that voting (and as he wrote on another occasion, writing history) was "not the Province of the Ladies."[2]

However, the war effort increased the influence of women in several ways. With so many men in uniform, women took over the management of countless farms, shops, and businesses, and they became involved in the handling of other day-to-day matters that men had normally conducted. Their experiences made both them, and in many cases their fathers and husbands, more aware of their ability to take on all sorts of work previously considered exclusively masculine in character. At the same time, women wanted to contribute to the winning of independence, and their efforts to do so made them conscious of their importance. Furthermore, the rhetoric of the Revolution, with its stress on liberty and equality, affected women in the same way that it caused many whites of both sexes to question the morality of slavery.

Attitudes toward the education of women also changed because of the Revolution. According to the best estimates, at least half the white women in America could not read or write as late as the 1780s. In a land of opportunity like the United States, women seemed particularly important, not only because they themselves were citizens, but because of their role in training the next generation. "You distribute 'mental nourishment' along with physical," one orator told the women of America in 1795. "The reformation of the world is in your power. . . . The solidity and stability of your country rest with you." The idea of female education began to catch on. Schools for girls were founded, and the level of female literacy gradually rose.

Growth of a National Spirit

The growth of American **nationalism** was an important result of the Revolution. Most modern revolutions have been *caused* by nationalism and have *resulted* in independence. In the case of the American Revolution, the desire to be free antedated any intense national feeling. The colonies entered into a political union not because they felt an overwhelming desire to bring all Americans under one rule but because unity offered the only hope of winning a war against Great Britain. That they remained

---

[2]Adams's distaste for women historians may have been based on the fact that in his friend Mercy Otis Warren's *History of the Rise, Progress, and Termination of the American Revolution* (1805) Warren claimed that Adams sometimes allowed his "prejudices" to distort his judgment.

united after throwing off British rule reflects the degree to which nationalism had developed during the conflict.

By the middle of the eighteenth century the colonists had begun to think of themselves as a separate society distinct from Europe and even from Britain. Benjamin Franklin described himself not as a British subject but as "an American subject of the King," and in 1750 a Boston newspaper could urge its readers to drink "American" beer in order to free themselves from being "beholden to Foreigners" for their alcoholic beverages. Little political nationalism existed before the Revolution, however, in part because most people knew little about life outside their own colony. When a delegate to the first Continental Congress mentioned "Colonel Washington" to John Adams soon after the Congress met, Adams had to ask him who this "Colonel Washington" was. He had never heard the name before.

The new nationalism arose from a number of sources and expressed itself in different ways. Common sacrifices in war certainly played a part; the soldiers of the Continental army fought in the summer heat of the Carolinas for the same cause that had led them to brave the ice floes of the Delaware in order to surprise the Hessians. Such men lost interest in state boundary lines; they became Americans.

The war caused many people to move from place to place. Soldiers traveled as the tide of war fluctuated; so too—far more than in earlier times—did prominent leaders. Members of Congress from every state had to travel to Philadelphia; in the process they saw much of the country and the people who inhabited it. Listening to their fellows and serving with them on committees almost inevitably broadened these men, most of them highly influential in their local communities.

With its thirteen stars and thirteen stripes representing the states, the American flag symbolized national unity and reflected the common feeling that such a symbol was necessary. Yet the flag had separate stars and stripes; local interests and local loyalties remained extremely strong, and these could be divisive when conflicts of interest arose.

Certain practical problems that demanded common solutions also drew the states together. No one seriously considered having thirteen postal systems or thirteen sets of diplomatic representatives abroad. Every new diplomatic appointment, every treaty of friendship or commerce signed, committed all to a common policy and thus bound them more closely together. And economic developments had a unifying effect. Deprived of English goods, Americans manufactured more things themselves, stimulating both interstate trade and national pride.

The Great Land Ordinances

The lands west of the Appalachians, initially a source of dispute, became a force for unity once they had been ceded to the national government. Everyone realized what a priceless national asset they were, and all now understood that no one state could determine the future of the West.

The politicians argued hotly about how these lands should be developed. Some advocated selling the land in township units in the traditional New England manner to groups or companies; others favored letting individual pioneers stake out farms in the helter-skelter manner common in the colonial South. The decision was a compromise. The Land Ordinance of 1785 provided for surveying the Western Territories into six-mile-square townships before sale. Every other township was to be further subdivided into thirty-six sections of 640 acres (one square mile) each. The land was sold at auction at a minimum price of $1 an acre. The law favored speculative land-development companies, for even the 640-acre units were far too large and expensive for the typical frontier family. But the fact that the land was to be surveyed and sold by the central government was a nationalizing force. It ensured orderly development of the West and simplified the task of defending the frontier in the event of Indian attack. Congress set aside the sixteenth section of every township for the maintenance of schools, another farsighted decision.

Still more significant was the **Northwest Ordinance** of 1787, which established governments for the West. As early as 1775 settlers in frontier districts were petitioning Congress to allow them to enter the Union as independent states, and in 1780 Congress had resolved that all lands ceded to the nation by the existing states should be "formed into distinct republican States" with "the same rights of sovereignty, freedom and independence" as the original

●●●─Read the Document

Northwest Ordinance, 1787 at
myhistorylab.com

thirteen. In 1784 a committee headed by Thomas Jefferson worked out a plan for doing this, and in 1787 it was enacted into law. The area bounded by the Ohio, the Mississippi, and the Great Lakes was to be carved into not fewer than three or more

The Land Ordinance of 1785 called for surveying and dividing the Western Territories into square mile subdivisions—640 acres. These were further subdivided and sold as forty-acre tracts. Few pieces of legislation have left a more visible imprint upon the landscape. Today's Midwest, as seen from an airplane, resembles a patchwork quilt of forty-acre squares, as in the section of Kansas shown here.

The Patriot

As the opening credits roll, Benjamin Martin (Mel Gibson) pries open a wooden box. It contains yellowing papers, a few medals, and a tomahawk. He lifts the tomahawk, fingers it gingerly, and stares at the blade. "I had long feared that my sins would revisit me," a voice intones, "and the cost is more than I can bear." The viewer suspects—rightly—that Martin's sins had something to do with hacking people apart. But at the outset of *The Patriot*, Hollywood's $100-million blockbuster, Martin is more pacifist than patriot. When the South Carolina legislature votes to go to war with Great Britain, he declares that his obligation is to his family: "I will not fight."

He soon changes his mind after the British capture Charleston (1780) which brings onto the scene a villainous British cavalry officer, Colonel Tavington. Ordered by General Cornwallis to subdue the insurrection, Tavington ransacks plantations, forces slaves into the king's service, and hounds the rebel militia. He also arrests Gabriel (Heath Ledger), Martin's oldest son, and orders the boy's execution as a spy. When Gabriel's younger brother tries to intervene, Tavington shoots the boy dead. Overcome with rage, Martin races to his room, grabs the hatchet, and proceeds to bury it—repeatedly—into the chests and skulls of countless British soldiers. He takes command of the militia, recruits more Patriots, and harries the British at every turn.

Tavington responds by intensifying his campaign against the rebels. His culminating barbarity is to round up the villagers of Wakefield (including Gabriel's fiancé), herd them into a church, and set it ablaze. All perish in unimaginable (and mercifully unfilmed) agony. Martin checks his rage long enough to plot the defeat of Cornwallis's army. This occurs at the Battle of Cowpens. When Tavington leads a cavalry charge, Martin reaches for the tomahawk. Tavington dies at Martin's hands, and Cornwallis is routed, too; the latter's subsequent surrender at Yorktown is now a foregone conclusion.

Historians have found much to criticize in the movie's retelling of the war in the South. There was no such person as Benjamin Martin, though elements of his story can be found in the exploits of guerrilla leaders such as Francis Marion ("the Swamp Fox"), Thomas Sumter, Andrew Pickens, and General Daniel Morgan, who commanded the Continentals at Cowpens. The movie's version of the Battle of Cowpens featured a glorious display of fireworks, though neither army's artillery in South Carolina was capable of firing explosive shells. Cornwallis was not humiliated at Cowpens because he was not there. The most serious deviation from the historical record was the incineration of the occupied church: It didn't happen. "*The Patriot* is to history what Godzilla was to biology," declared historian David Hackett Fischer.

However, *The Patriot* raises and addresses an important historical issue: How can any society reconcile peaceable virtues—love for family, neighborliness, cooperation—with the violence of war? In *The Patriot*, the dilemma is symbolized by Martin's tomahawk. This weapon helps free his captured son and vanquish the evil Tavington; and yet it is also a manifestation of Martin's savage, even pathological, rage.

Eighteenth-century Europeans struggled to reconcile the violence of war with the need for social order. Their particular refinement of the military arts was the ordered massing of musket fire. Because muskets were highly inaccurate, a troop of soldiers, dispersed and firing on their own, were unlikely to drive an enemy from the field. But when soldiers were brought together in concentrated formations and ordered to fire simultaneously, the enemy would be decimated. The technology of warfare required intense discipline; and the new penchant for order imposed seeming coherence upon the chaos of the battlefield.

The Patriot provides a vivid rendering of this juxtaposition. Soldiers in beautifully colored uniforms march in straight columns to the steady cadence of drums while officers

William Ranney's painting, *The Battle of Cowpens* (1845) anticipated an error of the movie, *The Patriot*. General Daniel Morgan's troops are shown in green uniforms while the British cavalry are wearing red. In fact the British commander, Banastre Tarleton, on whom Tavington was based, commanded the Green Dragoons, a name reflected in their uniform color. Source: William Ranney, *The Battle of Cowpens*. Oil on canvas. Photo by Sam Holland. Courtesy South Carolina State House.

Mel Gibson as Patriot leader Benjamin Martin with Jason Isaacs as Colonel Tavington, a barbarous British officer.

bark precise commands: "Circle right. Face forward. Lift weapons . . ." Then musket fire shatters the formations, low-velocity cannon balls decapitate soldiers, and bayonets pierce their chests.

Martin concludes that the British cannot be defeated in this type of battle. And they seldom were. Martin advocates guerrilla tactics, as did many southern Patriot militiamen. The British had good reason to doubt the legitimacy of this type of warfare. When men went wild on the battlefield, or fired their weapons and then hid among civilians, they were criminals. If such behavior were condoned, warfare would become barbarity.

During a truce, Martin confers with Cornwallis, who complains that the Patriot militia targeted British officers. Such behavior was inconsistent with "civilized warfare." Officers, as gentlemen, were bound by codes of honor. If they were killed, who would prevent the regular soldiers from reverting to a frenzy of terror and rage?

The movie's debate over "civilized" warfare parallels an ongoing debate at the time. At the outset of the war, British officers took an oath affirming the British Articles of War, which protected citizens and soldiers who had surrendered. The American Congress also adopted the British Articles of War. But with the outbreak of guerrilla warfare in the South, both sides frequently ignored these rules.

"Colonel Tavington" was based on Banastre Tarleton, the actual commander of the Green Dragoons. Tarleton became notorious after his soldiers raped plantation women and killed militiamen who had surrendered. This worried Cornwallis, who sent a dispatch that, while commending Tarleton's courage and zeal, also warned: "Use your utmost endeavors to prevent the troops under your command from committing irregularities." In a subsequent engagement at Waxhaws, however, Tarleton again lost control of his men, who stabbed and slashed vanquished foes.

British and American officers sought to affirm that the war could be civilized. But such high-minded notions were repeatedly subverted during tomahawk-wielding guerrilla warfare and by excessively zealous commanders. The question then remained, as it does today, whether unchecked aggression is, among soldiers, a virtue or a vice. *The Patriot* raises these issues but does not resolve them. Martin, surely, should have kept his tomahawk in its locked box; but if he had, would the Patriots have won?

Questions for Discussion

- Does the justice of a cause warrant the use of violence to attain it?
- Was guerrilla warfare in the South morally justified?
- In general, how can filmmakers contribute to understanding the past? How are they likely to alter the past to suit cinematic purposes?

than five territories. Until the adult male population of the entire area reached 5,000, it was to be ruled by a governor and three judges, all appointed by Congress. When 5,000 men of voting age had settled in the territory, the Ordinance authorized them to elect a legislature, which could send a nonvoting delegate to Congress. Finally, when 60,000 persons had settled in any one of the political subdivisions, it was to become a state. It could draft a constitution and operate in any way it wished, save that the government had to be "republican" and that slavery was prohibited.

Seldom has a legislative body acted more wisely. That the western districts must become states everyone conceded from the start. The people had had their fill of colonialism under British rule, and the rebellious temper of frontier settlers made it impossible even to consider maintaining the West in a dependent status. But it would have been unfair to turn the territories over to the first-comers, who would have been unable to manage such large domains and would surely have taken advantage of their priority to dictate to later arrivals. A period of tutelage was necessary, a period when the "mother country" must guide and nourish its growing offspring.

Thus the intermediate territorial governments corresponded almost exactly to the governments of British royal colonies. The appointed governors could veto acts of the assemblies and could "convene, prorogue, and dissolve" them at their discretion. The territorial delegates to Congress were not unlike colonial agents. Yet it was vital that this intermediate stage end and that its end be determined in advance so that no argument could develop over when the territory was ready for statehood.

The system worked well and was applied to nearly all the regions absorbed by the nation as it advanced westward. Together with the Ordinance of 1785, which branded its checkerboard pattern on the physical shape of the West, this law gave the growing country a unity essential to the growth of a national spirit.

National Heroes

The Revolution further fostered nationalism by giving the people their first commonly revered heroes. Benjamin Franklin was widely known before the break with Great Britain through his experiments with electricity, his immensely successful *Poor Richard's Almanack*, and his invention of the Franklin stove. His staunch support of the Patriot cause, his work in the Continental Congress, and his diplomatic successes in France, where he was extravagantly admired, added to his fame. Franklin demonstrated, to Europeans and to Americans themselves, that not all Americans need be ignorant rustics.

Stern, cold, a man of few words, Washington did not seem a likely candidate for hero worship. "My countenance never yet revealed my feelings," he himself admitted. Yet he had qualities that made people name babies after him and call him "the Father of His Country" long before the war was won: his personal sacrifices in the cause of independence, his integrity, and above all, perhaps, his obvious desire to retire to his Mount Vernon estate (for many Americans feared any powerful leader and worried lest Washington seek to become a dictator).

As a general, Washington was not a brilliant strategist like Napoleon. Neither was he a tactician of the quality of Caesar or Robert E. Lee. But he was a remarkable organizer and administrator—patient, thoughtful, conciliatory. In a way, his lack of genius made his achievements all the more impressive. He held his forces together in adversity, avoiding both useless slaughter and catastrophic defeat. People of all sections, from every walk of life, looked on Washington as the embodiment of American virtues: a man of deeds rather than words; a substantial citizen accustomed to luxury yet capable of enduring great hardships stoically and as much at home in the wilderness as an Indian; a bold Patriot, quick to take arms against British tyranny, yet eminently respectable. The Revolution might have been won without Washington, but it is unlikely that the free United States would have become so easily a true nation had he not been at its call.

Milestones

1774	Thomas Jefferson writes *A Summary View of the Rights of British America*	1777	Washington's troops win Battle of Princeton
	General Thomas Gage, commander-in-chief of British army in North America, is named governor of Massachusetts		American victory at Saratoga turns the tide and leads to alliance with France
1775	Colonists fight British in Battles of Lexington and Concord		British occupy Philadelphia after the Battle of Germantown
	Second Continental Congress names George Washington commander-in-chief (of Continental army)	1777–1778	Continental army winters at Valley Forge
		1778	British capture Savannah
	Gage is replaced as British commander by General Sir William Howe after the Battle of Bunker Hill	1780	British capture Charleston
		1781	States ratify Articles of Confederation
1776	Thomas Paine publishes *Common Sense*		General Cornwallis surrenders at Yorktown
	Washington's troops occupy Boston	1783	Great Britain recognizes independence of United States by signing the Peace of Paris
	Second Continental Congress issues Declaration of Independence		
	Washington's troops are defeated in Battle of Long Island	1785	Congress passes the Land Ordinance of 1785
	Washington evacuates New York City	1787	Northwest Ordinance establishes governments for the West
	Washington's victory at Battle of Trenton boosts morale		

✓●─Study and **Review** at www.myhistorylab.com

Review Questions

1. The introduction for this chapter states that the American victory over Britain was not inevitable. Do you agree?
2. Which of the following was the most important: Washington's morale-saving crossing of the Delaware and defeat of Hessian troops in Trenton, the surrender of Burgoyne at Saratoga, or the surrender of Cornwallis at Yorktown?
3. What were the main effects of the American Revolution on women? On relations between rich and poor?

Key Terms

Articles of
   Confederation   *130*
Common Sense   *117*
Continental army   *115*

Loyalists   *120*
nationalism   *135*
Northwest
   Ordinance   *137*

Second Continental
   Congress   *114*

The Federalist Era: Nationalism Triumphant

5

((•─[Hear the Audio Chapter 5 at myhistorylab.com

Do you illegally download?

WHEN THE PHONE RANG IN THE DORM ROOM OF BRITTANY KRUGER, a first-year student at Northern Michigan University, she had no idea that the Constitution of the United States was about to crash into her life. Kruger's dean was on the line. The dean informed Kruger that the nation's record companies had charged her with copyright infringement for having downloaded Guns N' Roses' "Welcome to the Jungle," Lynyrd Skynyrd's "Free Bird," and other popular songs. Because each copyright infringement carried a $150,000 penalty, Kruger was responsible for millions of dollars in fines. If she paid $8,100 immediately, the record companies would settle the claim. Kruger, who earned $4,500 working at a Dairy Queen, called her parents.

The record companies sued Joel Tenenbaum, a Boston University physics graduate student, for $4.5 million. He had downloaded and shared thirty songs. Instead of settling, Tenenbaum was among the first to seek his day in court. In 2009 a federal jury ordered Tenenbaum to pay $625,000; he said he would declare bankruptcy.

If the Articles of Confederation had remained the law of the land, Kruger, Tenenbaum, and the other 40,000 people charged with illegally downloading songs and games would have done nothing wrong. The Articles made no mention of copyright. But James Madison reasoned that if inventors did not "own" their inventions, they would have little incentive to invent. Authors, too, could expect no profit if their books could be freely reprinted. The economy would suffer from the lack of innovation and knowledge would languish. Thomas Jefferson, on the other hand, observed that in England copyright laws allowed businesses to monopolize inventions and books. This drove prices up and restricted dissemination of ideas. He argued that ideas, once divulged, should be made available to the public swiftly and freely. Jefferson had himself evaded Britain's copyright laws by stocking his library at Monticello with pirated books, printed on the cheap in Dublin.

Eventually the framers reached a compromise that became Article 1, Section 8 of the Constitution of the United States. It empowered Congress to "promote the Progress of Science and the Useful Arts" by providing "authors and inventors" the "exclusive right" to their creations; but this right would be for a "limited" time. Once the copyright had expired, the invention or book would become public property.

Polls today show that most Americans overwhelmingly endorse the United States Constitution (although some of those charged with illegal downloads may have second thoughts). In the 1780s, many Americans were satisfied with the federal government under the Articles of Confederation. Whatever its weaknesses, the government had negotiated the treaty ending the Revolutionary War, adopted humane and farsighted land policies, and established a rudimentary bureaucracy to manage routine affairs. If, as Washington said, that government had moved "on crutches . . . tottering at every step," it moved forward nevertheless. Yet the country's evolution placed demands on the national government that its creators had not anticipated. Dissatisfaction with the Articles mounted; the Founders sought solutions that through a process of conflict and compromise would finally result in the Constitution.

Inadequacies of the Articles of Confederation

Following the American Revolution and the Peace of Paris, the United States faced new challenges. The new nation struggled to achieve control of its own territory, to define the nature of its trade relationships with Europe, and to overcome crippling economic depression and the specter of inflation. If the Articles had proved adequate in achieving victory in the war, they proved less so in addressing these new concerns.

Both Great Britain and Spain stood in the way of the United States winning control of its borders. Although the British kept their promise to withdraw their troops from American soil promptly, they refused to abandon seven military posts beyond the periphery of the original thirteen states. The inability to eject the British seemed a national disgrace. In 1784, moreover, the Spaniards had closed the lower Mississippi River to American commerce. This harmed settlers beyond the Appalachians who depended on the Mississippi and its network of tributaries to get their corn, tobacco, and other products to eastern and European markets. Many reasoned that a stronger central government might have dealt with Britain and Spain more forcefully and effectively.

Another key problem concerned trade. After hostilities had ended, British merchants, eager to regain markets closed to them during the Revolution, poured low-priced manufactured goods of all kinds into the United States. Americans, long deprived of British products, rushed to take advantage of the bargains. Soon imports of British goods were approaching the levels of the early 1770s, while exports to the empire reached no more than half their earlier volume.

The influx of British goods aggravated the situation just when the economy was suffering as a result of the ending of the war. The inability of Congress to find money to pay the nation's debts undermined public confidence. Veterans who had still not been paid, and private individuals and foreign governments that had lent the government money during the Revolution, were clamoring for their due. In some regions crop failures compounded the difficulties.

An obvious way of dealing with these problems would have been to place tariffs on British goods in order to limit British imports, but the Confederation lacked the authority to do this. When individual states erected tariff barriers, British merchants easily got around them by bringing their goods in through states that did not. That the central government lacked the power to control commerce disturbed merchants, other businessmen, and the ever-increasing number of national-minded citizens in every walk of life.

Thus a movement developed to give the Confederation the power to tax imports, and in 1781 Congress sought authority to levy a 5 percent tariff duty. This would enable Congress to pay off some of its obligations and also put pressure on the British to relax their restrictions on American trade with the West Indies. Every state but Rhode Island agreed, but the measure required the unanimous consent of the states and therefore failed.

Defeat of the tariff pointed to the need for revising the Articles of Confederation, for here was a case where a large percentage of the states were ready to increase the power of the national government yet were unable to do so. Although many individuals in every region were worried about creating a centralized monster that might gobble up the sovereignty of the states, the practical needs of the times convinced many others that this risk must be taken.

Daniel Shays's "Little Rebellion"

Especially alarming to conservatives was an outbreak of violence in Massachusetts. The Massachusetts legislature was determined to pay off the state debt and maintain a sound currency. Taxes amounting to almost £1.9 million were levied between 1780 and 1786, the burden falling most heavily on those of moderate income. The average Massachusetts farmer paid about a third of every year's income in taxes. Bad times and deflation led to many foreclosures, and the prisons were crowded with honest debtors.

In the summer of 1786 mobs in the western communities began to stop foreclosures by forcibly preventing the courts from holding their sessions. Under the leadership of Daniel Shays, a veteran of Bunker Hill, Ticonderoga, and Saratoga, the "rebels" marched on Springfield and prevented the state supreme court from meeting. When the state government sent troops against them, the rebels attacked the Springfield arsenal. They were routed, and the uprising then collapsed. Shays fled to Vermont.

Most well-to-do Americans considered **Shays's rebellion** "Liberty run mad." "What, gracious God, is man! that there should be such inconsistency and perfidiousness in his conduct?" the usually unexcitable George Washington asked when news of the riots reached Virginia. "We are fast verging to anarchy and confusion!" During the crisis private persons had to subscribe funds to put the rebels down, and when Massachusetts had

Massachusetts militia crushing Shays's revolt in 1787.
Source: North Wind Picture Archives.

●●●┤**Read** the **Document**

Military Reports on Shays's at
myhistorylab.com

appealed to Congress for help there was little Congress could legally do. The lessons seemed plain: Liberty must not become an excuse for license; greater authority must be vested in the central government.

To Philadelphia, and the Constitution

If most people wanted to increase the power of Congress, they were also afraid to shift the balance too far lest they destroy the sovereignty of the states and the rights of individuals. The machinery for change established in the Articles of Confederation, which required the unanimous consent of the states for all amendments, posed a particularly delicate problem. Experience had shown it unworkable, yet to bypass it would be revolutionary and therefore dangerous.

The first fumbling step toward reform was taken in March 1785 when representatives of Virginia and Maryland suggested a conference of all the states to discuss common problems of commerce. In January 1786 the Virginia legislature sent out a formal call for such a gathering to be held in September at Annapolis. However, the Annapolis Convention disappointed advocates of reform; delegates from only five states appeared; even Maryland, supposedly the host state, did not send a representative. Being so few the group did not feel it worthwhile to propose changes.

Among the delegates was a young New York lawyer named Alexander Hamilton, a brilliant, imaginative, and daring man who was convinced that only drastic centralization would save the nation from disintegration. Hamilton described himself as a "nationalist."

This engraving by William Russell Birch shows Congress Hall (left) which was occupied by Congress from 1790 to 1800, when Philadelphia was capital of the nation. Here, too, was the site of President Washington's second inauguration in 1793 and President John Adams's inauguration in 1797.

While the war still raged he contrasted the virtues of "a great Federal Republic" with the existing system of "petty states with the appearance only of union, jarring, jealous, and perverse." Instead of giving up, he proposed calling another convention to meet at Philadelphia to deal generally with constitutional reform.

◉—View the Image

Alexander Hamilton-Portrait at **myhistorylab.com**

The Annapolis group approved Hamilton's suggestion, and Congress reluctantly endorsed it. This time all the states but Rhode Island sent delegates. On May 25, 1787, the convention opened its proceedings at the State House in Philadelphia and unanimously elected George Washington its president. When it adjourned four months later, it had drafted the Constitution.

The Great Convention

Collectively the delegates possessed a rare combination of talents. Most of them had considerable experience in politics, and the many lawyers among them were skilled in logic and debate. Furthermore, the times made them acutely aware of their opportunities. It was "a time when the greatest lawgivers of antiquity would have wished to live," an opportunity to "establish the wisest and happiest government that human wisdom can contrive," John Adams wrote. "We . . . decide for ever the fate of republican government," James Madison said during the deliberations.

If these remarks overstated the importance of their deliberations, they nonetheless represented the opinion of most of those present. They were boldly optimistic about their country. "We are laying the foundation of a great empire," Madison predicted. At the same time the delegates recognized the difficulties they faced. The ancient Roman republic was one model, and all knew that it had been overthrown by tyrants and eventually overrun by barbarians. The framers were familiar with Enlightenment thinkers such as John Locke, Thomas Hobbes, and Montesquieu, and also with the ideas that swirled around the great disputes between Parliament and the Stuart monarchs during the seventeenth century.

Fortunately, they were nearly all of one mind on basic questions. That there should be a federal system, with both independent state governments and a national government with limited powers to handle matters of common interest, was accepted by all but one or two of them. Republican government, drawing its authority from the people and remaining responsible to them, was a universal assumption. A measure of democracy followed inevitably from this principle, for even the most aristocratic delegates agreed that ordinary citizens should share in the process of selecting those who were to make and execute the laws.

All agreed that no group within society, no matter how numerous, should have unrestricted authority. People meant well and had limitless possibilities, the constitution makers believed, but they were selfish by nature and could not be counted on to respect the interests of others. The ordinary people—small farmers, artisans, any taxpayer—should have a say in government in order to be able to protect themselves against those who would exploit their weakness, and the majority must somehow be prevented from plundering the rich, for property must be secure or no government could be stable. Freedom, as Locke had maintained, rested on a right to property. No single state or section must be allowed to predominate, nor should the legislature be supreme over the executive or the courts. Power, in short, must be divided, and the segments must be balanced one against the other.

At the outset the delegates decided to keep the proceedings secret. That way no one was tempted to play to the gallery or seek some personal political advantage at the expense of the common good. Next they agreed to go beyond their instructions to revise the Articles of Confederation and draft an entirely new form of government. This was a bold, perhaps illegal act, but it was in no way irresponsible because nothing the convention might recommend was binding on anyone. Alexander Hamilton captured the mood of the gathering when he said, "We can only propose and recommend—the power of ratifying or rejecting is still in the States. . . . We ought not to sacrifice the public Good to narrow Scruples."

The Compromises That Produced the Constitution

The delegates voted on May 30, 1787, that "a national Government ought to be established." They then set to work hammering out a specific plan. The delegates believed that the national government should have separate executive and judicial branches as well as a legislature. But two big questions had to be answered. The first—*What powers should this national government be granted?*—occasioned relatively little discussion. The right to levy taxes and to regulate interstate and foreign commerce was assigned to the central government almost without debate, as was the power to raise and maintain an army and navy and to summon the militia of the states to enforce national laws and suppress insurrections. With equal absence of argument, the states were deprived of their rights to issue money, to make treaties, and to tax either imports or exports without the permission of Congress. Thus, in summary fashion, was brought about a massive shift of power.

The second major question—*Who shall control the national government?*—proved more difficult to answer in a manner satisfactory to all. Led by Virginia, the larger states pushed for representation in the national legislature based on population. The smaller states wished to maintain the existing system of equal representation for each state regardless of population. The large states rallied behind the **Virginia Plan**, drafted by James Madison and presented to the convention by Edmund Randolph, governor of the state. The small states supported the **New Jersey Plan**, prepared by William Paterson, a former attorney general of that state. The question was important; equal state representation would have been undemocratic, whereas a proportional system would have effectively destroyed the influence of all the states as states. But the delegates saw it in terms of combinations of large or small states, and this old-fashioned view was unrealistic: When the states combined, they did so on geographic, economic, or social grounds that seldom had anything to do with size. Nevertheless, the debate was long and heated, and for a time it threatened to disrupt the convention.

Day after day in the stifling heat of high summer, the weary delegates struggled to find a suitable compromise. July 2 was perhaps the most fateful day of the whole proceedings. "We are at full stop," said Roger Sherman of Connecticut, who had been one of the drafters of the Declaration of Independence. "If we do not concede on both sides," a North Carolina delegate warned, "our business must soon be at an end."

But the delegates did "concede on both sides," and the debates went on. Again on July 17 collapse threatened as the representatives of the larger states caucused to consider walking out of the convention. Fortunately they did not walk out, and the delegates adopted what is known as the Great Compromise. In the lower branch of the new legislature—the House of Representatives—places were to be assigned according to population and filled by popular vote. In the upper house—the Senate—each state was to have two members, elected by its legislature.

Then a complicated struggle took place between northern and southern delegates, occasioned by the institution of slavery and the differing economic interests of the regions. About one American in seven in the 1780s was a slave. Northerners contended that slaves should be counted in deciding each state's share of direct federal taxes. Southerners, of course, wanted to exclude slaves from the count. Yet Southerners wished to include slaves in determining each district's representation in the House of Representatives, although they had no intention of permitting the slaves to vote. In the **Three-Fifths Compromise** it was agreed that "three-fifths of all other Persons" should be counted for both purposes. Settlement of the knotty issue of the African slave trade was postponed by a clause making it illegal for Congress to outlaw the trade before 1808.

The final document, signed on September 17, established a legislature of two houses: an executive branch consisting of a president with wide powers and a vice president whose only function was to preside over the Senate; and a national judiciary consisting of a Supreme Court and such "inferior courts" as Congress might decide to create. The lower, popularly elected branch of the Congress—the House of Representatives— was supposed to represent especially the mass of ordinary citizens. It was given the sole right to introduce bills for raising revenue. The twenty-six-member Senate was looked on by many as a sort of advisory council similar to the upper houses of the colonial legislatures. Its consent was required before any treaty could go into effect and for major presidential appointments. The founders also intended the Senate to represent in Congress the interests not only of the separate states but of what Hamilton called "the rich and the well-born" as contrasted with "the great mass of the people."

The creation of a powerful president was the most drastic departure from past experience, and it is doubtful that the founders would have gone so far had everyone not counted on Washington, a man universally esteemed for character, wisdom, and impartiality, to be the first to occupy the office. Besides giving him general responsibility for executing the laws, the Constitution made the president commander-in-chief of the armed forces of the nation and general supervisor of its foreign relations. He was to appoint federal judges and other officials, and he might veto any law of Congress, although his veto could be overridden by a two-thirds majority of both houses. While not specifically ordered to submit a program of legislation to Congress, he was to deliver periodic reports on the "State of the Union" and recommend "such Measures as he shall judge necessary and expedient." Most modern presidents have interpreted this requirement as authorizing them to submit detailed legislative proposals and to use the full power and prestige of the office to get Congress to enact them.

Looking beyond Washington, whose choice was sure to come about under any system, the Constitution established a cumbersome method of electing presidents. Each state was to choose "electors" equal in number to its representation in Congress.

Table 5.1   Issues and Compromises that Produced the Constitution

Issue	Yes	No	Compromise
Debate 1785–1787			
Should Articles of Confederation be replaced?	Federalists	Antifederalists	Federalists win: All states but R.I. send delegates to Constitutional Convention at Philadelphia (1787)
Constitutional Convention Debates			
Should national government have broad powers?	Federalists	Antifederalists	Federalists win: National government imposes taxes, regulates trade, maintains army, issues money
Should seats in national legislature be unequal, based on a state's population?	Populous states	Small states	**Great Compromise:** Two-house legislature: In House of Representatives, delegates are apportioned by size of each state's population; in Senate, each state gets two senators

The electors, meeting separately in their own states, were to vote for two persons for president. Supposedly the procedure would prevent anyone less universally admired than Washington from getting a majority in the **Electoral College**, in which case the House of Representatives would choose the president from among the leading candidates, each state having but one vote. However, the swift rise of national political parties prevented the expected fragmentation of the electors' votes.

The national court system was set up to adjudicate disputes under the laws and treaties of the United States. No such system had existed under the Articles, a major weakness. Although the Constitution did not specifically authorize the courts to declare laws void when they conflicted with the Constitution, the courts soon exercised this right of **judicial review** in cases involving both state and federal laws.

That the Constitution reflected the commonly held beliefs of its framers is everywhere evident in the document. It greatly expanded the powers of the central government yet did not seriously threaten the independence of the states. Foes of centralization, at the time and ever since, have predicted the imminent disappearance of the states as sovereign bodies. But despite a steady trend toward centralization the states remain powerful political organizations that are sovereign in many areas of government.

The founders believed that since the new powers of government might easily be misused, each should be held within safe limits by some countervailing force. The Constitution is full of mechanisms ("checks and balances") whereby one power controls and limits another without reducing it to impotence. "Let Congress Legislate, let others execute, let others judge," John Jay suggested. This separation of legislative, executive, and judicial functions is the fundamental example of the principle. Other examples are the president's veto; Congress's power of impeachment, cleverly divided between the House and Senate; the Senate's power over treaties and appointments; and the balance between Congress's right to declare war and the president's control of the armed forces.

Ratifying the Constitution

Influenced by the widespread approval of the decision of Massachusetts to submit its state constitution of 1780 to the voters for ratification, the framers of the Constitution provided (Article VII) that their handiwork be ratified by special state conventions. This procedure gave the Constitution what Madison called "the highest source of authority"—the endorsement of the people, expressed through representatives chosen specifically to vote on it. The framers may also have been motivated by a desire to

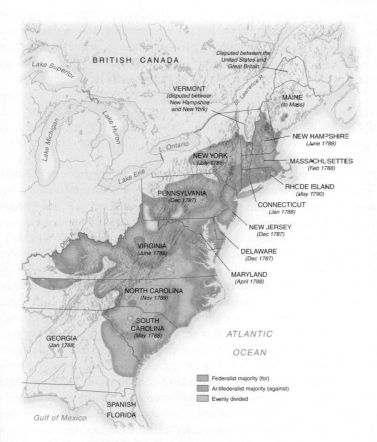

Ratification of the Federal Constitution, 1787–1790 Historian Jackson Turner Main argued that the debate over ratification of the Constitution was fundamentally a struggle between radical frontiersmen and conservative easterners. The Antifederalists were democratic populists; the Federalists sought to prevent further democratization of American society, or so Main claimed. The accompanying map showing the vote on ratification by congressional district provides support for Main's thesis. Kentucky and Tennessee were almost solidly opposed to the Constitution, along with most of the western sections of South Carolina, North Carolina, and Virginia. Western Pennsylvania and western Massachusetts were also mostly Antifederalists. Conversely, support for the Constitution was strongest in coastal regions of the Carolinas, the plantation districts of tidewater Virginia and the Chesapeake, as well as New Jersey, New York, Connecticut, and the New England coast. But such an explanation fails to explain why some districts in western Kentucky, Tennessee, Pennsylvania, and even Massachusetts, supported the Constitution. Some frontiersmen thought that a federal army could do better than state militias against Indian threats; and some sober citizens, even those living west of the Susquehanna, worried that society might devolve into anarchy if the Constitution were not approved.

bypass the state legislatures, where many members might resent the reductions being made in state authority. This was not of central importance because the legislatures could have blocked ratification by refusing to call conventions. Only Rhode Island did so, and since the Constitution was to go into operation when nine states had approved it, Rhode Island's stubbornness did no vital harm.

Such a complex and controversial document as the Constitution naturally excited argument throughout the country. Those who favored it called themselves **Federalists**, thereby avoiding the more accurate but politically unattractive label of Centralizers. Their opponents thus became the **Antifederalists**.

The Federalists tended to be substantial individuals, members of the professions, well-to-do, active in commercial affairs, and somewhat alarmed by the changes wrought by the Revolution. They were more interested, perhaps, in orderly and efficient government than in safeguarding the maximum freedom of individual choice.

The Antifederalists were more often small farmers, debtors, and persons to whom free choice was more important than power and who resented those who sought and held power. "Lawyers and men of learning and money men . . . expect to be the managers of the Const[itution], and get all the power and all the money into their own hands," a Massachusetts Antifederalist complained. "Then they will swallow up all us little folks . . . just as the whale swallowed up *Jonah*."

Many persons, including some who had been in the forefront of the struggle for independence, believed that a centralized republican system would not work in a country so large and with so many varied interests as the United States. Patrick Henry considered the Constitution "horribly frightful." It "squints toward monarchy," he added. That Congress could pass all laws "necessary and proper" to carry out the functions assigned it and legislate for the "general welfare" of the country seemed alarmingly all-inclusive.

Very little of the opposition to the Constitution grew out of economic issues. Most people wanted the national debt paid off; nearly everyone opposed an unstable currency; most favored uniform trade policies; most were ready to give the new government a chance if they could be convinced that it would not destroy the states. When backers agreed to add amendments guaranteeing the civil liberties of the people against challenge by the national government and reserving all unmentioned power to the states, much of the opposition disappeared. Sam Adams ended up voting for the Constitution in the Massachusetts convention after the additions had been promised.

The Constitution met with remarkably little opposition in most of the state ratifying conventions, considering the importance of the changes it instituted. Delaware acted first, ratifying unanimously on December 7, 1787. Pennsylvania followed a few days later, voting for the document by a 2 to 1 majority. New Jersey approved it unanimously on December 18, as did Georgia on January 2, 1788. A week later Connecticut fell in line, 128 to 40.

The Massachusetts convention provided the first close contest. Early in February, after an extensive debate, the delegates ratified by a vote of 187 to 168. In April, Maryland accepted the Constitution by nearly 6 to 1, and in May, South Carolina approved it, 149 to 73. New Hampshire came along on June 21, voting 57 to 47 for the Constitution. This was the ninth state, making the Constitution legally operative.

Before the news from New Hampshire had spread throughout the country, the Virginia convention debated the issue. Virginia, the largest state and the home of so many prestigious figures, was absolutely essential if the Constitution was to succeed. With unquestioned patriots like Richard Henry Lee and Patrick Henry opposed, the result was not easy to predict. But when the vote came on June 25, Virginia ratified, eighty-nine to seventy-nine. Aside from Rhode Island, this left only New York and North Carolina outside the Union.

New York politics presented a complex and baffling picture. Although New York was the third largest state, with a population rapidly approaching 340,000, it sided with the small states at Philadelphia, and two of its three delegates (Hamilton was the exception) walked out of the convention and took the lead in opposing ratification. A handful of great landowning and mercantile families dominated politics, but they were divided into shifting factions. In general, New York City, including most ordinary working people as well as the merchants, favored ratification and the rural areas were against it.

The Antifederalists, well-organized and competently led in New York by Governor George Clinton, won forty-six of the sixty-five seats at the ratifying convention. The New York Federalists had one great asset in the fact that so many states had already ratified and another in the person of Alexander Hamilton. Although contemptuous of the *weakness* of the Constitution, Hamilton supported it with all his energies as being incomparably stronger than the old government. Working with Madison and John Jay, he produced the **Federalist Papers**, a series of brilliant essays explaining and defending the new system. In his articles, Hamilton stressed the need for a strong federal executive, while Madison sought to allay fears that the new national government would have too much power by emphasizing the many checks and balances in the Constitution. The essays were published in the local press and later in book form. Although generations of judges and lawyers have treated them almost as parts of the Constitution, their impact on contemporary public opinion was probably slight. Open-minded members of the convention were undoubtedly influenced, but few delegates were open-minded.

•••─Read the **Document**

Madison Defends the Constitutions at **myhistorylab.com**

Hamilton became a kind of one-man army in defense of the Constitution, plying hesitating delegates with dinners and drinks, facing obstinate ones with the threat that New York City would secede from the state if the Constitution were rejected. Once New Hampshire and Virginia had ratified, opposition in New York became a good deal less intransigent. In the end, by promising to support a call for a second national convention to consider amendments, the Federalists carried the day, thirty to twenty-seven. With New York in the fold, the new government was free to get under way. North Carolina finally ratified in November 1789, and Rhode Island the following year in May 1790.

Washington as President

Elections took place in the states during January and February 1789, and by early April enough congressmen had gathered in New York, the temporary national capital, to commence operation. The ballots of the presidential electors were officially counted in the Senate on April 6, Washington being the unanimous choice. John Adams, with thirty-four electoral votes, won the vice-presidency.

Washington made a firm, dignified, conscientious, but cautious president. His acute sense of responsibility led him to face the task "with feelings not unlike those of a

◉ View the **Image**

Washington's Arrival in New
York City, 1789 at
myhistorylab.com

culprit who is going to the place of his execution." Each presidential action must of necessity establish a precedent. "The eyes of Argus are upon me," he complained, "and no slip will pass unnoticed." Hoping to make the presidency appear respectable in the eyes of the world, he saw to it that his carriage was drawn by six cream-colored horses, and when he rode (he was a magnificent horseman), he sat upon a great white charger, with the saddle of leopard skin and the cloth edged in gold.

Washington meticulously avoided treading on the toes of Congress, for he took seriously the principle of the separation of powers. Never would he speak for or against a candidate for Congress, nor did he think that the president should push or even propose legislation. When he knew a controversial question was to be discussed in Congress, he avoided the subject in his annual message. The veto, he believed, should be employed only when the president considered a bill unconstitutional.

Washington was a strong chief executive. As Hamilton put it, he "consulted much, pondered much, resolved slowly, resolved surely." His stress on the dignity of his office suited the needs of a new country whose people tended to be perhaps too informal. Because opponents of republican government predicted it must inevitably succumb to dictatorship and tyranny, Washington took scrupulous care to avoid overstepping the bounds of presidential power. Yet Washington's devotion to duty did not always come easily. Occasionally he exploded. Thomas Jefferson has left us a graphic description of the president at a Cabinet meeting, in a rage because of some unfair criticism, swearing that "by god he had rather be on his farm than to be made emperor of the world."

George Washington arriving by boat to New York City—the nation's capital—for his First Inaugural in 1789.
Source: North Wind Picture Archives.

Congress under Way

By September 1789 Congress had created the State, Treasury, and War Departments and passed a Judiciary Act establishing thirteen federal district courts and three circuit courts of appeal. The number of Supreme Court justices was set at six, and Washington named John Jay the chief justice.

True to Federalist promises—for a large majority of both houses were friendly to the Constitution—Congress prepared a list of a dozen amendments guaranteeing what Congressman James Madison, who drafted the amendments, called the "great rights of mankind." These amendments, known as the **Bill of Rights**, provided that Congress should make no law infringing freedom of speech, the press, or religion. The right of trial by jury was reaffirmed, and the right to bear arms guaranteed. No one was to be subject to "unreasonable" searches or seizures or compelled to testify against himself or herself in a criminal case. No one was to "be deprived of life, liberty, or property, without due process of law."

Despite Washington's reluctance to interfere with the activities of Congress, he urged acceptance of these amendments so that the "rights of freemen" would be "impregnably fortified." The Bill of Rights was unique; the English Bill of Rights of 1689 was much less broad-gauged and, being an act of Parliament, was subject to repeal by Parliament at any time. The Tenth Amendment—not, strictly speaking, a part of the Bill of Rights—was designed to mollify those who feared that the states would be destroyed by the new government. It provided that powers not delegated to the United States or denied specifically to the states by the Constitution were to reside either in the states or in the people.

The Bill of Rights did much to convince doubters that the new government would not become too powerful. More complex was the task of proving that it was powerful enough to deal with those national problems that the Confederation had not been able to solve: the threat to the West posed by the British, Spaniards, and Indians, the disruption of the pattern of American foreign commerce resulting from independence, and the collapse of the financial structure of the country.

Hamilton and Financial Reform

One of the first acts of Congress in 1789 was to employ its new power to tax. The simplest means of raising money seemed to be that first attempted by the British after 1763, a tariff on foreign imports. Congress levied a 5 percent tax on all foreign products entering the United States, applying higher rates to certain products, such as hemp, glass, and nails, as a measure of protection for American producers. The Tariff Act of 1789 also placed heavy taxes on foreign-owned ships, assessed by their weight, on entering

"To confess my weakness," Hamilton wrote when he was only 14, "my ambition is prevalent." This pastel drawing by James Sharples was made about 1796.

William Russell Birch painted this view of the capitol building, under construction, in Washington, DC. The site, located at the junction of two rivers, was chosen in part because it could be easily defended; this proved to be untrue during the War of 1812, when the capitol was burned.

American ports, a mercantilist measure designed to stimulate the American merchant marine.

Raising money for current expenses was a small and relatively simple aspect of the financial problem faced by Washington's administration. But the nation's debt from the revolutionary war was large, its credit shaky, and its economic future uncertain. In October 1789 Congress deposited on the slender shoulders of Secretary of the Treasury Hamilton the task of straightening out the fiscal mess and stimulating the country's economic development.

Hamilton admired aristocracy and disparaged the abilities of the common run of mankind who, he said, "seldom judge or determine right." Although granting that Americans must be allowed to govern themselves, he was as apprehensive of the "turbulence" of the masses as a small boy passing a graveyard in the dark. "No popular government was ever without its Catilines and its Caesars," he warned—a typical example of that generation's concern about the fate of the Roman republic.

The country, Hamilton insisted, needed a strong national government. "I acknowledge," he wrote in one of the *Federalist Papers*, "my aversion to every project that is calculated to disarm the government of a single weapon, which in any possible contingency might be usefully employed for the general defense and security." He avowed that government should be "a great Federal Republic," not "a number of petty states, with the appearance only of union, jarring, jealous, perverse, without any determined direction." He wished to reduce the states to mere administrative units, like English counties.

As secretary of the treasury, Hamilton proved to be a farsighted economic planner. The United States, a "Hercules in the cradle," needed capital to develop its untapped material and resources. To persuade investors to commit their funds in America, the country would have to convince them that it would meet every obligation in full. His *Report on the Public Credit* outlined a plan for the federal government to borrow money to pay all of its debts as well as those of the states.

While most members of Congress agreed, albeit somewhat grudgingly, that the debt should be paid in full, they had misgivings as to who should get those payments. Many of the soldiers, farmers, and merchants who had been forced to accept government securities in lieu of cash for goods and services, had sold their securities for a fraction of their face value to speculators; under Hamilton's proposal, the speculators—now paid for the full value of the securities—would make a killing. To the argument for divided payment, Hamilton answered coldly: "[The speculator] paid what the commodity was worth in the market, and took the risks. . . . He . . . ought to reap the benefit of his hazard."

Hamilton was essentially correct, and in the end Congress had to go along. After all, the speculators had not caused the securities to fall in value; indeed, as a group they had favored sound money and a strong government. The best way to restore the nation's credit was to convince investors that the government would honor all obligations in full. What infuriated his contemporaries and still attracts the scorn of many historians was Hamilton's motive. He deliberately intended his plan to give a special advantage to the rich. The government would be strong, he thought, only if well-to-do Americans enthusiastically supported it. What better way to win them over than to make it worth their while financially to do so?

In part, opposition to the funding plan was sectional, for citizens of the northern states held more than four-fifths of the national debt. The scheme for assuming the state debts aggravated the controversy, since most of the southern states had already paid off much of their Revolutionary War obligations. For months Congress was dead-locked. Finally, in July 1790, Hamilton worked out a compromise with Representative James Madison and Secretary of State Jefferson. The two Virginians swung a few south-ern votes, and Hamilton induced some of his followers to support the southern plan for locating the permanent capital of the Union on the Potomac River.

Jefferson later claimed that Hamilton had hoodwinked him. Having only recently returned from Europe, he said, "I was really a stranger to the whole subject." Hamilton had persuaded him to "rally around" by the false tale that "our Union" was threatened with dis-solution. This was nonsense; Jefferson agreed to the compromise because he expected that Virginia and the rest of the South would profit from having the capital so near at hand.

The assumption bill passed, and the entire funding plan was a great success. Soon the United States had the highest possible credit rating in the world's financial centers. Foreign capital poured into the country.

Hamilton next proposed that Congress charter a national bank. Such an institution would provide safe storage for government funds and serve as an agent for the govern-ment in the collection, movement, and expenditure of tax money. Most important, because of its substantial resources, a bank could finance new and expanding business enter-prises, greatly speeding the economic growth of the nation.

> •👂•🛑Read the Document
> Alexander Hamilton, *Bank* at
> myhistorylab.com

It would also be able to issue bank notes, thereby providing a vitally needed medium of exchange for the specie-starved economy. This **Bank of the United States** was to be partly owned by the government, but 80 percent of the $10 million stock issue was to be sold to private individuals.

The country had much to gain from such a bank, but again—Hamilton's cleverness was never more in evidence—the well-to-do commercial classes would gain still more. Government balances in the bank belonging to all the people would earn dividends for a handful of rich investors. Manufacturers and other capitalists would profit from the bank's credit facilities. Public funds would be invested in the bank, but control would remain in private hands, since the government would appoint only five of the twenty-five directors. Nevertheless, the bill creating the bank passed both houses of Congress with relative ease in February 1791.

President Washington, however, hesitated to sign it, for the bill's constitutionality had been questioned during the debate in Congress. Nowhere did the Constitution specifi-cally authorize Congress to charter corporations or engage in the banking business. As was his wont when in doubt, Washington called on Jefferson and Hamilton for advice.

Hamilton defended the legality of the bank by enunciating the doctrine of "implied powers." If a logical connection existed between the purpose of the bill and powers clearly stated in the Constitution, he wrote, the bill was constitutional.

> If the *end* be clearly comprehended within any of the specified powers, and if the measure have an obvious relation to that *end* . . . it may safely be deemed to come within the compass of the national authority. . . . A bank has a natural relation to the power of collecting taxes—to that of regulating trade—to that of providing for the common defence.

Jefferson disagreed. Congress could only do what the Constitution specifically authorized, he said. The "elastic clause" granting it the right to pass "all Laws which shall be necessary and proper" to carry out the specified powers must be interpreted literally or Congress would "take possession of a boundless field of power, no longer susceptible to any definition." Because a bank was obviously not necessary, it was not authorized.

Although not entirely convinced, Washington accepted Hamilton's reasoning and signed the bill. He could just as easily have followed Jefferson, for the Constitution is not clear. If one stresses *proper* in the "necessary and proper" clause in Article I, Section 8 of the Constitution, one ends up a Hamiltonian; if one stresses *necessary*, then Jefferson's view is correct. Historically politicians have nearly always adopted the "loose" Hamiltonian "implied powers" interpretation when they favored a measure and the "strict" Jeffersonian one when they do not.

In 1819 the Supreme Court officially sanctioned Hamilton's construction of the "necessary and proper" clause, and in general that interpretation has prevailed. Because the majority tends naturally toward an argument that increases its freedom of action, the pressure for this view has been continual and formidable. The Bank of the United States succeeded from the start. When its stock went on sale, investors snapped up every share in a matter of hours. People eagerly accepted its bank notes at face value. Business ventures of all kinds found it easier to raise new capital. Soon state-chartered banks entered the field. There were only three state banks in 1791; by 1801, there were thirty-two.

Hamilton had not finished. In December 1791 he submitted his *Report on Manufactures*, a bold call for economic planning. The pre-Revolutionary nonimportation agreements and wartime shortages had stimulated interest in manufacturing. Already a number of joint-stock companies had been founded to manufacture textiles, and an elaborate argument for economic diversification had been worked out by American economists such as Tench Coxe and Mathew Carey. Hamilton was familiar with these developments. In his *Report* he called for government tariffs, subsidies, and awards to encourage American manufacturing. He hoped to change an essentially agricultural nation into one with a complex, self-sufficient economy. Once again business and commercial interests in particular would benefit. They would be protected against foreign competition and otherwise subsidized, whereas the general taxpayer, particularly the farmer, would pay the bill in the form of higher taxes and higher prices on manufactured goods. Hamilton argued that in the long run every interest would profit, and he was undoubtedly sincere, being too much the nationalist to favor one section at the expense of another. A majority of the Congress, however, balked at so broad-gauged a scheme. Hamilton's *Report* was set aside, although many of the specific tariffs he recommended were enacted into law in 1792.

Nevertheless, the secretary of the treasury had managed to transform the financial structure of the country and to prepare the ground for an economic revolution. The constitutional reforms of 1787 had made this possible, and Hamilton turned possibility into reality.

The Ohio Country: A Dark and Bloody Ground

The western issues and those related to international trade proved more difficult because other nations were involved. The British showed no disposition to evacuate their posts on American soil simply because the American people had decided to strengthen their central government, nor did the western Indians suddenly agree to abandon their hunting grounds.

Trouble came swiftly when white settlers moved onto the land north of the Ohio River in large numbers. The Indians, determined to hold this country at all costs, struck hard at the invaders. In 1790 the Miami chief Little Turtle inflicted a double defeat on militia units commanded by General Josiah Harmar. The next year Little Turtle and his men defeated the forces of General Arthur St. Clair still more convincingly. Both Harmar and St. Clair resigned from the army, their careers ruined, but the defeats led Congress to authorize raising a regular army of 5,000 men.

By early 1792 the Indians had driven the whites into "beachheads" at Marietta and Cincinnati on the Ohio. Resentment of the federal government in the western counties of every state from New York to the Carolinas mounted, the people feeling that it was ignoring their interests. They were convinced that the British were inciting the Indians to attack them, yet the supposedly powerful national government seemed unable to force Great Britain to surrender its forts in the West.

Still worse, the Westerners believed, was the way the government was taxing them. In 1791, as part of his plan to take over the debts of the states, Hamilton had persuaded Congress to adopt a sales tax of 8 cents a gallon on American-made whiskey. Excise taxes were particularly disliked by most Americans. Westerners, who were heavy drinkers and who turned much of their grain into whiskey in order to cope with the high cost of transportation, were especially angered by the tax on whiskey.

But Hamilton was determined to enforce the law. To western complaints, he suggested that farmers drank too much to begin with. If they found the tax oppressive, they should cut down on their consumption. Of course this did nothing to reduce western opposition to the tax. Resistance was especially intense in western Pennsylvania, where treasury agents were forcibly prevented from collecting the tax.

Revolution in France

Momentous events in Europe influenced the situation. In 1789 the **French Revolution** erupted, and four years later war broke out between France and Great Britain and most of the rest of Europe. With France fighting Great Britain and Spain, there arose the question of America's obligations under the Alliance of 1778. That treaty required the United States to defend the French West Indies "forever against all other powers." Suppose the British attacked the French island of Martinique; must America declare war on Britain? Legally

In the summer of 1793, a yellow fever epidemic struck Philadelphia, killing nearly 4,000. Tens of thousands fled the city, including President Washington and much of the federal government. Absalom Jones, a religious leader, was among the free blacks who remained to take care of the sick and the dead. This portrait of Jones is by Raphaelle Peale.

the United States was so obligated, but no responsible American statesman urged such a policy. With the British in Canada and Spanish forces to the west and south, the nation would be in serious danger if it entered the war. Instead, in April 1793, Washington issued a proclamation of neutrality committing the United States to be "friendly and impartial" toward both sides in the war.

Meanwhile the French had sent a special representative, Edmond Charles Genet, to the United States to seek support. During its early stages, especially when France declared itself a republic in 1792, the revolution had excited much enthusiasm in the United States, for it seemed to indicate that American democratic ideas were already engulfing the world. The increasing radicalism in France tended to dampen some of the enthusiasm, yet when "Citizen" Genet landed at Charleston, South Carolina, in April 1793, the majority of Americans probably wished the revolutionaries well. As Genet, a charming, ebullient young man, made his way northward to present his credentials, cheering crowds welcomed him in every town. Quickly concluding that the proclamation of neutrality was "a harmless little pleasantry designed to throw dust in the eyes of the British," he began, in plain violation of American law, to license American vessels to operate as privateers against British shipping and to grant French military commissions to a number of Americans in order to mount expeditions against Spanish and British possessions in North America.

Washington received Genet coolly, and soon thereafter demanded that he stop his illegal activities. Genet, whose capacity for self-deception was monumental, appealed to public opinion over the president's head and continued to commission privateers. Washington then requested his recall. The incident ended on a ludicrous note. When Genet left France, he had been in the forefront of the Revolution. But events there had marched swiftly leftward, and the new leaders in Paris considered him a dangerous reactionary. His replacement arrived in America with an order for his arrest. To return might well mean the guillotine, so Genet asked the government that was expelling him for political asylum! Washington agreed, for he was not a vindictive man. A few months later the bold revolutionary married the daughter of the governor of New York and settled down as a farmer on Long Island, where he raised a large family and "moved agreeably in society."

The Genet affair was incidental to a far graver problem. Although the European war increased the foreign demand for American products, it also led to attacks on American shipping by both France and Great Britain. Each power captured American vessels headed for the other's ports whenever it could. In 1793 and 1794 about 600 United States ships were seized.

The British attacks caused far more damage, both physically and psychologically, because the British fleet was much larger than France's, and France at least professed to be America's friend and to favor freedom of trade for neutrals. In addition the British issued secret orders late in 1793 turning their navy loose on neutral ships headed for the French West Indies. Pouncing without warning, British warships captured about 250 American vessels and sent them off as prizes to British ports. The merchant marine, one American diplomat declared angrily, was being "kicked, cuffed, and plundered all over the Ocean."

The attacks roused a storm in America, reviving hatreds that had been smoldering since the Revolution. The continuing presence of British troops in the Northwest (in 1794 the British began to build a new fort in the Ohio country) and the restrictions imposed on American trade with the British West Indies raised tempers still further. To try to avoid a war, for he wisely believed that the United States should not become embroiled in the Anglo-French conflict, Washington sent Chief Justice John Jay to London to seek a settlement with the British.

Federalists and Republicans: The Rise of Political Parties

The furor over the violations of neutral rights focused attention on a new development, the formation of political parties. Why national political parties emerged after the ratification of a Constitution that made no provision for such organizations is a question that has long intrigued historians. Probably the main reason was the obvious one: By creating a strong central government the Constitution produced national issues and a focus on national discussion and settlement of these issues. Furthermore, by failing to create machinery for nominating candidates for federal offices, the Constitution left a vacuum, which informal party organizations filled. That the universally admired Washington headed the government was a force limiting partisanship, but his principal advisers, Hamilton and Jefferson, were in sharp disagreement, and they soon became the leaders around which parties coalesced.

In the spring of 1791 Jefferson and James Madison began to sound out other politicians about forming an informal political organization. Jefferson also appointed the poet Philip Freneau to a minor state department post and Freneau then began publishing a newspaper, the *National Gazette*, to disseminate the views of what became known as the Republican party. Hamilton organized his own followers in the Federalist party, the organ of which was John Fenno's *Gazette of the United States*.

The personal nature of early American political controversies goes far toward explaining why the party battles of the era were so bitter. So does the continuing anxiety that plagued partisans of both persuasions about the supposed frailty of a republican government. The United States was still very much an experiment; leaders who sincerely proclaimed their own devotion to its welfare suspected that their opponents wanted to undermine its institutions. Federalists feared that the Jeffersonians sought a dictatorship based on "mob rule," and Republicans feared that the Hamiltonians hid "under the mask of Federalism hearts devoted to monarchy."

At the start Hamilton had the ear of the president, and his allies controlled a majority in Congress. Jefferson, who disliked controversy, avoided a direct confrontation as long as he could. He went along with Hamilton's funding plan and traded the assumption of state debts for a capital on the Potomac. However, when Hamilton proposed the Bank of the United States, he dug in his heels. It seemed designed to benefit the northeastern commercial classes at the expense of southern and western farmers. He sensed a plot to milk the producing masses for the benefit of a few capitalists.

The growing controversy over the French Revolution and the resulting war between France and Great Britain widened the split between the parties. After the radicals in France executed Louis XVI and instituted the Reign of Terror, American conservatives were horrified. The Jeffersonians were also deeply shocked. However, they continued to defend the Revolution. Great southern landlords whose French counterparts were losing their estates—some their heads—extolled "the glorious successes of our Gallic brethren." In the same way the Federalists began to idealize the British, whom they considered the embodiment of the forces that were resisting French radicalism.

This created an explosive situation. Enthusiasm for a foreign country might tempt Americans to betray their own. Hamilton came to believe that Jefferson was so prejudiced in favor of France as to be unable to conduct foreign affairs rationally, and Jefferson could say contemptuously, "Hamilton is panick struck, if we refuse our breech to every kick which Great Britain may choose to give it." This, of course, was an exaggeration, but Hamilton was certainly predisposed toward England. As he put it to an English official, *"we think in English."*

In fact, Jefferson never lost his sense of perspective. When the Anglo-French war erupted, he recommended neutrality. In the Genet affair, although originally sympathetic to the young envoy, Jefferson cordially approved Washington's decision to send Genet packing. Hamilton perhaps went a little too far in his friendliness to Great Britain, but the real danger was that some of Hamilton's and Jefferson's excitable followers might become so committed as to forget the true interests of the United States.

1794: Crisis and Resolution

During the summer of 1794 several superficially unrelated events brought the partisan conflicts of the period to a peak. For the better part of two years the government had been unable to collect Hamilton's whiskey tax in the West. In Pennsylvania, mobs had burned the homes of revenue agents, and several men had been killed. Late in July, 7,000 "rebels" converged on Pittsburgh, threatening to set fire to the town. They were turned away by the sight of federal artillery and the liberal dispensation of whiskey by the frightened inhabitants.

Early in August President Washington was determined "to go to every length that the Constitution and laws would permit" to enforce the law. He mustered an enormous army of nearly 13,000 militiamen. This had the desired effect; when the troops arrived in western Pennsylvania, rebels were nowhere to be seen. The expected **Whiskey Rebellion** simply did not happen. Moderates in the region (not everyone, after all, was a distiller) agreed that even unpopular laws should be obeyed.

More important, perhaps, than the militia in pacifying the Pennsylvania frontier was another event that occurred while that army was being mobilized. This was the Battle of Fallen Timbers in Ohio near present-day Toledo, where the regular army troops of Major General "Mad Anthony" Wayne won a decisive victory over the

The United States and Its Territories, 1787–1802 In 1804 Georgia's cession became part of the Mississippi Territory. The seven British forts were evacuated as a result of Jay's Treaty (1795).

Indians. Wayne's victory opened the way for the settlement of the region. Some 2,000 of the whiskey tax rebels simply pulled up stakes and headed for Ohio after the effort to avoid the excise collapsed.

Jay's Treaty

Still more significant was the outcome of President Washington's decision to send John Jay to England to seek a treaty settling the conflicts between the two nations. The British genuinely wanted to reach an accommodation with the United States—as one minister quipped, the Americans "are so much in debt to this country that we scarcely dare to quarrel with them." The British also feared that the two new republics, France and the United States, would draw together in a battle against Europe's monarchies. On the other hand, the British were riding the crest of a wave of important victories in the war in Europe and were not disposed to make concessions to the Americans simply to avoid trouble.

The treaty that Jay brought home did contain a number of concessions. The British agreed to evacuate the posts in the West. They also promised to compensate American shipowners for seizures in the West Indies and to open up their colonies in Asia to

American ships. They conceded nothing, however, to American demands that the rights of neutrals on the high seas be respected; no one really expected them to do so in wartime. A provision opening the British West Indies to American commerce was so hedged with qualifications limiting the size of American vessels and the type of goods allowed that the United States refused to accept it.

Jay's Treaty also committed the United States to paying pre-Revolutionary debts still owed British merchants, a slap in the face to many states whose courts had been impeding their collection. Yet nothing was said about the British paying for the slaves they had "abducted" during the fighting in the South.

Although Jay might have driven a harder bargain, this was a valuable treaty for the United States. But it was also a humiliating one. Most of what the United States gained already legally belonged to it, and the treaty sacrificed principles of importance to a nation dependent on foreign trade. When the terms became known, they raised a storm of popular protest. It seemed possible that President Washington would repudiate the treaty or that if he did not, the Senate would refuse to ratify it.

1795: All's Well That Ends Well

Washington did not repudiate Jay's Treaty and after long debate the Senate ratified it in June 1795. After a bitter debate, with most Republicans opposing the measure, the House passed the requisite funding resolution. The treaty marked an important step toward the regularization of Anglo-American relations, which in the long run was essential for both the economic and political security of the nation. And the evacuation of the British forts in the Northwest was of enormous immediate benefit.

Still another benefit was totally unplanned. Unexpectedly, the Jay Treaty enabled the United States to solve its problems on its southeastern frontier. During the early 1790s Spain had entered into alliances with the Cherokee, Creek, and other Indian tribes hostile to the Americans and built forts on territory ceded to the United States by Great Britain in the Treaty of Paris. In 1795, however, Spain intended to withdraw from the European war against France. Fearing a joint Anglo-American attack on Louisiana and its other American possessions, it decided to improve relations with the United States. Therefore the king's chief minister, Manuel de Godoy, known as "the Prince of Peace," offered the American envoy Thomas Pinckney a treaty that granted the United States the free navigation of the Mississippi River and the right of deposit at New Orleans that western Americans so urgently needed. This Treaty of San Lorenzo, popularly known as Pinckney's Treaty, also accepted the American version of the boundary between Spanish Florida and the United States.

The Senate ratified the Jay Treaty in June. Pinckney signed the Treaty of San Lorenzo in October that same year. These agreements put an end, at least temporarily, to European pressures in the trans-Appalachian region. Between the signings, in August 1795, as an aftermath of the Battle of Fallen Timbers, twelve tribes signed the Treaty of Greenville. The Indians surrendered huge sections of their lands, thus ending a struggle that had consumed a major portion of the government's revenues for years.

After the events of 1794 and 1795, settlers poured into the West. "I believe scarcely anything short of a Chinese Wall or a line of Troops will restrain . . . the Incroachment of Settlers, upon the Indian Territory," President Washington explained in 1796.

Kentucky had become a state in 1792; now, in 1796, Tennessee was admitted. Two years later the Mississippi Territory was organized, and at the end of the century, the Indiana Territory was organized as well. The great westward flood reached full tide.

Washington's Farewell

Settlement of western problems did not, however, put an end to partisan strife. Even the sainted Washington was neither immune to attack nor entirely above the battle. On questions of finance and foreign policy he usually sided with Hamilton and thus increasingly incurred the anger of the Jeffersonians. But he was, after all, a Virginian. Only the most rabid partisan could think him a tool of northern commercial interests. He remained as he intended himself to be, a symbol of national unity. In September 1796 he announced his retirement in a **Farewell Address** to the nation.

●●●⊸ Read the **Document**

George Washington, *Farewell Addresss* at
myhistorylab.com

Washington found the acrimonious rivalry between Federalists and Republicans most disturbing. Hamilton advocated national unity, yet he seemed prepared to smash any individual or faction that disagreed with his vision of the country's future. Jefferson had risked his neck for independence, but he opposed the economic development needed to make America strong enough to defend that independence. Washington was less brilliant than either Hamilton or Jefferson, but wiser. He appreciated how important it was that the new nation should remain at peace with the rest of the world and with itself. In his farewell he deplored the "baneful effects of the spirit of party" that led honest people to use unscrupulous means to win a mean advantage over fellow Americans. He tried to show how the North benefited from the prosperity of the South, the South from that of the North, and the East and West also in reciprocal fashion.

Washington urged the people to avoid both "inveterate antipathies" and "passionate attachments" to any foreign nation. Nothing had alarmed him more than the sight of Americans dividing into "French" and "English" factions. Furthermore, France had repeatedly interfered in American domestic affairs. "Against the insidious wiles of foreign influence," Washington now warned, "the jealousy of a free people ought to be constantly awake." America should develop its foreign trade but steer clear of foreign political connections as far as possible. "Permanent alliances" should be avoided, although "temporary alliances for extraordinary emergencies" might sometimes be useful.

The Election of 1796

Washington's Farewell Address was destined to have a long and important influence on American thinking, but its immediate impact was small. He had intended it to cool political passions. Instead, in the words of Federalist congressman Fisher Ames, people took it as "a signal, like dropping a hat, for the party racers to start." By the time the 1796 presidential campaign had ended, many Federalists and Republicans were refusing to speak to one another.

Jefferson was the only Republican candidate seriously considered in 1796. The logical Federalist was Hamilton, but, as was to happen so often in American history with powerful leaders, he was not considered "available" because his controversial policies had made him many enemies. Gathering in caucus, the Federalists in Congress nominated Vice President John Adams for the top office and Thomas Pinckney of South Carolina, negotiator of the popular Spanish treaty, for vice president. In the election the Federalists were victorious.

Hamilton, hoping to run the new administration from the wings, preferred Pinckney to Adams. He arranged for some of the Federalist electors from South Carolina to vote only for Pinckney. (Pinckney, who was on the high seas at the time, did not even know he was running for vice president!) Catching wind of this, a number of New England electors retaliated by cutting Pinckney. As a result, Adams won in the electoral college, seventy-one to sixty-eight, over Jefferson, who thus became vice president. Pinckney got only fifty-nine electoral votes.

That Adams would now be obliged to work with a vice president who led the opposition seemed to presage a decline in partisanship. Adams actually preferred the Virginian to Pinckney for the vice presidency, while Jefferson said that if Adams would "relinquish his bias to an English constitution," he might make a fine chief executive. The two had in common a distaste for Hamilton—a powerful bond.

However, the closeness of the election indicated a trend toward the Republicans, who were making constant and effective use of the charge that the Federalists were "monocrats" (monarchists) determined to destroy American liberty. Without Washington to lead them, the Federalist politicians were already quarreling among themselves; honest, able, hardworking John Adams was too caustic and too scathingly frank to unite them. Everything seemed to indicate a Republican victory at the next election.

The XYZ Affair

At this point occurred one of the most remarkable reversals of public feeling in American history. French attacks on American shipping, begun out of irritation at the Jay Treaty and in order to influence the election, continued after Adams took office. Hoping to stop them, Adams appointed three commissioners to try to negotiate a settlement. They were instructed to seek a moderate settlement, to "terminate our differences . . . without referring to the merits."

Their mission was a fiasco. Talleyrand, the French foreign minister, sent an agent later spoken of as X to demand "something for the pocket," a "gratification,"—read a bribe—as the price of making a deal. Later two other Tallyrand agents, Y and Z, made the same demand. The Americans refused, more because they suspected Talleyrand's good faith than because of any particular distaste for bribery. "No, no, not a sixpence," Pinckney later told X. The talks broke up, and in April 1798 President Adams released the commissioners' reports.

They caused a sensation. Americans' sense of national honor, perhaps overly tender because the country was so young and insecure, was outraged. Pinckney's laconic refusal to pay a bribe was translated into the grandiose phrase "Millions for defense, but not one cent for tribute!" and broadcast throughout the land. John Adams, never a man with mass appeal, suddenly found himself a national hero. Federalist hotheads burned for a fight. Congress unilaterally abrogated the French Alliance, created a Navy

Department, and appropriated enough money to build forty-odd warships and triple the size of the army. Washington came out of retirement to lead the forces, with Hamilton, now a general, as second in command. On the seas American privateers began to attack French shipping.

Adams did not much like the French and he could be extremely stubborn. A declaration of war would have been immensely popular. But perhaps the famously prickly president did not want to be popular. Instead of calling for war, he contented himself with approving the buildup of the armed forces.

The Republicans, however, committed to friendship with France, did not appreciate Adams's moderation. Although angered by the **XYZ Affair**, they tried, one Federalist complained, "to clog the wheels of government" by opposing the military appropriations. John Daly Burk of the New York *Time Piece* called Adams a "mock Monarch" surrounded by a "court composed of tories and speculators," which of course was a lie. Many Federalists expected the Republicans to side with France if war broke out. Hysterical and near panic, they easily persuaded themselves that the danger of subversion was acute.

The Alien and Sedition Acts

Conservative Federalists saw in this situation a chance to smash the opposition. In June and July 1798 they pushed through Congress a series of repressive measures known as the **Alien and Sedition Acts**. The Alien Enemies Act gave the president the power to arrest or expel aliens in time of "declared war," but since the quasi-war with France was never declared, this measure had no practical importance. The Alien Act authorized the president to expel all aliens whom he thought "dangerous to the peace and safety of the United States." (Adams never invoked this law, but a number of aliens left the country out of fear that he might.)

Read the Document
The Alien and Sedition Acts at **myhistorylab.com**

Finally, there was the Sedition Act. Its first section, making it a crime "to impede the operation of any law" or to attempt to instigate a riot or insurrection, was reasonable enough; but the act also made it illegal to publish, or even to utter, any "false, scandalous and malicious" criticism of high government officials. This proviso rested, as James Madison said, on "the exploded doctrine" that government officials "are the masters and not the servants of the people."

Matthew Lyon of Vermont, holding tongs, and Roger Griswold of Connecticut, come to blows in Congress. After denouncing Adams' call for war against Spain, Lyon was convicted of violating the Alien and Sedition Acts. While serving a four-month jail sentence, he was re-elected.

The Kentucky and Virginia Resolves

While Thomas Jefferson did not object to state sedition laws, he believed that the Alien and Sedition Acts violated the First Amendment's guarantees of freedom of speech and the press and were an invasion of the rights of the states. In 1798 he and Madison decided to draw up resolutions arguing that the laws were unconstitutional. Madison's draft was presented to the Virginia legislature and Jefferson's to the legislature of Kentucky. (Although separate documents, historians refer to them collectively as the **Kentucky and Virginia Resolves**.)

•••-[Read the Document

The Virginia and Kentucky Resolutions at **myhistorylab.com**

Jefferson argued that since the Constitution was a compact made by sovereign states, each state had "an equal right to judge for itself" when the compact had been violated. Thus a state could declare a law of Congress unconstitutional. Madison's Virginia Resolves took an only slightly less forthright position.

Neither Kentucky nor Virginia tried to implement these resolves or to prevent the enforcement of the Alien and Sedition Acts. Jefferson and Madison were protesting Federalist high-handedness and firing the opening salvo of Jefferson's campaign for the presidency, not advancing a new constitutional theory of extreme states' rights. "Keep away all show of force," Jefferson advised his supporters.

This was sound advice, for events were again playing into the hands of the Republicans. Talleyrand had never wanted war with the United States. When he discovered how vehemently the Americans had reacted to his little attempt to replenish his personal fortune, he let Adams know that new negotiators would be properly received.

President Adams quickly grasped the importance of the French change of heart. Other leading Federalists, however, had lost their heads. By shouting about the French danger, they had roused the country against radicalism, and they did not intend to surrender this advantage tamely. Hamilton in particular wanted war at almost any price—if not against France, then against Spain. He saw himself at the head of the new American army sweeping first across Louisiana and the Floridas, then on to the South. "We ought to squint at South America," he suggested. "Tempting objects will be within our grasp."

But the puritan John Adams was a specialist at resisting temptation. At this critical point his intelligence, his moderate political philosophy, and his stubborn integrity stood him in good stead. He would neither go to war merely to destroy the political opposition in America nor follow "the fools who were intriguing to plunge us into an alliance with England . . . and wild expeditions to South America." Instead he submitted to the Senate the name of a new minister plenipotentiary to France, and when the Federalists tried to block the appointment, he threatened to resign. This would have made Jefferson president. So the furious Federalists had to give in, although they forced Adams to send three men instead of one.

Napoleon had taken over France by the time the Americans arrived, and he drove a harder bargain than Talleyrand would have. But in the end he signed an agreement (the Convention of 1800) abrogating the Franco-American treaties of 1778. Nothing was said about the damage done to American shipping by the French, but the war scare was over.

The Kentucky and Virginia Resolves, however, had raised an issue that would loom large in the next century. If Congress passed laws that particular states thought to be unconstitutional, did states have the right to ignore those laws—or to withdraw from the Constitution altogether?

Milestones

1781	States fail to approve Congress's tariff	1791	Philip Freneau's *National Gazette* and John Fenno's *Gazette of the United States* are founded
1786	Rhode Island Supreme Court upholds state legal tender act (*Trevett v. Weeden*)	1793	French revolutionaries execute King Louis XVI
	Shays's Rebellion collapses in Springfield, Massachusetts		Washington issues Declaration of Neutrality
	Only five states send delegates to Annapolis Convention	1794	"Mad Anthony" Wayne's troops defeat Indians at Battle of Fallen Timbers
1787	Delegates meet at Philadelphia Constitutional Convention		Washington's militiamen thwart Whiskey Rebellion in Pennsylvania
1787– 1788	All states but North Carolina and Rhode Island ratify Constitution	1795	Senate ratifies humiliating Jay's Treaty
1789	President Washington is inaugurated	1796	Washington announces his retirement in Farewell Address
	Storming of Paris Bastille begins French Revolution		John Adams is elected president
1790	Hamilton issues his *Report on Public Credit*	1798	French demand bribe during XYZ Affair
1791	Hamilton issues his *Report on Manufactures*		Congress passes Alien and Sedition Acts
	First Ten Amendments (Bill of Rights) to the Constitution are ratified	1798– 1799	Jefferson presents Kentucky Resolutions
	Republican and Federalist political parties are organized		Madison presents Virginia Resolutions

✓•⎯Study and **Review** at www.myhistorylab.com

Review Questions

1. The Articles of Confederation are famously known to have been "ineffective." What were their strengths?
2. Who were the winners and losers in the political compromises that resulted in the Constitution?
3. How did the Constitution expand the powers of the federal government?
4. The rise of the Federalists and Republicans constituted what some historians call the "First American Political Party System." What were the key points of dispute? Agreement?
5. How did the Alien and Sedition Acts exacerbate political tensions?
6. Did Washington succeed in bringing the country together, or was his toleration of division a reason for the rise of political factions?

Key Terms

Alien and Sedition
  Acts *167*
Antifederalists *152*
Bank of the United
  States *157*
Bill of Rights *155*
Electoral College *150*
Farewell Address *165*

Federalist Papers *153*
Federalists *152*
French Revolution *159*
Great Compromise *150*
Jay's Treaty *164*
judicial review *150*
Kentucky and Virginia
  Resolves *168*

New Jersey Plan *148*
Shays's rebellion *145*
Three-Fifths
  Compromise *149*
Virginia Plan *148*
Whiskey Rebellion *162*
XYZ Affair *167*

Jeffersonian Democracy

6

((•—Hear the Audio Chapter 6 at myhistorylab.com

Do you have too much debt?

DURING THEIR FIRST WEEK IN COLLEGE, FRESHMEN RECEIVE ON average eight applications for credit cards. Credit card companies target college students because they have a lifetime to acquire debt—and pay it off. The average freshman in 2008 finished the year with a credit card debt of $2,038, while graduating seniors owed $4,138— up 44 percent since 2004. Many students cope with debt by cutting expenses, taking jobs, or skipping school, while some do not cope. A 2006 documentary film described the plight of two college students in Oklahoma who, awash in credit card debt, committed suicide.

Many college students incur debt responsibly, most often to pay for college. In 2008 the average college graduate owed $23,000, mostly for college loans. But this investment usually pays off—literally: College graduates on average earned $57,200, while individuals with only a high school education earned $31,300.

Many of the founders of the nation were also entangled in personal debt. In 1798 Robert Morris, the financier who had devised the funded debt to pay and equip George Washington's army, was imprisoned for personal debt. He languished in the Prune Street debtor's prison in Philadelphia for three years. Thomas Jefferson, on paper one of the richest men in Virginia, owner of thousands of acres of land and 200 slaves, was also plagued by debt. His financial woes mounted as he built additions to Monticello, his home, and acquired more books for his library, one of the finest in the nation. Creditors harassed him. "I am miserable till I shall owe not a shilling," he wrote in 1787. When he died, he was bankrupt. His slaves were sold to pay creditors.

Jefferson's antipathy toward debt influenced his ideas about government. He opposed federal expenditures because they could lead to indebtedness. A weak government, too, was less likely to restrict individual freedoms, a doctrine that endures to this day. Few presidents have left a deeper imprint. His parsimony sometimes left the nation vulnerable to foreigners, whether high-handed European rulers or pirate states in northern Africa. On a few occasions—such as the chance to acquire the Louisiana territory—he splurged, but soon recanted. On leaving office he urged his successor to pay off the federal deficit.[1]

---

[1] After the 3,000-volume Library of Congress was destroyed by fire in 1814, Madison persuaded Congress to purchase Jefferson's 6,000-volume library for $23,950. This helped pay some of Jefferson's debts. At the time, some politicians grumbled that Jefferson's library had been overvalued. Many of his books, after all, were pirated (published by printers who had not paid copyright fees), that era's equivalent of an "illegal download."

Jefferson Elected President

Once the furor over war and subversion subsided, public attention focused on the presidential contest between Adams and Jefferson. Because of his stand for peace, Adams personally escaped the brunt of popular indignation against the Federalist party. His solid qualities had a strong appeal to conservatives, and fear that the Republicans would introduce radical "French" social reforms did not disappear when the danger of war with France ended. Many nationalist-minded voters worried that the Republicans, waving the banner of states' rights, would weaken the strong government established by the Federalists. The economic progress stimulated by Hamilton's financial reforms also seemed threatened. When the electors' votes were counted in February 1801, however, the Republicans were discovered to have won narrowly, seventy-three to sixty-five.

But which Republican was to be president? The Constitution did not distinguish between presidential and vice presidential candidates; it provided only that each elector vote for two candidates, the one with the most votes becoming president and the runner-up vice president. The development of national political parties made this system impractical. The vice presidential candidate of the Republicans was Aaron Burr of New York, a former senator and a rival of Hamilton in law and politics. But Republican party solidarity had been perfect; Jefferson and Burr received seventy-three votes each. Because of the tie, the Constitution required that the House of Representatives (voting by states) choose between them.

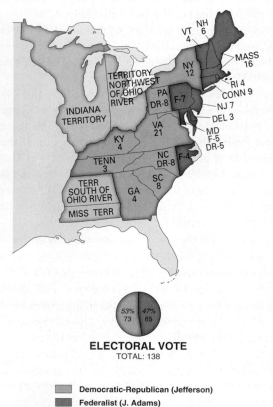

ELECTORAL VOTE
TOTAL: 138

53% 47%
73 65

◻ Democratic-Republican (Jefferson)
◼ Federalist (J. Adams)

In the House the Republicans could control only eight of the sixteen state delegations. On the first ballot Jefferson got these eight votes, one short of election, while six states voted for Burr. Two state delegations, being evenly split, lost their votes. Through thirty-five ballots the deadlock persisted; the Federalist congressmen, fearful of Jefferson's supposed radicalism, voted solidly for Burr.

In the end, Alexander Hamilton decided who would be the next president. Although he considered Jefferson "too much in earnest in his

The Wild Election of 1800 The election of 1800 was arguably the weirdest in the nation's history. When the electors' votes were counted in February 1801, the Republicans won New York State—and, seemingly, the election, seventy-three to sixty-five. But which Republican was to be president? The Republican electors held to the party line: Jefferson and Burr each received seventy-three votes. Because of the tie, the Constitution required that the House of Representatives (voting by states) choose between them. Jefferson ultimately prevailed.

democracy" and "not very mindful of truth," he detested Burr. He exerted his considerable influence on Federalist congressmen on Jefferson's behalf. Finally, on February 17, 1801, Jefferson was elected. Burr became vice president.

To make sure that this deadlock would never be repeated, the Twelfth Amendment was drafted, providing for separate balloting in the Electoral College for president and vice president. This change was ratified in 1804, shortly before the next election.

The Federalist Contribution

On March 4, 1801, in the new national capital on the Potomac River named in honor of George Washington, Thomas Jefferson took the presidential oath and delivered his inaugural address. His goal was to recapture the simplicity and austerity—the "pure republicanism"—that had characterized "the spirit of '76." The new president believed that a revolution as important as that heralded by his immortal Declaration of Independence had occurred, and for once most of his political enemies agreed with him.

●●●─Read the **Document**
Thomas Jefferson, *First Inaugural Address* at
myhistorylab.com

Jefferson erred, however, in calling this triumph a revolution. The real upheaval had been attempted in 1798; it was Federalist-inspired, and it failed. In 1800 the voters expressed a preference for individual freedom and limited national power. And Jefferson, despite Federalist fears that he would destroy the Constitution and establish a radical social order, presided instead over a regime that confirmed the great achievements of the Federalist era, chiefly, the creation and implementation of the Constitution itself.

What was most significant about the election of 1800 was that it was *not* a revolution. After a bitter contest, the Jeffersonians took power and proceeded to change the policy of the government. They did so peacefully. Thus American republican government passed a crucial test: Control of its machinery had changed hands in a democratic and orderly way. And only slightly less significant, the informal party system had demonstrated its usefulness. The Jeffersonians had organized popular dissatisfaction with Federalist policies, formulated a platform of reform, chosen leaders to put their plans into effect, and elected those leaders to office.

Thomas Jefferson: Political Theorist

Much as Jefferson worried that an indebted nation could become enslaved to its creditors, he feared banks because they, too, deprived debtors of true liberty. He believed *all* government a necessary evil at best, for by its nature it restricted the freedom of the individual. For this reason, he wanted the United States to remain a society of small independent farmers. Such a nation did not need much political organization.

Jefferson's main objection to Alexander Hamilton was that Hamilton wanted to commercialize and centralize the country; Hamilton embraced public debt so as to initiate public projects and promote investment. This Jefferson feared, for it would mean that financial speculators and creditors would acquire economic power. Moreover, a commercial economy would lead to the growth of cities, which would complicate society and hence require more regulation. "The mobs of great cities add just as much to the support of pure government," he said, "as sores do to the strength of the human body." Like Hamilton, he believed that city workers were easy prey for demagogues. "I consider the class of artificers as the panderers of vice, and the instruments by which the liberties of a country are usually overturned," he said. Like Hamilton, Jefferson thought human beings basically selfish. "Lions and tigers are mere lambs compared with men," he once said. Although he claimed to have some doubts about the subject, he suspected that blacks were "inferior to whites in the endowments both of body and mind." (Hamilton, who also owned slaves, stated flatly of blacks that "Their natural faculties are as good as ours.") Jefferson's pronouncements on race are yet more troubling in light of recent research, including DNA studies, that point to the likelihood that he fathered one or more children by Sally Hemings, one of his slaves.

Read the Document

Memoirs of a Monticello Slave at **myhistorylab.com**

Jefferson as President

The novelty of the new administration lay in its style and its moderation. Both were apparent in Jefferson's inaugural address. The new president's opening remarks showed that he was neither a demagogue nor a firebrand. "The task is above my talents," he said modestly, "and . . . I approach it with . . . anxious and awful presentiments." The people had spoken, and their voice must be heeded, but the rights of dissenters must be respected. "All . . . will bear in mind this sacred principle," he said, "that though the will of the majority is in all cases to prevail, that will to be rightful must be reasonable; that the minority possess their equal rights, which equal law must protect, and to violate would be oppression."

Jefferson spoke at some length about specific policies. He declared himself against "entangling alliances" and for economy in government, and he promised to pay off the national debt, preserve the government's credit, and stimulate both agriculture and its "handmaid" commerce. His main stress was on the cooling of partisan passions: "Every difference of opinion is not a difference of principle. We have called by different names brethren of the same principle. We are all Republicans—we are all Federalists." And he promised the country "a wise and frugal Government which shall restrain men from injuring one another" and "leave them otherwise free to regulate their own pursuits."

Read the Document

Reflections Upon Meeting Jefferson at **myhistorylab.com**

Jefferson quickly demonstrated the sincerity of his remarks. He saw to it that the whiskey tax and other Federalist excises were repealed, and he made sharp cuts in military and naval

This portrait of Thomas Jefferson, painted when he was thirty-seven years old, in 1800, the year before he was elected president, is considered an accurate likeness. Its artist, just twenty at the time, was the American painter, Rembrandt Peale. Rembrandt's father—the painter Charles Willson Peale—also named his other sons after painters: Rubens, Titian, Raphaelle, and Titian II.

expenditures to keep the budget in balance. The Naturalization Act of 1798 was repealed, and the old five-year residence requirement for citizenship restored. The Sedition Act and the Alien Act expired of their own accord in 1801 and 1802.

The changes were not drastic. Jefferson made no effort to tear down the fiscal structure that Hamilton had erected. "We can pay off his debt," the new president confessed, "but we cannot get rid of his financial system." Nor did the author of the Kentucky Resolves try to alter the balance of federal-state power.

Yet there was a different tone to the new regime. Jefferson had no desire to surround himself with pomp and ceremony; the excessive formality of the Washington and Adams administrations had been distasteful to him. From the moment of his election, he played down the ceremonial aspects of the presidency. He asked that he be notified of his election by mail rather than by a committee, and he would have preferred to have taken the oath at Charlottesville, near Monticello, his home, rather than at Washington. After the inauguration, he returned to his boardinghouse on foot and took dinner in his usual seat at the common table.

In the White House he often wore a frayed coat and carpet slippers, even to receive the representatives of foreign powers when they arrived. At social affairs he paid little heed to the status and seniority of his guests. During business hours congressmen, friends, foreign officials, and plain citizens coming to call took their turn in the order of their arrival. "The principle of society with us," Jefferson explained, "is the equal rights of all. . . . Nobody shall be above you, nor you above anybody, *pell-mell* is our law."

"Pell-mell" was also good politics, and Jefferson turned out to be a superb politician. He gave dozens of small stag dinner parties for congressmen, serving the food personally from a dumbwaiter connected with the White House kitchen. The guests, carefully chosen to make congenial groups, were seated at a round table to encourage general conversation, and the food and wine were first-class. These were ostensibly social occasions—shoptalk was avoided—yet they paid large political dividends. Jefferson learned to know every congressman personally, Democratic Republican and Federalist alike, and not only their political views but their strengths, their quirks, and their flaws as well. And he worked his personal magic on them, displaying the breadth of his knowledge, his charm and wit, and his lack of pomposity.

Jefferson made effective use of his close supporters in Congress and of Cabinet members as well, in persuading Congress to go along with his proposals. His state papers were models of reason, minimizing conflicts, stressing areas where all honest people must agree. After all, as he indicated in his inaugural address, nearly all Americans believed in having both a federal government and a republican system. No great principle divided them into irreconcilable camps. Jefferson set out to bring them all into *his* camp, and he succeeded so well in four years that when he ran for reelection against Charles Pinckney, he got 162 of the 176 electoral votes cast. Eventually even John Quincy Adams, son of the second president, became a Jeffersonian.

At the same time, Jefferson was anything but nonpartisan in the sense that Washington had been. His Cabinet consisted exclusively of men of his own party. He exerted almost continuous pressure on Congress to make sure that his legislative program was enacted into law. He did not remove many Federalist officeholders, and at one point he remarked ruefully that government officials seldom died and never resigned. But when he could, he used his power of appointment to reward his friends and punish his enemies.

Jefferson's Attack on the Judiciary

Although notably open-minded and tolerant, Jefferson had a few stubborn prejudices. One was against kings, another against the British system of government. A third was against judges, or rather, against entrenched judicial power. The biased behavior of Federalist judges during the trials under the Sedition Act had enormously increased this distrust, and it burst all bounds when the Federalist majority of the dying Congress rammed through the Judiciary Act of 1801.

The Judiciary Act created six new circuit courts, presided over by sixteen new federal judges and a small army of attorneys, marshals, and clerks. The expanding country needed the judges, but with the enthusiastic cooperation of President Adams, the Federalists made shameless use of the opportunity to fill all the new positions with conservative members of their own party. The new appointees were dubbed "midnight justices" because Adams had stayed up until midnight on March 3, his last day as president, feverishly signing their commissions.

The Republicans retaliated as soon as the new Congress met by repealing the Judiciary Act of 1801. But on taking office Jefferson had discovered that in the confusion of Adams's last hours, the commissions of a number of justices of the peace for the new District of Columbia had not been distributed. While these were small fry indeed, Jefferson was so angry that he ordered the commissions held up even though they had been signed by Adams.

One of the appointees, William Marbury, then petitioned the Supreme Court for a writ of mandamus (Latin for "we order") directing the new secretary of state, James Madison, to give him his commission.

The case of *Marbury v. Madison* (1803) placed Chief Justice John Marshall, one of Adams's "midnight" appointments, in an embarrassing position. Marbury had a strong claim; if Marshall refused to order Madison to give Marbury the job, everyone would say Marshall dared not stand up to Jefferson, and the prestige of the Court would suffer. If he ordered that Marbury be seated, however, he would place the Court in direct conflict with the President. Jefferson particularly disliked Marshall. He would probably tell Madison to ignore the order, and in the prevailing state of public opinion nothing could be done about it. This would be a still more staggering blow to the judiciary. If its decisions were ignored, would the Supreme Court have any purpose?

Marshall had studied law only briefly and had no previous judicial experience, but in this crisis he first displayed the genius that was to mark him as a great judge. By right Marbury should have his commission, Marshall announced. However, the Court could not require Madison to give it to him. Marbury's request for a court order had been based on an ambiguous clause in the Judiciary Act of 1789. That clause was unconstitutional, Marshall declared, and therefore void. Congress could not legally give the Supreme Court the right to issue such orders.

With the skill and foresight of a chess grand master, Marshall turned what had looked like a trap into a triumph. By sacrificing the pawn, Marbury, he established the power of the Supreme Court to invalidate federal laws that conflicted with the Constitution. Jefferson could not check him because Marshall had *refused* power instead of throwing an anchor ahead, as Jefferson had

●◆●[Read the Document

Opinion of the Supreme Court for Marbury v. Madison at **myhistorylab.com**

feared. Yet he had certainly grappled a "further hold for future advances of power," and the president could do nothing to stop him.

The Marbury case made Jefferson more determined to strike at the Federalist-dominated courts. He decided to press for the impeachment of some of the more partisan judges. First he had the House of Representatives bring charges against District Judge John Pickering. Pickering was clearly deranged—he had frequently delivered profane and drunken harangues from the bench—and the Senate quickly voted to remove him. Then Jefferson went after a much larger fish, Samuel Chase, associate justice of the Supreme Court.

Chase had been prominent for decades and active in the affairs of the Continental Congress. Washington had named him to the Supreme Court in 1796, and he had delivered a number of important opinions. But his handling of cases under the Sedition Act had been outrageously high-handed. Defense lawyers had become so exasperated as to throw down their briefs in disgust at some of his prejudiced rulings. However, the trial demonstrated that Chase's actions had not constituted the "high crimes and misdemeanors" required by the Constitution to remove a judge. Even Jefferson became disenchanted with the efforts of some of his more extreme followers and accepted Chase's acquittal with equanimity.

The Barbary Pirates

The North African Arab states of Morocco, Algiers, Tunis, and Tripoli had for decades made a business of piracy, seizing vessels all over the Mediterranean and holding crews and passengers for ransom. The European powers found it simpler to pay them annual protection money than to crush them. Under Washington and Adams, the United States joined in the payment of this tribute; while large, the sums were less than the increased costs of insurance for shippers when the protection was not purchased.

Such spinelessness ran against Jefferson's grain. "When this idea comes across my mind, my faculties are absolutely suspended between indignation and impatience," he said. When the pasha of Tripoli tried to raise the charges, Jefferson balked. Tripoli then declared war in May 1801, and Jefferson dispatched a squadron to the Mediterranean.

But the pirates were not overwhelmed, and a major American warship, the frigate *Philadelphia*, had to be destroyed after running aground off the Tripolitan coast. The payment of tribute continued until 1815. Just the same, America, though far removed from the pirate bases, was the only maritime nation that tried to resist the blackmail. Although the war failed to achieve Jefferson's purpose of ending the payments, the pasha agreed to a new treaty more favorable to the United States, and American sailors, led by Commodore Edward Preble, won valuable experience.

The Louisiana Purchase

The major achievements of Jefferson's first term had to do with the American West, and the greatest by far was the **Louisiana Purchase**, the acquisition of the huge area between the Mississippi River and the Rocky Mountains. In a sense the purchase of this region, called Louisiana, was fortuitous, an accidental by-product of

See the **Map**

The Louisiana Purchase at myhistorylab.com

This depicts New Orleans in 1803, when the city was acquired—along with much of the modern United States—in the Louisiana Purchase. It was known as the Crescent City because of the way it hugged a curved section of the Mississippi River. In 1803, New Orleans's population was about 8,000, including 4,000 whites, 2,700 slaves, and about 1,300 free "persons of color."
Source: P&S-1932.0018/Creator—Boqueto de Woieseri/Chicago History Museum.

European political adjustments and the whim of Napoleon Bonaparte. Certainly Jefferson had not planned it, for in his inaugural address he had expressed the opinion that the country already had all the land it would need "for a thousand generations." It was nonetheless the perfectly logical—one might almost say inevitable—result of a long series of events in the history of the Mississippi Valley.

Along with every other American who had even a superficial interest in the West, Jefferson understood that the United States must have access to the mouth of the Mississippi and the city of New Orleans or eventually lose everything beyond the Appalachians. "There is on the globe one single spot, the possessor of which is our natural and habitual enemy," he was soon to write. "It is New Orleans." Thus when he learned shortly after his inauguration that Spain had given Louisiana back to France, he was immediately on his guard. Control of Louisiana by Spain, a "feeble" country with "pacific dispositions," could be tolerated; control by a resurgent France dominated by Napoleon, the greatest military genius of the age, was entirely different.

Deeply worried, the president instructed his minister to France, Robert R. Livingston, to seek assurances that American rights in New Orleans would be respected and to negotiate the purchase of West Florida in case that area had also been turned over to France.

Jefferson's concern was well-founded; France was indeed planning new imperial ventures in North America. Immediately after settling its difficulties with the United States through the Convention of 1800, France signed a secret treaty with Spain, which returned Louisiana to France. Napoleon hoped to use this region as a breadbasket for the French West Indian sugar plantations, just as colonies like Pennsylvania and Massachusetts had fed the British sugar islands before the Revolution.

However, the most important French island, Saint Domingue (Hispaniola), at the time occupied entirely by the nation of Haiti, had slipped from French control. During the French Revolution, the slaves of the island had revolted. In 1793 they were granted personal freedom, but they fought on under the leadership of the "Black Napoleon," a self-taught genius named Toussaint L'Ouverture, and by 1801 the island was entirely in their hands. The original Napoleon, taking advantage of the slackening of war in Europe, dispatched an army of 20,000 men under General Charles Leclerc to reconquer it.

When Jefferson learned of the Leclerc expedition, he had no trouble divining its relationship to Louisiana. His uneasiness became outright alarm. In April 1802 he again urged Minister Livingston to attempt the purchase of New Orleans and Florida or, as an alternative, to buy a tract of land near the mouth of the Mississippi where a new port could be constructed. Of necessity, the mild-mannered, idealistic president now became an aggressive realist. "The day that France takes possession of New Orleans," he warned, "we must marry ourselves to the British fleet and nation."

In October 1802 the Spanish, who had not yet actually turned Louisiana over to France, heightened the tension by declaring that American boats plying the Mississippi could no longer deposit and store their goods in warehouses in New Orleans, the first step to exporting them to Europe. We now know that the French had no hand in this action, but it was beyond reason to expect Jefferson or the American people to believe it at the time. With the West clamoring for relief, Jefferson appointed his friend and

Toussaint L'Ouverture leading a revolt of slaves against the French in Haiti—the first and only successful slave rebellion in history.

disciple James Monroe minister plenipotentiary and sent him to Paris with instructions to offer up to $10 million for New Orleans and Florida. If France refused, he and Livingston should open negotiations for a "closer connection" with the British.

The tension broke before Monroe even reached France. General Leclerc's Saint Domingue expedition ended in disaster. Although Toussaint surrendered, Haitian resistance continued. Yellow fever raged through the French army; Leclerc himself fell to the fever, which wiped out practically his entire force.

When news of this calamity reached Napoleon early in 1803, he had second thoughts about reviving French imperialism in the New World. Without Saint Domingue, the wilderness of Louisiana seemed of little value. Napoleon was preparing a new campaign in Europe. He could no longer spare troops to recapture a rebellious West Indian island or to hold Louisiana against a possible British attack, and he needed money.

For some weeks the commander of the most powerful army in the world mulled the question without consulting anyone. Then, with characteristic suddenness, he made up his mind. On April 10 he ordered Foreign Minister Talleyrand to offer not merely New Orleans but all of Louisiana to the Americans. The next day Talleyrand summoned Livingston to his office on the rue du Bac and dropped this bombshell. Livingston was almost struck speechless but quickly recovered his composure. When Talleyrand asked what the United States would give for the province, he suggested the French equivalent of about $5 million. Talleyrand pronounced the sum "too low" and urged Livingston to think about the subject for a day or two.

Livingston faced a situation that no modern diplomat would ever have to confront. His instructions said nothing about buying an area almost as large as the entire United States, and there was no time to write home for new instructions. The offer staggered the imagination. Luckily, Monroe arrived the next day to share the responsibility. The two Americans consulted, dickered with the French, and finally agreed—they could scarcely have done otherwise—to accept the proposal. Early in May they signed a treaty. For 60 million francs—about $15 million—the United States was to have all of Louisiana.

No one knew exactly how large the region was or what it contained. When Livingston asked Talleyrand about the boundaries of the purchase, he replied, "I can give you no direction. You have made a noble bargain for yourselves, and I suppose you will make the most of it." Never, as the historian Henry Adams wrote, "did the United States government get so much for so little."

Napoleon's unexpected concession caused consternation in America, though there was never real doubt that the treaty would be ratified. Jefferson did not believe that the government had the power under the Constitution to add new territory or to grant American citizenship to the 50,000 residents of Louisiana by executive act, as the treaty required. He even drafted a constitutional amendment: "The province of Louisiana is incorporated with the United States and made part thereof." But his advisers convinced him that it would be dangerous to delay approval of the treaty until an amendment could be acted on by three-fourths of the states. Jefferson then suggested that the Senate ratify the treaty and submit an amendment afterward "confirming an act which the nation had not previously authorized." This idea was so obviously illogical that he quickly dropped it. Finally, he came to believe "that the less we say about constitutional difficulties the better." Since what he called "the good sense of our country" clearly wanted Louisiana, he decided to "acquiesce with satisfaction" while Congress overlooked the "metaphysical subtleties" of the problem and ratified the treaty.

Louisiana Purchase Jefferson bought the Louisiana region from Napoleon. No payments were made to the many Indians who had no idea that the world of their ancestors was owned by distant rulers

Some of the more partisan Federalists, who had been eager to fight Spain for New Orleans, attacked Jefferson for undermining the Constitution. One such critic described Louisiana contemptuously as a "Gallo-Hispano-Indian" col-

> •**Read** the **Document**
> *The Louisiana Purchase* at
> **myhistorylab.com**

lection of "savages and adventurers." Even Hamilton expressed hesitation about absorbing "this new, immense, unbounded world," though he had dreamed of seizing still larger domains himself. In the end Hamilton's nationalism reasserted itself, and he urged ratification of the treaty, as did such other important Federalists as John Adams and John Marshall. It was ironic—and a man as perceptive as Hamilton must surely have recognized the irony—that the acquisition of Louisiana ensured Jefferson's reelection and further contributed to the downfall of the Federalists. The

> •**Read** the **Document**
> *Fisher Ames on the*
> *Louisiana Purchase* at
> **myhistorylab.com**

purchase was popular even in the New England bastions of that party. While the negotiations were progressing in Paris, Jefferson had written the following of partisan political affairs: "If we can settle happily the difficulties of the Mississippi, I think we may promise ourselves smooth seas during our time." These words turned out to be no more accurate than most political predictions, but the Louisiana Purchase drove another spike into the Federalists' coffin.

The Federalists Discredited

As the election of 1804 approached, the West and South were solidly for Jefferson, and the North was rapidly succumbing to his charm. The addition of new western states would soon further reduce New England's power in national affairs.

These pistols were used in the duel between Aaron Burr and Alexander Hamilton. Before the duel Hamilton's lawyer drew up a contract specifying the terms: The duelists were to shoot at ten paces, and the barrels of the guns were to be no longer than 11 inches. Witnesses claimed that Hamilton never fired his fine pistol, but Burr took deadly aim, firing a .54-caliber ball that hit Hamilton in the chest. It ricocheted off his rib, punctured his liver, and lodged in his backbone. Hamilton died the next day.

So complete did the Republican triumph seem that a handful of diehard Federalists in New England began to think of secession. Led by former secretary of state Timothy Pickering, a group known as the Essex Junto organized in 1804 a scheme to break away from the Union and establish a "northern confederacy."

Even within the dwindling Federalist ranks the junto had little support. Nevertheless, Pickering and his friends pushed ahead, drafting a plan whereby, having captured political control of New York, they would take the entire Northeast out of the Union. Since they could not begin to win New York for anyone in their own ranks, they hit on the idea of supporting Vice President Aaron Burr, who was running against the "regular" Republican candidate for governor of New York. Although Burr did not promise to bring New York into their confederacy if elected, he encouraged them enough to win their backing. The foolishness of the plot was revealed in the April elections: Burr was overwhelmed by the regular Republican. The junto's scheme collapsed.

The incident, however, had a tragic aftermath. Hamilton had campaigned against Burr, whom he considered "an embryo Caesar." When he continued after the election to cast aspersions on Burr's character (not a very difficult assignment, since Burr, despite being a grandson of the preacher Jonathan Edwards, frequently violated both the political and sexual mores of the day), Burr challenged him to a duel. It was well known that Hamilton opposed dueling in principle, his own son having been slain in such an encounter, and he certainly had no need to prove his courage. But he believed that his honor was at stake. The two met with pistols on July 11, 1804, at Weehawken, New Jersey, across the Hudson from New York City. Hamilton made no effort to hit the challenger, but Burr took careful aim. Hamilton fell, wounded; he died the next day.

Thus a great, if enigmatic, man was cut off in his prime. His work, in a sense, had been completed, and his philosophy of government was being everywhere rejected, yet the nation's loss was large.

Lewis and Clark

While the disgruntled Federalists dreamed of secession, Jefferson was planning the exploration of Louisiana and the region beyond. He especially hoped to find a water route to connect the upper Mississippi or its tributaries with the Pacific Ocean. Early in 1803 he got $2,500 from Congress and obtained the permission of the French to send his exploring party across Louisiana. To command the expedition he appointed his private secretary, Meriwether Lewis, a young Virginian who had seen considerable service with the army in the West and who possessed, according to Jefferson, "a great mass of accurate information on all the subjects of nature." Lewis chose as his companion officer William Clark, another soldier (he had served with General Anthony Wayne at the Battle of Fallen Timbers) who had much experience in negotiating with Indians.

The country greeted the news of the explorers' return to St. Louis with delight. Besides locating several passes across the Rockies, Lewis and Clark had established friendly relations with a great many Indian tribes to whom they presented gifts, medals, American flags,

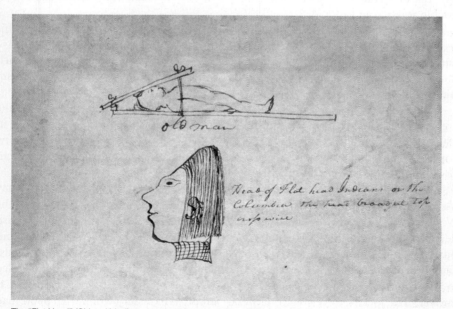

The "Flat Head" (Chinook) Indians acquired their name through shaping in infancy, as shown in a diagram from the Lewis and Clark journals. More remarkable to the explorers than the shape of the Indians' heads was the tribeswomen's open sexuality. "The young females are fond of the attention of our men and appear to meet the sincere approbation of their friends and connections for thus obtaining their favors," Captain Clark confided in his diary.

and a sales talk designed to promote peace and the fur trade. They brought back a wealth of data about the country and its resources. The journals kept by members of the group were published and, along with their accurate maps, became major sources for scientists, students, and future explorers.

The success of the **Lewis and Clark expedition** did not open the gates of Louisiana very wide. Other explorers sent out by Jefferson accomplished far less. Thomas Freeman, an Irish-born surveyor, led a small party up the Red River but ran into a powerful Spanish force near the present junction of Arkansas, Oklahoma, and Texas and was forced to retreat. Between 1805 and 1807 Lieutenant Zebulon Pike explored the upper Mississippi Valley and the Colorado region. (He discovered but failed to scale the peak south of Denver that bears his name.) Pike eventually made his way to Santa Fe and the upper reaches of the Rio Grande,

but he was not nearly so careful and acute an observer as Lewis and Clark were and consequently brought back much less information. By 1808 fur traders based at St. Louis were beginning to invade the Rockies, and by 1812 there were 75,000 people in the southern section of the new territory, which was admitted to the Union that year as the state of Louisiana. The northern region lay almost untouched until much later.

The Burr Conspiracy

Republican virtue seemed to have triumphed, but Jefferson soon found himself in trouble at home and abroad.

In part his difficulties arose from the extent of the Republican victory. In 1805 his Federalist opponents had no useful ideas, no intelligent leadership, and no effective numbers. They held only a quarter of the seats in Congress. As often happens in such situations, lack of opposition weakened party discipline and encouraged factionalism among the Republicans.

The Republican who caused Jefferson the most trouble was Aaron Burr, and the president was partly to blame for the difficulty. After their contest for the presidency in 1801, Jefferson pursued Burr vindictively, depriving him of federal patronage in New York and replacing him as the 1804 Republican vice presidential candidate with Governor George Clinton, Burr's chief rival in the state.

While still vice president, Burr began to flirt with treason. He approached Anthony Merry, the British minister in Washington, and offered to "effect a separation of the Western part of the United States." His price was £110,000 and the support of a British fleet off the mouth of the Mississippi. The British did not fall in with his scheme, but Burr went ahead nonetheless. Exactly what he had in mind has long been in dispute. Certainly he dreamed of acquiring a western empire for himself; whether he intended to wrest it from the United States or from Spanish territories beyond Louisiana is unclear. He joined forces with General James Wilkinson, whom Jefferson had appointed governor of the Louisiana Territory and was secretly in the pay of Spain.

The opening of the Ohio and Mississippi valleys had not totally satisfied land-hungry westerners. In 1806 Burr and Wilkinson had no difficulty raising a small force at a place called Blennerhassett Island, in the Ohio River. Some six dozen men began to move downriver toward New Orleans under Burr's command. Whether the objective was New Orleans or some part of Mexico, the scheme was clearly illegal. For some reason, however—possibly because he was incapable of loyalty to anyone[2]—Wilkinson betrayed Burr to Jefferson at the last moment. Burr tried to escape to Spanish Florida but was captured in February 1807, brought to Richmond, Virginia, under guard, and charged with high treason.

Any president will deal summarily with traitors, but Jefferson's attitude during Burr's trial reveals the depth of his hatred. He "made himself a party to the prosecution," personally sending evidence to the United States attorney who was handling the case and offering blanket pardons to associates of Burr who would agree to turn state's evidence. In stark contrast, Chief Justice Marshall, presiding at the trial in his capacity as judge of the circuit court, repeatedly showed favoritism to the prisoner.

In this contest between two great men at their worst, Jefferson as a vindictive executive and Marshall as a prejudiced judge, the victory went to the judge. Organizing "a military assemblage," Marshall declared on his charge to the jury, "was not a levying of war." To "advise or procure treason" was not in itself treason. Unless two independent witnesses testified to an overt act of treason as thus defined, the accused should be declared innocent. The jury, deliberating only twenty-five minutes, found Burr not guilty.

The Burr affair was a blow to Jefferson's prestige; it left him more embittered against Marshall and the federal judiciary, and it added nothing to his reputation as a statesman.

Napoleon and the British

Jefferson's difficulties with Burr may be traced at least in part to the purchase of Louisiana, which, empty and unknown, excited the greed of men like Burr and Wilkinson. But problems infinitely more serious were also related to Louisiana.

Napoleon had jettisoned Louisiana to clear the decks before resuming the battle for control of Europe. This war had the effect of stimulating the American economy, for the warring powers needed American goods and American vessels. Shipbuilding boomed and foreign trade, which had quintupled since 1793, nearly doubled again between 1803 and 1805. By the summer of 1807, however, the situation had changed: An unusual stalemate had developed in the war.

In October 1805 Britain's Horatio Nelson demolished the combined Spanish and French fleets in the Battle of Trafalgar, off the coast of Spain. Napoleon, now at the summit of his powers, quickly redressed the balance, smashing army after army thrown against him by Great Britain's continental allies. By 1807 he was master of Europe, while the British controlled the seas around the Continent. Neither nation could strike directly at the other.

They therefore resorted to commercial warfare, striving to disrupt each other's economy. Napoleon struck first with his Berlin Decree (November 1806), which made "all commerce and correspondence" with Great Britain illegal. The British retaliated with a series of edicts called Orders in Council, blockading most continental ports and barring from them all foreign vessels unless they first stopped at a British port and paid customs duties. Napoleon then issued his Milan Decree (December 1807), declaring any vessel that submitted to the British rules "to have become English property" and thus subject to seizure.

---

[2]John Randolph said that "Wilkinson is the only man that I ever saw who was from the bark to the very core a villain."

American traders in the exchange at a port in China.

When war first broke out between Britain and France in 1792, the colonial trade of both sides had fallen largely into American hands because the danger of capture drove many belligerent merchant vessels from the seas. This commerce had engaged Americans in some devious practices.

For example, American merchants carried sugar from the French colony of Martinique first to the United States, a legal peacetime voyage under French mercantilism. Then they reshipped it to France as American sugar. Since the United States was a neutral nation and sugar was not contraband of war, the Americans expected the British to let their ships pass with impunity. Continental products likewise reached the French West Indies by way of United States ports, and the American government encouraged the traffic in both directions by refunding customs duties on foreign products reshipped within a year.

This underhanded commerce irritated the British. Thus just when Britain and France were cracking down on direct trade by neutrals, Britain determined to halt the American reexport trade, thereby gravely threatening American prosperity.

The Impressment Controversy

More dismaying were the cruel indignities being visited on American seamen by the British practice of **impressment**. Under British law any able-bodied subject could be drafted for service in the Royal Navy in an emergency. Normally, when the commander of a warship found himself shorthanded, he put into a British port and sent a "press gang" ashore to round up the necessary men in harborside pubs. When far from home waters, he might hail any passing British merchant ship and commandeer the necessary men, though this practice was understandably unpopular in British maritime circles. He might also stop a *neutral* merchant vessel on the high seas and remove any British subject. Since the United States owned by far the largest merchant fleet among the neutrals, its vessels bore the brunt of this practice.

Many British captains made little effort to be sure they were impressing British subjects. Furthermore, there were legal questions in dispute. When did an English immigrant become an American? When he was naturalized, the United States claimed. Never, the British retorted: "once an Englishman, always an Englishman."

The Jefferson administration conceded the right of the British to impress their own subjects from American merchant ships. When naturalized Americans were impressed, however, the administration was irritated, and when native-born Americans were taken, it became incensed. Impressment, Secretary of State Madison said in 1807, was "anomalous in principle . . . grievous in practice, and . . . abominable in abuse." Between 1803 and 1812 at least 5,000 sailors were snatched from the decks of United States vessels and forced to serve in the Royal Navy. Most of them—estimates run as high as three out of every four—were Americans.

The combination of impressment, British interference with the reexport trade, and the general harassment of neutral commerce instituted by both Great Britain and France would have perplexed the most informed and hardheaded of leaders, and in dealing with these problems Jefferson was neither informed nor hardheaded. He believed it much wiser to stand up for one's rights than to compromise, yet he hated the very thought of war. Perhaps, being a Southerner, he was less sensitive than he might have been to the needs of New England commercial interests. While the American merchant fleet passed 600,000 tons and continued to grow at an annual rate of over 10 percent, Jefferson kept only a skeleton navy on active service, despite the fact that the great powers were fighting a worldwide, no-holds-barred war. Instead of building a navy that other nations would have to respect, he relied on a tiny fleet of frigates and a swarm of gunboats that were useless against the Royal Navy—"a macabre monument," in the words of one historian, "to his hasty, ill-digested ideas" about defense.[3]

The Embargo Act

The frailty of Jefferson's policy became obvious once the warring powers began to attack neutral shipping in earnest. Between 1803 and 1807 the British seized more than 500 American ships, Napoleon more than 200. The United States could do nothing.

---

[3]The gunboats had performed effectively against the Barbary pirates, but Jefferson was enamored of them mainly because they were cheap. A gunboat cost about $10,000 to build, a big frigate over $300,000.

The Ograbme ("embargo" spelled backward), a snapping turtle drawn by cartoonist Alexander Anderson, frustrates an American tobacco smuggler.
Source: Collection of The New-York Historical Society, [Neg. No. 7278].

The ultimate in frustration came on June 22, 1807, off Norfolk, Virginia. The American forty-six-gun frigate *Chesapeake* had just left port for patrol duty in the Mediterranean. Among its crew were a British sailor who had deserted from HMS *Halifax* and three Americans who had been illegally impressed by the captain of HMS *Melampus* and had later escaped. The *Chesapeake* was barely out of sight of land when HMS *Leopard* (fifty-six guns) approached and signaled it to heave to. Thinking that *Leopard* wanted to make some routine communication, Captain James Barron did so. A British officer came aboard and demanded that the four "deserters" be handed over to him. Barron refused, whereupon as soon as the officer was back on board, *Leopard* opened fire on the unsuspecting American ship, killing three sailors. Barron had to surrender. The "deserters" were seized, and then the crippled *Chesapeake* was allowed to limp back to port.

The attack was in violation of international law, for no nation claimed the right to impress sailors from warships. The British government admitted this, though it delayed making restitution for years. The American press clamored for war, but the country had nothing to fight with. Jefferson contented himself with ordering British warships out of American territorial waters. However, he was determined to put a stop to the indignities being heaped on the flag by Great Britain and France. The result was the **Embargo Act**.

The Embargo Act prohibited all exports. American vessels could not clear for any foreign port, and foreign vessels could do so only if empty. Although the law was sure to injure the American economy, Jefferson hoped that it would work in two ways to benefit the nation. By keeping U.S. merchant ships off the seas, it would end all chance of injury to them and to the national honor. By cutting off American goods and markets, it would

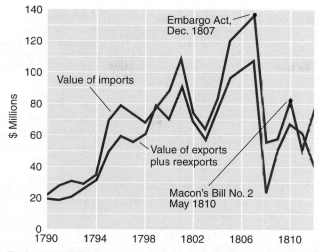

American Foreign Trade, 1790–1812 This graph shows the embargo's effects. The space between the upper (import) and the lower (export) line indicates a persistent foreign-trade deficit.

put great economic pressure on Britain and France to moderate policies toward American shipping.

Seldom has a law been so bitterly resented and resisted by a large segment of the public. It demanded of the maritime interests far greater sacrifices than they could reasonably be expected to make. Massachusetts-owned ships alone were earning over $15 million a year in freight charges by 1807, and Bay State merchants were making far larger gains from the buying and selling of goods. Foreign commerce was the most expansive force in the economy, the chief reason for the nation's prosperity. As John Randolph remarked in a typical sally, the administration was trying "to cure the corns by cutting off the toes."

The Embargo Act had catastrophic effects. Exports fell from $108 million in 1807 to $22 million in 1808, imports from $138 million to less than $57 million. Prices of farm products and manufactured goods reacted violently, seamen were thrown out of work, and merchants found their businesses disrupted.

Surely the embargo was a mistake. The United States ought either to have suffered the indignities heaped on its vessels for the sake of profits or, by constructing a powerful navy, made it dangerous for the belligerents to treat its merchant ships so roughly. Jefferson was too proud to choose the former alternative, too parsimonious to choose the latter. Instead he applied harsher and harsher regulations in a futile effort to accomplish his purpose. Jefferson refused to admit that the embargo was a fiasco and urge its repeal. Only in his last week in office did a leaderless Congress finally abolish it, substituting the Non-Intercourse Act, which forbade trade only with Great Britain and France and authorized the president to end the boycott against either power by proclamation when and if it stopped violating the rights of Americans.

Thus Jefferson's political career ended on a sour note. Several weeks after he had left office and returned to Monticello, he privately advised his successor, James Madison, to trust his own judgment to govern because the people readily succumbed to "the floating lies of the day."

Table 6.1   Jeffersonian Doctrine: Small Federal Government

Measure	Advantages	Disadvantages
Repealed whiskey and other taxes on imports (excise)	Reduced taxes	Lowered federal revenue
Curtailed military and naval spending	Reduction in federal debt	Weak navy: Foreign powers could "impress" American sailors and seize American ships
Embargo Act (1807): no export trade	End to humiliations at the hand of British and French warships	Collapse of foreign trade, weakening of economy, increased smuggling

Jeffersonian Democracy

Yet Jefferson completed the construction of the political institution known as the Republican party and the philosophy of government known as Jeffersonian democracy. In part his success was a matter of personality; he was perfectly in tune with the thinking of his times. The colonial American had practiced democracy without really believing in it, for example, the maintenance of property qualifications for voting in regions where nearly everyone owned property. Stimulated by the libertarian ideas of the Revolution, Americans were rapidly adjusting their beliefs to conform with their practices. However, it took Jefferson, possessed of the general prejudice in favor of the old-fashioned citizen rooted in the soil, yet deeply committed to majority rule, to oversee the transition.

Jefferson's marvelous talents as a writer help explain his success. He expounded his ideas in language that few people could resist. He had a remarkable facility for discovering practical arguments to justify his beliefs—as when he suggested that by letting everyone vote, elections would be made more honest because with large numbers going to the polls, bribery would become prohibitively expensive.

Jefferson prepared the country for democracy by proving that a democrat could establish and maintain a stable regime. The Federalist tyranny of 1798 was compounded of selfishness and stupidity, but it was also based in part on honest fears that an egalitarian regime would not protect the fabric of society from hotheads and crackpots. The impact of the French Revolution on conservative thinking in the mid-1790s cannot be overestimated. America had fought a seven-year revolution without executing a single Tory, yet during the few months that the Reign of Terror ravaged France, nearly 17,000 persons were officially put to death for political "crimes" and many thousands more were killed in civil disturbances. Worse, in the opinion of many, the French extremists had attempted to destroy Christianity, substituting for it a "cult of reason." Little wonder that many Americans feared that the Jeffersonians, lovers of France and of *liberté, égalité, fraternité*, would try to remodel American society in a similar way.

Jefferson calmed these fears. The most partisan Federalist was hard put to see a Robespierre, leader during the Reign of Terror in France, in the amiable Jefferson scratching out state papers at his desk or chatting with a Kentucky congressman at a

The storming of the Bastille in 1789. After the crowd seizes the fortification, they tear it down, stone by stone.

"republican" dinner party. Furthermore, Jefferson accepted Federalist ideas on public finance, even learning to live with Hamilton's bank. As a good democrat, he drew a nice distinction between his own opinions and the wishes of the majority, which he felt must always take priority. Even in his first inaugural address he admitted that manufacturing and commerce were, along with agriculture, the "pillars of our prosperity," and he accepted the principle that the government should protect them when necessary from "casual embarrassments." During his term the country grew and prospered, the commercial classes sharing in the bounty along with the farmers so close to Jefferson's heart.

Thus Jefferson undermined the Federalists all along the line. They had said that the country must pay a stiff price for prosperity and orderly government, and they demanded prompt payment in full, both in cash (taxes) and in the form of limitations on human liberty. Under Jefferson these much-desired goals had been achieved cheaply and without sacrificing freedom. A land whose riches could only be guessed at had been obtained without firing a shot and without burdening the people with new taxes. Order without discipline, security without a large military establishment, prosperity without regulatory legislation, freedom without license—truly the Sage of Monticello appeared to have led his fellow Americans into a golden age.

Jefferson insisted that one of his chief accomplishments had been to reduce the national debt from $83 million to $57 million. Writing from Monticello shortly after leaving office, he urged his successors to eliminate the remainder. "The discharge of the public debt," he warned Treasury Secretary Gallatin, "is vital to the destinies of our government."

Yet Jefferson had also learned the perils of an inadequately funded government. His unwillingness to build a real navy had rendered the nation vulnerable to foreign states. Conversely, he had exulted in the purchase of Louisiana, and he backed modest proposals for spending federal money on roads, canals, and other projects that, according to his political philosophy, ought to have been left to the states and private individuals. Debt, Jefferson accepted, was sometimes good policy.

Milestones

1801	Judiciary Act of 1801 allows Adams to appoint many Federalist judges	**1804–1806**	Lewis and Clark explore West
	Jefferson is elected president	**1806**	Aaron Burr schemes to take land in West during Burr Conspiracy
1801–1805	U.S. wages war against Barbary pirates in North Africa	**1806–1807**	Napoleon issues Berlin and Milan decrees in order to disrupt British shipping and economy
1803	Supreme Court declares part of Judiciary Act of 1789 unconstitutional (*Marbury v. Madison*)	**1807**	HMS *Leopard* attacks USS *Chesapeake*
	Jefferson negotiates Louisiana Purchase with France		Embargo Act prohibits all exports
1804	Aaron Burr kills Alexander Hamilton in duel	**1809**	Non-Intercourse Act forbids trade with Great Britain and France
	Jefferson is reelected		

✓•⌐**Study** and **Review** at www.myhistorylab.com

Review Questions

1. The Federalist vision of the nation largely prevailed during the 1790s. Why did it fade so rapidly during the 1800s? Was its decline caused by a failure of Federalist leadership or the successes of Jefferson?

2. What effect did the Napoleonic wars have on events in America? Why did Napoleon abandon his dreams of a French economic empire in the Americas?

3. What chief obstacle—literally—stood in the way of an all-water route across the United States connecting the Atlantic and Pacific Oceans?

4. The text asserts that the Embargo Act was "surely" a mistake, yet Jefferson was a savvy politician. How did he decide to propose it in the first place?

Key Terms

Embargo Act   *188*
impressment   *187*
Lewis and Clark expedition   *184*

Louisiana Purchase   *177*
Marbury v. Madison   *176*

National Growing Pains

((•─Hear the Audio Chapter 7 at myhistorylab.com

Does the government help you pay for college?

THE RECESSION THAT STRUCK IN 2008 HIT YOUNG ADULTS THE HARDEST.
By the end of the year, less than half (46 percent) of those aged eighteen to twenty-four
had jobs—the lowest rate on record.[1] Many of those who couldn't find jobs decided to go
to college. This influx produced another record in 2008: More young adults ages eighteen
to twenty-four were enrolled in either two- or four-year colleges than ever before. The chief
enrollment increase was in community colleges, whose costs (tuition, fees, books and
expenses) averaged $7,000, compared to four-year public colleges ($10,000) and four-year
private colleges ($27,000).

But how could young people pay for college during a severe recession? The federal
government provided the answer—through loans for college, chiefly Pell grants. By
2010, for example, nearly 8 million students received Pell grants averaging $3,700 with
a maximum grant of $5,500.

That the federal government would one day play so profound a role in the lives of its
people would have astonished the founding generation. Well into the nineteenth century,
the federal government failed to generate much income. In 1809 its total revenue fell short
of $8 million. Of that, $7 million came from taxes on imports (the tariff); the balance
came mostly from the sale of federal lands and postage stamps. Without income from the
tariff, the federal government could have done little more than deliver the mail.

From 1809 to 1828, Americans repeatedly expanded the role of the federal government. Armies and navies were raised to subdue the Indians and defend the nation from
European predators; highways were built to encourage trade and promote settlement
of the Louisiana territories. The federal budget tripled. The nation was growing, and the
federal government grew with it. The tariff inevitably increased as well. The 1828 "**Tariff
of Abominations**" was the highest to that time.

But the sharp increase in the tariff, and in the role of the federal government, sent
shock waves through American society. As the tariff raised the price of manufactured
goods, farmers had to pay more for clothing and farm implements. Worse, Britain and

---

[1]The federal government began tracking such data in 1948.

other foreign nations retaliated against high American tariffs by setting their own high tariffs on American imports—chiefly tobacco, cotton, wheat, and other foodstuffs mostly grown in the South and West. This angered southern farmers because it made their products more expensive—and so less desirable—in foreign markets.

The tariff pitted one section of the nation against another, especially North vs. South. The years from 1809 to 1828 were marked by growth and governmental expansion; but new problems—none more important than the question of slavery—loomed ever larger and more menacing.

Madison in Power

In his inaugural address, James Madison observed that the "present situation" of the United States was "full of difficulties" and that war continued to rage among European powers. Yet he assumed the presidency, he said, "with no other discouragement than what springs from my own inadequacy." The content of the speech was as modest as its delivery; virtually no one could hear it.

Read the Document

Madison, *First Inaugural Address* at **myhistorylab.com**

Madison was narrower in his interests than Jefferson but in many ways a deeper thinker. He was more conscientious in the performance of his duties and more consistent in adhering to his principles. Ideologically, however, they were as close as two active and intelligent people could be. Madison had no better solution to offer for the problem of the hour than had Jefferson. The Embargo Act had failed and its successor, the Non-Intercourse Act, proved difficult to enforce—once an American ship left port, there was no way to prevent the skipper from steering for England or France. The British continued to seize American vessels.

Because prudent captains remained in port, trade stagnated. Federal revenue through the tariff declined. In 1809, Secretary of the Treasury Gallatin was alarmed by the growing federal deficit. He urged Representative Nathaniel Macon of North Carolina to introduce legislation to remove all restrictions on commerce with France and Britain. Known as Macon's Bill No. 2, it authorized the president to reapply the principle of non-intercourse to either of the major powers if the other should "cease to violate the neutral commerce of the United States." This bill became law in May 1810.

The volume of U.S. commerce with the British Isles zoomed to pre-embargo levels. The mighty British fleet controlled the seas. Napoleon therefore announced that he had repealed his decrees against neutral shipping, seemingly fulfilling the provisions of Macon's Bill No. 2. Madison, seeking concessions from Britain, closed American ports to British ships and goods. Napoleon, despite his announcement to the contrary, continued to seize American ships and cargoes whenever it suited his purposes.

The British refused to modify the Orders in Council. Madison could not afford either to admit that Napoleon had deceived him or to reverse American policy still another time. Reluctantly he came to the conclusion that unless Britain repealed the Orders, the United States must declare war.

Tecumseh and Indian Resistance

There were other reasons for war with Britain besides its violations of neutral rights. The Indians were again restive, and western farmers believed that the British in Canada were egging them on. This had been true in the past but was no longer the case in 1811 and 1812.

As a young man Tecumseh was a superb hunter and warrior; his younger brother, Tenskwatawa, was awkward and inept with weapons; he accidentally gouged out his right eye with an arrow. In 1805 he had a religious vision, became known as "The Prophet," and inspired Tecumseh's warriors.

American domination of the southern Great Lakes region was no longer in question. Canadian officials had no desire to force a showdown between the Indians and the Americans, for that could have but one result. Aware of their own vulnerability, the Canadians wanted to preserve Indian strength in case war should break out between Great Britain and the United States.

•••▸Read the Document

Pennsylvania *Gazette*, "Indian hostilities" at myhistorylab.com

American political leaders tended to believe that Indians should be encouraged to become farmers and to copy the "civilized" ways of whites. However, no government had been able to control the frontiersmen, who by bribery, trickery, and force were driving the tribes back year after year from the rich lands of the Ohio Valley. General William Henry Harrison, governor of the Indiana Territory, kept constant pressure on them. He wrested land from one tribe by promising it aid against a traditional enemy, from another as a penalty for having murdered a white man, from others by corrupting a few chiefs. Harrison justified his sordid behavior by citing the end in view—that "one of the fairest portions of the globe" be secured as "the seat of civilization, of science, and of true religion." The "wretched savages" should not be allowed to stand in the path of this worthy objective. Unless something drastic was done, Harrison's aggressiveness, together with the corroding effects of white civilization, would soon obliterate the tribes.

Tecumseh, the Shawnee chief, made a bold and imaginative effort to reverse the trend by binding all the tribes east of the Mississippi into a great confederation. Traveling from the Wisconsin country to the Floridas, he persuaded tribe after tribe to join him.

To Tecumseh's political movement his brother Tenskwatawa, known as "The Prophet," added the force of a moral crusade. Instead of aping white customs, the Prophet said that Indians must give up white ways, white clothes, and white liquor and reinvigorate their own culture. Ceding lands to the whites must stop because the Great Spirit intended that the land be used in common by all.

The Prophet saw visions and claimed to be able to control the movement of heavenly bodies. Tecumseh, however, possessed true genius. A powerful orator and a great organizer, he had deep insight into the needs of his people. Harrison himself said of Tecumseh, "He is one of those uncommon geniuses which spring up occasionally to produce revolutions and overturn the established order of things." The two brothers made a formidable team. By 1811 thousands of Indians were organizing to drive the whites off Indian land.

With about a thousand soldiers, General Harrison marched against the brothers' camp at Prophetstown in Indiana. Tecumseh was away recruiting men, and the Prophet recklessly ordered an assault on Harrison's camp outside the village on November 7, 1811. When the white soldiers held their ground despite the Prophet's magic, the Indians lost confidence and fell back. Harrison then destroyed Prophetstown.

Unwilling as usual to admit that their own excesses were the chief cause of the trouble, the settlers directed their resentment at the British in Canada. "This combination headed by the Shawanese prophet is a British scheme," a resolution adopted by the citizens of Vincennes, Indiana, proclaimed. As a result, the cry for war with Great Britain rang along the frontier.

Depression and Land Hunger

Some westerners pressed for war because they were suffering an agricultural depression. The prices they received for their wheat, tobacco, and other products in the markets of New Orleans were falling, and they attributed the decline to the loss of foreign markets and the depredations of the British. American commercial restrictions had more to do with the western depression than the British, and in any case the slow and cumbersome transportation and distribution system that western farmers were saddled with was the major cause of their difficulties. But the farmers were no more inclined to accept these explanations than they were to absolve the British from responsibility for the Indian difficulties. If only the seas were free, they reasoned, costs would go down, prices would rise, and prosperity would return.

It was primarily because of Canada, nearby and presumably vulnerable, that westerners wanted war. President Madison probably regarded an attack on Canada as a way to force the British to respect neutral rights. Still more important in Madison's mind, if the United States conquered Canada, Britain's hope of obtaining food in Canada for its West Indian sugar islands would be shattered. Then it would have to end its hateful assaults and restrictions on American merchant ships or the islands' economy would collapse.

But westerners, and many easterners too, were more patriots than imperialists or merchants in 1811 and 1812. When the **War Hawks** (their young leaders in Congress) called for war against Great Britain, they did so because they saw no other way to defend the national honor and force repeal of the Orders in Council. The choice seemed to lie between war and surrender of true independence. As Madison put it, to bow to British policy would be to "recolonize" American foreign commerce.

Opponents of War

Large numbers of people, however, thought that a war against Great Britain would be a national calamity. No shipowner could view with equanimity the idea of taking on the largest navy in the world. Such persons complained sincerely enough about impressment and the Orders in Council, but war seemed worse to them by far. Self-interest led them to urge patience.

Such a policy would have been wise, for Great Britain did not represent a real threat to the United States. British naval officers were high-handed, officials in London complacent, British diplomats in Washington second-rate and obtuse. Yet language, culture, and strong economic ties bound the two countries. Napoleon, on the other hand, represented a tremendous potential danger. He had offhandedly turned over Louisiana, but even Jefferson, the chief beneficiary of his largesse, hated everything he stood for. Jefferson called Napoleon "an unprincipled tyrant who is deluging the continent of Europe with blood."

No one understood the Napoleonic danger to America more clearly than the British; part of the stubbornness and arrogance of their maritime policy grew out of their conviction that Napoleon was a threat to all free nations. The *Times* of London declared, "The Alps and the Apennines of America are the British Navy. If ever that should be removed, a short time will suffice to establish the headquarters of a [French] Duke-Marshal at Washington." Yet by going to war with Britain, the United States was aiding Napoleon.

What made the situation even more unfortunate was the fact that by 1812 conditions had changed in England in a way that made a softening of British maritime policy likely. A depression caused chiefly by the increasing effectiveness of Napoleon's Continental System was plaguing the country. Manufacturers, blaming the slump on the loss of American markets, were urging repeal of the Orders in Council. On June 23, after a change of ministries, the new foreign secretary, Lord Castlereagh, suspended the Orders. Five days earlier, alas, the United States had declared war.

The War of 1812

In the first phase of the war, 1812–1813, the United States attempted to invade Canada near Detroit, Buffalo, and Plattsburgh (New York); it failed. In the second phase, 1814, the British invaded the Chesapeake and burned Washington, DC. The final phase of the war occurred from November 1814 to early 1815, after the Treaty of Ghent was signed. British troops landed at the mouth of the Mississippi River and were defeated by General Andrew Jackson at New Orleans.

The illogic of the War Hawks in pressing for a fight was exceeded only by their ineffectiveness in planning and managing what would become the **War of 1812**. By what possible strategy could the ostensible objective of the war be achieved? To construct a navy capable of challenging the British fleet would have been the work of many years and a more expensive proposition than the War Hawks were willing to consider. Several hundred merchant ships lashed a few cannon to their decks and sailed off as privateers to attack British commerce. The navy's seven modern frigates, built during the war scare after the XYZ Affair, put to sea. But these forces could make no pretense of disputing Britain's mastery of the Atlantic.

For a brief moment the American frigates held center stage, for they were faster, tougher, larger, and more powerfully armed than their British counterparts. Barely two months after the declaration of war, Captain Isaac Hull of the USS *Constitution* chanced upon the HMS *Guerrière* mid-Atlantic, outmaneuvered the *Guerrière* brilliantly, and gunned it into submission. In October the USS *United States* caught the HMS *Macedonian* off the Madeiras, pounded it unmercifully at long range, and forced the British

The USS *Constitution*, restored in 1997.

ship to surrender. The *Macedonian* was taken into New London as a prize; over a third of the 300-man crew were casualties, while American losses were but a dozen. Then, in December, the *Constitution*, now under Captain William Bainbridge, took on the British frigate *Java* off Brazil. "Old Ironsides" shot away *Java's* mainmast and reduced it to a hulk too battered for salvage.

These victories had little influence on the outcome of the war. The Royal Navy had thirty-four frigates, seven more powerful ships of the line, and dozens of smaller vessels. As soon as these forces could concentrate against them, the American frigates were immobilized, forced to spend the war gathering barnacles at their moorings while powerful British squadrons ranged offshore. The privateering merchantmen were more effective because they were so numerous; they captured more than 1,300 British vessels during the war. The best of them—vessels like the *America* and the *True-Blooded Yankee*—were redesigned, given more sail to increase their speed, and formidably armed. The *America* captured twenty-six prizes valued at more than a million dollars. The *True-Blooded Yankee* took twenty-seven vessels and destroyed seven more in a Scottish harbor.

Great Britain's one weak spot seemed to be Canada. The colony had but half a million inhabitants to oppose 7.5 million Americans. Only 2,257 British regulars guarded the long border from Montréal to Detroit. The Canadian militia was feeble, and many of its members, being American-born, sympathized with the "invaders." According to the War Hawk congressman Henry Clay of Kentucky, the West was one solid horde of ferocious frontiersmen, armed to the teeth and thirsting for Canadian blood. Yet such talk was mostly brag and bluster; when Congress authorized increasing the army by 25,000 men, Kentucky produced 400 enlistments.

American military leadership proved extremely disappointing. Madison showed poor judgment by relying on officers who had served with distinction in the Revolution. Instead of a concentrated strike against Canada's St. Lawrence River lifeline, which would have isolated Upper Canada, the generals planned a complicated three-pronged attack. It failed dismally. In July 1812 General William Hull, veteran of the battles of Trenton, Saratoga, and Monmouth and now governor of the Michigan Territory, marched forth with 2,200 men against the Canadian positions facing Detroit. Hoping that the Canadian militia would desert, he delayed his assault, only to find his communications threatened by hostile Indians led by Tecumseh. Hastily he retreated to Detroit, and when the Canadians, under General Isaac Brock, pursued him, he surrendered the fort without firing a shot! In October

In the heat of the Battle of Lake Erie, Perry had to abandon his flagship, the *Lawrence*, which had been shot to pieces by enemy fire. (Over three-fourths of the ship's crew were killed or wounded.) He was rowed to the *Niagara*, from which he directed the rest of the engagement.

another force attempted to invade Canada from Fort Niagara. After an initial success it was crushed by superior numbers, while a large contingent of New York militiamen watched from the east bank of the Niagara River, unwilling to fight outside their own state.

The third arm of the American "attack" was equally unsuccessful. Major General Henry Dearborn, who had fought honorably in the Revolution from Bunker Hill to Yorktown, but who had now grown so fat that he needed a specially designed cart to get from place to place, set out from Plattsburgh, New York, at the head of an army of militiamen. Their objective was Montréal, but when they reached the border, the troops refused to cross. Dearborn meekly marched them back to Plattsburgh.

Meanwhile, the British had captured Fort Michilimackinac in northern Michigan, and the Indians had taken Fort Dearborn (now Chicago), massacring eighty-five captives. Instead of sweeping triumphantly through Canada, the Americans found themselves trying desperately to keep the Canadians out of Ohio.

Stirred by these disasters, westerners rallied somewhat in 1813. General Harrison, the victor of Tippecanoe, headed an army of Kentuckians in a series of inconclusive battles against British troops and Indians led by Tecumseh. He found it impossible to recapture Detroit because a British squadron controlling Lake Erie threatened his communications. President Madison therefore assigned Captain Oliver Hazard Perry to the task of building a fleet to challenge this force. In September 1813, at Put-in-Bay near the western end of the lake, Perry destroyed the British vessels in a battle in which 85 of the 103 men on Perry's flagship were casualties. "We have met the enemy and

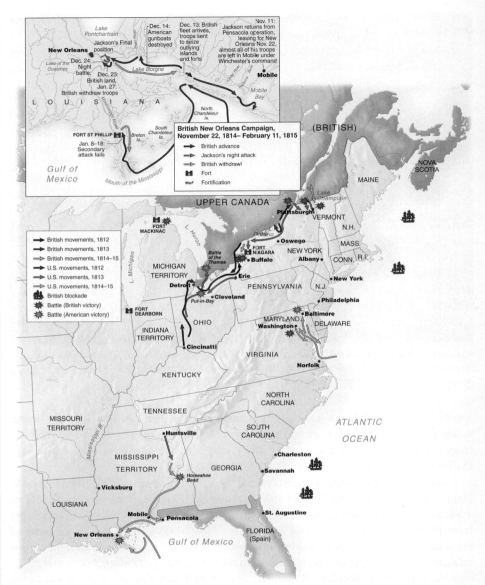

The War of 1812 In the first phase of the war, 1812–1813, the United States attempted to invade Canada near Detroit, Buffalo, and Plattsburgh (New York); it failed. In the second phase, 1814, the British invaded the Chesapeake and burned Washington, DC. The final phase of the war occurred from November 1814 to early 1815, after the Treaty of Ghent was signed. British troops landed at the mouth of the Mississippi River and were defeated by General Andrew Jackson at New Orleans.

they are ours," he reported. About a quarter of Perry's 400 men were blacks, which led him to remark that "the color of a man's skin" was no more an indication of his worth than "the cut and trimmings" of his coat. With the Americans in control of Lake Erie, Detroit became untenable for the British, and when they fell back, Harrison gave chase and defeated them at the Thames River, some 60 miles northeast of Detroit. Although little more than a skirmish, this battle had large repercussions. Tecumseh was among the dead and without him the Indians lost heart. But American attempts to win control of Lake Ontario and to invade Canada in the Niagara region were again thrown back. Late in 1813 the British captured Fort Niagara and burned the town of Buffalo. The conquest of Canada was as far from realization as ever.

The British fleet had intensified its blockade of American ports, extending its operations to New England waters previously spared to encourage the antiwar sentiments of local maritime interests. All along the coast, patrolling cruisers, contemptuous of Jefferson's puny gunboats, captured small craft, raided shore points to commandeer provisions, and collected ransom from port towns by threatening to bombard them. One captain even sent a detail ashore to dig potatoes for his ship's mess.

Britain Assumes the Offensive

Until 1814 the British put relatively little effort into the American war, being concerned primarily with the struggle against Napoleon. However, in 1812 Napoleon had invaded Russia and been thrown back; thereafter, one by one, his European satellites rose against him. Gradually he relinquished his conquests, and in April 1814 the Allies drove Napoleon from power. Then the British, free to strike hard at the United States, dispatched some 14,000 veterans to Canada.

By the spring of 1814 British strategists had devised a master plan for crushing the United States. One army, 11,000 strong, was to march from Montréal, tracing the route that General Burgoyne had followed to disaster in the Revolution. A smaller amphibious force was to make a feint at the Chesapeake Bay area, destroying coastal towns and threatening Washington and Baltimore. A third army was to assemble at Jamaica and sail to attack New Orleans and bottle up the West.

While the main British army was assembling in Canada, some 4,000 veterans under General Robert Ross sailed from Bermuda for the Chesapeake. After making a rendezvous with a fleet commanded by Vice Admiral Sir Alexander Cochrane and Rear Admiral Sir George Cockburn, which had been terrorizing the coast, they landed in Maryland at the mouth of the Patuxent River, southeast of Washington. A squadron of gunboats "protecting" the capital promptly withdrew upstream; when the British pursued, their commander ordered them blown up to keep them from being captured.

The British troops marched rapidly toward Washington. At Bladensburg, on the outskirts of the city, they came upon an army twice their number, commanded by General William H. Winder, a Baltimore lawyer who had already been captured and released by the British in the Canadian fighting. While President Madison and other officials watched, the British charged—and Winder's army turned tail almost without firing a shot. The British swarmed into the capital and put most public buildings to the torch. Before personally setting fire to the White House, Admiral Cockburn took one of the president's hats and a cushion from Dolley Madison's chair as souvenirs, and, finding the table set for dinner, derisively drank a toast to "Jemmy's health."

●●●[Read the Document
Dolley Payne Madison to Lucy Payne Todd at
myhistorylab.com

This was the sum of the British success. When they attempted to take Baltimore, they were stopped by a formidable line of defenses devised by General Samuel Smith, a militia officer. General Ross fell in the attack. The fleet then moved up the Patapsco

River and pounded Fort McHenry with its cannon, raining 1,800 shells upon it in a twenty-five-hour bombardment on September 13 and 14.

"The Star Spangled Banner"

While this attack was in progress, an American civilian, Francis Scott Key, who had been temporarily detained on one of the British ships, watched anxiously through the night. As twilight faded, Key had seen the Stars and Stripes flying proudly over the battered fort. During the night the glare of rockets and bursting of bombs proved that the defenders were holding out. Then, by the first light of the new day, Key saw again the flag, still waving over Fort McHenry. Drawing an old letter from his pocket, he dashed off the words to "The Star Spangled Banner," which, when set to music, was to become the national anthem of the United States.

To Key that dawn seemed a turning point in the war. He was roughly correct, for in those last weeks of the summer of 1814 the struggle began to move toward resolution. Unable to crack the defenses of Baltimore, the British withdrew to their ships; shortly after, they sailed to Jamaica to join the forces preparing to attack New Orleans.

The destruction of Washington had been a profound shock. Thousands came forward to enlist in the army. The new determination and spirit were strengthened by news from the northern front, where General Sir George Prevost had been leading the main British invasion force south from Montréal. At Plattsburgh, on the western shore of Lake Champlain, his 1,000 Redcoats came up against a well-designed defense line manned by 3,300 Americans under General Alexander Macomb. Prevost called up his

The Bombardment of Fort McHenry by John Bower, with the Stars and Stripes flying over the fort (center). The British fleet fired 1,800 bombs and red-glaring incendiary rockets. The fort did not return fire because the British ships were beyond the range of its cannon. Although "The Star Spangled Banner" celebrates the "home of the brave," the defenders of Fort McHenry sensibly fled the ramparts and took cover below during the bombardment; they sustained only thirty casualties.

supporting fleet of four ships and a dozen gunboats. An American fleet of roughly similar strength under Captain Thomas Macdonough came forward to oppose the British. On September 11, in a brutal battle at point-blank range, Macdonough destroyed the British ships and drove off the gunboats. With the Americans now threatening his flank, Prevost lost heart and retreated to Canada.

The Treaty of Ghent

The war might as well have ended with the battles of Plattsburgh, Washington, and Baltimore, for later military developments had no effect on the outcome. Earlier in 1814 both sides had agreed to discuss peace terms. Commissioners were appointed and negotiations begun during the summer at Ghent, in Belgium.

The talks at Ghent were drawn out and frustrating. The British were in no hurry to sign a treaty, believing that their three-pronged offensive in 1814 would swing the balance in their favor. But news of the defeat at Plattsburgh modified their ambitions, and when the Duke of Wellington advised that from a military point of view they had no case for territorial concessions so long as the United States controlled the Great Lakes, they agreed to settle for *status quo ante bellum*, to leave things as they were before the war. The other issues, everyone suddenly realized, had simply evaporated. The mighty war triggered by the French Revolution seemed finally over. The seas were free to all ships, and the Royal Navy no longer had need to snatch sailors from the vessels of the United States or of any other power. On Christmas Eve 1814 the treaty, which merely ended the state of hostilities, was signed. Although, like other members of his family, he was not noted for tact, John Quincy Adams rose to the spirit of the occasion. "I hope," he said, "it will be the last treaty of peace between Great Britain and the United States." And so it was.

●●●—Read the Document
The Treaty of Ghent at
myhistorylab.com

The Hartford Convention

Before news of the treaty could cross the Atlantic, two events took place that had important effects but that would not have occurred had the news reached America more rapidly. The first was the **Hartford Convention**, a meeting of New England Federalists held in December 1814 and January 1815 to protest the war and to plan for a convention of the states to revise the Constitution.

Sentiment in New England had opposed the war from the beginning. The governor of Massachusetts titled his annual address in 1813 "On the Present Unhappy War," and the General Court went on record calling the conflict "impolitic, improper, and unjust." The Federalist party had been quick to employ the discontent to revive its fortunes. Federalist-controlled state administrations refused to provide militia to aid in the fight and discouraged individuals and banks from lending money to the hard-pressed national government. Trade with the enemy flourished as long as the British fleet did not crack down on New England ports, and goods flowed across the Canadian line in as great or greater volume as during Jefferson's embargo.

Their attitude toward the war made the Federalists even more unpopular with the rest of the country, and this in turn encouraged extremists to talk of seceding from the Union. After Massachusetts summoned the meeting of the Hartford Convention, the fear was widespread that the delegates would propose a New England Confederacy, thereby striking at the Union in a moment of great trial.

Luckily for the country, moderate Federalists controlled the convention. They approved a statement that in the case of "deliberate, dangerous and palpable infractions of the Constitution" a state has the right "to interpose its authority" to protect itself. This concept, similar to that expressed in the Kentucky and Virginia resolutions by the Republicans when they were in the minority, was accompanied by a list of proposed constitutional amendments designed to weaken the federal government, reduce Congress's power to restrict trade, and limit presidents to a single term.

Nothing formally proposed at Hartford was treasonable, but the proceedings were kept secret, and rumors of impending secession were rife. In this atmosphere came the news from Ghent of an honorable peace. The Federalists had been denouncing the war and predicting a British triumph; now they were discredited.

The Battle of New Orleans and the End of the War

Still more discrediting to Federalists was the second event that would not have happened had communications been more rapid: the Battle of New Orleans. During the fall of 1814 the British had gathered an army at Negril Bay in Jamaica, commanded by Major General Sir Edward Pakenham, brother-in-law of the Duke of Wellington. Late in November an armada of sixty ships set out for New Orleans with 11,000 soldiers. Instead of sailing directly up from the mouth of the Mississippi as the Americans expected, Pakenham approached the city by way of Lake Borgne, to the east. Proceeding through a maze of swamps and bayous, he advanced close to the city's gates before being detected. Early on the afternoon of December 23, three mud-spattered local planters burst into the headquarters of General Andrew Jackson, commanding the defenses of New Orleans, with the news.

For once in this war of error and incompetence the United States had the right man in the right place at the right time. After his Revolutionary War experiences, Jackson had studied law, then moved west, settling in Nashville, Tennessee. He served briefly in both houses of Congress and was active in Tennessee affairs. Jackson was a hard man and fierce-tempered, frequently involved in brawls and duels, but honest and, by western standards, a good public servant. When the war broke out, he was named major general of volunteers. Almost alone among nonprofessional troops during the conflict, his men won impressive victories, savagely crushing the Creek Indians in a series of battles in Alabama.

Following these victories, Jackson was assigned the job of defending the Gulf Coast against the expected British strike. Although he had misjudged Pakenham's destination, he was ready when the news of the British arrival reached him. "By the Eternal," he vowed, "they shall not sleep on our soil." "Gentlemen," he told his staff officers, "the British are below, we must fight them tonight."

While the British rested and awaited reinforcements, planning to take the city the next morning, Jackson rushed up men and guns. At 7:30 PM on December 23 he attacked, taking the British by surprise. But Pakenham's veterans rallied quickly, and the battle was inconclusive. With Redcoats pouring in from the fleet, Jackson fell back to a point five miles below New Orleans and dug in.

He chose his position wisely. On his right was the Mississippi, on his left an impenetrable swamp, to the front an open field. On the day before Christmas (while the commissioners in Ghent were signing the peace treaty), Jackson's army, which included a segregated unit of free black militiamen, erected an earthen parapet about ten yards behind a dry canal bed. Here the Americans would make their stand.

General Andrew Jackson, on the horse, exhorts his men to throw back the advancing British; they succeed, and Jackson becomes a war hero.

For two weeks Pakenham probed the American line. Jackson strengthened his defenses daily. At night, patrols of silent Tennesseans slipped out with knives and toma-hawks to stalk British sentries. They called this grim business "going hunting." On January 8, 1815, Pakenham ordered an all-out frontal assault. The American position was formidable, but these were men who had defeated Napoleon. At dawn, through the lowland mists, the Redcoats moved forward with fixed bayonets. Pakenham assumed that the undisciplined Americans—about 4,500 strong—would run at the sight of bare steel.

The Americans did not run. Perhaps they feared the wrath of their commander more than enemy bayonets. Artillery raked the advancing British, and when the range closed to about 150 yards, the riflemen opened up. Jackson had formed his men in three ranks behind the parapet. One rank fired, then stepped down as another took its place. By the time the third had loosed its volley, the first had reloaded and was ready to fire again. Nothing could stand against this rain of lead. General Pakenham was wounded twice, then killed by a shell fragment while calling up his last reserves. During the battle a single brave British officer reached the top of the parapet. When retreat was finally sounded, the British had suffered almost 2,100 casualties, including nearly 300 killed. Thirteen Americans lost their lives, and fifty-eight more were wounded or missing.

Word of Jackson's magnificent triumph reached Washington almost simultaneously with the good news from Ghent. People found it easy to confuse the chronology and con-sider the war a victory won on the battlefield below New Orleans instead of the standoff it had been. Jackson became the "Hero of New Orleans"; his proud fellow citizens rated his military abilities superior to those of the Duke of Wellington. The nation rejoiced. One sour Republican complained that the Federalists of Massachusetts had fired off more pow-der and wounded more men celebrating the victory than they had during the whole course of the conflict. The Senate ratified the peace treaty unanimously, and the frustrations and failures of the past few years were forgotten. Moreover, American success in holding off Great Britain despite internal frictions went a long way toward convincing European nations that both the United States and its republican form of government were here to stay. The powers might accept these truths with less pleasure than the Americans, but accept them they did.

Anglo-American Rapprochement

There remained a few matters to straighten out with Great Britain, Spain, and Europe generally. Since no territory had changed hands at Ghent, neither signatory had reason to harbor a grudge. For years no serious trouble marred Anglo-American relations. The war had taught the British to respect Americans, if not to love them.

In this atmosphere the two countries worked out peaceful solutions to a number of old problems. American trade was becoming ever more important to the British, that of the sugar islands less so. In July 1815 they therefore signed a commercial convention ending discriminatory duties and making other adjustments favorable to trade. Boundary difficulties also moved toward resolution. At Ghent the diplomats had created several joint commissions to settle the disputed boundary between the United States and Canada. Many years were to pass before the line was finally drawn, but establishing the principle of defining the border by negotiation was important. In time, a line extending over 3,000 miles was agreed to without the firing of a single shot.

Immediately after the war the British reinforced their garrisons in Canada and began to rebuild their shattered Great Lakes fleet. The United States took similar steps. But both nations found the cost of rearming more than they cared to bear. When the United States suggested demilitarizing the lakes, the British agreed. The Rush-Bagot Agreement of 1817 limited each country to one 100-ton vessel armed with a single eighteen-pounder on Lake Champlain and another on Lake Ontario. The countries were to have two each for all the other Great Lakes.

Gradually, as an outgrowth of this decision, the entire border was demilitarized, a remarkable achievement. In the Convention of 1818 the two countries agreed to the forty-ninth parallel as the northern boundary of the Louisiana Territory between the Lake of the Woods and the Rockies, and to the joint control of the Oregon country for ten years. The question of the rights of Americans in the Labrador and Newfoundland fisheries, which had been much disputed during the Ghent negotiations, was settled amicably.

The Transcontinental Treaty

The acquisition of Spanish Florida and the settlement of the western boundary of Louisiana were also accomplished as an aftermath of the War of 1812, but in a far different spirit. Spain's control of the Floridas was feeble. West Florida had passed into American hands by 1813, and frontiersmen in Georgia were eyeing East Florida greedily. Indians struck frequently into Georgia from Florida, then fled to sanctuary across the line. American slaves who escaped across the border could not be recovered. In 1818 James Monroe, who had been elected president in 1816, ordered General

Andrew Jackson to clear raiding Seminole Indians from American soil and to pursue them into Florida if necessary. Seizing on these instructions, Jackson marched into Florida and easily captured two Spanish forts.

Although Jackson eventually withdrew from Florida, the impotence of the Spanish government made it obvious even in Madrid that if nothing were done, the United States would soon fill the power vacuum by seizing the territory. The Spanish minister in Washington, Luis de Onís, set out in December 1817 to negotiate a treaty with John Quincy Adams, Monroe's secretary of state. Adams pressed the minister mercilessly on the question of Louisiana's western boundary and eventually the minister agreed to accept a boundary that followed the Sabine, Red, and Arkansas Rivers to the Continental Divide and the forty-second parallel to the Pacific, thus abandoning Spain's claim to a huge area beyond the Rockies that had no connection at all with the Louisiana Purchase. The United States obtained Florida in return for a mere $5 million.

This **Transcontinental Treaty** was signed in 1819, although ratification was delayed until 1821. Most Americans at the time thought the acquisition of Florida the most important part of the treaty, but Adams, whose vision of America's future was truly continental, knew better. "The acquisition of a definite line of boundary to the [Pacific] forms a great epoch in our history," he recorded in his diary.

The Monroe Doctrine

Concern with defining the boundaries of the United States did not reflect a desire to limit expansion; rather, most Americans felt that quibbling and quarreling with foreign powers might prove a distraction from the great task of

•⊷Read the **Document**

Monroe Doctrine at **myhistorylab.com**

national development. The classic enunciation of this point of view, the completion of America's withdrawal from Europe, was the **Monroe Doctrine**.

Two separate strands met in this pronouncement. The first led from Moscow to Alaska and down the Pacific coast to the Oregon country. Beginning with the explorations of Vitus Bering in 1741, the Russians had maintained an interest in fishing and fur trading along the northwest coast of North America. In 1821 the czar extended his claim south to the fifty-first parallel and forbade the ships of other powers to enter coastal waters north of that point. This announcement was disturbing.

The second strand ran from the courts of the European monarchs to Latin America. Between 1817 and 1822 practically all of the region from the Rio Grande to the southernmost tip of South America had won its independence. Spain, former master of all the area except Brazil, was too weak to win it back by force, but Austria, Prussia, France, and Russia decided at the Congress of Verona in 1822 to try to regain the area for Spain in the interests of "legitimacy." There was talk of sending a large French army to South America. This possibility also caused grave concern in Washington.

To the Russian threat, Monroe and Secretary of State Adams responded with a terse warning: "The American continents are no longer subjects for any new European colonial establishments." This statement did not impress the Russians, but they had no intention of colonizing the region. In 1824 they signed a treaty with the United States abandoning all claims below the present southern limit of Alaska (54°40'; north latitude) and removing their restrictions on foreign shipping.

HARBOUR of NEW ARCHANGEL in SITCA or NORFOLK SOUND.

The harbor of New Archangel in Sitka, Alaska, part of the Russian empire's expansive claims to North America.

The Latin American problem was more complex. The United States was not alone in its alarm at the prospect of a revival of French or Spanish power in that region. Great Britain, having profited greatly from the breakup of the mercantilist Spanish empire by developing a thriving commerce with the new republics, had no intention of permitting a restoration of the old order. But the British monarchy preferred not to recognize the new revolutionary South American republics, for England itself was only beginning to recover from a period of social upheaval as violent as any in its history. Bad times and high food prices had combined to cause riots, conspiracies, and angry demands for parliamentary reform.

In 1823 the British foreign minister, George Canning, suggested to the American minister in London that the United States and Britain issue a joint statement opposing any French interference in South America, pledging that they themselves would never annex any part of Spain's old empire, and saying nothing about recognition of the new republics. This proposal of joint action with the British was flattering to the United States but scarcely in its best interests. The United States had already recognized the new republics, and it had no desire to help Great Britain retain its South American trade. As Secretary Adams pointed out, to agree to the proposal would be to abandon the possibility of someday adding Cuba or any other part of Latin America to the United States. America should act independently, Adams urged.

Monroe heartily endorsed Adams's argument and decided to include a statement of American policy in his annual message to Congress in December 1823. "The American continents," he wrote, "by the free and independent condition which they have assumed and maintain, are henceforth not to be considered as subjects for future colonization by any European powers." Europe's political system was "essentially

The United States, 1819 As American settlers ventured farther westward, the United States government sought to extend the nation's boundaries, negotiating with Spain for control of Florida and border sections of the Southwest, and with Britain for the Oregon Country.

different" from that developing in the New World, and the two should not be mixed. The United States would not interfere with existing European colonies in North or South America and would avoid involvement in strictly European affairs, but any attempt to extend European control to countries in the hemisphere that had already won their independence would be considered, Monroe warned, "the manifestation of an unfriendly disposition toward the United States" and consequently a threat to the nation's "peace and safety."

This policy statement—it was not dignified with the title Monroe Doctrine until decades later—attracted little notice in Europe or Latin America and not much more at home. European statesmen dismissed Monroe's message as "arrogant" and "blustering," worthy only of "the most profound contempt." Latin Americans, while appreciating the intent behind it, knew better than to count on American aid in case of attack from European powers.

Nevertheless, the principles laid down by President Monroe so perfectly expressed the wishes of the people of the United States that when the country grew powerful enough to enforce them, there was little need to alter or embellish his pronouncement. However understood at the time, the doctrine may be seen as the final stage in the evolution of American independence.

From this perspective, the famous Declaration of 1776 merely began a process of separation and self-determination. The peace treaty ending the Revolutionary War was a further step, and Washington's Declaration of Neutrality in 1793 was another, demonstrating as it did the capacity of the United States to determine its own best interests despite the treaty of alliance with France. The removal of British troops from the northwest forts, achieved by the otherwise ignominious Jay Treaty, marked the next stage. Then the Louisiana Purchase made a further advance toward true independence by ensuring that the Mississippi River could not be closed to the commerce so vital to the development of the western territories.

The standoff War of 1812 ended any lingering British hope of regaining control of America, the Latin American revolutions further weakened colonialism in the Western Hemisphere, and the Transcontinental Treaty pushed the last European power from the path of westward expansion. Monroe's "doctrine" was a kind of public announcement that the sovereign United States had completed its independence and wanted nothing better than to be left alone to concentrate on its own development. Better yet, Europe should be made to allow the entire hemisphere to follow its own path.

The Era of Good Feelings

The person who gave his name to the so-called Monroe Doctrine was an unusually lucky man. James Monroe lived a long life in good health and saw close up most of the great events in the history of the young republic. At the age of 18 he shed his blood for liberty at the Battle of Trenton. He was twice governor of Virginia, a United States senator, and a Cabinet member. He was at various times the nation's representative in Paris, Madrid, and London. Elected president in 1816, his good fortune continued. The world was finally at peace, the country united and prosperous. A person of good feeling who would keep a steady hand on the helm and hold to the present course seemed called for, and Monroe possessed exactly the qualities that the times required. "He is a man whose soul might be turned wrongside outwards, without discovering a blemish," Jefferson said, and John Quincy Adams, a harsh critic of public figures, praised Monroe's courtesy, sincerity, and sound judgment.

By 1817 the divisive issues of earlier days had vanished. Monroe dramatized their disappearance by beginning his first term with a goodwill tour of New England, heartland of the opposition. The tour was a triumph. Everywhere the president was greeted with tremendous enthusiasm. After he visited Boston, once the headquarters and now the graveyard of Federalism, a Federalist newspaper, the *Columbian Centinel*, gave the age its name. Pointing out that the celebrations attending Monroe's visit had brought together in friendly intercourse many persons "whom party politics had long severed," it dubbed the times the **Era of Good Feelings**.

The people of the period had good reasons for thinking it extraordinarily harmonious. Peace, prosperity, liberty, and progress all flourished in 1817 in the United States. The heirs of Jefferson had accepted, with a mixture of resignation and enthusiasm, most of the economic policies advocated by the Hamiltonians.

The Jeffersonian balance between individual liberty and responsible government, having survived both bad management and war, had justified itself to the opposition. The new unity was symbolized by the restored friendship of Jefferson and John Adams. Although they continued to disagree vigorously about matters of philosophy and government, the bitterness between them disappeared entirely. By Monroe's day, Jefferson was writing long letters to "my dear friend," and receiving equally warm and voluminous replies. "Whether you or I were right," Adams wrote amiably to Jefferson, "Posterity must judge."

When political divisions appeared again, as they soon did, it was not because the old balance had been shaky. Few of the new controversies challenged Republican principles or revived old issues. Instead, these controversies were children of the present and the future, products of the continuing growth of the country. From 1790 to 1820, the area of the United States doubled, but very little of the Louisiana Purchase had been settled. More significant, the population of the nation had more than doubled, from 4 million to 9.6 million. The pace of the westward movement had also quickened; by 1820 the moving edge of the frontier ran in a long, irregular curve from Michigan to Arkansas.

New Sectional Issues

The War of 1812 and the depression that struck the country in 1819 had shaped many controversies. The tariff question was affected by both. Before the War of 1812 the level of duties averaged about 12.5 percent of the value of dutiable products, but to meet the added expenses occasioned by the conflict, Congress doubled all tariffs. In 1816, when the revenue was no longer needed, a new act kept duties close to wartime levels. Infant industries that had grown up during the years of embargo, non-intercourse, and war were able to exert considerable pressure. The act especially favored textiles because the British were dumping cloth in America at bargain prices in their attempt to regain lost markets. Unemployed workers and many farmers became convinced that prosperity would return only if American industry were shielded against foreign competition.

At first every section endorsed high duties, but with the passage of time the South rejected protection almost completely. Besides increasing the cost of nearly everything they bought, Southerners exported most of their cotton and tobacco and high duties on imports would limit the foreign market for southern staples by inhibiting international exchange. As this fact became clear, the West tended to divide on the tariff question: The Northwest and much of Kentucky, which had a special interest in protecting its considerable hemp production, favored high duties; the Southwest, where cotton was the major crop, favored low duties.

National banking policy was another important political issue affected by the war and the depression. Presidents Jefferson and Madison had managed to live with the Bank of the United States despite its dubious constitutionality, but its charter was not renewed when it expired in 1811. Aside from the constitutional question, the major opposition to recharter came from state banks eager to take over the business of the Bank for themselves. The fact that English investors owned most of the Bank's stock was also used as an argument against recharter.

Many more state banks were created after 1811, and most extended credit recklessly. When the British raid on Washington and Baltimore in 1814 sent panicky depositors scurrying to convert their deposits into gold or silver, the overextended financiers could not oblige them. All banks outside New England suspended specie payments; that is, they stopped exchanging their bank notes for hard money on demand.

Table 7.1 Key Sectional Issues

Issue	West	South	North
Favorite leaders	Henry Clay (Kentucky)	John Calhoun (South Carolina), William Crawford (Georgia), Andrew Jackson (Tennessee)	John Quincy Adams (Massachusetts), Daniel Webster (Massachusetts), Martin Van Buren (New York)
Should import taxes (tariffs) be high?	Yes and no, depending on the region	No, because high tariffs increased the cost of manufactured goods and harmed export trade (cotton, tobacco)	Yes, because manufacturers and factory workers wanted protection from inexpensive foreign-made products; the exception: New England, because high tariffs harmed trade
Should federal government support construction of roads and canals?	Yes, to reduce transportation costs of products from western farms	No, because this would require more federal revenue—and thus an increase in the tariff	Yes and no, depending on the locality
Should federally owned lands be sold as cheaply as possible?	Yes, because pioneers and farmers needed cheap land	No, because income from land sales would reduce the need for tariffs to raise money; and the products of cheap western farms would compete with southern farms	No, because cheap land in the west would drain off surplus labor and increase labor costs in the East
Should slavery be allowed in the new states being created in the West?	Yes and no, but generally yes because much of the West was economically tied to the South, which supported slavery	Yes, because slaveowners were moving into western regions and were entitled to keep their "property"	No, because new "slave states" would give the South more power in the Senate and because free labor could not fairly compete with a slave system

The shaded boxes indicate the critical issue for each region.

Paper money immediately fell in value; a paper dollar was soon worth only eighty-five cents in coin in Philadelphia, less in Baltimore. Government business also suffered from the absence of a national bank. In October 1814 Secretary of the Treasury Alexander J. Dallas submitted a plan for a second Bank of the United States, and after considerable wrangling over its precise form, the institution was authorized in April 1816.

The new Bank was much larger than its predecessor, being capitalized at $35 million. However, unlike Hamilton's creation, it was badly managed at the start. Its first president, William Jones, a former secretary of the treasury, allowed his institution to join in the irresponsible creation of credit. By the summer of 1818 the Bank's eighteen branches had issued notes in excess of ten times their specie reserves, far more than was prudent, considering the Bank's responsibilities. When depression struck the country in 1819, the Bank of the United States was as hard pressed as many of the state banks. Jones resigned.

The new president, Langdon Cheves of South Carolina, was as rigid as Jones had been permissive. During the bad times, when easy credit was needed, he pursued a policy of stern curtailment. The Bank thus regained a sound position at the expense of hardship to borrowers. "The Bank was saved," the contemporary economist William Gouge wrote somewhat hyperbolically, "and the people were ruined." Indeed, the bank reached a low point in public favor. Irresponsible state banks resented it, as did the advocates of hard money.

Regional lines were less sharply drawn on the Bank issue than on the tariff. Northern congressmen voted against the Bank fifty-three to forty-four in 1816—many of them because they objected to the particular proposal, not because they were against any national bank. Those from other sections favored it, fifty-eight to thirty. The collapse occasioned by the Panic of 1819 produced further opposition to the institution in the West.

Land policy in the West also caused sectional controversy. No one wished to eliminate the system of survey and sale, but there was continuous pressure to reduce the price of public land and the minimum unit offered for sale. The Land Act of 1800 set $2 an acre as the minimum price and 320 acres (a half section) as the smallest unit. In 1804 the minimum was cut to 160 acres, which could be had for about $80 down, roughly a quarter of what the average artisan could earn in a year.

Sectional attitudes toward the public lands were fairly straightforward. The West wanted cheap land; the North and South tended to look on the national domain as an asset that should be converted into as much cash as possible. Northern manufacturers feared that cheap land in the West would drain off surplus labor and force wages up, while southern planters were concerned about the competition that would develop when the virgin lands of the Southwest were put to the plow to make cotton. The West, however, was ready to fight to the last line of defense over land policy, while the other regions would usually compromise on the issue to gain support for their own vital interests.

The most divisive sectional issue was slavery. After the compromises affecting the "peculiar institution" made at the Constitutional Convention, it caused remarkably little conflict in national politics before 1819. Although the importation of blacks rose in the 1790s, Congress abolished the African slave trade in 1808 without major incident. As the nation expanded, free and slave states were added to the Union in equal numbers with Ohio, Indiana, and Illinois being balanced by Louisiana, Mississippi, and Alabama. In 1819 there were twenty-two states, eleven slave and eleven free. The expansion of slavery occasioned by the cotton boom led Southerners to support it more aggressively, which tended to irritate many Northerners, but most persons considered slavery mainly a local issue. To the extent that it was a national question, the North opposed it and the South defended it ardently. The West leaned toward the southern point of view, for in addition to the southwestern slave states, the Northwest was sympathetic, partly because much of its produce was sold on southern plantations and partly because at least half of its early settlers came from Virginia, Kentucky, and other slave states.

New Leaders

By 1824 the giants of the Revolutionary generation had completed their work. Washington, Hamilton, Franklin, Samuel Adams, Patrick Henry, and most of their peers were dead. John Adams (88), Thomas Jefferson (81), and James Madison (73) were passing their declining years quietly on their ancestral acres, full of memories and sage advice, but no longer active in national affairs. In every section new leaders had come forward, men shaped by the past but chiefly concerned with the present. Quite suddenly, between the war and the panic, they had inherited power. They would shape the future of the United States.

In the North, John Quincy Adams was the best-known of the new political leaders. Just completing his brilliant work as secretary of state under Monroe, highlighted by his negotiation of the Transcontinental Treaty and his design of the Monroe Doctrine, he had behind him a record of public service dating to the Confederation period.

Adams was farsighted, imaginative, hardworking, and extremely intelligent, but he was inept in personal relations. He had all the virtues and most of the defects

Samuel Morse, chiefly famous for his work on the telegraph and Morse code, was also a talented painter. His *House of Representatives* (1822–1823) shows the legislators at work at night, a symbolic expression of their commitment to the nation.

Source: Samuel F.B. Morse, *The House of Representatives*. 1822–23. oil on Canvas. 86 $7/8$ × 130 $5/8$. Corcoran Gallery of Art, Museum Purchase, Gallery Fund.

Eyes like "anthracite furnaces," the Scottish historian Thomas Carlyle remarked of Daniel Webster; this is the "Black Dan" portrait by Francis Alexander (1835).
Source: Hood Museum of Art, Dartmouth College, Hanover, New Hampshire, Gift of George C. Shattuck, Class of 1803.

of the puritan, being suspicious both of others and of himself. He suffered in two ways from being his father's child: As the son of a president he was under severe pressure to live up to the Adams name, and his father expected a great deal of him. When the boy was only seven, John Adams wrote the following to his wife: "Train [the children] to virtue. Habituate them to industry, activity, and spirit. Make them consider vice as shameful and unmanly. Fire them with ambition to be useful."

Like his father, John Quincy Adams was a strong nationalist. While New England still opposed high tariffs, he was at least open-minded on the subject. Unlike most easterners, he believed that the federal government should spend freely on roads and canals in the West. To slavery he was, like most New Englanders, personally opposed. As Monroe's second term drew toward its close, Adams seemed one of the most likely candidates to succeed him, and at this period his ambition to be president was his great failing. It led him to make certain compromises with his principles, which in turn plagued his oversensitive conscience and had a corrosive effect on his peace of mind.

Daniel Webster, a congressman from Massachusetts, was recognized as one of the coming leaders of New England. He owed much of his reputation to his formidable presence and his oratorical skill. Dark, broad-chested, large-headed, and craggy of brow, he projected a remarkable appearance of heroic power and moral strength. His thunderous voice, his resourceful vocabulary, and his manner—all backed by the mastery of every oratorical trick—made him unique.

New York's man of the future was a sandy-haired politico named Martin Van Buren. The Red Fox, as he was called, was one of the most talented politicians ever to play a part in American affairs. He was clever and hardworking, but his mind and his energy were always devoted to some political purpose. From 1812 to 1820 he served in the state legislature; in 1820 he was elected United States senator.

Van Buren had great charm and immense tact. By nature affable, he never allowed partisanship to mar his personal relationships with other leaders. The members of his political machine, known as the Albany Regency, were almost fanatically loyal to him, but even his enemies could seldom dislike him as a person.

The most prominent southern leader was William H. Crawford, Monroe's secretary of the treasury. After being elected to the Senate from Georgia, he became controversial. Many of his contemporaries considered him no more than a cynical spoilsman, although his administration of the treasury department was first-rate. Yet he had many friends. His ambition was vast, his power great. Fate, however, was about to strike Crawford a crippling blow.

John C. Calhoun, the other outstanding southern leader, was born in South Carolina in 1782 and graduated from Yale in 1804. After serving in the South Carolina legislature, he was elected to Congress in 1811. He took a strong nationalist position on all the issues of the day. In 1817 Monroe made him secretary of war.

Calhoun, a well-to-do planter, was devoted to the South and its institutions, but he took the broadest possible view of political affairs. John Quincy Adams, seldom charitable in his private opinions of colleagues (he called Crawford "a worm" and Henry Clay a "gamester" with an "undigested system of ethics"), praised Calhoun's "enlarged philosophic views" and considered him "above all sectional and factional prejudices."

The outstanding western leader of the 1820s was Henry Clay of Kentucky, one of the most charming and colorful of American statesmen. On the platform he ranked with Webster; behind the political scenes he was the peer of Van Buren. In every environment he was warm and open—what a modern political scientist might call a charismatic personality. Clay loved to drink, swear, tell tales, and play poker. He was a reasonable man, skilled at arranging political compromises, but he possessed a reckless streak: Twice in his career he challenged men to duels for having insulted him. Fortunately, all concerned were poor shots.

Clay was elected to Congress in 1810. He led the War Hawks in 1811 and 1812 and was Speaker of the House from 1811 to 1820 and from 1823 to 1825.

In the early 1820s he was just developing his **American System**. In return for eastern support of a policy of federal aid in the construction of roads and canals, the West would back the protective tariff. He justified this deal on the widest national grounds. America has a "great diversity of interests," ranging from agriculture and fishing to manufacturing, shipbuilding, and commerce. "The good of each . . . and of the whole should be carefully consulted. This is the only mode by which we can preserve, in full vigor, the harmony of the whole Union." Stimulating manufacturing, for example, would increase the demand for western raw materials, while western prosperity would lead to greater consumption of eastern manufactured goods.

Although himself a slaveowner, Clay called slavery the "greatest of human evils." He favored freeing the slaves and "colonizing" them in Africa, which could, he said, be accomplished gradually and at relatively minor cost.

The Missouri Compromise

The sectional concerns of the 1820s repeatedly influenced politics. The depression of 1819–1822 increased tensions by making people feel more strongly about the issues of the day. For example, manufacturers who wanted high tariffs in 1816 were more vehemently in favor of protection in 1820 when their business fell off. Even when economic conditions improved, geographic alignments on key issues tended to solidify.

One of the first and most critical of the sectional questions concerned the admission of Missouri as a slave state. When Louisiana entered the Union in 1812, the rest of the Louisiana Purchase was organized as the Missouri Territory. Building on a nucleus of Spanish and French inhabitants, the region west and north of St. Louis grew rapidly, and in 1817 the Missourians petitioned for statehood. A large percentage of the settlers—the population exceeded 60,000 by 1818—were Southerners who had moved into the valleys of the Arkansas and Missouri rivers. Since many of them owned slaves, Missouri would become a slave state.

The admission of new states had always been a routine matter in keeping with the admirable pattern established by the Northwest Ordinance. But during the debate on the Missouri Enabling Act in February 1819, Congressman James Tallmadge of New York introduced an amendment prohibiting "the further introduction of slavery" and providing that all slaves born in Missouri after the territory became a state should be freed at age 25.

While Tallmadge was merely seeking to apply in the territory the pattern of race relations that had developed in the states immediately east of Missouri, his amendment represented, at least in spirit, something of a revolution. The Northwest Ordinance had prohibited slavery in the land between the Mississippi and the Ohio, but that area had only a handful of slaveowners in 1787 and little prospect of attracting more. Elsewhere no effort to restrict the movement of slaves into new territory had been attempted. If one assumed (as whites always had) that the slaves themselves should have no say in the matter, it appeared democratic to

•**•**—⌐Read the Document
Missouri Enabling Act at
myhistorylab.com

let the settlers of Missouri decide the slavery question for themselves. Nevertheless, the Tallmadge amendment passed the House, the vote following sectional lines closely. The Senate, however, resoundingly rejected it. The less populous southern part of Missouri was then organized separately as the Arkansas Territory, and an attempt to bar slavery there was stifled. The Missouri Enabling Act failed to pass before Congress adjourned.

When the next Congress met in December 1819, the Missouri issue came up at once. The vote on Tallmadge's amendment had shown that the rapidly growing North controlled the House of Representatives. Southerners thought it vital to preserve a balance in the Senate. Yet Northerners objected to the fact that Missouri extended hundreds of miles north of the Ohio River, which they considered slavery's natural boundary. Angry debate raged in Congress for months.

The debate did not turn on the morality of slavery or the rights of blacks. Northerners objected to adding new slave states because under the Three-Fifths Compromise these states would be overrepresented in Congress (60 percent of their slaves would be counted in determining the size of the states' delegations in the House of Representatives) and because they did not relish competing with slave labor. Since the question was political influence rather than the rights and wrongs of slavery, a compromise was worked out in 1820. Missouri entered the Union as a slave state and Maine, having been separated from Massachusetts, was admitted as a free state to preserve the balance in the Senate.

To prevent further conflict, Congress adopted the proposal of Senator Jesse B. Thomas of Illinois, that "forever prohibited" slavery in all other parts of the Louisiana Purchase north of 36°300' latitude, the westward extension of Missouri's southern boundary. Although this division would keep slavery out of most of the territory, Southerners accepted it cheerfully. The land south of the line, the present states of Arkansas and Oklahoma, seemed ideally suited for the expanded plantation economy, and most persons considered the treeless northern regions little better than a desert.

The **Missouri Compromise** did not end the crisis. When Missouri submitted its constitution for approval by Congress (the final step in the admission process), the document, besides authorizing slavery and prohibiting the emancipation of any slave without the consent of the owner, required the state legislature to pass a law barring free blacks and mulattos from entering the state "under any pretext whatever." This provision plainly violated Article IV, Section 2, of the U.S. Constitution: "The Citizens of each State shall be entitled to all Privileges and Immunities of Citizens in the several States." It did not, however, represent any more of a break with established racial patterns, North or South, than the Tallmadge amendment; many states east of Missouri barred free blacks without regard for the Constitution.

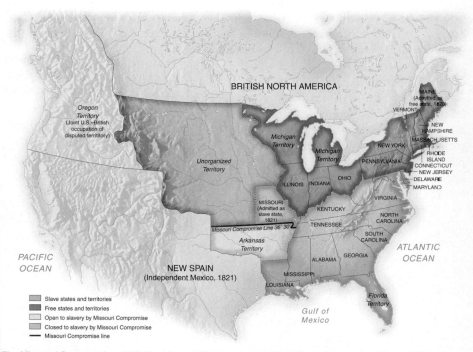

The Missouri Compromise, 1820 The Missouri Compromise admitted Missouri as a slave state, and Maine as a free state, retaining a balance in the Senate: Half of the nation's 24 states allowed slavery; half did not. The Compromise also drew an imaginary line along the 36°30' latitude (northern boundary of Arkansas): Slavery would be allowed in the lands to the south of the line.

Nevertheless, northern congressmen hypocritically refused to accept the Missouri constitution. Once more the debate raged. Again, since few Northerners cared to defend the rights of blacks, the issue was compromised. In March 1821 Henry Clay found a face-saving formula: Out of respect for the "supreme law of the land," Congress accepted the Missouri constitution with the demurrer that no law passed in conformity to it should be construed as contravening Article IV, Section 2.

Every thinking person recognized the political dynamite inherent in the Missouri controversy. The sectional lineup had been terrifyingly compact. Moreover, despite the timidity and hypocrisy of the North, everyone realized that the rights and wrongs of slavery lay at the heart of the conflict. "We have the wolf by the ears, and we can neither safely hold him, nor safely let him go," Jefferson wrote a month after Missouri became a state. The dispute, he said, "like a fire bell in the night, awakened and filled me with terror." Jefferson knew that the compromise had not quenched the flames ignited by the Missouri debates. "This is a reprieve only," he said. John Quincy Adams called it the "title page to a great tragic volume." Yet one could still hope that the fire bell was only a false alarm, that Adams's tragic volume would remain unread.

The Election of 1824

The tariff continued to divide the country. When a new, still higher tariff was enacted in 1824, the slave states voted almost unanimously against it, the North and Northwest in favor, and New England remained of two minds. Webster (after conducting a poll of business leaders before deciding how to vote) made a powerful speech against the act, but the measure passed without creating a major storm.

The presidential fight was waged on personal grounds, although the heat generated by the contest began the process of reenergizing party politics. Besides Calhoun the candidates were Andrew Jackson (hero of the battle of New Orleans), Crawford, Adams, and Clay. The maneuvering among them was complex, the infighting savage. In March 1824, Calhoun, who was young enough to wait for the White House, withdrew and declared for the vice presidency, which he won easily. Crawford, who had the support of many congressional leaders, seemed the likely winner, but he suffered a series of paralytic strokes that gravely injured his chances.

Despite the bitterness of the contest, it attracted relatively little public interest; barely a quarter of those eligible took the trouble to vote. In the Electoral College Jackson led with ninety-nine, Adams had eighty-four, Crawford forty-one, and Clay thirty-seven. Since no one had a majority, the contest was thrown into the House of Representatives, which, under the Constitution, had to choose from among the three leaders, each state delegation having one vote. By employing his great influence in the House, Clay swung the balance. Not wishing to advance the fortunes of a rival westerner like Jackson and feeling, with reason, that Crawford's health made him unavailable, Clay gave his support to Adams, who was thereupon elected.

John Quincy Adams as President

Adams, elected in 1824, hoped to use the national authority to foster all sorts of useful projects. He asked Congress for a federal program of internal improvements so vast that even Clay boggled when he realized its scope. He came out for aid to manufacturing and agriculture, for a national university, and even for a government astronomical observatory. For a nationalist of unchallengeable Jeffersonian origins like Clay or Calhoun to have pressed for so extensive a program would have been politically risky. For the son of John Adams to do so was disastrous; every doubter remembered his Federalist background and decided that he was trying to overturn the glorious "Revolution of 1800."

•••—Read the Document

John Quincy Adams, *Inaugural Address* at **myhistorylab.com**

Adams proved to be his own worst enemy, for he was an inept politician. To persuade Americans, who were almost pathological on the subject of monarchy, to support his road building program, he cited with approval the work being done abroad by "the nations of Europe and . . . their rulers," which revived fears that all Adamses were royalists at heart. He was insensitive to the ebb and flow of public feeling; even when he wanted to move with the tide, he seldom managed to dramatize and publicize his stand effectively. Many Americans, for example, endorsed a federal bankruptcy law to protect poor debtors; Adams agreed, but instead of describing himself as a friend of debtors, he called for the "amelioration" of the "often oppressive codes relating to insolvency" and buried the recommendation at the tail end of a dull state paper.

Calhoun's *Exposition and Protest*

The tariff question added to the president's troubles. An increasingly powerful federal government required higher revenues—and higher duties—culminating in what became known as the record-high 1828 "Tariff of Abominations." This exacerbated sectional divisions.

Vice President Calhoun was especially upset; he believed that the new tariff would impoverish the South. His essay, *The South Carolina Exposition and Protest*, repudiated the nationalist philosophy he had previously championed.

The South Carolina legislature released this document to the country in December 1828, along with eight resolutions denouncing the protective tariff as unfair and unconstitutional. The theorist Calhoun, however, was not content with outlining the case against the tariff. His *Exposition* provided an ingenious defense of the right of the people of a state to reject a law of Congress. Starting with John Locke's revered concept of government as a contractual relationship, he argued that since the states had created the Union, logic dictated that they be the final arbiters of the meaning of the Constitution. If a special state convention, representing the sovereignty of the people, decided that an act of Congress violated the Constitution, it could interpose its authority and "nullify" the law within its boundaries. Calhoun did not seek to implement this theory in 1828, for he hoped that the next administration would lower the tariff and make nullification unnecessary.

The Meaning of Sectionalism

The sectional issues that occupied the energies of politicians and strained the ties between the people of the different regions were produced by powerful forces that actually bound the sections together. Growth caused differences that sometimes led to conflict, but growth itself was the product of prosperity. People were drawn to the West by the expectation that life would be better there, as more often than not it was, at least in the long run.

Another force unifying the nation was patriotism; the increasing size and prosperity of the nation made people proud to be part of a growing, dynamic society. Still another was the uniqueness of the American system of government and the people's knowledge that their immediate ancestors had created it. John Adams and Thomas Jefferson died on the same day, July 4, 1826, the fiftieth anniversary of the signing of the Declaration of Independence. People took this not as a remarkable coincidence, but as a sign from the heavens, an indication that God looked with favor on the American experiment. Many believed that patriotism and providence would transcend the intensifying sectionalism. They would be proven wrong.

John Lewis Krimmel's painting of the *Fourth of July in Centre Square Philadelphia* (1812). Note the diversity of those who've assembled to observe the festivities.

Source: Courtesy of the Pennsylvania Academy of Fine Arts, Philadelphia. Pennsylvania Academy purchase (from the estate of Paul Beck, Jr.).

Milestones

1808	James Madison is elected president
1810	Macon's Bill No. 2 removes all restrictions on commerce with Britain and France
1811	Battle of Tippecanoe shatters Indian confederation
1812	James Madison is reelected president
	Congress declares war on Great Britain
	USS *Constitution* and *United States* win naval victories
1813	Captain Oliver Hazard Perry destroys British fleet in Battle of Lake Erie
	General William Henry Harrison defeats British in Battle of the Thames
	Tecumseh dies at Battle of the Thames
1814	British burn Washington, DC
	Francis Scott Key writes "The Star Spangled Banner" during the bombardment of Fort McHenry
	New England Federalists meet at Hartford Convention
	Treaty of Ghent officially ends War of 1812
1815	General Andrew Jackson defeats British at Battle of New Orleans
1816	James Monroe is elected president
1817	Rush-Bagot Agreement limits American and British forces on Lake Champlain and Great Lakes
1819	United States signs Transcontinental Treaty with Spain
1819–1822	United States experiences economic depression
1820	James Monroe is reelected president
1820–1821	Missouri Compromise closes Missouri Territory to slavery, but opens Arkansas Territory to slavery
1820–1850	Cities and manufacturing grow rapidly
1823	Monroe Doctrine says United States will consider future European colonization in Western Hemisphere a threat to American peace and safety
1824–1825	House of Representatives decides election of 1824 in favor of John Quincy Adams, leading to claims of a "corrupt bargain" with Henry Clay
1828	Congress passes Tariff of Abominations, leading to nullification debate

✓●─Study and **Review** at www.myhistorylab.com

Review Questions

1. The period covered in this chapter saw a steady increase in federal power. During that time, the Democratic party, which opposed federal power, was dominant. What explains this seeming contradiction?
2. Before 1812, who sought war against the British and who opposed it? Why?

3. What accounted for the military reverses during the war and its one major success?
4. What factors led to the Missouri Compromise and what were its main provisions?

Key Terms

American System   *216*
Era of Good
   Feelings   *210*
Hartford
   Convention   *203*

Missouri
   Compromise   *218*
Monroe Doctrine   *207*
Tariff of
   Abominations   *193*

Transcontinental
   Treaty   *207*
War Hawks   *196*
War of 1812   *197*

8 Toward a National Economy

((•—Hear the Audio Chapter 8 at myhistorylab.com

Are you wearing anything made in the United States?

IF YOU'RE WEARING SOCKS, THEY WERE LIKELY MADE IN DATANG, China, a small city near the Vietnamese border. Datang manufactures eight billion socks annually, about one-third of the world's output. Within Datang, companies specialize in different aspects of sock production: some buy yarn, dye it, or weave it into cloth; some sew in toes or heels; some press the socks or bind them with metal clips; some put socks into packages. Because of the huge scale and specialization, Datang manufactures a pair of socks for twenty-five cents, about half the cost of socks made in the United States.

That a single city provides socks for much of the world illustrates the global character of the modern economy. The emergence of a global economy has been going on for centuries. A global market for Asian spices was well-established at the time of Columbus, a reason for his voyage in 1492 (see the introduction to Chapter 1, p. 14).

As late as the 1700s, American farmers still produced much of what they needed—food, soap, candles, clothing, and even their socks. Farm women working in their homes spun locally produced flax, wool, and cotton into thread and yarn; knitted the yarn into fabric; and sewed the pieces into socks.

But by the early 1800s the "Age of Homespun" was waning. Manufactured products, often produced in distant factories, increasingly supplanted home-made goods. Historians still debate whether the shift from rural self-sufficiency to a specialized market economy occurred over a few pivotal decades during the early 1800s or whether it evolved slowly, over a longer period of time.

Nearly all agree, though, that after 1810 a cluster of changes imparted a new dynamism to the American economy: the growing demand for high-quality, store-bought goods; the rise of the factory system; the recruitment and training of a cheap labor force; the emergence of corporations; the revival of the Southern economy based on slavery and cotton production; the development of improved transportation that facilitated the exchange of farm and factory goods; and the creation of legal structures that promoted economic growth.

By the mid-nineteenth century, most Americans had been contributors to and consumers of an economic system that, while not yet fully global, had become national in scope. Most Americans wore socks that were manufactured in a handful of cities in Massachusetts, New York, and Pennsylvania. Thus while political tendencies tended to pull the nation apart, especially the growing dispute over the future of slavery in the territories, Americans were becoming more interdependent economically.

Gentility and the Consumer Revolution

The democratic revolution that led to the founding of the American nation was accompanied by widespread emulation of aristocratic behavior. Sometimes the most ardent American democrats proved the most susceptible to the allure of European gentility. Thus young John Adams, while lampooning "the late Refinements in modern manners," nevertheless advised his future wife, Abigail, to be more attentive to posture: "You very often hang your Head like a Bulrush, and you sit with your legs crossed to the ruin of the figure." On his trip to Paris in

Watch the **Video**

Coming of Age in 1833 (a great period of change/ reinvention in the world) at **myhistorylab.com**

1778 on behalf of the Continental Congress, he denounced the splendor of the houses, furniture, and clothing. "I cannot help suspecting that the more Elegance, the less Virtue," he concluded. Yet despite the exigencies of war, on returning to America, Adams bought a three-story mansion and furnished it with Louis XV chairs and, among other extravagances, an ornate wine cooler from Vincennes.

Among aristocratic circles in Europe, gentility was the product of ancestry and cultivated style; but in America it was largely defined by possession of material goods. By the mid-eighteenth century the "refinement of America" had touched the homes of some Southern planters and urban merchants; but a half century later porcelain plates

Americans enshrined the simple life and a homespun equality; yet they coveted the cultural markers of aristocracy, such as imported porcelain tea services. This one, made in France, was given to Alexander Hamilton. Gentility spread, historian Richard Bushman writes, "because people longed to be associated with the 'best society.'"

made by English craftsman Josiah Wedgwood and mahogany washstands by Thomas Chippendale were appearing even in frontier communities. Americans were demanding more goods than such craftsmen could turn out. Everywhere producers sought to expand their workshops, hire and train more artisans, and acquire large stocks of materials and labor-saving machines.

But first they had to locate the requisite capital, find ways to supervise large numbers of workers, and discover how to get raw materials to factories and products to customers. The solutions to these problems, taken together, constituted the "market revolution" of the early nineteenth century. The "industrial revolution" came on its heels.

Birth of the Factory

By the 1770s British manufacturers, especially those in textiles, had made astonishing progress in mechanizing their operations, bringing workers together in buildings called factories where waterpower, and later steam, supplied the force to run new spinning and weaving devices that increased productivity and reduced labor costs.

Because machine-spun cotton was cheaper and of better quality than that spun by hand, producers in other countries were eager to adopt British methods. Americans had depended on Great Britain for such products until the Revolution cut off supplies; then the new spirit of nationalism gave impetus to the development of local industry. A number of state legislatures offered bounties to anyone who would introduce the new machinery. The British, however, guarded their secrets vigilantly. It was illegal to export any of the new machines or to send their plans abroad. Workers skilled in their construction and use were forbidden to leave the country. These restrictions were effective for a time; the principles on which the new machines were based were simple enough, but to construct workable models without plans was another matter. Although a number of persons tried to do so, it was not until Samuel Slater installed his machines in Pawtucket, Rhode Island, that a successful factory was constructed.

Slater, born in England, was more than a skilled mechanic. Attracted by stories of the rewards offered in the United States, he slipped out of England in 1789. Not daring to carry any plans, he depended on his memory and his mechanical sense for the complicated specifications of the necessary machines. Moses Brown brought Slater to Rhode Island to help run his textile-manufacturing operation. Working in secrecy with a carpenter who was "under bond not to steal the patterns nor disclose the nature of the work," Slater built and installed his machinery. In December 1790 the first American factory began production.

It was a humble beginning indeed. Slater's machines made only cotton thread, which Brown's company sold in its Providence store and "put out" to individual artisans, who, working for wages, wove it into cloth in their homes. The machines were tended by a labor force of nine children, for the work was simple and the pace slow. The young operatives' pay ranged from thirty-three to sixty-seven cents a week, about what a youngster could earn in other occupations. The factory was profitable from the start. Slater soon branched out on his own, and others trained by him opened their own establishments. By 1800 seven mills possessing 2,000 spindles were in operation; by 1815, after production had been stimulated by the War of 1812, there were 130,000 spindles turning in 213 factories.

Before long the Boston Associates, a group of merchants headed by Francis Cabot Lowell, added a new dimension to factory production. Beginning at Waltham, Massachusetts, where the Charles River provided the necessary waterpower, between 1813 and 1850 they revolutionized textile production. Some early factory owners had set up hand looms in their plants, but the weavers could not keep pace with the spinning jennies. After an extensive study of British mills, Lowell smuggled the plans for an efficient power loom into America. His Boston Manufacturing Company at Waltham, capitalized at $300,000, combined machine production, large-scale operation, efficient management, and centralized marketing procedures. It concentrated on the mass production of a standardized product.

Lowell's cloth, though plain and rather coarse, was durable and cheap. His profits averaged almost 20 percent a year during the Era of Good Feelings. In 1823 the Boston Associates began to harness the power of the Merrimack River, setting up a new $600,000 corporation at the sleepy village of East Chelmsford, Massachusetts (population 300), where there was a fall of thirty-two feet in the river. Within three years the town, appropriately renamed Lowell, had 2,000 inhabitants.

An Industrial Proletariat?

As machines displaced skilled labor, the ability of laborers to influence working conditions declined. If skilled, they either became employers and developed entrepreneurial and managerial skills, or they descended into the mass of wage earners. Simultaneously, the changing structure of production widened the gap between owners and workers and blurred the distinction between skilled and unskilled labor.

These trends might have been expected to generate hostility between workers and employers. To some extent they did. There were strikes for higher wages and to protest work speedups throughout the 1830s and again in the 1850s. Efforts to found unions and to create political organizations dedicated to advancing the interests of workers were also undertaken. But well into the 1850s Americans displayed less evidence of the class solidarity common among European workers.

Why America did not produce a self-conscious working class is a question that has long intrigued historians. Some historians argue that the existence of the frontier siphoned off displaced and dissatisfied workers. The number of urban laborers who went west could not have been large, but the fact that the expanding economy created many opportunities for laborers to rise out of the working class was surely another reason why so few of them developed strong class feelings.

Other historians believe that ethnic and racial differences kept workers from seeing themselves as a distinct class with common needs and common enemies. The influx of needy immigrants willing to accept almost any wage was certainly resented by native-born workers. The growing number of free blacks in Northern cities—between 1800 and 1830 the number tripled in Philadelphia and quadrupled in New York—also inhibited the development of a self-identified working class.

These answers help explain the relative absence of class conflict during the early stages of the industrial revolution in America, but so does the fact that conditions in

Slater's Mill, in Pawtucket, Rhode Island.
Source: N. Carter/North Wind Picture Archives.

the early shops and factories represented an improvement for the people who worked in them. This was the case with nearly all European immigrants, though less so for urban free blacks, since in the South many found work in the skilled trades.

Most workers in the early textile factories were drawn from outside the regular labor market. Relatively few artisan spinners and weavers became factory workers; indeed, some of them continued to work as they had, for it was many years before the factories could even begin to satisfy the ever-increasing demand for cloth. Nor did immigrants attend the new machines. Instead, the mill owners relied chiefly on women and children. They did so because machines lessened the need for skill and strength and because the labor shortage made it necessary to tap unexploited sources. By the early 1820s about half the cotton textile workers in the factories were under sixteen years of age.

Most people of that generation reasoned that the work was easy and that it kept youngsters busy at useful tasks while providing their families with extra income. Roxanna Foote, whose daughter, Harriet Beecher Stowe, wrote *Uncle Tom's Cabin*, came from a solid, middle-class family in Guilford, Connecticut. Nevertheless, she worked full-time before her marriage in her grandfather's small spinning mill. "This spinning-mill was a favorite spot," a relative recalled many years later. "Here the girls often received visitors, or read or chatted while they spun." Roxanna explained her daily regimen as a mill girl matter-of-factly: "I generally rise with the sun, and, after breakfast, take my wheel, which is my daily companion, and the evening is generally devoted to reading, writing, and knitting."

This seems like an idealized picture, or perhaps working for one's grandfather made a difference. Another young girl, Emily Chubbock, later a well-known writer, had a less pleasant recollection of her experience as an eleven-year-old factory hand earning

$1.25 a week: "My principal recollections . . . are of noise and filth, bleeding hands and aching feet, and a very sad heart." In any case, a society accustomed to seeing the children of fairly well-to-do farmers working full-time in the fields was not shocked by the sight of children working all day in mills. In factories where laborers were hired in family units, no member earned very much, but with a couple of adolescent daughters and perhaps a son of nine or ten helping out, a family could take home enough to live decently. For most working Americans, that was success enough.

Lowell's Waltham System: Women as Factory Workers

Instead of hiring children, the Boston Associates developed the "Waltham System" of employing young, unmarried women in their new textile mills. For a generation after the opening of the Merrimack Manufacturing Company in 1823, the thriving factory towns of Lowell, Chicopee, and Manchester provided the background for a remarkable industrial idyll. Young women came from farms all over New England to work for a year or two in the mills. They were lodged in company boardinghouses, which, like college dormitories, became centers of social life. Unlike modern college dormitories, the boardinghouses were strictly supervised; straitlaced New Englanders did not hesitate to permit their daughters to live in them. The regulations laid down by one company, for example, required that all employees "show that they are penetrated by a laudable love of temperance and virtue." "Ardent spirits" were banished from company property, and "games of hazard and cards" prohibited. A 10 PM curfew was strictly enforced.

The women earned between $2.50 and $3.25 a week, about half of which went for room and board. Some of the remainder they sent home, the rest (what there was of it) they could spend as they wished.

Most of these young women did not have to support themselves. They worked to save for a trousseau, to help educate a younger brother, or simply for the experience and excitement of meeting new people and escaping the confining environment of the farm. Anything but an industrial proletariat, they filled the windows of the factories with flowering plants, organized sewing circles, edited their own literary periodicals, and attended lectures on edifying subjects. That such activity was possible on top of a seventy-hour work week is a commentary on both the resiliency of youth and the leisurely pace of these early factories.

Life in the mills was nevertheless demanding. Although they made up 85 percent of the workforce, women were kept out of supervisory positions. In 1834 workers in several mills "turned out" to protest cuts in their wages and a hike in what they paid for board. This work stoppage did not force a reversal of management policy. Another strike two years later in response to a work speedup was somewhat more successful. But when a drop in prices in the 1840s led the owners to introduce new rules designed to increase production, workers lacked the organizational strength to block them. By then young women of the kind that had flocked to the mills in the 1820s and 1830s were beginning to find work as schoolteachers and clerks. Mill owners turned increasingly to Irish immigrants to operate their machines.

> **Read the Document**
> Regarding Life in the Mills at
> myhistorylab.com

Irish and German Immigrants

Between 1790 and 1820 the population of the United States had more than doubled to 9.6 million. The most remarkable feature of this growth was that it resulted almost entirely from natural increase. The birthrate in the early nineteenth century exceeded fifty per 1,000 population, a rate as high as that of any country in the world today. Fewer than 250,000 immigrants entered the United States between 1790 and 1820. European wars, the ending of the slave trade, and doubts about the viability of the new republic slowed the flow of humanity across the Atlantic to a trickle.

But soon after the final defeat of Napoleon in 1815, immigration picked up. In the 1820s, some 150,000 European immigrants arrived; in the 1830s, 600,000; and in the 1840s, 1.7 million. The 1850 census, the first to make the distinction, estimated that of the nation's population of 23 million, more than 10 percent were foreign-born. In the Northeast the proportion exceeded 15 percent.

Most of this human tide came from Germany and Ireland, but substantial numbers also came from Great Britain and the Scandinavian countries. As with earlier immigrants, most were drawn to America by what are called "pull" factors: the prospect of abundant land, good wages, and economic opportunity generally, or by the promise of political and religious freedom. But many came because of "push" factors: To stay where they were meant to face starvation. This was particularly true of those from Ireland, where a potato blight triggered the flight of tens of thousands. This Irish exodus continued; by the end of the century there were more people of Irish origin in America than in Ireland.

Once ashore in New York, Boston, or Philadelphia, most relatively prosperous immigrants pushed directly westward. Others found work in the new factory towns

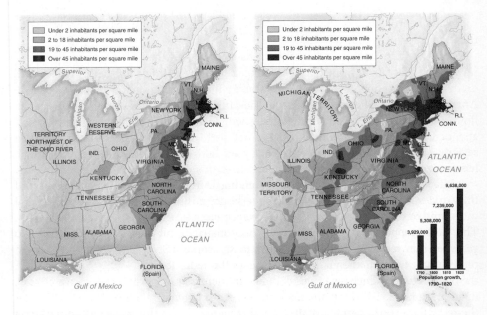

Population Density, 1790 Then, as now, the most densely populated part of the nation was the coastal region from Virginia to Massachusetts.

Population Density, 1820 The thirty years from 1790 to 1820 saw a sizable increase in population, especially along the Ohio and Mississippi River valleys.

along the route of the Erie Canal, in the lower Delaware Valley southeast of Philadelphia, or along the Merrimack River north of Boston. But most of the Irish immigrants, "the poorest and most wretched population that can be found in the world," one of their priests called them, lacked the means to go west. Like it or not, they had to settle in the eastern cities.

Viewed in historical perspective, this massive wave of immigration stimulated the American economy. In the short run, the influx of the 1830s and 1840s depressed living standards and strained the social fabric. For the first time the nation had acquired a culturally distinctive, citybound, and propertyless class. The poor Irish immigrants had to accept whatever wages employers offered them. By doing so they caused resentment among native workers—resentment exacerbated by the unfamiliarity of the Irish with city ways and by their Roman Catholic faith, which the Protestant majority associated with European authoritarianism and corruption.

The Persistence of the Household System

Since technology affected American industry unevenly, contemporaries found the changes difficult to evaluate. Interchangeable firing pins for rifles did not lead at once even to matching pairs of shoes. More than fifteen years passed after John Fitch built and launched the world's first regularly scheduled steamboat in 1790 before it was widely accepted. Few people in the 1820s appreciated how profound the impact of the factory system would be. The city of Lowell seemed remarkable and important but not necessarily a herald of future trends.

Yet in nearly every field apparently minor changes were being made. Beginning around 1815, small improvements in the design of waterwheels, such as the use of leather transmission belts and metal gears, made possible larger and more efficient machinery in mills and factories. Iron production advanced beyond the stage of the blacksmith's forge and the small foundry only slowly; nevertheless, by 1810 machines were stamping out nails at a third of the cost of the hand-forged type. At about this time the puddling process for refining pig iron made it possible to use coal for fuel instead of expensive charcoal.

Rise of Corporations

Mechanization required substantial capital investment, and capital was chronically in short supply. The modern method of organizing large enterprises, the corporation, was slow to develop. Between 1781 and 1801 only 326 corporations were chartered by the states, and only a few of them were engaged in manufacturing.

The general opinion was that only quasi-public projects, such as roads and waterworks, were entitled to the privilege of incorporation. Anyone interested in organizing a corporation had to obtain a special act of a state legislature. And even among businessmen there was a tendency to associate corporations with monopoly, with corruption, and with the undermining of individual enterprise. In 1820 the economist Daniel Raymond wrote, "The very object . . . of the act of incorporation is to produce inequality, either in rights, or in the division of property. Prima facie, therefore all money corporations are detrimental to national wealth. They are always created for the benefit of the rich. . . ." Such feelings help explain why as late as the 1860s most manufacturing was being done by unincorporated companies.

While the growth of industry did not suddenly revolutionize American life, it reshaped society in various ways. For a time it lessened the importance of foreign commerce. Some relative decline from the lush years immediately preceding Jefferson's embargo was no doubt inevitable, especially in the fabulously profitable reexport trade. But American industrial growth reduced the need for foreign products and thus the business of merchants. Only in the 1850s, when the wealth and population of the United States were more than three times what they had been in the first years of the century, did the value of American exports climb back to the levels of 1807. As the country moved closer to self-sufficiency (a point it never reached), nationalistic and isolationist sentiments were subtly augmented. During the embargo and the War of 1812 a great deal of capital had been transferred from commerce to industry; afterward new capital continued to prefer industry, attracted by the high profits and growing prestige of manufacturing. The rise of manufacturing affected farmers too, for as cities grew in size and number, the need to feed the populace caused commercial agriculture to flourish.

Cotton Revolutionizes the South

By far the most important indirect effect of industrialization occurred in the South, which soon began to produce cotton to supply the new textile factories of Great Britain and New England. Beginning in 1786, "sea-island" cotton was grown successfully in the mild, humid lowlands and offshore islands along the coasts of Georgia and South Carolina. This was a high-quality cotton, silky and long-fibered like the Egyptian kind. But its susceptibility to frost severely limited the area of its cultivation. Elsewhere in the South, "green-seed," or upland, cotton flourished, but this plant had little commercial value because the seeds could not be easily separated from the lint. When sea-island cotton was passed between two rollers, its shiny black seeds simply popped out; with upland cotton the seeds were pulled through with the lint and crushed, the oils and broken bits destroying the value of the fiber. To remove the seeds by hand was laborious; a slave working all day could clean scarcely a pound of the white fluff. This made it an uneconomical crop. In 1791 the usually sanguine Hamilton admitted in his *Report on Manufactures* that "the extensive cultivation of cotton can, perhaps, hardly be expected."

Early American cotton manufacturers used the sea-island variety or imported the foreign fiber, in the latter case paying a duty of 3 cents a pound. However, the planters of South Carolina and Georgia, suffering from hard times after the Revolution, needed a new cash crop. Rice production was not expanding, and indigo, the other staple of the area, had ceased to be profitable when it was no longer possible to claim the British bounty. Cotton seemed an obvious answer. Farmers were experimenting hopefully with varieties of the plant and mulling the problem of how upland cotton could be more easily deseeded.

Generations of American schoolchildren—and college students—have been taught that over the course of two weeks in 1793 Eli Whitney, a Yankee who had never seen a

In 2005 historian Angela Lakwete used this print as the cover of *Inventing the Cotton Gin. Machine and Myth in Antebellum America* to show that devices similar to that "invented" by Eli Whitney in 1793 had long been in use in the South. The human details in the image are revealing as well.

cotton plant, invented a machine that instantly revolutionized the production of cotton. His cotton gin (engine) consisted of a cylinder covered with rows of wire teeth rotating in a box filled with cotton. As the cylinder turned, the teeth passed through narrow slits in a metal grating. Cotton fibers were caught by the teeth and pulled through the slits. The seeds, too thick to pass through the openings, were left behind. A second cylinder, with brushes rotating in the opposite direction to sweep the cotton from the wires, prevented matting and clogging.

In fact, as the lithograph on this page suggests, Southern cotton planters had for decades used a roller gin, which operated according to similar principles—tugging cotton through meshed teeth to pull out seeds without harming the fibers. Many regarded Whitney's design as an improvement, but it took nearly three decades before it replaced the roller gins. The expansion of cotton production did not rise sharply until the 1820s.

Upland cotton would grow wherever there were 200 consecutive days without frost and twenty-four inches of rain. The crop engulfed Georgia and South Carolina and spread north into parts of Virginia. After Andrew Jackson defeated the southeastern Indians during the War of 1812, the rich "Black Belt" area of central Alabama and northern Mississippi and the delta region along the lower Mississippi River were rapidly taken over by the fluffy white staple. In 1821 Alabama alone raised 40,000 bales. Central Tennessee also became important cotton country.

Cotton stimulated the economy of the rest of the nation as well. Most of it was exported, the sale paying for much-needed European products. The transportation,

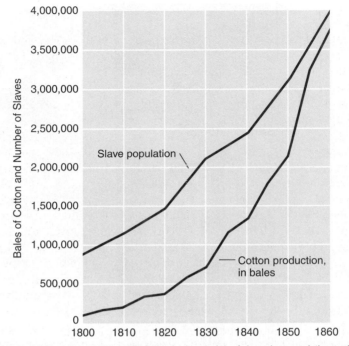

Cotton Production and Slave Population, 1800–1860 As the number of slaves increased, the production of cotton increased also.

insurance, and final disposition of the crop fell largely into the hands of Northern merchants, who profited accordingly. And the surplus corn and hogs of western farmers helped feed the slaves of the new cotton plantations. Cotton was the major force in the economy for a generation, beginning about 1815.

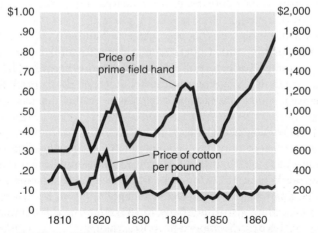

Prices for Cotton and for Slaves, 1802–1860 These prices for cotton and field slaves appear in New Orleans records. The left axis shows the price of cotton; the right, the price of a slave. The rising trend of slave prices (especially from 1850 to 1860), and a growing slave population, show the continuing profitability and viability of slavery up to 1860.

Revival of Slavery

Amid the national rejoicing over this prosperity, one aspect both sad and ominous was easily overlooked. Slavery, a declining or at worst stagnant institution in the decade of the Revolution, was revitalized in the following years.

Libertarian beliefs inspired by the Revolution ran into the roadblock of race prejudice as soon as some of the practical aspects of freedom for blacks became apparent. As disciples of John Locke, the Revolutionary generation had a deep respect for property rights; in the last analysis most white Americans placed these rights ahead of the personal liberty of black Americans. Forced abolition of slavery therefore attracted few recruits. Moreover, the rhetoric of the Revolution had raised the aspirations of blacks. Increasing signs of rebelliousness appeared among them, especially after the slave uprising in Saint Domingue, which culminated, after a great bloodbath, in the establishment of the black Republic of Haiti in 1804. This example of a successful slave revolt filled white Americans with apprehension. Their fears were irrational (Haitian blacks outnumbered whites and mulattos combined by seven to one), but nonetheless real. And fear led to repression; the exposure in 1801 of a plot to revolt in Virginia resulted in some three dozen executions even though no actual uprising had occurred.

The mood of the Revolutionary decade had led a substantial number of masters to free their slaves. Unfortunately this led many other whites to have second thoughts about ending slavery. "If the blacks see all of their color slaves, it will seem to them a disposition of Providence, and they will be content," a Virginia legislator claimed. "But if they see others like themselves free . . . they will repine." As the number of free blacks rose, restrictions on them were everywhere tightened.

In the 1780s many opponents of slavery began to think of solving the "Negro problem" by colonizing freed slaves in some distant region—in the western districts or perhaps in Africa. The colonization movement had two aspects. The first one was a manifestation of an embryonic black nationalism that reflected the disgust of black Americans with local racial attitudes and their interest in African civilization. Paul Cuffe, a Massachusetts Quaker, managed to finance the emigration of thirty-eight of his fellow blacks to British Sierra Leone in 1815, but few others followed. Most influential Northern blacks, the most conspicuous among them the Reverend Richard Allen, bishop of the African Methodist Church, opposed the idea vigorously.

The other colonization movement, led by whites, was paternalistic. Some white colonizationists genuinely abhorred slavery. Others could not stomach living with free blacks; to them colonization was merely a polite word for deportation. Most white colonizationists were conservatives who considered themselves realists.

The colonization idea became popular in Virginia in the 1790s, but nothing was achieved until after the founding of the **American Colonization Society** in 1817. The society purchased African land and established the Republic of Liberia. However, despite the cooperation of a handful of black nationalists and the patronage of many important white Southerners, including Presidents Madison and Monroe and Chief Justice Marshall, it accomplished little. Although some white colonizationists expected ex-slaves to go to Africa as Christian missionaries to convert and "civilize" the natives, few blacks wished to migrate to a land so alien to their own experience. Only about 12,000 went to Liberia, and the toll taken among them by tropical diseases was large. As late as 1850 the black American population of Liberia was only 6,000.

The cotton boom of the early nineteenth century acted as a brake on the colonization movement. As cotton production expanded, the need for labor in the South grew apace. The price of slaves doubled between 1795 and 1804. As it rose, the inclination of even the most kindhearted masters to free their slaves began to falter. Although the importation of slaves from abroad had been outlawed by all the states, perhaps 25,000 were smuggled into the country in the 1790s. In 1804 South Carolina reopened the trade, and between that date and 1808, when the constitutional prohibition of importation became effective, some 40,000 were brought in. Thereafter the miserable traffic in human beings continued clandestinely, though on a lesser scale.

The cotton boom triggered an internal trade in slaves that frequently ripped black families apart. While it had always been legal for owners to transport their own slaves to a new state if they were settling there, many states forbade, or at least severely restricted, interstate commercial transactions in human flesh. A Virginia law of 1778, for example, prohibited the importation of slaves for purposes of sale, and persons entering the state with slaves had to swear that they did not intend to sell them. Once cotton became important, these laws were either repealed or systematically evaded. There was a surplus of slaves in one part of the United States and an acute shortage in another. A migration from the upper South to the cotton lands quickly sprang up. Slaves from "free" New York and New Jersey and even from New England began to appear on the auction blocks of Savannah and Charleston. Early in the Era of Good Feelings, newspapers in New Orleans were carrying reports such as, "Jersey negroes appear to be particularly adapted to this market. . . . We have the right to calculate on large importations in the future, from the success which hitherto attended the sale."

The lot of African Americans in the Northern states was almost as bad as that of Southern free blacks. Except in New England, where there were few blacks to begin with, most were denied the vote, either directly or by extralegal pressures. They could not testify in court, intermarry with whites, obtain decent jobs or housing, or get even a rudimentary education. Most states segregated blacks in theaters, hospitals, churches, and on public transportation facilities. They were barred from hotels and restaurants patronized by whites.

Northern blacks could at least protest and try to convince the white majority of the injustice of their treatment. These rights were denied their Southern brethren. They could and did publish newspapers and pamphlets, organize for political action, and petition legislatures and Congress for redress of grievance—in short, they applied methods of peaceful persuasion in an effort to improve their position in society.

Roads to Market

Inventions and technological improvements were extremely important in the settlement of the West. On superficial examination, this may not seem to have been the case, for the hordes of settlers who struggled across the mountains immediately after the War of 1812 were no better equipped than their ancestors who had pushed up the eastern slopes in previous generations. Many plodded on foot over hundreds of miles, dragging crude carts laden with their meager possessions. More

See the **Map**

Expanding America and Internal Improvements at myhistorylab.com

This stagecoach has just passed over a solid road made of tree trunks, but it must now continue traveling across a dirt road. Already its wheels have sunk several inches into the mud.

Source: George Tattersall, English, 1817–1849 (active U.S. 1836), *Album of Western Sketches: Highways and Byeways of the Forest*, a Scene on "the Road", 1836. Pen and brown ink with brush and brown wash, heightened with white gouache, over graphite pencil, on gray paper. 21.0 x 29.8 cm (8 1/4 x 11 3/4 in.) Museum of Fine Arts, Boston. Gift of Maxim Karolik for the M. and M. Karolik Collection of American Watercolors and Drawings, 1800–1875, 56.400.11. Photograph © 2011 Museum of Fine Arts, Boston.

fortunate pioneers traveled on horseback or in heavy, cumbersome wagons, the best known being the canvas-topped Conestoga "covered wagons," pulled by horses or oxen.

In many cases the pioneers followed trails and roads no better than those of colonial days—quagmires in wet weather, rutted and pitted with potholes a good part of the year. When they settled down, their way of life was no more advanced than that of the Pilgrims. At first they were creatures of the forest, feeding on its abundance, building their homes and simple furniture with its wood, clothing themselves in the furs of forest animals. They usually planted the first crop in a natural glade; thereafter, year by year, they pushed back the trees with ax and saw and fire until the land was cleared. Until the population of the territory had grown large enough to support town life, settlers were as dependent on crude household manufacturers as any earlier pioneer.

The spread of settlement into the Mississippi Valley created challenges that required technological advances if they were to be met. In the social climate of that age in the United States, these advances were not slow in coming. Most were related to transportation, the major problem for westerners. Everyone recognized that an efficient transportation network would increase land values, stimulate domestic and foreign trade, and strengthen the entire economy. The Mississippi River and its tributaries provided a natural highway for western commerce and communication, but it was one that had grave disadvantages. Farm products could be floated down to New Orleans on rafts and flatboats, but the descent along the Ohio River from Pittsburgh to the Mississippi took at least a month. In any case, the natural flow of trade was between the East and West. That is why, from early in the westward movement, much attention was given to building roads linking the Mississippi Valley to the eastern seaboard.

Constructing decent roads over the rugged Appalachians was a formidable task. The steepest grades had to be reduced by cutting through hills and filling in low places, all without modern blasting and earth-moving equipment. Drainage ditches were essential if the roads were not to be washed out by the first rains, and a firm foundation of stones had to be provided if they were to stand up under the pounding of heavy wagons. The skills required for building roads of this quality had been developed in Great Britain and France, and the earliest American examples, constructed in the 1790s, were similar to good European highways. The first such road, connecting Philadelphia and Lancaster, Pennsylvania, opened to traffic in 1794.

Transportation and the Government

Most of the improved highways and many bridges were built as business ventures by private interests. Promoters charged tolls, the rates being set by the states. Tolls were collected at gates along the way; hinged poles suspended across the road were turned back by a guard after receipt of the toll. Hence these thoroughfares were known as turnpikes, or simply pikes.

The profits earned by a few early turnpikes, such as the one between Philadelphia and Lancaster, caused the boom in private road building, but even the most fortunate of the turnpike companies did not make much money. Maintenance was expensive, and traffic spotty. (Ordinary public roads paralleling turnpikes were sometimes called "shunpikes" because penny-pinching travelers used them to avoid the tolls.) Some states bought stock to bolster weak companies, and others built and operated turnpikes as public enterprises. Local governments everywhere provided considerable support, for every town was eager to develop efficient communication with its neighbors.

Despite much talk about individual self-reliance and free enterprise, local, state, and national governments contributed heavily to the development of what in the jargon of the day were called "internal improvements." They served as "primary entrepreneurs," supplying capital for risky but socially desirable enterprises with the result that a fascinating mixture of private and public energy went into the building of these institutions. At the federal level even the parsimonious Jeffersonians became deeply involved. In 1808 Secretary of the Treasury Albert Gallatin drafted a comprehensive plan for constructing much-needed roads at a cost of $16 million. This proposal was not adopted, but the government poured money in an erratic and unending stream into turnpike companies and other organizations created to improve transportation.

Logically, the major highways, especially those over the mountains, should have been built by the national government. Strategic military requirements alone would have justified such a program. One major artery, the Old National Road, running from Cumberland, Maryland, to Wheeling, in western Virginia, was constructed by the United States between 1811 and 1818. In time it was extended as far west as Vandalia, Illinois. However, further federal road building was hampered by political squabbles in Congress, usually phrased in constitutional terms but in fact based on sectional rivalries and other economic conflicts. Thus no comprehensive highway program was undertaken in the nineteenth century.

While the National Road, the New York Pike, and other, rougher trails such as the Wilderness Road into the Kentucky country were adequate for the movement of settlers, they did not begin to answer the West's need for cheap and efficient transportation.

Wagon freight rates averaged at least thirty cents a ton-mile around 1815. At such rates, to transport a ton of oats from Buffalo to New York would have cost twelve times the value of the oats! To put the problem another way, four horses could haul a ton and a half of oats about eighteen or twenty miles a day over a good road. If they could obtain half their feed by grazing, the horses would still consume about fifty pounds of oats a day. It requires little mathematics to figure out how many pounds of oats would be left in the wagon when it reached New York City, almost 400 miles away.

Until the coming of the railroad, which was just being introduced in England in 1825, the cost of shipping bulky goods by land over the great distances common in America was prohibitive. Businessmen and inventors concentrated instead on improving water transport, first by designing better boats and then by developing artificial waterways.

Development of Steamboats

Rafts and flatboats were adequate for downstream travel, but the only practical solution to upstream travel was the steamboat. After John Fitch's work around 1790, a number of others made important contributions to the development of steam navigation. One early enthusiast was John Stevens, a wealthy New Jerseyite, who designed an improved steam boiler for which he received one of the first patents issued by the United States. Stevens got his brother-in-law, Robert R. Livingston, interested in the problem, and the latter used his political influence to obtain an exclusive charter to operate steamboats on New York waters. In 1802, while in France trying to buy New Orleans from Napoleon, Livingston got to know Robert Fulton, a young American artist and engineer who was experimenting with steam navigation, and agreed to finance his work. In 1807, after returning to New York, Fulton constructed the *North River Steam Boat*, famous to history as the *Clermont*.

The *Clermont* was 142 feet long, 18 feet abeam, and drew 7 feet of water. With its towering stack belching black smoke, its side wheels could push it along at a steady five miles an hour. Nothing about it was radically new, but Fulton brought the essentials— engine, boiler, paddle wheels, and hull—into proper balance and thereby produced an efficient vessel.

No one could patent a steamboat; soon the new vessels were plying the waters of every navigable river from the Mississippi east. After 1815 steamers were making the run from New Orleans as far as Ohio. By 1820 at least sixty vessels were operating between New Orleans and Louisville, and by the end of the decade there were more than 200 steamers on the Mississippi.

The day of the steamboat had dawned, and although the following generation would experience its high noon, even in the 1820s its major effects were clear. The great Mississippi Valley, in the full tide of its development, was immensely enriched. Produce poured down to New Orleans, which soon ranked with New York and Liverpool among the world's great ports. From 1816–1817, only 80,000 tons of freight was shipped down the Mississippi to New Orleans; but by 1840–1841, that freight arriving in New Orleans had increased to 542,000 tons. Upriver traffic was affected even more spectacularly. Freight charges plummeted, in some cases to a tenth of what they had been after the War of 1812. Around 1818 coffee cost sixteen cents a pound more in Cincinnati than in

New Orleans, a decade later less than three cents more. The Northwest emerged from self-sufficiency with a rush and became part of the national market.

Steamboats were far more comfortable than any contemporary form of land transportation, and competition soon led builders to make them positively luxurious. The *General Pike*, launched in 1819 and set the fashion. Marble columns, thick carpets, mirrors, and crimson curtains adorned its cabins and public rooms. Soon the finest steamers were floating palaces where passengers could dine, drink, dance, and gamble in luxury as they sped smoothly to their destinations. Yet raft and flatboat traffic increased. Farmers, lumbermen, and others with goods from upriver floated down in the slack winter season and returned in comfort by steamer after selling their produce and their rafts as well, for lumber was in great demand in New Orleans. Every January and February New Orleans teemed with westerners and Yankee sailors, their pockets jingling, bent on a fling before going back to work. The shops displayed everything from the latest Paris fashions to teething rings made of alligator teeth mounted in silver. During the carnival season the city became one great festival, where every human pleasure could be tasted, every vice indulged.

The Canal Boom

While the steamboat was conquering western rivers, canals were being constructed that further improved the transportation network. Since the midwestern rivers all emptied into the Gulf of Mexico, they did not provide a direct link with the eastern seaboard. If an artificial waterway could be cut between the great central valley and some navigable stream flowing into the Atlantic, all sections would profit immensely.

Canals were more expensive than roads, but so long as the motive power used in overland transportation was the humble horse, they offered enormous economic advantages to shippers. Because there is less friction to overcome, a team plodding along a towpath could pull a canal barge with a 100-ton load and make better time over long distances than it could pulling a single ton in a wagon on the finest road.

Although canals were as old as Egypt, only about 100 miles of them existed in the United States as late as 1816. Construction costs aside, in a rough and mountainous country canals presented formidable engineering problems. To link the Mississippi Valley and the Atlantic meant somehow circumventing the Appalachian Mountains. Most people thought this impossible.

Mayor DeWitt Clinton of New York believed that such a project was feasible in New York State. In 1810, while serving as state canal commissioner, he traveled across central New York and convinced himself that it would be practicable to dig a canal from Buffalo, on Lake Erie, to the Hudson River. The Mohawk Valley cuts through the Appalachian chain just north of Albany, and at no point along the route to Buffalo does the land rise more than 570 feet above the level of the Hudson. Marshaling a mass of technical, financial, and commercial information and using his political influence cannily, Clinton placed his proposal before the New York legislature. In its defense he was eloquent and farsighted:

> As an organ of communication between the Hudson, the Mississippi, the
> St. Lawrence, the great lakes of the north and west, and their tributary rivers,
> [the canal] will create the greatest inland trade ever witnessed. The most fertile

and extensive regions of America will avail themselves of its facilities for a market. All their surplus . . . will concentrate in the city of New York. . . . That city will, in the course of time, become the granary of the world, the emporium of commerce, the seat of manufactures, the focus of great moneyed operations. . . . And before the revolution of a century, the whole island of Manhattan, covered with habitations and replenished with a dense population, will constitute one vast city.

The legislators were convinced, and in 1817 the state began construction along a route 363 miles long, most of it across densely forested wilderness. At the time the longest canal in the United States ran less than twenty-eight miles!

The construction of the Erie Canal, as it was called, was a remarkable accomplishment. The chief engineer, Benjamin Wright, a surveyor-politician from Rome, New York, had had almost no experience with canal building. Fortunately, Wright proved to be a good organizer and a fine judge of engineering talent. He quickly spotted young men of ability among the workers and pushed them forward. One of his finds, Canvass White, was sent to study British canals. White became an expert on the design of locks; he also discovered an American limestone that could be made into waterproof cement, a vital product in canal construction that had previously been imported at a substantial price from England. Another of Wright's protégés, John B. Jervis, began as an axman, rose in two years to resident engineer in charge of a section of the project, and went on to become perhaps the outstanding American civil engineer of his time. Workers who learned the business digging the "Big Ditch" supervised the construction of dozens of canals throughout the country in later years.

((•—[Hear the Audio
Erie Canal at
myhistorylab.com

The Erie, completed in 1825, was an immediate financial success. Together with the companion Champlain Canal, which linked Lake Champlain and the Hudson, it brought in over half a million dollars in tolls in its first year. Soon its entire $7 million cost had been recovered, and it was earning profits of about $3 million a year. The effect of this prosperity on New York State was enormous. Buffalo, Rochester, Syracuse, and half a dozen lesser towns along the canal flourished.

New York City: Emporium of the Western World

New York City had already become the largest city in the nation, thanks chiefly to its merchants who had established a reputation for their rapid and orderly way of doing business. In 1818 the Black Ball Line opened the first regularly scheduled freight and passenger service between New York and England. Previously shipments might languish in port for weeks while a skipper waited for additional cargo. Now merchants on both sides of the Atlantic could count on the Black Ball packets to move their goods between Liverpool and New York on schedule whether or not the transporting vessel had a full cargo. This improvement brought much new business to the port.

Now the canal cemented New York's position as the national metropolis. Most European-manufactured goods destined for the Mississippi Valley entered the country at New York and passed on to the West over the canal. The success of the Erie also sparked a nationwide canal-building boom. Most canals were constructed either by the states, as in the case of the Erie, or as "mixed enterprises" that combined public and private energies.

Nicolino V. Calyo's painting, *Burning of the Merchant's Exchange* (1835) in New York.
The entire block was rebuilt within a year.
Source: Museum of the City of New York.

No state profited as much from this construction as New York, for none possessed New York's geographic advantages. The rocky hills of New England discouraged all but fanatics. Canals were built connecting Worcester and Northampton, Massachusetts, with the coast, but they were financial failures. The Delaware and Hudson Canal, running from northeastern Pennsylvania across northern New Jersey and lower New York to the Hudson, was completed by private interests in 1828. It managed to earn respectable dividends by barging coal to the eastern seaboard, but it made no attempt to compete with the Erie for the western trade. Pennsylvania, desperate to keep up with New York, engaged in an orgy of construction. In 1834 it completed a complicated system, part canal and part railroad, over the mountains to Pittsburgh. This Mainline Canal cost a staggering sum for that day. With its 177 locks and cumbersome "inclined-plane railroad" it was slow and expensive to operate and never competed effectively with the Erie. Efforts in Maryland to link Baltimore with the West by water failed utterly.

Beyond the mountains there was even greater zeal for canal construction in the 1820s and still more in the 1830s. Once the Erie opened the way across New York, farmers in the Ohio country demanded that links be built between the Ohio River and the Great Lakes so that they could ship their produce by water directly to the East. Local feeder canals seemed equally necessary; with corn worth 20 cents a bushel at Columbus selling for 50 cents at Marietta, on the Ohio, the value of cheap transportation became obvious to Ohio farmers.

Even before the completion of the Erie, Ohio had begun construction of the Ohio and Erie Canal running from the Ohio River to Cleveland. Another, from Toledo to Cincinnati, was begun in 1832. Meanwhile, Indiana had undertaken the 450-mile Wabash and Erie Canal. These canals were well conceived, but the western states overextended themselves building dozens of feeder lines, trying, it sometimes seemed, to supply all farmers west of the Appalachians with water connections from their barns to the New York docks. Politics made such programs almost inevitable, for in order to win support for their pet projects, legislators had to back the schemes of their fellows. The result was frequently financial disaster. There was not enough traffic to pay for all the waterways that were dug. By 1844, $60 million in state "improvement" bonds were in default. Nevertheless, the canals benefited both western farmers and the national economy.

The Marshall Court

The most important legal advantages bestowed on business in the period were the gift of Chief Justice John Marshall. His particular combination of charm, logic, and force-fulness made the Court during his long reign remarkably submissive to his view of the Constitution. Marshall's belief in a powerful central government explains his tendency to hand down decisions favorable to manufacturing and business interests. He also thought that "the business community was the agent of order and progress" and tended to interpret the Constitution in a way that would advance its interests.

Many important cases came before the Court between 1819 and 1824, and in each one Marshall's decision was applauded by most of the business community. The cases involved two major principles: the "sanctity" of contracts and the supremacy of federal legislation over the laws of the states. Marshall shared the conviction of the Revolutionary generation that property had to be protected against arbitrary seizure if liberty was to be preserved. Contracts between private individuals and between individu-

> **Read the Document**
>
> *Martin v. Hunter's Lessee* at myhistorylab.com

als and the government must be strictly enforced, he believed, or chaos would result. He therefore gave the widest possible application to the constitutional provision that no state could pass any law "impairing the Obligation of Contracts."

In **Dartmouth College v. Woodward** (1819), which involved an attempt by New Hampshire to alter the charter granted to Dartmouth by King George III in 1769, Marshall held that such a charter was a contract which could not be canceled or altered without the consent of both parties. The state had sought not to destroy the college but to change it from a private to a public institution, yet Marshall held that to do so would violate the contract clause.

Marshall's decisions concerning the division of power between the federal government and the states were even more important. The question of the constitutionality of a national bank, first debated by Hamilton and Jefferson, had not been submitted to the courts during the life of the first Bank of the United States. By the time of the second Bank there were many state banks, and some of them felt that their interests were threatened by the national institution. Responding to pressure from local banks, the Maryland legislature placed an annual tax of $15,000 on "foreign" banks, including the Bank of the United States! The Maryland branch of the Bank of the United States refused to pay, whereupon the state brought suit against its cashier, John W McCulloch. **McCulloch v. Maryland** was crucial to the Bank, for five other states had levied taxes on its branches, and others would surely follow suit if the Maryland law were upheld.

Marshall extinguished the threat. The Bank of the United States was constitutional, he announced in phrases taken almost verbatim from Hamilton's 1791 memorandum to Washington on the subject; its legality was implied in many of the powers specifically granted to Congress. Full "discretion" must be allowed Congress in deciding exactly how its powers "are to be carried into execution." Since the Bank was legal, the Maryland tax was unconstitutional. Marshall found a "plain repugnance" in the thought of "conferring on one government a power to control the constitutional measures of another." He put this idea in the simplest possible language: "The power to tax involves the power to destroy . . . the power to destroy may defeat and render useless the power to create." The long-range significance of the decision lay in its strengthening of the implied powers of Congress and its confirmation of the "loose" interpretation of the Constitution. By establishing the legality of the Bank, it also aided the growth of the economy.

In 1824 Marshall handed down an important decision involving the regulation of interstate commerce. This was the "steamboat case," **Gibbons v. Ogden**. In 1815 Aaron Ogden, former U.S. senator and governor of New Jersey, had purchased the right to operate a ferry between Elizabeth Point, New Jersey, and New York City from Robert Fulton's backer, Robert R. Livingston, who held a New York monopoly of steamboat navigation on the Hudson. When Thomas Gibbons, who held a federal coasting license, set up a competing line, Ogden sued him. Ogden argued in effect that Gibbons could operate his boat on the New Jersey side of the Hudson but had no right to cross into New York waters. After complicated litigation in the lower courts, the case reached the Supreme Court on appeal. Marshall decided in favor of Gibbons, effectively destroying the New York monopoly. A state can regulate commerce that begins and ends in its own territory but not when the transaction involves crossing a state line; then the national authority takes precedence. "The act of Congress," he said, "is supreme; and the law of the state . . . must yield to it."

This decision threw open the interstate steamboat business to all comers, and since an adequate 100-ton vessel could be built for as little as $7,000, dozens of small operators were soon engaged in it. More important in the long run was the fact that in order to include the ferry business within the federal government's power to regulate interstate commerce, Marshall had given the word the widest possible meaning: "Commerce, undoubtedly, is traffic, but it is something more,—it is intercourse." By construing the "commerce" clause so broadly, he made it easy for future generations of judges to extend its coverage to include the control of interstate electric power lines and even radio and television transmission.

•••—[Read the **Document**

McCulloch v. Maryland at **myhistorylab.com**

Many of Marshall's decisions aided the economic development of the country in specific ways, but his chief contribution lay in his broadly national view of economic affairs. When he tried consciously to favor business by making contracts inviolable, his influence was important but limited—and, as it worked out, impermanent. In the steamboat case and in *McCulloch v. Maryland*, where he was really deciding between rival property interests, his work was more truly judicial in spirit and far more lasting. In such matters his nationalism enabled him to add form and substance to Hamilton's vision of the economic future of the United States.

Marshall and his colleagues firmly established the principle of judicial limitation on the power of legislatures and made the Supreme Court a vital part of the American system of government. In an age plagued by narrow sectional jealousies, Marshall's contribution was of immense influence and significance, and on it rests his claim to greatness.

John Marshall died in 1835. Two years later, in the *Charles River Bridge* case, the court handed down another decision that aided economic development. The state of Massachusetts had built a bridge across the Charles River between Boston and Cambridge that drew traffic from an older, privately owned toll bridge nearby. Since no

Table 8.1   Supreme Court Decisions and Economic Growth

	Specific Issue	Marshall Court Ruled—	Economic Consequences
Dartmouth College v. Woodward (1819)	NH sought to revoke the charter of Dartmouth College, a private school, and turn it into a public institution	For Dartmouth College: Contracts cannot be overturned	Ensured the security and regularity of business agreements and protected property rights
McCullough v. Maryland (1819)	Maryland proposed to tax the Baltimore branch of the Bank of the United States; McCullough, cashier for the bank, refused to pay Maryland tax	For federal government: States cannot tax the federal government	Ensured the supremacy of federal government over states; also strengthened the Bank of the United States and promoted economic growth
Gibbons v. Ogden (1824)	NJ steamboat operator sought to run a ferry across the Hudson River between New Jersey and New York (City), challenging a company that had a New York monopoly on such ferries	For the competing ferry: States cannot make laws that impede interstate commerce	Encouraged interstate commerce and fully national markets
Charles River Bridge Case (1837)	Operators of a company that had a contract to run a ferry across the Charles River sued Massachusetts for building a bridge that ruined the company— thereby rendering its contract worthless	For Massachusetts: The needs of the community transcend contract rights (Note: Marshall had died by time of decision)	Promoted new economic initiatives

tolls were collected from users of the state bridge after construction costs were recovered, owners of the older bridge sued for damages on the ground that the free bridge made the stock in their company worthless. They argued that in building the bridge, Massachusetts had violated the contract clause of the Constitution.

The Court, however, now speaking through the new Chief Justice, Roger B. Taney, decided otherwise. The state had a right to place "the comfort and convenience" of the whole community over that of a particular company, Taney declared. "Improvements" that add to public "wealth and property" take precedence. Like most of the decisions of the Court that were made while Marshall was chief justice, the *Charles River Bridge* case advanced the interests of those who favored economic development. Whether they were pursuing political or economic advantage, the Americans of the early nineteenth century seemed committed to a policy of compromise and accommodation.

Milestones

1790	Samuel Slater sets up first American factory
1793	Eli Whitney is widely—but wrongly—credited for inventing the cotton gin
1794	Philadelphia–Lancaster turnpike is built
1807	Robert Fulton constructs the *North River Steam Boat* (the *Clermont*)
1808	Constitutional prohibition of importation of slaves goes into effect
1813	Boston Manufacturing Company opens in Waltham, Massachusetts
1816	Second Bank of the United States is created
1817	American Colonization Society is founded in order to establish Republic of Liberia for freed slaves
1819	Chief Justice John Marshall asserts "sanctity" of contracts in *Dartmouth College v. Woodward*
	Chief Justice Marshall strengthens implied powers of Congress in *McCulloch v. Maryland* (Bank of United States)
1824	Chief Justice Marshall defends supremacy of federal government over states in *Gibbons v. Ogden* (steamboat case)
1825	Erie Canal is completed
1837	Chief Justice Roger B. Taney rules in favor of the whole community over a particular company in *Charles River Bridge v. Warren Bridge*

✓•—Study and **Review** at www.myhistorylab.com

Review Questions

1. That we live in a global economy is obvious; Americans in the early 1800s similarly perceived that their economy was undergoing substantial changes. Historians chiefly debate whether this transformation from self-sufficient farms to a market economy was sudden—revolutionary—or whether it was more gradual. What evidence can be cited in support of both positions?
2. How did cotton "revolutionize" the South?
3. How did the Marshall Court stimulate economic development?

Key Terms

American Colonization Society *235*
Dartmouth College v. Woodward *243*

Gibbons v. Ogden *244*
McCulloch v. Maryland *243*

Jacksonian Democracy

9

((•─Hear the **Audio** Chapter 9 at myhistorylab.com

Do you vote?

THE 2008 OBAMA CAMPAIGN BROUGHT THE INTERNET REVOLUTION TO American politics. By election night Obama had 7 million friends on Facebook and 1 million on MySpace. Some 137,573 followed his every move on Twitter ("Traveling through PA today & asking folks to vote for change!") Obama's YouTube site logged 15 million viewer-hours. Yet this high-tech media blitz had little impact on the young voters it was supposed to mobilize. Fewer than half of the registered voters aged eighteen to twenty-four cast ballots, an increase of only 2 percent over 2004. And the young-voter turnout (49 percent) remained below the turnout for all age groups—64 percent.

By contrast, the political revolution inaugurated by Andrew Jackson in 1828 energized voters like nothing before or since. Prior to 1828, only one in four eligible voters cast ballots on average during a presidential election. But Jackson transformed his supporters—called Jacksonians—into a well-structured Democratic party, built a rudimentary bureaucracy to manage its affairs, and appealed directly—and effectively—to masses of voters. In 1828 more than 1.1 million ballots were cast by 58 percent of the eligible voters, more than doubling the turnout of previous elections.

Jackson won in a landslide. During the next few decades, his opponents had little choice but to imitate his techniques and build a rival mass party—the Whigs. A new type of politics emerged, which some historians call the "Second American Party System." Its central feature was the mass mobilization of the electorate, characterized by a consistent turnout of over half of all voters.

Almost from the start, Jackson's more inclusive politics encountered new challenges and obstacles. Victorious campaign workers clamored for government jobs. Energized voters, seeking cheap land, ignored the plight of the Indians, not to mention legal rights secured by treaties. As more people voted, too, politicians were obliged to "represent" a vast electorate, which made it difficult to broker deals. Sectional tensions became more intractable. The new politics of democratic engagement were not without costs; within several decades, these would include civil war.

"Democratizing" Politics

At 11 AM on March 4, 1829, a bright sunny day, Andrew Jackson, hatless and dressed severely in black, left his quarters at Gadsby's Hotel. Accompanied by a few close associates, he walked up Pennsylvania Avenue to the Capitol. At a few minutes after noon he emerged on the East Portico with the justices of the Supreme Court and other dignitaries. Before a throng of more than 15,000 people he delivered an almost inaudible and thoroughly commonplace inaugural address and then took the presidential oath. The first man to congratulate him was Chief Justice Marshall, who had administered the oath. The second was "Honest George" Kremer, a Pennsylvania congressman who led the cheering crowd that brushed past the barricade and scrambled up the Capitol steps to wring the new president's hand.

●●●─┤Read the **Document**

Jackson, *First Annual Message to Congress* at **myhistorylab.com**

Jackson shouldered his way through the crush, mounted a splendid white horse, and rode off to the White House. A reception had been announced, to which "the officially and socially eligible as defined by precedent" had been invited. As Jackson rode down Pennsylvania Avenue, the crowds that had turned out to see the Hero of New Orleans followed—on horseback, in rickety wagons, and on foot. Nothing could keep them out of the executive mansion, and the result was chaos. Jackson was pressed back helplessly as men tracked mud across valuable rugs and clambered up on delicate chairs to catch a glimpse of him. The White House shook with their shouts. Glassware splintered, furniture was overturned, women fainted.

Jackson was a thin old man despite his toughness, and soon he was in danger. Fortunately, friends formed a cordon and managed to extricate him through a rear door. The new president spent his first night in office at Gadsby's Hotel.

Jackson's inauguration, and especially this celebration in the White House, symbolized the triumph of "democracy," the achievement of place and station by "the common man." Having been taught by Jefferson that all men are created equal, the Americans of Jackson's day (conveniently ignoring black males, to say nothing of women, regardless of color) found it easy to believe that every person was as competent and as politically important as his neighbor.

The difference between **Jacksonian democracy** and the Jefferson variety was more one of attitude than of practice. Jefferson had believed that ordinary citizens could be educated to determine what was right. Jackson insisted that they knew what was right by instinct. Jefferson's pell-mell encouraged the average citizen to hold up his head; by the time of Jackson, the "common man" gloried in ordinariness and made mediocrity a virtue. The slightest hint of distinctiveness or servility became suspect. While most middle-class families could still hire people to do their cooking and housework, the word *servant* itself fell out of fashion, replaced by the egalitarian *help*.

The Founders had not foreseen all the implications of political democracy for a society like the one that existed in the United States. They believed that the ordinary man should have political power in order to protect himself against the superior man, but they assumed that the latter would always lead. The people would naturally choose the best men to manage public affairs. In Washington's day and even in Jefferson's this was generally the case, but the inexorable logic of democracy gradually produced a change. The new western states, unfettered by systems created in a less democratic age, drew up constitutions that eliminated property qualifications for voting and holding office. Many more public offices were made elective rather than appointive. The eastern states revised their own frames of government to accomplish the same purposes.

Even the presidency, designed to be removed from direct public control by the Electoral College, felt the impact of the new thinking. By Jackson's time only two states, Delaware and South Carolina, still provided for the choice of presidential electors by the legislature; in all others they were selected by popular vote. The system of permitting the congressional caucus to name the candidates for the presidency came to an end before 1828. Jackson and Adams were put forward by state legislatures, and soon thereafter the still more democratic system of nomination by national party conventions was adopted.

Certain social changes reflected a new way of looking at political affairs. The final disestablishment of churches further reveals the dislike of special privilege. The beginnings of the free-school movement, the earliest glimmerings of interest in adult education, and the slow spread of secondary education all bespeak a concern for improving the knowledge and judgment of the ordinary citizen. The rapid increase in the number of newspapers, their declining prices, and their ever-greater concentration on political affairs indicate an effort to bring political news to the common man's attention.

All these changes emphasized the idea that every citizen was equally important and the conviction that all should participate in government. Officeholders began to stress the fact that they were *representatives* as well as leaders and to appeal more openly and much more intensively for votes. The public responded. At each succeeding presidential election, more people went to the polls. Eight times as many people voted in 1840 as in 1824.

As voting became more important, so did competition among candidates, and this led to changes in the role and structure of political parties. Running campaigns and getting out the vote required money, people, and organized effort. Party managers, often holders of relatively minor offices, held rallies, staged parades, dreamed up catchy slogans, and printed broadsides, party newspapers, and ballots containing the names of the party's nominees for distribution to their supporters. Parties became powerful institutions that instilled loyalty among adherents.

1828: The New Party System in Embryo

The new system could scarcely have been imagined in 1825 while John Quincy Adams ruled over the White House; Adams was not well equipped either to lead King Mob or to hold it in check. Indeed, it was the battle to succeed Adams that caused the system to develop. The campaign began almost on the day of his selection by the House of Representatives. Jackson felt that he, the man who had received the largest number of votes, had been cheated of the presidency in 1824 by "the corrupt bargain" that he believed Adams had made with Henry Clay, and he sought vindication.

Relying heavily on his military reputation and on Adams's talent for making enemies, Jackson avoided taking a stand on issues where his views might displease one or another faction. The political situation thus became chaotic, one side unable to marshal support for its policies, the other unwilling to adopt policies for fear of losing support.

Rachel Jackson, wife of Andrew Jackson. At seventeen she had married Lewis Robards, but the marriage failed and after two years she returned to her family in Natchez, Mississippi. Robards sued for divorce in Virginia. Several months later, Rachel married Jackson in Mississippi, unaware that Robards would not finalize the divorce until a year later. In defending Rachel's honor from a charge of bigamy, Jackson killed a man in a duel. During the 1824 and 1828 presidential campaigns, critics denounced their marriage as immoral. Rachel died in December 1828, several weeks before her husband was inaugurated.

The campaign was disgraced by character assassination and lies of the worst sort. Administration supporters denounced Jackson as a bloodthirsty military tyrant, a drunkard, and a gambler. His wife Rachel, ailing and shy, was dragged into the campaign by an Adams pamphleteer who branded her a "convicted adulteress."

Furious, the Jacksonians (now calling themselves Democrats) replied in kind. Discovering that Adams had purchased a chess set and a billiard table for the White House, they accused him of squandering public money on gambling devices. They translated his long and distinguished public service into the statistic that he had received over the years a sum equal to $16 for every day of his life in government pay. The great questions of the day were largely ignored.

All this was inexcusable, and both sides must share the blame. But as the politicians noticed when the votes were counted, their efforts had certainly brought out the electorate. *Each* candidate received far more votes than all four candidates had received in the preceding presidential election.

The Jacksonian Appeal

Although Jackson's supporters liked to cast him as the political heir of Jefferson, he was in many ways like the conservative Washington: a soldier first, an inveterate speculator in western lands, the owner of a fine plantation and of many slaves, a man with few intellectual interests, and only sketchily educated.

Nor was Jackson quite the rough-hewn frontier character he sometimes seemed. True, he could not spell (again, like Washington), he possessed the unsavory habits of the tobacco chewer, and he had a violent temper. But his manners and lifestyle were those of a southern planter. "I have always felt that he was a perfect savage," Grace Fletcher Webster, wife of Senator Daniel Webster, explained. "But," she added, "his manners are very mild and gentlemanly." Jackson's judgment was intuitive yet usually

1828

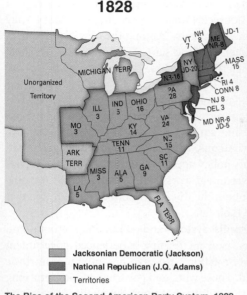

Jacksonian Democratic (Jackson)
National Republican (J.Q. Adams)
Territories

The Rise of the Second American Party System, 1828
Jackson's enormous turnout in 1828 heralded a new era in
mass political participation. In the past, Federalists tended
to take New England, and Democrats, the South. But in
1832 Jackson shattered his fragmented opposition.

Andrew Jackson as president.

sound; his frequent rages were often feigned, designed to accomplish some carefully
thought-out purpose. Once, after scattering a delegation of protesters with an exhibi-
tion of wrath, he turned to an observer and said impishly, "They thought I was mad."

Whatever his personal convictions, Jackson stood as the symbol for a new,
democratically oriented generation. That he was both a great hero and in many ways a
most extraordinary person helps explain his mass appeal. He had defeated a mighty
British army and killed many Indians, but he acted on hunches and not always
consistently, put loyalty to old comrades above efficiency when making appointments,
and distrusted "aristocrats" and all special privilege. Perhaps he was rich, perhaps
conservative, but he was a man of the people, born in a frontier cabin, and familiar with
the problems of the average citizen.

For these reasons Jackson drew support from every section and every social class:
western farmers and southern planters, urban workers and bankers, and merchants.
In this sense he was profoundly democratic. He believed in equality of opportunity,
distrusted entrenched status of every sort, and rejected no free American because of
humble origins or inadequate education.

The Spoils System

Jackson took office with the firm intention of punishing the "vile wretches" who had
attacked him so viciously during the campaign. (Rachel Jackson died shortly after the
election, and her devoted husband was convinced that the indignities heaped on her by

Adams partisans had hastened her decline.) The new concept of political office as a reward for victory seemed to justify a housecleaning in Washington. Henry Clay captured the fears of anti-Jackson government workers. "Among the official corps here there is the greatest solicitude and apprehension," he said. "The members of it feel something like the inhabitants of Cairo when the plague breaks out; no one knows who is next to encounter the stroke of death."

Eager for the "spoils," an army of politicians invaded Washington. Such invasions were customary, for the principle of filling offices with one's partisans was almost as old as the republic. However, the long lapse of time since the last real political shift, and the recent untypical example of John Quincy Adams, who rarely removed or appointed anyone for political reasons, made Jackson's policy appear revolutionary. His removals were not entirely unjustified, for many government workers had grown senile and others corrupt. Jackson was determined to root out the thieves. Even Adams admitted that some of those Jackson dismissed deserved their fate.

Aside from going along with the **spoils system** and eliminating crooks and incompetents, Jackson advanced another reason for turning experienced government employees out of their jobs: the principle of rotation. "No man has any more intrinsic right to official station than another," he said. Those who hold government jobs for a long time "are apt to acquire a habit of looking with indifference upon the public interests and of tolerating conduct from which an unpracticed man would revolt." By "rotating" jobholders periodically, more citizens could participate in the tasks of government, and the danger of creating an entrenched bureaucracy would be eliminated. The problem was that the constant replacing of trained workers by novices was not likely to increase the efficiency of the government. Jackson's response to this argument was typical: "The duties of all public officers are . . . so plain and simple that men of intelligence may readily qualify themselves for their performance."

Contempt for expert knowledge and the belief that ordinary Americans can do anything they set their minds to became fundamental tenets of Jacksonian democracy. To apply them to present-day government would be to court disaster, but in the early nineteenth century it was not so preposterous, because the role that government played in American life was simple and nontechnical.

President of All the People

President Jackson was not cynical about the spoils system. As a strong man who intuitively sought to increase his authority, the idea of making government workers dependent on him made excellent sense. His opponents had pictured him as a simple soldier fronting for a rapacious band of politicians, but he soon proved he would exercise his authority directly. Except for Martin Van Buren, the secretary of state, his Cabinet was not distinguished, and he did not rely on it for advice. He turned instead to an informal "Kitchen Cabinet," which consisted of the influential Van Buren and a few close friends. But these men were advisers, not directors; Jackson was clearly master of his own administration.

More than any earlier president, he conceived of himself as the direct representative of all the people and therefore the embodiment of national power. From Washington to John Quincy Adams, his predecessors together had vetoed only nine bills, all on the ground that they believed the measures unconstitutional. Jackson vetoed a dozen, some simply because he thought the legislation inexpedient. Yet he had no ambition to expand the scope of federal authority at the expense of the states. Basically he was a Jeffersonian; he favored a "frugal," constitutionally limited national government. Furthermore, he was a poor administrator, given to penny-pinching and lacking in imagination. His strong prejudices and his contempt for expert advice, even in fields such as banking where his ignorance was almost total, did him no credit and the country considerable harm.

Sectional Tensions Revived

In office Jackson had to say something about western lands, the tariff, and other issues. He tried to steer a moderate course, urging a slight reduction of the tariff and "constitutional" internal improvements. He suggested that once the rapidly disappearing federal debt had been paid off, the surplus revenues of the government might be "distributed" among the states.

So complex were the interrelations of sectional disputes that even these cautious proposals caused conflict. If the federal government turned its expected surplus over to the states, it could not afford to reduce the price of public land without going into the red. This disturbed westerners, notably Senator Thomas Hart Benton of Missouri, and western concern suggested to southern opponents of the protective tariff an alliance of South and West. The Southerners argued that a tariff levied only to raise revenue would increase the cost of foreign imports, bring more money into the treasury, and thus make it possible to reduce the price of public land.

The question came up in the Senate in December 1829, when Senator Samuel A. Foot of Connecticut suggested restricting the sale of government land. Benton promptly denounced the proposal. On January 19, 1830, Senator Robert Y. Hayne of South Carolina, a spokesman for Vice President Calhoun, supported Benton vigorously, suggesting an alliance of South and West based on cheap land and low tariffs. Daniel Webster then rose to the defense of northeastern interests, cleverly goading Hayne by accusing South Carolina of advocating disunionist policies. Responding to this attack, the South Carolinian launched into an impassioned exposition of the states' rights doctrine.

Webster then took the floor again and for two days, before galleries packed with the elite of Washington society, cut Hayne's argument to shreds. The Constitution was a compact of the American people, not merely of the states, he insisted, the Union perpetual and indissoluble. Webster made the states' rights position appear close to treason; his "second reply to Hayne" effectively prevented the formation of a West–South alliance and made Webster a presidential candidate.

Jackson: "The Bank . . . I Will Kill It!"

In the fall of 1832 Jackson was reelected president, handily defeating Henry Clay. The main issue in this election, aside from Jackson's personal popularity, was the president's determination to destroy the Second Bank of the United States. In this **Bank war**, Jackson won a complete victory, yet the effects of his triumph were anything but beneficial to the country.

After *McCulloch v. Maryland* had presumably established its legality and the conservative Langdon Cheves had gotten it on a sound footing, the Bank of the United States had flourished. In 1823 Cheves was replaced as president by Nicholas Biddle, who managed it brilliantly. A talented Philadelphian, Biddle realized that his institution could act as a rudimentary central bank, regulating the availability of credit throughout the nation by

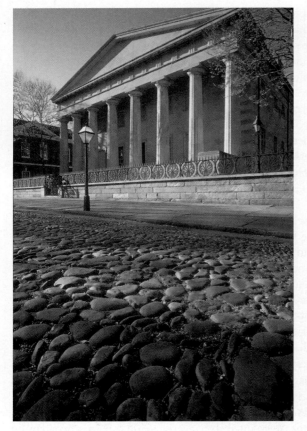

With its simple lines and perfect symmetry, the Second Bank of the United States was a symbol of Classical architecture. Jackson thought its internal workings were less simple and transparent.

controlling the lending policies of the state banks. Small banks, possessing limited amounts of gold and silver, sometimes overextended themselves in making large amounts of bank notes available to borrowers in order to earn interest. All this paper money was legally convertible into hard cash on demand, but in the ordinary run of business people seldom bothered to convert their notes so long as they thought the issuing bank was sound.

Bank notes passed freely from hand to hand and from bank to bank in every section of the country. Eventually much of the paper money of the local banks came across the counter of one or another of the twenty-two branches of the Bank of the United States. By collecting these notes and presenting them for conversion into coin, Biddle could compel the local banks to maintain adequate reserves of gold and silver—in other words, make them hold their lending policies within bounds. "The Bank of the United States," he explained, "has succeeded in keeping in check many institutions which might otherwise have been tempted into extravagant and ruinous excesses."

Biddle's policies in the 1820s were good for the Bank of the United States (which earned substantial profits), for the state banks, and probably for the country. Pressures on local bankers to make loans were enormous. The nation had an insatiable need for capital, and the general mood of the people was optimistic. Everyone wanted to borrow, and everyone expected values to rise, as in general they did. But by making liberal loans to produce merchants, for example, rural bankers indirectly stimulated farmers to expand their output beyond current demand, which eventually led to a decline in prices and an agricultural depression. In every field of economic activity, reckless lending caused inflation and greatly exaggerated the ups and downs of the business cycle. (This lesson was hammered home to Americans during the financial meltdown of 2008, when lending for home mortgages spiraled out of control and the mortgage market crashed.)

Biddle's policies acted to stabilize the economy, and many interests, including a substantial percentage of state bankers, supported them. They also provoked a great deal of opposition. In part the opposition originated in pure ignorance: Distrust of paper money did not disappear, and people who disliked all paper saw the Bank as merely the largest (and thus the worst) of many bad institutions. At the other extreme, some bankers chafed under Biddle's restraints because by discouraging them from lending freely, he was limiting their profits.

Finally, some people objected to the Bank because it was a monopoly. Distrust of chartered corporations as agents of special privilege tended to focus on the Bank, which had a monopoly of public funds but was managed by a private citizen and controlled by a handful of rich men. Biddle's wealth and social position intensified this feeling. Like many brilliant people, he sometimes appeared arrogant. He was unused to criticism and disdainful of ignorant and stupid attacks, failing to see that they were sometimes the most dangerous.

Jackson's Bank Veto

This formidable opposition to the Bank was diffuse and unorganized until Andrew Jackson brought it together. When he did, the Bank was quickly destroyed. Jackson can be included among the ignorant enemies of the institution, a hard-money man suspicious of all commercial banking. "I think it right to be perfectly frank with you," he told Biddle in 1829. "I do not dislike your Bank any more than all banks. But ever since I read the history of the South Sea Bubble I have been afraid of banks."

Jackson's attitude dismayed Biddle. It also mystified him, since the Bank was the country's best defense against a speculative mania like the eighteenth-century South Sea Bubble, in which hundreds of naive British investors had been fleeced. Bankers usually *opposed* government restraints on lending. Almost against his will, Biddle found himself gravitating toward Clay and the new National Republican party, offering advantageous loans and retainers to politicians and newspaper editors in order to build up a following. Thereafter, events moved inevitably toward a showdown, for the president's combative instincts were easily aroused. "The Bank," he told Van Buren, "is trying to kill me, *but I will kill it!*"

Henry Clay, Daniel Webster, and other prominent National Republicans hoped to use the Bank controversy against Jackson. They reasoned that the institution was so important to the country that Jackson's opposition to it would undermine his popularity. They therefore urged Biddle to ask Congress to renew the Bank's charter. The charter would not expire until 1836, but by pressing the issue

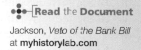

•••— Read the Document

Jackson, *Veto of the Bank Bill* at myhistorylab.com

before the 1832 presidential election, they could force Jackson either to approve the recharter bill or to veto it (which would give candidate Clay a lively issue in the campaign). The banker yielded to this strategy and a recharter bill passed Congress early in July 1832. Jackson promptly vetoed it.

Jackson's message explaining why he had rejected the bill was immensely popular, but it adds nothing to his reputation as a statesman. Being a good Jeffersonian—and no friend of John Marshall—he insisted that the Bank was unconstitutional. (*McCulloch v. Maryland* he brushed aside, saying that as president he had sworn to uphold the Constitution as *he* understood it.) The Bank was inexpedient, he argued. A dangerous private monopoly that allowed a handful of rich men to accumulate "many millions" of dollars, the Bank was making "the rich richer and the potent more powerful."

Furthermore, many of its stockholders were foreigners: "If we must have a bank . . . it should be *purely American.*"[1]

Buttressed by his election triumph, Jackson acted swiftly. He ordered the withdrawal of government funds from the Bank, but his own secretary of the treasury thought it unwise and refused to do so. Jackson replaced him with Attorney General Roger B. Taney, who had been advising him closely on Bank affairs. Taney carried out the order by depositing new federal receipts in seven state banks in eastern cities while continuing to meet government expenses with drafts on the Bank of the United States.

Set on winning the Bank war, Jackson lost sight of his fear of unsound paper money. Taney, however, knew exactly what he was doing. One of the state banks receiving federal funds was the Union Bank of Baltimore. Taney owned stock in this institution, and its president was his close friend. Little wonder that Jackson's enemies were soon calling the favored state banks "pet" banks.

When Taney began to remove the deposits, the government had $9,868,000 to its credit in the Bank of the United States; within three months the figure fell to about $4 million. Faced with the withdrawal of so much cash, Biddle had to contract his operations. He decided to exaggerate the contraction, pressing the state banks hard by presenting all their notes and checks that came across his counter for conversion into specie and drastically limiting his own bank's business loans. He hoped that the resulting shortage of credit would be blamed on Jackson and that it would force the president to return the deposits.

For a time the strategy appeared to be working. Paper money became scarce, specie almost unobtainable. A serious panic threatened. New York banks were soon refusing to make any loans at all. "Nobody buys; nobody can sell," a French visitor to the city observed. Petitions poured in on Congress. Worried and indignant delegations of businessmen began trooping to Washington seeking "relief." Clay, Webster, and John C. Calhoun thundered against Jackson in the Senate.

The president would not budge. "I am fixed in my course as firm as the Rockey Mountain," he wrote Vice President Van Buren. No "frail mortals" who worshiped "the golden calf" could change his mind. To others he swore he would sooner cut off his right arm and "undergo the torture of ten Spanish inquisitions" than restore the deposits. When delegations came to him, he roared, "Go to Nicholas Biddle . . . . Biddle has all the money!" And in the end—because he was right—business leaders began to take the old general's advice. Pressure on Biddle mounted swiftly, and in July 1834 he suddenly reversed his policy and began to lend money freely. The artificial crisis ended.

Jackson versus Calhoun

The Webster-Hayne debate had revived discussion of Calhoun's argument about nullification. Although southern-born, Jackson had devoted too much of his life to fighting for the entire United States to countenance disunion. Therefore, in April 1830,

---

[1]The country needed all the foreign capital it could attract. Foreigners owned only $8 million of the $35 million stock, and in any case they could not vote their shares.

when the states' rights faction invited him to a dinner to celebrate the anniversary of Jefferson's birth, he came prepared. The evening reverberated with speeches and toasts of a states' rights tenor, but when the president was called on to volunteer a toast, he raised his glass, fixed his eyes on John C. Calhoun, and said, "Our *Federal* Union: It must be preserved!" Calhoun took up the challenge at once. "The Union," he retorted, "next to our liberty, most dear!"

It is difficult to measure the importance of the animosity between Jackson and Calhoun in the crisis to which this clash was a prelude. Calhoun wanted very much to be president. He had failed to inherit the office from John Quincy Adams and had accepted the vice presidency again under Jackson in the hope of succeeding him at the end of one term, if not sooner, for Jackson's health was known to be frail. Yet Old Hickory showed no sign of passing on or retiring. Jackson also seemed to place special confidence in the shrewd Van Buren, who, as secretary of state, also had claim to the succession.

A silly social fracas in which Calhoun's wife appeared to take the lead in the systematic snubbing of Peggy Eaton, wife of the secretary of war, had estranged Jackson and Calhoun. (Peggy was supposed to have had an affair with Eaton while she was still married to another man, and Jackson, undoubtedly sympathetic because of the attacks he and Rachel had endured, stoutly defended her good name.) Then, shortly after the Jefferson Day dinner, Jackson discovered that in 1818, when he had invaded Florida, Calhoun, then secretary of war, had recommended to President Monroe that Jackson be summoned before a court of inquiry and charged with disobeying orders. Since Calhoun had repeatedly led Jackson to believe that he had supported him at the time, the revelation convinced the president that Calhoun was not a man of honor.

The personal difficulties are worth stressing because Jackson and Calhoun were not far apart ideologically except on the ultimate issue of the right of a state to overrule federal authority. Jackson was a strong president, but he did not believe that the area of national power was large or that it should be expanded. His interests in government economy, in the distribution of federal surpluses to the states, and in interpreting the powers of Congress narrowly were all similar to Calhoun's. Like most westerners, he favored internal improvements, but he preferred that local projects be left to the states.

Indian Removals

The president also took a states' rights position in the controversy that arose between the Cherokee Indians and Georgia. The Cherokee inhabited a region coveted by whites because it was suitable for growing cotton. Since most Indians preferred to maintain their tribal ways, Jackson pursued a policy of removing them from the path of white settlement. This policy seems heartless to modern critics, but since few Indians were willing to adopt the white way of life, most contemporary whites considered removal the only humane solution if the nation was to continue to expand. Jackson insisted that the Indians receive fair prices for their lands and that the government bear the expense of resettling them. He believed that moving them beyond the Mississippi would protect them from the "degradation and destruction to which they were rapidly hastening . . . in the States."

Many tribes resigned themselves to removal without argument. Between 1831 and 1833, some 15,000 Choctaw migrated from their lands in Mississippi to the region west of the Arkansas Territory.

In *Democracy in America*, the French writer Alexis de Tocqueville described "the frightful sufferings that attend these forced migrations," and he added sadly that the migrants "have no longer a country, and soon will not be a people." He vividly described a group of Choctaw crossing the Mississippi River at Memphis in the dead of winter:

> The cold was unusually severe; the snow had frozen hard upon the ground, and the river was drifting huge masses of ice. The Indians had their families with them, and they brought in their train the wounded and the sick, with children newly born and old men upon the verge of death. They possessed neither tents nor wagons, but only their arms and some provisions. I saw them embark to pass the mighty river, and never will that solemn spectacle fade from my remembrance. No cry, no sob, was heard among the assembled crowd; all were silent.

A few tribes, such as Black Hawk's Sac and Fox in Illinois and Osceola's Seminole in Florida, resisted removal and were subdued by troops. One Indian nation, the Cherokee, sought to hold on to their lands by adjusting to white ways. They took up farming and cattle raising, developed a written language, drafted a constitution, and tried to establish a state within a state in northwestern Georgia. Several treaties with the United States seemed to establish the legality of their government. But Georgia would not recognize the Cherokee Nation. It passed a law in 1828 declaring all Cherokee laws void and the region part of Georgia.

The Indians challenged this law in the Supreme Court. In *Cherokee Nation v. Georgia* (1831), Chief Justice John Marshall had ruled that the Cherokee were "not a foreign state, in the sense of the Constitution" and therefore could not sue in a U.S. court. However, in *Worcester v. Georgia* (1832), a case involving two missionaries to the Cherokee who had not procured licenses required by Georgia law, he ruled that the state could not control the Cherokee or their territory. Later, when a Cherokee named Corn Tassel, convicted in a Georgia court of the murder of another Indian, appealed on the ground that the crime had taken place in Cherokee territory, Marshall agreed and declared the Georgia action unconstitutional.

Jackson backed Georgia's position. No independent nation could exist within the United States, he insisted. Georgia thereupon hanged Corn Tassel. In 1838, after Jackson had left the White House, the United States forced 15,000 Cherokee to leave

Osceola had led the Seminole Indians' resistance to their forced removal from Florida to lands west of the Mississippi. He was seized during a truce parlay and imprisoned at Fort Moultrie, South Carolina. George Catlin, incensed by this treatment, became friends with Osceola and then painted this picture.

Osceola's Rebellion Osceola, a young warrior, refused to accept tribal elders' decision to cede Seminole land in Florida and move to Oklahoma. In 1835 he murdered the tribal leader who had accepted removal and spearheaded Seminole resistance. Seminole warriors, augmented by African Americans who had escaped from slavery, proved to be astute tacticians in guerrilla warfare. During the next seven years, the federal government spent $20 million, an immense sum, and lost 1,500 soldiers in the war to force the remaining Seminole from Florida. When Osceola hoisted a white flag to negotiate with federal officers, they seized him and put him in prison. He died shortly after George Catlin completed his portrait. Because of his courageous resistance and the treacherous manner of his capture, Osceola became famous after his death.

Georgia for Oklahoma. At least 4,000 of them died on the way; the route has been aptly named the **Trail of Tears**.

Jackson's willingness to allow Georgia to ignore decisions of the Supreme Court persuaded extreme southern states' righters that he would not oppose the doctrine of nullification should it be formally applied to a law of Congress. They deceived themselves egregiously. Jackson did not challenge Georgia because he approved of the state's position. He spoke of "the poor deluded . . . Cherokees" and called William Wirt, the distinguished lawyer who defended

⊙ See the Map

Native American Removal at **myhistorylab.com**

their cause, a "truly wicked" man. Jackson was not one to worry about being inconsistent. When South Carolina revived the talk of nullification in 1832, he acted in quite a different manner.

The Nullification Crisis

The proposed alliance of South and West to reduce the tariff and the price of land had not materialized, partly because Webster had discredited the South in the eyes of western patriots and partly because the planters of South Carolina and Georgia, fearing the competition of fertile new cotton lands in Alabama and Mississippi, opposed the rapid exploitation of the West almost as vociferously as northern manufacturers did. When a new tariff law was passed in 1832, it lowered duties much less than the Southerners desired. At once talk of nullifying it began to be heard in South Carolina.

In addition to the economic woes of the up-country cotton planters, the great planter-aristocrats of the rice-growing Tidewater, though relatively prosperous, were troubled by northern criticisms of slavery. In the rice region, blacks outnumbered whites two to one; it was the densest concentration of blacks in the United States. Usually controlled by overseers of the worst sort, the slaves seemed to their masters like savage beasts straining to rise up against their oppressors. In 1822 the exposure in Charleston of a planned revolt organized by Denmark Vesey, who had bought his freedom with money won in a lottery, had alarmed many whites. News of a far more serious uprising in Virginia led by the slave Nat Turner in 1831, just as the tariff controversy was coming to a head, added to popular concern. Radical South Carolinians saw protective tariffs and agitation against slavery as the two sides of one coin; against both aspects of what appeared to them the tyranny of the majority, nullification seemed the logical defense. Yield on the tariff, editor Henry L. Pinckney of the influential *Charleston Mercury* warned, and "abolition will become the order of the day."

Endless discussions of Calhoun's doctrine after the publication of his *Exposition and Protest* in 1828 had produced much interesting theorizing without clarifying the issue. Plausible at first glance, it was based on false assumptions: that the Constitution was subject to definitive interpretation; that one party could be permitted to interpret a compact unilaterally without destroying it; that a minority of the nation could reassume its sovereign independence but that a minority of a state could not.

President Jackson was in this respect Calhoun's exact opposite. The South Carolinian's mental gymnastics he brushed aside; intuitively he realized the central reality: If a state could nullify a law of Congress, the Union could not exist. "Tell . . . the Nullifiers from me that they can talk and write resolutions and print threats to their hearts'

View along the East Battery, Charleston by Samuel Bernard (1831). Many whites feared a slave uprising in South Carolina where African Americans outnumbered whites.

content," he warned a South Carolina representative when Congress adjourned in July 1832. "But if one drop of blood be shed there in defiance of the laws of the United States, I will hang the first man of them I can get my hands on to the first tree I can find."

The warning was not taken seriously in South Carolina. In October the state legislature provided for the election of a special convention, which, when it met, contained a solid majority of nullifiers. On November 24, 1832, the convention passed an ordinance of **nullification** prohibiting the collection of tariff duties in the state after February 1, 1833. The legislature then authorized the raising of an army and appropriated money to supply it with weapons.

Jackson quickly began military preparations of his own, telling friends that he would have 50,000 men ready to move in a little over a month. He also made a statesmanlike effort to end the crisis peaceably. First he suggested to Congress that it lower the tariff further. On December 10 he delivered a "Proclamation to the People of South Carolina." Nullification could only lead to the destruction of the Union: "The laws of the United States must be executed. I have no discretionary power on the subject. . . . Those who told you that you might peaceably prevent their execution deceived you." Old Hickory added sternly, "Disunion by armed force is *treason*. Are you really ready to incur its guilt?" If South Carolina did not back down, the president's threat to use force would mean civil war and possibly the destruction of the Union he claimed to be defending.

Calhoun sought desperately to control the crisis. By prearrangement with Senator Hayne, he resigned as vice president and was appointed to replace Hayne in the Senate, where he led the search for a peaceful solution. Having been defeated in his campaign for the presidency, Clay was a willing ally. In addition, many who admired Jackson nonetheless, as Van Buren later wrote, "distrusted his prudence," fearing that he would "commit some rash act." They believed in dealing with the controversy by discussion and compromise.

As a result, administration leaders introduced both a new tariff bill and a Force Bill granting the president additional authority to execute the revenue laws. Jackson was perfectly willing to see the tariff reduced but insisted that he was determined to enforce the law. As the February 1 deadline approached, he claimed that he could raise 200,000 men if needed to suppress resistance. "Union men, fear not," he said. "*The Union will be preserved.*"

Jackson's determination sobered the South Carolina radicals. Their appeal for the support of other southern states fell on deaf ears: All rejected the idea of nullification. The unionist minority in South Carolina added to the radicals' difficulties by threatening civil war if federal authority were defied.

Ten days before the deadline, South Carolina postponed nullification pending the outcome of the tariff debate. Then, in March 1833, Calhoun and Clay pushed a compromise tariff through Congress. As part of the agreement Congress also passed the Force Bill, mostly as a face-saving device for the president.

The compromise reflected the willingness of the North and West to make concessions in the interest of national harmony. And so the Union weathered the storm. Having stepped to the brink of civil war, the nation had drawn hastily back. The South Carolina legislature professed to be satisfied with the new tariff (in fact it made few immediate reductions, providing for a gradual lowering of rates over a ten-year period) and repealed the Nullification Ordinance. But the radical South Carolina planters were becoming convinced that only secession would protect slavery. The nullification fiasco had proved that they could not succeed without the support of other slave states. Thereafter they devoted themselves ceaselessly to obtaining it.

Boom and Bust

During 1833 and 1834 Secretary of the Treasury Taney insisted that the pet banks maintain large reserves. But other state banks began to offer credit on easy terms, aided by a large increase in their reserves of gold and silver resulting from causes unconnected with the policies of either the government or Biddle's Bank. A decline in the Chinese demand for Mexican silver led to increased exports of the metal to the United States, and the rise of American interest rates attracted English capital into the country. Heavy English purchases of American cotton at high prices also increased the flow of specie into American banks. These developments caused bank notes in circulation to jump from $82 million in January 1835 to $120 million in December 1836. Bank deposits rose even more rapidly.

Much of the new money flowed into speculation in land; a mania to invest in property swept the country. The increased volume of currency caused prices to soar 15 percent in six months, buoying investors' spirits and making them ever more optimistic about the future. By the summer of 1835 one observer estimated that in New York City, which had about 250,000 residents, enough house lots had been laid out and sold to support a population of 2 million. Chicago at this time had only 2,000 to 3,000 inhabitants, yet most of the land for twenty-five miles around had been sold and resold in small lots by speculators anticipating the growth of the area. Throughout the West farmers borrowed money from local banks by mortgaging their land, used the money to buy more land from the government, and then borrowed still more money from the banks on the strength of their new deeds.

So long as prices rose, the process could be repeated endlessly. In 1832, while the Bank of the United States still regulated the money supply, federal income from the sale of land was $2.6 million; in 1834 it was $4.9 million; and in 1835, $14.8 million. In 1836 it rose to $24.9 million, and the government found itself totally free of debt and with a surplus of $20 million!

Finally Jackson became alarmed by the speculative mania. In the summer of 1836 he issued the **Specie Circular,** which provided that purchasers must henceforth pay for public land in gold or silver. At once the rush to buy land came to a halt. As demand slackened, prices sagged. Speculators, unable to dispose of lands mortgaged to the banks, had to abandon them to the banks, but the banks could not realize enough on the foreclosed property to recover their loans. Suddenly the public mood changed. Commodity prices tumbled 30 percent between February and May. Hordes of depositors sought to withdraw their money in the form of specie, and soon the banks exhausted their supplies. Panic swept the country in the spring of 1837 as every bank in the nation was forced to suspend specie payments. The boom was over.

Major swings in the business cycle can never be attributed to the actions of a single person, however powerful, but there is no doubt that Jackson's war against the Bank exaggerated the swings of the economic pendulum, not so much by its direct effects as by the impact of the president's ill-considered policies on popular thinking. His Specie

Circular did not prevent speculators from buying land—at most it caused purchasers to pay a premium for gold or silver. But it convinced potential buyers that the boom was going to end and led them to make decisions that in fact ended it. Old Hickory's combination of impetuousness, combativeness, arrogance, and ignorance rendered the nation he loved so dearly a serious disservice.

The Jacksonians

Jackson's personality had a large impact on the shape and tone of American politics and thus with the development of the **second party system**. When he came to office, nearly everyone professed to be a follower of Jefferson. By 1836 being a Jeffersonian no longer meant much; what mattered was how one felt about Andrew Jackson. He had ridden to power at the head of a diverse political army, but he left behind him an organization with a fairly cohesive, if not necessarily consistent, body of ideas. This Democratic party contained rich citizens and poor, easterners and westerners, abolitionists as well as slaveholders. It was not yet a close-knit national organization, but the Jacksonians agreed on certain underlying principles. These included suspicion of special privilege and large business corporations, both typified by the Bank of the United States; freedom of economic opportunity, unfettered by private or governmental restrictions; absolute political freedom, at least for white males; and the conviction that any ordinary man is capable of performing the duties of most public offices.

Jackson's ability to reconcile his belief in the supremacy of the Union with his conviction that national authority should be held within narrow limits tended to make the Democrats the party of those who believed that the powers of the states should not be diminished. Tocqueville caught this aspect of Jackson's philosophy perfectly: "Far from wishing to extend Federal power," he wrote, "the president belongs to the party that wishes to limit that power."

Although the radical Locofoco[2] wing of the party championed the idea, nearly all Jacksonians, like their leader, favored giving the small man his chance—by supporting public education, for example, and by refusing to place much weight on a person's origin, dress, or manners. "One individual is as good as another" (for accuracy we must insert the adjective *white*) was their axiom. This attitude helps explain why immigrants, Catholics, and other minority groups usually voted Democratic. However, the Jacksonians showed no tendency either to penalize the wealthy or to intervene in economic affairs to aid the underprivileged. The motto "That government is best which governs least" graced the masthead of the chief Jacksonian newspaper, the *Washington Globe*, throughout the era.

Rise of the Whigs

The opposition to Jackson was far less cohesive. Henry Clay's National Republican party provided a nucleus, but Clay never dominated that party as Jackson dominated the Democrats. Its orientation was basically anti-Jackson. It was as though the

---

[2]A locofoco was a type of friction match. The name was first applied in politics when a group of New York Jacksonians used these matches to light candles when a conservative faction tried to break up their meeting by turning off the gaslights.

American people were a great block of granite from which some sculptor had just fashioned a statue of Jackson, the chips scattered about the floor of the studio representing the opposition.

While Jackson was president, the impact of his personality delayed the formation of a true two-party system, but as soon as he surrendered power, the opposition, taking heart, began to coalesce. Many Democrats could not accept the odd logic of Jacksonian finance. As early as 1834 they (together with the Clay element, the extreme states' righters who followed Calhoun, and other dissident groups) were calling themselves **Whigs**. The name harkened back to the Revolution. It implied patriotic distaste for too-powerful executives, expressed specifically as resistance to the tyranny of "King Andrew."

This coalition possessed great resources of wealth and talent. Anyone who understood banking was almost obliged to become a Whig unless he was connected with one of Jackson's "pets." Those spiritual descendants of Hamilton who rejected the administration's refusal to approach economic problems from a broadly national perspective also joined in large numbers. Those who found the coarseness and "pushiness" of the Jacksonians offensive were another element in the new party. The anti-intellectual and antiscientific bias of the administration (Jackson rejected proposals for a national university, an observatory, and a scientific and literary institute) drove many ministers, lawyers, doctors, and other well-educated people into the Whig fold.

The philosopher Ralph Waldo Emerson was no doubt thinking of these types when he described the Whigs as "the enterprizing, intelligent, well-meaning & wealthy part of the people," but Whig arguments also appealed to ordinary voters who were predisposed to favor strong governments that would check the "excesses" of unrestricted individualism.

Table 9.1 Second American Party System: Democrats and Whigs, 1828–1850s

	Democrats	Whigs
Leaders	Andrew Jackson, Martin Van Buren, John Calhoun, James Polk	Henry Clay, Daniel Webster
Key issue	For: "the common man"	Against: "King Andrew" (Jackson)
Bank of United States	Oppose	Favor
Federal support for internal improvements (roads, canals)	Oppose	Favor
Removal of Indians	Favor	Oppose
Tariffs	Favor low	Favor high
States' rights vs. strong central government	Endorse states' rights	Endorse strong federal government

The Whigs were slow to develop effective party organization. They had too many generals and not enough troops. The issues that defined the Whigs varied from one state to another. For the most part, the sole unifying principle was opposition to Jackson. Furthermore, they stood in conflict with the major trend of the age: the glorification of the common man.

Lacking a dominant leader in 1836, the Whigs relied on "favorite sons," hoping to throw the presidential election into the House of Representatives. Daniel Webster ran in New England. For the West and South, Hugh Lawson White of Tennessee, a former friend who had broken with Jackson, was counted on to carry the fight. General William Henry Harrison was supposed to win in the Northwest and to draw support everywhere from those who liked to vote for military heroes. This sorry strategy failed; Jackson's handpicked candidate, Martin Van Buren, won a majority of both the popular and the electoral votes.

Martin Van Buren: Jacksonianism without Jackson

Van Buren's brilliance as a political manipulator—the Red Fox, the Little Magician— has tended to obscure his statesmanlike qualities and his engaging personality. He made a powerful argument, for example, that political parties were a force for unity, not for partisan bickering. In addition, high office sobered him, and improved his judgment. He fought the Bank of the United States as a monopoly, but he also opposed irresponsible state banks. New York's Safety Fund System (requiring all banks to contribute to a fund) supervised by the state (to be used to redeem the notes of any member bank that failed) was established largely through his efforts. Van Buren believed in public construction of internal improvements, but he favored state rather than national programs, and he urged a rational approach: Each project must stand on its own as a useful and profitable public utility.

Van Buren had outmaneuvered Calhoun easily in the struggle to succeed Jackson, winning the old hero's confidence and serving him well. In 1832 he was elected vice president and thereafter was conceded to be the "heir apparent." In 1835 the Democratic National Convention unanimously nominated him for president.

((•●┤**Hear** the **Audio**

Van Buren at
myhistorylab.com

Van Buren took office just as the Panic of 1837 struck the country. Its effects were frightening but short-lived. When the banks stopped converting paper money into gold and silver, they outraged conservatives but in effect eased the pressure on the money market: Interest rates declined and business loans again became relatively easy to obtain. In 1836, at the height of the boom in land sales, Congress had voted to "distribute" the new treasury surplus to the states, and this flow of money, which the states promptly spent, also stimulated the revival. Late in 1838 the banks resumed specie payments.

But in 1839 a bumper crop caused a sharp decline in the price of cotton. Then a number of state governments that had overextended themselves in road- and canal-building projects were forced to default on their debts. This discouraged investors, particularly foreigners. A general economic depression ensued that lasted until 1843.

Van Buren was not responsible for the panic or the depression, but his manner of dealing with economic issues was scarcely helpful. He saw his role as being concerned only with problems plaguing the government, ignoring the economy as a whole.

DAVY CROCKETT

Davy Crockett, the myth, is known better than the man, who was born David Crockett in 1786 in a cabin in hardscrabble east Tennessee. John Crockett, his father, borrowed money to buy cheap frontier land and seldom repaid his creditors. When a passing Dutchman said he needed help to drive his cattle to market in Virginia, John proposed he take on David as a "bound boy" to help out. David was twelve.

After delivering the cattle to Virginia, the driver declared that David's term of service was not over. The boy pretended to accept the arrangement, but after several weeks he sneaked away in a snowstorm; two months later he was back home in Tennessee.

The next fall his father enrolled David at a small country school. But after beating up another boy, he played hooky, fearing the wrath of the schoolmaster. When his father learned of his son's truancy, he came after the boy with a hickory stick. David hightailed it into the woods.

He was gone for over two years, wandering through Tennessee, North Carolina, Virginia, and Maryland. He moved from town to town "to see what sort of place it was, and what sort of folks lived there." He mostly did odd jobs on farms for twenty-five cents a day. When he showed up back home two years later, his father, near bankruptcy, bartered David's labor to settle the debts with various creditors.

This 1839 engraving of Davy Crockett was based on an earlier painting.

Soon young Crockett's thoughts turned to girls, few of whom had much interest in such an uncouth boy. Crockett could not even write his name. So he broke free from his father and made his own deal with a local schoolteacher, bartering his labor for board and instruction. The arrangement lasted for six months, Crockett's only formal schooling.

Shortly afterward he attended a "stomp down"—a community-wide harvest festival with games, music, and dancing—where he met Polly Finley, "a very pretty" Irish girl. Within a few months they were married. Polly's parents gave the couple two cows. Crockett rented a nearby farm.

But Crockett proved to be a poor farmer. Time and again he fell into debt, lost his farm, and moved to cheaper land farther west. "I found that I was better at increasing my family than my fortune," he observed: He and his wife had three children. In 1813 they took possession of land deep in Creek territory, near the Alabama border.

The timing was poor. By then, the War of 1812 had spread to the frontier, as Tecumseh, the Indian leader, incited Indian uprisings throughout the West. In Alabama, Creeks attacked and overran Fort Mims, killing hundreds of soldiers and settlers. In response Crockett enlisted in the Tennessee militia. He served under

Andrew Jackson, participating in the slaughter of scores of Indians. "We shot them like dogs," Crockett noted.

After returning to Tennessee, he was elected magistrate for Lawrence County, a rough frontier district. Again, his farm failed; but the woodsy region was thick with game and Crockett was accurate with a long rifle. He killed deer, wolves, panthers, alligators and, in one winter alone, 105 bear. Soon tales of Crockett's hunting prowess spread throughout the region.

In 1821 Crockett was elected to the Tennessee legislature, the first of many victories. Once, accused of telling lies about an opponent, Crockett conceded that he had. But therein lay the difference, he explained, for he truthfully admitted his lies while his opponent did not. The crowd roared. In 1826 Crockett was elected to the House of Representatives.

Newspapermen delighted in the spectacle of the rough frontiersman in the nation's capital. They reported that at a White House dinner Crockett drank from the finger bowls and accused a waiter of trying to steal his food.

In Congress, Crockett's key issue—indeed, the only one he pursued with much passion—was cheap land for frontier farmers. "The rich require but little legislation," he said. "We should, at least occasionally, legislate for the poor." Such positions aligned him with the Jacksonian Democrats.

But in 1830 Crockett broke with Jackson over the removal of Indians from the South. Although Crockett readily acknowledged that he had fought to "kill up Indians," he thought it wrong that "the poor remnants of a once powerful people" should be driven from their homes. He voted against the Indian removal bill. In the next election Jackson, furious, campaigned against Crockett, who lost.

But by then his fame had spread. Newspaper editors seized on the story of the rough-hewn, bear-killing frontiersman. An 1831 play entitled *The Lion of the West,* based on Crockett, was performed in New York and London. Publishers found an eager audience for books about Crockett: some celebrated him, others lampooned him, but all exaggerated his exploits. The *Crockett Almanacs*—the first comic books—told of how Crockett rode his pet alligator up Niagara Falls, skinned Indians "the natural way, with his teeth," and indulged in insatiable and exotic sexual appetites. Tens of thousands were sold.

After seeing others make money off his celebrity, Crockett published several books of his own. In 1833 he was reelected to Congress. There was talk of his running for president on a Whig ticket, allowing that party to steal the "common man" claims of the Jacksonians. In 1835, however, Crockett was defeated for reelection to Congress by several hundred votes. Thereafter, always on the lookout for cheaper land, he told the voters of Tennessee, "you may all go to hell and I will go to Texas."

Several months later, toting his long rifle, Crockett rode into the Alamo in Texas, then a part of Mexico. Thirteen days later history caught up with the legend of Davy Crockett—and perhaps surpassed it. (See Re-Viewing the Past, *The Alamo*, pp. 320–321.)

Questions for Discussion

■ Davy Crockett was arguably the first American to become famous for his fame. What explains the appeal of Crockett to Americans in the 1830s?

■ Davy Crockett symbolized the frontier as violent, savage, and uncouth. How did his life sustain that image? And how did it undermine it?

"The less government interferes with private pursuits the better for the general prosperity," he pontificated. As Daniel Webster scornfully pointed out, Van Buren was following a policy of "leaving the people to shift for themselves," one that many Whigs rejected.

Van Buren's chief goal was finding a substitute for the state banks as a place to keep federal funds. He soon settled on the idea of "divorcing" the government from all banking activities. His independent treasury bill called for the construction of government-owned vaults where federal revenues could be stored until needed. To ensure absolute safety, all payments to the government were to be made in hard cash. After a battle that lasted until the summer of 1840, the Independent Treasury Act passed both the House and the Senate.

Opposition to the Independent Treasury Act had been bitter, and not all of it was partisan. Bankers and businessmen objected to the government's withholding so much specie from the banks because they needed all the hard money they could get to support loans that were the lifeblood of economic growth. It seemed irresponsible for the federal government to turn its back on the banks, which so obviously performed a semipublic function. These criticisms made good sense, but through a lucky combination of circumstances, the system worked reasonably well for many years.

By creating suspicion in the public mind, officially stated distrust of banks acted as a damper on their tendency to overexpand. No acute shortage of specie developed because heavy agricultural exports and the investment of much European capital in American railroads beginning in the mid-1840s brought in large amounts of new gold and silver. After 1849 the discovery of gold in California added another important source of specie. The supply of money and bank credit kept pace roughly with the growth of the economy, but through no fault of the government. "Wildcat" banks proliferated. Fraud and counterfeiting were common, and the operation of everyday business affairs was inconvenienced in countless ways. The disordered state of the currency remained a grave problem until corrected by Civil War banking legislation.

The Log Cabin Campaign

It was not his financial policy that led to Van Buren's defeat in 1840. The depression naturally hurt the Democrats, and the Whigs were far better organized than in 1836. The Whigs also adopted a different strategy. The Jacksonians had come to power on the coattails of a popular general whose views on public questions they concealed or ignored. They had maintained themselves by shouting the praises of the common man. Now the Whigs seized on these techniques and carried them to their logical—or illogical—conclusion. Not even bothering to draft a program, and passing over Clay and Webster, whose views were known and therefore controversial, they nominated General William Henry Harrison for president. To "balance" the ticket, the Whigs chose a former Democrat, John Tyler of Virginia, an ardent supporter of states' rights, as their vice presidential candidate.

The Democrats used the same methods as the Whigs and were equally well organized, but they had little heart for the fight. The best they could come up with was the fact that their vice presidential candidate, Richard Mentor Johnson, had killed Tecumseh, not merely defeated him. Van Buren tried to focus public attention on issues, but his voice could not be heard above the huzzahs of the Whigs.

A huge turnout (four-fifths of the eligible voters) carried Harrison to victory by a margin of almost 150,000. The electoral vote was 234 to 60.

The Whigs continued to repeat history by rushing to gather the spoils of victory. Washington was again flooded by office seekers, the political confusion was monumental. Harrison had no ambition to be an aggressive leader. He believed that Jackson had misused the veto and professed to put as much emphasis as had Washington on the principle of the separation of legislative and executive powers. This delighted the Whig leaders in Congress, who had had their fill of the "executive usurpation" of Jackson. Either Clay or Webster seemed destined to be the real ruler of the new administration, and soon the two were squabbling over their old general like sparrows over a crust.

At the height of their squabble, less than a month after his inauguration, Harrison fell gravely ill. Pneumonia developed, and on April 4 he died. John Tyler of Virginia, honest and conscientious but doctrinaire, became president of the United States. The political climate of the country was changed dramatically. Events began to march in a new direction.

Milestones

1828	Andrew Jackson is elected president	1831–1838	Chief Justice Marshall rules in Cherokees' favor in *Worcester v. Georgia*
1829	Crowds cause chaos at Jackson's White House inaugural reception		Jackson is reelected president
	Jackson relies on his "Kitchen Cabinet"	1833	Treasury Secretary Roger B. Taney orders Treasury funds removed from Bank of the United States
1830	Daniel Webster, in his "Second Reply to Hayne," calls Union perpetual and indissoluble		Calhoun and Clay push through Compromise Tariff
	Jackson vetoes the Maysville Road Bill	1836	Jackson issues Specie Circular to control speculation
1831	Nat Turner leads slave rebellion in Virginia		Martin Van Buren is elected president
	Chief Justice Marshall denies Cherokee rights in *Cherokee Nation v. Georgia*	1837–1838	Panic sweeps nation, ending boom
1831–1838	Southern Indians are removed to Oklahoma	1838	4,000 Cherokee die on Trail of Tears to Oklahoma
	South Carolina defends states' rights in Ordinance of Nullification	1840	"Log Cabin" Campaign is first to use "hoopla"
	Force Bill grants president authority to execute revenue laws		William Henry Harrison is elected president
	Jackson vetoes Bank Recharter Bill	1841	Harrison dies one month after inauguration; John Tyler becomes president

✓●⌐**Study** and **Review** at www.myhistorylab.com

Review Questions

1. How did the Jacksonian Democrats agree with the principles of the Jeffersonian Democrats? How did they disagree?

2. How did Jackson generate so high a turnout in the election of 1828? How did the opponents of the Jacksonian Democrats respond to Jackson's success?

3. How did the Second Bank of the United States restrain local banks from loaning too much money? Why did President Jackson seek to "kill"

the Bank of the United States? Was this policy wise?

4. Why did Jackson insist on the removal of Indians from the Southeast? Was the policy justified? Were there alternatives?

5. The Jacksonian Democrats stood for "states' rights" on many issues. Why did Jackson break so vociferously with fellow Democrat Calhoun's claim that states had the right to "nullify" federal laws with which they disagreed?

Key Terms

Bank war   *253*
Jacksonian
   democracy   *248*
nullification   *261*

second party
   system   *263*
Specie Circular   *262*
spoils system   *252*

Trail of Tears   *259*
Whigs   *264*

The Making of
Middle-Class America

10

((•—[Hear the Audio Chapter 10 at myhistorylab.com

Who is your family?

FEARS ABOUT A "CRISIS" IN THE FAMILY HAVE GENERATED HEADLINES since the early 1900s, when divorce rates began to rise. Nowadays defenders of the traditional family cite a set of familiar statistics: Nearly a third of all children are born to unwed mothers; half of all marriages end in divorce; a third of all families are headed by a single parent; more than half of all single mothers with children younger than six work outside the home. Some even redefine marriage itself. By 2010 state legislatures and judges in New Hampshire, Iowa, Massachusetts, Vermont, and Connecticut allowed same sex marriages. Yet when the issue was put directly to the electorate, the voters of thirty-five states rejected it.

If ever the traditional "ideal" prevailed in America, it was among white families in the 1820s and 1830s. Divorce was rare; the overwhelming majority of families had two parents; only one woman in fifteen worked outside the home.

Whether such families were "happier" or "stronger" than now is a different matter. Divorce was rare partly because so few could obtain it. South Carolina recognized no legal grounds for divorce. Many other states granted divorce only if a spouse committed adultery. Many couples thus endured loveless, unhappy marriages.

Nevertheless the family after 1820 was perceived as a new and dynamic force in American society. Middle-class women, especially those freed from the drudgery of farm chores, were especially influential. Sarah Hale, the leading female journalist of the era, pronounced women to be "God's appointed agents of morality." Such women organized religious revivals, spearheaded efforts to improve prisons and mental asylums, and campaigned for temperance, abolition, and women's rights. Young middle-class women, too, were avid readers, and their patronage stimulated publication of countless books and magazines. These women shaped society and culture even more directly by serving as teachers in the common schools that extended public education to much of the nation.

The reformers of the era decried the pessimism of their Calvinist forebears. Romanticism in the arts and literature affirmed that Americans and their institutions could—and would—grow and change for the better.

Tocqueville: Democracy in America

On May 12, 1831, two French aristocrats, Alexis de Tocqueville and Gustave de Beaumont, arrived in New York City from Le Havre. Their official purpose was to make a study of American prisons for the French government. But they really came, as Tocqueville explained, "to see what a great republic is like."

Tocqueville and Beaumont believed that Europe was passing from its aristocratic past into a democratic future. How better to prepare for the change, they believed, than by studying the United States, where democracy was already the "enduring and normal state" of the land. The visit provided the material for Tocqueville's classic *De la Démocratie en Amérique*, published in France in 1835 and a year later in an English translation. *Democracy in America* has been the starting point for virtually all subsequent writers who have tried to describe what Tocqueville called "the creative elements" of American institutions.

The gist of *Democracy in America* is contained in the book's first sentence: "No novelty in the United States struck me more vividly during my stay there than the equality of conditions." Tocqueville meant not that Americans lived in a state of total equality, but that the inequalities that did exist among white Americans were not enforced by institutions or supported by public opinion. "In America," he concluded, "men are nearer equality than in any other country in the world."

This sweeping generalization, however comforting to Americans then and since, is an oversimplification. Few modern students of Jacksonian America would accept it without qualification. In the 1830s and 1840s a wide and growing gap existed between the rich and poor in the eastern cities. According to one study, the wealthiest 4 percent of the population of New York controlled about half the city's wealth in 1828, about two-thirds in 1845. The number of New Yorkers worth $100,000 or more tripled in that period. A similar concentration of wealth was occurring in Philadelphia and Boston. Moreover, Tocqueville failed to observe the many poor people in Jacksonian America. Particularly in the cities, bad times forced many unskilled laborers and their families into dire poverty. Tocqueville took little notice of such inequalities, in part because he was so captivated by the theme of American equality.

Despite his blind spots, Tocqueville realized that America was undergoing some fundamental social changes. These changes, he wrote, were being made by "an innumerable crowd who are . . . not exactly rich nor yet quite poor [and who] have enough property to want order and

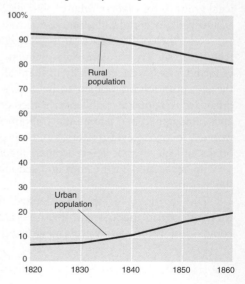

Rural versus Urban Population, 1820–1860 As the balance of rural and urban population began to shift during the years from 1820 to 1860, the number of cities with populations over 100,000 grew from one in 1820—New York—to nine in 1870, including southern and western cities like New Orleans and San Francisco.

not enough to excite envy." In his notes he put it even more succinctly: "The whole society seems to have turned into one middle class."

The Family Recast

Tocqueville was particularly struck by the character of the family. Americans, he wrote, showed an "equal regard" for husbands and wives, but defined their roles differently. This was made possible by the growth of the market economy, which undermined the importance of home and family as the unit of economic production. More and more people did their work in shops, in offices, or on factory floors. Whether a job was skilled or unskilled, white-collar or blue-collar, or strictly professional, it took the family breadwinner out of the house during working hours six days a week. This did not mean that the family necessarily ceased to be an economic unit. But the labor of the father and any children with jobs came home in the form of cash, thus at least initially in the custody of the individual earners. The social consequences of this change were enormous for the traditional "head of the family" and for his wife and children.

Because he was away so much, the husband had to surrender to his wife some of the power in the family that he had formerly exercised, if for no other reason than the fact that she was always there. Noah Webster explained that the ideal father's authority was "like the mild dominion of a limited monarch, and not the iron rule of an austere tyrant." It certainly explains why Tocqueville concluded that "a sort of equality reigns around the domestic hearth" in America.

••••⌐**Read** the **Document**
Carey *Rules for Husbands and Wives* at **myhistorylab.com**

The new power and prestige that wives and mothers enjoyed were not obtained without cost. Since they were exercising day-to-day control over household affairs, they were expected to tend only to those affairs. Expanding their interest to other fields of human endeavor was frowned on. Where the typical wife had formerly been a partner in a family enterprise, she now left earning a living entirely to her husband. She was certainly not encouraged to have an independent career as, say, a lawyer or doctor. Time spent away from home or devoted to matters unrelated to

Lilly Martin Spencer's *Young Husband: First Marketing* (1854). Note that passersby are amused at this husband's inept attempt to do "women's work."
Source: *Young Husband: First Marketing,* 1854 by Lilly Martin Spencer. The Metropolitan Museum of Art, New York, NY, U.S.A. Image copyright © The Metropolitan Museum of Art.

the care of husband and family was, according to the new normative doctrine of "separate spheres," time misappropriated.

This trend widened the gap between the middle and lower classes. For a middle-class wife and mother to take a job or, still worse, to devote herself to any "frivolous" activity outside the home was considered a dereliction of duty. Such an attitude could not possibly develop in lower-class families where everyone had to work simply to keep food on the table.

Some women objected to the **Cult of True Womanhood**: By placing an ideal on so high a pedestal, all real women would fall short. Others escaped its more suffocating aspects by forming close friendships with other women. But most women, including such forceful proponents of women's rights as Hale and the educator Catharine Beecher, subscribed to the view that a woman's place was in the home. "The formation of the moral and intellectual character of the young is committed mainly to the female hand," Beecher wrote in *A Treatise on Domestic Economy for the Use of Young Ladies* (1841). "The mother forms the character of the future man."

●◆●─┤Read the Document

Beecher, from *A Treatise on Domestic Economy* at **myhistorylab.com**

Another reason for the shift in domestic influence from husbands to wives was that women began to have fewer children. People married later than in earlier periods. Long courtships and broken engagements were common, probably because prospective marriage partners were becoming more selective. On average, women began having their children two or three years later than their mothers had, and they stopped two or three years sooner. Apparently many middle-class couples made a conscious effort to limit family size, even when doing so required sexual abstinence.

As families became smaller, relations within them became more caring. Parents ceased to think of their children mostly as future workers. The earlier tendency even among loving parents to keep their children at arm's length, yet within reach of the strap, gave way to more intimate relationships. Gone was the puritan notion that children possessed "a perverse will, a love of what's forbid," and with it the belief that parents were responsible for crushing all juvenile resistance to their authority. In its place arose the view described by Lydia Maria Child in *The Mother's Book* (1831) that children "come to us from heaven, with their little souls full of innocence and peace." Mothers "should not interfere with the influence of angels," Child advised her readers.

●◆●─┤Read the Document

Mother's Magazine at **myhistorylab.com**

The Second Great Awakening

The basic goodness of children contradicted the Calvinist doctrine of infant damnation, to which most American Protestant churches formally subscribed. "Of all the impious doctrines which the dark imagination of man ever conceived," Bronson Alcott wrote in his journal, "the worst [is] the belief in original and certain depravity of infant nature." Alcott was far from alone in thinking infant damnation a "debased doctrine," despite its standing as one of the central tenets of orthodox Calvinism. Mothers enshrined infancy and childhood; they became increasingly active and vocal in church. They scathingly indicted the concept of infant damnation.

The inclination to set aside other Calvinist tenets, such as predestination, became more pronounced as a new wave of revivalism took shape in the 1790s. This **Second Great Awakening** began as a counteroffensive to the deistic thinking and other forms of "infidelity" that New England Congregationalists and southern Methodists alike identified with the French Revolution. Prominent New England ministers, who considered themselves traditionalists but also revivalists (men such as Yale's president, Timothy Dwight, and Dwight's student, the Reverend Lyman Beecher) placed less stress in their sermons on God's arbitrary power over mortals, and more on the promise of the salvation of sinners because of God's mercy and "disinterested benevolence." When another of Dwight's students, Horace Bushnell, declared in a sermon on "Christian nurture" in 1844 that Christian parents should prepare their children "for the skies," he meant that parents could contribute to their children's salvation.

Calvinism came under more direct assault from Charles Grandison Finney, probably the most effective of a number of charismatic Evangelists who brought the Second Great Awakening to its crest. In 1821 Finney abandoned a promising career as a lawyer and became an itinerant preacher. His most spectacular successes occurred during a series of revivals conducted in towns along the Erie Canal, a region Finney called "the burned-over district" because it had been the site of so many revivals before his own. From Utica, where his revival began in 1826, to Rochester, where it climaxed in 1831, he exhorted his listeners to take their salvation into their own hands. He insisted that people could control their own fate. He dismissed Calvinism as a "theological fiction." Salvation was available to anyone. But the day of judgment was just around the corner; there was little time to waste.

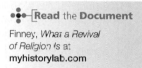

Read the Document
Finney, *What a Revival of Religion Is* at
myhistorylab.com

During and after Finney's efforts in Utica, conversions increased sharply. In Rochester, church membership doubled in six months. Elsewhere in the country, churches capitalized on the efforts of other Evangelists to fill their pews. In 1831 alone, church membership grew by 100,000, an increase, according to a New England minister, "unparalleled in the history of the church." The success of the Evangelists of the Second Great Awakening stemmed from the timeliness of their assault on Calvinist doctrine and even more from their methods. Finney, for example, consciously set out to be entertaining as well as edifying. The singing of hymns and the solicitation of personal testimonies provided his meetings with emotional release and human interest. Prominent among his innovations was the "anxious bench," where leading members of the community awaited the final prompting from within before coming forward to declare themselves saved.

Economic changes and their impact on family life also contributed to the Second Awakening. The growth of industry and commerce that followed the completion of the Erie Canal in 1825, along with the disappearance of undeveloped farmland, led hundreds of young men to leave family farms to seek their fortunes in Utica and other towns along the canal. There, uprooted, uncertain, and buffeted between ambition, hope, and anxiety, they found it hard to resist the comfort promised by the revivalists to those who were saved.

Women, and especially the wives of the business leaders of the community, felt particularly responsible for the Christian education of their children, which fell within

Lily Spenser Martin's painting, *Domestic Happiness* (1844), reflects the change in attitudes toward infants. Parents such as these could not believe that God had consigned their angelic babies to eternal damnation.
Source: *Domestic Happiness*, 1849 (oil on canvas), Spencer, Lilly Martin (1827–1902)/Detroit Institute of Arts, USA/Gift of Dr. and Mrs. James Cleland Jr./The Bridgeman Art Library International.

their separate sphere. Many women had servants and thus had time and energy to devote to their own and their offsprings' salvation.

Paradoxically, this caused many of them to venture out of that sphere and in doing so they moved further out of the shadow of their husbands. They founded the Oneida County Female Missionary Society, an association that did most of the organizing and a good deal of the

Watch the Video
Evangelical Religion & Politics, Then and Now at **myhistorylab.com**

financing of the climactic years of the Second Awakening. The Female Missionary Society raised more than $1,000 a year (no small sum at that time) to support the revival in Utica, in its environs, and throughout the burned-over district. Apparently without consciously intending to do so, women challenged the authority of the paternalistic, authoritarian churches they so fervently embraced. Then, by mixtures of exhortation, example, and affection, they set out to save the souls of their loved ones, first their children and ultimately their husbands too.

The Era of Associations

Alongside the recast family and the "almost revolutionized" church, a third pillar of the emerging American middle class was the voluntary association. Unlike the other two, it had neither colonial precedents nor contemporary European equivalents. The voluntary association of early nineteenth-century America was unique. "In France," Tocqueville wrote of this phenomenon, "if you want to proclaim a truth or propagate some feeling . . . you would find the government or in England some territorial magnate." In America, however, "you are sure to find an association."

The leaders of these associations tended to be ministers, lawyers, or merchants, but the rank and file consisted of tradesmen, foremen, clerks, and especially their wives. Some of these associations were formed around a local cause that some townspeople wished to advance, such as the provision of religious instruction for orphaned children; others were affiliated with associations elsewhere for the purposes of combating some national evil, such as drunkenness. Some, such as the American Board of Commissioners of Foreign Missions, founded in Boston in 1810, quickly became large and complex enterprises. (By 1860 the board had sent 1,250 missionaries into the "heathen world" and raised $8 million to support them.) Others lasted only as long as it took to accomplish a specific good work, such as the construction of a school or a library.

In a sense the associations were assuming functions previously performed in the family, such as caring for old people and providing moral guidance to the young, but without the paternalistic discipline of the old way. They constituted a "benevolent empire," eager to make society over into their members' idea of how God wanted it to be.

Backwoods Utopias

Americans frequently belonged to several associations at the same time and more than a few made reform their life's work. The most adventuresome tested their reform theories by withdrawing from workaday American society and establishing experimental communities. The communitarian point of view aimed at "commencing a wholesale social reorganization by first establishing and demonstrating its principles completely on a small scale." The first communitarians were religious reformers. In a sense the Pilgrims fall into this category, along with a number of other groups in colonial times, but only in the nineteenth century did the idea flourish.

One of the most influential of the earlier communities were the **Shakers**, founded by an Englishwoman, Ann Lee, who came to America in 1774. Mother Ann, as she was called, saw visions that convinced her that Christ would come to earth again as a woman and that she was that woman. With a handful of followers she founded a community near Albany, New York. The group grew rapidly, and after Ann Lee's death in 1784 her movement continued to expand. By the 1830s her followers had established about twenty successful communities.

Watch the **Video**
Religious Troublemakers of the Nineteenth Century at **myhistorylab.com**

The Shakers practiced celibacy; believing that the millennium was imminent, they saw no reason for perpetuating the human race. Each group lived in a large Family House, the sexes strictly segregated. Property was held in common but controlled by a ruling hierarchy. So much stress was placed on equality of labor and reward and on voluntary acceptance of the rules, however, that the system does not seem to have been oppressive.

The Shaker religion, joyful and fervent, was marked by much group singing and dancing, which provided the members with emotional release from their tightly controlled regimen. An industrious, skillful people, they made a special virtue of simplicity; some of their designs for buildings and, especially, furniture achieved a classic beauty seldom equaled among untutored artisans. Despite their customs, the Shakers were universally tolerated and even admired.

The most important of the religious communitarians were the Mormons. A remarkable Vermont farm boy, Joseph Smith, founded the religion in western New York in the 1820s. Smith saw visions; he claimed to have discovered and translated an ancient text, the Book of Mormon, which described the adventures of a tribe of Israelites that had populated America from biblical times until their destruction in a great war in 400 CE. With a small band of followers, Smith established a community in Ohio in 1831. The Mormons' dedication and economic efficiency attracted large numbers of converts, but their unorthodox religious views and their exclusivism, a product of their sense of being a chosen people, caused resentment among unbelievers. The Mormons were forced to move first to Missouri and then back to Illinois, where in 1839 they founded the town of Nauvoo.

In 1839 Mary Cragin, 29, became a convert to John Humphrey Noyes's "communism of love" and persuaded her husband to move with her to the commune. In 1846, after having an affair with another member of the commune, she and Noyes developed an attachment. After a meeting of the church, Noyes proposed that he and Cragin's husband share each other's wives. In an understatement, he called the arrangement a "complex marriage."

Nauvoo flourished—by 1844 it was the largest city in the state, with a population of 15,000—but once again the Mormons ran into local trouble. They quarreled among themselves, especially after Smith secretly authorized polygamy and a number of other unusual rites for members of the "Holy Order," the top leaders of the church.[1] They created a paramilitary organization, the Nauvoo Legion, headed by Smith, envisaging themselves as a semi-independent state within the Union. Smith announced that he was a candidate for president of the United States. Rumors circulated that the Mormons intended to take over the entire Northwest for their "empire." Once again local "gentiles" rose against them. Smith was arrested, then murdered by a mob.

Under a new leader, Brigham Young, the Mormons sought a haven beyond the frontier. In 1847 they marched westward, pressing through the mountains until they reached the desolate wilderness on the shores of the Great Salt Lake. There, at last, they established their Zion and began to make their truly significant impact on American history. Irrigation made the desert flourish, precious water wisely being treated as a community asset. Hard, cooperative, intelligently directed effort spelled growth and prosperity; more than 11,000 people were living in the area when it became part of the Utah Territory in 1850. In time the communal Mormon settlement broke down, but the religion has remained—known as the Church of Latter-Day Saints, a major force in the shaping of the West. The Mormon Church is still by far the most powerful single influence in Utah and is a thriving organization in many other parts of the United States and in Europe.

The religious communities had some influence on reformers who wished to experiment with social organization. When Robert Owen, a British **utopian** socialist who believed in economic as well as political equality and who considered competition debasing, decided to create an ideal community in America, he purchased the Rappite settlement at New Harmony, Indiana. Owen's advocacy of free love and "enlightened atheism" did not add to the stability of his group or to its popularity among outsiders. The colony was a costly failure.

The American followers of Charles Fourier, a French utopian socialist who proposed that society should be organized in cooperative units called phalanxes, fared

---

[1]One justification of polygamy, paradoxically, was that marriage was a sacred, eternal state. If a man remarried after his wife's death, eventually he would have two wives in heaven. Therefore why not on earth?

New England Roots of Utopian Communities The shaded section represents areas that were settled predominantly by people from New England. It suggests that communitarian sentiments were strongly influenced by New England culture.

better. Fourierism did not seek to tamper with sexual and religious mores. Its advocates included important journalists such as Horace Greeley of the *New York Tribune* and Parke Godwin of the *New York Evening Post.* In the 1840s several dozen Fourierist colonies were established in the northern and western states. Members worked at whatever tasks they wished and only as much as they wished. As might be expected, none of the communities lasted very long.

> **See the Map**
>
> *Utopian Communities before the Civil War* at **myhistorylab.com**

The Age of Reform

The communitarians were the most colorful of the reformers, their proposals the most spectacular. More effective, however, were the many individuals who took on themselves responsibility for caring for the physically and mentally disabled and for the rehabilitation of criminals. The work of Thomas Gallaudet in developing methods for educating deaf people reflects the spirit of the times. Gallaudet's school in Hartford, Connecticut, opened its doors in 1817; by 1851 similar schools for the deaf had been established in fourteen states.

Dr. Samuel Gridley Howe did similar work with the blind, devising means for making books with raised letters (Louis Braille's system of raised dots was not introduced until later in the century) that the blind could "read" with their fingers. Howe headed a school for the blind in Boston, the pioneering Perkins Institution, which opened in 1832. Of all that Charles Dickens observed in America, nothing so favorably impressed him as Howe's success in educating twelve-year-old Laura Bridgman, who was deaf, mute, and blind. Howe was also interested in trying to educate the mentally disabled and in other causes, including antislavery. "Every creature in human shape should command our respect," he insisted. "The strong should help the weak, so that the whole should advance as a band of brethren."

One of the most striking aspects of the reform movement was the emphasis reformers placed on establishing special institutions for dealing with social problems. In the colonial period, orphans, indigent persons, the insane, and the feebleminded were usually cared for by members of their own families or boarded in a neighboring household. They remained part of the community. Even criminals were seldom "locked away" for extended jail terms; punishment commonly consisted of whipping, being placed in stocks in the town square, or (for serious crimes) execution. But once persuaded that people were primarily shaped by their surroundings, reformers demanded that deviant and dependent members of the community be taken from their present corrupting circumstances and placed in specialized institutions where they could be trained or rehabilitated. Almshouses, orphanages, reformatories, prisons, and "lunatic asylums" sprang up throughout the United States like mushrooms in a forest after a summer rain.

Eastern State Penitentiary, opened in 1829 in Philadelphia, sought to reform prisoners by enforcing a solitary life to promote reflection.

The rationale for this movement was scientific; elaborate statistical reports attested to the benefits that such institutions would bring to both inmates and society as a whole. The motivating spirit of the founders of these asylums was humane, although many of the institutions seem anything but humane to the modern eye. The highly regarded Philadelphia prison system was based on strict solitary confinement, which was supposed to lead culprits to reflect on their sins and then reform their ways. The prison was literally a penitentiary, a place to repent. In fact, the system drove some inmates mad, and soon a rival Auburn system was introduced in New York State, which allowed for some social contact among prisoners and for work in shops and stone quarries. Absolute silence was required at all times. The prisoners were herded about in lockstep and punished by flogging for the slightest infraction of the rules. Regular "moral and religious instruction" was provided, which the authorities believed would lead inmates to reform their lives. Tocqueville and Beaumont, in their report on American prisons, concluded that the Philadelphia system produced "the deepest impression on the soul of the convict," while the Auburn system made the convict "more conformable to the habits of man in society."

The hospitals for mental patients were intended to cure inmates, not merely to confine them. The emphasis was on isolating them from the pressures of society; on order, quiet, routine; and on control—but not on punishment. The unfortunates were seen as *de*ranged; the task was to *ar*range their lives in a rational manner. In practice, shortages of trained personnel, niggardly legislative appropriations, and the inherent difficulty of managing violent and irrational patients often produced deplorable conditions in the asylums.

This situation led Dorothea Dix, a woman of almost saintlike selflessness, to devote thirty years of her life to a campaign to improve the care of the insane. She traveled to every state in the Union, and as far afield as Turkey and Japan, inspecting asylums and poorhouses. Insane persons in Massachusetts, she wrote in a memorial intended to shock state legislators into action, were being kept in cages and closets, "*chained, naked, beaten with rods, and lashed into obedience!*" Her reports led to some improvement in conditions in Massachusetts and other states, but in the long run the bright hopes of the reformers were never realized. Institutions founded to uplift the deviant and dependent all too soon became places where society's "misfits" might safely be kept out of sight.

"Demon Rum"

Women did much of the work in all antebellum reforms, but they were especially active in the **temperance movement**. The husband who squandered his earnings on booze, or who came home drunk and debauched, imperiled the family. Thus middle-class women who believed that a woman's place was in the home were obliged to take on a public role to protect the family.

Alcohol—"demon rum"—was perhaps foremost among those threats. By the 1820s Americans were consuming prodigious amounts of alcohol, more than ever before or since. Not that the colonists had been teetotalers. Liquor, mostly in the form of rum or hard apple cider, was cheap and everywhere available; taverns were an integral part of colonial society.

Watch the Video

Drinking & the Temperance Movement in Nineteenth-Century America at **myhistorylab.com**

There were alcoholics in colonial America, but because neither political nor religious leaders considered drinking dangerous, there was no alcohol "problem." Most doctors recommended the regular consumption of alcohol as healthy. John Adams, certainly the soul of propriety, drank a tankard of hard cider every day for breakfast. Dr. Benjamin Rush's *Inquiry into the Effects of Ardent Spirits* (1784), which questioned the medicinal benefits of alcohol, fell on deaf ears.

However, alcohol consumption increased markedly in the early years of the new republic, thanks primarily to the availability of cheap corn and rye whiskey distilled in the new states of Kentucky and Tennessee. In the 1820s the per capita consumption of hard liquor reached five gallons, well over twice what it is today. Since small children and many grown people did not drink that much, others obviously drank a great deal more.

The foundation of the American Temperance Union in 1826 signaled the start of a national crusade against drunkenness. Employing lectures, pamphlets, rallies, essay contests, and other techniques, the union set out to persuade people to "sign the pledge" not to drink liquor. Primitive sociological studies of the effects of drunkenness (reformers were able to show a high statistical correlation between alcohol consumption and crime) added to the effectiveness of the campaign.

●●●─|Read the Document

Beecher, *Six Sermons on Intemperance* at myhistorylab.com

Revivalist ministers like Charles Grandison Finney argued that alcohol was one of the great barriers to conversion, which helps explain why Utica, a town of fewer than 13,000 residents in 1840, supported four separate temperance societies in that year. Employers all over the country also signed on, declaring their businesses henceforward to be "cold-water" enterprises. Soon the temperance movement claimed a million members.

The temperance people aroused bitter opposition, particularly after they moved beyond calls for restraint to demands for prohibition of all alcohol. German and Irish immigrants, for the most part Catholics, and also members of Protestant sects that used wine in their religious services, objected to being told by reformers that their drinking would have to stop. But by the early 1840s the reformers had secured legislation in many states that imposed strict licensing systems and heavy liquor taxes. Local option laws permitted towns and counties to ban the sale of alcohol altogether.

In 1851 Maine passed the first effective law prohibiting the manufacture and sale of alcoholic beverages. The leader of the campaign was Mayor Neal Dow of Portland, a businessman who became a prohibitionist after seeing the damage done by drunkenness among workers in his tannery. By 1855 a dozen other states had passed laws based on the Maine statute, and the nation's per capita consumption of alcohol had plummeted to two gallons a year.

The Abolitionist Crusade

No reform movement of this era was more significant, more ambiguous, or more provocative of later historical investigation than **abolitionism**—the drive to abolish slavery. That slavery should have been a cause of indignation to reform-minded Americans was inevitable. Humanitarians were outraged by the master's whip and by the practice of disrupting families. Democrats protested the denial of political and civil rights to slaves. Perfectionists of all stripes deplored the fact that slaves had no chance to improve themselves. However, well into the 1820s, the abolitionist cause attracted few followers because there seemed to be no way of getting rid of slavery short of revolution. While a few theorists argued that the Fifth Amendment, which provides that no one may be "deprived of life, liberty, or property, without due process of law," could be interpreted to mean that the Constitution outlawed slavery, the great majority believed that the institution was not subject to federal control.

Particularly in the wake of the Missouri Compromise, antislavery Northerners neatly compartmentalized their thinking. Slavery was wrong; they would not tolerate it in their own communities. But since the Constitution obliged them to tolerate it in states where it existed, they felt no responsibility to fight it. The issue was explosive enough even when limited to the question of the expansion of slavery into the territories. People who advocated any kind of forced abolition in states where it was legal were judged irresponsible in the extreme. Most critics of slavery therefore confined themselves to urging "colonization" or persuading slaveowners to treat their property humanely.

More provocative and less accommodating to local sensibilities were people such as William Lloyd Garrison of Massachusetts, who called for "immediate" abolition. When his extreme position made continued residence in Baltimore impossible, he returned to Boston, where in 1831 he established his own newspaper, *The Liberator*. "I am in earnest," he announced in the first issue. "I will not equivocate—I will not excuse—I will not retreat a single inch—and I will be heard."

•••⸻Read the Document

Garrison, First Issue of *The Liberator* at **myhistorylab.com**

Garrison's position, and that espoused by the New England Anti-Slavery Society, which he organized in 1831, was absolutely unyielding: Slaves must be freed immediately and treated as equals; compensated emancipation was unacceptable, colonization unthinkable. Because the U.S. government countenanced slavery, Garrison refused to engage in political activity to achieve his ends. Burning a copy of the Constitution—that "agreement with hell"—became a regular feature at Society-sponsored public lectures.

Few white Americans found Garrison's line of argument convincing, and many were outraged by his confrontational tactics. In 1833 a Garrison meeting in New York City was broken up by colonizationists. Two years later a mob dragged Garrison through the streets of his own Boston. That same day a mob broke up the convention of the New York Anti-Slavery Society in Utica. In 1837 Elijah Lovejoy, a Garrisonian newspaper editor in Alton, Illinois, first saw his press destroyed by fire and then was himself murdered by a mob. When the proprietors of Philadelphia's Pennsylvania Hall booked an abolitionist meeting in 1838, a mob burned the hall to the ground to prevent the meeting from taking place.

In the wake of this violence some of Garrison's backers had second thoughts about his call for an immediate end to slavery. The wealthy New York businessmen Arthur and Lewis Tappan, who had subsidized *The Liberator*, turned instead to Theodore Dwight Weld, a young minister who was part of Charles Grandison Finney's "holy band" of revivalists. Weld and his followers spoke of "immediate" emancipation "gradually" achieved, and they were willing to engage in political activity to achieve that goal.

In 1840 the Tappans and Weld broke with Garrison over the issue of involvement in politics and the participation of female abolitionists as public lecturers. Garrison, mindful of women's central role in other reforms, supported the women. "The destiny of the slaves is in the hands of American women," he declared in 1833. Weld thought women lecturers would needlessly antagonize would-be supporters. The Tappans then organized the Liberty party, which nominated as its presidential candidate James G. Birney, a Kentucky slaveholder who had been converted to evangelical Christianity and abolitionism by Weld. Running on a platform of universal emancipation to be gradually brought about through legislation, Birney received only 7,000 votes.

Many blacks were abolitionists long before the white movement began to attract attention. In 1830 some fifty black antislavery societies existed, and thereafter these groups grew in size and importance, being generally associated with the Garrisonian wing. White abolitionists eagerly sought out black speakers, especially runaway slaves, whose heartrending accounts of their experiences aroused sympathies and who, merely by speaking clearly and with conviction, stood as living proof that blacks were neither animals nor fools.

The first prominent black abolitionist was David Walker, whose powerful *Appeal to the Coloured Citizens of the World* (1829) is now considered one of the roots of the modern black nationalist movement. Walker was born free and had experienced American racism extensively in both the South and the North. He denounced white talk of democracy and freedom as pure hypocrisy and predicted that when God finally brought justice to America white "tyrants will wish they were never born!"

Frederick Douglass, a former slave who had escaped from Maryland, was one of the most remarkable Americans of his generation. While a bondsman he had received a full portion of beatings and other indignities, but he had been allowed to learn to read and write and to master a trade, opportunities denied the vast majority of slaves.

A photo of Frederick Douglass in 1847, having escaped from slavery nine years earlier. He attracted large audiences as an antislavery lecturer, though his white supporters worried that he neither looked nor sounded like a former slave. Lest audiences think him an imposter, William Lloyd Garrison counseled him to not sound too "learned." Another thought it would be better if he had "a little of the plantation in his speech." Douglass rejected such suggestions.

Settling in Boston, he became an agent of the Massachusetts Anti-Slavery Society and a featured speaker at its public meetings.

Douglass was a tall, majestically handsome man who radiated determination and indignation. Slavery, he told white audiences, "brands your republicanism as a sham, your humanity as a base pretense, your Christianity as a lie." In 1845 he published his *Narrative of the Life of Frederick Douglass*, one of the most gripping autobiographical accounts of a slave's life ever written. Douglass insisted that freedom for blacks required not merely emancipation but full equality, social and economic as well as political. Not many white Northerners accepted his reasoning, but few who heard him or read his works could afterward maintain the illusion that all blacks were dull-witted or resigned to inferior status.

•••—Read the **Document**

Passages from *The Autobiography of Frederick Douglass* at **myhistorylab.com**

At first Douglass was, in his own words, "a faithful disciple" of Garrison, prepared to tear up the Constitution and destroy the Union to gain his ends. In the late 1840s, however, he changed his mind, deciding that the Constitution, created to "establish Justice, insure domestic Tranquility . . . and secure the Blessings of Liberty," as its preamble states, "could not well have been designed at the same time to maintain and perpetuate a system of rapine and murder like slavery." Thereafter he fought slavery and race prejudice from within the system, something Garrison was never willing to do.

Garrison's importance cannot be measured by the number of his followers, which was never large. Unlike more moderately inclined enemies of slavery, he recognized that abolitionism was a revolutionary movement, not merely one more middle-class reform. He also understood that achieving racial equality, not merely "freeing" the slaves, was the only way to reach the abolitionists' professed objective: full justice for blacks. And he saw clearly that few whites, even among abolitionists, believed that blacks were their equals.

Both Garrison's insights into the limits of northern racial egalitarianism and his blind contempt for southern whites led him to the conclusion that American society was rotten to the core. Thus he refused to make any concession to the existing establishment, religious or secular. He was hated in the North as much for his explicit denial of the idea that a constitution that supported slavery merited respect as for his implicit denial of the idea that a professed Christian who tolerated slavery for even an instant could hope for salvation. He was, in short, a perfectionist, a trafficker in moral absolutes who wanted his Kingdom of Heaven in the here and now. By contrast, most other American reformers were willing to settle for perfection on the installment plan.

Women's Rights

The question of slavery was related to another major reform movement of the era, the crusade for women's rights. Superficially, the connection can be explained in this way: Women were as likely as men to find slavery offensive and to protest against it. When they did so, they ran into even more adamant resistance: the prejudices of those who objected to abolitionists being reinforced by their feelings that women should not speak in public or participate in political affairs. Thus female abolitionists, driven by the urgencies of conscience, were almost forced to become advocates of women's rights. "We have good cause to be

{•}—Watch the **Video**

The Women's Rights Movement in Nineteenth-Century America at **myhistorylab.com**

Single women worth at least 50 pounds were allowed to vote in New Jersey from 1775 to 1807.

grateful to the slave," the feminist Abby Kelley wrote. "In striving to strike his irons off, we found most surely, that we were manacled ourselves."

At a more profound level, the reference that abolitionists made to the Declaration of Independence to justify their attack on slavery radicalized women with regard to their own place in society. Were only all men created equal and endowed by God with unalienable rights? For many women the question was a consciousness-raising experience; they began to believe that, like African Americans, they were imprisoned from birth in a caste system, legally subordinated and assigned menial social and economic roles that prevented them from developing their full potentialities. Such women considered themselves in a sense worse off than blacks, who had at least the psychological advantage of confronting an openly hostile and repressive society rather than one concealed behind the cloying rhetoric of romantic love.

With the major exception of Margaret Fuller, whose book *Women in the Nineteenth Century* (1844) made a frontal assault on all forms of sexual discrimination, the leading advocates of equal rights for women began their public careers in the abolitionist movement. Among the first were Sarah and Angelina Grimké, South Carolinians who abandoned their native state and the domestic sphere to devote themselves to speaking out against slavery. Male objections to the Grimkés' activities soon made them advocates of women's rights. Similarly, the refusal of delegates to the World Anti-Slavery Convention held in London in 1840 to let women participate in their debates precipitated the decision of two American abolitionists, Lucretia Mott and Elizabeth Cady Stanton, to turn their attention to the women's rights movement.

As Lydia Child, a popular novelist noted, the subordination of women was as old as civilization. The attack on it came not because of any new discrimination but for the same reasons that motivated reformers against other forms of injustice: belief in progress, a sense of personal responsibility, and the conviction that institutions could be changed and that the time for changing them was limited.

When women sought to involve themselves in reform, they became aware of perhaps the most serious handicap that society imposed on them—the conflict between their roles as wives and mothers and their urge to participate in the affairs of the larger world. Elizabeth Cady Stanton has left a striking description of this dilemma. She lived in the 1840s in Seneca Falls, a small town in central New York. Her husband was frequently away on business; she had a brood of growing children and little domestic help. When, stimulated by her interest in abolition and women's rights, she sought to become active in the movements, her family responsibilities made it almost impossible even to read about them.

"I now fully understood the practical difficulties most women had to contend with," she recalled in her autobiography *Eighty Years and More* (1898):

> The general discontent I felt with woman's portion as wife, mother, housekeeper, physician, and spiritual guide, the chaotic condition into which everything fell without her constant supervision, and the wearied, anxious look of the majority of women, impressed me with the strong feeling that some active measures should be taken.

Active measures she took. Together with Lucretia Mott and a few others of like mind, she organized a meeting, the **Seneca Falls Convention** (July 1848), and drafted a Declaration of Sentiments patterned on the Declaration of Independence. "We hold these truths to be self-evident: that all men and women are created equal," it stated, and it went on to list the "injuries and usurpations" of men, just as Jefferson had outlined those of George III.

●●●—Read the **Document**

Stanton, *Declaration of Sentiments* at myhistorylab.com

From this seed the movement grew. During the 1850s a series of national conventions was held, and more and more reformers, including William Lloyd Garrison, joined the cause. Of the recruits, Susan B. Anthony was the most influential, for she was the first to see the need for thorough organization if effective pressure was to be brought to bear on male-dominated society. Her first campaign, mounted in 1854 and 1855 in behalf of a petition to the New York legislature calling for reform of the property and divorce laws, accumulated 6,000 signatures. But the petition did not persuade the legislature to act. Indeed, the feminists achieved very few practical results during the Age of Reform. Their leaders, however, were persevering types, most of them extraordinarily long-lived. Their major efforts lay in the future.

Despite the aggressiveness of many reformers and the extremity of some of their proposals, little social conflict blighted these years. Although Americans argued about everything from prison reform to vegetarianism, from women's rights to phrenology (a pseudoscience much occupied with developing the diagnostic possibilities of measuring the bumps on people's heads), they seldom came to blows. Even the abolitionist movement might not have caused serious social strife if the territorial expansion of the late 1840s had not dragged the slavery issue back into politics. When that happened, politics again assumed center stage, public discourse grew embittered, and the first great Age of Reform came to an end.

The Romantic View of Life

The spreading belief that human institutions were improving had a profound effect on the arts and literature. In the Western world, it gave rise to **romanticism**, a revolt against the bloodless logic of the Age of Reason. It was a noticeable if unnamed point of view in Germany, France, and England as early as the 1780s and in America a generation later; by the second quarter of the nineteenth century, few intellectuals were unmarked by it. "Romantics" believed that change and growth were the essence of life, for individuals and for institutions. They valued feeling and intuition over pure thought, and they stressed the differences between individuals and societies rather than the similarities. Ardent love of country characterized the movement; individualism, optimism, ingenuousness, and emotion were its bywords. Romanticism, too, drew much from the religious sensibilities of mothers. Children were innately good; pernicious influences led to their corruption.

The romantic way of thinking found its greatest American expression in **transcendentalism**, a New England creation that is difficult to describe because it emphasized the indefinable and the unknowable. It was a mystical, intuitive way of looking at life that subordinated facts to feelings. Its literal meaning was "to go beyond the world of the senses," by which the transcendentalists meant the material and observable world. To the transcendentalists, human beings were truly divine because they were part of nature, itself the essence of divinity. Peoples' intellectual capacities

Frederic Edwin Church conveyed the romantic sensibility in *Twilight in the Wilderness* (1860). The clouds glow with religious portent, and their reflected light pervades Nature.

did not define their capabilities, for they could "transcend" reason by having faith in themselves and in the fundamental benevolence of the universe. Transcendentalists were complete individualists, seeing the social whole as no more than the sum of its parts. Organized religion, indeed all institutions, were unimportant if not counterproductive; what mattered was the single person and that people aspire, stretch *beyond* their known capabilities.

Emerson and Thoreau

The leading transcendentalist thinker was Ralph Waldo Emerson. Born in 1803 and educated at Harvard, Emerson became a minister, but in 1832 he gave up his pulpit, deciding that "the profession is antiquated." After traveling in Europe he settled in Concord, Massachusetts, where he had a long career as an essayist, lecturer, and sage.

Emerson's philosophy was at once buoyantly optimistic, rigorously intellectual, self-confident, and conscientious. In "The American Scholar," a notable address he delivered at Harvard in 1837, he urged Americans to put aside their devotion to things European and seek inspiration in their immediate surroundings. Emerson saw himself as pitting "spiritual powers" against "the mechanical powers and the mechanical philosophy of this time." The new industrial society of New England disturbed him profoundly.

Because he put so much emphasis on self-reliance, Emerson disliked powerful governments. "The less government we have the better," he said. In a sense he was the prototype of some modern alienated intellectuals, so repelled by the world as it was that he would not actively try to change it. Nevertheless he thought strong leadership essential. Emerson also had a strong practical streak. He made his living

●●●—Read the **Document**

Emersor, *The Concord Hymn* at **myhistorylab**.com

by lecturing, tracking tirelessly across the country, talking before every type of audience for fees ranging from $50 to several hundreds.

Closely identified with Emerson was his Concord neighbor Henry David Thoreau. After graduating from Harvard in 1837, Thoreau taught school for a time and helped out in a small pencil-making business run by his family. He was a strange man, content to absorb the beauties of nature almost intuitively, yet stubborn and individualistic to the point of selfishness. The hectic scramble for wealth that Thoreau saw all about him he found disgusting and alarming, for he believed it was destroying both the natural and the human resources of the country.

Like Emerson, Thoreau objected to many of society's restrictions on the individual. "That government is best which governs not at all," he said, surpassing both Emerson and the Jeffersonians. He was perfectly prepared to see himself as a majority of one. "When were the good and the brave ever in a majority?" Thoreau asked. "If a man does not keep pace with his companions," he wrote on another occasion, "perhaps it is because he hears a different drummer."

In 1845 Thoreau decided to put to the test his theory that a person need not depend on society for a satisfying existence. He built a cabin at Walden Pond on some property owned by Emerson and lived there alone for two years. The best fruit of this period was that extraordinary book *Walden* (1854). Superficially, *Walden* is the story of Thoreau's experiment, movingly and beautifully written. It is also an indictment of the social behavior of the average American, an attack on unthinking conformity, on subordinating one's own judgment to that of the herd.

Walden Pond, where Henry David Thoreau lived from 1845 to 1847: "I went to the woods because I wished to live deliberately, to front only the essential facts of life, and see if I could not learn what it had to teach, and not, when I came to die, to discover that I had not lived."

The most graphic illustration of Thoreau's confidence in his own values occurred while he was living at Walden. At that time the Mexican War was raging. Thoreau considered the war immoral because it advanced the cause of slavery. To protest, he refused to pay his Massachusetts poll tax. For this he was arrested and lodged in jail, although only for one night because an aunt promptly paid the tax for him. His essay "Civil Disobedience," explaining his view of the proper relation between the individual and the state, resulted from this experience. Like Emerson, however, Thoreau refused to participate in practical reform movements. "I love Henry," one of his friends said, "but I cannot like him; and as for taking his arm, I should as soon think of taking the arm of an elm tree."

Edgar Allan Poe

The work of all the imaginative writers of the period reveals romantic influences, and it is possibly an indication of the affinity of the romantic approach to American conditions that a number of excellent writers of poetry and fiction first appeared in the 1830s and 1840s. Edgar Allan Poe, one of the most remarkable, seems almost a caricature of the romantic image of the tortured genius. Poe was born in Boston in 1809, the son of poor actors who died before he was three years old. He was raised by a wealthy Virginian, John Allan.

Few persons as neurotic as Poe have been able to produce first-rate work. In college he ran up debts of $2,500 in less than a year and had to withdraw. He won an appointment to West Point but was discharged after a few months for disobedience and "gross neglect of duty." He was a lifelong alcoholic and an occasional taker of drugs. He married a child of thirteen.

Poe responded strongly to the lure of romanticism. His works abound with examples of wild imagination and fascination with mystery, fright, and the occult. If he did not invent the detective story, he perfected it; his tales "The Murders in the Rue Morgue" and "The Purloined Letter" stressed the thought processes of a clever detective in solving a mystery by reasoning from evidence.

Although dissolute in his personal life, when Poe touched pen to paper, he became a disciplined craftsman. The most fantastic passages in his works are the result of careful, reasoned selection; not a word, he believed, could be removed without damage to the whole. And despite his rejection of most of the values prized

An image of Edgar Allan Poe on a cigar box. In 1845, impoverished and an alcoholic, Poe was living in the "greatest wretchedness." His young wife was dying of tuberculosis. That same year he wrote, "The Raven," a poem about an ill-omened bird that intrudes on a young man's grief over the death of his beloved. "Take thy beak from out my heart," the man screams. Quoth the raven— famously—"Nevermore."

by middle-class America, Poe was widely read in his own day. His poem "The Raven" won instantaneous popularity when it was published in 1845. Had he been a little more stable, he might have made a good living with his pen—but in that case he might not have written as he did.

Nathaniel Hawthorne

Another product of the prevailing romanticism was Nathaniel Hawthorne, born in 1804 in Salem, Massachusetts. When Hawthorne was a small child, his father died and his grief-stricken mother became a recluse. Left largely to his own devices, he grew to be a lonely, introspective person. Wandering about New England by himself in summertime, he soaked up local lore, which he drew on in writing short stories.

Hawthorne's early stories, originally published in magazines, were brought together in *Twice-Told Tales* (1837). They made excellent use of New England culture and history for background but were concerned chiefly with the struggles of individuals with sin, guilt, and especially the pride and isolation that often afflict those who place too much reliance on their own judgment. His greatest works were two novels written after the Whigs turned him out of his government job in 1849. *The Scarlet Letter* (1850), a grim yet sympathetic analysis of adultery, condemned not the woman, Hester Prynne, but the people who presumed to judge her. *The House of the Seven Gables* (1851) was a gripping account of the decay of an old New England family brought on by the guilty feelings of the current owners of the house, caused by the way their ancestors had cheated the original owners of the property.

Like Poe, Hawthorne was appreciated in his own day and widely read; unlike Poe, he made a modest amount of money from his work. Yet he was never very comfortable in the society he inhabited. He had no patience with the second-rate. And despite his success in creating word pictures of a somber, mysterious world, he considered America too prosaic a country to inspire good literature. "There is no shadow, no antiquity, no mystery, no picturesque and gloomy wrong, nor anything but a commonplace prosperity," he complained.

Herman Melville

In 1850, while Hawthorne was writing *The House of the Seven Gables*, his publisher introduced him to another writer who was in the midst of a novel. The writer was Herman Melville and the book, *Moby-Dick*. Hawthorne and Melville became good friends at once, for despite their dissimilar backgrounds, they had a great deal in common. Melville was a New Yorker, born in 1819, one of eight children of a merchant of distinguished lineage. His father, however, lost all his money and died when the boy was twelve. Melville left school at fifteen, worked briefly as a bank clerk, and in 1837 went to sea. For eighteen months, in 1841 and 1842, he was crewman on the whaler *Acushnet*. Then he jumped ship in the South Seas. For a time he lived among a tribe of cannibals in the Marquesas; later he made his way to Tahiti, where he idled away nearly a year. After another year at sea he returned to America in the fall of 1844.

Experience made Melville too aware of the evil in the world to be a transcendentalist. His dark view of human nature culminated in *Moby-Dick* (1851). This book, Melville said, was "broiled in hellfire." Against the background of a whaling voyage he dealt subtly and symbolically with the problems of good and evil, of courage and cowardice, of faith, stubbornness, and pride. In Captain Ahab, driven relentlessly to hunt down the huge white whale Moby Dick, which had destroyed his leg, Melville created one of the great figures of literature; in the book as a whole, he produced one of the finest novels written by an American, comparable to the best in any language.

As Melville's work became more profound, it lost its appeal to the average reader, and its originality and symbolic meaning escaped most of the critics. *Moby-Dick*, his masterpiece, received little attention and most of that unfavorable. He kept on writing until his death in 1891 but was virtually ignored. Only in the 1920s did the critics rediscover him and give him his merited place in the history of American literature.

Walt Whitman

Walt Whitman, whose *Leaves of Grass* (1855) was the last of the great literary works of this brief outpouring of genius, was the most romantic and by far the most distinctly American writer of his age. He was born on Long Island, outside New York City, in 1819. At thirteen he left school and worked for a printer; thereafter he held a succession of newspaper jobs in the metropolitan area.

●●●─[**Read** the **Document**

Whitman, Preface to *Leaves of Grass* at **myhistorylab.com**

Although genuinely a "common man," thoroughly at home among tradesmen and laborers, he was surely not an ordinary man. During the early 1850s, while employed as a carpenter and composing the poems that made up *Leaves of Grass*, he regularly carried a book of Emerson in his lunch box. "I was simmering, simmering, simmering," he later recalled. "Emerson brought me to a boil." The transcendental idea that inspiration and aspiration are at the heart of all achievement captivated him. Poets could best

Some scholars regard Walt Whitman as a poet of nature, and others, a poet of the body—a reference to erotic lines such as: "Without shame the man I like knows and avows the deliciousness of his sex. Without shame the woman I like knows and avows hers." Whitman's Leaves of Grass had every leaf in nature, complained critic E. P. Whipple, except the fig leaf.

express themselves, he believed, by relying uncritically on their natural inclinations without regard for rigid metrical forms.

Leaves of Grass consisted of a preface, in which Whitman made the extraordinary statement that Americans had "probably the fullest poetical nature" of any people in history, and twelve poems in free verse: rambling, uneven, appearing to most readers shocking both in the commonplace nature of the subject matter and the coarseness of the language. Emerson, Thoreau, and a few others saw a fresh talent in these poems, but most readers and reviewers found them offensive. Indeed, the work was so undisciplined and so much of it had no obvious meaning that it was easy to miss the many passages of great beauty and originality.

Part of Whitman's difficulty arose because there was much of the charlatan in his makeup; often his writing did not ring true. He loved to use foreign words and phrases, and since he had no more than a smattering of any foreign language, he sounded pretentious and sometimes downright foolish when he did so. In reality a sensitive, gentle person, he tried to pose as a great, rough character. (Later in his career he bragged of fathering no less than six illegitimate children, which was assuredly untrue.) He never married, and his work suggests that his strongest emotional ties were with men. Thomas Carlyle once remarked shrewdly that Whitman thought he was a big man because he lived in a big country.

Whitman's work was more authentically American than that of any contemporary. His egoism—he titled one of his finest poems "Song of Myself"—was tempered by his belief that he was typical of all humanity:

I celebrate myself and sing myself
And what I assume you shall assume,
For every atom belonging to me as good belongs to you.

Source: Walt Whitman "Song of Myself."

He had a remarkable ear for rendering common speech poetically, for employing slang, and for catching the breezy informality of Americans and their faith in themselves:

> *Earth! you seem to look for something at my hands,*
> *Say, old top-knot, what do you want?*
> *I bequeath myself to the dirt to grow from the grass I love,*
> *If you want me again look for me under your boot-soles.*

Source: Walt Whitman "Song of Myself."

Because of these qualities and because in his later work, especially during the Civil War, he occasionally struck a popular chord, Whitman was never as neglected as Melville. When he died in 1892, he was, if not entirely understood, at least widely appreciated.

Reading and the Dissemination of Culture

As the population grew and became more concentrated, and as society, especially in the North, was permeated by a middle-class point of view, popular concern for "culture" in the formal sense increased. A largely literate people, committed to the idea of education but not generally well-educated, set their hearts on being "refined" and "cultivated." Industrialization made it easier to satisfy this new demand for culture, though the new machines also tended to make the artifacts of culture more stereotyped.

Improved printing techniques reduced the cost of books, magazines, and newspapers. In the 1850s one publisher sold a fifty-volume set of Sir Walter Scott for $37.50. The first penny newspaper was the *New York Sun* (1833), but James Gordon Bennett's *New York Herald*, founded in 1835, brought the cheap new journalism to perfection. The *Boston Daily Times* and the *Philadelphia Public Ledger* soon followed. The penny newspapers depended on sensation, crime stories, and society gossip to attract readers, but they covered important national and international news too.

The desire for knowledge and culture in America is well illustrated by the success of the mutual improvement societies known as **lyceums**. The movement began in Great Britain; in the United States its prime mover was Josiah Holbrook, an itinerant lecturer and sometime schoolmaster from Connecticut. Holbrook founded the first lyceum in 1826 at Millbury, Massachusetts; within five years there were over a thousand scattered across the country. The lyceums conducted discussions, established libraries, and lobbied for better schools. Soon they began to sponsor lecture series on topics of every sort. Many of the nation's political and intellectual leaders, such as Webster, Emerson, Melville, and Lowell, regularly graced their platforms. So did other less famous lecturers who in the name of culture pronounced on subjects ranging from "Chemistry Applied to the Mechanic Arts" to a description of the tombs of the Egyptian pharaohs.

Education for Democracy

Except on the edge of the frontier and in the South, most youngsters between the ages of five and ten attended a school for at least a couple of months of the year. These schools, however, were privately run and charged fees. Attendance was not required and fell off sharply once children learned to read and do their sums well enough to get along in day-to-day life. The teachers were usually young men waiting for something better to turn up.

All this changed with the rise of the common school movement. At the heart of the movement was the belief, widely expressed in the first days of the republic, that a government based on democratic rule must provide the means, as Jefferson put it, to "diffuse knowledge throughout the mass of the people." This meant free tax-supported schools that all children were expected to attend. It also came to mean that such an educational system should be administered on a statewide basis and that teaching should become a profession that required formal training.

The two most effective leaders of the common school movement were Henry Barnard and Horace Mann. Both were New Englanders, Whigs, trained in the law, and in other ways conservative types. They shared an unquenchable faith in the improvability of the human race through education. Mann drafted the 1837 Massachusetts law creating a state school board and then became its first secretary. Over the next decade Mann's annual reports carried the case for common schools to every corner of the land. Seldom given to understatement, Mann called common schools "the greatest discovery ever made by man." He encouraged young women to become teachers while commending them to school boards by claiming that they could get along on lower salaries than men.

••••[**Read** the **Document**

Mann, *Report of the Massachusetts Board of Education* at **my**historylab.com

Young women heeded the call. By 1860, women comprised 78 percent of the common school teachers in Massachusetts, a trend that prefigured developments elsewhere. The influx of young women invigorated the common schools and brought to the enterprise the zeal of a missionary. Harriet Beecher Stowe, who once taught at the Hartford Seminary, explained that men teachers lacked the "patience, the long-suffering, and gentleness necessary to superintend the formation of character."

By the 1850s every state outside the South provided free elementary schools and supported institutions for training teachers. Many extended public education to include high schools, and Michigan and Iowa even established publicly supported colleges.

Historians differ in explaining the success of the common school movement. Some stress the arguments Mann used to win support from employers by appealing to their need for trained and well-disciplined workers. Others see the schools as designed to "Americanize" the increasing numbers of non-English and non-Protestant immigrants who were flooding into the country. (Supporting this argument is the fact that Catholic bishops in New York and elsewhere opposed laws requiring Catholic children to attend these "Protestant" schools and set up their own private, parochial schools.)

Still other scholars argue that middle-class reformers favored public elementary schools on the theory that they would instill the values of hard work, punctuality, and submissiveness to authority in children of the laboring classes. All these reasons played a part in advancing the cause of the common schools. Yet it remains the case that the most compelling argument for common schools was cultural; more effectively than any other institution, they brought Americans of different economic circumstances and ethnic backgrounds into early and mutually beneficial contact with one another. They served the two roles that Mann assigned to them: "the balance wheel of the social machinery" and "the great equalizer."

[◉]Watch the **Video**

Who Was Horace Mann and Why Are So Many Schools Named After Him? at **my**historylab.com

The State of the Colleges

Unlike common schools, with their democratic overtones, private colleges had at best a precarious place in Jacksonian America. For one thing, there were too many of them. Any town with pretensions of becoming a regional center felt it had to have a college. Ohio had twenty-five in the 1850s, and Tennessee sixteen. Many of these institutions were short-lived. Of the fourteen colleges founded in Kentucky between 1800 and 1850, only half were still operating in 1860.

Watch the Video

What Was the Progressive Education Movement? at **myhistorylab.com**

The problem of supply was compounded by a demand problem—too few students. Enrollment at the largest, Yale, never topped 400 until the mid-1840s. On the eve of the Civil War the largest state university, North Carolina, had fewer than 500. Higher education was beyond the means of the average family. Although most colleges charged less than half the $55 tuition required by Harvard, that was still too much for most families. So desperate was the shortage that colleges accepted applicants as young as eleven and twelve and as old as thirty.

The typical college curriculum, dominated by the study of Latin and Greek, had almost no practical relevance except for future clergymen. The Yale faculty, most of them ministers, defended the classics as admirably providing for both "the discipline and the furniture of the mind," but these subjects commended themselves to college officials chiefly because they did not require costly equipment or a faculty that knew anything else. Professors spent most of their time in and out of the classroom trying to maintain a semblance of order, "to the exclusion of any great literary undertakings to which their choice might lead them," one explained. "Our country is yet too young for old professors," a Bostonian informed a foreign visitor in the 1830s, "and, besides, they are too poorly paid to induce first rate men to devote themselves to the business of lecturing. . . . We consider professors as secondary men."

Fortunately for the future of higher education, some college officials recognized the need for a drastic overhaul of their institutions. President Francis Wayland of Brown University used his 1842 address, "On the Present Collegiate System," to call for a thorough revamping of the curriculum to make it responsive to the economic realities of American society. This meant more courses in science, economics (where Wayland's own *Elements of Political Economy* might be used), modern history, and applied mathematics; and fewer in Hebrew, biblical studies, Greek, and ancient history.

Yale established a separate school of science in 1847, which it hoped would attract serious-minded students and research-minded professors. At Harvard, which also opened a scientific school, students were allowed to choose some of their courses and were compelled to earn grades as a stimulus to study. Colleges in the West and the South began to offer mechanical and agricultural subjects relevant to their regional economies. Oberlin enrolled four female students in 1837, and the first women's college, the Georgia Female College, opened its doors in 1839.

These reforms slowed the downward spiral of colleges; they did not restore them to the honored place they had enjoyed in the Revolutionary era. Of the first six presidents of the United States, only Washington did not graduate from college. Beginning in 1829, seven of the next eleven did not. In this Presidents Jackson, Van Buren, Harrison, Taylor, Fillmore, Lincoln, and Johnson were like 98 of every 100 white males, all blacks and Indians, and all but a handful of white women in mid-nineteenth-century America. Going to college had yet, in Wayland's words, to "commend itself to the good sense and patriotism of the American people."

Milestones

1774	Mother Ann Lee founds first Shaker community	**1843**	Dorothea Dix exposes treatment of the insane in *Memorial to the Legislature of Massachusetts*
1784	Dr. Benjamin Rush's *Inquiry into the Effects of Ardent Spirits* questions alcohol's benefits	**1844**	Margaret Fuller condemns sexual discrimination in *Women in the Nineteenth Century*
1826	American Temperance Union begins campaign against drunkenness		Nauvoo mob murders Joseph Smith
1829	Black abolitionist David Walker publishes *Appeal to the Coloured Citizens of the World*	**1845**	Frederick Douglass describes slave life in *Narrative of the Life of Frederick Douglass*
1830s	Second Great Awakening stresses promise of salvation	**1847**	Brigham Young leads Mormon migration to Great Salt Lake
	Prison reformers debate Auburn versus Philadelphia system	**1848**	Elizabeth Cady Stanton and Lucretia Mott organize Seneca Falls Convention and draft Declaration of Sentiments
1830–1850	Utopian communities flourish		
1830	Joseph Smith shares his "vision" in *Book of Mormon*	**1850**	Nathaniel Hawthorne publishes *The Scarlet Letter*
1831	Abolitionist William Lloyd Garrison founds *The Liberator* and New England Anti-Slavery Society	**1851**	Maine bans alcoholic beverages
			Herman Melville publishes *Moby-Dick*
1831–1832	Alexis de Tocqueville and Gustave de Beaumont tour America	**1854–1855**	Susan B. Anthony leads petition campaign against New York property and divorce laws
1832	Perkins Institution for the Blind opens in Boston	**1854**	Henry David Thoreau attacks conformity in *Walden*
1837	Illinois abolitionist Elijah Lovejoy is murdered	**1855–1892**	Walt Whitman publishes *Leaves of Grass* (various editions)
	Ralph Waldo Emerson delivers "The American Scholar" at Harvard		
	Horace Mann and Henry Barnard call for common schools		

✔●─ **Study** and **Review** at www.myhistorylab.com

Review Questions

1. The introduction to this chapter suggests that the "traditional" family was far more common in the mid-nineteenth century than nowadays. What were its strengths and limitations?

2. Many institutions were created during the years from 1820 to 1850; many remain a part of contemporary life. Prisons are an obvious example. What other institutions were established during this period that exist today? Does their persistence prove their value to society or the difficulty of eliminating outmoded institutions?

3. How did the changing attitudes toward marriage and children influence the rise of reform movements during the first half of the nineteenth century? How did the Great Awakening contribute to the social reforms of the era?

4. The campaign for women's rights and woman suffrage gained momentum during this period. Did these new ideas of women's roles in society stimulate the structural transformation of the family (fewer children, for example), or did the smaller families free women to undertake new initiatives such as reform and woman's suffrage?

5. Why did the great writers of the age—Emerson, Thoreau, Melville, Hawthorne, Whitman—fail to find large audiences?

Key Terms

abolitionism *282*

Cult of True Womanhood *274*

lyceums *294*

romanticism *288*

Second Great Awakening *275*

Seneca Falls Convention *287*

Shakers *277*

temperance movement *281*

transcendentalism *288*

utopian *278*

Westward Expansion

((•—[Hear the Audio Chapter 11 at myhistorylab.com

Has your family crossed borders?

IN 2010 ADRIANA CARILLO, A MEMBER OF THE MEXICAN SENATE, DERIDED President Barack Obama's plans to strengthen the 700-mile fence between the United States and Mexico. She explained that Spanish-speaking peoples, many of them of Mexican descent, constituted a third of the population of New Mexico, California, Texas, and Arizona. No fence, she declared, should separate the southwestern United States and Mexico, a region bound by economic and cultural ties. On the other side of the fence—literally and rhetorically—U.S. Senator Lamar Smith of San Antonio, Texas, complained that Obama was not doing enough to stem the flood of illegal immigrants into the United States.

As the debate raged, few noted that the United States had built the fence to prevent Mexicans from passing into lands that had once belonged to Mexico. In 1821, when Mexico secured its independence from Spain, the American Southwest became Mexican territory. But the heavy influx of American settlers into the Mexican state of Texas prompted Mexico to restrict further American immigration. Yet the "illegal" immigrants kept coming into Texas; some talked of independence and in 1836 secured it by war. In 1845 Texas became part of the United States; California (1850), New Mexico (1912) and Arizona (1912) would follow. Mexicans who entered the region were trespassing; in time, they would become illegal immigrants.

The acquisition of the Southwest by the United States had several important (if unintended) consequences. The most important concerned slavery. The annexation of Texas as a slave state raised the question of slavery throughout the Southwest. Would the "peculiar institution" eventually span the entire continent, stretching all the way to California? And, if the federal government disallowed slavery in some of the western regions, why not all of them? A crisis of inconceivable dimensions loomed.

Tyler's Troubles

John Tyler, who became president in 1841 after the death of William Henry Harrison, was a thin, rather delicate-appearing man. Courteous, tactful, and soft-spoken, he gave the impression of being weak, an impression reinforced by his professed belief that the president should defer to Congress in the formulation of policy. This was a false impression; John Tyler was stubborn and proud, and these characteristics combined with an almost total lack of imagination to make him worship consistency. He had turned away from Jackson because of the aggressive way the president had used his powers of appointment and the veto, but he also disagreed with Henry Clay and the northern Whigs about the Bank, protection, and federal internal improvements. Being a states' rights Southerner, he considered such measures unconstitutional. Nevertheless, he was prepared to cooperate with Clay as the leader of what he called the "more immediate representatives" of the people, the members of Congress. But he was not prepared to be Clay's puppet. He asked all of Harrison's Cabinet to remain in office.

Tyler and Clay did not get along, and for this Clay was chiefly to blame. He behaved in an overbearing manner that was out of keeping with his nature, probably because he resented having been passed over by the Whigs in 1840. He considered himself the real head of the Whig party and intended to exercise his leadership.

In Congress, Clay announced a comprehensive federal program that ignored Tyler's states' rights view of the Constitution. Most important was his plan to set up a new Bank of the United States. When Congress passed the new Bank bill, Tyler vetoed it. The entire Cabinet except Secretary of State Daniel Webster thereupon resigned in protest.

Abandoned by the Whigs, Tyler attempted to build a party of his own. He failed to do so, and for the remainder of his term the political squabbling in Washington was continuous.

The Webster-Ashburton Treaty

Webster's decision to remain in the Cabinet was motivated in part by his desire to settle the boundary between Maine and New Brunswick. The intent of the peace treaty of 1783 had been to award the United States all land in the area drained by rivers flowing into the Atlantic rather than into the St. Lawrence, but the wording was obscure and the old maps conflicting. In 1842 the British sent a new minister, Lord Ashburton, to the United States to try to settle all outstanding disputes. Ashburton and Webster easily worked out a compromise boundary. The British needed only a small part of the territory to build a military road connecting Halifax and Quebec. Webster, who thought any settlement desirable simply to eliminate a possible cause of war, willingly agreed.

Webster solved the problem of placating Maine and Massachusetts, both of which wanted every acre of the land in dispute, in an extraordinary manner. During the peace negotiations ending the Revolution, Franklin had marked the boundary between Maine and Canada on a map with a heavy red line, but no one could find the Franklin map. Webster obtained an old map of the area and had someone mark off in red a line that followed the British version of the boundary. He showed this document to representatives of Maine and Massachusetts, convincing them that they had better agree to his compromise before the British got wind of it and demanded the whole region! It later came out that the British had a true copy of the Franklin map, which showed that the entire area rightfully belonged to the United States.

Nevertheless, Webster's generosity made excellent sense. Lord Ashburton, gratified by having obtained the strategic territory, made concessions elsewhere along the Canadian and American border. British dependence on foreign foodstuffs was increasing; America's need for British capital was rising. War, or even unsettled affairs, would have injured vital business relations and produced no compensating gains. The **Webster-Ashburton Treaty** was regarded as a diplomatic triumph.

The Texas Question

The settlement with Great Britain won support in every section of the United States, but the same could not be said for Tyler's attempt to annex the Republic of Texas, for this involved the question of slavery. In the Transcontinental Treaty of 1819 with Spain the boundary of the United States had been drawn in such a way as to exclude Texas. This seemed unimportant at the time, yet within months of the treaty's ratification in February 1821, Americans led by Stephen F. Austin had begun to settle in the area. Almost simultaneously Mexico threw off the last vestiges of Spanish rule and secured its independence. Texas was now part of Mexico.

Cotton flourished on the fertile Texas plains, and for a time, the new Mexican authorities offered free land and something approaching local autonomy to groups of settlers from the United States. By 1830 there were some 20,000 white Americans in Texas, about 2,000 slaves, and only a few thousand Mexicans.

President John Quincy Adams had offered Mexico $1 million for Texas, and Jackson was willing to pay $5 million, but Mexico would not sell. Nevertheless, by the late 1820s, the flood of American settlers was giving the Mexican authorities second thoughts. The immigrants apparently felt no loyalty to Mexico. Most were Protestants, though Mexican law required that all immigrants be Catholics; few attempted to learn more than a few words of Spanish. When Mexico outlawed slavery in 1829, American settlers evaded the law by "freeing" their slaves and then signing them to lifetime contracts as indentured servants. In 1830 Mexico prohibited further immigration of Americans into Texas, though again the law proved impossible to enforce.

As soon as the Mexican government began to restrict them, the Texans began to seek independence. In 1835 a series of skirmishes escalated into a full-scale rebellion. The Mexican president, Antonio López de Santa Anna, marched north with over 5,000 soldiers to subdue the rebels. Late in February 1836 he reached San Antonio.

A force of 187 men under Colonel William B. Travis held the city. They took refuge behind the stout walls of a former mission called the Alamo. For nearly two weeks they held off Santa Anna's assaults, inflicting terrible casualties on the attackers. Finally, on March 6, the Mexicans breached and scaled the walls. Once inside they killed everyone, even the wounded. Among the dead were the legendary Davy Crockett and Jim Bowie, inventor of the Bowie knife. (See Re-Viewing the Past, *The Alamo*, pp. 320–321.)

●●●─Read the Document

Travis, *Letter from the Alamo* at **myhistorylab.com**

After the Alamo and the slaughter of another garrison at Goliad, southeast of San Antonio, peaceful settlement of the dispute between Texas and Mexico was impossible. Meanwhile, on March 2, 1836, Texas had declared its independence. Sam Houston, a former congressman and governor of Tennessee and an experienced Indian fighter, was placed in charge of the rebel army. For a time Houston retreated before Santa Anna's troops, who greatly outnumbered his own. At the San Jacinto River he took a stand. On April 21, 1836, shouting "Forward! Charge! Remember the Alamo! Remember Goliad!" his troops routed the Mexican army, which soon retreated across the Rio Grande. In October, Houston was elected president of the Republic of Texas, and a month later a plebiscite revealed that an overwhelming majority favored annexation by the United States.

President Jackson hesitated. To take Texas might lead to war with Mexico. Assuredly it would stir up the slavery controversy. On his last day in office he recognized the republic, but he made no move to accept it into the Union, nor did his successor, Van Buren. Texas thereupon went its own way, which involved developing friendly ties with Great Britain. An independent Texas suited British tastes perfectly, for it could provide an alternative supply of raw cotton and a market for manufactures unfettered by tariffs.

Sam Houston—and his horse—earned this heroic tribute. At the Battle of San Jacinto, a musket ball shattered Houston's right ankle; his horse, hit by five bullets, fell dead.
Source: San Jacinto Museum of History, Houston.

These events caused alarm in the United States, especially among Southerners, who dreaded the possibility that a Texas dominated by Great Britain might abolish slavery. As a Southerner, Tyler shared these feelings; as a beleaguered politician, spurned by the Whigs and held in contempt by most Democrats, he saw in annexation a chance to revive his fortunes. When Webster resigned as secretary of state in 1843, Tyler replaced him with a fellow Virginian, Abel P. Upshur, whom he ordered to seek a treaty of annexation. The South was eager to take Texas, and in the West and even the Northeast the patriotic urge to add such a magnificent new territory to the national domain was great. Upshur negotiated a treaty in February 1844, but before he could sign it he was killed by the accidental explosion of a cannon on USS *Princeton* during a weapons demonstration.

To ensure the winning of Texas, Tyler appointed John C. Calhoun secretary of state. This was a blunder; by then Calhoun was so closely associated with the South and with slavery that his appointment alienated thousands of Northerners who might otherwise have welcomed annexation. Suddenly Texas became a hot political issue. Clay and Van Buren, who seemed assured of the 1844 Whig and Democratic presidential nominations, promptly announced that they opposed annexation, chiefly on

> **Watch the Video**
> *The Annexation of Texas*
> at myhistorylab.com

the ground that it would probably lead to war with Mexico. With a national election in the offing, northern and western senators refused to vote for annexation, and in June the Senate rejected the treaty, 35 to 16. The Texans were angry and embarrassed, the British eager again to take advantage of the situation.

Manifest Destiny

The Senate, Clay, and Van Buren had all misinterpreted public opinion. John C. Calhoun, whose world was so far removed from that of the average citizen, in this case anticipated the mood of the country.

After 200 years of westward expansion, Americans perceived their destined goal: *The whole continent was to be theirs!* A New York journalist, John L. O'Sullivan, captured the new mood in a sentence. Nothing must interfere, he wrote in 1845, with "the fulfillment of our *manifest destiny* to overspread the continent allotted by Providence for the free development of our yearly multiplying millions."

> **Read the Document**
> John O'Sullivan, *Annexation* at
> myhistorylab.com

The expansion, stimulated by the natural growth of the population and by a revived flood of immigration, was going on in every section and with little regard for political boundaries. New settlers rolled westward in hordes to fulfill their **manifest destiny**. The politicians did not sense the new mood in 1844; even Calhoun, who saw the acquisition of Texas as part of a broader program, was thinking of balancing sectional interests rather than of national expansion.

Life on the Trail

The romantic myths attached by later generations to this mighty human tide have obscured the adjustments forced on the pioneers and focused attention on the least significant of the dangers they faced and the hardships they endured. For example, Indians could of course be deadly enemies, but pioneers were more likely to complain that

In *American Progress* (1872), John Gast depicts a feminized (and eroticized) America moving westward, a school book in one hand, a telegraph wire in the other. Confronted with the onslaught of "civilization," the buffalo flee and the Indians cringe.

the Indians they encountered were dirty, lazy, and pitiably poor than to worry about the danger of Indian attack.

The greater dangers were accidents on the trail, particularly to children, and also unsanitary conditions and exposure to the elements. "Going west" had always been laborious, but in the 1840s the distances covered were longer by far and the comforts and conveniences of "civilization" that had to be left behind, being more extensive than those available to earlier generations, tended to be more painful to surrender.

Travel on the plains west of the Mississippi was especially taxing for women. Some assumed tasks traditionally performed by men. "I keep close to my gun and dog," a woman from Illinois wrote in her diary. But most found the experience disillusioning. Guidebooks promised them that "regular exercise, in the open air . . . gives additional vigor and strength." But the books did not prepare women for collecting dried buffalo dung for fuel, for the heat and choking dust of summer, for the monotony, the dirt, the cramped quarters. Caring for an infant or a two-year-old in a wagon could be torture week after week on the trail.

California and Oregon

By 1840 many Americans had settled far to the west in California, which was unmistakably Mexican territory, and in the Oregon country, jointly claimed by the United States and Great Britain; and it was to these distant regions that the pioneers traveled in increasing numbers as the decade progressed. California was a sparsely settled land of some 7,000 Spanish-speaking ranchers and a handful of "Anglo" settlers from the United States. Until the 1830s, when their estates were broken up by the anticlerical Mexican government, twenty-one Catholic missions, stretching north from San Diego to San Francisco, controlled more than 30,000 Indian converts, who were little better off than slaves.

Oregon, a vaguely defined area between California and Russian Alaska, proved still more alluring to Americans. Captain Robert Gray had sailed up the Columbia River in 1792, and Lewis and Clark had visited the region on their great expedition. In 1811 John Jacob Astor's Pacific Fur Company had established trading posts on the Columbia. Two decades later Methodist, Presbyterian, and Catholic missionaries began to find their way into the Willamette Valley, a green land of rich soil, mild climate, and tall forests teeming with game. Gradually a small number of settlers followed, until by 1840 there were about 500 Americans in the Willamette area.

In the early 1840s, fired by the spirit of manifest destiny, the country suddenly burned with "Oregon fever." In dozens upon dozens of towns, societies were founded to collect information and organize groups to make the march to the Pacific. Land hunger (stimulated by glowing reports from the scene) drew the new migrants most powerfully, but the patriotic concept of manifest destiny gave the trek across the 2,000 miles of wilderness separating Oregon from the western edge of American settlement in Missouri the character of a crusade. In 1843 nearly 1,000 pioneers made the long trip.

The Oregon Trail began at the western border of Missouri and followed the Kansas River and the muddy Platte past Fort Laramie to the Rockies. It crossed the Continental Divide by the relatively easy South Pass, veered south to Fort Bridger (on Mexican soil), and then ran north and west through the valley of the Snake River and

Ada McColl gathers buffalo chips, used for fuel, in western Nebraska.
Source: Kansas State Historical Society.

eventually, by way of the Columbia, to Fort Vancouver, a British post guarding the entrance to the Willamette Valley.

Over this tortuous path wound the canvas-covered caravans with their scouts and their accompanying herds. Each group became a self-governing community on the march, with regulations democratically agreed on "for the purpose of keeping good order and promoting civil and military discipline." Most of the travelers consisted of young families, some from as far away as the East Coast cities, more from towns and farms in the Ohio Valley. Few could be classified as poor because the cost of the trip for a family of four was about $600, no small sum at that time. (The faster and less fatiguing trip by ship around South America cost about $600 per person.)

For large groups Indians posed no great threat (though constant vigilance was necessary), but the five-month trip was full of labor, discomfort, and uncertainty. "It became so monotonous after a while that I would have welcomed an Indian fight if awake," one man wrote. And at the end lay the regular tasks of pioneering. The spirit of the trailblazers is caught in an entry from the diary of James Nesmith:

> Friday, October 27.—Arrived at Oregon City at the falls of the Willamette.
> Saturday, October 28.—Went to work.

Trails West The Old Spanish Trail was the earliest of the trails west. Part of it was mapped in 1776 by a Franciscan missionary. The Santa Fe Trail came into use after 1823. The Oregon Trail was pioneered by trappers and missionaries. The Mormon Trail was first traversed in 1847, while the Oxbow Route, developed under a federal mail contract, was used from 1858 to 1861.

Behind the dreams of the Far West as an American Eden lay the commercial importance of the three major West Coast harbors: San Diego, San Francisco, and the Strait of Juan de Fuca leading into Puget Sound. Eastern merchants considered these harbors the keys to the trade of the Orient. That San Diego and San Francisco were Mexican and the Puget Sound district was claimed by Great Britain only heightened their desire to possess them. As early as 1835, Jackson tried to buy the San Francisco region. Even Calhoun called San Francisco the future New York of the Pacific and proposed buying all of California from Mexico.

The Election of 1844

In the spring of 1844 expansion did not seem likely to affect the presidential election. The Whigs nominated Clay unanimously and ignored Texas in their party platform. When the Democrats gathered in convention at Baltimore in May, Van Buren appeared to have the nomination in his pocket. He too wanted to keep Texas out of the campaign. John C. Calhoun, however, was determined to make Texas a campaign issue.

That a politician of Van Buren's caliber, controlling the party machinery, could be upset at a national convention seemed unthinkable. But upset he was, for the southern delegates rallied round the Calhoun policy of taking Texas to save it for slavery. "I can beat Clay and Van Buren put together on this issue," Calhoun boasted. "They are behind the age." James K. Polk of Tennessee, who favored expansion, swept the convention.

Polk was a good Jacksonian; his supporters called him "Young Hickory." He opposed high tariffs and was dead set against establishing another national bank. But he believed in taking Texas. The Democratic platform demanded that Texas be "reannexed" (implying that it had been part of the Louisiana Purchase) and that all of Oregon be "reoccupied" (suggesting repeal of the joint occupation of the region with Great Britain, which had been agreed to in the Convention of 1818).

Texas was now in the campaign. When Clay sensed the new expansionist sentiment of the voters, he tried to hedge on his opposition to annexation, but by doing so he probably lost as many votes as he gained. The election was extremely close. The campaign followed the pattern established in 1840, with stress on parades, mass meetings, and slogans. Polk carried the country by only 38,000 of 2.7 million votes. In the Electoral College the vote was 170 to 105. Polk's victory was nevertheless taken as a mandate for expansion. Tyler promptly called on Congress to take Texas by joint resolution, which was done a few days before Tyler left the White House. Under the resolution, if the new state agreed, as many as four new states might be carved from its territory. Polk accepted this arrangement, and in December 1845 Texas became a state.

Polk as President

Polk was uncommonly successful in doing what he set out to do as president. He persuaded Congress to lower the tariff of 1842 and to restore the independent treasury. He opposed federal internal improvements and managed to have his way. He made himself the spokesman of American expansion by committing himself to obtaining, in addition to Texas, both Oregon and the great Southwest. Here again, he succeeded.

Oregon was the first order of business. In his inaugural address Polk stated the American claim to the entire region in the plainest terms, but he informed the British minister in Washington, Richard Pakenham, that he would accept a boundary following the forty-ninth parallel to the Pacific. Pakenham rejected this proposal without submitting it to London, and Polk thereupon decided to insist again on the whole area. When Congress met in December 1845, he asked for authority to give the necessary one year's notice for withdrawing from the 1818 treaty of joint occupation. Following considerable discussion, Congress complied and in May 1846 Polk notified Great Britain that he intended to terminate the joint occupation.

The British then decided to compromise. Officials of the Hudson's Bay Company had become alarmed by the rapid growth of the American settlement in the Willamette Valley. By 1845 some 5,000 people had poured into the region, whereas the country north of the Columbia contained no more than 750 British subjects. The company decided to shift its base from the Columbia to Vancouver Island. And British experts outside the company reported that the Oregon country could not possibly be defended in case of war. Thus, when Polk accompanied the one-year notice with a hint that he would again consider a compromise, the British foreign secretary, Lord Aberdeen, hastily suggested Polk's earlier proposal, dividing the Oregon territory along the forty-ninth parallel. Polk agreed. The treaty followed that line from the Rockies to Puget Sound, but Vancouver Island, which extends below the line, was left entirely to the British, so that both nations retained free use of the Strait of Juan de Fuca. Although some northern Democrats accused Polk of treachery because he had failed to fight for all of Oregon, the treaty so obviously accorded with the national interest that the Senate approved it by a large majority in June 1846. Polk was then free to take up the Texas question in earnest.

War with Mexico

One reason for the popularity of the Oregon compromise was that the country was already at war with Mexico and wanted no trouble with Great Britain. The **Mexican War** had broken out in large measure because of the expansionist spirit, and the confidence born of its overwhelming advantages of size and wealth certainly encouraged the United States to bully Mexico. In addition, Mexico had defaulted on debts owed the United States, which caused some people to suggest using force to obtain the money. But Mexican pride was also involved. Texas had been independent for the better part of a decade, and Mexico had made no serious effort to reconquer it; nevertheless, Mexico never recognized its independence and promptly broke off diplomatic relations when the United States annexed the republic.

Polk then ordered General Zachary Taylor into Texas to defend the border. However, the location of that border was in dispute. Texas claimed the Rio Grande; Mexico insisted that the boundary was the Nueces River, which emptied into the Gulf of Mexico about 150 miles to the north. Taylor reached the Nueces in July 1845 with about 1,500 troops and crossed into the disputed territory. He stopped on the southern bank at Corpus Christi, not wishing to provoke the Mexicans by marching to the Rio Grande.

In November, Polk sent an envoy, John Slidell, on a secret mission to Mexico to try to obtain the disputed territory by negotiation. He authorized Slidell to

The War with Mexico, 1846–1848 The war with Mexico required considerable coordination of far-flung military and naval operations.

cancel the Mexican debt in return for recognition of the annexation of Texas and acceptance of the Rio Grande boundary. The president also empowered Slidell to offer as much as $30 million if Mexico would sell the United States all or part of New Mexico and California.

It would probably have been to Mexico's advantage, at least in the short run, to have made a deal with Slidell. The area Polk wanted, lying in the path of American expansion, was likely to be engulfed as Texas had been, without regard for the actions of the American or Mexican governments. But the Mexican government refused to receive Slidell. Amid a wave of anti-American feeling, a military coup occurred and General Mariano Paredes, the new head of state, promptly reaffirmed his country's claim to all of Texas. Slidell returned to Washington convinced that the Mexicans would not give an inch until they had been "chastised."

Polk had already ordered Taylor to advance to the Rio Grande. By late March 1846 the army, which swelled to about 4,000, had taken up positions near the Mexican town of Matamoros. The Mexicans crossed the river on April 25 and attacked an American mounted patrol. They were driven back easily, but when news of the fighting reached Washington, Polk asked Congress to declare war. He treated the matter as a *fait accompli*: "War exists," he stated flatly. Congress accepted this reasoning and without actually declaring war voted to raise and supply an additional 50,000 troops.

From the first battle, the outcome of the Mexican War was never in doubt. At Palo Alto, north of the Rio Grande, 2,300 Americans scattered a Mexican force more than twice their number. Then, 1,700 Americans routed 7,500 Mexicans at Resaca de la Palma near what is now Brownsville, Texas. Fewer than 50 U.S. soldiers lost their lives in these engagements, while Mexican losses in killed, wounded, and captured exceeded 1,000. Within a week of the outbreak of hostilities, the Mexicans had been driven across the Rio Grande and General Taylor had his troops firmly established on the southern bank.

To the Halls of Montezuma

President Polk insisted not only on directing grand strategy but on supervising hundreds of petty details, down to the purchase of mules and the promotion of enlisted men. But he allowed party considerations to control his choice of generals. This partisanship caused unnecessary turmoil in army ranks. He wanted, as Thomas Hart Benton said, "a small war, just large enough to require a treaty of peace, and not large enough to make military reputations dangerous for the presidency."

•••⌐Read the Document

Thomas Corwin, *Against the Mexican War* at **myhistorylab.com**

Unfortunately for Polk, both Taylor and Winfield Scott, the commanding general in Washington, were Whigs. Polk, who tended to suspect the motives of anyone who disagreed with him, feared that one or the other would make political capital of his popularity as a military leader. The examples of his hero, Jackson, and of General Harrison loomed large in Polk's thinking.

Polk's attitude was narrow, almost unpatriotic, but not unrealistic. Zachary Taylor was not a brilliant soldier. He had joined the army in 1808 and made it his whole life. He cared so little for politics that he had never bothered to cast a ballot in an election. Polk believed that he lacked the "grasp of mind" necessary for high command, and

American soldiers—some of them regulars in deep blue uniforms, others in buckskin cowboy outfits—fight in the streets to drive Mexicans from a Spanish mission in Monterrey, California, in 1846.

General Scott complained of his "comfortable, laborsaving contempt for learning of every kind." But Taylor commanded the love and respect of his men, and he knew how to deploy them in the field. He had won another victory against a Mexican force three times larger than his own at Buena Vista in February 1847.

The dust had barely settled on the field of Buena Vista when Whig politicians began to pay Taylor court. "Great expectations and great consequences rest upon you," a Kentucky politician explained to him. "People everywhere begin to talk of converting you into a political leader, when the War is done."

Polk's concern was heightened because domestic opposition to the war was growing. Many Northerners feared that the war would lead to the expansion of slavery. Others—among them an obscure Illinois congressman named Abraham Lincoln—felt that Polk had misled Congress about the original outbreak of fighting and that the United States was the aggressor. The farther from the Rio Grande one went in the United States, the less popular "Mr. Polk's war" became; in New England opposition was almost as widespread as it had been to "Mr. Madison's war" in 1812.

Polk's design for prosecuting the war consisted of three parts. First, he would clear the Mexicans from Texas and occupy the northern provinces of Mexico. Second, he would take possession of California and New Mexico. Finally, he would march on Mexico City. Proceeding west from the Rio Grande, Taylor swiftly overran Mexico's northern provinces. In June 1846, American settlers in the Sacramento Valley seized Sonoma and raised the Bear Flag of the Republic of California. Another group, headed by Captain John C. Frémont, leader of an American exploring party that happened to be in the area, clashed with the Mexican authorities around Monterey, California, and then joined with the Sonoma rebels. A naval squadron under Commodore John D. Sloat captured Monterey and San Francisco in July 1846, and a squadron of cavalry joined the other American units in mopping-up operations around San Diego and Los Angeles. By February 1847 the United States had won control of nearly all of Mexico north of the capital city.

The campaign against Mexico City was the most difficult of the war. Fearful of Taylor's growing popularity and entertaining certain honest misgivings about his ability to oversee a complicated campaign, Polk put Winfield Scott in charge of the offensive.

About Scott's competence no one entertained a doubt. But he seemed even more of a threat to the Democrats than Taylor, because he had political ambitions as well as military ability. In 1840 the Whigs had considered him for president. Scion of an old Virginia family, Scott was intelligent, even-tempered, and cultivated, if somewhat pompous. After a sound but not spectacular record in the War of 1812, he had added to his reputation by helping modernize military administration and strengthen the professional training of officers. On the record, and despite the politics of the situation, Polk had little choice but to give him this command.

Scott landed his army south of Veracruz, Mexico, on March 9, 1847, laid siege to the city, and obtained its surrender in less than three weeks with the loss of only a handful of his 10,000 men. Marching westward through hostile country, he maintained effective discipline, avoiding atrocities that might have inflamed the countryside against him. Finding his way blocked by well-placed artillery and a large army at Cerro Gordo, where the National Road rose steeply toward the central highlands, Scott outflanked the Mexican position and then carried it by storm, capturing more than 3,000 prisoners and much equipment. By mid-May he had advanced to Puebla, only eighty miles southeast of Mexico City.

After delaying until August for the arrival of reinforcements, he pressed on, won two hard-fought victories at the outskirts of the capital, and on September 14 hammered his way into the city. In every engagement the American troops had been outnumbered, yet they always exacted a far heavier toll from the defenders than they themselves were forced to pay. In the fighting on the edge of Mexico City, for example, Scott's army sustained about 1,000 casualties, for the Mexicans defended their capital bravely. But 4,000 Mexicans were killed or wounded in the engagements, and 3,000 (including eight generals, two of them former presidents of the republic) were taken prisoner. No less an authority than the Duke of Wellington, the conqueror of Napoleon, called Scott's campaign the most brilliant of modern times.

The Treaty of Guadalupe Hidalgo

Following the fall of Mexico City, the Mexican government was in turmoil. Polk had authorized payment of $30 million for New Mexico, upper and lower California, and the right of transit across Mexico's narrow isthmus of Tehuantepec. Now, observing the disorganized state of Mexican affairs, he began to consider demanding more territory and paying less for it. He recalled his chief negotiator, Nicholas P. Trist, who ignored the order. Trist realized that unless a treaty was arranged soon, the Mexican government might disintegrate, leaving no one in authority to sign a treaty. He dashed off a sixty-five-page letter to the president, in effect refusing to be recalled, and continued to negotiate. Early in February the **Treaty of Guadalupe Hidalgo** was completed. By its terms Mexico accepted the Rio Grande as the boundary of Texas and ceded New Mexico and upper California to the United States. In return the United States agreed to pay Mexico $15 million and to take on the claims of American citizens against Mexico, which by that time amounted to another $3.25 million.

When he learned that Trist had ignored his orders, the president ordered that he be fired from the State Department and placed under arrest. Yet Polk had no choice but to submit the treaty to the Senate, for to have insisted on more territory would have meant more fighting, and the war had become increasingly unpopular. The relatively easy military victory made some people ashamed that their country was crushing a weaker neighbor. Abolitionists, led by William Lloyd Garrison, called it an "invasion . . . waged solely for the detestable and horrible purpose of extending and perpetuating American slavery." The Senate, subject to the same pressures as the president, ratified the agreement by a vote of thirty-eight to fourteen.

The Fruits of Victory: Further Enlargement of the United States

See the **Map**

U.S. Territorial Expansion in the 1850s at **myhistorylab.com**

The Mexican War, won quickly and at relatively small cost in lives and money, brought huge territorial gains. The Pacific coast from south of San Diego to the forty-ninth parallel and all the land between the coast and the Continental Divide had become the property of the American people.

Immense amounts of labor and capital would have to be invested before this new territory could be made to yield its bounty, but the country clearly had the capacity to accomplish the job.

In this atmosphere came what seemed a sign from the heavens. In January 1848, while Scott's veterans rested on their victorious arms in Mexico City, a mechanic named James W. Marshall was building a sawmill on the American River in the Sacramento Valley east of San Francisco. One day, while supervising the deepening of the millrace, he noticed a few flecks of yellow in the bed of the stream. These he gathered up and tested. They were pure gold.

Other strikes had been made in California and been treated skeptically or as matters of local curiosity; since the days of Jamestown, too many pioneers had run fruitlessly in search of El Dorado, and too much fool's gold had been passed off as the real thing. Yet this discovery produced an international sensation. The gold was real and plentiful—$200 million of it was extracted in four years—but equally important was the fact that everyone was ready to believe the news. The **gold rush** reflected the heady confidence inspired by Guadalupe Hidalgo; it seemed the ultimate justification of manifest destiny. Surely an era of continental prosperity and harmony had dawned.

Slavery: Storm Clouds Gather

Prosperity came in full measure but harmony did not, for once again expansion brought the nation face to face with the divisive question of slavery. The future of this giant chunk of North America, most of it vacant, was soon to be determined—slave or free? The question, in one sense, seems hardly worth the national crisis it provoked. Slavery appeared to have little future in New Mexico and California, and none in Oregon. Why did the South fight so hard for the right to bring slaves into a region that seemed so poorly suited to their exploitation?

Slavery raised a moral question. Most Americans tried to avoid confronting this truth; as patriots they assumed that any sectional issue could be solved by compromise. However, while the majority of whites had little respect for blacks, slave or free, few persons, northern or southern, could look upon the ownership of one human being by another as simply an alternative form of economic organization and argue its merits as they would those of the protective tariff or a national bank. Twist the facts as they might, slavery was either right or it was wrong; being on the whole honest and moral, they could not, having faced that truth, stand by unconcerned while the question was debated.

Slavery had complicated the Texas problem from the start, and it beclouded the future of the Southwest even before the Mexican flag had been stripped from the staffs at Santa Fe and Los Angeles. The northern, Van Burenite wing of the Democratic party had become increasingly uneasy about the proslavery cast of Polk's policies, which were unpopular in that part of the country. Once it became likely that the war would bring new territory into the Union, these Northerners felt compelled to try to check the president and to assure their constituents that they would resist the admission of further slave territory. On August 8, 1846, during the debate on a bill appropriating money for the conduct of the war, Democratic Congressman David Wilmot of Pennsylvania introduced an amendment that provided "as an express and fundamental condition to the acquisition of any territory from the Republic of Mexico" that "neither slavery nor involuntary servitude shall ever exist in any part of said territory."

Southerners found the **Wilmot Proviso** particularly insulting. Nevertheless, it passed the House, where northern congressmen outnumbered southern. But it was defeated in the Senate, where Southerners held the balance. To counter the Proviso, Calhoun, once again serving as senator from South Carolina, introduced resolutions in 1846 arguing that Congress had no right to bar slavery from any territory; because territories belonged to all the states, slave and free, all should have equal rights in them. From this position it was only a step (soon taken) to demanding that Congress guarantee the right of slave owners to bring slaves into the territories and establish federal slave codes in the territories. Most Northerners considered this proposal as repulsive as Southerners found the Wilmot Proviso.

To resolve the territorial problem, two compromises were offered. One, eventually backed by President Polk, would extend the Missouri Compromise line to the Pacific. The majority of Southerners were willing to go along with this scheme, but most Northerners would no longer agree to the reservation of *any* new territory for slavery. The other possibility, advocated by Senator Lewis Cass of Michigan, called for organizing new territories without mention of slavery, thus leaving it to local settlers, through their territorial legislatures, to determine their own institutions. Cass's **popular sovereignty**, known more vulgarly as "squatter sovereignty," had the superficial merit of appearing to be democratic. Its virtue for the members of Congress, however, was that it allowed them to escape the responsibility of deciding the question themselves.

The Election of 1848

One test of strength occurred in August, before the 1848 presidential election. After six months of acrimonious debate, Congress passed a bill barring slavery from Oregon. The test, however, proved little. If it required half a year to settle the question for Oregon, how could an answer ever be found for California and New Mexico? Plainly the time had come, in a democracy, to go to the people. The coming presidential election seemed to provide an ideal opportunity.

The opportunity was missed. The politicians of the parties hedged, fearful of losing votes in one section or another. With the issues blurred, voters had no real choice. That the Whigs should behave in such a manner was perhaps to be expected. In 1848 they nominated Zachary Taylor for president, despite his lack of political sophistication and even after he had flatly refused to state his opinion on any current subject. The party offered no platform. Taylor's contribution to the campaign was so naive as to be pathetic. "I am a Whig, *but not an ultra Whig.* . . . If elected . . . I should feel bound to administer the government untrammeled by party schemes."

The Democratic party had little better to offer. All the drive and zeal characteristic of it in the Jackson period had gradually seeped away. Polk's espousal of Texas's annexation had driven many Northerners from its ranks. The party members finally nominated Lewis Cass, the father of popular sovereignty, but they did not endorse that or any other solution to the territorial question. The Van Buren wing of the Democratic party could not stomach Cass's willingness to countenance the extension of slavery into new territories. Combining with the antislavery Liberty party, they formed the **Free Soil party** and nominated Van Buren.

The Free Soil party polled nearly 300,000 votes, about 10 percent of the total, in a very dull campaign. Offered a choice between the honest ignorance of Taylor and the cynical opportunism of Cass, the voters—by a narrow margin—chose the former, Taylor receiving 1.36 million votes to Cass's 1.22 million. Taylor carried eight of the fifteen slave states and seven of the fifteen free states, proof that the sectional issue

AN AVAILABLE CANDIDATE.

According to this Democratic cartoon, the only qualification of General Zachary Taylor, the Whig candidate for president in 1848, is that he killed many Mexicans.

had been avoided. The chief significance of the election was the growing strength of the antislavery forces; in the next decade, this would bring about the collapse of the second party system.

The Gold Rush

The question of slavery in the territories could no longer be deferred. The discovery of gold had brought an army of prospectors into California. By the summer of 1848 San Francisco had become almost a ghost town, and an estimated two-thirds of the adult males of Oregon had hastened south to the gold fields. After President Polk confirmed the "extraordinary character" of the strike in his annual message of December 1848, there was no containing the gold seekers. During 1849, some 25,000 Americans made their way to California from the East by ship; more than 55,000 others crossed the continent by overland routes. About 8,000 Mexicans, 5,000 South Americans, and numbers of Europeans joined the rush.

The rough limits of the gold country had been quickly marked out. For 150 miles and more along the western slope of the Sierra stretched the great mother lode. Along the expanse any stream or canyon, or any ancient gravel bed might conceal a treasure in nuggets, flakes, or dust. Between 1849 and 1860 about 200,000 people, nearly all of them males, crossed the Rockies to California and thousands more reached California by ship via Cape Horn. Disregarding justice and reason alike, the newcomers from the East, as one observer noted, "regarded every man but a native [North] American as an interloper." They referred to people of Latin American origin as "greasers" and sought by law and by violence to keep them from mining for gold. Even the local Californians (now American citizens) were discriminated against. The few free blacks in California and the several thousand more who came in search of gold were treated no better. As for the far larger Indian population, it was almost wiped out. There were about 150,000 Indians in California in the mid-1840s but only 35,000 in 1860.

●●●┤Read the Document

Burrum, from *Six Months in the Gold Mines* at
myhistorylab.com

The ethnic conflict was only part of the problem. Rough, hard men, separated from women, lusted for gold in a strange, wild country where fortunes could be made in a day, gambled away in an hour, or stolen in an instant. The situation demanded the establishment of a territorial government. President Taylor appreciated this, and in his gruff, simple-hearted way he suggested an uncomplicated answer: Admit California directly as a state, letting the Californians decide for themselves about slavery. The rest of the Mexican cession could be formed into another state. No need for Congress, with its angry rivalries, to meddle at all, he believed. In this way the nation could avoid the divisive effects of sectional debate.

The Californians reacted favorably to Taylor's proposal. They were overwhelmingly opposed to slavery, though not for humanitarian reasons. On the contrary, they tended to look on blacks as they did Mexicans and feared that if slavery were permitted, white gold seekers would be disadvantaged. By October 1849 they had drawn up a constitution that outlawed slavery, and by December the new state government was functioning.

Taylor was the owner of a large plantation and more than 100 slaves; Southerners had assumed (without bothering to ask) that he would fight to keep the territories open to slavery. But being a military man, he was above all a nationalist; he disliked the divisiveness that partisan discussion of the issue was producing. Southerners were horrified by the president's reasoning. To admit California would destroy the balance between free and slave states in the Senate; to allow all the new land to become free would doom the South to wither in a corner of the country, surrounded by hostile free states. Radicals were already saying that the South would have to choose between secession and surrender. Taylor's plan played into the hands of extremists.

The Compromise of 1850

This was no longer a squabble over territorial governments. With the Union itself at stake, Henry Clay rose to save the day. He had been as angry and frustrated when the Whigs nominated Taylor as he had been when they passed him over for Harrison. Now, well beyond age seventy and in poor health, he put away his ambition and his resentment and for the last time concentrated his remarkable vision on a great, multifaceted national problem. On

•:•[Read the **Document**

Clay, *Speech to the U.S. Senate* at **myhistorylab.com**

January 29, 1850, he laid his proposal, "founded upon mutual forbearance," before the Senate. A few days later he defended it on the floor of the Senate in the last great speech of his life.

California should be brought directly into the Union as a free state, he argued. The rest of the Southwest should be organized as a territory without mention of slavery: The Southerners would retain the right to bring slaves there, while in fact none would do so. "You have got what is worth more than a thousand Wilmot Provisos," Clay pointed out to his northern colleagues. "You have nature on your side." Empty lands in dispute along the Texas border should be assigned to the New Mexico Territory, Clay continued, but in exchange the United States should take over Texas's preannexation debts. The slave trade should be abolished in the District of Columbia (but not slavery itself), and a more effective federal fugitive slave law should be enacted and strictly enforced in the North.

Clay's proposals occasioned one of the most magnificent debates in the history of the Senate. Every important member had his say. Calhoun, perhaps even more than Clay, realized that the future of the nation was at stake and that his own days were numbered (he died four weeks later). He was so feeble that he could not deliver his speech himself. He sat impassive, wrapped in a great cloak, gripping the arms of his chair, while Senator James M. Mason of Virginia read it to the crowded Senate. Calhoun thought his plan would save the Union, but his speech was an argument for secession; he demanded that the North yield completely on every point, ceasing even to discuss the question of slavery. Clay's compromise was unsatisfactory; he himself had no other to offer. If you will not yield, he said to the northern senators, "let the States . . . agree to separate and part in peace. If you are unwilling we should part in peace, tell us so, and we shall know what to do."

Three days later, on March 7, Daniel Webster took the floor. He too had begun to fail. Years of heavy drinking and other forms of self-indulgence had taken their toll. The brilliant volubility and the thunder were gone, and when he spoke his face was bathed in sweat and there were strange pauses in his delivery. But his argument was lucid. Clay's proposals should be adopted. Since the future of all the territories had already been fixed by geographic and economic factors, the Wilmot Proviso was unnecessary. The North's constitutional obligation to yield fugitive slaves, he said, braving the wrath of New England abolitionists, was "binding in honor and conscience." The Union, he continued, could not be sundered without bloodshed. At the thought of that dread possibility, the old fire flared: "Peaceable secession!" Webster exclaimed, "Heaven forbid! Where is the flag of the republic to remain? Where is the eagle still to tower?" The debate did not end with the aging giants. Every possible viewpoint was presented, argued, rebutted, rehashed.

•••—[Read the Document

Webster, *Speech to the U.S. Senate* at **myhistorylab.com**

The majority clearly favored some compromise, but nothing could have been accomplished without the death of President Taylor on July 9, 1850. Obstinate, probably resentful because few people paid him half the heed they paid Clay and other prominent members of Congress, the president had insisted on his own plan to bring both California and New Mexico directly into the Union. When Vice President Millard Fillmore, who was a politician, not an ideologue, succeeded Taylor, the deadlock between the White House and Capitol Hill was broken.

In the Senate and then in the House, tangled combinations pushed through the separate measures, one by one. California became the thirty-first state. The rest of the Mexican cession was divided into two territories, New Mexico and Utah, each to be admitted to the Union when qualified, "with or without slavery as [its] constitution may prescribe." Texas received $10 million to pay off its debt in return for accepting a narrower western boundary. The slave trade in the District of Columbia was abolished as of January 1, 1851. The **Fugitive Slave Act** of 1793 was amended to provide for the appointment of federal commissioners with authority to issue warrants, summon posses, and compel citizens under pain of fine or imprisonment to assist in the capture of fugitives. Commissioners who decided that an accused person was a runaway received a larger fee than if they declared the person legally free. The accused could not testify in their own defense. They were to be returned to the South without jury trial merely on the submission of an affidavit by their "owner."

Only four senators and twenty-eight representatives voted for all these bills. The two sides did not meet somewhere in the middle as is the case with most compromises. Each bill passed because those who preferred it outnumbered those opposed. In general, the Democrats gave more support to the **Compromise of 1850** than the Whigs, but party lines never held firmly. In the Senate, for example, seventeen Democrats and fifteen Whigs voted to admit California as a free state. A large number of congressmen absented themselves when parts of the settlement unpopular in their home districts came to a vote; twenty-one senators and thirty-six representatives failed to commit themselves on the new fugitive slave bill.

•••—[Read the Document

The Fugitive Slave Act (1850) at **myhistorylab.com**

In this piecemeal fashion the Union was preserved. The credit belongs mostly to Clay, whose original conceptualization of the compromise enabled lesser minds to understand what they must do.

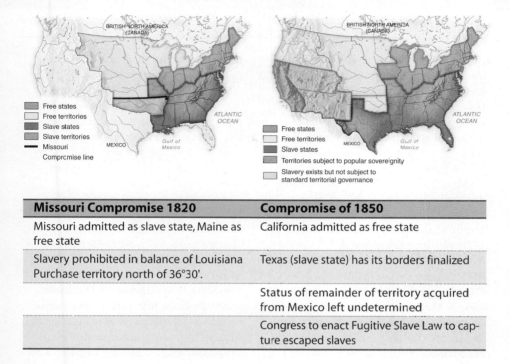

Missouri Compromise 1820	Compromise of 1850
Missouri admitted as slave state, Maine as free state	California admitted as free state
Slavery prohibited in balance of Louisiana Purchase territory north of 36°30'.	Texas (slave state) has its borders finalized
	Status of remainder of territory acquired from Mexico left undetermined
	Congress to enact Fugitive Slave Law to capture escaped slaves

Everywhere sober and conservative citizens sighed with relief. Mass meetings throughout the country "ratified" the result. Hundreds of newspapers gave the compromise editorial approval. In Washington patriotic harmony reigned. When Congress met again in December it seemed that party discord had been buried forever. "I have determined never to make another speech on the slavery question," Senator Stephen A. Douglas of Illinois told his colleagues. "Let us cease agitating, stop the debate, and drop the subject." If this were done, he predicted, the compromise would be accepted as a "final settlement." With this bit of wishful thinking the year 1850 passed into history.

The Alamo

Alamo, Pearl Harbor, 9/11: Each of these syllables has been seared into the national consciousness. Each galvanized Americans to go to war; and each has persisted in memory.

Two movies entitled *The Alamo* have influenced how Americans remember the event: John Wayne directed the 1960 movie by that name, and also starred in it as Davy Crockett. The second was a 2004 release by director John Lee Hancock. Both movies briskly establish the historical context: Mexico secures independence from Spain in 1821, with Texas as a state within the Mexican federation. Antonio Lopez de Santa Anna, a Mexican general who regarded himself as the "Napoleon of the West," becomes dictator of Mexico. The American settlers in Texas seize several of Santa Anna's garrisons, including the Alamo, a fortified Spanish mission near San Antonio.

Neither movie explains that, up to this time, Santa Anna had been razing Zacatecas, a Mexican state that had also opposed his rule. Early in 1836, though, he marched an army of several thousand soldiers north to crush the Texas rebels. Late in February, his advance units entered San Antonio and took up positions outside the Alamo. Both movies show the Texans sending riders to get reinforcements from the fledgling Texas government at Washington-on-the-Brazos, far to the east. There Sam Houston tried but failed to find a way to relieve the beleaguered garrison.

At the Alamo, the defenders, probably fewer than 200, were divided into three sets of volunteers and a fourth group, consisting of the "regular" soldiers of the Texas government, commanded by William B. Travis, a twenty-six-year-old cavalryman. One of the volunteer groups was led by Jim Bowie, an Indian fighter known for his long-bladed knife. David Crockett, the bear-hunter-turned-Congressman-turned-celebrity led the second group of volunteer fighters. (See Chapter 9, American Lives, "Davy Crockett.") The third group of volunteers consisted of Mexicans seeking to restore the Mexican republic.

Both movies ended with the battle that began on March 6, the thirteenth day of the siege. Within an hour, resistance had been silenced. All of the defenders were dead; some 500–600 Mexicans were killed, many caught in their own crossfire as they converged upon the Alamo.

Both movies *mostly* adhere to these facts. The 1960 movie added many fanciful plot elements: John Wayne's Crockett spends his nights stealing Mexican cattle, destroying their cannon, and romancing their prettiest senorita. There is no evidence for any of this. Both movies also show Santa Anna pounding the Alamo with artillery fusillades. In fact, Santa Anna had no big cannon. Some of his generals urged him to postpone the attack until heavier cannon had arrived; they would reduce the Alamo to rubble, sparing the heavy losses of a frontal assault. (Santa Anna, eager for victory in battle, refused to wait.) The 1960 movie also contends, wrongly, that Bowie wanted to abandon the Alamo while Travis insisted on staying. In fact, both men thought it essential to hold the Alamo. Sam Houston, by contrast, thought it was unwise for the commanders to have allowed their men to be "forted up" and destroyed.

The main question—for historians and movie makers—concerns the motivations of the defenders. Why did they persist against impossible odds? Santa Anna had signaled his intention to take no prisoners—certainly reason enough to fight on—but there was an alternative. Until the final forty-eight hours or so, escape was possible. Messengers and even small groups of men slipped through Santa Anna's lines at night. Some historians contend that the defenders remained at their posts because they expected to be rescued, but the defenders of the Alamo were not fools. The impossibility of their situation was clear. Why, then, did most choose to remain and die?

John Wayne as Crockett.

Billy Bob Thornton as Crockett.

John Wayne's movie provided a simple answer. Wayne's Crockett is fighting for freedom: "Republic. I like the sound of that word. Means people can live free, talk free. Go or come, buy or sell. Republic is one of the words that makes you tight in the throat, same tightness he gets when his baby takes his first step."

Such words made sense to Wayne's audience in 1960s America, then embroiled in a "cold war" against Communism. Santa Anna, a "tyrannical ruler," was akin to Soviet Communism, and the defenders of the Alamo were freedom fighters. But this analogy makes little historical sense. Mexico had outlawed slavery while the Texas rebels drafted a constitution that legalized slavery and prohibited the immigration of free blacks. From that perspective, Mexico stood for freedom, Texas for slavery.

The 2004 movie offered an alternative explanation of the defenders' self-sacrifice, citing the words of Travis: "We will show the world what patriots are made of." This notion of a death for posthumous honor was most strikingly scripted in the character of Davy Crockett, played by Billy Bob Thornton. As the prospects for reinforcement fade, Thornton's Crockett muses about escaping:

If it was just simple old me, David, from Tennessee, I might drop over the wall some night and take my chances. But this Davy Crockett feller, they are all watching him. He's been fightin' on this wall every day of his life.

This resonates with what we know about the real Crockett. Similarly, the actual Travis, who had abandoned his wife and neglected his children, wrote a letter before the final battle hoping that he would leave his boy "the proud recollection that he is the son of a man who died for his country."

Much the same could have been said of the others at the Alamo. Most had grown up beneath the long shadow of the Revolutionary generation that had fought and died to found a great nation. As the men of the Alamo looked upon a horizon darkened by enemy troops, they perhaps realized that their deaths would assure their own immortality. The Alamo would not be forgotten, although doubtless none could have imagined the malleability of memory centuries later.

Questions for Discussion

■ How was the rebellion of the Texas settlers against Santa Anna comparable to the Founders' battle against the British in 1776? How did it differ?

■ Why do some events and people leave a deep imprint upon subsequent generations?

Milestones

1835	Alamo falls to Santa Anna's Mexican army		1845	John L. O'Sullivan coins the expression *manifest destiny*
1836	Sam Houston routs Santa Anna at Battle of San Jacinto		1846	United States and Britain settle Oregon boundary dispute
1837	United States recognizes Republic of Texas		1846–1848	United States wages "Mr. Polk's War" with Mexico
1840	Richard Henry Dana describes voyage to California in *Two Years Before the Mast*		1846	House of Representatives adopts Wilmot Proviso prohibiting slavery in Mexican cession, but Senate defeats it
	William Henry Harrison is elected president		1847	General Winfield Scott captures Mexico City
1841	William Henry Harrison dies; Vice President John Tyler becomes president		1848	James W. Marshall discovers gold at Sutter's Mill, California
	Preemption Act grants "squatters' rights" in West			Treaty of Guadalupe Hidalgo brings United States huge territorial gains
				Zachary Taylor is elected president
1842	Webster-Ashburton Treaty determines Maine boundary		1850	Taylor dies; Vice President Millard Fillmore becomes president
1843	Oregon Trail opens			Henry Clay's Compromise of 1850 preserves Union
1844	James K. Polk is elected president			
1845	United States annexes Texas			

✓—[Study and **Review** at www.myhistorylab.com

Review Questions

1. From the Louisiana Purchase (1803) until the war with Mexico in 1845 the United States only added Florida (1819) to the national domain. But in the next three years, with the addition of Texas, California, and much of the Southwest, the nation increased in size 50 percent. What accounts for this sudden expansionism?

2. Why did the United States go to war with Mexico and what were its consequences politically?

3. How did the frontier undermine traditional gender roles? How did it reinforce those roles?

4. What was the relationship between slavery and manifest destiny?

Key Terms

Compromise of 1850 *318*
Free Soil party *315*
Fugitive Slave Act *318*
gold rush *313*

manifest destiny *303*
Mexican War *308*
popular sovereignty *314*

Treaty of Guadalupe Hidalgo *312*
Webster-Ashburton Treaty *301*
Wilmot Proviso *314*

The Sections Go Their Own Ways

12

((•—[Hear the Audio Chapter 12 at myhistorylab.com

What do you do when someone curses at you?

YOUR RESPONSE MAY DEPEND ON WHERE YOU'RE FROM. IN 2009 Malcolm Gladwell, author of the non-fiction bestseller *The Tipping Point*, described a psychology test in which researchers asked male students at the University of Michigan to complete questionnaires and, one-by-one, to take them to an office down a narrow corridor past a row of file cabinets. As each student neared the office, a researcher posing as a clerk opened a file drawer, forcing the student to squeeze past. As he did, the "clerk" slammed the drawer and muttered, "Asshole." The student, after delivering his questionnaire, was asked to provide a technician with a saliva sample. It turned out that the saliva of students from the South showed heightened levels of cortisol and testosterone—chemicals released as part of a person's fight response; but the saliva of students from northern states showed no such elevation. Gladwell regarded this as proof that cultural legacies persist "virtually intact" over many generations. Today's southern men, even though attending a northern university, were behaving much as had their great-great-grandfathers 180 years earlier. When confronted with a challenge to their honor, their psychic defenses readied them to fight, or so Gladwell contended.

This thesis is speculative: Over the past 200 years, countless peoples have washed over the regions of the United States; how distinctive cultural patterns could have been continually imprinted upon such different peoples is unclear. Yet nowadays many people still speak of distinctive regional cultures; and a glance at the political maps in this book illustrates the persistence of regional voting patterns: Over the past forty-six presidential elections, for example, Massachusetts and South Carolina have voted for the same candidate only thirteen times.

If regional cultural variations have become an enduring trait in American life, this was largely a consequence of changes that gained momentum during the three decades after 1830. Each section of the country was shaped by distinctive economic systems and workforces. Industrialization took hold of much of the Northeast, attracting immigrants who found work in factories in the burgeoning cities and factory towns. To the West, farming became more commercial and productive, attracting immigrant and other forms of free (if lowly paid) labor. The South was characterized in large part by the production of cash crops, especially cotton, and by its unwilling immigrants, the slaves.

But countervailing forces after 1830 also reduced the differences among regions. The Northeast and the West became economically interdependent, linked by an increasingly elaborate network of canals and railroads. The South, whose transportation infrastructure lagged, nevertheless benefited from the improvements in international transportation and trade. By the 1850s the nation remained divided—chiefly between the slave economy of the South and the nominally "free" labor of the North. But as the nation was knit together more tightly, the incompatibility of those diverse economic systems could no longer be ignored.

The South

The South was less affected than other sections by urbanization, European immigration, the transportation revolution, and industrialization. The region remained predominantly agricultural; cotton was still king, slavery the most distinctive southern institution. But important changes were occurring. Cotton continued to march westward, until by 1859 fully 1.3 million of the 4.3 million bales grown in the United States came from beyond the Mississippi. In the upper South, Virginia held its place as the leading tobacco producer, but states beyond the Appalachians were raising more than half the crop. The introduction of Bright Yellow, a mild variety of tobacco that grew best in poor soil, gave a great stimulus to production. The older sections of Maryland, Virginia, and North Carolina shifted to the kind of diversified farming usually associated with the Northeast. By 1849 the wheat crop of Virginia was worth twice as much as the tobacco crop.

The Economics of Slavery

The increased importance of cotton in the South strengthened the hold of slavery on the region. The price of slaves rose until by the 1850s a prime field hand was worth as much as $1,800, roughly three times the cost in the 1820s. While the prestige value of owning this kind of property affected prices, the rise chiefly reflected the increasing value of the South's agricultural output. "Crop value per slave" jumped from less than $15 early in the century to more than $125 in 1859.

In the cotton fields of the Deep South slaves brought several hundred dollars per head more than in the older regions; thus the tendency to sell them "down the river" continued. Mississippi took in some 10,000 slaves a year throughout the period; by 1830 the black population of the state exceeded the white. The westward shift of cotton cultivation was accompanied by the forcible transfer of more than a million African American slaves from the seaboard states to the dark, rich soil of regions watered by the Mississippi and Arkansas rivers and their tributaries. This "second great migration" of blacks far surpassed the original uprooting of blacks from Africa to the United States.

The impact of the trade on the slaves was frequently disastrous. Husbands were often separated from wives, and parents from children. This was somewhat less likely to happen on large, well-managed plantations than on small farms, but it was common enough everywhere. According to one study, one-third of all slave first "marriages" in the upper South were broken by forced separation and nearly half of all children were separated from at least one parent. Families were torn apart less frequently in the lower South, where far more slaves were bought than sold.

A woman in a net on a Congo shore. Although the importation of slaves was illegal after 1807, historians William Cooper and Thomas Terrill estimate in *The American South* (2009) that 50,000 were smuggled into the United States between 1808 and 1860.

As blacks became more expensive, the ownership of slaves became more concentrated. In 1860 only about 46,000 of the 8 million white residents of the slave states had as many as twenty slaves. When one calculates the cost of twenty slaves and the land to keep them profitably occupied, it is easy to understand why this figure is so small. The most efficient size of a plantation worked by gangs of slaves ranged between 1,000 and 2,000 acres. In every part of the South the majority of farmers cultivated no more than 200 acres, and in many sections fewer than 100 acres. On the eve of the Civil War only one white family in four in the South owned any slaves at all. A few large plantations and many small farms—this was the pattern.

There were few genuine economies of scale in southern agriculture. Small farmers grew the staple crops; and many of them owned a few slaves, often working beside them in the fields. These yeomen farmers were hardworking, self-reliant, and moderately prosperous, quite unlike the poor whites of the Appalachians who scratched a meager subsistence from substandard soils.

Well-managed plantations yielded annual profits of 10 percent and more, and, in general, money invested in southern agriculture earned at least a modest return. Considering the way the workforce was exploited, this is hardly surprising. Recent estimates indicate that after allowing for the cost of

Read the Document

Overseer's Report from Chicora Wood Plantation at **myhistorylab.com**

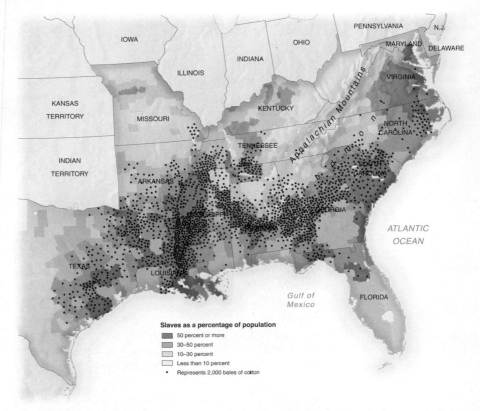

Cotton and Slaves in the South, 1860 Not surprisingly, the areas of greatest cotton production were also the areas with the highest proportion of slaves in the population. Note the concentrations of both in the Piedmont, the Alabama Black Belt, and the lower Mississippi Valley, and the relative absence of both in the Appalachian Mountains.

land and capital, the average plantation slave "earned" cotton worth $78.78 in 1859. It cost masters about $32 a year to feed, clothe, and house a slave. In other words, almost 60 percent of the product of slave labor was expropriated by the masters.

The South failed to develop locally owned marketing and transportation facilities, and for this slavery was at least partly responsible. In 1840 *Hunt's Merchant Magazine* estimated that it cost $2.85 to move a bale of cotton from the farm to a seaport and that additional charges for storage, insurance, port fees, and freight to a European port exceeded $15. Middlemen from outside the South commonly earned most of this money. New York capitalists gradually came to control much of the South's cotton from the moment it was picked, and a large percentage of the crop found its way into New York warehouses before being sold to manufacturers. The same middlemen supplied most of the foreign goods that the planters purchased with their cotton earnings.

Southerners complained about this state of affairs but did little to correct it. Capital tied up in the ownership of labor could not be invested in anything else, and social pressures in the South militated against investment in trade and commerce. Ownership of land and slaves yielded a kind of psychic income not available to any middleman. As one British visitor pointed out, the southern blacks were "a nonconsuming class." Still more depressing, under slavery the enormous reservoir of intelligence and skill that the blacks represented was almost entirely wasted. Many slave artisans worked on the plantations, and a few free blacks made their way in the South remarkably well, but the amount of talent unused, energy misdirected, and imagination smothered can only be guessed.

Foreign observers in New England frequently noted the alertness and industriousness of ordinary laborers and attributed this, justifiably, to the high level of literacy. Nearly everyone in New England could read and write. Correspondingly, the stagnation and inefficiency of southern labor could be attributed in part to the high degree of illiteracy, for over 20 percent of *white* Southerners could not read or write, another tragic squandering of human resources.

Antebellum Plantation Life

The "typical" plantation did not exist, but it is possible to describe, in a general way, what a medium-to-large operation employing twenty or more slaves was like in the two decades preceding the Civil War. Such a plantation was more like a small village than a northern-type agricultural unit, and in another way more like a self-sufficient colonial farm than a nineteenth-century commercial operation, although its major activity involved producing cotton or some other cash crop.

Slaveholding families were also quite different from northern families of similar status, in part because they were engaged in agriculture and in part because of their so-called peculiar institution. Husbands and wives did not function in separate spheres to nearly the same extent, although their individual functions were different and gender-related.

The master was in general charge and his word was law—the system was literally paternalistic. But his wife nearly always had immense responsibilities. Running the household meant supervising the servants (and sometimes punishing them, which often meant wielding a lash), nursing the sick, taking care of the vegetable and flower gardens, planning meals, and seeing to the education of her own children and the training of young slaves. It could also involve running the entire plantation on the frequent occasions when her husband was away on business. At the same time, her role entailed being a "southern lady": refined, graceful, and supposedly untroubled by worldly affairs.

The majority of the slaves of both sexes were field hands who labored on the land from dawn to dusk. Household servants and artisans, indeed any slave other than small children and the aged and infirm, might be called on for such labor when needed. Slave women were expected to cook for their own families and do other chores after working in the fields.

Children, free and slave, were cared for by slaves, the former by household servants, the latter usually by an elderly woman, perhaps with the help of a girl only a little older than the children. Infants were brought to their mothers in the fields for nursing several times a day, for after a month or two at most, slave mothers were required to go back to work. Slave children were not put to work until they were six or seven years old, and until they were about ten they were given only small tasks such as feeding the chickens or minding a smaller child. Black and white youngsters played together and were often cared for by the same nursemaid.

Slave cabins were simple and crude; most consisted of a single room, dark, with a fireplace for cooking and heat. Usually the flooring was raised above ground level, though some were set on the bare earth. In 1827 Basil Hall, a British naval officer, reported that in a large South Carolina plantation, 140 slaves lived in twenty-eight cottages or huts. These were "uncommonly neat and comfortable, and might have shamed those of many countries I have seen." Yet Hall dismissed the claims of whites that slaves were happier than the peasantry of England. Slavery was, above all, a "humiliation" imposed upon "the whole mass of the labouring population" of the South.

The Sociology of Slavery

It is difficult to generalize about the peculiar institution because so much depended on the individual master's behavior. Although some ex-slaves told of masters who refused to whip them, Bennet Barrow of Louisiana, a harsh master, averaged one whipping a month. "The great secret of our success," another planter recalled years later, "was the great motive power contained in that little instrument." Overseers were commonly instructed to give twenty lashes for ordinary offenses, such as shirking work or stealing, and thirty-nine for more serious offenses, such as running away. Sometimes slaves were whipped to death; by 1821, however, all southern states had passed laws allowing a master to be charged with murder if he caused a slave's death from excessive punishment. Conviction normally resulted in a fine. In 1840 a South Carolina woman convicted of killing a slave was fined $214.28.

On balance, it is significant that the United States was the only nation in the Western Hemisphere where the slave population grew by natural increase. After the

This slave burial service, painted by John Antrobus in 1860, reflects an inversion of power relations, a slave preacher leads the mourners while the white overseer and the plantation owners watch uneasily, shunted (literally) to the sides.

ending of the slave trade in 1808, the black population increased at nearly the same rate as the white. Put differently, during the entire period from the founding of Jamestown to the Civil War, only a little more than half a million slaves were imported into the country, about 5 percent of the number of Africans carried by slavers to the New World. Yet in 1860 there were about 4 million blacks in the United States.

Most owners felt responsibilities toward their slaves, and slaves were dependent on and in some ways imitative of white values. However, powerful fears and resentments, not always recognized, existed on both sides. The plantation environment forced the two races to live in close proximity. From this circumstance could arise every sort of human relationship. One planter, using the appropriate pseudonym Clod Thumper, could write, "Africans are nothing but brutes, and they will love you better for whipping, whether they deserve it or not." Another, describing a slave named Bug, could say, "No one knows but myself what feeling I have for him. Black as he is we were raised together." One southern white woman tended a dying servant with "the kindest and most unremitting attention." Another, discovered crying after the death of a slave she had repeatedly abused, is said to have explained her grief by complaining that she "didn't have nobody to whip no more."

Slaves were without rights; they developed a distinctive way of life by attempting to resist oppression and injustice while accommodating themselves to the system. Their marriages had no legal status, but their partnerships seem to have been loving and stable. Even families whose members were sold to different masters often maintained close ties over considerable distances.

Slave religion, on the surface an untutored form of Christianity tinctured with some African infusions, seemed to most slave owners a useful instrument for teaching meekness and resignation and for providing harmless emotional release, which it sometimes was and did. However, religious meetings, secret and open, provided slaves with the opportunity to organize, which led at times to rebellions and more often to less drastic ways of resisting white domination. Religion also sustained the slaves' sense of their own worth as beings made in the image of God, and it taught them, therefore, that while human beings can be enslaved in body, their spirits cannot be enslaved without their consent.

((•—[Hear the Audio

When the Roll Is Called up Yonder at **myhistorylab.com**

•••—[Read the Document

A Catechism for Slaves at **myhistorylab.com**

Observing that slaves often seemed happy and were only rarely overtly rebellious, whites persuaded themselves that most blacks accepted the system without resentment and indeed preferred slavery to the uncertainties of freedom. There was much talk about "loyal and faithful servants." The Civil War, when slaves flocked to the Union lines once assured of freedom and fair treatment, would disabuse them of this illusion.

As the price of slaves rose and as northern opposition to the institution grew more vocal, the system hardened perceptibly. White Southerners made much of the danger of insurrection. When a plot was uncovered or a revolt took place, instant and savage reprisals resulted. In 1811, Charles Deslondes led a rebellion of several hundred slaves, armed with tools, who burned a handful of plantations and marched toward New Orleans before being routed by the United States Army. Over fifty slaves were slaughtered immediately; a tribunal of plantation owners ordered the execution of several dozen more. In 1822, after the conspiracy of Denmark Vesey was exposed by informers, thirty-seven slaves were executed and another thirty-odd deported, although no overt act of rebellion had occurred.

The Nat Turner revolt in Virginia in 1831 was the most sensational of the slave uprisings; fifty-seven whites lost their lives before it was suppressed. White Southerners treated runaways almost as brutally as rebels, although they posed no real threat to whites. The authorities tracked down fugitives with bloodhounds and subjected captives to merciless lashings.

•••⎡Read the **Document**

Turner, *The Confessions of Nat Turner* at **myhistorylab.com**

After the Nat Turner revolt, interest in doing away with slavery vanished in the white South. The southern states made it increasingly difficult for masters to free their slaves; during 1859 only about 3,000 in a slave population of nearly 4 million were given their freedom.

Slavery did not flourish in urban settings, and cities did not flourish in societies where slavery was important. Most southern cities were small, and within them, slaves made up a small fraction of the labor force. The existence of slavery goes a long way toward explaining why the South was so rural and why it had so little industry. Slaves were much harder to supervise and control in urban settings. Individual slaves were successfully employed in southern manufacturing plants, but they made up only an insignificant fraction of the South's small industrial labor supply.

Southern whites considered the existence of free blacks undesirable, no matter where they lived. The mere fact that they could support themselves disproved the notion that African Americans were by nature childlike and shiftless, unable to work efficiently without white guidance. From the whites' point of view, free blacks set a bad example for slaves. In a petition calling for the expulsion of free blacks from the state, a group of South Carolinians noted that slaves

> continualy [sic] have before their eyes, persons of the same color . . . freed from the control of masters, working where they please, going where they please, and expending their money how they please.

Many southern states passed laws aimed at forcing free blacks to emigrate, but these laws were not well enforced. There is ample evidence that the white people of, say, Maryland, would have liked to get rid of the state's large free-black population. Free blacks were barred from occupations in which they might cause trouble—no free black could be the captain of a ship, for example—and they were required by law to find a "respectable" white person who would testify as to their "good conduct and character." But whites, who needed slave labor, did not try very hard to expel them.

Psychological Effects of Slavery

The injustice of slavery needs no proof; less obvious is the fact that it had a corrosive effect on the personalities of Southerners, slave and free alike. By "the making of a human being an animal without hope," the system bore heavily on all slaves' sense of their own worth. Some found the condition absolutely unbearable. They became the habitual runaways who collected whip scars like medals, the "loyal" servants who struck out in rage against a master knowing that the result would be certain death, and the leaders of slave revolts.

Table 12.1 **Major Slave Rebellions**

Rebellion	Year	Description	Backlash against slaves	Legislative response
New York Slave Revolt	1712	Several buildings burned; whites attacked	Twenty-one African Americans executed, including free blacks	Slaves prohibited from carrying firearms and free blacks from owning land; slave owners obliged to pay tax for freeing slaves
Gabriel's Rebellion	1800	Conspiracy to rebel near Richmond, Virginia	Over two dozen slaves hanged, including Gabriel	Restrictions placed on owner's right to free slaves; free blacks not allowed to congregate freely on Sundays
Deslondes' Rebellion	1811	Burned plantations near New Orleans	Nearly 100 slaves killed, including Deslondes	Restrictions on right of free blacks to congregate
Denmark Vesey's Rebellion	1822	Plot to free blacks, kill whites, flee to Haiti	Thirty-five slaves hanged, including Vesey	Municipal guard established in Charleston, South Carolina
Nat Turner's Rebellion	1831	Fifty-five whites killed in Virginia	Over 100 slaves killed, including Turner	Virginia legislature prohibited teaching literacy to blacks, slave and free alike, and required the presence of white ministers during slave religious meetings

Denmark Vesey of South Carolina, even after buying his freedom, could not stomach the subservience demanded of slaves by the system. When he saw Charleston slaves step into the gutter to make way for whites, he taunted them: "You deserve to remain slaves!" For years he preached resistance to his fellows, drawing his texts from the Declaration of Independence and the Bible and promising help from black Haiti. So vehemently did he argue that some of his followers claimed they feared Vesey more than their masters, even more than God. He planned his uprising for five years, patiently working out the details, only to see it aborted at the last moment when a few of his recruits lost their nerve and betrayed him. For Denmark Vesey, death was probably preferable to living with such rage as his soul contained.

Yet Veseys were rare. Most slaves appeared at least resigned to their fate. Many seemed even to accept the whites' evaluation of their inherent abilities and place in society. Of course in most instances it is impossible to know whether this apparent subservience was feigned in order to avoid trouble.

Slaves had strong family and group attachments and a complex culture of their own, maintained, so to speak, under the noses of their masters. By a mixture of subterfuge, accommodation, and passive resistance, they erected subtle defenses against exploitation, achieving a sense of community that helped sustain the psychic integrity of individuals. But slavery discouraged, if it did not extinguish, independent judgment and self-reliance.

SOJOURNER TRUTH

Isabella was born in 1797, or perhaps 1799, in Ulster County, New York. She was a slave. Her owner was Colonel Ardinburgh, a Dutch farmer, who grew tobacco, corn, and flax. Because he could make use of only a handful of slaves, he sold most of the slave children, including Isabella's brother and sister. When Ardinburgh died in 1807, his heirs sold his "slaves, horses, and other cattle" at auction. A local farmer of English descent bought Isabella for $100. Isabella's parents, too old to work, were freed. Destitute, they soon died.

Isabella, who spoke only Dutch, found herself at odds with her new English master and family. "If they sent me for a frying pan, not knowing what they meant, perhaps I carried them the pot hooks," she recalled. Once, for failing to obey an order she did not understand, her master whipped her with a bundle of rods, scarring her back permanently.

In 1810 she was sold to John Dumont, a farmer. Though she came to regard him "as a God," she claimed that his wife subjected her to cruel and "unnatural" treatment. What exactly transpired, she refused "from motives of delicacy" to say. In 1815 Dumont arranged for Isabella to marry another of his slaves. Isabella had no say in the matter. She had five children by him.

Isabella labored in the fields, sowing and harvesting crops. She also cooked and cleaned the house. In recognition of her diligence, Dumont promised to set her free on July 4, 1826, exactly one year prior to the date set by the New York State legislature to end slavery. But on the proposed date, Dumont reneged. Soon thereafter Isabella heard the voice of God tell her to leave. She picked up her baby and walked to the house of a neighbor. When Dumont showed up to bring her back, the neighbor paid him $25 for Isabella and the baby and set them free.

But Isabella learned that her five-year-old son, Peter, had been sold to a planter in Alabama, which had no provision for ending slavery. She angrily confronted the Dumonts, who scoffed at her concern for "a paltry nigger." "I'll have my child again," Isabella retorted. She consulted a Quaker lawyer. He filed suit in her behalf and won. In 1828 the boy was returned.

Now on her own, Isabella went to New York City, then awash in religious ferment. Isabella, whose views on religion were a complex amalgam of African folkways, spiritualism, temperance, and dietary asceticism, was attracted to various unorthodox religious leaders. The most curious of these was Robert Matthews, a bearded, thundering tyrant who claimed to be the Old Testament prophet Matthias. Matthews acquired a house in the town of Sing Sing, housed nearly a dozen converts, and ruled it with an iron hand. Isabella was among those who joined the commune. In 1834, local authorities, who had heard stories of sexual and other irregularities, arrested Matthews.

Isabella had by this time become a preacher. Tall and severe in manner, she jabbed at the air with bony fingers and demanded the obedience she had formerly given to others. She changed her name to Sojourner Truth, a messenger conveying God's true spirit, and embarked on a career of antislavery feminism.

Sojourner Truth

Questions for Discussion
- In what ways did Sojourner Truth's life likely differ from that of a slave on a plantation in the Deep South?
- How did religion contribute to Sojourner Truth's self-empowerment?

These qualities are difficult enough to develop in human beings under the best of circumstances; when every element in white society encouraged slaves to let others do their thinking for them, to avoid questioning the status quo, to lead a simple life, many did so willingly enough. Was this not slavery's greatest shame?

Whites, too, were harmed by the slave system. Associating working for others with servility discouraged many poor whites from hiring out to earn a stake. Slavery provided the weak, the shiftless, and the unsuccessful with a scapegoat that made their own miserable state easier to bear but harder to escape.

More subtly, the patriarchal nature of the slave system reinforced the already existing tendency toward male dominance over wives and children typical of the larger society. For men of exceptional character, the responsibilities of ownership could be ennobling, but for hotheads, alcoholics, or others with psychological problems, the power could be brutalizing, with terrible effects on the whole plantation community, whites and blacks alike.

Aside from its fundamental immorality, slavery caused basically decent people to commit countless petty cruelties. "I feel badly, got very angry and whipped Lavinia," one Louisiana woman wrote in her diary. "O! for government over my temper." But for slavery, she would surely have had better self-control. The finest white Southerners were often warped by the institution. Even those who abhorred slavery sometimes let it corrupt their thinking: "I consider the labor of a breeding woman as no object, and that a child raised every 2 years is of more profit than the crop of the best laboring man." This cold calculation came from the pen of Thomas Jefferson, author of the Declaration of Independence, a man who, it now seems likely, fathered at least one child by a slave.

Manufacturing in the South

Although the temper of southern society discouraged business and commercial activities, considerable manufacturing developed.

The availability of the raw material and the abundance of waterpower along the Appalachian slopes made it possible to manufacture textiles profitably. By 1825 a thriving factory was functioning at Fayetteville, North Carolina, and soon others sprang up elsewhere in North Carolina and in adjoining states. William Gregg's factory, at Graniteville, South Carolina, established in 1846, was employing about 300 people by 1850. An able propagandist as well as a good businessman, Gregg saw the textile business not only as a source of profit but also as a device for improving the lot of the South's poor whites. He worked hard to weaken the southern prejudice against manufacturing and made his plant a model of benevolent paternalism similar to that of the early mills of Lowell, Massachusetts. As with every other industry, however, southern textile manufacturing amounted to very little when compared with that of the North. While Gregg was employing 300 textile workers in 1850, the whole state of South Carolina had fewer than 900. In 1860 Lowell, Massachusetts had more spindles turning cotton into yarn than the entire South.

Less than 15 percent of all the goods manufactured in the United States in 1860 came from the South; the region did not really develop an industrial society. Its textile manufacturers depended on the North for machinery, for skilled workers and technicians, for financing, and for insurance. When the English geologist Charles Lyell visited New Orleans in 1846, he was astounded to discover that the thriving city supported not a single book publisher. Even a local guidebook that he purchased bore a New York imprint.

The Northern Industrial Juggernaut

The most obvious change in the North in the decades before the Civil War was the rapid growth of industry. The best estimates suggest that immediately after the War of 1812 the United States was manufacturing less than $200 million worth of goods annually. In 1859 the northeastern states alone produced $1.27 billion of the national total of almost $2 billion.

Manufacturing expanded in so many directions that it is difficult to portray or to summarize its evolution. The factory system made great strides. The development of rich anthracite coal fields in Pennsylvania was particularly important in this connection. The coal could be floated cheaply on canals to convenient sites and used to produce both heat for smelting and metalworking and steam power to drive machinery. Steam permitted greater flexibility in locating factories and in organizing work within them, and since waterpower was already being used to capacity, steam was essential for the expansion of output.

American industry displayed a remarkable receptivity to technological change. The list of inventions and processes developed between 1825 and 1850, included—besides such obviously important items as the sewing machine, the vulcanization of rubber, and the cylinder press—the screw-making machine, the friction match, the lead pencil, and an apparatus for making soda water.

By 1850 the United States led the world in the manufacture of goods that required the use of precision instruments, and in certain industries the country was well on the way toward modern mass production methods. American clocks, pistols, rifles, and locks were outstanding.

Industrial growth led to a great increase in the demand for labor. The effects, however, were mixed. Skilled artisans, technicians, and toolmakers earned good wages and found it relatively easy to set themselves up first as independent craftsmen, later as small manufacturers. The expanding frontier drained off much agricultural labor that might otherwise have been attracted to industry, and the thriving new towns of the West absorbed large numbers of eastern artisans of every kind. At the same time, the pay of an unskilled worker was never enough to support a family decently, and the new machines weakened the bargaining power of artisans by making skill less important.

Many other forces acted to stimulate the growth of manufacturing. Immigration increased rapidly in the 1830s and 1840s. By 1860 Irish immigrants alone made up more than 50 percent of the labor force of the New England mills. An avalanche of strong backs, willing hands, and keen minds descended on the country from Europe. European investors poured large sums into the booming American economy, and the savings of millions of Americans and the great hoard of new California gold added to the supply of capital. Improvements in transportation, population growth, the absence of internal tariff barriers, and the relatively high per capita wealth all meant an ever expanding market for manufactured goods.

A Nation of Immigrants

Rapid industrialization influenced American life in countless ways, none more significant than its effect on the character of the workforce and consequently on the structure of society. The jobs created by industrial expansion attracted European immigrants by the tens of thousands. It is a truism that America is a nation of immigrants—recall that even the ancestors of the Indians came to the New World from Asia.

Read the **Document**

Foreign Immigration at myhistorylab.com

But only with the development of nationalism, that is, with the establishment of the independent United States, did the word *immigrant*, meaning a foreign-born resident, come into existence.

The "native" population (native in this case meaning those whose ancestors had come from Europe rather than native Americans, the Indians) tended to look down on immigrants, and many of the immigrants, in turn, developed prejudices of their own. The Irish, for example, disliked blacks, with whom they often competed for work. Antiblack prejudice was less noticeable among other immigrant groups but by no means absent; most immigrants adopted the views of the local majority, which was often unfriendly to African Americans.

Social and racial rivalries aside, the infusion of unskilled immigrants into the factories of New England speeded the disintegration of the system of hiring young farm women. Already competition and technical advances in the textile industry were increasing the pace of the machines and reducing the number of skilled workers needed to run them. Fewer young farm women were willing to work under these conditions. Recent immigrants replaced the women in large numbers. By 1860 Irish immigrants alone made up more than 50 percent of the labor force in the New England mills.

How Wage Earners Lived

The influx of immigrants does not entirely explain the low standard of living of industrial workers during this period. Low wages and the crowding that resulted from the swift expansion of city populations produced slums that would make the most noisome modern ghetto seem a paradise. In New York tens of thousands of the poor lived in dark, rank cellars, those in the waterfront districts often invaded by high tides. Tenement houses rose back to back, each with many windowless rooms and often without heat or running water.

Out of doors, city life for the poor was almost equally squalid. Slum streets were littered with garbage and trash. Recreational facilities were almost nonexistent. Police and fire protection in the cities were pitifully inadequate. "Urban problems" were less critical than a century later only because they affected a smaller part of the population; for those who experienced them, they were, all too often, crushing.

In 1851 the editor Horace Greeley's *New York Tribune* published a minimum weekly budget for a family of five. The budget, which allowed nothing for savings, medical bills, recreation, or other amenities (Greeley did include 12 cents a week for newspapers), came to $10.37. Since the weekly pay of a factory hand seldom reached $5, the wives and children of most male factory workers also had to labor in the factories merely to survive. And child labor in the 1850s differed fundamentally

A girl stares blankly as the manager of an employment agency suggests her suitability as a maid or housekeeper. The lady, seated, ponders whether the girl will do. The sign on the wall reads, "Agent for Domestics: Warranted Honest." This painting is by William Henry Burr, 1849.
Source: Assession no. 1959.46 Collection of The New-York Historical Society.

from child labor in the 1820s. The pace of the machines had become much faster by then, and the working environment more debilitating.

Relatively few workers belonged to unions, but federations of craft unions sprang up in some cities, and during the boom that preceded the Panic of 1837, a National Trades Union representing a few northeastern cities managed to hold conventions. Early in the Jackson era, "workingmen's" political parties enjoyed a brief popularity, occasionally electing a few local officials. These organizations were made up mostly of skilled craftsmen, professional reformers, and even businessmen. They soon expired, destroyed by internal bickering over questions that had little or nothing to do with working conditions.

The depression of the late 1830s led to the demise of most trade unions. Nevertheless, skilled workers improved their lot somewhat in the 1840s and 1850s. The working day declined gradually from about twelve and a half hours to ten or eleven hours. Many states passed ten-hour laws and laws regulating child labor, but they were poorly enforced. Most states, however, enacted effective mechanic's lien laws, giving workers first call on the assets of bankrupt and defaulting employers, and the Massachusetts court's decision in the case of *Commonwealth v. Hunt* (1842), establishing the legality of labor unions, became a judicial landmark when other state courts followed the precedent.

The flush times of the early 1850s caused the union movement to revive. Many strikes occurred, and a few new national organizations appeared. However, most unions were local institutions, weak and with little control over their membership. The Panic of 1857 dealt the labor movement another body blow. Thus there was no trend toward the general unionization of labor between 1820 and the Civil War.

For this the workers themselves were partly responsible: Craftsmen took little interest in unskilled workers except to keep them down. Few common laborers considered themselves part of a permanent working class with different objectives from those of their employers. Although hired labor had existed throughout the colonial period, it was only with the growth of factories and other large enterprises that significant numbers of people worked for wages. To many people, wage labor seemed almost un-American, a violation of the republican values of freedom and independence that had triumphed in the Revolution. Jefferson's professed dislike of urban life was based in part on his fear that people who worked for wages would be so beholden to their employers that they could not act independently.

This republican value system, along with the fluidity of society, the influx of job-hungry immigrants, and the widespread employment of women and children in unskilled jobs made labor organization difficult. The assumption was that nearly anyone who was willing to work could eventually escape from the wage-earning class. "If any continue through life in the condition of the hired laborer," Abraham Lincoln declared in 1859, "it is . . . because of either a dependent nature which prefers it, or improvidence, folly, or singular misfortune."

Progress and Poverty

Any investigation of American society before the Civil War reveals a paradox that is obvious but difficult to resolve. The United States was a land of opportunity, a democratic society with a prosperous, expanding economy and few class distinctions. Its people had a high standard of living in comparison with the citizens of European countries. Yet within this rich, confident nation there existed a class of miserably underpaid and depressed unskilled workers, mostly immigrants, who were worse off materially than nearly any southern slave. In 1848 more than 56,000 New Yorkers, about a quarter of the population, were receiving some form of public relief. A police drive in that city in 1860 brought in nearly 500 beggars.

The middle-class majority seemed indifferent to or at best unaware of these conditions. Reformers conducted investigations, published exposés, and labored to help the victims of urbanization and industrialization. They achieved little. Great fires burned in these decades to release the incredible energies of America. The poor were the ashes, sifting down silent and unnoticed beneath the dazzle and the smoke. Industrialization produced poverty and riches (in Marxian terminology, a proletarian class and an aristocracy of capitalists).

Economic opportunities were great, and taxation was minimal. Little wonder that as the generations passed, the rich got richer. Industrialization accelerated the process and, by stimulating the immigration of masses of poor workers, skewed the social balance still further. By the mid-nineteenth century Americans were convinced that all men were equal, and indeed all *white* men had equal political rights. Socially and economically, however, the distances between top and bottom were widening. This situation endured for the rest of the century, and in some respects it still endures.

Foreign Commerce

Changes in the pattern of foreign commerce were less noticeable than those in manufacturing but were nevertheless significant. After increasing erratically during the 1820s and 1830s, both imports and exports leapt forward in the next twenty years. The nation remained primarily an exporter of raw materials and an importer of manufactured goods, and in most years it imported more than it exported. Cotton continued to be the most valuable export, in 1860 accounting for a record $191 million of total exports of $333 million. Despite America's own thriving industry, textiles still held the lead among imports, with iron products second. As in earlier days, Great Britain was both the best customer of the United States and its leading supplier.

The increase in the volume and value of trade and its concentration at larger ports had a marked effect on the construction of ships. By the 1850s the average vessel was three times the size of those built thirty years earlier. Startling improvements in design, culminating in the long, sleek, white-winged clipper ships, made possible speeds previously undreamed of. Appearing just in time to supply the need for fast transportation to the

The American clipper ship, *Red Jacket*, off Cape Horn, sails from Australia to Liverpool, England in 1854.

California gold fields, the clippers cut sailing time around Cape Horn to San Francisco from five or six months to three, the record of eighty-nine days being held jointly by *Andrew Jackson* and Donald McKay's famous *Flying Cloud.* To achieve such speeds, cargo capacity had to be sacrificed, making clippers uneconomical for carrying the bulky produce that was the mainstay of commerce. But for specialty goods, in their brief heyday the clippers were unsurpassed.

Steam Conquers the Atlantic

The reign of the clipper ship was short. Like so many other things, ocean commerce was being mechanized. Steamships conquered the high seas more slowly than the rivers because early models were unsafe in rough waters and uneconomical. A riverboat could take on fuel along its route, whereas an Atlantic steamer had to carry tons of coal across the ocean, thereby reducing its capacity for cargo. However, by the late 1840s, steamships were capturing most of the passenger traffic, mail contracts, and first-class freight. These vessels could not keep up with the clippers in a heavy breeze, but their average speed was far greater, especially on the westward voyage against the prevailing winds. Steamers were soon crossing the Atlantic in less than ten days.

The steamship, and especially the iron ship, which had greater cargo-carrying capacity and was stronger and less costly to maintain, took away the advantages that American shipbuilders had held since colonial times. American lumber was cheap, but the British excelled in iron technology. Although the United States invested about $14.5 million in subsidies for the shipping industry, the funds were not employed intelligently and did little good. In 1858 government efforts to aid shipping were abandoned.

The combination of competition, government subsidy, and technological advance drove down shipping rates from one cent to about a third of a cent. Transatlantic passengers could obtain the best accommodations on the fastest ships for under $200, good accommodations on slower packets for as little as $75.

Rates were especially low for European emigrants willing to travel to America on cargo vessels. By the 1840s at least 4,000 ships were engaged in carrying bulky American cotton and Canadian lumber to Europe. On their return trips with manufactured goods they had unoccupied space, which they converted into rough quarters for passengers. Conditions on these ships were crowded, gloomy, and foul. Frequently epidemics took a fearful toll among steerage passengers. On one crossing of the ship *Lark,* 158 of 440 passengers died of typhus.

Yet without this cheap means of transportation, thousands of poor immigrants would simply have remained at home. Bargain freight rates also help explain the clamor of American manufacturers for high tariffs, for transportation costs added relatively little to the price of European goods.

Canals and Railroads

Another dramatic change was the shift in the direction of the nation's internal commerce and its immense increase. From the time of the first settlers in the Mississippi Valley, the Great River had controlled the flow of goods from farm to market. The completion of the Erie Canal in 1825 heralded a shift. In 1830 there were 1,277 miles of canal in the United States; by 1840 there were 3,326 miles.

Each year saw more western produce moving to market through the canals. In 1845 the Erie Canal was still drawing over two-thirds of its west to east traffic from within New York, but by 1847, despite the fact that this local business held steady, more than half of its traffic came from west of Buffalo, and by 1851 more than two-thirds. The volume of western commerce over the Erie Canal in 1851 amounted to more than twenty times what it had been in 1836, while the value of western goods reaching New Orleans in this period increased only two and a half times.

The expanding traffic and New York's enormous share of it caused businessmen in other eastern cities whose canal projects had been unsuccessful to respond promptly when a new means of transport, the railroad, became available. The first railroads were built in England in the 1820s. In 1830 the first American line, the ambitiously named Baltimore and Ohio Railroad, carried 80,000 passengers over a thirteen-mile stretch of track. By 1833 Charleston, South Carolina, had a line reaching 136 miles to Hamburg, on the Savannah River. Two years later the cars began rolling on the Boston and Worcester Railroad. The Panic of 1837 slowed construction, but by 1840 the United States had 3,328 miles of track, equal to the canal mileage and nearly double the railroad mileage of all Europe.

The first railroads did not compete with the canals for intersectional traffic. The through connections needed to move goods economically over great distances materialized slowly. Of the 6,000 miles of track operating in 1848, nearly all lay east of the Appalachians, and little of it had been coordinated into railroad systems. The intention of most early builders had been to monopolize the trade of surrounding districts, not to establish connections with competing centers. Frequently, railroads used tracks of different widths deliberately to prevent other lines from tying into their tracks.

Between 1848 and 1852 railroad mileage nearly doubled. Three years later it had doubled again, and by 1860 the nation had 30,636 miles of track. During this extraordinary burst of activity, four companies drove lines of gleaming iron from the Atlantic seaboard to the great interior valley. In 1851 the Erie Railroad, the longest road in the world with 537 miles of track, linked the Hudson River north of New York City with Dunkirk on Lake Erie. Late the next year the Baltimore and Ohio reached the Ohio River at Wheeling, and in 1853 a banker named Erastus Corning consolidated eight short lines connecting Albany and Buffalo to form the New York Central Railroad. Finally, in 1858 the Pennsylvania Railroad completed a line across the mountains from Philadelphia to Pittsburgh.

In the states beyond the Appalachians, building went on at an even more feverish pace. By 1855 passengers could travel from Chicago or St. Louis to the east coast at a cost of $20 to $30, the trip taking, with luck, less than forty-eight hours. A generation earlier such a trip had required two to three weeks. Construction was slower in the South: Mississippi laid about 800 miles of track, and Alabama about 600.

Financing the Railroads

Railroad building required immense amounts of labor and capital at a time when many other demands for these resources existed. Immigrants or (in the South) slaves did most of the heavy work. Raising the necessary money proved a more complex task.

Private investors supplied about three-quarters of the money invested in railroads before 1860, more than $800 million in the 1850s alone. Much of this capital came from local merchants and businessmen and from farmers along the proposed rights-of-way. Funds were easy to raise because subscribers seldom had to lay out the full price of their stock at one time; instead they were subject to periodic "calls" for a percentage of their commitment as construction progressed. If the road made money, much of the additional mileage could be paid for out of earnings from the first sections built.

But many railroads that failed to find enough investors sought public money. Towns, counties, and the states themselves lent money to railroads and invested in their stock. Special privileges, such as exemption from taxation and the right to condemn property, were often granted, and in a few cases states built and operated roads as public corporations.

As with earlier internal improvement proposals, federal financial aid to railroads was usually blocked in Congress by a combination of eastern and southern votes. But in 1850 a scheme for granting federal lands to the states to build a line from Lake Michigan to the Gulf of Mexico passed both houses. The main beneficiary was the Illinois Central Railroad, which received a 200-foot right-of-way and alternate strips of land along the track one mile wide and six miles deep, a total of almost 2.6 million acres. By mortgaging this land and by selling portions of it to farmers, the Illinois Central raised nearly all the $23.4 million it spent on construction. The success of this operation led to additional grants of almost 20 million acres in the 1850s, benefiting more than forty railroads. Far larger federal grants were made after the Civil War, when the transcontinental lines were built.

•◦•⌐Read the Document

Senate Report on the Railroads at **myhistorylab.com**

Frequently, the capitalists who promoted railroads were more concerned with making money out of the construction of the lines than with operating them.

Others in the business were unashamedly crooked and avidly took advantage of the public passion for railroads. Some officials issued stock to themselves without paying for it and then sold the shares to gullible investors. Others manipulated the books of their corporations and set up special construction companies and paid them exorbitant returns out of railroad assets. These practices did not become widespread until after the Civil War, but all of them first sprang up in the decades preceding the war. At the same time that the country was first developing a truly national economy, it was also producing its first really big-time crooks.

Railroads and the Economy

The effects of so much railroad construction were profound. Although the main reason that farmers put more land under the plow was an increase in the price of agricultural products, the railroad helped determine just what land was used and how profitably it could be farmed. Much of the fertile prairie through which the Illinois Central ran had been available for settlement for many years before 1850, but development had been slow because it was remote from navigable waters and had no timber. In 1840 the three counties immediately northeast of Springfield had a population of about 8,500. They produced about 59,000 bushels of wheat and 690,000 bushels of corn. In the next decade the region grew slowly by the standards of that day: The three counties had about 14,000 people in 1850 and produced 71,000 bushels of wheat and 2.2 million bushels of corn. Then came the railroad and with it an agricultural revolution. By 1860 the population of the three counties had soared to over 38,000, wheat production had topped 550,000 bushels, and corn 5.7 million bushels.

Access to world markets gave the farmers of the upper Mississippi Valley an incentive to increase output. Land was plentiful and cheap, but farm labor was scarce; consequently agricultural wages rose sharply, especially after 1850. New tools and machines appeared in time to ease the labor shortage. First came the steel plowshare, invented by John Deere, a Vermont-born blacksmith who had moved to Illinois in 1837. In 1839 Deere turned out ten such plows in his little shop in Moline, Illinois. By 1857 he was selling 10,000 a year.

Still more important was the perfection of the mechanical reaper, for wheat production was limited more by the amount that farmers could handle during the brief harvest season than by the acreage they could plant and cultivate. The major figure in the development of the reaper was Cyrus Hall McCormick. McCormick's horse-drawn reaper bent the grain against the cutting knife and then deposited it neatly on a platform, whence it could easily be raked into windrows. With this machine, two workers could cut fourteen times as much wheat as with scythes.

The railroad had an equally powerful impact on American cities. The eastern seaports benefited, and so did countless intermediate centers, such as Buffalo and Cincinnati. But no city was affected more profoundly by railroads than Chicago. In 1850 not a single line had

Railroads, 1860 Major trunk lines carrying long-distance traffic crisscrossed the area east of the Mississippi. The North had a more extensive rail grid than the South; the North and West were linked, while the South was not as tightly connected to the national economy.

reached there; five years later it was terminal for 2,200 miles of track and controlled the commerce of an imperial domain. By extending half a dozen lines west to the Mississippi, it drained off nearly all the river traffic north of St. Louis. The Illinois Central sucked the expanding output of the prairies into Chicago as well. Most of this freight went eastward over the new railroads or on the Great Lakes and the Erie Canal. Nearly 350,000 tons of shipping plied the lakes by 1855.

The railroads, like the textile industry, stimulated other kinds of economic activity. They transformed agriculture; both real estate values and the buying and selling of land increased whenever the iron horse puffed into a new district. The railroads spurred regional concentration of industry and an increase in the size of business units. Their insatiable need for capital stimulated the growth of investment banking. Their massive size required the creation of complex structures and the employment of salaried managers.

Agriculture, 1860 Cotton was central to the southern economy, while tobacco was the primary crop in Virginia, Tennessee, and Kentucky. Wheat was the key crop in the upper Midwest, and corn was grown nearly everywhere.

The proliferation of trunk lines and the competition of the canal system led to a sharp decline in freight and passenger rates. Cheap transportation had a revolutionary effect on western agriculture. Farmers in Iowa could now raise grain to feed the factory workers of Lowell and even of Manchester, England. Two-thirds of the meat consumed in New York City was soon arriving by rail from beyond the Appalachians. The center of American wheat production shifted westward to Illinois, Wisconsin, and Indiana. When the Crimean War (1853–1856) and European crop failures increased foreign demand, these regions boomed. Success bred success for farmers and for the railroads. Profits earned from carrying wheat enabled the roads to build feeder lines that opened up still wider areas to commercial agriculture and made it easy to bring in lumber, farm machinery, household furnishings, and the settlers themselves at low cost.

Railroads and the Sectional Conflict

Increased production and cheap transportation boosted the western farmer's income and standard of living. The days of isolation and self-sufficiency, even for the family on the edge of the frontier, rapidly disappeared. Pioneers quickly became operators of businesses and, to a far greater extent than their forebears, consumers, buying all sorts of manufactured articles that their ancestors had made for themselves or done without. These changes had their costs. Like southern planters, they now became dependent on middlemen and lost some of their feeling of self-reliance. Overproduction became a problem. Buying a farm began to require more capital, for as profits increased, so did the price of land. Machinery was an additional expense. The proportion of farm laborers and tenants increased.

The linking of the East and West had fateful effects on politics. The increased ease of movement from section to section and the ever more complex social and economic integration of the East and West stimulated nationalism and thus became a force for the preservation of the Union. Without the railroads and canals, Illinois and Iowa would scarcely have dared to side against the South in 1861. When the Mississippi ceased to be essential to them, citizens of the upper valley could afford to be more hostile to slavery and especially to its westward extension. Economic ties with the Northeast reinforced cultural connections.

The South might have preserved its influence in the Northwest if it had pressed forward its own railroad-building program. It failed to do so. There were many southern lines but nothing like a southern system. As late as 1856 one could get from Memphis to Richmond or Charleston only by very indirect routes. As late as 1859 the land-grant road extending the Illinois Central to Mobile, Alabama, was not complete, nor did any economical connection exist between Chicago and New Orleans.

This state of affairs could be accounted for in part by the scattered population of the South, the paucity of passenger traffic, the seasonal nature of much of the freight business, and the absence of large cities. Southerners placed too much reliance on the Mississippi: The fact that traffic on the river continued to be heavy throughout the 1850s blinded them to the precipitous rate at which their relative share of the nation's trade was declining. But the fundamental cause of the South's backwardness in railroad construction was the attitude of its leaders. Southerners of means were no more interested in commerce than in industry; their capital found other outlets.

The Economy on the Eve of Civil War

Between the mid-1840s and the mid-1850s the United States experienced one of the most remarkable periods of growth in the history of the world. Every economic indicator surged forward: manufacturing, grain and cotton production, population, railroad mileage, gold production, sales of public land. The building of the railroads stimulated business, and by making transportation cheaper, the completed lines energized the nation's economy. The American System that Henry Clay had dreamed of arrived with a rush just as Clay was passing from the scene.

Inevitably, this growth caused dislocations that were aggravated by the boom psychology that once again infected the popular mind. In 1857 there was a serious collapse. The return of Russian wheat to the world market after the Crimean War caused grain prices to fall. This checked agricultural expansion, which hurt the railroads and cut down on the demand for manufactures. Unemployment increased. Frightened depositors started runs on banks, most of which had to suspend specie payments.

People called this abrupt downturn the Panic of 1857. Yet the vigor of the economy was such that the bad times did not last long. The upper Mississippi Valley suffered most, for so much new land had been opened up that supplies of farm produce greatly exceeded demand. Elsewhere conditions improved rapidly.

The South, somewhat out of the hectic rush to begin with, was affected very little by the collapse of 1857, for cotton prices continued to be high. This gave planters the false impression that their economy was immune to such violent downturns. Some began to argue that the South would be better off out of the Union.

Before a new national upward swing could become well established, however, the sectional crisis between North and South shook people's confidence in the future. Then the war came, and a new set of forces shaped economic development.

Milestones

1808	Congress bans further importation of slaves	1840–1857	Economy surges during boom in manufacturing, railroad construction, and foreign commerce
1822	Thirty-seven slaves are executed when Denmark Vesey's "conspiracy" is exposed	1842	Massachusetts declares unions legal in *Commonwealth v. Hunt*
1825	Erie Canal is completed, connecting the East and the Midwest	1846	Elias Howe invents sewing machine
1830	Baltimore and Ohio Railroad begins operation	1850	Congress grants land to aid construction of Illinois Central Railroad
1831	Nat Turner's slave uprising kills fifty-seven whites	1854	Clipper ship *Flying Cloud* sails from New York to San Francisco in eighty-nine days
1837	Cyrus Hall McCormick invents reaper to harvest wheat	1857	Brief economic depression (Panic of 1857) collapses economy
1839	John Deere begins manufacturing steel plows		

✓•⌐**Study** and **Review**   at **www.myhistorylab.com**

Review Questions

1. This chapter explores two tendencies: an increasing economic and cultural gap between the South and the rest of the country; and a tighter integration of the nation through spreading transportation systems. In 1860, was the United States breaking into different economic and cultural systems, or did politicians exaggerate the significance of regional variations?

2. The harshness of the slave system was everywhere apparent. In what ways did slaves succeed in fashioning their own culture?

3. Southerners often insisted that immigrants who toiled in northern factories were subjected to far worse conditions than southern slaves. What arguments can be used to support and reject this thesis?

4. During these decades, southern cities sought militia units and armories to help defend against slave insurrections. Northern cities sought such protections to defend against industrial worker insurrections. Which was the greater threat?

The Coming of the Civil War

((•—[Hear the Audio Chapter 13 at myhistorylab.com

Do you space out during political debates?

IN LATE JULY 2008 PRESIDENTIAL CANDIDATE JOHN MCCAIN, BEHIND IN the polls, ran a 30-second TV ad attacking Barack Obama. "He's the biggest celebrity in the world," the narrator declared, as the camera moved from Obama's beaming face to a crowd shouting, "Obama! Obama!" "But is he ready to lead?" the narrator intoned, with a quick cut to glamour shots of Britney Spears and Paris Hilton. Obama retaliated with an attack ad of his own: "John McCain. Same old politics. Same failed policies." By the time the 2008 campaign was over, Obama had placed 553,629 television ads, McCain 287,090. The great majority of these ads were negative.

Many pundits claimed that politics had devolved into little more than name-calling. It had been different 150 years earlier, they said, when Abraham Lincoln squared off against Stephen A. Douglas in a series of debates that framed the national discussion over slavery.

In fact, though, Lincoln and Douglas tore into each other. "Mr. Lincoln has not character enough for integrity and truth," Douglas declared in the first debate. Lincoln responded in kind: "I don't want to quarrel with him—to call him a liar—but when I come square up to him I don't know what else to call him."

If the tone of politics has changed little over the past century and a half, its substance is of an entirely different character. Each of the seven Lincoln-Douglas debates lasted three hours: For the first debate Douglas spoke for one hour. Lincoln's reply lasted ninety minutes, and Douglas concluded with another thirty minute speech. The order of speakers was reversed in subsequent debates. Such a debate nowadays is unimaginable. Most viewers would soon be reaching for the remote.

But during the 1850s audiences stood for hours to hear candidates debate the issues at the heart of this chapter: the morality of the Fugitive Slave Act; the accuracy of Harriet Beecher Stowe's description of slavery in *Uncle Tom's Cabin*; the question of whether "bleeding Kansas" should be admitted to the Union as a slave or free state; the Supreme Court's inflammatory decision in the Dred Scott case; John Brown's manic crusade to free the slaves by force. Most knew, or at least sensed, that the fate of the nation depended on the outcome of these debates. The drumbeat of words came faster and louder. The din culminated in the superheated rhetoric of the 1860 presidential campaign and the secession of the South. Soon words would be drowned out by the roar of cannon.

Slave-Catchers Come North

The political settlement between the North and South that Henry Clay designed—the Compromise of 1850—lasted only four years (see Chapter 11). Its central provisions inevitably sparked controversy. Allowing new territories to decide the question of slavery themselves ensured that the issue would resurface. Americans continued to migrate westward by the thousands, and as long as slaveholders could carry their human property into federally controlled territories, northern resentment would smolder. The Fugitive Slave Act, another part of the Compromise of 1850, imposed fines for hiding or rescuing fugitive slaves. Abolitionists fought against the law and expanded the **underground railroad**, a secret network to help escaped slaves make their way to freedom.

Watch the Video
Underground Railroad at
myhistorylab.com

When two Georgians came to Boston to reclaim William and Ellen Craft, admitted fugitives, a "vigilance committee" hounded them through the streets shouting "slave hunters, slave hunters," and forced them to return home empty-handed. The Crafts prudently—or perhaps in disgust—decided to leave the United States for

This painting by Thomas S. Noble describes the story of Margaret Garner, a slave who escaped with her family across the frozen Ohio River to Cincinnati. When apprehended by slavecatchers, she killed her daughter rather than return her to slavery. Garner's story inspired Toni Morrison's Pulitzer Prize-winning novel *Beloved* (1987).

Free Blacks in 1850 The existence of so many free blacks caused many slaves to question their own servitude and facilitated the attempts of others to escape from bondage.

England. Early in 1851 a Virginia agent captured Frederick "Shadrach" Jenkins, a waiter in a Boston coffeehouse. While Jenkins was being held for deportation, a mob of African Americans broke into the courthouse and hustled him off to Canada. That October a slave named Jerry, who had escaped from Missouri, was arrested in Syracuse, New York. Within minutes the whole town had the news. Crowds surged through the streets, and when night fell, a mob smashed into the building where Jerry was being held and spirited him away to safety in Canada.

●●●—Read the Document

Drew, from *Narratives of Fugitive Slaves in Canada* at **myhistorylab.com**

Such incidents exacerbated sectional feelings. White Southerners accused the North of reneging on one of the main promises made in the Compromise of 1850, while the sight of harmless human beings being hustled off to a life of slavery disturbed many Northerners who were not abolitionists.

However, most white Northerners were not prepared to interfere with the enforcement of the Fugitive Slave Act themselves. Of the 332 blacks put on trial under the law, about 300 were returned to slavery, most without incident. Nevertheless, enforcing the law in the northern states became steadily more difficult.

Uncle Tom's Cabin

Tremendously important in increasing sectional tensions and bringing home the evils of slavery to still more people in the North was Harriet Beecher Stowe's novel *Uncle Tom's Cabin* (1852). Stowe was neither a professional writer nor an abolitionist, and she had almost no firsthand knowledge of slavery. But her conscience had been roused by the Fugitive Slave Act. In gathering material for the book, she depended heavily on abolitionist writers, many of whom she knew. *Uncle Tom's Cabin* was an enormous success: 10,000 copies were sold in a week, and 300,000 in a year. It was translated into dozens of languages. Dramatized versions were staged in countries throughout the world.

•••⌐Read the Document

Stowe, *Uncle Tom's Cabin* at **myhistorylab.com**

Harriet Beecher Stowe was hardly a distinguished writer; it was her approach to the subject that explains the book's success. Her tale of the pious, patient slave Uncle Tom, the saintly white child Eva, and the callous slave driver Simon Legree appealed to an audience far wider than that reached by the abolitionists. She avoided the self-righteous, accusatory tone of most abolitionist tracts and did not seek to convert readers to belief in racial equality. Many of her southern white characters were fine, sensitive people, while the cruel Simon Legree was a transplanted Connecticut Yankee. There were many heart-rending scenes of pain, self-sacrifice, and heroism. The story proved especially effective on the stage: The slave Eliza crossing the frozen Ohio River to freedom, the death of Eva, Eva and Tom ascending to Heaven—these scenes left audiences in tears.

◉⌐Watch the Video

Harriet Beecher Stowe & The Making of Uncle Tom's Cabin at **myhistorylab.com**

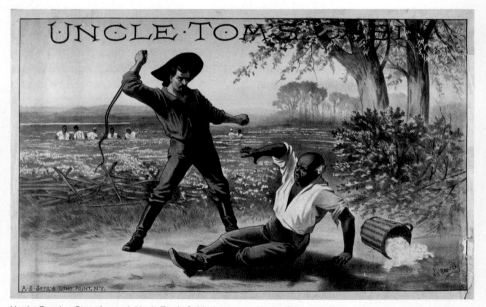

Harriet Beecher Stowe's novel, *Uncle Tom's Cabin*, became a staple of the mid-nineteenth-century theater. This poster shows Simon Legree whipping a blameless Uncle Tom.

Southern critics pointed out, correctly enough, that Stowe's picture of plantation life was distorted, her slaves atypical. They called her a "coarse, ugly, long-tongued woman" and accused her of trying to "awaken rancorous hatred and malignant jealousies" that would undermine national unity. Most Northerners, having little basis on which to judge the accuracy of the book, tended to discount southern criticism as biased. In any case, *Uncle Tom's Cabin* raised questions that transcended the issue of accuracy. Did it matter if every slave was not as kindly as Uncle Tom, as determined as George Harris? What if only one white master was as evil as Simon Legree? No earlier white American writer had looked at slaves as people.

Uncle Tom's Cabin touched the hearts of millions. Some became abolitionists; others, still hesitating to step forward, asked themselves as they put the book down, "Is slavery just?"

Diversions Abroad: The "Young America" Movement

Clearly a distraction was needed to help keep the lid on sectional troubles. Some people hoped to find one in foreign affairs. The spirit of manifest destiny explains this in large part; once the United States had reached the Pacific, expansionists began to think of transmitting the dynamic, democratic U.S. spirit to other countries by aiding local revolutionaries, opening new markets, or perhaps even annexing foreign lands. This became known as the **Young America movement**, whose adherents were confident that democracy would triumph everywhere, even if by conquest.

One of those who dreamt of conquest was an adventurer named William Walker. In 1855 Walker, backed by an American company engaged in transporting migrants to California across Central America, seized control of Nicaragua and elected himself president. He was ousted two years later but made repeated attempts to regain control until, in 1860, when he died before a Honduran firing squad. There were reasons unrelated to slavery why Central America suddenly seemed important. The rapid development of California created a need for improved communication with the West Coast. A canal across Central America would cut weeks from the sailing time between New York and San Francisco. In 1850 Secretary of State John M. Clayton and the British minister to the United States, Henry Lytton Bulwer, negotiated a treaty providing for the demilitarization and joint Anglo-American control of any canal across the isthmus.

As this area assumed strategic importance to the United States, the desire to obtain Cuba grew stronger. In 1854 President Franklin Pierce instructed his minister to Spain to offer $130 million for the island. The State Department prepared a confidential dispatch suggesting that if Spain refused to sell Cuba, "the great law of self-preservation" might justify "wresting" it from Spain by force.

News of the dispatch—known as the **Ostend Manifesto**—leaked out, and it had to be published. Northern opinion was outraged by this "slaveholders' plot" to add another slave state to the Union. Europeans claimed to be shocked by such "dishonorable" and "clandestine" diplomacy. The government had to disavow the manifesto, and any hope of obtaining Cuba or any other territory in the Caribbean vanished.

The expansionist mood of the moment also explains President Fillmore's dispatching an expedition under Commodore Matthew C. Perry to try for commercial concessions in the isolated kingdom of Japan in 1854. Perry's expedition was a great success. The Japanese, impressed by American naval power, agreed to establish diplomatic relations. In 1858 an American envoy, Townsend Harris, negotiated a commercial treaty that opened to American ships six Japanese ports heretofore closed to foreigners. President Pierce's negotiation of a Canadian reciprocity treaty with Great Britain in 1854 and an unsuccessful attempt, also made under Pierce, to annex the Hawaiian Islands are further demonstrations of the assertive foreign policy of the period.

Stephen Douglas: "The Little Giant"

The most prominent spokesman of the Young America movement was Stephen A. Douglas. The senator from Illinois was the Henry Clay of his generation. Like Clay at his best, Douglas was able to see the needs of the nation in the broadest perspective. He held a succession of state offices before being elected to Congress in 1842 at the age of twenty-nine. After only two terms in the House, he was chosen to be a United States senator.

The foundations of Douglas's politics were expansion and popular sovereignty. He had been willing to fight for all of Oregon in 1846, and he supported the Mexican War to the hilt, in sharp contrast to his one-term Illinois colleague in Congress, Abraham Lincoln. That local settlers should determine their own institutions was, to his way of thinking, axiomatic. Since he believed that arguments over the future of slavery in the territories were a foolish waste of energy and time, he was convinced that natural conditions would keep the institution out of the West.

The main thing, he insisted, was to get on with the development of the United States. Let the nation build railroads, acquire new territory, expand its trade. He believed slavery "a curse beyond computation" for both blacks and whites, but he refused to admit that any moral issue was involved. He cared not, he boasted, whether slavery was voted up or voted down. This was not really true, but the question was interfering with the rapid exploitation of the continent. Douglas wanted it settled so that the country could concentrate on more important matters.

Douglas's success in steering the Compromise of 1850 through Congress added to his reputation. In 1851, he set out to win the Democratic presidential nomination, reasoning that since he was the brightest, most imaginative, and hardest-working Democrat around, he had every right to press his claim.

This brash aggressiveness proved his undoing. He expressed open contempt for James Buchanan and said of his other chief rival, Lewis Cass, who had won considerable fame while serving as minister to France, that his "reputation was beyond the C."

At the 1852 Democratic convention Douglas had no chance. Cass and Buchanan killed each other off, and the delegates finally chose a dark horse, Franklin Pierce of New Hampshire. The Whigs, rejecting the colorless Fillmore, nominated General Winfield Scott, who was known as "Old Fuss and Feathers" because of his "punctiliousness in dress and decorum." In the campaign both sides supported the Compromise of 1850. The Democrats won an easy victory, 254 electoral votes to 42.

So handsome a triumph seemed to ensure stability, but in fact it was a prelude to political chaos. The Whig party was crumbling fast. The "Cotton" Whigs of the South, alienated by the antislavery sentiments of their northern brethren, were flocking into the Democratic fold. In the North the Whigs, divided between an antislavery wing ("conscience Whigs") and another that was undisturbed by slavery, found themselves more and more at odds with each other. Congress fell overwhelmingly into the hands of proslavery southern Democrats, a development profoundly disturbing to northern Democrats as well as to Whigs.

The Kansas-Nebraska Act

Franklin Pierce appeared a youthful forty-eight years old when he took office. He was generally well-liked by politicians. His career had included service in both houses of Congress. Alcohol had become a problem for him in Washington, however, and in 1842 he had resigned from the Senate and returned home to try to best the bottle, a struggle in which he was successful. His law practice boomed,

⊙ See the **Map**

The Compromise of 1850 and the Kansas-Nebraska Act at **myhistorylab.com**

This engraving of Franklin Pierce shows him on his horse during the Mexican War. In actuality, he did not remain there long. During one battle, Pierce was thrown from his horse and sustained pelvic and knee injuries. While leading his men the next day, he fainted. Another officer assumed that Pierce was drunk. For years, Whigs attacked Pierce's military record, calling him "hero of many a bottle."

and he added to his reputation by serving as a brigadier general during the Mexican War. Although his nomination for president came as a surprise, once made, it had appeared perfectly reasonable. Great things were expected of his administration, especially after he surrounded himself with men of all factions: To balance his appointment of a radical states' rights Mississippian, Jefferson Davis, as secretary of war, for example, he named a conservative Northerner, William L. Marcy of New York, as secretary of state.

Only a strong leader, however, can manage a ministry of all talents, and that President Pierce was not. The ship of state was soon drifting; Pierce seemed incapable of holding firm the helm.

This was the situation in January 1854 when Senator Douglas, chairman of the Committee on Territories, introduced what looked like a routine bill organizing the land west of Missouri and Iowa as the Nebraska Territory. Since settlers were beginning to trickle into the area, the time had arrived to set up a civil administration. But besides his expansionist motives, Douglas also acted because a territorial government was essential to railroad development. As a director of the Illinois Central line and as a land speculator, he hoped to make Chicago the terminus of a transcontinental railroad, but construction could not begin until the route was cleared of Indians and brought under some kind of civil control.

The railroad question aside, Nebraska would presumably become a free state, for it lay north of latitude 36°30' in a district from which slavery had been excluded by the Missouri Compromise. Under pressure from the Southerners, led by Senator David R. Atchison of Missouri, Douglas agreed first to divide the region into two territories, Kansas and Nebraska, and then—a fateful concession—to repeal the part of the Missouri Compromise that excluded slavery from land north of 36°30'. Whether the new territories should become slave or free, he argued, should be left to the decision of the settlers in accordance with the democratic principle of popular sovereignty. The fact that he might advance his presidential ambitions by making concessions to the South must have influenced Douglas too, as must the local political situation in Missouri, where slaveholders feared being "surrounded" on three sides by free states.

Douglas's miscalculation of northern sentiment was monumental. It was one thing to apply popular sovereignty to the new territories in the Southwest, but quite another to apply it to a region that had been part of the United States for half a century and free soil for thirty-four years. A group of abolitionist congressmen issued what they called their "Appeal of the Independent Democrats" (actually, all were Free Soilers and Whigs) denouncing the Kansas-Nebraska bill as "a gross violation of a sacred pledge" and calling for a campaign of letter writing, petitions, and public meetings to prevent its passage. The unanimity and force of the northern public's reaction was like nothing in America since the days of the Stamp Act and the Intolerable Acts.

But protests could not defeat the bill. Southerners in both houses backed it regardless of party. Douglas, at his best when under attack, pushed it with all his power. The authors of the "Appeal," he charged, were "the pure unadulterated representatives of Abolitionism, Free Soilism, [and] Niggerism." President Pierce added whatever force the administration could muster. As a result, the northern Democrats split and the **Kansas-Nebraska Act** was passed late in May 1854. In this manner the nation took the greatest single step in its march toward the abyss of secession and civil war.

The repeal of the Missouri Compromise struck the North like a slap in the face—at once shameful and challenging. Presumably the question of slavery in the territories had been settled forever; now, seemingly without justification, it had been reopened. On May 24, two days after the Kansas-Nebraska bill passed the House of Representatives, Anthony Burns, a slave who had escaped from Virginia by stowing away on a ship, was arrested in Boston. Massachusetts abolitionists brought suit against Burns's former master, charging false arrest. They also organized a protest meeting at which they inflamed the crowd into attacking the courthouse where Burns was being held. The mob broke into the building and a guard was killed, but federal marshals drove off the attackers.

President Pierce ordered the Boston district attorney to "incur any expense" to enforce the law. He also sent a federal ship to Boston to carry Burns back to Virginia. Thus Burns was returned to his master, but it required two companies of soldiers and 1,000 police and marines to get him aboard ship. As the grim parade marched past buildings festooned with black crepe, the crowd screamed "Kidnappers! Kidnappers!" at the soldiers. Estimates of the cost of returning this single slave to his owner ran as high as $100,000. A few months later, northern sympathizers bought Burns his freedom—for a few hundred dollars.

In previous cases Boston's conservative leaders, Whig to a man, had tended to hold back; after the Burns incident, they were thoroughly radicalized. "We went to bed one night old fashioned . . .Whigs," one of them explained, "and waked up stark mad Abolitionists."

Know-Nothings, Republicans, and the Demise of the Two-Party System

There were ninety-one free-state Democrats in the House of Representatives when the Kansas-Nebraska Act was passed, only twenty-five after the next election. With the Whig party already moribund, dissidents flocked to two new parties.

One was the American party, or **Know-Nothing party**, so called because it grew out of a secret society whose members used the password "I don't know." The Know-Nothings were primarily nativists—immigration was soaring in the early 1850s, and the influx of poor foreigners was causing genuine social problems. Crime was on the rise in the cities along with drunkenness and other "diseases of poverty."

Several emotion-charged issues related to the fact that a large percentage of the immigrants were Irish and German Catholics also troubled the Know-Nothings. Questions such as public financing of parochial schools, lay control of church policies, the prohibition of alcoholic beverages, and increasing the time before an immigrant could apply for citizenship (the Know-Nothings favored twenty-one years) were matters of major importance to them. Since these were divisive issues, the established political parties tried to avoid them—hence the development of the new party.

The American party was important in the South as well as in the North, and while most Know-Nothings disliked blacks and considered them inherently inferior beings, they tended to adopt the dominant view of slavery in whichever section they were located. In the North most opposed the Kansas-Nebraska Act.

Operating often in tacit alliance with the antislavery forces (dislike of slavery did not prevent many abolitionists from being prejudiced against Catholics and immigrants), the northern Know-Nothings won a string of local victories in 1854 and elected more than forty congressmen.

Far more significant in the long run was the formation of the Republican party, which was made up of former Free Soilers, Conscience Whigs, and "Anti-Nebraska" Democrats. The American party was a national organization, but the **Republican party** was purely sectional. It sprang up spontaneously throughout the Old Northwest and caught on with a rush in New England.

Republicans presented themselves as the party of freedom. They were not abolitionists (though most abolitionists were soon voting Republican), but they insisted that slavery be kept out of the territories. They believed that if America was to remain a land of opportunity, free white labor must have exclusive access to the West. Thus the party appealed not only to voters who disapproved of slavery, but also to those who wished to keep blacks—free or slave—out of their states. In 1854 the Republicans won more than a hundred seats in the House of Representatives and control of many state governments.

The Whig party had almost disappeared in the northern states and the Democratic party had been gravely weakened, but it was unclear how these two new parties would fare. The Know-Nothing party had the superficial advantage of being a nationwide organization, but where slavery was concerned, this was anything but advantageous. And many Northerners who disliked slavery were troubled by the harsh Know-Nothing policies toward immigrants and Catholics. If the Know-Nothings were in control, said former Whig congressman Abraham Lincoln in 1855, the Declaration of Independence would read "all men are created equal, except negroes, *and foreigners, and catholics.*"

"Bleeding Kansas"

The furor over slavery might have died down if settlement of the new territories had proceeded in an orderly manner. Almost none of the settlers who flocked to Kansas owned slaves and relatively few of them were primarily interested in the slavery question. Most had a low opinion of blacks. Like nearly all frontier settlers, they wanted land and local political office, lucrative government contracts, and other business opportunities.

When Congress opened the gates to settlement in May 1854, none of the land in the territory was available for sale. Treaties extinguishing Indian titles had yet to be ratified, and public lands had not been surveyed. In July Congress authorized squatters to occupy unsurveyed federal lands, but much of this property was far to the west of the frontier and practically inaccessible. The situation led to confusion over property boundaries, to graft and speculation, and to general uncertainty, thereby exacerbating the difficulty of establishing an orderly government.

The legal status of slavery in Kansas became the focus of all these conflicts. Both northern abolitionists and southern defenders of slavery were determined to have Kansas. They made of the territory first a testing ground and then a battlefield, thus exposing the fatal flaw in the Kansas-Nebraska Act and the idea of popular sovereignty. The law said that the people of Kansas were "perfectly free" to decide the slavery question. But the citizens of territories were not entirely free because territories were not sovereign political units. The Act had created a political vacuum, which its vague statement that the settlers must establish their domestic institutions "subject. . . to the Constitution" did not begin to fill. The virtues of the time-tested system of congressional control established by the Northwest Ordinance became fully apparent only when the system was discarded.

In November 1854 an election was held in Kansas to pick a territorial delegate to Congress. A large band of Missourians crossed over specifically to vote for a proslavery candidate and elected him easily. In March 1855 some 5,000 "border ruffians" again descended on Kansas and elected a territorial legislature. A census had recorded 2,905 eligible voters, but 6,307 votes were cast. The legislature promptly enacted a slave code and laws prohibiting abolitionist agitation. Antislavery settlers refused to recognize this regime and held elections of their own. By January 1856 two governments existed in Kansas: one based on fraud, the other extralegal.

"Bleeding Kansas" In the late 1850s, one Kansas government (located in Topeka) abolished slavery; the other (located in Lecompton) legalized slavery. As proslavery settlers poured into Kansas from Missouri, and antislavery settlers from the North, clashes were inevitable.

By denouncing the free-state government located at Topeka, President Pierce encouraged the proslavery settlers to assume the offensive. In May, 800 of them sacked the antislavery town of Lawrence. An extremist named John Brown then took the law into his own hands in retaliation. By his reckoning, five Free Soilers had been killed by proslavery forces. In May 1856, together with six companions (four of them his sons), Brown stole into a settlement on Pottawatomie Creek in the dead of night. They dragged five unsuspecting men from their cabins and murdered them. This slaughter brought men on both sides to arms by the hundreds. Marauding bands came to blows and terrorized homesteads, first attempting to ascertain the inhabitants' position on slavery.

Brown and his followers escaped capture and were never indicted for the murders, but pressure from federal troops eventually forced him to go into hiding. He finally left Kansas in October 1856. By that time some 200 persons had lost their lives.

A certain amount of violence was normal in any frontier community, but it suited the political interests of the Republicans to make the situation in Kansas seem worse than it was. Exaggerated accounts of "bleeding Kansas" filled the pages of northern newspapers. The Democrats were also partly to blame, for although residents of nearby states often tried to influence elections in new territories, the actions of the border ruffians made a mockery of the democratic process.

However, the main responsibility for the Kansas tragedy must be borne by the Pierce administration. Under popular sovereignty the national government was supposed to see that elections were orderly and honest. Instead, the president acted as a partisan. When the first governor of the territory objected to the manner in which the proslavery legislature had been elected, Pierce replaced him with a man who backed the southern group without question.

Senator Sumner Becomes a Martyr for Abolitionism

As counterpoint to the fighting in Kansas there arose an almost continuous clamor in the halls of Congress. Epithets like "liar" were freely tossed about. Prominent in these angry outbursts was a new senator, Charles Sumner of Massachusetts. Brilliant, learned, and articulate, Sumner had made a name for himself in New England as a reformer interested in the peace movement, prison reform, and the abolition of slavery. His unyielding devotion to his principles was less praiseworthy than it seemed on casual examination, for it resulted from his complete lack of respect for the principles of others. Reform movements evidently provided him with a kind of emotional release; he became combative and totally lacking in objectivity when espousing a cause.

In the Kansas debates Sumner displayed an icy disdain for his foes. Colleagues threatened him with assassination, called him a "filthy reptile" and a "leper." He was impervious to such hostility. In the spring of 1856 he loosed a dreadful blast titled "The Crime Against Kansas." Characterizing administration policy as tyrannical, imbecilic, absurd, and infamous, he demanded that Kansas be admitted to the Union at once as a free state. Then he began a long and intemperate attack on both Douglas and the elderly Senator Andrew P. Butler of South Carolina, who was not present to defend himself.

SOUTHERN CHIVALRY — ARGUMENT versus CLUB'S.

In this cartoon Charles Sumner of Massachusetts is caned on the floor of the Senate by Preston Brooks of South Carolina.

Source: J. L. Magee, *Southern Chivalry-Argument Versus Clubs*, 1856. Lithograph. Weitenkampf Collection #745, Prints Collection: Miriam and Ira D. Wallach Division of Art, Prints and Photographs, The New York Public Library, Astor, Lenox, and Tilden Foundations.

Sumner described Butler as a "Don Quixote" who had taken "the harlot, slavery" as his mistress, and he spoke scornfully of "the loose expectoration" of Butler's speech. This was an inexcusable reference to the uncontrollable drooling to which the elderly senator was subject. While he was still talking, Douglas, who shrugged off most political name-calling as part of the game, was heard to mutter, "That damn fool will get himself killed by some other damn fool."

Such a "fool" quickly materialized in the person of Congressman Preston S. Brooks of South Carolina, a nephew of Senator Butler. Since Butler was absent from Washington, Brooks, who was probably as mentally unbalanced as Sumner, assumed the responsibility of defending his kinsman's honor. A southern romantic par excellence, he decided that caning Sumner would reflect his contempt more effectively than challenging him to a duel. Two days after the speech, Brooks entered the Senate as it adjourned. Sumner remained at his desk writing. Waiting until a talkative woman in the lobby had left so that she would be spared the sight of violence, Brooks then walked up to Sumner and rained blows on his head with a cane until Sumner fell, unconscious and bloody, to the floor. "I. . . gave him about 30 first-rate stripes," Brooks later boasted. "Towards the last he bellowed like a calf. I wore my cane out completely but saved the head which is gold." The physical damage suffered by Sumner was not life-threatening, but the incident so affected him psychologically that he was unable to return to his seat in Congress until 1859.

Both sides made much of this disgraceful incident. When the House censured him, Brooks resigned, returned to his home district, and was triumphantly reelected. A number of well-wishers sent him souvenir canes. Northerners viewed the affair as illustrating the brutalizing effect of slavery on southern whites and made a hero of Sumner.

Buchanan Tries His Hand

Such was the atmosphere surrounding the 1856 presidential election. The Republican party now dominated much of the North. It nominated John C. Frémont, "the Pathfinder," one of the heroes of the conquest of California during the war with Mexico. Frémont fit the Whig tradition of presidential candidates: a popular military man with almost no political experience. Unlike Taylor and Scott, however, he was articulate on the issue of slavery in the territories. Although citizens of diverse interests had joined the party, Republicans expressed their objectives in one simple slogan: "Free soil, free speech, and Frémont."

The Democrats cast aside the ineffectual Pierce, but they did not dare nominate Douglas because he had raised such a storm in the North. They settled on James Buchanan, chiefly because he had been out of the country serving as minister to Great Britain during the long debate over Kansas! The American party nominated former president Millard Fillmore, a choice the remnants of the Whigs endorsed.

In the campaign, the Democrats concentrated on denouncing the Republicans as a sectional party that threatened to destroy the Union. On this issue they carried the day. Buchanan won only a minority of the popular vote, but he had strength in every section. He got 174 electoral votes to Frémont's 114 and Fillmore's 8. The significant contest took place in the populous states just north of slave territory—Pennsylvania, Ohio, Indiana, and Illinois. Of these, Buchanan carried all but Ohio, although by narrow margins.

No one could say that James Buchanan lacked political experience. Elected to the Pennsylvania legislature in 1815 when he was only twenty-four years old, he served for well over twenty years in Congress and had served as minister to Russia, as secretary of state, and as minister to Great Britain.

Personally, Buchanan was a bundle of contradictions. Dignified in bearing and by nature cautious, he could consume enormous amounts of liquor without showing the slightest sign of inebriation. He wore a very high collar to conceal a scarred neck, and because of an eye defect he habitually carried his head to one side and slightly forward, which gave him, as his biographer says, "a perpetual attitude of courteous deference and attentive interest" that sometimes led individuals to believe they had won a greater share of his attention and support than was actually the case. In fact he was extremely stubborn and sometimes vindictive.

The Dred Scott Decision

Before Buchanan could fairly take the Kansas problem in hand, an event occurred that drove another deep wedge between North and South. Back in 1834 Dr. John Emerson of St. Louis joined the army as a surgeon and was assigned to duty at Rock Island, Illinois. Later he was transferred to Fort Snelling, in the Wisconsin Territory. In 1838 he returned to Missouri. Accompanying him on these travels was his body servant, Dred Scott, a slave. In 1846, after Emerson's death, Scott and his wife Harriet, whom he had married while in Wisconsin, brought suit in the Missouri courts for their liberty with the help of a friendly lawyer. They claimed that residence in Illinois, where slavery was barred under the Northwest Ordinance, and in the Wisconsin Territory, where the Missouri Compromise outlawed it, had made them free.

Watch the Video
Dred Scott & The Crises that led to the Civil War at **myhistorylab.com**

The future of Dred and Harriet Scott mattered not at all to the country or the courts; at issue was the question of whether Congress or the local legislatures had the power to outlaw slavery in the territories. After many years of litigation, the case reached the Supreme Court of the United States. On March 6, 1857, two days after Buchanan's inauguration, the high tribunal acted, issuing what is known as the **Dred Scott decision**. Free or slave, the Court declared, blacks were not citizens; therefore, Scott could not sue in a federal court. This was dubious legal logic because many blacks were accepted as citizens in some states when the Constitution was drafted and ratified, and Article IV, Section 2, says that "the citizens of each state shall be entitled to all privileges and immunities of citizens in the several states." But the decision settled Scott's fate.

However, the Court went further. Since the plaintiff had returned to Missouri, the laws of Illinois no longer applied to him. His residence in the Wisconsin Territory—this was the most controversial part of the decision—did not make him free because the Missouri Compromise was unconstitutional. According to the Bill of Rights (the Fifth Amendment), the federal government cannot deprive any person of life, liberty, or property without due process of law.[1] Therefore, Chief Justice Roger B. Taney reasoned, "an Act of Congress which deprives a person . . . of his liberty or property merely because he

---

[1]Some state constitutions had similar provisions, but the slave states obviously did not.

Dred Scott and his wife and children are featured on the cover of *Frank Leslie's Illustrated Newspaper*. Historian Joshua Brown argues in *Beyond the Lines* (2002) that this publication was the precursor to today's popular newsmagazines. Its plentiful pictures were made possible by the new technology of mass-produced wood engraving.

came himself or brought his property into a particular Territory. . . could hardly be dignified with the name of due process of law." The Missouri Compromise had deprived Dr. Emerson of his "property"—his slaves—and thus was unconstitutional!

In addition to invalidating the already repealed Missouri Compromise, the decision threatened Douglas's principle of popular sovereignty, for if Congress could not exclude slaves from a territory, how could a mere territorial legislature do so? Until statehood was granted, slavery seemed as inviolate as freedom of religion or speech or any other civil liberty guaranteed by the Constitution. Where formerly freedom (as guaranteed in the Bill of Rights) was a national institution and slavery a local one, now, according to the Court, slavery was nationwide, excluded only where states had specifically abolished it.

Read the Document
Opinion of the Supreme Court for Dred Scott v. Sanford at **myhistorylab.com**

The irony of employing the Bill of Rights to keep blacks in chains did not escape northern critics. Now slaves could be brought into the Minnesota Territory, even into Oregon. In his inaugural address Buchanan had urged the people to accept the forthcoming ruling, "whatever this may be," as a final settlement. Many assumed (indeed, it was true) that he had put pressure on the Court to act as it did and that he knew in advance of his speech what the decision would be. The Dred Scott decision convinced thousands that the South was engaged in an aggressive attempt to extend the peculiar institution so far that it could no longer be considered peculiar.

The Proslavery Lecompton Constitution

Kansas soon provided a test for northern suspicions. The proslavery leaders in Kansas had managed to convene a constitutional convention at Lecompton, but the Free Soil forces had boycotted the election of delegates. When this rump body drafted a proslavery constitution and then refused to submit it to a fair vote of all the settlers, Kansas governor Robert J. Walker denounced its work and hurried back to Washington to explain the situation to Buchanan.

The president refused to face reality. His prosouthern advisers were clamoring for him to "save" Kansas. Instead of rejecting the **Lecompton constitution**, he asked Congress to admit Kansas to the Union with this document as its frame of government.

Buchanan's decision brought him head-on against Stephen A. Douglas, and the repercussions of their clash shattered the Democratic party. Principle and self-interest forced Douglas to oppose the leader of his party. If he stood aside while Congress admitted Kansas, he not only would be abandoning popular sovereignty, but he would be committing political suicide as well. He was up for reelection to the Senate in 1858. All but one of the fifty-six newspapers in Illinois had declared editorially against the Lecompton constitution; if Douglas supported it, his defeat was certain. In a dramatic confrontation at the White House, he and Buchanan argued the question at length, tempers rising. Finally, the president tried to force him into line. "Mr. Douglas," he said, "I desire you to remember that no Democrat ever yet differed from an Administration of his own choice without being crushed." "Mr. President," Douglas replied contemptuously, "I wish you to remember that General Jackson is dead!" And he stalked out of the room.

Buchanan then compounded his error by putting tremendous political pressure on Douglas, cutting off his Illinois patronage on the eve of his reelection campaign. Of course Douglas persisted, openly joining the Republicans in the fight. Congress rejected the Lecompton bill.

Meanwhile, the extent of the fraud perpetrated at Lecompton became clear. In October 1857 a new legislature had been chosen in Kansas, antislavery voters participating in the balloting. It ordered a referendum on the Lecompton constitution in January 1858. This time the proslavery settlers boycotted the vote and the constitution was overwhelmingly rejected. When Buchanan persisted in pressing Congress to admit Kansas under the Lecompton constitution, Congress ordered another referendum. To slant the case in favor of approval, the legislators stipulated that if the constitution were voted down, Kansas could not be admitted into the Union until it had a population of 90,000. Nevertheless, the Kansans rejected it by a ratio of six to one.

The Emergence of Lincoln

Dissolution threatened the Union. To many Americans, Stephen A. Douglas seemed to offer the best hope of preserving it. For this reason unusual attention was focused on his campaign for reelection to the Senate in 1858. The importance of the contest and Douglas's national prestige put great pressure on the Republicans of Illinois to nominate someone who would make a good showing against him. The man they chose was Abraham Lincoln.

After a towering figure has passed from the stage, it is always difficult to discover what he was like before his rise to prominence. This is especially true of Lincoln, who changed greatly when power, responsibility, and fame came to him. Lincoln was not unknown in 1858, but his public career had not been distinguished. He was born in Kentucky in 1809, and the story of his early life can be condensed, as he once said himself, into a single line from Gray's *Elegy*: "The short and simple annals of the poor." His illiterate father, Thomas Lincoln, was a typical frontier wanderer. When Abraham was seven years old, the family moved to Indiana. In 1830 they pushed west again into southern Illinois. The boy received almost no formal schooling.

However, Lincoln had a good mind, and he was extremely ambitious.[2] In 1834, when barely twenty-five, he won a seat in the Illinois legislature as a Whig. Meanwhile, he studied law and was admitted to the bar in 1836.

Lincoln remained in the legislature until 1842, displaying a perfect willingness to adopt the Whig position on all issues. In 1846 he was elected to Congress. After one term in Congress, marked by his partisan opposition to Polk's Mexican policy, his political career petered out. He seemed fated to pass his remaining years as a small-town lawyer.

Even during this period Lincoln's personality was extraordinarily complex. His bawdy sense of humor and his endless fund of stories and tall tales made him a legend first in Illinois and then in Washington. He was thoroughly at home with toughs like the "Clary's Grove Boys" of New Salem and in the convivial atmosphere of a party caucus. But in a society where most men drank heavily, he never touched liquor. And he was subject to periods of profound melancholy. He wrote of himself in the early 1840s, "I am now the most miserable man living. If what I felt were equally distributed to the whole human family, there would not be one cheerful face on earth."

The revival of the slavery controversy in 1854 stirred Lincoln deeply. No abolitionist, he had tried to take a "realistic" view of the problem. The Kansas-Nebraska bill led him to see the moral issue more clearly. "If slavery is not wrong, nothing is wrong," he stated with the directness and simplicity of expression for which he later became famous. Yet unlike most Free Soilers, he did not blame the Southerners for slavery. "They are just what we would be in their situation," he confessed.

Thus Lincoln was at once compassionate toward the slave owner and stern toward the institution. "A house divided against itself cannot stand," he warned. "I believe this government cannot endure permanently half slave and half free." Without minimizing the difficulties or urging a hasty or ill-considered solution, Lincoln demanded that the people look toward a day, however remote, when not only Kansas but the entire country would be free.

---

[2]His law partner, William Herndon, said that Lincoln's ambition was "a little engine that knows no rest."

The Lincoln-Douglas Debates

As Lincoln developed these ideas his reputation grew. In 1855 he almost won the Whig nomination for senator. He became a Republican shortly thereafter, and in June 1856, at the first Republican National Convention, he received 110 votes for the vice-presidential nomination. He seemed the logical man to pit against Douglas in 1858. The Lincoln-Douglas debates were well-attended and widely reported, for the idea of a direct confrontation between candidates for an important office captured the popular imagination.

The choice of the next senator lay, of course, in the hands of the Illinois legislature. Technically, Douglas and Lincoln were campaigning for candidates for the legislature who were pledged to support them for the Senate seat. The two employed different political styles, each calculated to project a particular image. Douglas epitomized efficiency and success. Ordinarily he arrived in town in a private railroad car, to be met by a brass band, then to ride at the head of a parade to the appointed place.

Lincoln appeared before the voters as a man of the people. He wore ill-fitting black suits and a stovepipe hat that exaggerated his great height. He presented a worn and rumpled appearance, partly because he traveled from place to place on day coaches, accompanied by only a few advisers. When local supporters came to meet him at the station, he preferred to walk with them through the streets to the scene of the debate.

●●●▪[Read the **Document**

Douglas, *Debate at Galesburg, Illinois* at **myhistorylab.com**

Lincoln and Douglas maintained a high intellectual level in their speeches, but these were political debates. Both tailored their arguments to appeal to local audiences—more antislavery in the northern counties, more proslavery in the southern. They also tended to exaggerate their differences,

Abraham Lincoln speaks as Stephen Douglas gazes at the audience—mostly standing—during the debate in Charleston, Illinois in 1858, as painted by Robert Root.

which were not in fact enormous. Neither wanted to see slavery in the territories or thought it economically efficient, and neither sought to abolish it by political action or by force. Both believed blacks congenitally inferior to whites, although Douglas took more pleasure in expounding on supposed racial differences than Lincoln did.

Douglas's strategy was to make Lincoln look like an abolitionist. He accused the Republicans of favoring racial equality and refusing to abide by the decision of the Supreme Court in the Dred Scott case. Himself he pictured as a heroic champion of democracy, attacked on one side by the "black" Republicans and on the other by Buchanan supporters, yet ready to fight to his last breath for popular sovereignty.

Lincoln tried to picture Douglas as proslavery and a defender of the Dred Scott decision. "Slavery is an unqualified evil to the negro, to the white man, to the soil, and to the State," he said. "Judge Douglas," he also said, "is blowing out the moral lights around us, when he contends that whoever wants slaves has a right to hold them."

However, Lincoln often weakened the impact of his arguments, being perhaps too eager to demonstrate his conservatism. "All men are created equal," he would say on the authority of the Declaration of Independence, only to add, "I am not, nor ever have been, in favor of bringing about in any way the social and political equality of the white and black races." He opposed allowing blacks to vote, to sit on juries, to marry whites, even to be citizens. He predicted the "ultimate extinction" of slavery, but when pressed he predicted that it would not occur "in less than a hundred years at the least."

In the debate at Freeport, a town northwest of Chicago near the Wisconsin line, Lincoln asked Douglas if, considering the Dred Scott decision, the people of a territory could exclude slavery before the territory became a state. Unhesitatingly Douglas replied that they could, simply by not passing the local laws essential for holding blacks in bondage. "It matters not what way the Supreme Court may hereafter decide as to the abstract question," Douglas said. "The people have the lawful means to introduce or exclude it as they please, for the reason that slavery cannot exist. . . unless it is supported by local police regulations."

This argument saved Douglas in Illinois. The Democrats carried the legislature by a narrow margin, whereas it is almost certain that if Douglas had accepted the Dred Scott decision outright, the balance would have swung to the Republicans. But the so-called Freeport Doctrine cost him heavily two years later when he made his bid for the Democratic presidential nomination. "It matters not what way the Supreme Court may hereafter decide"—southern extremists would not accept a man who suggested that the Dred Scott decision could be circumvented, although in fact Douglas had only stated the obvious.

Probably Lincoln had not thought beyond the senatorial election when he asked the question; he was merely hoping to keep Douglas on the defensive and perhaps injure him in southern Illinois, where considerable proslavery sentiment existed. In any case, defeat did Lincoln no harm politically. He had more than held his own against one of the most formidable debaters in politics, and his distinctive personality and point of view had impressed themselves on thousands of minds. Indeed, the defeat revitalized his political career.

The campaign of 1858 marked Douglas's last triumph, Lincoln's last defeat. Elsewhere the elections in the North went heavily to the Republicans. When the old Congress reconvened in December, northern-sponsored economic measures (a higher tariff, the transcontinental railroad, river and harbor improvements, a free homestead bill) were all blocked by southern votes.

Whether the South could continue to prevent the passage of this legislation in the new Congress was problematical. In early 1859 even many moderate Southerners were uneasy about the future. The radicals, made panicky by Republican victories and their own failure to win in Kansas, spoke openly of secession if a Republican were elected president in 1860. Lincoln's "house divided" speech was quoted out of context, while Douglas's Freeport Doctrine added to southern woes. When Senator William H. Seward of New York spoke of an "irrepressible conflict" between freedom and slavery, white Southerners became still more alarmed.

John Brown's Raid

In October 1859, John Brown, the scourge of Kansas, made his second contribution to the unfolding sectional drama. Gathering a group of eighteen followers, white and black, he staged an attack on Harpers Ferry, Virginia, a town on the Potomac River upstream from Washington. Having boned up on guerrilla tactics, he planned to seize the federal arsenal there; arm the slaves, whom he thought would flock to his side; and then establish a black republic in the mountains of Virginia.

Simply by overpowering a few night watchmen, Brown and his men occupied the arsenal and a nearby rifle factory. They captured several hostages, one of them Colonel Lewis Washington, a great-grandnephew of George Washington. But no slaves came forward to join them. Federal troops commanded by Robert E. Lee soon trapped Brown's men in an engine house of the Baltimore and Ohio Railroad. After a two-day siege in which the attackers picked off ten of his men, Brown was captured.

After John Brown's capture, Emerson called him "a martyr" who would "make the gallows as glorious as the cross." Brown's principled radicalism found favor during the Depression decade of the 1930s. John Stewart Curry's mural, completed in 1943, depicted the demented John Brown in the pose of Christ on the cross. The image offended the Kansas legislature, which had commissioned Curry to portray Kansas history in a "sane and sensible manner."
Source: Kansas State Historical Society, Copy and Reuse Restrictions apply.

No incident so well illustrates the role of emotion and irrationality in the sectional crisis as does John Brown's raid. Over the years before his Kansas escapade, Brown had been a drifter, horse thief, a swindler, and several times a bankrupt, a failure in everything he attempted. After his ghastly Pottawatomie murders it should have been obvious to anyone that he was both a fanatic and mentally unstable: Some of the victims were hacked to bits with a broadsword. Yet numbers of high-minded Northerners, including Emerson and Thoreau, had supported Brown and his antislavery "work" after 1856. White Southerners reacted to Harpers Ferry with equal irrationality, some with a rage similar to Brown's. Dozens of hapless Northerners in the southern states were arrested, beaten, or driven off. One, falsely suspected of being an accomplice of Brown, was lynched.

Brown's fate lay in the hands of the Virginia authorities. Ignoring his obvious derangement, they charged him with treason, conspiracy, and murder. He was speedily convicted and sentenced to death by hanging.

Yet "Old Brown" had still one more contribution to make to the developing sectional tragedy. Despite the furor he had created, cool heads everywhere called for calm and denounced his attack. Most Republican politicians repudiated him. Even execution would probably not have made a martyr of Brown had he behaved like a madman after his capture. Instead, an enormous dignity descended on him as he lay in his Virginia jail awaiting death. Whatever his faults, he truly believed in racial equality. He addressed blacks who worked for him as "Mister" and arranged for them to eat at his table and sit with his family in church.

This conviction served him well in his last days. "If it is deemed necessary that I should forfeit my life for the furtherance of the ends of justice, and mingle my blood further with the blood of. . . millions in this slave country whose rights are disregarded by wicked, cruel, and unjust enactments," he said before the judge pronounced sentence, "I say, let it be done."

•••⌐Read the **Document**
John Brown's Address Before Sentencing at **myhistorylab.com**

This John Brown, with his patriarchal beard and sad eyes, so apparently incompatible with the bloody terrorist of Pottawatomie and Harpers Ferry, led thousands in the North to ignore his past and treat him almost as a saint.

And so Brown, hanged on December 2, 1859, became to the North a hero and to the South a symbol of northern ruthlessness. Soon, as the popular song had it, Brown's body lay "a-mouldering in the grave," and the memory of his bloody act did indeed go "marching on."

The Election of 1860

By 1860 the nation was teetering on the brink of disunion. Radicals in the North and South were heedlessly provoking one another.

Extremism was more evident in the South, and to any casual observer that section must have seemed the aggressor in the crisis. Yet even in demanding the reopening of the African slave trade, southern radicals believed that they were defending themselves against attack. They felt surrounded by hostility. The North was growing at a much faster rate; if nothing was done, they feared, a flood of new free states would soon be able to amend the Constitution and emancipate the slaves. John Brown's raid, with its threat of an insurrection like Nat Turner's, reduced them to a state of panic.

That politics was always a rough business is shown in this cartoon, which shows Lincoln, assisted by an African American (who carries a basket of liquor bottles) while Douglas is backed by some Irish pols, who have a basket overflowing with cash. John Breckinridge thumbs his nose at the combatants as he hustles up the hill toward the White House.

When legislatures in state after state in the South cracked down on freedom of expression, made the manumission of slaves illegal, banished free blacks, and took other steps that Northerners considered blatantly provocative, the advocates of these policies believed that they were only defending the status quo. Perhaps, by seceding from the Union, the South could raise a dike against the tide of abolitionism. Secession also provided an emotional release, a way of dissipating tension by striking back at criticism.

Stephen A. Douglas was probably the last hope of avoiding a rupture between North and South. But when the Democrats met at Charleston, South Carolina, in April 1860 to choose a presidential candidate, the southern delegates would not support him unless he promised not to disturb slavery in the territories. Indeed, they went further in their demands. The North, William L. Yancey of Alabama insisted, must accept the proposition that slavery was not merely tolerable but right. When southern proposals were voted down, most of the delegates from the Deep South walked out and the convention adjourned without naming a candidate.

In June the Democrats reconvened at Baltimore. Again they failed to reach agreement. The two wings then met separately, the Northerners nominating Douglas, the Southerners John C. Breckenridge of Kentucky, Buchanan's vice president. On the question of slavery in the territories, the Northerners promised to "abide by the decision of the Supreme Court," which meant, in effect, that they stood for Douglas's Freeport Doctrine. The Southerners announced their belief that neither Congress nor any territorial government could prevent citizens from settling "with their property" in any territory.

Meanwhile, the Republicans, who met in Chicago in mid-May, had drafted a platform attractive to all classes and all sections of the northern and western states.

Presidential Election, 1860 This map shows clearly the North-South electoral divide, and the fracturing of the Democratic party.

For manufacturers they proposed a high tariff, for farmers a homestead law providing free land for settlers. Internal improvements "of a National character," notably a railroad to the Pacific, should receive federal aid. No restrictions should be placed on immigration. As to slavery in the territories, the Republicans did not equivocate: "The normal condition of all the territory of the United States is that of freedom." Neither Congress nor a local legislature could "give legal existence to Slavery in any Territory."

In choosing a presidential candidate the Republicans displayed equally shrewd political judgment. Senator Seward was the front-runner, but he had taken too extreme a stand and appeared unlikely to carry the crucial states of Pennsylvania, Indiana, and Illinois. He led on the first ballot but could not get a majority. Then the delegates began to look closely at Abraham Lincoln. His thoughtful and moderate views on the main issue of the times and his formidable debating skills attracted many, and so did his political personality. "Honest Abe," the "Railsplitter," a man of humble origins (born in a log cabin), self-educated, self-made, a common man but by no means an ordinary man—the combination seemed unbeatable.

On the second ballot Lincoln drew shoulder to shoulder with Seward, on the third he was within two votes of victory. Before the roll could be called again, delegates began to switch their votes, and in a landslide, soon made unanimous, Lincoln was nominated.

A few days earlier the remnants of the American and Whig parties had formed the Constitutional Union party and nominated John Bell of Tennessee for president. "It is both the part of patriotism and of duty," they resolved, "to recognize no political principle

Table 13.1   Descent into War: The 1850s

Harriet Beecher Stowe's, *Uncle Tom's Cabin*	1852	Best-selling novel fuels abolitionist sentiment and enrages Southerners.
Kansas-Nebraska Act	1854	Opens Kansas and Nebraska Territories for settlement and repeals Missouri Compromise of 1820 by allowing residents to determine whether the new states would be slave or free.
Lecompton Constitution	1857	Proslavery constitution drafted by proslavery "government" of Kansas: It is accepted by President James Buchanan but rejected by Congress.
Dred Scott Case	1857	Supreme Court rules that Congress lacked the authority to ban slavery from the territories; slavery is legal everywhere unless states prohibit it.
John Brown's Raid at Harpers Ferry, Virginia	1859	Brown attacks federal arsenal in order to initiate slave rebellion; Brown's execution angers abolitionists; the martyrdom of Brown infuriates Southerners.
Election of 1860	1860	The Democrats, divided over slavery, disintegrate. Lincoln wins presidency but receives no electoral votes from South.

other than the Constitution of the country, the union of the states, and the enforcement of the laws." Ostrichlike, the Constitutional Unionists ignored the conflicts rending the nation. Only in the border states, where the consequences of disunion were sure to be most tragic, did they have any following.

With four candidates in the field, no one could win a popular majority, but it soon became clear that Lincoln was going to be elected. Breckenridge had most of the slave states in his pocket and Bell would run strong in the border regions, but the populous northern and western states had a majority of the electoral votes, and there the choice lay between the Republicans and the Douglas Democrats. In such a contest the Republicans, with their attractive economic program and their strong stand against slavery in the territories, were sure to come out on top.

Lincoln avoided campaigning and made no public statements. Douglas, recognizing the certainty of Lincoln's victory, accepted his fate and for the first time in his career rose above ambition. "We must try to save the Union," he said. "I will go South." In the heart of the Cotton Kingdom, he appealed to the voters to stand by the Union regardless of who was elected. He was the only candidate to do so; the others refused to remind the people that their election might result in secession and civil war.

When the votes were counted, Lincoln had 1.866 million, almost a million fewer than the combined total of his three opponents, but he swept the North and West, which gave him 180 electoral votes and the presidency. Douglas received 1.383 million votes, so distributed that he carried only Missouri and part of New Jersey. Breckenridge, with 848,000 popular votes, won most of the South; Bell, with 593,000, carried Virginia,

Tennessee, and Kentucky. Lincoln was thus a minority president, but his title to the office was unquestionable. Even if his opponents could have combined their popular votes in each state, Lincoln would have won.

The Secession Crisis

Only days after Lincoln's victory, the South Carolina legislature ordered an election of delegates to a convention to decide the state's future course. On December 20 the convention voted unanimously to secede, basing its action on the logic of Calhoun. "The State of South Carolina has resumed her position among the nations of the world," the delegates announced. By February 1, 1861, the six other states of the lower South had followed suit. A week later, at Montgomery, Alabama, a provisional government of the Confederate States of America was established. Virginia, Tennessee, North Carolina, and Arkansas did not leave the Union but announced that if the federal government attempted to use force against the Confederacy, they too would secede.

•••—Read the Document
South Carolina Declaration of the Causes of Secession at myhistorylab.com

Why were white Southerners willing to wreck the Union their forebears had put together with so much love and labor? No simple explanation is possible. Lincoln had assured them that he would respect slavery where it existed. The Democrats had retained control of Congress in the election; the Supreme Court was firmly in their hands as well. If the North did try to destroy slavery, secession would perhaps be a logical tactic, but why not wait until the threat materialized? To leave the Union meant abandoning the very objectives for which the South had been contending for over a decade: a share of the federal territories and an enforceable fugitive slave law.

One reason why the South rejected this line of thinking was the tremendous economic energy generated in the North, which seemed to threaten the South's independence.

Secession, white Southerners argued, would "liberate" the South and produce the kind of balanced economy that was proving so successful in the North. Moreover, the mere possibility of emancipation was a powerful force for secession. "We must either submit to degradation, and to the loss of property worth four billions," the Mississippi convention declared, "or we must secede."

Although states' rights provided the rationale for leaving the Union, and Southerners expounded the strict constructionist interpretation of the Constitution with great ingenuity, the economic and emotional factors were far more basic. The lower South decided to go ahead with secession regardless of the cost. "Let the consequences be what they may," an Atlanta newspaper proclaimed. "Whether the Potomac is crimsoned in human gore, and Pennsylvania Avenue is paved ten fathoms in depth with mangled bodies . . . the South will never submit."

Not every slave owner could contemplate secession with such bloodthirsty equanimity. Some believed that the risks of war and slave insurrection were too great. Others retained a profound loyalty to the United States. Many accepted secession only after the deepest examination of conscience. Lieutenant Colonel Robert E. Lee of Virginia was typical of thousands. "I see only that a fearful calamity is upon us," he wrote during the secession crisis. "There is no sacrifice I am not ready to

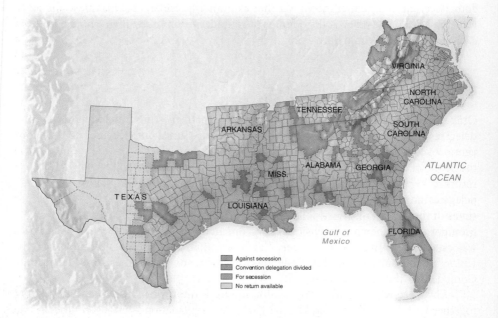

Secession of the South, 1860–1861 A comparison of this map with the one on page 326 shows the minimal support for secession in the nonslave mountain areas of the Appalachians. The strong antisecession sentiment in the mountainous areas of Virginia eventually led several counties there to break from Virginia in 1863 and form the new state of West Virginia.

make for the preservation of the Union save that of honour. If a disruption takes place, I shall go back in sorrow to my people & share the misery of my native state."

In the North there was a foolish but understandable reluctance to believe that the South really intended to break away. President-elect Lincoln was inclined to write off secession as a bluff designed to win concessions he was determined not to make. He also showed lamentable political caution in refusing to announce his plans or to cooperate with the outgoing Democratic administration before his inauguration.

In the South there was an equally unrealistic expectation that the North would not resist secession forcibly. The "Yankees" were timid materialists who would neither bear the cost nor risk their lives to prevent secession. President Buchanan recognized the seriousness of the situation but professed himself powerless. Secession, he said, was illegal, but the federal government had no legal way to prevent it. He urged making concessions to the South yet lacked the forcefulness to take the situation in hand.

Of course he faced unprecedented difficulties. His term was about to run out—Lincoln's inauguration day was March 4—and since he could not commit to his successor, his influence was minuscule. Yet a bolder president would have denounced secession in uncompromising terms. Instead Buchanan vacillated between compromise and aimless drift.

Appeasers, well-meaning believers in compromise, and those prepared to fight to preserve the Union were alike—incapable of effective action. A group of moderates headed by Henry Clay's disciple, Senator John J. Crittenden of Kentucky, proposed a constitutional amendment in which slavery would be "recognized as existing" in all territories south of latitude 36°30'. Crittenden had a special reason for seeking to avoid a conflict. His oldest son was about to become a southern general, another son a northern general. His amendment also promised that no future amendment would tamper with the institution in the slave states and offered other guarantees to the South. But Lincoln refused to consider any arrangement that would open new territory to slavery. "On the territorial question," he wrote, "I am inflexible." The **Crittenden Compromise** got nowhere.

The new southern Confederacy set vigorously to work drafting a constitution, choosing Jefferson Davis as provisional president, seizing arsenals and other federal property within its boundaries, and preparing to dispatch diplomatic representatives to enlist the support of foreign powers. Buchanan bumbled helplessly in Washington. And out in Illinois, Abraham Lincoln juggled Cabinet posts and grew a beard.

Watch the Video
What Caused the Civil War? at **myhistorylab**.com

Milestones

1850	Compromise of 1850 preserves Union; United States and Great Britain sign Clayton-Bulwer Treaty on interoceanic canal	**1856**	John Brown and followers murder five proslavery men in Pottawatomie Massacre
1851– 1860	Northerners resist enforcement of Fugitive Slave Act		South Carolina's Preston Brooks canes Senator Charles Sumner of Massachusetts on Senate floor
1852	Harriet Beecher Stowe publishes *Uncle Tom's Cabin*, a novel depicting slavery		James Buchanan is elected president
		1857	U.S. Supreme Court issues decision in Dred Scott case, declaring slaves are not citizens
	Franklin Pierce is elected president		
1854	United States disavows secret Ostend Manifesto on Cuba		Panic of 1857 collapses economy
	Kansas-Nebraska Act repeals Missouri Compromise	**1858**	Abraham Lincoln loses Senate race to Stephen Douglas after Lincoln-Douglas Debates, but wins national attention
	Commodore Matthew Perry forces Japan to open its ports to U.S. trade	**1859**	John Brown raids Harpers Ferry, Virginia, arsenal
	Senate ratifies Gadsden Purchase of Mexican territory	**1860**	Abraham Lincoln is elected president
			South Carolina secedes from Union
1855	William Walker seizes power in Nicaragua	**1861**	Seven southern states establish Confederate States of America
1856– 1858	Proslavery forces oppose Free Soilers in "Bleeding Kansas" Territory		Lincoln rejects Crittenden Compromise, last peaceful attempt to save Union

✓●─Study and **Review** at www.myhistorylab.com

Review Questions

1. The introduction to this chapter claims that Americans in the 1850s paid close attention to the issues that culminated in the election of Lincoln and the secession of the South. If political agitation can precipitate such anger and even war, is it always a good thing? Can there be such a thing as too much democracy—too much "popular sovereignty"? Should leaders refrain from raising questions that will elicit passionate responses?

2. What events during the 1850s reduced the prospects of finding a political compromise between North and South?

3. Were the economic divisions—free vs. slave labor—more consequential than the moral ones—freedom vs. slavery?

4. The 1858 Lincoln-Douglas debate largely turned on Lincoln's assertion that the United States could not endure half-slave and half-free. But for over seventy years, Douglas replied, the United States under the Constitution had done just that; compromise remained a possibility. Who was right?

Key Terms

Crittenden
   Compromise *373*
Dred Scott
   decision *360*
Kansas-Nebraska
   Act *354*

Know-Nothing
   party *355*
Lecompton
   constitution *362*
Ostend Manifesto *351*
Republican party *356*

underground
   railroad *348*
Young America
   movement *351*

The War to Save the Union

14

Are you a Northerner or a Southerner?

ON FEBRUARY 22, 2006, SUNNI MUSLIMS OVERWHELMED THE CARETAKER and staff of the Mosque of the Golden Dome in Samarra, sixty miles north of Baghdad, Iraq. The mosque was among the most revered Shiite shrines in the Middle East, visited by more than a million Muslims each year. Sunni and Shiite Muslims differed in their interpretation of Islam. Sunni insurgents placed explosives at the base of the dome and left the building. Moments later, an explosion collapsed the dome, shattering its 72,000 golden tiles. By sunset, Shiite militiamen had destroyed twenty-seven Sunni mosques and killed three imams—Islamic holy men. Over the next twelve months, the violence escalated, resulting in the deaths of over 34,000 Iraqi civilians. "The gates of hell are open in Iraq," declared Amr Moussa, head of the Arab League.

In 2009 President Barack Obama visited Iraq after a spate of bombings had destroyed another Shiite shrine and killed scores of Muslims. Obama called on Iraqis to end "this senseless violence."

But no civil war makes much sense, as Americans learned in 1861. Then, brother fought brother; men intent on destroying each other prayed to the same God. The horrors of the war eclipsed any good that might attend victory, or so it seemed.

The U.S. Civil War moved forward, impelled by its own terrible momentum. The first inconclusive battle led to others. More men were called to arms, often against their will. Farms and factories were diverted to the war effort. Lincoln emancipated some slaves to weaken the South. The strains of the war fractured the political consensus. When the guns at last fell silent, a half million men lay dead, and millions more were casualties. While touring a hospital ward after another gruesome battle, President Lincoln despaired at the horror of it all. "If there is a place worse than hell, I am in it."

Lincoln's Cabinet

The nomination of Lincoln had succeeded brilliantly for the Republicans, but was his election a good thing for the country? Honest Abe was a clever politician who had spoken well about the central issue of the times, but would he act decisively in this crisis? People remembered uneasily that he had never held executive office, that his congressional career had been short and undistinguished. When he finally uprooted himself from Springfield in February 1861, his occasional speeches en route to Washington were vague, almost flippant. Some people thought it downright cowardly that he let himself be spirited in the dead of night through Baltimore, where feeling against him ran high.

Everyone waited tensely to see whether Lincoln would oppose secession with force, but Lincoln seemed concerned only with organizing his Cabinet. The final slate was not ready until the morning of inauguration day, March 4, and shrewd observers found it alarming, for the new president had chosen to construct a "balanced" Cabinet representing a wide range of opinion instead of putting together a group of harmonious advisers who could help him face the crisis.

William H. Seward, the secretary of state, was the ablest and best known of the appointees. Despite his reputation for radicalism, Seward hoped to conciliate the South and was thus in bad odor with the radical wing of the Republican party. In time Seward proved himself Lincoln's strong right arm, but at the start he underestimated the president and expected to dominate him. Senator Salmon P. Chase, an antislavery leader from Ohio whom Lincoln named secretary of the treasury, represented the radicals. Chase was humorless and vain but able; he detested Seward. Many of the president's other selections worried thoughtful people.

Lincoln's inaugural address was conciliatory but firm. Southern institutions were in no danger from his administration. Secession, however, was illegal, and the Union

●◀●─[Read the **Document**

Lincoln, *First Inaugural Address* at **myhistorylab.com**

"perpetual." "A husband and wife may be divorced," Lincoln said, "but the different parts of our country cannot." His tone was calm and warm. His concluding words catch the spirit of the inaugural perfectly:

> I am loath to close. We are not enemies, but friends. We must not be enemies. Though passion may have strained, it must not break, our bonds of affection. The mystic chords of memory, stretching from every battlefield and patriot grave to every living heart . . . will yet swell the chorus of the Union when again touched, as surely they will be, by the better angels of our nature.

Fort Sumter: The First Shot

While denying the legality of secession, Lincoln had not decided what to do next. The Confederates had seized most federal property in the Deep South. Lincoln admitted frankly that he would not attempt to reclaim this property. However, two strongholds, Fort Sumter, on an island in Charleston harbor, and Fort Pickens, at Pensacola, Florida, were still in loyal Union hands. Most Republicans did not want to surrender them without a show of resistance. To do so, one wrote, would be to convert the American eagle into a "debilitated chicken."

Yet to reinforce the forts might mean bloodshed that would make reconciliation impossible. After weeks of indecision, Lincoln took the moderate step of sending a naval expedition to supply the beleaguered Sumter garrison with food. Unwilling to permit this, the Confederates opened fire on the fort on April 12 before the supply ships arrived. After holding out for thirty-four hours, Major Robert Anderson and his men surrendered.

This lithograph by Currier and Ives gives an erroneous impression of the "battle." Major Robert Anderson, commander of Ft. Sumter, did not want to expose his men to the looping mortar shells and artillery of the Confederates, so he manned only the cannon on the lowest floor, just above the water. The top two levels of guns were seldom fired.

The attack precipitated an outburst of patriotic indignation in the North. Lincoln issued a call for 75,000 volunteers; his request prompted Virginia, North Carolina, Arkansas, and Tennessee to secede. After years of crises and compromises, the nation chose to settle the great quarrel between the sections by force of arms.

Lincoln took the position that secession was a rejection of democracy. If the South could refuse to abide by the result of an election in which it had freely participated, then everything that monarchists and other conservatives had said about the instability of republican governments would be proved true. "The central idea of secession is the essence of anarchy," he said. The United States must "demonstrate to the world" that "when ballots have been fairly and constitutionally decided, there can be no successful appeal except to ballots themselves, at succeeding elections."

This was the proper ground to take. A war against slavery would not have been supported by a majority of Northerners. Slavery was the root cause of secession but not of the North's determination to resist secession, which resulted from the people's commitment to the Union. Although abolition was to be one of the major results of the Civil War, the war was fought for nationalistic reasons, not to destroy slavery. Lincoln made this plain when he wrote in response to an editorial by Horace Greeley urging immediate emancipation: "I would save the Union. . . . If I could save the Union without freeing any slave, I would do it; and if I could save it by freeing all the slaves, I would do it; and if I could do it by freeing some and leaving others alone, I would also do that." He added, however, "I intend no modification of my oft-expressed personal wish that all men, everywhere, could be free."

The Blue and the Gray

In any test between the United States and the Confederacy, the former possessed tremendous advantages. There were more than 20 million people in the northern states (excluding Kentucky and Missouri, where opinion was divided) but only 9 million in the South, including 3.5 million slaves whom the whites hesitated to trust with arms. The North's economic capacity to wage war was even more preponderant. It was manufacturing nine times as much as the Confederacy (including 97 percent of the nation's firearms) and had a far larger and more efficient railroad system than the South. Northern control of the merchant marine and the navy made possible a blockade of the Confederacy, a particularly potent threat to a region so dependent on foreign markets.

The Confederates discounted these advantages. Many doubted that public opinion in the North would sustain Lincoln if he attempted to meet secession with force. Northern manufacturers needed southern markets, and merchants depended heavily on southern business. Many western farmers still sent their produce down the Mississippi. War would threaten the prosperity of all these groups, Southerners maintained. Should the North try to cut Europe off from southern cotton, the European powers, particularly Great Britain, would descend on the land in their might, force open southern ports, and provide the Confederacy with the means of defending itself forever. Moreover, the South provided nearly three-fourths of the world's cotton, essential for most textile mills. "You do not dare to make war on cotton," Senator Hammond of South Carolina had taunted his northern colleagues in 1858. "No power on earth dares to make war upon it. Cotton is king."

The Confederacy also counted on certain military advantages. The new nation need only hold what it had; it could fight a defensive war, less costly in men and material and of great importance in maintaining morale and winning outside sympathy. Southerners would be defending not only their social institutions but also their homes and families.

Luck played a part too; the Confederacy quickly found a great commander, while many of the northern generals in the early stages of the war proved either bungling or indecisive. In battle after battle

Why did these young volunteers of the First Virginia Militia join the Confederate army in 1861? "It is better to spend our all in defending our country than to be subjugated and have it taken away from us," one explained, a sentiment that appeared often in the letters of Confederate soldiers. Soldiers on both sides believed that their cause was righteous.

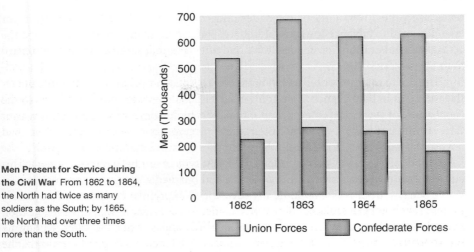

Men Present for Service during the Civil War From 1862 to 1864, the North had twice as many soldiers as the South; by 1865, the North had over three times more than the South.

Union armies were defeated by forces of equal or smaller size. There was little to distinguish the enlisted men of the two sides. Both, conscious of their forefathers of 1776, fought for liberty, though they interpreted the concept in different ways.

Both sides faced massive difficulties in organizing for a war long feared but never properly anticipated. After southern defections, the regular Union army consisted of only 13,000 officers and enlisted men, far too few to absorb the 186,000 who had joined the colors by early summer, much less the additional 450,000 who had volunteered by the end of the year. Recruiting was left to the states, each being assigned a quota; there was little central organization. Unlike later conflicts in which men from all parts of the country were mixed in each regiment, Civil War units were recruited locally. Few knew even the rudiments of soldiering. The hastily composed high command, headed by the elderly Winfield Scott, debated grand strategy endlessly while regimental commanders lacked decent maps of Virginia.

> ●●●—Read the Document
>
> Davis, *Address to the Provisional Congress* at **myhistorylab.com**

Lincoln's strength lay in his ability to think problems through. When he did, he acted unflinchingly. Anything but a tyrant by nature, he boldly exceeded the conventional limits of presidential power in the emergency: expanding the army without congressional authorization, suspending the writ of habeas corpus (which entitles those seized by the government to go before a court to see if their arrest were warranted), even emancipating the slaves when he thought military necessity demanded that action. Yet he also displayed remarkable patience and depth of character: He would willingly accept snubs and insults in order to advance the cause.

Gradually Lincoln's stock rose—first with men like Seward, who saw him close up and experienced both his steel and his gentleness, and then with the people at large, who sensed his compassion, his humility, and his wisdom. He was only fifty-two when he became president, and already people were calling him Old Abe. Before long they would call him Father Abraham.

The Confederacy faced far greater problems than the North, for it had to create an entire administration under pressure of war with the additional handicap of the states' rights philosophy to which it was committed. The Confederate constitution explicitly recognized the sovereignty of the states and contained no broad authorization for laws designed to advance the general welfare. State governments repeatedly defied the central administration, located at Richmond after Virginia seceded, even with regard to military affairs.

The call to arms produced a turnout in the Confederacy perhaps even more impressive than that in the North; by July 1861 about 112,000 men were under arms. As in the North, men of every type enlisted, and morale was high. Some wealthy recruits brought slave servants with them to care for their needs in camp, cavalrymen supplied their own horses, and many men arrived with their own shotguns and hunting rifles.

President Jefferson Davis represented the best type of southern planter, noted for his humane treatment of his slaves. In politics he had pursued a somewhat unusual course. While senator from Mississippi, he opposed the Compromise of 1850 and became a leader of the southern radicals. After Pierce made him secretary of war, however, he took a more nationalistic position, one close to that of Douglas. After the 1860 election he supported secession only reluctantly, preferring to give Lincoln a chance to prove that he meant the South no harm.

Davis was courageous, industrious, and intelligent, but he was too reserved and opinionated to make either a good politician or a popular leader. As president he devoted too much time to details, failed to delegate authority, and (unlike Lincoln) was impatient with garrulous and dull-witted people, types political leaders frequently have to deal with. Being a graduate of West Point, he fancied himself a military expert, but he was a mediocre military thinker. Unlike Lincoln, he quarreled frequently with his subordinates, held grudges, and allowed personal feelings to distort his judgment.

The Test of Battle: Bull Run

"Forward to Richmond!" "On to Washington!" Such shouts propelled the armies into battle long before either was properly trained. On July 21 at Manassas Junction, Virginia, some

👁️ See the **Map**

The Civil War, Part I: 1861–1862
at myhistorylab.com

twenty miles below Washington, on a branch of the Potomac called Bull Run, 30,000 Union soldiers under General Irvin McDowell attacked a roughly equal force of Confederates commanded by the "Napoleon of the South," Pierre G. T. Beauregard. McDowell swept back the Confederate left flank. Victory seemed sure. Then a Virginia brigade under Thomas J. Jackson rushed to the field by rail from the Shenandoah Valley in the nick of time and checked the advance.

The Southerners then counterattacked, driving the Union soldiers back. As often happens with green troops, retreat quickly turned to rout. McDowell's men fled toward the defenses of Washington, abandoning their weapons, stumbling through lines of supply wagons, trampling foolish sightseers who had come out to watch the battle. Panic engulfed Washington. Richmond exulted. Both sides expected the northern capital to fall within hours.

The inexperienced southern troops were too disorganized to follow up their victory. Casualties on both sides were light, and the battle had little direct effect on anything but morale. Southern confidence soared, while the North began to realize how immense the task of subduing the Confederacy would be.

Eighteen-year-olds were the largest age group in the first year of the war in both armies. Soldiers were universally called "the boys"; and officers, even in their thirties, were called "old men." One of the most popular war songs was "Just Before the Battle, Mother."

After Bull Run, Lincoln devised a broader, more systematic strategy for winning the war. The navy would clamp a tight blockade on all southern ports. In the West Union generals made plans to gain control of the Mississippi. (This was part of General Scott's **Anaconda Plan**, designed to starve the South into submission.) More important, a new army would be mustered at Washington to invade Virginia. Congress promptly authorized the enlistment of 500,000 three-year volunteers. To lead this army and—after General Scott's retirement in November—to command the Union forces, Lincoln appointed a thirty-four-year-old major general, George B. McClellan.

McClellan was the North's first military hero. After graduating from West Point second in his class in 1846, he had served in the Mexican War. During the Crimean War he spent a year in the field, talking with British officers and studying fortifications. He was a talented administrator and organizer. He liked to concoct bold plans and dreamed of striking swiftly at the heart of the Confederacy to capture Richmond, Nashville, even New Orleans. Yet he was sensible enough to insist on massive logistic support, thorough training for the troops, iron discipline, and meticulous staff work before making a move.

Paying for the War

After Bull Run, this policy was exactly right. By the fall of 1861 a real army was taking shape along the Potomac: disciplined, confident, adequately supplied. Northern shops and factories were producing guns, ammunition, wagons, uniforms, shoes, and the countless other supplies needed to fight a great war. Most manufacturers operated on a small scale, but with the armed forces soon wearing out 3 million pairs of shoes and 1.5 million uniforms a year and with men leaving their jobs by the hundreds of thousands to fight, the tendency of industry to mechanize and to increase the size of the average manufacturing unit became ever more pronounced.

At the beginning of the war Secretary of the Treasury Salmon P. Chase underestimated how much it would cost. He learned quickly. In August 1861 Congress passed an income tax law and assessed a direct tax on the states. Loans amounting to $140 million were authorized. As the war dragged on and expenses mounted, new excise taxes on every imaginable product and service were passed, and still further borrowing was necessary. In 1863 the banking system was overhauled.

During the war the federal government borrowed a total of $2.2 billion and collected $667 million in taxes, slightly over 20 percent of its total expenditures. These unprecedented large sums proved inadequate. Some debts were repaid by printing paper money unredeemable in coin. About $431 million in **greenbacks**—the term distinguished this fiat money from the redeemable yellowback bills—were issued during the conflict. Public confidence in all paper money vacillated with each change in the fortunes of the Union armies, but by the end of the war the cost of living in the North had doubled.

Politics as Usual

Partisan politics was altered by the war but not suspended. The secession of the southern states left the Republicans with large majorities in both houses of Congress. Most Democrats supported measures necessary for the conduct of the war but objected to the way the Lincoln administration was conducting it. The sharpest conflicts came when slavery and race relations were under discussion. The Democrats adopted a conservative stance, as reflected in the slogan "The Constitution as it is; the Union as it was; the Negroes where they are." The Republicans divided into Moderate and Radical wings. Political divisions on economic issues such as tariffs and land policy tended to cut across party lines and, so far as the Republicans were concerned, to bear little relation to slavery and race. As the war progressed, the Radical faction became increasingly influential.

In 1861 the most prominent Radical senator was Charles Sumner, finally recovered from his caning by Preston Brooks and brimful of hatred for slaveholders. In the House, Thaddeus Stevens of Pennsylvania was the rising power. Sumner and Stevens were uncompromising on all questions relating to slaves; they insisted not merely on abolition but on granting full political and civil rights to blacks. Moderate Republicans objected vehemently to treating blacks as equals and opposed making abolition a war aim, and even many of the so-called **Radical Republicans** disagreed with Sumner and Stevens on race relations. Senator Benjamin Wade of Ohio, for example, was a lifelong opponent of slavery, yet he disliked blacks (whom he called by a racial slur). But prejudice, he maintained, gave no one the right "to do injustice to anybody"; he insisted that blacks were at least as intelligent as whites and were entitled not merely to freedom but to full political equality.

At the other end of the political spectrum stood the so-called Peace Democrats. These **Copperheads** (apparently a reference to a time when some hard-money Democrats wore copper pennies around their necks) opposed all measures in support of the war. They hoped to win control of Congress and force a negotiated peace. Few were actually disloyal, but their activities at a time when thousands of men were risking their lives in battle infuriated many Northerners.

The most notorious domestic foe of the administration was the Peace Democrat Congressman Clement L. Vallandigham of Ohio, who was sent to prison by a military court. There were two rebellions in progress, Vallandigham claimed, "the Secessionist Rebellion" and "the Abolitionist Rebellion." "I am against both," he added. But Lincoln ordered him released and banished to the Confederacy. Once at liberty Vallandigham moved to Canada, from which refuge he ran unsuccessfully for governor of Ohio.

"Perish offices," he once said, "perish life itself, but do the thing that is right." In 1864 he returned to Ohio. Although he campaigned against Lincoln in the presidential election, he was not arrested. Lincoln was no dictator.

Behind Confederate Lines

The South also revised its strategy after Bull Run. Although it might have been wiser to risk everything on a bold invasion of the North, President Davis relied primarily on a strong defense to wear down the Union's will to fight. In 1862 the Confederate Congress passed a conscription act that permitted the hiring of substitutes and exempted many classes of people (including college professors, druggists, and mail carriers) whose work could hardly have been deemed essential. A provision deferring one slave owner or overseer for every plantation of twenty or more slaves led many to grumble about "a rich man's war and a poor man's fight."

Finance was the Confederacy's most vexing problem. The blockade made it impossible to raise much money through tariffs. The Confederate Congress passed an income tax together with many excise taxes but all told they covered only 2 percent of its needs by taxation. The most effective levy was a tax in kind, amounting to one-tenth of each farmer's production. The South borrowed as much as it could (S712 million), even mortgaging cotton undeliverable because of the blockade, in order to gain European credits. But it relied mainly on printing paper currency; over $1.5 billion poured from the presses during the war. Considering the amount issued, this currency held its value well until late in the war, when the military fortunes of the Confederacy began to decline. Then the bottom fell out, and by early 1865 the Confederate dollar was worth less than 2 cents in gold.

Outfitting the army strained southern resources to the limit. Large supplies of small arms (some 600,000 weapons during the entire war) came from Europe through the blockade, along with other valuable military supplies. As the blockade became more efficient, however, it became increasingly difficult to obtain European goods. The Confederates did manage to build a number of munitions plants, and they captured huge amounts of northern arms. No battle was lost because of a lack of guns or other military equipment, although shortages of shoes and uniforms handicapped the Confederate forces on some occasions.

Foreign policy loomed large in Confederate thinking, for the "cotton is king" theory presupposed that the great powers would break any northern blockade to get cotton for their textile mills. Southern expectations were not realized, however. The European nations would have been delighted to see the United States broken up, but none was prepared to support the Confederacy directly. The attitude of Great Britain was decisive.

The cutting off of cotton did not hit the British as hard as the South had hoped. They had a large supply on hand when the war broke out, and when that was exhausted, alternative sources in India and Egypt took up part of the slack. Furthermore, British crop failures necessitated the importation of large amounts of northern wheat, providing a powerful reason for not antagonizing the United States. The fact that most ordinary people in Great Britain favored the North also influenced British policy.

War in the West: Shiloh

After Bull Run no battles were fought until early 1862. Then, while McClellan continued his deliberate preparations to attack Richmond, important fighting occurred far to the west. Most of the Plains Indians sided with the Confederacy, principally because of their resentment of the federal government's policies toward them. White settlers from Colorado to California were mostly Unionists. In March 1862 a Texas army advancing beyond Santa Fe clashed with a Union force in the Battle of Glorieta Pass. The battle was indecisive, but a Union unit destroyed the Texans' supply train. The Texans felt compelled to retreat to the Rio Grande, thus ending the Confederate threat to the Far West.

Meanwhile, far larger Union forces, led by a shabby, cigar-smoking West Pointer named Ulysses S. Grant, had invaded Tennessee from a base at Cairo, Illinois. Making effective use of armored gunboats, Grant captured Fort Henry and Fort Donelson, strongholds on the Tennessee and Cumberland rivers, taking 14,000 prisoners. Next he marched toward Corinth, Mississippi, an important railroad junction.

To check Grant's advance, the Confederates massed 40,000 men under Albert Sidney Johnston. On April 6, while Grant slowly concentrated his forces, Johnston struck suddenly at Shiloh, twenty miles north of Corinth. Some Union soldiers were caught half-dressed, others in the midst of brewing their morning coffee. A few died in their blankets. "We were more than surprised," one Illinois officer later admitted. "We were astonished." However, Grant's men stood their ground. At the end of a day of ghastly carnage the Confederates held the advantage, but fresh Union troops poured in during the night, and on the second day of battle the tide turned. The Confederates fell back toward Corinth, exhausted and demoralized.

Grant, shaken by the unexpected attack and appalled by his losses, allowed the enemy to escape. This cost him the fine reputation he had won in capturing Fort Henry and Fort Donelson. He was relieved of his command. Although Corinth eventually fell and New Orleans was captured by a naval force under the command of Captain David Farragut, Vicksburg, key to control of the Mississippi, remained firmly in Confederate hands. A great opportunity had been lost.

Shiloh had other results. The staggering casualties shook the confidence of both belligerents. More Americans fell there in two days than in all the battles of the Revolution, the War of 1812, and the Mexican War combined. Union losses exceeded 13,000 out of 63,000 engaged; the Confederates lost 10,699, including General Johnston. Technology in the shape of more accurate guns that could be fired far more rapidly than the muskets of earlier times and more powerful artillery were responsible for the carnage. Gradually the generals began to reconsider their tactics and to experiment with field fortifications and other defensive measures. And the people, North and South, stopped thinking of the war as a romantic test of courage and military guile.

Battles in the West The Anaconda Plan called for the North to gain control of the Mississippi River. To that end, in the spring of 1862 Grant seized western Kentucky and Tennessee and won a major battle at Shiloh, just north of Corinth. Farragut, attacking by sea from the Gulf of Mexico, moved up the mouth of the Mississippi, seizing New Orleans and Baton Rouge. But the South retained Vicksburg: The Confederacy had not been sliced in two.

McClellan: The Reluctant Warrior

In Virginia, General McClellan, after unaccountable delays, was finally moving against Richmond. Instead of trying to advance across the difficult terrain of northern Virginia, he transported his army by water to the tip of the peninsula formed by the York and James rivers in order to attack Richmond from the southeast. After the famous battle on March 9, 1862, between the USS *Monitor* and the Confederate *Merrimack*, the first fight in history between armored warships, control of these waters was securely in northern hands.

While McClellan's plan alarmed many congressmen because it seemed to leave Washington relatively unprotected, it simplified the problem of keeping the army supplied in hostile country. But McClellan now displayed the weaknesses that eventually ruined his career. His problems were both intellectual and psychological. Basically he approached tactical questions in the manner of a typical eighteenth-century general. He considered war a kind of gentlemanly contest in which maneuver, guile, and position determined victory. He believed it more important to capture Richmond than to destroy the army protecting it. With their capital in northern hands, surely the Southerners would acknowledge defeat and agree to return to the Union. The idea of crushing the South seemed to him wrongheaded and uncivilized.

McClellan began the Peninsular campaign in mid-March. Proceeding deliberately, he floated an army of 112,000 men down the Potomac. Landing near Yorktown, he prepared to besiege the Confederates, much as Washington had done against Cornwallis in 1781. But in early May the Confederate army slipped away and McClellan pursued them nearly to Richmond. A swift thrust might have ended the war quickly, but McClellan delayed, despite the fact that he had 80,000 men in striking position and large reserves. As he pushed forward slowly, the Confederates caught part of his force separated from the main body by the rain-swollen Chickahominy River and attacked. The Battle of Seven Pines was indecisive yet resulted in more than 10,000 casualties.

At Seven Pines, General Joseph E. Johnston, the Confederate commander, was severely wounded; leadership of the Army of Northern Virginia then passed to Robert E. Lee. Although a reluctant supporter of secession, Lee was a superb soldier. During the Mexican War his gallantry under fire inspired General Scott to call him the bravest man in the army. He also had displayed an almost instinctive mastery of tactics. Admiral Raphael Semmes, who accompanied Scott's army on the march to Mexico City, recalled in 1851 that Lee "seemed to receive impressions intuitively, which it cost other men much labor to acquire."

Lee was McClellan's antithesis. McClellan seemed almost deliberately to avoid understanding his foes, acting as though every southern general was a genius. Lee, a master psychologist on the battlefield, took the measure of each Union general and devised his tactics accordingly. Where McClellan was complex, egotistical, perhaps even unbalanced, Lee was courtly, tactful, and entirely without McClellan's vainglorious belief that he was a man of destiny. Yet on the battlefield Lee's boldness skirted the edge of foolhardiness.

To relieve the pressure on Richmond, Lee sent General "Stonewall" Jackson, soon to be his most trusted lieutenant, on a diversionary raid in the Shenandoah Valley, west of Richmond and Washington. Jackson struck swiftly at scattered Union forces in the region, winning a number of battles and capturing vast stores of equipment. Lincoln dispatched 20,000 reserves to the Shenandoah to check him—to the dismay of McClellan, who wanted the troops to attack Richmond from the north. But after Seven Pines, Lee ordered Jackson back to Richmond. While Union armies streamed toward the valley, Jackson slipped stealthily between them. On June 25 he reached Ashland, directly north of the Confederate capital.

Before that date McClellan had possessed clear numerical superiority yet had only inched ahead; now the advantage lay with Lee, and the very next day he attacked. From June 25 to July 1 (the Seven Days' Battles) Lee repeatedly struck different parts of McClellan's lines. The full weight of his force never hit the northern army at any one time. Nevertheless, the shock was formidable. McClellan, who excelled in defense, fell back, his lines intact, exacting a fearful toll. Under difficult conditions he managed to transfer his troops to a new base on the James River at Harrison's Landing, where the guns of the navy could shield his position. Again the loss of life was terrible: Northern casualties totaled 15,800, and those of the South nearly 20,000 in the Seven Days' Battle for Richmond.

●●●[**Read** the **Document**

McClellan to Abraham Lincoln (July 7, 1862) at myhistorylab.com

War in the East, 1861–1862 In the spring of 1862, McClellan seized Yorktown on the Virginia Peninsula (Peninsular Campaign). But he failed to take Richmond and his army was recalled to the Potomac. That fall, McClellan halted Lee's northern advance into Maryland at Antietam. By the end of 1862, the situation in the East was much as it had been a year earlier, except for the nearly 100,000 casualties.

Lee Counterattacks: Antietam

McClellan was still within striking distance of Richmond, in an impregnable position with secure supply lines and 86,000 soldiers ready to resume battle. Lee had absorbed heavy losses without winning any significant advantage. Yet Lincoln was exasperated with McClellan for having surrendered the initiative and, after much deliberation, reduced his authority by placing him under General Henry W. Halleck. Halleck called off the Peninsular campaign and ordered McClellan to move his army from the James to the Potomac, near Washington. He was to join General John Pope, who was gathering a new army between Washington and Richmond.

If McClellan had persisted and captured Richmond, the war might have ended and the Union been restored without the abolition of slavery, since at that point the North was still fighting for union, not for freedom for the slaves. By prolonging the war, Lee inadvertently enabled it to destroy slavery along with the Confederacy, though no one at the time looked at the matter this way.

For the president to have lost confidence in McClellan was understandable. Nevertheless, to allow Halleck to pull back the troops was a bad mistake. When they withdrew, Lee seized the initiative. With typical decisiveness and daring, he marched rapidly north. Late in August his Confederates drove General Pope's confused troops from the same ground, Bull Run, where the first major engagement of the war had been fought.

While McClellan was regrouping the shaken Union Army, Lee once again took the offensive. He realized that no number of individual southern triumphs could destroy the enormous material advantages of the North. Unless some dramatic blow, delivered on northern soil, persuaded the people of the United States that military victory was impossible, the South would surely be crushed in the long run. Lee therefore marched rapidly northwest around the defenses of Washington.

Acting with even more than his usual boldness, Lee divided his army of 60,000 into a number of units. One, under Jackson, descended on weakly defended Harpers Ferry, capturing more than 11,000 prisoners. Another pressed as far north as Hagerstown, Maryland, nearly to the Pennsylvania line. McClellan pursued with his usual deliberation until a captured dispatch revealed to him Lee's dispositions. Then he moved a bit more swiftly, forcing Lee to stand and fight on September 17 at Sharpsburg, Maryland, between the Potomac and Antietam Creek. On a field that offered Lee no room to maneuver, 70,000 Union soldiers clashed with 40,000 Confederates. When darkness fell, more than 22,000 lay dead or wounded on the bloody field.

Although casualties were evenly divided and the Confederate lines remained intact, Lee's position was perilous. His men were exhausted. McClellan had not yet thrown in his reserves, and new federal units were arriving hourly. A bold northern general would have continued the fight without respite through the night. One of ordinary aggressiveness would have waited for first light and then struck with every soldier who could hold a rifle, for with the Potomac at his back, Lee could not retreat under fire without inviting disaster. McClellan, however, did nothing. For an entire day, while Lee scanned the field in futile search of some weakness in the Union lines, he held his fire. That night the Confederates slipped back across the Potomac into Virginia.

Lee's invasion had failed; his army had been badly mauled; the gravest threat to the Union in the war had been checked. But McClellan had let victory slip through his fingers. Soon Lee was back behind the defenses of Richmond, rebuilding his army.

Once again, this time finally, Lincoln dismissed McClellan from his command.

The Emancipation Proclamation

Antietam, though hardly the victory he had hoped for, gave Lincoln the excuse he needed to take a step that changed the character of the war decisively. When the fighting started, fear of alienating the border states was reason enough for not making emancipation of the slaves a war aim. Lincoln even insisted on enforcing the Fugitive Slave Act for this reason. However, pressures to act against the South's "peculiar institution" mounted steadily. Slavery had divided the nation; now it was driving Northerners to war within themselves. Love of country led them to fight to save the

Union, but fighting aroused hatreds and caused many to desire to smash the enemy. Sacrifice, pain, and grief made abolitionists of many who had no love for blacks—they sought to free the slave only to injure the master.

To make abolition an object of the war might encourage the slaves to revolt, but Lincoln disclaimed this objective. Nevertheless, the possibility existed. Already the slaves seemed to be looking to the North for freedom: Whenever Union troops invaded Confederate territory, slaves flocked into their lines.

As the war progressed, the Radical faction in Congress gradually chipped away at slavery. In April 1862 the Radicals pushed through a bill abolishing slavery in the District of Columbia; two months later another measure outlawed it in the territories; in July the Confiscation Act "freed" all slaves owned by persons in rebellion against the United States. In fighting for these measures and in urging general emancipation, some Radicals made statements harshly critical of Lincoln; but while he carefully avoided being identified with them or with any other faction, the president was never very far from their position. He resisted emancipation because he feared it would divide the country and injure the war effort, not because he personally disapproved. Indeed, he frequently cited Radical pressure as an excuse for doing what he wished to do on his own.

When Union troops pushed toward Richmond in June of 1862, these slaves crossed the Rappahannock River heading north toward freedom. But McClellan's offensive failed and the Union army withdrew to Washington. Whether these slaves made it to Maryland in time is unknown.

Lincoln would have preferred to see slavery done away with by state law, with compensation for slave owners and federal aid for former slaves willing to leave the United States. He tried repeatedly to persuade the loyal slave states to adopt this policy, but without success. By the summer of 1862 he was convinced that for military reasons and to win the support of liberal opinion in Europe, the government should make abolition a war aim. "We must free the slaves or be ourselves subdued," he explained to a member of his Cabinet. He delayed temporarily, fearing that a statement in the face of military reverses would be taken as a sign of weakness. The "victory" at Antietam Creek gave him his opportunity, and on September 22 he made public the **Emancipation Proclamation**. After January 1, 1863, it said, all slaves in areas in rebellion against the United States "shall be then, thenceforward, and forever free."

•●•⌐Read the **Document**

The Emancipation Proclamation
at **myhistorylab.com**

No single slave was freed directly by Lincoln's announcement, which did not apply to the border states or to those sections of the Confederacy, like New Orleans and Norfolk, Virginia, already controlled by federal troops. The proclamation differed in philosophy, however, from the Confiscation Act in striking at the institution, not at the property of rebels. Henceforth every Union victory would speed the destruction of slavery without regard for the attitudes of individual masters.

Southerners considered the Emancipation Proclamation an incitement to slave rebellion—as one of them put it, an "infamous attempt to . . . convert the quiet, ignorant, and dependent black son of toil into a savage incendiary and brutal murderer." Most antislavery groups thought it did not go far enough. Lincoln "is only stopping on the edge of Niagara, to pick up a few chips," one abolitionist declared. "He and they will go over together." Foreign opinion was mixed: Liberals tended to applaud, conservatives to react with alarm or contempt.

As Lincoln anticipated, the proclamation had a subtle but continuing impact in the North. Its immediate effect was to aggravate racial prejudices. Millions of whites disapproved of slavery yet abhorred the idea of equality for blacks. David Wilmot, for example, insisted that his famous proviso was designed to preserve the territories for whites rather than to weaken slavery, and as late as 1857 the people of Iowa had rejected black suffrage by a vote of 49,000 to 8,000.

The Democrats spared no effort to make political capital of these fears and prejudices even before Lincoln's Emancipation Proclamation, and they made large gains in the 1862 election, especially in the Northwest. So strong was antiblack feeling that most of the Republican politicians who defended emancipation did so with racist arguments. Far from encouraging southern blacks to move north, they claimed, the ending of slavery would lead to a mass migration of northern blacks to the South.

When the Emancipation Proclamation began actually to free slaves, the government pursued a policy of "containment," that is, of keeping the former slaves in the South. Panicky fears of an inundation of blacks subsided in the North. Nevertheless, emancipation remained a cause of social discontent. In March 1863, volunteering having fallen off, Congress passed the Conscription Act. The law applied to all men between ages twenty and forty-five, but it allowed draftees to hire substitutes and even to buy exemption for $300, provisions that were patently unfair to the poor. During the remainder of the war 46,000 men were actually drafted, whereas 118,000 hired substitutes, and another 161,000 "failed to report." Conscription represented an enormous expansion of national authority, since in effect it gave the government the power of life and death over individual citizens.

The Draft Riots

After the passage of the Conscription Act, draft riots erupted in a number of cities. By far the most serious disturbance occurred in New York City in July 1863. Many workers resented conscription in principle and were embittered by the $300 exemption fee (which represented a year's wages). The idea of being forced to risk their lives to free slaves who would then, they believed, compete with them for jobs infuriated them. On July 13 a mob attacked the office where the names of conscripts were being drawn. For four days the city was an inferno. Public buildings, shops, and private residences were put to the torch. What began as a protest against the draft became an assault on blacks and the well-to-do. It took federal troops and the temporary suspension of the draft in the city to put an end to the rioting. By the time order was restored more than a hundred people had lost their lives.

Most white Northerners did not surrender their comforting belief in black inferiority, and Lincoln was no exception. Yet Lincoln was evolving. He talked about deporting freed slaves to the tropics, but he did not send any there. And he began to receive black leaders in the White House and to allow black groups to hold meetings on the grounds.

Many other Americans were changing too. The brutality of the New York riots horrified many white citizens. Over $40,000 was swiftly raised to aid the victims, and some conservatives were so appalled by the Irish rioters that they began to talk of giving blacks the vote.

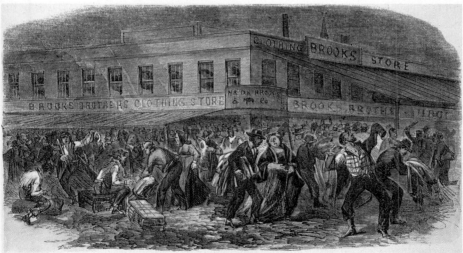

SACKING BROOKS'S CLOTHING STORE.

This lithograph of the New York draft riots, 1863, shows that although the rioters mainly targeted blacks, they also attacked homes and businesses of prominent Republicans: Brooks Brothers, Horace Greeley's newspaper, and the *Times*.

The Emancipated People

To blacks, both slave and free, the Emancipation Proclamation served as a beacon. Even if it failed immediately to liberate one slave or to lift the burdens of prejudice from one black back, it stood as a promise of future improvement. "I took the proclamation for a little more than it purported," Frederick Douglass recalled in his autobiography, "and saw in its spirit a life and power far beyond its letter." Lincoln was by modern standards a racist, but his most militant black contemporaries respected him deeply. Douglass said of him, "Lincoln was not . . . either our man or our model. In his interests, in his association, in his habits of thought and in his prejudices, he was a white man." Nevertheless, Douglass described Lincoln as "one whom I could love, honor, and trust without reserve or doubt."

As for the slaves of the South, after January 1, 1863, whenever the "Army of Freedom" approached, they laid down their plows and hoes and flocked to the Union lines in droves. Such behavior came as a shock to the owners. "[The slaves] who loved us best—as we thought—were the first to leave us," one planter mourned. Talk of slave "ingratitude" increased. Instead of referring to their workers as "servants" or "my black family," many owners began to describe them as "slaves" or "niggers."

African American Soldiers

A revolutionary shift occurred in white thinking about using black men as soldiers. Although they had fought in the Revolution and in the Battle of New Orleans during the War of 1812, a law of 1792 barred blacks from the army. During the early stages of the rebellion, despite the eagerness of thousands of free blacks to enlist, the prohibition remained in force. By 1862, however, the need for manpower was creating pressure for change. In August Secretary of War Edwin M. Stanton authorized the military government of the captured South Carolina sea islands to enlist slaves in the area. After the Emancipation Proclamation specifically authorized the enlistment of blacks, the governor of Massachusetts moved to organize a black regiment, the famous Massachusetts 54th. (See Re-Viewing the Past, *Glory*, pp. 404–405.) Swiftly thereafter, other states began to recruit black soldiers, and in May 1863 the federal government established a Bureau of Colored Troops to supervise their enlistment. By the end of the war one soldier in eight in the Union army was black.

Enlisting so many black soldiers changed the war from a struggle to save the Union to a kind of revolution. "Let the black man . . . get an eagle on his button and a musket on his shoulder," wrote Frederick Douglass, "and there is no power on earth which can deny that he has won the right to citizenship."

At first black soldiers received only $7 a month, about half what white soldiers were paid. But they soon proved themselves in battle; of the 178,000 who served in the Union army, 37,000 were killed, a rate of loss about 40 percent higher than that among white troops. The Congressional Medal of Honor was awarded to twenty-one blacks.

The higher death rates among black soldiers were partly due to the fury of Confederate soldiers. Many black captives were killed on the spot. After overrunning the garrison of Fort Pillow on the Mississippi River, the Confederates massacred several dozen black soldiers, along with their white commander. Lincoln was tempted to order reprisals, but he and his advisers realized that to do so would have been both morally wrong (two wrongs never make a right) and likely to lead to still more atrocities. "Blood can not restore blood," Lincoln said in his usual direct way.

Antietam to Gettysburg

It was well that Lincoln seized on Antietam to release his proclamation; had he waited for a more impressive victory, he would have waited nearly a year. To replace McClellan, he chose General Ambrose E. Burnside, best known to history for his magnificent side-whiskers (originally called burnsides, later, at first jokingly, sideburns). Burnside was a good corps commander, but he lacked the self-confidence essential to anyone who takes responsibility for major deci-

sions. He knew his limitations and tried to avoid high command, but patriotism and his sense of duty compelled him, when pressed, to accept leadership of the Army of the Potomac. He prepared to march on Richmond.

Unlike McClellan, Burnside was aggressive—too aggressive. He planned to ford the Rappahannock River at Fredericksburg. Supply problems and bad weather delayed him until mid-December, giving Lee time to concentrate his army in impregnable positions behind the town. Although he had more than 120,000 men against Lee's 75,000, Burnside should have called off the attack when he saw Lee's advantage; instead he ordered the troops forward. Crossing the river over pontoon bridges, his divisions occupied Fredericksburg. Then, in wave after wave, they charged the Confederate defense line while Lee's artillery riddled them from nearby Marye's Heights.

On December 14, the day following this futile assault, General Burnside, tears streaming down his cheeks, ordered the evacuation of Fredericksburg. Shortly thereafter General Joseph Hooker replaced him.

Unlike Burnside, "Fighting Joe" Hooker was ill-tempered, vindictive, and devious. He proved no better than his predecessor, but his failings were more like McClellan's than Burnside's. By the spring of 1863 he had 125,000 men ready for action. Late in April he forded the Rappahannock and quickly concentrated at Chancellorsville, about ten miles west of Fredericksburg. His army outnumbered the Confederates by more than two to one; he should have forced a battle at once. Instead he delayed, and while he did, Lee sent Jackson's corps of 28,000 men across tangled countryside to a position directly athwart Hooker's unsuspecting flank. At 6 PM on May 2, Jackson attacked.

Completely surprised, the Union right crumbled, brigade after brigade overrun before it could wheel to meet Jackson's charge. At the first sound of firing, Lee had struck along the entire front to impede Union troop movements. If the battle had begun earlier in the day, the Confederates might have won a decisive victory; as it happened, nightfall brought a lull, and the next day the Union troops rallied and held their ground. Heavy fighting continued until May 5, when Hooker abandoned the field and retreated in good order behind the Rappahannock.

Gettysburg Campaign, 1863 As Lee's main army advanced north, Meade paralleled his movements to the east, preventing Lee from attacking Baltimore or Philadelphia. When the armies converged at Gettysburg, Lee was for the first time soundly defeated. Jeb Stuart, Lee's calvary commander, had been marauding to the east and missed the decisive engagement.

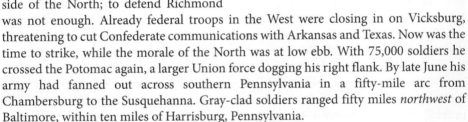

Chancellorsville cost the Confederates dearly, for their losses, in excess of 12,000, were almost as heavy as the North's and harder to replace. They also lost Stonewall Jackson, struck down by the bullets of his own men while returning from a reconnaissance. Nevertheless, the Union army had suffered another fearful blow to its morale.

Lee knew that time was still on the side of the North; to defend Richmond was not enough. Already federal troops in the West were closing in on Vicksburg, threatening to cut Confederate communications with Arkansas and Texas. Now was the time to strike, while the morale of the North was at low ebb. With 75,000 soldiers he crossed the Potomac again, a larger Union force dogging his right flank. By late June his army had fanned out across southern Pennsylvania in a fifty-mile arc from Chambersburg to the Susquehanna. Gray-clad soldiers ranged fifty miles *northwest* of Baltimore, within ten miles of Harrisburg, Pennsylvania.

As Union soldiers had been doing in Virginia, Lee's men destroyed property and commandeered food, horses, and clothing wherever they could find them. They even seized a number of blacks and sent them south to be sold as slaves. On July 1 a Confederate division looking for shoes in the town of Gettysburg clashed with two brigades of Union cavalry northwest of the town. Both sides sent out calls for reinforcements. Like iron filings drawn to a magnet, the two armies converged. The Confederates won control of the town, but the Union army, now commanded by General George G. Meade, took a strong position on Cemetery Ridge, a hook-shaped stretch of high ground just to the south. Lee's men occupied Seminary Ridge, a parallel position.

On this field the fate of the Union was probably decided. For two days the Confederates attacked Cemetery Ridge, pounding it with the heaviest artillery barrage ever seen in America and sweeping bravely up its flanks in repeated assaults. During General George E. Pickett's famous charge, a handful of his men actually reached the Union lines, but reserves drove them back. By nightfall on July 3 the Confederate army was spent, the Union lines unbroken.

The following day was the Fourth of July. The two weary forces rested on their arms. Had the Union army attacked in force, the Confederates might have been crushed, but just as McClellan had hesitated after Antietam, Meade let opportunity pass. On July 5 Lee retreated to safety. For the first time he had been clearly bested on the field of battle.

Lincoln Finds His General: Grant at Vicksburg

On Independence Day, a day after Gettysburg, federal troops won another great victory far to the west. When General Halleck was called east in July 1862, Ulysses S. Grant resumed command of the Union troops. Grant was one of the most controversial officers in the army. During the Mexican War he served well, but when he was later assigned to a lonely post in the West, he took to drink and was forced to resign his commission. Thereafter he was by turns a farmer, a real estate agent, and a clerk in a leather goods store. In 1861, approaching age forty, he seemed well into a life of frustration and mediocrity.

The war gave him a second chance. Back in service, however, his reputation as a ne'er-do-well and his unmilitary bearing worked against him, as did the heavy casualties suffered by his troops at Shiloh. Yet the fact that he knew how to manage a large army and win battles did not escape Lincoln. According to tradition, when a gossip tried to poison the president against Grant by referring to his drinking, Lincoln retorted that if he knew what brand Grant favored, he would send a barrel of it to some of his other generals.

Grant's major aim was to capture Vicksburg, a city of tremendous strategic importance. Together with Port Hudson, a bastion north of Baton Rouge, Louisiana, it guarded a 150-mile stretch of the Mississippi. The river between these points was inaccessible to federal gunboats. So long as Vicksburg remained in southern hands, the trans-Mississippi region could send men and supplies to the rest of the Confederacy.

Vicksburg sits on a bluff overlooking a sharp bend in the river. When it proved unapproachable from either the west or the north, Grant devised an audacious scheme for getting at it from the east. He descended the Mississippi from Memphis to a point a few miles north of the city. Then, leaving part of his force behind to create the impression that he planned to attack from the north, he crossed the west bank and slipped quickly southward. Recrossing the river below Vicksburg, he abandoned his communications and supply lines and struck at Jackson, the capital of Mississippi. In a series of swift engagements his troops captured Jackson, cutting off the army of General John C. Pemberton, defending Vicksburg, from other Confederate units. Turning next on Pemberton, Grant defeated him in two decisive battles, Champion's Hill and Big Black River, and drove him inside the Vicksburg fortifications. By mid-May the city was under siege. Grant applied relentless pressure, and on July 4 Pemberton surrendered. With Vicksburg in Union hands, federal gunboats could range the entire length of the Mississippi. Texas and Arkansas were for all practical purposes lost to the Confederacy.

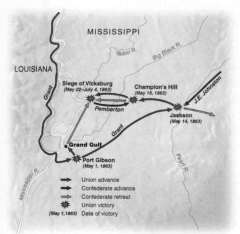

Vicksburg Campaign Unable to seize Vicksburg by direct assault, Grant swept to the south, crossed the Mississippi near Port Gibson, and then took Vicksburg from the east.

Lincoln had disliked Grant's plan for capturing Vicksburg. Now he generously confessed his error and placed Grant in command of all federal troops west of the Appalachians. Grant promptly took charge of the fighting around Chattanooga, Tennessee, where Confederate advances, beginning with the Battle of Chickamauga (September 19–20), were threatening to develop into a major disaster for the North. Shifting corps commanders and bringing up fresh units, he won another decisive victory at Chattanooga in a series of battles ending on November 25, 1863. This cleared the way for an invasion of Georgia. Suddenly this unkempt man emerged as the military leader the North had been so desperately seeking. In March 1864 Lincoln summoned him to Washington, named him lieutenant general, and gave him supreme command of the armies of the United States.

Economic and Social Effects, North and South

Although much blood would yet be spilled, by the end of 1863 the Confederacy was on the road to defeat. Northern military pressure, gradually increasing, was eroding the South's most precious resource: manpower. An ever-tightening naval blockade was reducing its economic strength. Shortages developed that, combined with the flood of currency pouring from the presses, led to drastic inflation. By 1864 an officer's coat cost $2,000 in Confederate money, cigars sold for $10 each, butter was $25 a pound, and flour went for $275 a barrel. Wages rose too, but not nearly as rapidly.

The southern railroad network was gradually wearing out, the major lines maintaining operations only by cannibalizing less vital roads. Imported products such as coffee disappeared; even salt became scarce. Efforts to increase manufacturing were only moderately successful because of the shortage of labor, capital, and technical knowledge. In general, southern prejudice against centralized authority prevented the Confederacy from making effective use of its scarce resources.

In the North, after a brief depression in 1861 caused by the uncertainties of the situation and the loss of southern business, the economy flourished: Government purchases greatly stimulated certain lines of manufacturing, the railroads operated at close to capacity and with increasing efficiency, the farm machinery business boomed because so many farmers left their fields to serve in the army, and bad harvests in Europe boosted agricultural prices.

Congress passed a number of economic measures long desired but held up in the past by southern opposition. The **Homestead Act (1862)** gave 160 acres to any settler who would farm the land for five years. The Morrill Land Grant Act of the same year provided the states with land at the rate of 30,000 acres for each member of Congress to support state agricultural colleges. Various tariff acts raised the duties on manufactured goods to an average rate of 47 percent in order to protect domestic manufacturers from foreign competition. The Pacific Railway Act (1862) authorized subsidies in land and money for the construction of a transcontinental railroad. And the National Banking Act of 1863 gave the country, at last, a uniform currency.

Although the economy grew, it did so more slowly during the 1860s than in the decades preceding and following. Prices soared beginning in 1862, averaging about 80 percent over the 1860 level by the end of the war. As in the South, wages did not keep pace. This did not make for a healthy economy. As the war dragged on and the continuing inflation eroded purchasing power, resentment on the part of workers deepened. During the 1850s iron molders, cigar makers, and some other skilled workers had formed national unions. This trend continued through the war years. There were many strikes. Inflation and shortages encouraged speculation and fostered a selfish, materialistic attitude toward life. Many contractors took advantage of wartime confusion to sell the government shoddy goods. By 1864 cotton was worth $1.90 a pound in New England. It could be had for twenty cents a pound in the South. Although it was illegal to traffic in the staple across the lines, unscrupulous operators did so and made huge profits.

Yet the war undoubtedly hastened industrialization and laid the basis for many other aspects of modern civilization. It posed problems of organization and planning, both military and civilian, that challenged the talents of creative persons and thus led to a more complex and efficient economy. The mechanization of production, the growth of large corporations, the creation of a better banking system, and the emergence of business leaders attuned to these conditions would surely have occurred in any case, for industrialization was under way long before the South seceded. Nevertheless, the war greatly speeded all these changes.

Civilian participation in the war effort was far greater than in earlier conflicts. Some churches split over the question of emancipation, but in North and South, church directors took the lead in recruitment drives and in charitable activities aimed at supporting the armed forces. In the North a Christian Commission raised the money and coordinated the personnel needed to provide Union soldiers with half a million Bibles, several million religious tracts, and other books, along with fruit, coffee, and spare clothing.

Women in Wartime

Many southern women took over the management of farms and small plantations when their menfolk went off to war. Others became volunteer nurses, and after an initial period of resistance, the Confederate army began to enlist women in the medical corps. At least two female nurses, Captain Sally Tompkins and Kate Cumming, left records of their experiences that throw much light on how the wounded were treated during the war. Other southern women worked as clerks in newly organized government departments.

Southern "ladyhood" more generally was yet another casualty of the war. The absence or death of husbands or other male relations changed attitudes toward gender roles. When her husband obeyed a military order to abandon Atlanta to the advancing Union armies, Julia Davidson, about to give birth, denounced the "men of Atlanta" for having "run and left Atlanta" and their homes. Such women learned to fend for themselves. "Necessity," Davidson later wrote her husband, would "make a different woman of me."

Large numbers of women also contributed to the northern war effort. As in the South, farm women went out into fields to plant and harvest crops, aided in many instances by new farm machinery. Many others took jobs in textile factories; in establishments making shoes, uniforms, and other supplies for the army; and in government agencies. But as was usually the case, the low wages traditionally paid women acted as a brake on wage increases for their male colleagues.

Besides working in factories and shops and on farms, northern women, again like their southern counterparts, aided the war effort more directly. Elizabeth Blackwell, the

Sarah Rosetta Wakeman, a.k.a. Private Lyons Wakeman of the 153rd Regiment of New York, and Janeta Velasquez, a.k.a. Lt. Harry T. Buford of the Confederate army, disguised themselves as men to fight.

first American woman doctor of medicine, had already founded the New York Infirmary for Women and Children. After war broke out she helped set up what became the U.S. **Sanitary Commission**, an organization of women similar to the Christian Commission dedicated to improving sanitary conditions at army camps, supplying hospitals with volunteer nurses, and raising money for medical supplies. Many thousands of women volunteers took part in Sanitary Commission and related programs.

An additional 3,000-odd women served as regular army nurses during the conflict. At the start the high command of both armies resisted the efforts of women to help, but

Read the Document

Barton, *Memoirs About Medical Life at the Battlefield* at **myhistorylab.com**

necessity and a grudging recognition of the competence of these women gradually brought the generals around. Clara Barton, a schoolteacher and government clerk, was among the first women to dress wounds at forward stations on the battlefield. After she ran out of bandages at Antietam, she dressed wounds with green corn leaves. The chief surgeon declared her to be "the angel of the battlefield." The "proper sphere" of American women was expanding, another illustration of the modernizing effect of the war.

Grant in the Wilderness

Grant's strategy as supreme commander was simple, logical, and ruthless. He would attack Lee and try to capture Richmond, Virginia. General William Tecumseh Sherman would drive from Chattanooga toward Atlanta, Georgia. Like a lobster's claw,

Toward Lee's Surrender in Virginia, 1864–1865
During the final year of the war in the East, Grant kept driving toward Richmond, and Lee kept blocking his way, like two whirling wrestlers locked in a hold. His army battered and bloodied, Lee surrendered at Appomattox Courthouse on April 9, 1865.

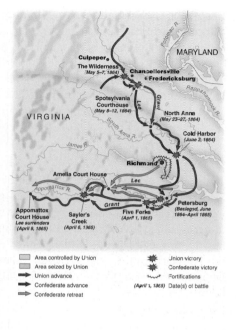

the two armies could then close to crush all resistance. Early in May 1864 Grant and Sherman commenced operations, each with more than 100,000 men.

Grant marched the Army of the Potomac directly into the tangled wilderness area south of the Rappahannock, where Hooker had been routed a year earlier. Lee, having only 60,000 men, forced the battle in the roughest possible country, where Grant found it difficult to make efficient use of his larger force. For two days (May 5–6) the Battle of the Wilderness raged. When it was over, the North had sustained another 18,000 casualties, far more than the Confederates. But unlike his predecessors, Grant did not fall back after being checked, nor did he expose his army to the kind of devastating counterattack at which Lee was so expert. Instead he shifted his troops to the southeast, attempting to outflank the Confederates. Divining his intent, Lee rushed his divisions southeastward and disposed them behind hastily erected earthworks in well-placed positions around Spotsylvania Court House. Grant attacked. After five more days, at a cost to the Union army of another 12,000 men, the Confederate lines were still intact.

Grant had grasped the fundamental truth that the war could be won only by grinding the South down beneath the weight of numbers. His own losses of men and equipment could be replaced; Lee's could not. When critics complained of the cost, he replied doggedly that he intended to fight on in the same manner if it took all summer. Once more he pressed southeastward in an effort to outflank the enemy. At Cold Harbor, nine miles from Richmond, he found the Confederates once more in strong defenses. He attacked. It was a battle as foolish and nearly as one-sided as General Pakenham's assault on Jackson's line outside New Orleans in 1815. "At Cold Harbor," the forthright Grant confessed in his memoirs, "no advantage whatever was gained to compensate for the heavy losses we sustained."

Sixty thousand casualties in less than a month! The news sent a wave of dismay through the North. There were demands that "Butcher" Grant be removed from command. Lincoln, however, stood firm. Although the price was fearfully high, Grant was gaining his objective. At Cold Harbor, Lee had to fight without a single regiment in general reserve while Grant's army was larger than at the start of the offensive. When Grant next swung around his flank, striking south of the James River toward Petersburg, Lee had to rush his troops to that city to hold him.

As the Confederates dug in, Grant put Petersburg under siege. Soon both armies had constructed complicated lines of breastworks and trenches, running for miles in a great arc south of Petersburg, much like the fortifications that would be used in France in World War I. Methodically the Union forces extended their lines, seeking to weaken the Confederates and cut the rail connections supplying Lee's troops and the city of Richmond. Grant could not overwhelm him, but by late June, Lee was pinned to earth. Moving again would mean having to abandon Richmond.

Sherman in Georgia

The summer of 1864 saw the North submerged in pessimism. The Army of the Potomac held Lee at bay but appeared powerless to defeat him. In Georgia, General Sherman inched forward methodically against the wily Joseph E. Johnston, but when he tried a direct assault at Kennesaw Mountain on June 27, he was thrown back with heavy casualties. In July Confederate raiders under General Jubal Early dashed suddenly across the Potomac from the Shenandoah Valley to within five miles of Washington before being turned back. A draft call for 500,000 additional men did not improve the public temper. Huge losses and the absence of a decisive victory were taxing the northern will to continue the fight.

In June, Lincoln had been renominated on a National Union ticket, with the Tennessee Unionist Andrew Johnson, a former Democrat, as his running mate. He was under attack not only from the Democrats, who nominated General McClellan and came out for a policy that might almost be characterized as peace at any price, but also from the Radical Republicans, many of whom had wished to dump him in favor of Secretary of the Treasury Chase.

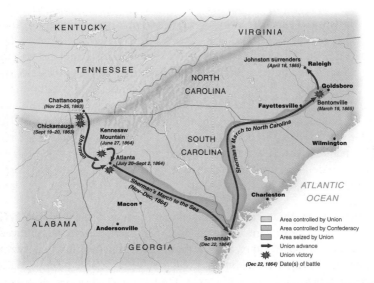

Sherman Pierces the Heart of the South, 1864–1865 After slogging through tenacious Confederate resistance in the Appalachians, Sherman finally broke through and seized Atlanta in September, 1864; he then marched "to the sea" to Savannah and in 1865 drove north through South Carolina and into North Carolina.

Table 14.1 Turning Points in the War

Pivotal Battles	Date	Outcome	Consequence
Ft. Sumter	April, 1861	Confederates fire on Ft. Sumter; Union garrison surrenders	Civil War commences
First Bull Run	July, 1861	Confederate victory	Northerners sobered, Southerners exhilarated; no swift ending to war likely
Shiloh	April, 1862	Tactical Union victory	23,000 casualties stagger everyone: Was the war worth such a high cost?
Antietam	September, 1862	Lee's advance northward halted	Lincoln, confidence regained, issues Emancipation Proclamation freeing slaves in rebel areas
Chancellorsville	May, 1863	Lee defeats Union army that had crossed into Virginia	Emboldened by victory, Lee invades North in search of decisive victory
Gettysburg	July, 1863	Confederate defeat; Lee retreats to Virginia	Confederate hopes dashed
Vicksburg	July, 1863	Grant seizes control of lower Mississippi River	Texas and Arkansas cut off from the Confederacy
Wilderness and Cold Harbor	May and June, 1864	Lee inflicts staggering losses on Union troops	Though criticized as a butcher, Grant perseveres, backed by Lincoln: War becomes battle of attrition
Sherman's March	November, 1864 through March, 1865	Sherman drives through Georgia and South Carolina	Demoralizes South
Siege of Petersburg	June 1864 through April 1865	Lee's defenses exhausted	South surrenders

Then, almost overnight, the whole atmosphere changed. On September 2, General Sherman's army fought its way into Atlanta. When the Confederates countered with an offensive northward toward Tennessee, Sherman did not follow. Instead he abandoned his communications with Chattanooga and marched unopposed through Georgia, "from Atlanta to the sea."

Sherman was in some ways like Grant. He was a West Pointer who resigned his commission only to fare poorly in civilian occupations. Back in the army in 1861, he suffered a brief nervous breakdown. After recovering he fought well under Grant at Shiloh and the two became close friends. "He stood by me when I was crazy," Sherman later recalled, "and I stood by him when he was drunk." Far more completely than most military men of his generation, Sherman believed in total war—in appropriating or destroying everything that might help the enemy continue the fight.

The march through Georgia had many objectives besides conquering territory. One obvious one was economic, the destruction of southern resources. "[We] must make old and young, rich and poor feel the hard hand of war," Sherman said.

Another object of Sherman's march was psychological. "If the North can march an army right through the South," he told General Grant, Southerners will take it "as proof positive that the North can prevail." This was certainly true of Georgia's blacks, who flocked to the invaders by the thousands, women and children as well as men, all cheering mightily when the soldiers put their former masters' homes to the torch. "They pray and shout and mix up my name with Moses," Sherman explained.

Sherman's victories staggered the Confederacy and the anti-Lincoln forces in the North. In November the president was easily reelected, 212 electoral votes to 21. The country was determined to carry on the struggle.

At last the South's will to resist began to crack. Sherman entered Savannah on December 22, having denuded a strip of Georgia sixty miles wide. Early in January 1865 he marched northward, leaving behind "a broad black streak of ruin and desolation—the fences all gone; lonesome smoke-stacks,

●◦●─Read the **Document**

Sherman, *The March Through Georgia* at **myhistorylab.com**

surrounded by dark heaps of ashes and cinders, marking the spots where human habitations had stood." In February his troops captured Columbia, South Carolina. Soon they were in North Carolina, advancing relentlessly. In Virginia, Grant's vise grew tighter day by day while the Confederate lines became thinner and more ragged.

These photos are of Lincoln, when he became president, and shortly before he was assassinated.
Source: (left) ICHi-20265/Photo by Alexander Hesler/Chicago Historical Society.

To Appomattox Court House

On March 4 Lincoln took the presidential oath and delivered his second inaugural address. Photographs taken at about this time show how four years of war had marked him. Somehow he had become both gentle and steel-tough, both haggard and inwardly calm. With victory sure, he spoke for tolerance, mercy, and reconstruction. "Let us judge not," he said after stating again his personal dislike of slavery, "that we be not judged." He urged all Americans to turn without malice to the task of mending the damage and to make a just and lasting peace between the sections.

Now the Confederate troops around Petersburg could no longer withstand the federal pressure. Desperately Lee tried to pull his forces back to the Richmond and Danville Railroad at Lynchburg, but the swift wings of Grant's army enveloped them. Richmond fell on April 3. With fewer than 30,000 men to oppose Grant's 115,000, Lee recognized the futility of further resistance. On April 9 he and Grant met by prearrangement at Appomattox Court House.

It was a scene at once pathetic and inspiring. Lee was noble in defeat; Grant, despite his rough-hewn exterior, was sensitive and magnanimous in victory. "I met you once before, General Lee, while we were serving in Mexico," Grant said after they had shaken hands. "I have always remembered your appearance, and I think I should have recognized you anywhere." They talked briefly of that earlier war, and then, acting on Lincoln's instructions, Grant outlined his terms. All that would be required was that the Confederate soldiers lay down their arms. They could return to their homes in peace. When Lee hinted that his men would profit greatly if allowed to retain possession of their horses, Grant agreed to let them do so.

Winners, Losers, and the Future

And so the war ended in 1865. It had cost the nation more than 600,000 lives, nearly as many as in all other American wars combined. The story of one of the lost thousands must stand for all, Union and Confederate. Jones Budbury, a tall, nineteen-year-old redhead, was working in a Pennsylvania textile mill when the war broke out, and he enlisted at once. His regiment first saw action at Bull Run. He took part in McClellan's Peninsular campaign. He fought at Second Bull Run, at Chancellorsville, and at Gettysburg. A few months after Gettysburg he was wounded in the foot and spent some time in an army hospital. By the spring of 1864 he had risen through the ranks to first sergeant and his hair had turned gray. In June he was captured and sent to Andersonville military prison, near Macon, Georgia, but he fell ill and the Confederates released him. In March 1865 he was back with his regiment in the lines besieging Richmond. On April 6, three days before Lee's surrender, Jones Budbury was killed while pursuing Confederate units near Sayler's Creek, Virginia.

The war also caused enormous property losses, especially in the Confederacy. All the human and material destruction explains the corrosive hatred and bitterness that the war implanted in millions of hearts. The corruption, the gross materialism, and the selfishness generated by wartime conditions were other disagreeable by-products of the conflict. Such sores fester in any society, but the Civil War bred conditions that inflamed and multiplied them. The war produced many examples of

Glory

Glory (1989) tells the story of the 54th Massachusetts Volunteer Infantry, a black regiment, from its establishment in the fall of 1862 through its attack on Fort Wagner, South Carolina, on July 18, 1863.

"Historical accuracy," director Edward Zwick declared, was "the goal of everyone involved in the production." Filmmakers commonly make such assertions, but Zwick proved that he had attended to the historical record. The peak of Shaw's cap was dyed the exact shade of medium green used by officers of the Massachusetts 54th; and when shoes were distributed to the recruits, there were no "lefts" or "rights": Shoes were to shape themselves to either foot from wear.

Zwick's evident commitment to history makes his deviations all the more interesting. The movie begins with a panoramic shot of rolling hills, dotted with tents. Fog blankets the valley and softens the morning light. Then the quiet is shattered by explosions: Soldiers hasten to form ranks, trot toward a battlefield, and charge across it, a young officer in the vanguard. (He is Captain Robert Gould Shaw, played by Matthew Broderick.) The attackers are decimated. Shaw is hit and loses consciousness.

Shaw is sent home to Boston to convalesce. At a reception, Governor Andrew offers the young officer command of the Massachusetts 54th, a black regiment being raised in Boston. Shaw hesitates for a moment. Then he confers privately with another officer, who is appalled.

"I knew how much you'd like to be a colonel, but a colored regiment?"

"I'm gonna do it," Shaw replies.

"You're not serious."

"Yeah."

These scenes contain truths without being entirely truthful. Governor Andrew did offer the commission and Shaw accepted it. But at the time Shaw was in Virginia. Andrew, in Boston, conveyed it through Shaw's father and young Shaw initially refused. Zwick has compressed the story chronologically, squeezing weeks into minutes; and he has

rearranged it geographically to enable Andrew and young Shaw to meet. Such modifications are common in "reel history," and these do not impair historical understanding.

But *Glory* deviates from the historical record in more significant ways. It suggests, for example, that the Massachusetts 54th was composed mostly of former slaves. In fact, most of its volunteers were from northern states and had never been slaves.

The fiction that they had been slaves, however, made it possible for Zwick to examine a larger truth. Of the 178,000 blacks who served in the Union army, fewer than one-fifth were from the North; the great majority *were* former slaves. Nearly 100,000 were recruited from Louisiana, Mississippi, or Tennessee, among the first states occupied by the Union army. *Glory* thus merges the story of the free blacks of the Massachusetts 54th with that of former slaves who were recruited from the Deep South.

Zwick exploited the dramatic potential of the latter groups. How did slaves respond when, having just received their freedom, they were placed under the absolute power of white officers?

Glory develops the question chiefly through the character of Trip (Denzel Washington), a former slave who hates all whites, including Shaw. Shaw illuminates the other side of the question. An abolitionist, he reluctantly decides that former slaves must be whipped (literally) into shape. When Trip sneaks off one night and is captured for desertion, Shaw orders him flogged. When Trip's back is bared, Shaw sees that it is laced with scars from whippings by slave masters. During the flogging, Trip fixes Shaw with a hateful stare, a powerful scene that underscores the movie's central irony: To end slavery, Shaw has become Trip's master while Trip has again become a slave.

Whatever its dramatic merits, the scene is ahistorical. In 1861 Congress had outlawed flogging in the military. Disobedient soldiers were tied in a crouched position, or they were

Matthew Broderick as Robert Gould Shaw, and Denzel Washington as the former slave recruit Trip, in the movie *Glory*.

suspended by their thumbs, toes just touching the ground.

Physical punishment was, in fact, one of the chief sources of contention between ex-slave soldiers and white officers. "I am no slave to be driven," one black recruit informed a brutish commander. When an officer of the 38th Colored Infantry tied a black recruit up by the thumbs, his friends cut him down and forced the officers back with bayonets: "No white son of a bitch can tie a man up here," they declared. The blacks were charged with mutiny and several were executed, an incident that shows that former slaves did not willingly submit to army discipline tainted with racism. Though African Americans constituted only 8 percent of the Union army, 80 percent of those executed for mutiny were black. Many white officers, as the movie suggests, did assert that former slaves must be treated as slaves.

Could such soldiers—black recruits and white officers alike—have been good ones? The movie answers the question by recreating the actual attack on Fort Wagner, the first step in the offensive on Charleston. It shows the blacks of the Massachusetts 54th marching to the front of the line, and forming up along a narrow beach. On Shaw's command, they charge forward. Unlike the white troops in the opening scene, the blacks follow him to the ramparts; when he falls, they continue onward until they are wiped out.

Were the actual soldiers of the Massachusetts 54th as courageous as those in the movie? Shortly after the battle, Lieutenant Iredell Jones, a Confederate officer, reported,

"The negroes fought gallantly, and were headed by as brave a colonel as ever lived." Of the 600 members of the 54th Massachusetts, 40 percent were casualties on that day, an extraordinarily high ratio. But did ex-slaves fight as courageously as the free blacks of the 54th? The answer to this question came not at Fort Wagner, but at other, less publicized battles. A few weeks earlier, for example, several companies of the Louisiana (Colored) Infantry, composed of former slaves who had been in the army only for several weeks, fought off a furious Confederate assault at Milliken's Bend near Vicksburg. The Confederate general was astonished when whites in the Union army fled but the blacks held their ground despite sustaining staggering casualties—45 percent— the highest of any single battle in the war.

Thus while *Glory* is a fictional composite— of free black and ex-slave recruits, and of the assault on Fort Wagner and Milliken's Bend—it conveys a broader truth about black soldiers. Howell Cobb, a Confederate senator from Georgia, declared, "If the black can make a good soldier, our whole system of government is wrong." *Glory* shows that although white officers and black recruits did not form a harmonious team, they together proved that slavery was doomed.

Questions for Discussion
- Was conscription during the Civil War a form of slavery?
- Would free blacks or former slaves more likely have been the better soldiers?

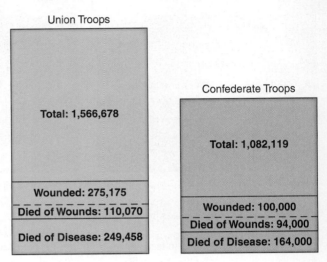

Casualities of the Civil War The Union death rate was 23 percent, the Confederate 24 percent. Twice as many soldiers were killed by disease as were killed by bullets.

Union Troops

Total: 1,566,678

Wounded: 275,175

Died of Wounds: 110,070

Died of Disease: 249,458

Confederate Troops

Total: 1,082,119

Wounded: 100,000

Died of Wounds: 94,000

Died of Disease: 164,000

charity, self-sacrifice, and devotion to duty as well, yet if the general moral atmosphere of the postwar generation can be said to have resulted from the experiences of 1861 to 1865, the effect overall was bad.

What had been obtained at this price? Slavery was dead. Paradoxically, while the war had been fought to preserve the Union, after 1865 the people tended to see the United States not as a union of states but as a nation. After Appomattox, secession was almost literally inconceivable. In a strictly political sense, as Lincoln had predicted from the start, the northern victory heartened friends of republican government and democracy throughout the world. A better-integrated society and a more technically advanced and productive economic system also resulted from the war.

The Americans of 1865 estimated the balance between cost and profit according to their individual fortunes and prejudices. Only the wisest realized that no final accounting could be made until the people had decided what to do with the fruits of victory. That the physical damage would be repaired no one could reasonably doubt; that even the loss of human resources would be restored in short order was equally apparent. But would the nation make good use of the opportunities the war had made available? What would the former slaves do with freedom? How would whites, northern and southern, react to emancipation? To what end would the new technology and social efficiency be directed? Would the people be able to forget the recent past and fulfill the hopes for which so many brave soldiers had given their "last full measure of devotion"?

Watch the Video

The Meaning of the Civil War for Americans at myhistorylab.com

Milestones

1861	Confederates attack Fort Sumter; Lincoln calls for 75,000 volunteers	**1862**	Lincoln's Emancipation Proclamation frees slaves in "areas of rebellion"
	First Battle of Bull Run (Virginia) boosts Confederate morale		Congress passes Homestead, Morrill Land Grant, and Pacific Railway acts
	Lincoln appoints George B. McClellan Union commander	**1863**	Congress passes Conscription and National Banking acts
	Supreme Court rules against Lincoln's suspension of habeas corpus in *Ex parte Merryman*		Federal troops subdue draft riots in New York City
1862	Confederate Congress passes Conscription Act		Union army defeats Confederates at turning point Battle of Gettysburg, Pennsylvania
	USS *Monitor* defeats Confederate *Merrimack* in first battle between ironclads		Union siege and capture of Vicksburg, Mississippi, gives Union control of entire Mississippi River
	Battle of Shiloh, Tennessee, leaves 23,000 dead, wounded, or missing	**1864**	Grant pushes deep into Virginia in costly Battles of the Wilderness, Spotsylvania Court House, and Cold Harbor
	Robert E. Lee assumes command of Confederate Army of Northern Virginia		Sherman captures Atlanta, Georgia; marches to sea; captures Savannah
	Lee and Stonewall Jackson defeat huge Union army at Seven Days' Battle for Richmond		Lincoln is reelected president
	Lee and Jackson defeat Union army at Second Battle of Bull Run	**1864– 1865**	Grant takes Petersburg, Virginia, after ten-month siege
	Lee's northern advance is stopped at Battle of Antietam; 22,000 casualties	**1865**	Sherman captures Columbia, South Carolina
			Lee surrenders to Grant at Appomattox Court House, Virginia

✓•–Study and **Review** at www.myhistorylab.com

Review Questions

1. The introduction to this chapter notes that civil wars, in retrospect, often seem senseless. If the American people had known in advance the terrible cost of its civil war, would it have been fought? Why did each side think it could win?

2. Dwight D. Eisenhower, U.S. general during World War II and subsequently President, once declared that "every war is going to astonish you in the way it occurred and the way it is carried out." What were the astonishing aspects of the Civil War?

3. How did Lincoln's war aims evolve? What were the reasons for and consequences of Lincoln's Emancipation Proclamation?
4. What factors on the home front influenced the course of war?

5. The table on page 401 summarizes the "turning points" during the Civil War. Which one was the most important?
6. How did the Civil War strengthen the American nation? Was the nation stronger after the war than before?

Key Terms

Anaconda Plan   *381*
Copperheads   *382*
Emancipation Proclamation   *390*
greenbacks   *382*

Homestead Act (1862)   *396*
Radical Republicans   *382*
Sanitary Commission   *398*

Reconstruction and the South

Has your family overcome adversity?

WITH NEARLY $3 BILLION IN ASSETS, OPRAH WINFREY IS THE RICHEST self-made woman in America. Her great-great-grandfather, Constantine Winfrey, was an illiterate slave in Sanford, Mississippi. On gaining his freedom in 1865, he owned little more than a strong back and a knowledge of cotton farming. But within fifteen years, he had learned to read and write and was owner of several farms and over 100 acres of land.

Whoopi Goldberg, another prominent black woman TV host and actress, is the great-great-granddaughter of William Washington and Elsa Tucker, slaves who were living in Alachua County, Florida when Lee surrendered at Appomattox. Over the next decade, the couple fulfilled the demanding provisions of the Southern Homestead Act, passed by the Republican-dominated Congress in 1866.

Chris Rock, comedian and actor, is the great-great-grandson of Julius Caesar Tingman, a slave in South Carolina. In March 1865, a few weeks after Sherman had marched through South Carolina, Tingman joined the U.S. Colored Troops in the Union army. Three years later, at the age of twenty-four, he was elected to the "reconstructed" South Carolina legislature.

Such accounts add another dimension to the usual narrative of the Reconstruction era (1865–1877). The period began with the liberal readmission of southern states to the Union as proposed by Lincoln and his successor, Andrew Johnson. Once readmitted, southern states restricted the rights of former slaves through a series of "**Black Codes.**" A furious Republican Congress overturned white southern rule through a series of laws and constitutional amendments that empowered former slaves—and their Republican allies. A white backlash, often violent, followed Republican rule.

•••─Read the Document
The Mississippi Black Code, at **myhistorylab.com**

Ultimately, white political power was restored, and a corrupt bargain secured the presidency for the Republican, Hayes. When Hayes removed Union troops from the South in 1877, Reconstruction was over.

Deprived of federal assistance, former slaves were obliged to make do on their own. Many failed. Only 10 percent of freed slaves acquired farms. But the ancestors of Oprah Winfrey, Whoopi Goldberg, Chris Rock, and many others prove that *some* former slaves succeeded, almost entirely through their own efforts. Harvard historian Louis Henry

Gates, Jr., whose *In Search of Our Roots* (2009) recounted their stories and many similar ones, hoped that someday such accounts would move history "from our kitchens or parlors into the texts, ultimately changing the official narrative of American history itself." This chapter describes the era's bitter wrangles and recriminations, its political failures and disappointments, but it also shows that many survived and even flourished during these difficult years.

The Assassination of Lincoln

On April 5, 1865, Abraham Lincoln visited Richmond. The fallen capital lay in ruins, sections blackened by fire, but the president was able to walk the streets unmolested and almost unattended. Everywhere African Americans crowded around him worshipfully; some fell to their knees as he passed, crying "Glory, Hallelujah," hailing him as a messiah. Even white townspeople seemed to have accepted defeat without resentment.

A few days later, in Washington, Lincoln delivered an important speech on Reconstruction, urging compassion and open-mindedness. On April 14 he held a Cabinet meeting at which postwar readjustment was considered at length. That evening, while Lincoln was watching a performance of the play *Our American Cousin* at Ford's Theater, an actor, John Wilkes Booth, slipped into his box and shot him in the back of the head with a small pistol. Early the next morning, without having regained consciousness, Lincoln died.

Richmond, Virginia lies in ruins in April, 1865 at the time of Lincoln's visit—and a few days before his assassination.

The murder was part of a complicated plot organized by die-hard pro-Southerners. One of Booth's accomplices went to the home of Secretary of State William Seward and stabbed him—Seward recovered from his wounds. A third conspirator, assigned to kill Vice President Andrew Johnson, changed his mind and fled Washington. Seldom have fanatics displayed so little understanding of their own interests, for with Lincoln perished the South's best hope for a mild peace. After his body had been taken home to Illinois, the national mood hardened; apparently the awesome drama was still unfolding—retribution and a final humbling of the South were inevitable.

Presidential Reconstruction

Despite its bloodiness, the Civil War had caused less intersectional hatred than might have been expected. The legal questions related to bringing the defeated states back into the Union, however, were extremely complex. Since Southerners believed that secession was legal, logic should have compelled them to argue that they were out of the Union and would thus have to be formally readmitted. Northerners should have taken the contrary position, for they had fought to prove that secession was illegal. Yet the people of both sections did just the opposite. Senator Charles Sumner and Congressman Thaddeus Stevens, who in 1861 had been uncompromising expounders of the theory that the Union was indissoluble, now insisted that the Confederate states had "committed suicide" and should be treated like "conquered provinces."

The process of readmission began in 1862, when Lincoln reappointed provisional governors for those parts of the South that had been occupied by federal troops. On December 8, 1863, he issued a proclamation setting forth a general policy. With the exception of high Confederate officials and a few other special groups, all Southerners could reinstate themselves as United States citizens by taking a simple loyalty oath. When, in any state, a number equal to 10 percent of those voting in the 1860 election had taken this oath, they could set up a state government. Under this **Ten Percent Plan**, such governments had to be republican in form, must recognize the "permanent freedom" of the slaves, and must provide for black education. The plan, however, did not require that blacks be given the right to vote.

President Andrew Johnson poses regally with carefully manicured fingernails. Although Johnson hated southern aristocrats, he sometimes craved their approval.

The Ten Percent Plan reflected Lincoln's lack of vindictiveness and his political wisdom. He realized that any government based on such a small minority of the population would be, as he put it, merely "a tangible nucleus which the remainder . . . may rally around as fast as it can," a sort of puppet regime, like the paper government established in those sections of Virginia under federal control.[1] The regimes established under this plan in Tennessee, Louisiana, and Arkansas bore, in the president's mind, the same relation to finally reconstructed states that an egg bears to a chicken. "We shall sooner have the fowl by hatching it than by smashing it," he remarked. He knew that eventually representatives of the southern states would again be sitting in Congress, and he wished to lay the groundwork for a strong Republican party in the section. Yet he realized that Congress had no intention of seating representatives from the "10 percent" states at once.

The Radicals in Congress disliked the Ten Percent Plan, partly because of its moderation and partly because it enabled Lincoln to determine Union policy toward the recaptured regions. In July 1864 they passed the **Wade-Davis Bill**, which provided for constitutional conventions only after a majority of the others in a southern state had taken a loyalty oath. Confederate officials and anyone who had "voluntarily borne arms against the United States" were barred from voting in the election or serving at the convention. Besides prohibiting slavery, the new state constitutions would have to repudiate Confederate debts. Lincoln disposed of the Wade-Davis Bill with a pocket veto and that's where matters stood when Andrew Johnson became president following the assassination.

Lincoln had picked Johnson for a running mate in 1864 because he was a border-state Unionist Democrat and something of a hero as a result of his courageous service as military governor of Tennessee. His political strength came from the poor whites and yeomen farmers of eastern Tennessee, and he was fond of extolling the common man and attacking "stuck-up aristocrats."

Johnson was a Democrat, but because of his record and his reassuring penchant for excoriating southern aristocrats, the Republicans in Congress were ready to cooperate with him. "Johnson, we have faith in you," said Senator Ben Wade, author of the Wade-Davis Bill, the day after Lincoln's death. "By the gods, there will be no trouble now in running the government!"

Johnson's reply, "Treason must be made infamous," delighted the Radicals, but the president proved temperamentally unable to work with them. Like Randolph of Roanoke, his antithesis intellectually and socially, opposition was his specialty; he soon alienated every powerful Republican in Washington.

Radical Republicans listened to Johnson's diatribes against secessionists and the great planters and assumed that he was anti-southern. Nothing could have been further from the truth. He had great respect for states' rights and he shared most of his poor white Tennessee constituents' contempt of blacks. "Damn the negroes, I am fighting these traitorous aristocrats, their masters," he told a friend during the war. "I wish to God," he said on another occasion, "every head of a family in the United States had one slave to take the drudgery and menial service off his family."

The new president did not want to injure or humiliate all white Southerners. He issued an amnesty proclamation only slightly more rigorous than Lincoln's. It assumed, correctly

---

[1]By approving the separation of the western counties that had refused to secede, this government had provided a legal pretext for the creation of West Virginia in 1863.

enough, that with the war over most southern voters would freely take the loyalty oath; thus it contained no 10 percent clause. More classes of Confederates, including those who owned taxable property in excess of $20,000, were excluded from the general pardon. By the time Congress convened in December 1865, all the southern states had organized governments, ratified the **Thirteenth Amendment** abolishing slavery, and elected senators and representatives. Johnson promptly recommended these new governments to the attention of Congress.

Republican Radicals

Peace found the Republicans in Congress no more united than they had been during the war. A small group of "ultra" Radicals were demanding immediate and absolute civil and political equality for blacks; they should be given, for example, the vote, a plot of land, and access to a decent education. Senator Sumner led this faction. A second group of Radicals, headed by Thaddeus Stevens in the House and Ben Wade in the Senate, agreed with the ultras' objectives but were prepared to accept half a loaf if necessary to win the support of less radical colleagues.

Nearly all Radicals distinguished between the "natural" God-given rights described in the Declaration of Independence, and social equality. The moderate Republicans wanted to protect the former slaves from exploitation and guarantee their basic rights but were unprepared to push for full political equality. A handful of Republicans sided with the Democrats in support of Johnson's approach, but all the rest insisted at least on the minimal demands of the moderates. Thus Johnsonian Reconstruction was doomed.

Johnson's proposal had no chance in Congress for reasons having little to do with black rights. The Thirteenth Amendment had the effect of increasing the representation of the southern states in Congress because it made the Three-fifths Compromise meaningless (see Chapter 5). Henceforth those who had been slaves would be counted as whole persons in apportioning seats in the House of Representatives. If Congress seated the Southerners, the balance of power might swing to the Democrats. To expect the Republicans to surrender power in such a fashion was unrealistic. Former Copperheads gushing with extravagant praise for Johnson put them instantly on guard.

Congress Rejects Johnsonian Reconstruction

The Republicans in Congress rejected Johnsonian Reconstruction. Quickly they created a joint committee on Reconstruction, headed by Senator William P. Fessenden of Maine, a moderate, to study the question of readmitting the southern states.

The committee held public hearings that produced much evidence of the mistreatment of blacks. Colonel George A. Custer, stationed in Texas, testified: "It is of weekly, if not of daily occurrence that Freedmen are murdered." The nurse Clara Barton told a gruesome tale about a pregnant woman who had been brutally whipped. Others described the intimidation of blacks by poor whites. The hearings strengthened the Radicals, who had been claiming all along that the South was perpetuating slavery under another name.

President Johnson's attitude speeded the swing toward the Radical position. While the hearings were in progress, Congress passed a bill expanding and extending the **Freedmen's Bureau**, which had been established in March 1865 to care for refugees. The bureau, a branch of the war department, was already exercising considerable coercive and supervisory power in the South. Now Congress sought to add to its authority in order to protect the black population. Although the bill had wide support, Johnson vetoed it, arguing that it was an unconstitutional extension of military authority in peacetime. Congress then passed a Civil Rights Act that, besides declaring specifically that blacks were citizens of the United States, denied the states the power to restrict their rights to testify in court, to make contracts for their labor, and to hold property. In other words, it put teeth in the Thirteenth Amendment.

Once again the president refused to go along, although his veto was sure to drive more moderates into the arms of the Radicals. On April 9, 1866, Congress repassed the Civil Rights Act by a two-thirds majority, the first time in American history that a major piece of legislation became law over the veto of a president. This event marked a revolution in the history of Reconstruction. Thereafter Congress, not President Johnson, had the upper hand.

In the clash between the president and Congress, Johnson was his own worst enemy. His language was often intemperate, his handling of opponents inept, his analysis of southern conditions incorrect. He had assumed that the small southern farmers who made up the majority in the Confederacy shared his prejudices against the planter class. They did not, as their choices in the postwar elections demonstrated.

The president also misread northern opinion. He believed that Congress had no right to pass laws affecting the South before southern representatives had been readmitted to Congress. However, in the light of the refusal of most southern whites to grant any real power or responsibility to the freedmen (an attitude that Johnson did not condemn), the public would not accept this point of view. Johnson placed his own judgment over that of the overwhelming majority of northern voters, and this was a great error, morally and tactically. By encouraging white Southerners to resist efforts to improve the lot of blacks, Johnson played into the hands of the Radicals.

Read the Document
Southern Skepticism of the Freedmen's Bureau at
myhistorylab.com

The Radicals encountered grave problems in fighting for their program. Northerners might object to the Black Codes and to seating "rebels" in Congress, but few believed in racial equality. Between 1865 and 1868, Wisconsin, Minnesota, Connecticut, Nebraska, New Jersey, Ohio, Michigan, and Pennsylvania all rejected bills granting blacks the vote.

The Radicals were in effect demanding not merely equal rights for freedmen but extra rights; not merely the vote but special protection of that right against the pressure that southern whites would surely apply to undermine it. This idea flew in the face of conventional American beliefs in equality before the law and individual self-reliance. Such protection would involve interference by the federal government in local affairs, a concept at variance with American practice. Events were to show that the Radicals were correct—that what amounted to a political revolution in state–federal relations was essential if blacks were to achieve real equality. But in the climate of that day their proposals encountered bitter resistance, and not only from white Southerners.

Thus, while the Radicals sought partisan advantage in their battle with Johnson and sometimes played on war-bred passions in achieving their ends, they were taking large political risks in defense of genuinely held principles.

The Fourteenth Amendment

In June 1866 Congress submitted to the states a new amendment to the Constitution. The **Fourteenth Amendment** was, in the context of the times, a truly radical measure. Never before had newly freed slaves been granted significant political rights. For example, in the British Caribbean sugar islands, where slavery had been abolished in the 1830s, stiff property qualifications and poll taxes kept freedmen from voting. The Fourteenth Amendment was also a milestone along the road to the centralization of political power in the United States because it reduced the power of all the states. In this sense it confirmed the great change wrought by the Civil War: the growth of a more complex, more closely integrated social and economic structure requiring closer national supervision. Few people understood this aspect of the amendment at the time.

•**⦂• Read the Document**

13th, 14th, and 15th Amendments at **myhistorylab.com**

First the amendment supplied a broad definition of American citizenship: "All persons born or naturalized in the United States, and subject to the jurisdiction thereof, are citizens of the United States and of the State wherein they reside." Obviously this included blacks. Then it struck at discriminatory legislation like the Black Codes: "No State shall make or enforce any law which shall abridge the privileges or immunities of citizens of the United States; nor shall any State deprive any person of life, liberty, or property, without due process of law." The next section attempted to force the southern states to permit blacks to vote. If a state denied the vote to any class of its adult male citizens, its representation was to be reduced proportionately. Under another clause, former federal officials who had served the Confederacy were barred from holding either state or federal office unless specifically pardoned by a two-thirds vote of Congress. Finally, the Confederate debt was repudiated.

While the amendment did not specifically outlaw segregation or prevent a state from disenfranchising blacks, the southern states would have none of it. Without them the necessary three-fourths majority of the states could not be obtained.

President Johnson vowed to make the choice between the Fourteenth Amendment and his own policy the main issue of the 1866 congressional elections. He embarked on "a swing around the circle" to rally the public to his cause. He failed dismally. Northern women objected to the implication in the amendment that black men were more fitted to vote than white women, but a large majority of northern voters was determined that African Americans must have at least formal legal equality. The Republicans won better than two-thirds of the seats in both houses, together with control of all the northern state governments. Johnson emerged from the campaign discredited, the Radicals stronger and determined to have their way. The southern states, Congressman James A. Garfield of Ohio said in February 1867, have "flung back into our teeth the magnanimous offer of a generous nation. It is now our turn to act."

The Reconstruction Acts

Had the southern states been willing to accept the Fourteenth Amendment, coercive measures might have been avoided. Their recalcitrance and continuing indications that local authorities were persecuting blacks finally led to the passage, on March 2, 1867, of the First Reconstruction Act. This law divided the former Confederacy— exclusive of Tennessee, which had ratified the Fourteenth Amendment—into five military districts, each controlled by a major general. It gave these officers almost dictatorial power to protect the civil rights of "all persons," maintain order, and supervise the administration of justice. To rid themselves of military rule, the former states were required to adopt new state constitutions guaranteeing blacks the right to vote and disenfranchising broad classes of ex-Confederates. If the new constitutions proved satisfactory to Congress, and if the new governments ratified the Fourteenth Amendment, their representatives would be admitted to Congress and military rule ended. Johnson's veto of the act was easily overridden.

Although drastic, the Reconstruction Act was so vague that it proved unworkable. Military control was easily established. But in deference to moderate Republican views, the law had not spelled out the process by which the new constitutions were to be drawn up. Southern whites preferred the status quo, even under army control, to enfranchising blacks and retiring their own respected leaders. They made no effort to follow the steps laid down in the law. Congress therefore passed a second act, requiring the military authorities to register voters and supervise the election of delegates to constitutional conventions. A third act further clarified procedures.

👁️ **See the Map**

Reconstruction at
myhistorylab.com

Still white Southerners resisted. The laws required that the constitutions be approved by a majority of the registered voters. Simply by staying away from the polls, whites prevented ratification in state after state. At last, in March 1868, a full year after the First Reconstruction Act, Congress changed the rules again. The constitutions were to be ratified by a majority of the voters. In June 1868 Arkansas, having fulfilled the requirements, was readmitted to the Union, and by July a sufficient number of states had ratified the Fourteenth Amendment to make it part of the Constitution. But it was not until July 1870 that the last southern state, Georgia, qualified to the satisfaction of Congress.

Congress Supreme

To carry out this program in the face of determined southern resistance required a degree of single-mindedness over a long period seldom demonstrated by an American legislature. The persistence resulted in part from the suffering and frustrations of the war years. The refusal of the South to accept the spirit of even the mild reconstruction designed by Johnson goaded the North to ever more overbearing efforts to bring the ex-Confederates to heel. President Johnson's stubbornness also influenced the Republicans. They became obsessed with the need to defeat him. The unsettled times and the large Republican majorities, always threatened by the possibility of a Democratic resurgence if "unreconstructed" southern congressmen were readmitted, sustained their determination.

These considerations led Republicans to attempt a kind of grand revision of the federal government, one that almost destroyed the balance between judicial, executive, and legislative power established in 1789. A series of measures passed between 1866 and 1868 increased the authority of Congress over the army, over the process of amending the Constitution, and over Cabinet members and lesser appointive officers. Even the Supreme Court was affected. Its size was reduced and its jurisdiction over civil rights cases limited. Finally, in a showdown caused by emotion more than by practical considerations, the Republicans attempted to remove President Johnson from office.

The chief issue was the Tenure of Office Act of 1867, which prohibited the president from removing officials who had been appointed with the consent of the Senate without first obtaining Senate approval. In February 1868 Johnson "violated" this act by dismissing Secretary of War Edwin M. Stanton, who had been openly in sympathy with the Radicals for some time. The House, acting under the procedure set up in the Constitution for removing the president, promptly impeached him before the bar of the Senate, Chief Justice Salmon P. Chase presiding.

In the trial, Johnson's lawyers easily established that he had removed Stanton only in an effort to prove the Tenure of Office Act unconstitutional. They demonstrated that the act did not protect Stanton to begin with, since it gave Cabinet members tenure "during the term of the President by whom they may have been appointed," and Stanton had been appointed in 1862, during Lincoln's first term!

Nevertheless the Radicals pressed the charges (eleven separate articles) relentlessly. Tremendous pressure was applied to the handful of Republican senators who were unwilling to disregard the evidence.

Seven of them resisted to the end, and the Senate failed by a single vote to convict Johnson. This was probably fortunate. The trial weakened the presidency, but if Johnson had been forced from office on such flimsy grounds, the independence of the executive might have been permanently undermined. Then the legislative branch would have become supreme.

The Fifteenth Amendment

The failure of the impeachment did not affect the course of Reconstruction. The president was acquitted on May 16, 1868. A few days later, the Republican National Convention nominated General Ulysses S. Grant for the presidency. At the Democratic convention Johnson had considerable support, but the delegates nominated Horatio Seymour, a former governor of New York. In November Grant won an easy victory in the Electoral College, 214 to 80, but the popular vote was close: 3 million to 2.7 million. Although he would probably have carried the Electoral College in any case, Grant's margin in the popular vote was supplied by southern blacks enfranchised under the Reconstruction acts, about 450,000 of whom supported him. A majority of white voters probably preferred Seymour. Since many citizens undoubtedly voted Republican because of personal admiration for General Grant, the election statistics suggest that a substantial white majority opposed the policies of the Radicals.

The Reconstruction acts and the ratification of the Fourteenth Amendment achieved the purpose of enabling black Southerners to vote. The Radicals, however, were

Thomas Waterman Wood, a Northerner, painted this hopeful interpretation of Reconstruction, *His First Vote* (1868).

not satisfied; despite the unpopularity of the idea in the North, they wished to guarantee the right of blacks to vote in every state. Another amendment seemed the only way to accomplish this objective, but passage of such an amendment appeared impossible. The Republican platform in the 1868 election had smugly distinguished between blacks voting in the South.

However, after the election had demonstrated how important the black vote could be, Republican strategy shifted. Grant had carried Indiana by fewer than 10,000 votes and lost New York by a similar number. If blacks in these and other closely divided states had voted, Republican strength would have been greatly enhanced.

Suddenly Congress blossomed with suffrage amendments. After considerable bickering over details, the **Fifteenth Amendment** was sent to the states for ratification in February 1869. It forbade all the states to deny the vote to anyone "on account of race, color, or previous condition of servitude." Once again nothing was said about denial of the vote on the basis of sex, which caused feminists, such as Elizabeth Cady Stanton, to be even more outraged than they had been by the Fourteenth Amendment.

Most southern states, still under federal pressure, ratified the amendment swiftly. The same was true in most of New England and in some western states. Bitter battles were waged in Connecticut, New York, Pennsylvania, and the states immediately north of the Ohio River, but by March 1870 most of them had ratified the amendment and it became part of the Constitution.

When the Fifteenth Amendment went into effect, President Grant called it "the greatest civil change and . . . the most important event that has occurred since the nation came to life." The American Anti-Slavery Society formally dissolved itself, its work apparently completed. "The Fifteenth Amendment confers upon the African race the care of its own destiny," Radical Congressman James A. Garfield wrote proudly after the amendment was ratified.

"Black Republican" Reconstruction: Scalawags and Carpetbaggers

The Radicals had at last succeeded in imposing their will on the South. Throughout the region former slaves had real political influence; they voted, held office, and exercised the "privileges" and enjoyed the "immunities" guaranteed them by the Fourteenth Amendment. Nearly all voted Republican.

The spectacle of blacks not five years removed from slavery in positions of power and responsibility attracted much attention. But the real rulers of the "black Republican" governments were white: the **scalawags**—Southerners willing to cooperate with the Republicans because they accepted the results of the war and wished to advance their own interests—and the **carpetbaggers**—Northerners who went to the South as idealists to help the freed slaves as employees of the federal government, or more commonly as settlers hoping to improve themselves.

Although scalawags were by far the more numerous, the carpetbaggers were a particularly varied lot. Most had mixed motives for coming south and personal gain was certainly among them. But so were opposition to slavery and the belief that blacks deserved to be treated decently and given a chance to get ahead in the world.

Many northern blacks became carpetbaggers: former Union soldiers, missionaries from northern black churches, and also teachers, lawyers, and other members of the small northern black professional class. Many of these became officeholders, but like southern black politicians their influence was limited.

That blacks should fail to dominate southern governments is certainly understandable. They lacked experience in politics and were mostly poor and uneducated. They were nearly everywhere a minority. Those blacks who held office during Reconstruction tended to be better educated and more prosperous than most southern blacks.

In South Carolina and elsewhere, blacks proved in the main to be able and conscientious public servants. Even at the local level, where the quality of officials was usually poor, there was little difference in the degree of competence displayed by white and black officeholders. In power, the blacks were not vindictive; by and large they did not seek to restrict the rights of ex-Confederates.

Not all black legislators and administrators were paragons of virtue. In South Carolina, despite their control of the legislature, they broke up into factions repeatedly and failed to press for laws that would improve the lot of poor black farm workers. Waste and corruption were common during Reconstruction governments. Half the budget of Louisiana in some years went for salaries and "mileage" for representatives and their staffs. A South Carolina legislator was voted an additional $1,000 in salary after he lost that sum betting on a horse race.

However, the corruption must be seen in perspective. The big thieves were nearly always white; blacks got mostly crumbs. Furthermore, graft and callous disregard of the public interest characterized government in every section and at every level during the decade after Appomattox. Big-city bosses in the North embezzled sums that dwarfed the most brazen southern frauds. The New York City Tweed Ring probably made off with more money than all the southern thieves, black and white, combined. While the

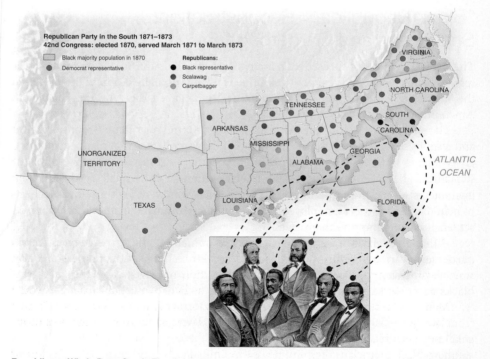

Republicans Win in Deep South The six black members of the House of Representatives in 1871 are from left to right: Benjamin Turner, Robert De Large, Josiah Wells, Jefferson Long, Joseph Rainey, Robert Brown Elliott. Each is linked to his district; the member in the blue coat—center—is not connected to a "black" dot. A special Republican primary replaced him with a scalawag.

evidence does not justify the southern corruption, it suggests that the unique features of Reconstruction politics—black suffrage, military supervision, and carpetbagger and scalawag influence—do not explain it.

In fact, the Radical southern governments accomplished a great deal. They spent money freely but not entirely wastefully. Tax rates zoomed, but the money financed the repair and expansion of the South's dilapidated railroad network, rebuilt crumbling levees, and expanded social services. Before the Civil War, southern planters possessed a disproportionate share of political as well as economic power, and they spent relatively little public money on education and public services of all kinds.

During Reconstruction an enormous gap had to be filled, and it took money to fill it. The Freedmen's Bureau made a major contribution. Northern religious and philanthropic organizations also did important work. Eventually, however, the state governments established and supported hospitals, asylums, and systems of free public education that, while segregated, greatly benefited everyone, whites as well as blacks. Much state money was also spent on economic development: land reclamation, repairing and expanding the war-ravaged railroads, maintaining levees.

> **Watch the Video**
>
> *The Schools that the Civil War & Reconstruction created* at **myhistorylab.com**

The Ravaged Land

The South's grave economic problems complicated the rebuilding of its political system. The section had never been as prosperous as the North, and wartime destruction left it desperately poor by any standard. In the long run the abolition of slavery released immeasurable quantities of human energy previously stifled, but the immediate effect was to create confusion. Freedom to move without a pass, to "see the world," was one of the former slaves' most cherished benefits of emancipation. Understandably, many at first equated legal freedom with freedom from having to earn a living, a tendency reinforced for a time by the willingness of the Freedmen's Bureau to provide rations and other forms of relief in war-devastated areas. Most, however, soon accepted the fact that they must earn a living; a small plot of land of their own ("40 acres and a mule") would complete their independence.

This objective was forcefully supported by the relentless Congressman Thaddeus Stevens, whose hatred of the planter class was pathological. "The property of the chief rebels should be seized," he stated. If the lands of the richest "70,000 proud, bloated and defiant rebels" were confiscated, the federal government would obtain 394 million acres. Every adult male ex-slave could easily be supplied with 40 acres. The beauty of his scheme, Stevens insisted, was that "nine-tenths of the [southern] people would remain untouched." Dispossessing the great planters would make the South "a safe republic," its lands cultivated by "the free labor of intelligent citizens." If the plan drove the planters into exile, "all the better."

Although Stevens's figures were faulty, many Radicals agreed with him. "We must see that the freedmen are established on the soil," Senator Sumner declared. "The great plantations, which have been so many nurseries of the rebellion, must be broken up, and the freedmen must have the pieces." Stevens, Sumner, and others who wanted to give land to the freedmen weakened their case by associating it with the idea of punishing the former rebels; the average American had too much respect for property rights to support a policy of confiscation.

The former slaves had either to agree to work for their former owners or strike out on their own. White planters, influenced by the precipitous decline of sugar production in Jamaica and other Caribbean islands that had followed the abolition of slavery there, expected freed blacks to be incapable of self-directed effort. If allowed to become independent farmers, they would either starve to death or descend into barbarism. Of course the blacks did neither. True, the output of cotton and other southern staples declined precipitously after slavery was abolished. Observers soon came to the conclusion that a free black produced much less than a slave had produced. "You can't get only about two-thirds as much out of 'em now as you could when they were slaves," an Arkansas planter complained.

View the Image

Five Generations of a Slave Family at **myhistorylab.com**

However, the decline in productivity was not caused by the inability of free blacks to work independently. They simply chose no longer to work like slaves. They let their children play instead of forcing them into the fields. Mothers devoted more time to childcare and housework, less to farm labor. Elderly blacks worked less.

Noting these changes, white critics spoke scornfully of black laziness and shiftlessness. "You cannot make the negro work without physical compulsion," was the common view. Even General Oliver O. Howard, head of the Freedmen's Bureau, used the phrase "wholesome compulsion" in describing the policy of forcing blacks to sign exploitive labor contracts. Moreover, studies show that emancipated blacks earned almost 30 percent more than the value of the subsistence provided by their former masters.

Sharecropping and the Crop-Lien System

Before the passage of the Reconstruction acts, plantation owners tried to farm their land with gang labor, the same system as before, only now paying wages to the former slaves. But blacks did not like working for wages because it kept them under the direction of whites and thus reminded them of slavery. They wanted to be independent, to manage not merely their free time but their entire lives for themselves.

Quite swiftly, a new agricultural system known as **sharecropping** emerged. Instead of cultivating the land by gang labor as in antebellum times, planters broke up their estates into small units and established on each a black family. The planter provided housing, agricultural implements, draft animals, seed, and other supplies, and the family provided labor. The crop was divided between them, usually on a fifty-fifty basis. If the landlord supplied only land and housing, the laborer got a larger share. This was called share tenancy.

Read the Document

A Sharecrop Contract at **myhistorylab.com**

Sharecropping gave blacks the day-to-day control of their lives that they craved and the hope of earning enough to buy a small farm. Many former slaves succeeded, as evidenced by the accounts narrated at the outset of this chapter. Oprah Winfrey's great-great-grandfather bought several plots of land and eventually moved a schoolhouse to his property so that black children in Sanford, Mississippi, could get an education. But not all managed to climb the first rungs into the middle class. As late as 1880 blacks owned less than 10 percent of the agricultural land in the South, although they made up more than half of the region's farm population.

Many white farmers in the South were also trapped by the sharecropping system and by white efforts to keep blacks in a subordinate position. New fencing laws kept them from grazing livestock on undeveloped land, a practice common before the Civil War. But the main cause of southern rural poverty for whites as well as for blacks was the lack of enough capital to finance the sharecropping system. Like their colonial ancestors, the landowners had to borrow against October's harvest to pay for April's seed. Thus the **crop-lien system** developed.

Under the crop-lien system, both landowner and sharecropper depended on credit supplied by local bankers, merchants, and storekeepers for everything from seed, tools, and fertilizer to overalls, coffee, and salt. Crossroads stores proliferated, and a new class of small merchants appeared. The prices of goods sold on credit were high, adding to the burden borne by the rural population. The small southern merchants were almost equally victimized by the system, for they also lacked capital, bought goods on credit, and had to pay high interest rates.

Seen in broad perspective, the situation is not difficult to understand. The South, drained of every resource by the war, was competing for funds with the North and West, both vigorous and expanding and therefore voracious consumers of capital. Reconstruction, in the literal sense of the word, was accomplished chiefly at the expense of the standard of living of the producing classes. The crop-lien system and the small

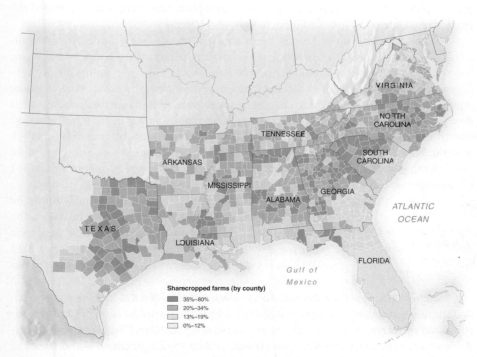

Sharecropped farms (by county)

- 35%–80%
- 20%–34%
- 13%–19%
- 0%–12%

Sharecropping, 1880 Sharecropping became especially common in areas outside of the cotton belt—eastern Texas, upland Alabama, and North Carolina.

storekeeper were only agents of an economic process dictated by national, perhaps even worldwide, conditions.

Compared with the rest of the country, progress was slow. Just before the Civil War cotton harvests averaged about 4 million bales. During the conflict, output fell to about half a million, and the former Confederate states did not enjoy a 4-million-bale year again until 1870. In contrast, national wheat production in 1859 was 175 million bushels and in 1878, 449 million. About 7,000 miles of railroad were built in the South between 1865 and 1879; in the rest of the nation nearly 45,000 miles of track were laid.

But in the late 1870s, cotton production revived. It soon regained, and thereafter long retained, its title as "king" of the southern economy. This was true in large measure because of the crop-lien system.

The White Backlash

Radical southern governments could sustain themselves only as long as they had the support of a significant proportion of the white population, for except in South Carolina and Louisiana, the blacks were not numerous enough to win elections alone. The key to survival lay in the hands of the wealthy merchants and planters, mostly former Whigs. People of this sort had nothing to fear from black economic competition. Taking a broad view, they could see that improving the lot of the former slaves would benefit all classes.

Southern white Republicans used the Union League of America, a patriotic club founded during the war, to control the black vote. Employing secret rituals, exotic symbols, and other paraphernalia calculated to impress unsophisticated people, they enrolled the freedmen in droves and marched them to the polls en masse.

Powerless to check the League by open methods, dissident Southerners established a number of secret terrorist societies, bearing such names as the **Ku Klux Klan**, the Knights of the White Camelia, and the Pale Faces. The most notorious of these organizations was the Klan, which originated in Tennessee in 1866. At first it was purely a social club, but by 1868 it had been taken over by vigilante types dedicated to driving blacks out of politics, and it was spreading rapidly across the South. Sheet-clad nightriders roamed the countryside, frightening the impressionable and chastising the defiant. Klansmen, using a weird mumbo jumbo and claiming to be the ghosts of Confederate soldiers, spread horrendous rumors and published broadsides designed to persuade the freedmen that it was unhealthy for them to participate in politics.

When intimidation failed, the Klansmen resorted to force. After being whipped by one group in Tennessee, a recently elected justice of the peace reported, "They said they had nothing particular against me . . . but they did not intend any nigger to hold office." In hundreds of cases the KKK murdered their opponents, often in the most gruesome manner.

•••⁌Read the Document

Accounts from Victims of the Ku Klux Klan at myhistorylab.com

Congress struck at the Klan with three **Force Acts** (1870–1871), which placed elections under federal jurisdiction and imposed fines and prison sentences on persons convicted of interfering with any citizen's exercise of the franchise. Troops were dispatched to areas where the Klan was strong, and by 1872 the federal authorities had arrested enough Klansmen to break up the organization.

Nevertheless the Klan contributed substantially to the destruction of Radical regimes in the South. Its depredations weakened the will of white Republicans (few of whom really believed in racial equality), and it intimidated many blacks. The fact that the army had to be called in to suppress it was a glaring illustration of the weakness of the Reconstruction governments.

Gradually it became respectable to intimidate black voters. Beginning in Mississippi in 1874, terrorism spread through the South. Instead of hiding behind masks and operating in the dark, these terrorists donned red shirts, organized into military companies, and paraded openly. Mississippi redshirts seized militant blacks and whipped them publicly. Killings were frequent. When blacks dared to fight back, heavily armed whites put them to rout. In other states similar results followed.

Before long the blacks learned to stay home on election day. One by one, "Conservative" parties—Democratic in national affairs—took over southern state governments. Intimidation was only a partial explanation of this development. The increasing solidarity of whites, northern and southern, was equally significant.

The North had subjected the South to control from Washington while preserving state sovereignty in the North itself. In the long run this discrimination proved unworkable. Many Northerners had supported the Radical policy only out of irritation with President Johnson. After his retirement their enthusiasm waned. The war was fading into the past and with it the worst of the anger it had generated.

Northern voters could still be stirred by references to the sacrifices Republicans had made to save the Union and by reminders that the Democratic party was the organization of rebels, Copperheads, and the Ku Klux Klan. "If the Devil himself were at the helm of the ship of state," wrote the novelist Lydia Maria Child in 1872, "my conscience would not allow me to aid in removing him to make room for the Democratic party." Yet emotional appeals could not convince Northerners that it was still necessary to maintain a large army in the South. In 1869 the occupying forces were down to 11,000 men. After Klan disruption and intimidation had made a farce of the 1874 elections in Mississippi, Governor Ames appealed to Washington for help. President Grant's attorney general, Edwards Pierrepont, refused to act. "The whole public are tired out with these autumnal outbreaks in the South," he told Ames. "Preserve the peace by the forces of your own state."

Nationalism was reasserting itself. Had not Washington and Jefferson been Virginians? Was not Andrew Jackson Carolina-born? Since most Northerners had little real love or respect for African Americans, their interest in racial equality flagged once they felt reasonably certain that blacks would not be re-enslaved if left to their own devices in the South.

Another, much subtler force was also at work. The prewar Republican party had stressed the common interest of workers, manufacturers, and farmers in a free and mobile society, a land of equal opportunity where all could work in harmony. Southern whites had insisted that laborers must be disciplined if large enterprises were to be run efficiently. By the 1870s, as large industrial enterprises developed in the northern states, the thinking of business leaders changed—the southern argument began to make sense to them, and they became more sympathetic to the southern demand for more control over "their" labor force.

An 1872 Grant campaign poster of "Our Three Great Presidents" at best got it about two-thirds right.

Grant as President

Other matters occupied the attention of northern voters. The expansion of industry and the rapid development of the West, stimulated by a new wave of railroad building, loomed more important to many than the fortunes of the former slaves. Beginning in 1873, when a stock market panic struck at public confidence, economic difficulties plagued the country and provoked another debate over the tariff.

Grant's most serious weakness as president was his failure to deal effectively with economic and social problems, what injured him and the Republicans most was his inability to cope with government corruption. The worst of the scandals did not become public knowledge during Grant's first term. However, in 1872 Republican reformers, alarmed by rumors of corruption and disappointed by Grant's failure to press for civil service reform, organized the Liberal Republican party and nominated Horace Greeley, the able but eccentric editor of the *New York Tribune*, for president.

The Liberal Republicans were mostly well-educated, socially prominent types—editors, college presidents, economists, along with a sprinkling of businessmen and politicians. Their liberalism was of the laissez-faire variety; they were for low tariffs and sound money, and against what they called "class legislation," meaning measures benefiting particular groups, whether labor unions or railroad companies or farm organizations. Nearly all had supported Reconstruction at the start, but by the early 1870s most were including southern blacks among the special interests that ought to be left to their own devices. Their observation of urban corruption and of unrestricted immigration led them to disparage universal suffrage, which, one of them said, "can only mean in plain English the government of ignorance and vice."

The Democrats also nominated Greeley in 1872, although he had devoted his political life to flailing the Democratic party in the *Tribune*. That surrender to expediency, together with Greeley's temperamental unsuitability for the presidency, made the campaign a fiasco for the reformers. Grant triumphed easily, with a popular majority of nearly 800,000.

Nevertheless, the defection of the Liberal Republicans hurt the Republican party in Congress. In the 1874 elections, no longer hampered as in the presidential contest by Greeley's notoriety and Grant's fame, the Democrats carried the House of Representatives. It was clear that the days of military rule in the South were ending. By the end of 1875 only three southern states—South Carolina, Florida, and Louisiana—were still under Republican control.

The Republican party in the South was "dead as a doornail," a reporter noted. He reflected the opinion of thousands when he added, "We ought to have a sound sensible republican . . . for the next President as a measure of safety; but only on the condition of absolute noninterference in Southern local affairs, for which there is no further need or excuse."

The Disputed Election of 1876

Against this background the presidential election of 1876 took place. Since corruption in government was the most widely discussed issue, the Republicans passed over their most attractive political personality, the dynamic James G. Blaine, Speaker of the House of Representatives, who had been connected with some chicanery involving railroad securities. Instead they nominated Governor Rutherford B. Hayes of Ohio, a former general with an untarnished reputation. The Democrats picked Governor Samuel J. Tilden of New York, a wealthy lawyer who had attracted national attention for his part in breaking up the Tweed Ring in New York City.

In November early returns indicated that Tilden had carried New York, New Jersey, Connecticut, Indiana, and all the southern states, including Louisiana, South Carolina, and Florida, where Republican regimes were still in control. This seemed to give him 203 electoral votes to Hayes's 165, and a popular plurality in the neighborhood of 250,000 out of more than 8 million votes cast. However, Republican leaders had anticipated the possible loss of Florida, South Carolina, and Louisiana and were prepared to use their control of the election machinery in those states to throw out sufficient Democratic ballots to alter the results if doing so would change the national outcome. Realizing that the electoral votes of those states were exactly enough to elect their man, they telegraphed their henchmen on the scene, ordering them to go into action. The local Republicans then invalidated Democratic ballots in wholesale lots and filed returns showing Hayes the winner. Naturally the local Democrats protested vigorously and filed their own returns.

The Constitution provides (Article II, Section 1) that presidential electors must meet in their respective states to vote and forward the results to "the Seat of the Government." There, it adds, "the President of the Senate shall, in the Presence of the Senate and House of Representatives, open all the Certificates, and the Votes shall then be counted." But who was to do the counting? The House was Democratic, the Senate Republican; neither would agree to allow the other to do the job. On January 29, 1877, scarcely a month before inauguration day, Congress created an electoral commission to decide the disputed cases. The commission consisted of five senators (three Republicans and two Democrats), five representatives (three Democrats and two Republicans), and five justices of the Supreme Court (two Democrats, two Republicans, and one "independent" judge, David Davis).

Since it was a foregone conclusion that the others would vote for their party no matter what the evidence, Davis would presumably swing the balance in the interest of fairness.

But before the commission met, the Illinois legislature elected Davis senator. He had to resign from the Court and the commission. Since independents were rare even on the Supreme Court, no neutral justice was available to replace him. The vacancy went to Associate Justice Joseph P. Bradley of New Jersey, a Republican.

Evidence presented before the commission revealed a disgraceful picture of corruption. On the one hand, in all three disputed states Democrats had clearly cast a majority of the votes; on the other, it was unquestionable that many blacks had been forcibly prevented from voting.

In truth, both sides were shamefully corrupt. The governor of Louisiana was reported

1876

ELECTORAL VOTE
TOTAL: 369

50% 185 | 50% 184

POPULAR VOTE
TOTAL: 8,340,783

48% 4,036,298 | 51% 4,300,590

MINOR
1%
93,895

- Republican (Hayes)
- Democratic (Tilden)
- Territories

The Republicans Gain the Presidency, the White South Loses the Union Army, 1877 By 1876 white Democrats had regained political control in much of the South, giving Tilden 203 electoral votes to the Republican Hayes's 185. But Republican election officials in South Carolina, Florida, and Louisiana invalidated thousands of Democratic votes, which seemingly gave the election to Tilden. In 1877 a congressional commission finalized a deal giving the presidency to Hayes, who would withdraw the Union army from the South.

willing to sell his state's electoral votes for $200,000. The Florida election board was supposed to have offered itself to Tilden for the same price. "That seems to be the standard figure," Tilden remarked ruefully.

The Democrats had some hopes that Justice Bradley would be sympathetic to their case, for he was known to be opposed to harsh Reconstruction policies. On the eve of the commission's decision in the Florida controversy, he was apparently ready to vote in favor of Tilden. But the Republicans subjected him to tremendous political pressure. When he read his opinion on February 8, it was for Hayes. Thus, by a vote of eight to seven, the commission awarded Florida's electoral votes to the Republicans.

Grant, a Republican and a Union war hero, won easily in 1868 and 1872 because ex-Confederates, many of whom had voted Democratic, were barred from the polls. By 1876, however, white Democrats had regained political control in much of the South, creating the electoral stalemate that led to the Compromise of 1877.

The rest of the proceedings was routine. The commission assigned all the disputed electoral votes (including one in Oregon where the Democratic governor had seized on a technicality to replace a single Republican elector with a Democrat) to Hayes.

Democratic institutions, shaken by the South's refusal to go along with the majority in 1860 and by the suppression of civil rights during the rebellion, and further weakened by military intervention and the intimidation of blacks in the South during Reconstruction, seemed now a farce. According to Tilden's campaign manager, angry Democrats in fifteen states, chiefly war veterans, were readying themselves to march on Washington to force the inauguration of Tilden. Tempers flared in Congress, where some spoke ominously of a filibuster that would prevent the recording of the electoral vote and leave the country, on March 4, with no president at all.

The Compromise of 1877

Forces for compromise had been at work behind the scenes in Washington for some time. Although northern Democrats threatened to fight to the last ditch, many southern Democrats were willing to accept Hayes if he would promise to remove the troops and allow the southern states to manage their internal affairs by themselves. Ex-Whig planters and merchants who had reluctantly abandoned the carpetbag governments and who sympathized with Republican economic policies hoped that by supporting Hayes they might contribute to the restoration of the two-party system that had been destroyed in the South during the 1850s.

Tradition has it that a great compromise between the sections was worked out during a dramatic meeting at the Wormley Hotel[2] in Washington on February 26. Actually the negotiations were drawn out and informal, and the Wormley conference was but one of many. With the tacit support of many Democrats, the electoral vote was counted by the president of the Senate on March 2, and Hayes was declared elected, 185 votes to 184.

Like all compromises, the **Compromise of 1877** was not entirely satisfactory; like most, it was not honored in every detail. Hayes recalled the last troops from South Carolina and Louisiana in April. He appointed a former Confederate general, David M. Key of Tennessee, postmaster general and delegated to him the congenial task of finding Southerners willing to serve their country as officials of a Republican administration. But the alliance of ex-Whigs and northern Republicans did not flourish; the South remained solidly Democratic. The major significance of the compromise, one of the great intersectional political accommodations of American history, was that it ended Reconstruction and inaugurated a new political order in the South. More than the Constitutional amendments and federal statutes, this new regime would shape the destinies of the four million freedmen.

For many former slaves, this future was to be bleak. Forgotten in the North, manipulated and then callously rejected by the South, rebuffed by the Supreme Court, voiceless in national affairs, they and their descendants were condemned in the interests of sectional harmony to lives of poverty, indignity, and little hope. But many other former slaves managed to thrive during the last third of the nineteenth century. Their hard work, discipline, and financial savvy elevated them into a property-owning middle class whose existence—more than Union armies—marked the end of slavery.

Watch the Video

The Promise and Failure of Reconstruction at
myhistorylab.com

---

[2]Ironically, the hotel was owned by James Wormley, reputedly the wealthiest black person in Washington.

Table 15.1 Two Phases of Reconstruction: 1863–1877

Phase	Measure	Consequence
1. Presidential Reconstruction: Accommodation with white South		
	Lincoln's Ten-Percent Plan (1863)	Re-admits Southern states when 10 percent of 1860 voters profess loyalty to Union
	Lincoln vetoes Wade-Davis Bill (1864)	Retains 10 percent "easy-admission" policy
	Andrew Johnson pardons many Confederates and recommends admission of all former Confederate states	By 1866, all southern states are readmitted
	Southern states pass Black Codes (1864–1865) sharply restricting rights of former slaves	Outrages Republicans
2. Radical Reconstruction: Republicans gain power in Congress		
	Thirteenth Amendment (1865)	Ends Slavery
	Freedmen's Bureau (1865) established as branch of war department	Promotes education and economic opportunities for former slaves and destitute whites
	Congress passes Civil Rights Act over Johnson's veto (1866)	Republicans in Congress dominate federal government Washington
	Reconstruction Act of 1867	Divides South into five military districts, each under command of Union general
	Tenure of Office Act (1867)	Prohibits president from removing high officials
	Johnson impeached for firing Secretary of State Stanton	Johnson is tried but not removed from office

Table 15.1   Two Phases of Reconstruction: 1863–1877 (Continued)

Fourteenth Amendment (passed 1866, ratified 1868)	Requires that all citizens have "equal protection" of laws
Republican Grant elected president (1868)	Further increases Republican domination
Fifteenth Amendment (passed 1869, ratified 1870)	Prohibits voting restrictions on basis of race
Force Acts (1870-1871)	Federal control of elections in South

Milestones

1863	Lincoln announces "Ten Percent Plan" for Reconstruction
1865	Federal government sets up Freedmen's Bureau to ease transition from slavery to freedom
	General Lee surrenders at Appomattox Court House
	Abraham Lincoln is assassinated
	Andrew Johnson becomes president
	Johnson issues amnesty proclamation
	States ratify Thirteenth Amendment abolishing slavery
1865–1866	Southern states enact Black Codes
1866	Civil Rights Act passes over Johnson's veto
	Johnson campaigns for his Reconstruction policy
1867	First Reconstruction Act puts former Confederacy under military rule
	Tenure of Office Act protects Senate appointees
1868	House of Representatives impeaches Johnson

1868	Fourth Reconstruction Act requires a majority of Southern voters to ratify state constitutions
	Senate acquits Johnson
	States ratify Fourteenth Amendment extending rights to freed slaves
	Ulysses S. Grant is elected president
	Ku Klux Klan uses intimidation and force throughout South
1870	States ratify Fifteenth Amendment granting black suffrage
1870–1871	Force Act destroys Ku Klux Klan
1872	Liberal Republican party nominates Horace Greeley for president
	Grant is reelected president
1876	Rutherford B. Hayes runs against Samuel Tilden in disputed presidential election
1877	Electoral Commission awards disputed votes to Rutherford B. Hayes who becomes president
	Hayes agrees to Compromise of 1877 ending Reconstruction

✔•⌐Study and **Review** at www.myhistorylab.com

Review Questions

1. The introduction to this chapter—which cites the success of some randomly-chosen figures during Reconstruction—can be easily dismissed: Extraordinary people can prevail against any odds. What gains did most former slaves achieve during Reconstruction? Which federal policies and actions promoted their prospects?

2. What strategies did white Southerners use to control slaves after the Thirteenth Amendment had ended slavery?

3. Why did the Republicans in Congress disagree with Lincoln? With Andrew Johnson? In what sense did the Republican Congress come to "dominate" the political process?

4. What were the economic consequences of Reconstruction?

5. How did Reconstruction come to an end?

Key Terms

Black Codes *409*
carpetbaggers *419*
Compromise
    of 1877 *429*
crop-lien system *423*
Fifteenth
    Amendment *419*
Force Acts *424*

Fourteenth
    Amendment *415*
Freedmen's
    Bureau *414*
Ku Klux Klan *424*
Radical
    Republicans *412*
scalawags *419*

sharecropping *422*
Ten Percent Plan *411*
Thirteenth
    Amendment *413*
Wade-Davis Bill *412*

APPENDIX: The Declaration of Independence

In Congress, July 4, 1776

The Unanimous Declaration of the Thirteen United States of America,

When, in the course of human events, it becomes necessary for one people to dissolve the political bonds which have connected them with another, and to assume, among the powers of the earth, the separate and equal station to which the laws of nature and of nature's God entitle them, a decent respect to the opinions of mankind requires that they should declare the causes which impel them to the separation.

We hold these truths to be self-evident: That all men are created equal; that they are endowed by their Creator with certain unalienable rights; that among these are life, liberty, and the pursuit of happiness; that, to secure these rights, governments are instituted among men, deriving their just powers from the consent of the governed; that whenever any form of government becomes destructive of these ends, it is the right of the people to alter or to abolish it, and to institute new government, laying its foundation on such principles, and organizing its powers in such form, as to them shall seem most likely to effect their safety and happiness. Prudence, indeed, will dictate that governments long established should not be changed for light and transient causes; and accordingly all experience hath shown that mankind are more disposed to suffer, while evils are sufferable, than to right themselves by abolishing the forms to which they are accustomed. But when a long train of abuses and usurpations, pursuing invariably the same object, evinces a design to reduce them under absolute despotism, it is their right, it is their duty, to throw off such government, and to provide new guards for their future security. Such has been the patient sufferance of these colonies; and such is now the necessity which constrains them to alter their former systems of government. The history of the present King of Great Britain is a history of repeated injuries and usurpations, all having in direct object the establishment of an absolute tyranny over these states. To prove this, let facts be submitted to a candid world.

He has refused his assent to laws, the most wholesome and necessary for the public good.

He has forbidden his governors to pass laws of immediate and pressing importance, unless suspended in their operation till his assent should be obtained; and, when so suspended, he has utterly neglected to attend to them.

He has refused to pass other laws for the accommodation of large districts of people, unless those people would relinquish the right of representation in the legislature, a right inestimable to them, and formidable to tyrants only.

He has called together legislative bodies at places unusual, uncomfortable, and distant from the depository of their public records, for the sole purpose of fatiguing them into compliance with his measures.

He has dissolved representative houses repeatedly, for opposing, with manly firmness, his invasions on the rights of the people.

He has refused for a long time, after such dissolutions, to cause others to be elected; whereby the legislative powers, incapable of annihilation, have returned to the people at large for their exercise; the state remaining, in the mean time, exposed to all the dangers of invasions from without and convulsions within.

He has endeavored to prevent the population of these states; for that purpose obstructing the laws for naturalization of foreigners; refusing to pass others to encourage their migration hither, and raising the conditions of new appropriations of lands.

He has obstructed the administration of justice, by refusing his assent to laws for establishing judiciary powers.

He has made judges dependent on his will alone, for the tenure of their offices, and the amount and payment of their salaries.

He has erected a multitude of new offices, and sent hither swarms of officers to harass our people and eat out their substance.

He has kept among us, in times of peace, standing armies, without the consent of our legislatures.

He has affected to render the military independent of, and superior to, the civil power.

He has combined with others to subject us to a jurisdiction foreign to our constitution, and unacknowledged by our laws, giving his assent to their acts of pretended legislation:

For quartering large bodies of armed troops among us;

For protecting them, by a mock trial, from punishment for any murder which they should commit on the inhabitants of these states;

For cutting off our trade with all parts of the world;

For imposing taxes on us without our consent;

For depriving us, in many cases, of the benefits of trial by jury;

For transporting us beyond seas, to be tried for pretended offenses;

For abolishing the free system of English laws in a neighboring province, establishing therein an arbitrary government, and enlarging its boundaries, so as to render it at once an example and fit instrument for introducing the same absolute rule into these colonies;

For taking away our charters, abolishing our most valuable laws, and altering fundamentally the forms of our governments;

For suspending our own legislatures, and declaring themselves invested with power to legislate for us in all cases whatsoever.

He has abdicated government here, by declaring us out of his protection and waging war against us.

He has plundered our seas, ravaged our coasts, burned our towns, and destroyed the lives of our people.

He is at this time transporting large armies of foreign mercenaries to complete the works of death, desolation, and tyranny already begun with circumstances of cruelty and perfidy scarcely paralleled in the most barbarous ages, and totally unworthy the head of a civilized nation.

He has constrained our fellow-citizens, taken captive on the high seas, to bear arms against their country, to become the executioners of their friends and brethren, or to fall themselves by their hands.

He has excited domestic insurrection among us, and has endeavored to bring on the inhabitants of our frontiers the merciless Indian savages, whose known rule of warfare is an undistinguished destruction of all ages, sexes, and conditions.

In every stage of these oppressions we have petitioned for redress in the most humble terms; our repeated petitions have been answered only by repeated injury. A prince, whose character is thus marked by every act which may define a tyrant, is unfit to be the ruler of a free people.

Nor have we been wanting in our attentions to our British brethren. We have warned them, from time to time, of attempts by their legislature to extend an unwarrantable jurisdiction over us. We have reminded them of the circumstances of our emigration and settlement here. We have appealed to their native justice and magnanimity; and we have conjured them, by the ties of our common kindred, to disavow these usurpations, which would inevitably interrupt our connections and correspondence. They, too, have been deaf to the voice of justice and of consanguinity. We must, therefore, acquiesce in the necessity which denounces our separation, and hold them, as we hold the rest of mankind, enemies in war, in peace friends.

We, therefore, the representatives of the United States of America, in General Congress assembled, appealing to the Supreme Judge of the world for the rectitude of our intentions, do, in the name and by the authority of the good people of these colonies, solemnly publish and declare, that these United Colonies are, and of right ought to be, FREE AND INDEPENDENT STATES; that they are absolved from all allegiance to the British crown, and that all political connection between them and the state of Great Britain is, and ought to be, totally dissolved; and that, as free and independent states, they have full power to levy war, conclude peace, contract alliances, establish commerce, and do all other acts and things which independent states may of right do. And for the support of this declaration, with a firm reliance on the protection of Divine Providence, we mutually pledge to each other our lives, our fortunes, and our sacred honor.

John Hancock

New Hampshire
Josiah Bartlett
William Whipple
Matthew Thornton

Massachusetts
John Adams
Samuel Adams
Robert Treat Paine
Elbridge Gerry

New York
William Floyd
Philip Livingston
Francis Lewis
Lewis Morris

Rhode Island
Stephen Hopkins
William Ellery

New Jersey
Richard Stockton
John Witherspoon
Francis Hopkinson
John Hart
Abraham Clark

Pennsylvania
Robert Morris
Benjamin Rush
Benjamin Franklin
John Morton
George Clymer
James Smith
George Taylor
James Wilson
George Ross

Delaware
Caeser Rodney
George Read
Thomas McKean

Maryland
Samuel Chase
William Paca
Thomas Stone
Charles Carroll
of Carrollton

North Carolina
William Hooper
Joseph Hewes
John Penn

Virginia
George Wythe
Richard Henry Lee
Thomas Jefferson
Benjamin Harrison
Thomas Nelson, Jr.
Francis Lightfoot Lee
Carter Braxton

South Carolina
Edward Rutledge
Thomas Heyward, Jr.
Thomas Lynch, Jr.
Arthur Middleton

Connecticut
Roger Sherman
Samuel Huntington
William Williams
Oliver Wolcott

Georgia
Button Gwinnett
Lyman Hall
George Walton

The Constitution of the United States of America

Preamble

We the People of the United States, in Order to form a more perfect Union, establish Justice, insure domestic Tranquility, provide for the common defence, promote the general Welfare, and secure the Blessings of Liberty to ourselves and our Posterity, do ordain and establish this Constitution for the United States of America.

Article I

Section 1

All legislative Powers herein granted shall be vested in a Congress of the United States, which shall consist of a Senate and House of Representatives.

Section 2

The House of Representatives shall be composed of Members chosen every second Year by the People of the several States, and the Electors in each State shall have the Qualifications requisite for Electors of the most numerous Branch of the State Legislature.

No Person shall be a Representative who shall not have attained to the Age of twenty five Years, and been seven Years a Citizen of the United States, and who shall not, when elected, be an inhabitant of that State in which he shall be chosen.

Representatives and direct Taxes shall be apportioned among the several States which may be included within this Union, according to their respective Numbers, *which shall be determined by adding to the whole Number of free Persons, including those bound to Service for a Term of Years, and excluding Indians not taxed, three fifths of all other Persons.** The actual Enumeration shall be made within three Years after the first Meeting of the Congress of the United States, and within every subsequent Term of ten Years, in such Manner as they shall by Law direct. The Number of Representatives shall not exceed one for every thirty Thousand, but each State shall have at Least one Representative; *and until such enumeration shall be made, the State of New Hampshire shall be entitled to chuse three, Massachusetts eight, Rhode-Island and Providence Plantations one, Connecticut five, New York six, New Jersey four, Pennsylvania eight, Delaware one, Maryland six, Virginia ten, North Carolina five, South Carolina five, and Georgia three.*

When vacancies happen in the Representation from any State, the Executive Authority thereof shall issue Writs of Election to fill such Vacancies.

The House of Representatives shall chuse their Speaker and other Officers; and shall have the sole Power of Impeachment.

---

*Passages no longer in effect are printed in italic type.

Section 3

The Senate of the United States shall be composed of two Senators from each State, *chosen by the Legislature thereof*, for six Years; and each Senator shall have one Vote.

Immediately after they shall be assembled in Consequence of the first Election, they shall be divided as equally as may be into three Classes. The Seats of the Senators of the first Class shall be vacated at the Expiration of the second Year, of the second Class at the Expiration of the fourth Year, and of the third Class at the Expiration of the sixth Year so that one third may be chosen every second Year; and if Vacancies happen by Resignation, or otherwise, during the Recess of the Legislature of any state, the Executive thereof may make temporary Appointments until the next Meeting of the Legislature, which shall then fill such Vacancies.

No Person shall be a Senator who shall not have attained to the Age of thirty Years, and been nine Years a Citizen of the United States, and who shall not, when elected, be an Inhabitant of that State for which he shall be chosen.

The Vice President of the United States shall be President of the Senate, but shall have no Vote, unless they be equally divided.

The Senate shall chuse their other Officers, and also a President *pro tempore*, in the Absence of the Vice President, or when he shall exercise the Office of President of the United States.

The Senate shall have the sole Power to try all Impeachments. When sitting for that Purpose, they shall be on Oath or Affirmation. When the President of the United States is tried the Chief Justice shall preside: And no Person shall be convicted without the Concurrence of two thirds of the Members present.

Judgment in Cases of Impeachment shall not extend further than to removal from Office, and disqualification to hold and enjoy any Office of honor, Trust or Profit under the United States: but the Party convicted shall nevertheless be liable and subject to Indictment, Trial, Judgment and Punishment, according to Law.

Section 4

The Times, Places and Manner of holding Elections for Senators and Representatives, shall be prescribed in each State by the Legislature thereof; but the Congress may at any time by Law make or alter such Regulations, except as to the Places of chusing Senators.

The Congress shall assemble at least once in every Year, *and such Meeting shall be on the first Monday in December, unless they shall by Law appoint a different Day.*

Section 5

Each House shall be the Judge of the Elections, Returns and Qualifications of its own Members, and a Majority of each shall constitute a Quorum to do Business; but a smaller Number may adjourn from day to day, and may be authorized to compel the Attendance of absent Members, in such Manner, and under such Penalties as each House may provide.

Each House may determine the Rules of its Proceedings, punish its Members for disorderly Behaviour, and, with the Concurrence of two thirds, expel a Member.

Each House shall keep a Journal of its Proceedings, and from time to time publish the same, excepting such Parts as may in their Judgment require Secrecy; and the Yeas and Nays of the Members of either House on any question shall, at the Desire of one fifth of those Present, be entered on the Journal.

Neither House, during the Session of Congress, shall, without the Consent of the other, adjourn for more than three days, nor to any other Place than that in which the two Houses shall be sitting.

Section 6

The Senators and Representatives shall receive a Compensation for their Services, to be ascertained by Law, and paid out of the Treasury of the United States. They shall in all Cases, except Treason, Felony and Breach of the Peace, be privileged from Arrest during their Attendance at the Session of their respective Houses, and in going to and returning from the same; and for any Speech or Debate in either House, they shall not be questioned in any other Place.

No Senator or Representative shall, during the Time for which he was elected, be appointed to any civil Office under the Authority of the United States, which shall have been created, or the Emoluments whereof shall have been encreased during such time, and no Person holding any Office under the United States, shall be a Member of either House during his Continuance in Office.

Section 7

All Bills for raising Revenue shall originate in the House of Representatives; but the Senate may propose or concur with Amendments as on other Bills.

Every Bill which shall have passed the House of Representatives and the Senate, shall, before it become a Law, be presented to the President of the United States; If he approve he shall sign it, but if not he shall return it, with his Objections to the House in which it shall have originated, who shall enter the Objections at large on their Journal, and proceed to reconsider it. If after such Reconsideration two thirds of that House shall agree to pass the Bill, it shall be sent, together with the Objections, to the other House, by which it shall likewise be reconsidered, and if approved by two thirds of that House, it shall become a Law. But in all such Cases the Votes of both Houses shall be determined by yeas and Nays, and the Names of the Persons voting for and against the Bill shall be entered on the Journal of each House respectively. If any Bill shall not be returned by the President within ten Days (Sundays excepted) after it shall have been presented to him, the Same shall be a Law, in like Manner as if he had signed it, unless the Congress by their Adjournment prevent its Return, in which Case it shall not be a Law.

Every Order, Resolution, or Vote to which the Concurrence of the Senate and House of Representatives may be necessary (except on a question of Adjournment) shall be presented to the President of the United States; and before the Same shall take Effect, shall be approved by him, or being disapproved by him, shall be repassed by two thirds of the Senate and House of Representatives, according to the Rules and Limitations prescribed in the Case of a Bill.

Section 8

The Congress shall have Power To lay and collect Taxes, Duties, Imposts and Excises, to pay the Debts and provide for the common Defence and general Welfare of the United States; but all Duties, Imposts and Excises shall be uniform throughout the United States;

To borrow Money on the credit of the United States;

To regulate Commerce with foreign Nations, and among the several States, and with the Indian Tribes;

To establish an uniform Rule of Naturalization, and uniform Laws on the subject of Bankruptcies throughout the United States;

To coin Money, regulate the Value thereof, and of foreign Coin, and fix the Standard of Weights and Measures;

To provide for the Punishment of counterfeiting the Securities and current Coin of the United States;

To establish Post Offices and post Roads;

To promote the Progress of Science and useful Arts, by securing for limited Times to Authors and Inventors the exclusive Right to their respective Writings and Discoveries;

To constitute Tribunals inferior to the supreme Court;

To define and punish Piracies and Felonies committed on the high Seas, and Offences against the Law of Nations;

To declare War, grant Letters of Marque and Reprisal, and make Rules concerning Captures on Land and Water;

To raise and support Armies, but no Appropriation of Money to that Use shall be for a longer Term than two Years;

To provide and maintain a Navy;

To make Rules for the Government and Regulation of the land and naval Forces;

To provide for calling forth the Militia to execute the Laws of the Union, suppress Insurrections and repel Invasions;

To provide for organizing, arming, and disciplining, the Militia, and for governing such Part of them as may be employed in the Service of the United States, reserving to the States respectively, the Appointment of the Officers, and the Authority of training the Militia according to the discipline prescribed by Congress;

To exercise exclusive Legislation in all Cases whatsoever, over such District (not exceeding ten Miles square) as may, by Cession of particular States, and the Acceptance of Congress, become the Seat of the Government of the United States, and to exercise like Authority over all Places purchased by the Consent of the Legislature of the State in which the Same shall be, for the Erection of Forts, Magazines, Arsenals, dock-Yards, and other needful Buildings;—And

To make all Laws which shall be necessary and proper for carrying into Execution the foregoing Powers, and all other Powers vested by this Constitution in the Government of the United States, or in any Department of Officer thereof.

Section 9

The Migration or Importation of such Persons as any of the States now existing shall think proper to admit, shall not be prohibited by the Congress prior to the Year one thousand eight hundred and eight, but a Tax or duty may be imposed on such Importation, not exceeding ten dollars for each Person.

The Privilege of the Writ of Habeas Corpus shall not be suspended, unless when in Cases of Rebellion or Invasion the public Safety may require it.

No Bill of Attainder or ex post facto Law shall be passed.

No Capitation, or other direct, Tax shall be laid, unless in Proportion to the Census or Enumeration herein before directed to be taken.

No Tax or Duty shall be laid on Articles exported from any State.

No Preference shall be given by any Regulation of Commerce or Revenue to the Ports of one State over those of another: nor shall Vessels bound to, or from, one State, be obliged to enter, clear, or pay Duties in another.

No Money shall be drawn from the Treasury, but in Consequence of Appropriations made by Law; and a regular Statement and Account of the Receipts and Expenditures of all public Money shall be published from time to time.

No Title of Nobility shall be granted by the United States: And no Person holding any Office of Profit or Trust under them, shall, without the Consent of the Congress, accept of any present, Emolument, Office, or Title, of any kind whatever, from any King, Prince, or foreign State.

Section 10

No State shall enter into any Treaty, Alliance, or Confederation; grant Letters of Marque and Reprisal; coin Money; emit Bills of Credit; make any Thing but gold and silver Coin a Tender in Payment of Debts; pass any Bill of Attainder, ex post facto Law, or Law impairing the obligation of Contracts, or grant any Title of Nobility.

No State shall, without the Consent of the Congress, lay any Imposts or Duties on Imports or Exports, except what may be absolutely necessary for executing its inspection Laws: and the net Produce of all Duties and Imposts, laid by any State on Imports or Exports, shall be for the Use of the Treasury of the United States; and all such Laws shall be subject to the Revision and Controul of the Congress.

No State shall, without the Consent of Congress, lay any Duty of Tonnage, keep Troops, or Ships of War in time of Peace, enter into any Agreement or Compact with another State, or with a foreign Power, or engage in War, unless actually invaded, or in such imminent Danger as will not admit of delay.

Article II

Section 1

The executive Power shall be vested in a President of the United States of America. He shall hold his Office during the Term of four Years, and, together with the Vice President, chosen for the same Term, be elected, as follows:

Each State shall appoint, in such Manner as the Legislature thereof may direct, a Number of Electors, equal to the whole Number of Senators and Representatives to which the State may be entitled in the Congress: but no Senator or Representative, or Person holding an Office of Trust or Profit under the United States, shall be appointed an Elector.

The Electors shall meet in their respective States, and vote by Ballot for two Persons, of whom one at least shall not be an Inhabitant of the same State with themselves. And they shall make a List of all the Persons voted for, and of the Number of Votes for each; which List they shall sign and certify, and transmit sealed to the Seat of the Government of the United States, directed to the President of the Senate. The President of the Senate shall, in the Presence of the Senate and House of Representatives, open all the Certificates, and the Votes shall then be counted. The Person having the greatest Number of Votes shall be the President, if such Number be a Majority of the whole number of Electors appointed; and if there be more than one who have such Majority, and have an equal Number of Votes, then the House of Representatives shall immediately chuse by Ballot one of them for President; and if no Person have a Majority, then from the five highest on the List the said House shall in like Manner chuse the President. But in chusing the President, the Votes shall be taken by States, the Representation from each State having one Vote; A quorum for this Purpose shall consist of a Member or Members from two thirds of the States, and a Majority of all the States shall be necessary to a Choice. In every Case, after the Choice of the President, the Person having the greatest Number of Votes of the Electors shall be the Vice President. But if there should remain two or more who have equal Votes, the Senate shall chuse from them by Ballot the Vice President.

The Congress may determine the time of chusing the Electors, and the Day on which they shall give their Votes; which Day shall be the same throughout the United States.

No person except a natural born Citizen, *or a Citizen of the United States, at the time of the Adoption of this Constitution,* shall be eligible to the Office of

President; neither shall any Person be eligible to that Office who shall not have attained to the Age of thirty five Years, and been fourteen Years a Resident within the United States.

In Case of the Removal of the President from Office, or of his Death, Resignation, or Inability to discharge the Powers and Duties of the said Office, the Same shall devolve on the Vice President, and the Congress may by Law provide for the Case of Removal, Death, Resignation or Inability, both of the President and Vice President, declaring what Officer shall then act as President, and such Officer shall act accordingly, until the Disability be removed, or a President shall be elected.

The President shall, at stated Times, receive for his Services, a Compensation, which shall neither be encreased nor diminished during the Period for which he shall have been elected, and he shall not receive within that period any other Emolument from the United States, or any of them.

Before he enter on the Execution of his Office, he shall take the following Oath or Affirmation:—"I do solemnly swear (or affirm) that I will faithfully execute the Office of President of the United States, and will to the best of my Ability, preserve, protect and defend the Constitution of the United States."

Section 2

The President shall be Commander in Chief of the Army and Navy of the United States, and of the Militia of the several States, when called into the actual Service of the United States; he may require the Opinion, in writing, of the principal Officer in each of the executive Departments, upon any Subject relating to the Duties of their respective Offices, and he shall have Power to grant Reprieves and Pardons for Offences against the United States, except in Cases of Impeachment.

He shall have Power, by and with the Advice and Consent of the Senate, to make Treaties, provided two thirds of the Senators present concur; and he shall nominate, and by and with the Advice and Consent of the Senate, shall appoint Ambassadors, other public Ministers and Consuls, Judges of the supreme Court, and all other Officers of the United States, whose Appointments are not herein otherwise provided for, and which shall be established by Law: but the Congress may by Law vest the Appointment of such inferior Officers, as they think proper in the President alone, in the Courts of Law, or in the Heads of Departments.

The President shall have Power to fill up all Vacancies that may happen during the Recess of the Senate, by granting Commissions which shall expire at the End of their next Session.

Section 3

He shall from time to time give to the Congress Information of the State of the Union, and recommend to their Consideration such Measures as he shall judge necessary and expedient; he may, on extraordinary Occasions, convene both Houses, or either of them, and in Case of disagreement between them, with Respect to the Time of Adjournment, he may adjourn them to such Time as he shall think proper; he shall receive Ambassadors and other public Ministers; he shall take Care that the Laws be faithfully executed, and shall Commission all the officers of the United States.

Section 4

The President, Vice President and all civil Officers of the United States, shall be removed from Office on Impeachment for, and Conviction of, Treason, Bribery or other high Crimes and Misdemeanors.

Article III

Section 1

The judicial Power of the United States, shall be vested in one supreme Court, and in such inferior Courts as the Congress may from time to time ordain and establish. The Judges, both of the supreme and inferior Courts, shall hold their offices during good Behaviour, and shall, at stated Times, receive for their Services, a Compensation, which shall not be diminished during their Continuance in Office.

Section 2

The judicial Power shall extend to all Cases, in Law and Equity, arising under this Constitution, the Laws of the United States, and Treaties made, or which shall be made, under their Authority;—to all Cases affecting Ambassadors, other public Ministers and Consuls;—to all Cases of admiralty and maritime Jurisdiction;—to Controversies to which the United States shall be a Party;—to Controversies between two or more States;— *between a State and Citizens of another State;*—between Citizens of different States;— between Citizens of the same State claiming Lands under Grants of different States, and between a State, or the Citizens thereof, and foreign States, Citizens or Subjects.

In all Cases affecting Ambassadors, other public Ministers and Consuls, and those in which a State shall be Party, the supreme Court shall have original Jurisdiction. In all the other Cases before mentioned, the supreme Court shall have appellate Jurisdiction, both as to Law and Fact, with such Exceptions, and under such Regulations as the Congress shall make.

The Trial of all Crimes, except in Cases of Impeachment, shall be by Jury; and such Trial shall be held in the State where the said Crimes shall have been committed, but when not committed within any State, the Trial shall be at such Place or Places as the Congress may by Law have directed.

Section 3

Treason against the United States, shall consist only in levying War against them, or in adhering to their Enemies, giving them Aid and Comfort. No person shall be convicted of Treason unless on the Testimony of two Witnesses to the same overt Act, or on Confession in open Court.

The Congress shall have Power to declare the Punishment of Treason, but no Attainder of Treason shall work Corruption of Blood, or Forfeiture except during the Life of the Person attainted.

Article IV

Section 1

Full Faith and Credit shall be given in each State to the public Acts, Records, and judicial Proceedings of every other State. And the Congress may by general Laws prescribe the Manner in which such Acts, Records and Proceedings shall be proved, and the Effect thereof.

Section 2

The Citizens of each State shall be entitled to all Privileges and Immunities of Citizens in the several States.

A Person charged in any State with Treason, Felony, or other Crime, who shall flee from Justice, and be found in another State, shall on Demand of the executive

Authority of the State from which he fled, be delivered up, to be removed to the State having Jurisdiction of the Crime.

No Person held to Service or Labour in one State, under the Laws thereof, escaping into another, shall, in Consequence of any Law or Regulation therein, be discharged from such Service or Labour, but shall be delivered up on Claim of the Party to whom such Service or Labour may be due.

Section 3

New States may be admitted by the Congress into this Union; but no new State shall be formed or erected within the Jurisdiction of any other State; nor any State be formed by the Junction of two or more States, or Parts of States, without the Consent of the Legislatures of the States concerned as well as of the Congress.

The Congress shall have Power to dispose of and make all needful Rules and Regulations respecting the Territory or other Property belonging to the United States; and nothing in this Constitution shall be so construed as to Prejudice any Claims of the United States, or of any particular States.

Section 4

The United States shall guarantee to every State in this Union a Republican Form of Government, and shall protect each of them against Invasion; and on Application of the Legislature, or of the Executive (when the Legislature cannot be convened) against domestic violence.

Article V

The Congress, whenever two thirds of both Houses shall deem it necessary, shall propose Amendments to this Constitution, or, on the Application of the Legislatures of two thirds of the several States, shall call a Convention for proposing Amendments, which, in either Case, shall be valid to all Intents and Purposes, as Part of this Constitution, when ratified by the Legislatures of three fourths of the several States, or by Conventions in three fourths thereof, as the one or the other Mode of Ratification may be proposed by the Congress; Provided *that no Amendment which may be made prior to the Year One thousand eight hundred and eight shall in any Manner affect the first and fourth Clauses in the Ninth Section of the first Article;* and that no State, without its Consent, shall be deprived of its equal Suffrage in the Senate.

Article VI

All Debts contracted and Engagements entered into, before the Adoption of this Constitution, shall be as valid against the United States under this Constitution, as under the Confederation.

This Constitution, and Laws of the United States which shall be made in Pursuance thereof; and all Treaties made, or which shall be made, under the Authority of the United States, shall be the supreme Law of the Land; and the Judges in every State shall be bound thereby, any Thing in the Constitution or Laws of any State to the Contrary notwithstanding.

The Senators and Representatives before mentioned, and the Members of the several State Legislatures, and all executive and Judicial Officers, both of the United States and of the several States, shall be bound by Oath or Affirmation, to support this Constitution; but no religious Test shall ever be required as a Qualification to any Office of public Trust under the United States.

Article VII

The Ratification of the Conventions of nine States, shall be sufficient for the Establishment of this Constitution between the States so ratifying the Same.

Done in Convention by the Unanimous Consent of the States present the Seventeenth Day of September in the Year of our Lord one thousand seven hundred and Eighty seven and of the Independence of the United States of America the Twelfth[†] IN WITNESS whereof We have hereunto subscribed our Names,

George Washington
President and Deputy from Virginia

Delaware
George Read
Gunning Bedford, Jr.
John Dickinson
Richard Bassett
Jacob Broom

Maryland
James McHenry
Daniel of St. Thomas
Jenifer
Daniel Carroll

Virginia
John Blair
James Madison, Jr.

North Carolina
William Blount
Richard Dobbs Spraight
Hugh Williamson

South Carolina
John Rutledge
Charles Cotesworth
Pinckney
Charles Pinckney
Pierce Butler

Georgia
William Paterson
William Few
Abraham Baldwin

New Hampshire
John Langdon
Nicholas Gilman

Massachusetts
Nathaniel Gorham
Rufus King

Connecticut
William Samuel Johnson
Roger Sherman

New York
Alexander Hamilton

New Jersey
William Livingston
David Brearley
Jonathan Dayton

Pennsylvania
Benjamin Franklin
Thomas Mifflin
Robert Morris
George Clymer
Thomas FitzSimons
Jared Ingersoll
James Wilson
Gouverneur Morris

[†]The Constitution was submitted on September 17, 1787, by the Constitutional Convention, was ratified by the Convention of several states at various dates up to May 29, 1790, and became effective on March 4, 1789.

Amendments to the Constitution

Amendment I

Congress shall make no law respecting an establishment of religion, or prohibiting the free exercise thereof; or abridging the freedom of speech, or of the press; or the right of the people peaceably to assemble, and to petition the Government for a redress of grievances.

Amendment II

A well regulated Militia being necessary to the security of a free State, the right of the people to keep and bear Arms, shall not be infringed.

Amendment III

No Soldier shall, in time of peace be quartered in any house, without the consent of the Owner, nor in time of war, but in a manner to be prescribed by law.

Amendment IV

The right of the people to be secure in their persons, houses, papers, and effects, against unreasonable searches and seizures, shall not be violated, and no Warrants shall issue, but upon probable cause, supported by Oath or affirmation, and particularly describing the place to be searched, and the persons or things to be seized.

Amendment V

No person shall be held to answer for a capital, or otherwise infamous crime, unless on a presentment or indictment of a Grand Jury, except in cases arising in the land or naval forces, or in the Militia, when in actual service in time of War or public danger; nor shall any person be subject for the same offense to be twice put in jeopardy of life or limb; nor shall be compelled in any criminal case to be a witness against himself, nor be deprived of life, liberty, or property, without due process of law; nor shall private property be taken for public use, without just compensation.

Amendment VI

In all criminal prosecutions, the accused shall enjoy the right to a speedy and public trial, by an impartial jury of the State and district wherein the crime shall have been committed, which district shall have been previously ascertained by law, and to be informed of the nature and cause of the accusation; to be confronted with the witnesses against him; to have compulsory process for obtaining witnesses in his favor, and to have the Assistance of Counsel for his defence.

Amendment VII

In Suits at common law, where the value in controversy shall exceed twenty dollars, the right of trial by jury shall be preserved, and no fact tried by a jury, shall be otherwise re-examined in any Court of the United States, than according to the rules of the common law.

Amendment VIII

Excessive bail shall not be required, nor excessive fines imposed, nor cruel and unusual punishments inflicted.

Amendment IX

The enumeration in the Constitution, of certain rights, shall not be construed to deny or disparage others retained by the people.

Amendment X*

The powers not delegated to the United States by the Constitution, nor prohibited by it to the States, are reserved to the States respectively, or to the people.

Amendment XI

[Adopted 1798]

The Judicial power of the United States shall not be construed to extend to any suit in law or equity, commenced or prosecuted against one of the United States by Citizens of another State, or by Citizens or Subjects of any Foreign State.

Amendment XII

[Adopted 1804]

The Electors shall meet in their respective states, and vote by ballot for President and Vice President, one of whom, at least, shall not be an inhabitant of the same state with themselves; they shall name in their ballots the person voted for as President, and in distinct ballots the person voted for as Vice President, and they shall make distinct lists of all persons voted for as President, and of all persons voted for as Vice President, and of the number of votes for each, which lists they shall sign and certify, and transmit sealed to the seat of the government of the United States, directed to the President of the Senate;—The President of the Senate shall, in the presence of the Senate and House of Representatives, open all the certificates and the votes shall then be counted;—The person having the greatest number of votes for President, shall be the President, if such number be a majority of the whole number of Electors appointed; and if no person have such majority, then from the persons having the highest numbers not exceeding three

---

*The first ten amendments (the Bill of Rights) were ratified and their adoption was certified on December 15, 1791.

on the list of those voted for as President, the House of Representatives shall choose immediately, by ballot, the President. But in choosing the President, the votes shall be taken by states, the representation from each state having one vote; a quorum for this purpose shall consist of a member or members from two-thirds of the states, and a majority of all the states shall be necessary to a choice. And if the House of Representatives shall not choose a President whenever the right of choice shall devolve upon them, before *the fourth day of March* next following, then the Vice President shall act as President, as in the case of the death or other constitutional disability of the President.—The person having the greatest number of votes as Vice President, shall be the Vice President, if such number be a majority of the whole number of Electors appointed, and if no person have a majority, then from the two highest numbers on the list, the Senate shall choose the Vice President; a quorum for the purpose shall consist of two-thirds of the whole number of Senators, and a majority of the whole number shall be necessary to a choice. But no person constitutionally ineligible to the office of President shall be eligible to that of Vice President of the United States.

Amendment XIII

[Adopted 1865]

Section 1

Neither slavery nor involuntary servitude, except as a punishment for crime whereof the party shall have been duly convicted, shall exist within the United States, or any place subject to their jurisdiction.

Section 2

Congress shall have power to enforce this article by appropriate legislation.

Amendment XIV

[Adopted 1868]

Section 1

All persons born or naturalized in the United States, and subject to the jurisdiction thereof, are citizens of the United States and of the State wherein they reside. No State shall make or enforce any law which shall abridge the privileges or immunities of citizens of the United States; nor shall any State deprive any person of life, liberty, or property, without due process of law; nor deny to any person within its jurisdiction the equal protection of the laws.

Section 2

Representatives shall be apportioned among the several States according to their respective numbers, counting the whole number of persons in each State, excluding Indians not taxed. But when the right to vote at any election for the choice of electors for President and Vice President of the United States, Representatives in Congress, the Executive and Judicial officers of a State, or the members of the Legislature thereof, is denied to any of the male inhabitants of such State, being twenty-one years of age, and citizens of the United States, or in any way abridged, except for participation in rebellion, or other crime, the basis of representation therein shall be reduced in the proportion which the number of such male citizens shall bear to the whole number of male citizens twenty-one years of age in such State.

Section 3

No person shall be a Senator or Representative in Congress, or elector of President and Vice President, or hold any office, civil or military, under the United States, or under any State, who, having previously taken an oath, as a member of Congress, or as an officer of the United States, or as a member of any State legislature, or as an executive or judicial officer of any State, to support the Constitution of the United States, shall have engaged in insurrection or rebellion against the same, or given aid or comfort to the enemies thereof. But Congress may by a vote of two-thirds of each House, remove such disability.

Section 4

The validity of the public debt of the United States, authorized by law, including debts incurred for payment of pensions and bounties for services in suppressing insurrection or rebellion, shall not be questioned. But neither the United States nor any State shall assume or pay any debt or obligation incurred in aid of insurrection or rebellion against the United States, or any claim for the loss or emancipation of any slave; but all such debts, obligations and claims shall be held illegal and void.

Section 5

The Congress shall have power to enforce, by appropriate legislation, the provisions of this article.

Amendment XV

[Adopted 1870]

Section 1

The right of citizens of the United States to vote shall not be denied or abridged by the United States or by any State on account of race, color, or previous condition of servitude.

Section 2

The Congress shall have power to enforce this article by appropriate legislation.

Amendment XVI

[Adopted 1913]

The Congress shall have power to lay and collect taxes on incomes, from whatever source derived, without apportionment among the several States, and without regard to any census or enumeration.

Amendment XVII

[Adopted 1913]

The Senate of the United States shall be composed of two Senators from each State, elected by the people thereof, for six years; and each Senator shall have one vote. The electors in each State shall have the qualifications requisite for electors of the most numerous branch of the State legislatures.

When vacancies happen in the representation of any State in the Senate, the executive authority of such State shall issue writs of election to fill such vacancies: *Provided,*

That the legislature of any State may empower the executive thereof to make temporary appointments until the people fill the vacancies by election as the legislature may direct.

This amendment shall not be so construed as to affect the election or term of any Senator chosen before it becomes valid as part of the Constitution.

Amendment XVIII

[Adopted 1919, repealed 1933]

Section 1

After one year from the ratification of this article the manufacture, sale, or transportation of intoxicating liquors within, the importation thereof into, or the exportation thereof from the United States and all territory subject to the jurisdiction thereof for beverage purposes is hereby prohibited.

Section 2

The Congress and the several States shall have concurrent power to enforce this article by appropriate legislation.

Section 3

This article shall be inoperative unless it shall have been ratified as an amendment to the Constitution by the legislatures of the several States, as provided in the Constitution, within seven years from the date of the submission hereof to the States by the Congress.

Amendment XIX

[Adopted 1920]

The right of citizens of the United States to vote shall not be denied or abridged by the United States or by any State on account of sex.

Congress shall have power to enforce this article by appropriate legislation.

Amendment XX

[Adopted 1933]

Section 1

The terms of the President and Vice President shall end at noon on the 20th day of January, and the terms of Senators and Representatives at noon on the 3d day of January, of the years in which such terms would have ended if this article had not been ratified and the terms of their successors shall then begin.

Section 2

The Congress shall assemble at least once in every year, and such meeting shall begin at noon on the 3d day of January, unless they shall by law appoint a different day.

Section 3

If, at the time fixed for the beginning of the term of the President, the President elect shall have died, the Vice President elect shall become President. If a President shall not have been chosen before the time fixed for the beginning of his term, or if the President elect shall have failed to qualify, then the Vice President elect shall act as President until a President shall have qualified; and the Congress may by law provide for the case wherein neither a President elect nor a Vice President elect shall have qualified, declaring who shall then act as President, or the manner in which one who is to act shall be selected, and such person shall act accordingly until a President or Vice President shall have qualified.

Section 4

The Congress may by law provide for the case of the death of any of the persons from whom the House of Representatives may choose a President whenever the right of choice shall have devolved upon them, and for the case of the death of any of the persons from whom the Senate may choose a Vice President whenever the right of choice shall have devolved upon them.

Section 5

Sections 1 and 2 shall take effect on the 15th day of October following the ratification of this article.

Section 6

This article shall be inoperative unless it shall have been ratified as an amendment to the Constitution by the legislatures of three fourths of the several States within seven years from the date of its submission.

Amendment XXI

[Adopted 1933]

Section 1

The eighteenth article of amendment to the Constitution of the United States is hereby repealed.

Section 2

The transportation or importation into any State, Territory, or possession of the United States for delivery or use therein of intoxicating liquors in violation of the laws thereof, is hereby prohibited.

Section 3

This article shall be inoperative unless it shall have been ratified as an amendment to the Constitution by conventions in the several States, as provided in the Constitution, within seven years from the date of the submission hereof to the States by the Congress.

Amendment XXII

[Adopted 1951]

Section 1

No person shall be elected to the office of the President more than twice, and no person who has held the office of President, or acted as President, for more than two years of a term to which some other person was elected President shall be elected to the office of the President more than once. But this Article shall not apply to any person holding the office of President when this Article was proposed by the Congress, and shall not prevent any person who may be holding the office of President, or acting as President, during the term within which this Article becomes operative from holding the office of President or acting as President during the remainder of such term.

Section 2

This article shall be inoperative unless it shall have been ratified as an amendment to the Constitution by the legislatures of three-fourths of the several States within seven years from the date of its submission to the States by the Congress.

Amendment XXIII

[Adopted 1961]

Section 1

The District constituting the seat of Government of the United States shall appoint in such manner as the Congress shall direct:

A number of electors of President and Vice President equal to the whole number of Senators and Representatives in Congress to which the District would be entitled if it were a State, but in no event more than the least populous State; they shall be in addition to those appointed by the States, but they shall be considered, for the purposes of the election of President and Vice President, to be electors appointed by a State; and they shall meet in the District and perform such duties as provided by the twelfth article of amendment.

Section 2

The Congress shall have power to enforce this article by appropriate legislation.

Amendment XXIV

[Adopted 1964]

Section 1

The right of citizens of the United States to vote in any primary or other election for President or Vice President, for electors for President or Vice President, or for Senator or Representative in Congress, shall not be denied or abridged by the United States or any state by reason of failure to pay any poll tax or other tax.

Section 2

The Congress shall have the power to enforce this article by appropriate legislation.

Amendment XXV

[Adopted 1967]

Section 1

In case of the removal of the President from office or his death or resignation, the Vice President shall become President.

Section 2

Whenever there is a vacancy in the office of the Vice President, the President shall nominate a Vice President who shall take the office upon confirmation by a majority vote of both houses of Congress.

Section 3

Whenever the President transmits to the President pro tempore of the Senate and the Speaker of the House of Representatives his written declaration that he is unable to discharge the powers and duties of his office, and until he transmits to them a written declaration to the contrary, such powers and duties shall be discharged by the Vice President as Acting President.

Section 4

Whenever the Vice President and a majority of either the principal officers of the executive departments or of such other body as Congress may by law provide, transmit to the President pro tempore of the Senate and the Speaker of the House of Representatives their written declaration that the President is unable to discharge the powers and duties of his office, the Vice President shall immediately assume the powers and duties of the office as Acting President.

Thereafter, when the President transmits to the President pro tempore of the Senate and the Speaker of the House of Representatives his written declaration that no inability exists, he shall resume the powers and duties of his office unless the Vice President and a majority of either the principal officers of the executive department or of such other body as Congress may by law provide, transmit within four days to the President pro tempore of the Senate and the Speaker of the House of Representatives their written declaration that the President is unable to discharge the powers and duties of his office. Thereupon Congress shall decide the issue, assembling within 48 hours for that purpose if not in session. If the Congress, within 21 days after receipt of the latter written declaration, or, if Congress is not in session, within 21 days after Congress is required to assemble, determines by two-thirds vote of both houses that the President is unable to discharge the powers and duties of his office, the Vice President shall continue to discharge the same as Acting President; otherwise, the President shall resume the powers and duties of his office.

Amendment XXVI

[Adopted 1971]

Section 1

The right of citizens of the United States, who are 18 years of age or older, to vote shall not be denied or abridged by the United States or any state on account of age.

Section 2

The Congress shall have the power to enforce this article by appropriate legislation.

Amendment XXVII

[Adopted 1992]

No law, varying the compensation for the services of the Senators and Representatives shall take effect, until an election of Representatives shall have intervened.

Glossary

abolitionism (p. 282) Worldwide movement to end slavery. In the United States the term chiefly applies to the antebellum reformers whose cause culminated in the Civil War.

acquired immunodeficiency syndrome (AIDS) (p. 821) A deadly, and very often sexually transmitted disease that emerged in the 1980s and that at first spread chiefly among injection drug users and gay male populations, but soon affected all communities. The disease is a complex of deadly pathologies resulting from infection with the **human immunodeficiency virus (HIV)**. By 2000, AIDS deaths in the United States had surpassed 40,000.

Agricultural Adjustment Act (AAA) (p. 681) New Deal legislation that raised farm prices by restricting output of staple crops. It restricted production and paid subsidies to growers; declared unconstitutional in 1936.

Albany Plan (p. 87) A proposal, drafted in Albany, New York, in 1754 by Benjamin Franklin of Pennsylvania, for a "plan of union" for the collective defense of the British colonies. Because it held the potential for unifying the colonies against its rule, the British government never adopted the plan.

Alien and Sedition Acts (p. 167) Four laws passed by the Federalist-dominated Congress in 1798 directed against sympathizers to the **French Revolution**—chiefly Thomas Jefferson and his **Republican party**. The laws, which stifled dissent and made it more difficult for immigrants to gain citizenship, had lapsed by 1802.

Allied Powers (p. 603) The military alliance during World War I, chiefly consisting of Britain, France, Russia, and Italy, that opposed the **Central Powers**, chiefly Germany, Austria-Hungary, and Turkey.

Allies (p. 718) In the context of United States history, a term that refers to the nations that opposed the **Axis Powers**, chiefly Nazi Germany, Italy, and Japan, during World War II. The Allies included Britain, France (except during the Nazi occupation, 1940–1944), the Soviet Union (1941–1945), the United States (1941–1945), and China.

American Colonization Society (p. 235) An organization, founded in 1816, that proposed to solve the "Negro problem" by transporting freed slaves from the United States to Africa. Although the society purchased land in Africa (Liberia), few African Americans chose to resettle there.

American Federation of Labor (AFL) (p. 472) A union, formed in 1886, that organized skilled workers along craft lines. It focused on workplace issues rather than political or social reform.

American System (p. 216) Kentucky Senator Henry Clay's plan for national economic development; it included protective tariffs, a national bank, and federal subsidies for railroad and canal construction.

Anaconda Plan (p. 381) General Winfield Scott's strategy for defeating the Confederacy; its central elements included a naval blockade and seizure of the Mississippi River valley.

Antifederalists (p. 152) Critics of the Constitution who initially opposed its ratification. By the late 1790s, they generally endorsed states' rights and sought limitations on federal power.

antinomianism (p. 35) A religious doctrine that affirmed that individuals who possessed saving grace were exempt from the rules of good behavior and from the laws of the community. In puritan New England, such beliefs were generally regarded as heresy.

Arminianism (p. 30) A religious doctrine that held that good works and faith could lead to salvation. In puritan New England, this was regarded as heresy akin to Catholicism because it implied that God's will was contingent on the acts of man.

Articles of Confederation (p. 130) The charter establishing the first government of the United States, ratified in 1781. The Articles placed the coercive powers to tax and regulate trade within the individual state governments; the national government, widely criticized for being weak, was superseded by the government established by the Constitution of the United States, effective in 1789.

Ashcan School (p. 545) Artists in the early twentieth century who used as their subject matter the things and people found in city streets and slums. Ashcan artists often supported progressive political and social reform.

Atlanta Compromise (p. 529) A social policy, propounded by black leader Booker T. Washington in 1895, advocating that blacks concentrate on learning useful skills rather than agitate over segregation, disfranchisement, and discrimination. In Washington's view, black self-help and self-improvement was the surest way to economic advancement.

axis of evil (p. 844) A pejorative phrase, coined by President George W. Bush in 2002, referring to states that supported terrorism and sought weapons of mass destruction. He specifically identified Iraq, Iran, and North Korea.

Axis Powers (p. 702) A term for the alliance between Nazi Germany and Italy after 1936 and, after 1940, Japan.

Bacon's Rebellion (p. 59) An armed uprising in 1676, led by Nathaniel Bacon, against Virginia governor Sir William Berkeley. Initially the rebels attacked Indian settlements but later moved against Berkeley's political faction and burned Jamestown, capital of the colony. After Bacon's death that year, the rebellion collapsed.

Bank of the United States (p. 157) Established as a joint public and private venture in 1791 at the behest of Secretary of Treasury Alexander Hamilton, the Bank of the United States served as a depository of government funds, collected and expended government revenue, and issued notes to serve as a national medium of exchange. The bank's charter expired in 1811. A Second Bank of the United States was chartered in 1816.

Bank war (p. 253) The political dispute over whether to renew the charter of the Second Bank of the United States. In 1832, Congress voted to recharter the bank but President Andrew Jackson vetoed the measure and the charter expired in 1836. He argued that the Bank was unconstitutional, a dangerous monopoly, and vulnerable to control by foreign investors.

Bay of Pigs fiasco (p. 762) A military debacle in April 1961, during an American-organized effort to invade Cuba and drive Fidel Castro, the communist ruler, from power. The invasion force of some 1,500 Cuban exiles was routed at the Bay of Pigs, a major embarrassment for President John F. Kennedy.

beat school (p. 771) Also known as "beats," "beatniks," or the "beat generation"—nonconformists in the late 1950s who rejected conventional dress and sexual standards and cultivated avant-garde literature and music.

Berlin airlift (p. 738) U.S. effort to deliver supplies including 2 million tons of food and coal by air to West Berlin in 1948–1949 in response to the Soviet blockade of the city.

Berlin wall (p. 762) Erected by East Germany in 1961 and torn down by a Dutch company in 1989, the wall isolated West Berlin from the surrounding areas in communist controlled East Berlin and East Germany.

Bill of Rights (p. 155) The first ten amendments to the United States Constitution (adopted in 1791); they protected individual liberties and states' rights against the power of the national government.

Black Codes (p. 409) Special laws passed by southern state and municipal governments after the Civil War that denied free blacks many rights of citizenship.

Bland-Allison Silver Purchase Act (p. 534) An 1878 compromise law that that provided for the limited coinage of silver.

***Blitzkrieg* (p. 701)** A German tactic in World War II, translated as "lightning war," involving the coordinated attack of air and armored firepower.

Bonus Army (p. 673) A gathering of 20,000 Great War veterans in Washington, DC in June

1932, to demand immediate payment of their "adjusted compensation" bonuses voted by Congress in 1924. Congress rejected their demands, and President Hoover ordered U.S. troops to drive them from the capital.

Boston Massacre (p. 106) A violent confrontation between British troops and a Boston mob on March 5, 1770; the soldiers opened fire and killed five, an incident that inflamed sentiment against the British.

Brown v. Board of Education of Topeka **(p. 753)** The 1954 Supreme Court decision that held that racially segregated education, which prevailed in much of the South, was unconstitutional. The ruling overturned the doctrine of "separate but equal" that had provided the legal justification for racial segregation ever since the 1896 *Plessy v. Ferguson* Supreme Court decision.

Camp David Accords (p. 792) A 1978 peace treaty between Egypt and Israel, mediated by President Jimmy Carter, signed at Camp David, a presidential retreat near Washington, DC.

carpetbaggers (p. 419) A pejorative term for Northerners who went to the South after the Civil War to exploit the new political power of freed blacks and the disenfranchisement of former Confederates.

Central Powers (p. 603) Germany and its World War I allies—Austria-Hungary, Turkey, and Bulgaria.

Chinese Exclusion Act (p. 434) A law passed by Congress in 1882 that prohibited Chinese immigration to the United States; it was overturned in 1943.

Civil Rights Act of 1964 (p. 767) Legislation outlawing discrimination in public accommodations and employment on the basis of race, skin color, sex, religion, or national origin.

civil rights cases (p. 526) A group of cases in 1883 in which the U.S. Supreme Court declared unconstitutional the Civil Rights Act of 1875, which had prohibited racial discrimination in hotels, theaters, and other privately owned facilities. The Court ruled that the **Fourteenth Amendment** barred state governments from discriminating on the basis of race but did not prevent private individuals, businesses, or organizations from doing so.

Civilian Conservation Corps (CCC) (p. 680) A **New Deal** program to provide government jobs in reforestation, flood control, and other conservation projects to young men between ages eighteen and twenty-five.

Clayton Antitrust Act (p. 566) Legislation that strengthened antitrust laws. Passed in 1914, it outlawed interlocking directorates, exempted labor unions from antitrust laws, and limited the use of injunctions in labor disputes.

Coercive Acts (p. 108) A series of laws passed by Parliament in 1774 to punish Boston and Massachusetts for the destruction of tea during the "Boston Tea Party." Many colonists, who regarded these and similar laws as "intolerable," moved closer toward war.

Columbian Exchange (p. 23) The transfer of plants, animals, and diseases from Europe, Africa, and Asia to and from the Americas after Columbus's fateful voyage in 1492.

Common Sense **(p. 117)** An influential tract, published by Thomas Paine in January 1776, calling for American independence from Great Britain and establishment of a republican government.

Compromise of 1850 (p. 318) Several laws that together sought to settle several outstanding issues involving slavery. They banned the slave trade, but not slavery in Washington, DC; admitted California as a free state; applied popular sovereignty to the remaining Mexican Cession territory; settled the Texas-New Mexico boundary dispute; and passed a more stringent **Fugitive Slave Act**.

Compromise of 1877 (p. 429) A brokered arrangement whereby Republican and Democratic leaders agreed to settle the disputed 1876 presidential election. Democrats allowed returns that ensured the election of Republican Rutherford B. Hayes; and Republicans agreed to withdraw federal troops from the South, ensuring an end to Reconstruction.

Comstock Lode (p. 441) The first major vein of silver ore in the United States, discovered in the late 1850s, near Virginia City, Nevada.

conquistadores **(p. 17)** The Spanish term for "conquerors," specifically the explorers, adventurers, and soldiers who crushed the native peoples of the Americas.

Conservation (p. 561) The efficient management and use of natural resources, such as forests, grasslands, and rivers; it represents a "middle-of-the-road" policy as opposed to the uncontrolled exploitation of such resources or the preservation those resources from any human exploiters.

Continental army (p. 115) The regular or professional army authorized by the **Second Continental Congress**, mostly under the command of General George Washington during the Revolutionary War.

Contract with America (p. 837) A pledge, signed by many Republicans running for Congress in 1994, to support conservative reforms limiting federal power and expenditures. Championed by House Speaker Newt Gingrich, it contributed to a Republican electoral victory; but opposition by President William Clinton, a Democrat, prevented passage of much of the contract's legislative agenda.

Copperheads (p. 382) Term that initially applied to northern Democrats who resisted Republican war measures and advocated negotiation with the Confederacy. Later in the Civil War, the term became tantamount to an accusation of treason against the Union.

Crittenden Compromise (p. 373) Legislation proposed by Kentucky Senator John Crittenden during the Secession Crisis in 1860–1861. It called for a constitutional amendment recognizing slavery in all territory south of 36°30' (the "Missouri Compromise line") and an iron-clad amendment guaranteeing slavery in slave states. President-elect Lincoln and the Republicans rejected the proposals.

crop-lien system (p. 423) A system of agriculture in which local landowners and merchants loaned money to farm workers in return for a portion of the harvest of cash crops. By forcing farmers to plant cash crops, the system discouraged diversified agriculture in the South.

Cuban missile crisis (p. 763) The showdown between the United States and the Soviet Union during October 1962, after the Soviet Union had sneaked medium-range nuclear missiles into communist Cuba. After President John F. Kennedy publicly demanded their removal and ordered the blockade of Cuba, Soviet leader

Nikita Khrushchev agreed to do so, averting a nuclear war.

Cult of True Womanhood (p. 274) An ideal of middle-class womanhood in the early nineteenth century that asserted that women were naturally pious, pure, and submissive; exemplars of Christian precepts; and best-suited to supervise the moral development of the family.

D-Day (p. 720) June 6, 1944, the day Allied troops crossed the English Channel, landed on the coast of Normandy, and opened a second front in Western Europe during World War II. The "D" stands for "disembarkation"—to leave a ship and go ashore.

***Dartmouth College v. Woodward* (p. 243)** The 1819 Supreme Court case that held that a state charter—in this case, to Dartmouth College—was a contract and that contracts could not be canceled or altered without the consent of both parties, a ruling that strengthened corporations and encouraged investment.

Dawes Severalty Act of 1887 (p. 439) An 1887 law terminating tribal ownership of land and allotting some parcels of land to individual Indians with the remainder of the land left open for white settlement. It included provisions for Indian education and eventual citizenship. The law led to corruption, exploitation, and the weakening of Indian tribal culture. It was reversed in 1934.

détente (p. 778) A French term, meaning the relaxation of tensions, applied to an easing of Cold War antagonisms during the 1970s. Under President Richard Nixon and foreign affairs adviser Henry Kissinger, détente was a strategy to allow the United States to weaken the bonds between the Soviet Union and communist China.

dollar diplomacy (p. 597) A policy of President William Taft to promote American economic penetration to underdeveloped nations, especially in Latin America; it sought to strengthen American influence without requiring the presence of U.S. troops.

Dred Scott decision (p. 360) The 1857 Supreme Court ruling that held that blacks were not citizens and could not sue in a federal court, and, most important, that Congress had exceeded its constitutional authority in banning slavery from the territories. By declaring the Missouri

Compromise unconstitutional, and making future compromises even more difficult, the decision pushed the nation closer to civil war.

Electoral College (p. 150) An assembly of delegates representing each of the states who choose the president of the United States. This mechanism, established by the U.S. Constitution, was regarded as less volatile than allowing voters to elect the president directly.

Emancipation Proclamation (p. 390) A decree by President Abraham Lincoln that freed all slaves in Confederate states that remained in active rebellion on January 1, 1863, when the proclamation went into effect.

Embargo Act (p. 188) A law passed by Congress in 1807 prohibiting all American exports. President Thomas Jefferson, who proposed the law, sought to pressure Britain and France—then at war with each other—into recognizing neutral rights.

encomienda **system (p. 18)** A feudal labor arrangement, imposed in the Spanish colonies of the Americas, by which Spanish settlers were granted a certain number of Indian subjects who were obliged to pay tribute in goods and labor.

Enlightenment (p. 88) An intellectual movement of the eighteenth century that celebrated human reason and scientific advances and expressed doubts about the truth claims of sacred texts.

Environmental Protection Agency (EPA) (p. 780) A federal agency created in 1970 to oversee environmental monitoring and cleanup programs.

Equal Rights Amendment (ERA) (p. 817) A proposed amendment to the U.S. Constitution to outlaw discrimination on the basis of sex. Although first proposed in 1923, the amendment was not passed by Congress until 1972; but the ratification movement fell short and the ERA was not added to the Constitution.

Era of Good Feelings (p. 210) A period from 1817 to 1823 in which the disappearance of the **Federalists** enabled the Republicans to govern in a spirit of seemingly nonpartisan harmony.

Espionage Act (p. 614) A law passed in 1917 that made it a crime to obstruct the nation's effort to win World War I.

Fair Deal (p. 739) President Harry Truman's 1949 program for expanded economic opportunity and civil rights.

Farewell Address (p. 165) President Washington's influential 1796 speech in which he deplored the rise of political factions and warned against "permanent alliances" with foreign nations.

Federal Reserve Act (p. 566) A 1913 law establishing a Federal Reserve Board, which controlled the rediscount rate and thus the money supply; this helped regularize the national banking system.

Federalist Papers **(p. 153)** A series of essays, chiefly written by Alexander Hamilton, James Madison, and John Jay, explaining and defending the national government proposed by the Constitutional Convention of 1787.

Federalists (p. 152) Advocates of a strong national government; they supported ratification of the Constitution and subsequently supported measures to expand federal revenues and functions.

Fifteenth Amendment (p. 419) An amendment (1870), championed by the Republican party, that sought to guarantee the vote to blacks in the South following the Civil War.

First Continental Congress (p. 109) An assembly comprised of delegates from twelve colonies that met in Philadelphia in 1774. It denied Parliament's authority to legislate for the colonies, adopted the Declaration of Rights and Grievances, created a Continental Association to enforce a boycott of British imports, and endorsed a call to take up arms against Britain.

Force Acts (p. 424) Three laws passed by the Republican-dominated Congress in 1870–1871 to protect black voters in the South. The laws placed state elections under federal jurisdiction and imposed fines and imprisonment on those guilty of interfering with any citizen exercising his right to vote.

Fourteen Points (p. 620) A comprehensive plan, proposed by President Woodrow Wilson in January 1918, to negotiate an end to World War I. It called for freedom of the seas, free trade, arms reduction, national self-determination and an end to colonial rule and secret diplomacy.

Fourteenth Amendment (p. 415) An amendment, passed by Congress in 1866 and ratified in 1868, that prohibited states from depriving citizens of the due process or the equal protection of the laws. Although the amendment was a response to discriminatory laws against blacks in the South, it figured prominently in the expansion of individual rights and liberties during the last half of the twentieth century.

Free Soil party (p. 315) A party that emerged in the 1840s in opposition to the expansion of slavery into the territories. Formally organized in 1848, it nominated Martin Van Buren for president. In 1856, Free Soil party members joined with former **Whigs** and other disaffected voters to form the **Republican party**.

Freedmen's Bureau (p. 414) A federal refugee agency to aid former slaves and destitute whites after the Civil War. It provided them food, clothing, and other necessities as well as helped them find work and set up schools.

French and Indian War (p. 92) Fourth in the series of great wars between Britain and France, this conflict (1754–1763) had its focal point in North America and pitted the French and their Indian allies against the British and their Indian allies. Known in Europe as the **Seven Years' War**, this struggle drove the French government from much of North America.

French Revolution (p. 159) The massive and violent social and political upheaval commencing in 1789 that ended the French monarchy, established a republic, expropriated the land and property of the Catholic Church, and culminated in a bloody reign of terror.

Fugitive Slave Act (p. 318) Initially, a 1793 law to encourage the return of runaway slaves; this law was amended, as part of the **Compromise of 1850**, so as to authorize federal commissioners to compel citizens to assist in the return of runaway (fugitive) slaves. The law offended Northerners and its nonenforcement offended Southerners.

Gibbons v. Ogden **(p. 244)** Supreme Court ruling (1824) that held that no state could pass laws affecting interstate trade, thereby ensuring the federal government's supremacy in interstate commerce.

Glorious Revolution (p. 66) The peaceful accession of William II, a Protestant, and Queen Mary to the British throne in 1688, ending the Catholic rule of James II. Many colonists rebelled against governors who had been appointed by James II and demanded greater political rights.

gold rush (p. 313) Term for the gold-mining boom in the U.S. western territories in the late 1840s and 1850s.

"good neighbor" (p. 665) President Herbert Hoover's policy to promote better relations between the United States and nations in the Western Hemisphere; it declared America's intention to disclaim the right to intervention pronounced in the **Platt Amendment** and the **Roosevelt Corollary**.

Great Awakening (p. 85) A widespread evangelical revival movement of the 1740s and 1750s, sparked by the tour of the English evangelical minister George Whitefield. The Awakening spread religious fervor but weakened the authority of established churches.

Great Compromise (p. 150) Resolved the differences between the New Jersey and Virginia delegations to the Constitutional Convention by providing for a bicameral legislature: the Senate, with equal representation for each state, and the House of Representatives, apportioned by population.

Great Society (p. 767) The sweeping legislative agenda of President Lyndon Johnson; it sought to end poverty, promote civil rights, and improve housing, health care, and education. The program was criticized as costly and ineffective.

greenbacks (p. 382) Paper currency issued by the Union government during the Civil War, resulting in inflation. Whether to continue the issue of greenbacks became a key political issue in the decades after the Civil War.

Gulf of Tonkin Resolution (p. 772) Congressional action, undertaken at President Johnson's request, giving the President the authority to deploy U.S. troops to repel aggression in Southeast Asia. This provided congressional sanction for the escalation of the Vietnam war.

Half-Way Covenant (p. 65) A modification of puritan practice, adopted by many Congregational churches during the 1650s and afterwards, that allowed baptized puritans who had not experienced saving grace to acquire partial church membership and receive sacraments.

Harlem Renaissance (p. 650) A modern artistic and literary movement that celebrated African American life and culture in early twentieth-century Harlem, New York. Among its key figures were Langston Hughes, Richard Wright, and Zora Neale Hurston (literature); Duke Ellington (music); Jacob Lawrence (painting); and Aaron Douglas (sculpture).

Hartford Convention (p. 203) A gathering of New England **Federalists** from December 1814 through January 1815 to channel opposition to Thomas Jefferson and the **War of 1812**. Some participants may have regarded the meeting as preparatory to a secession movement by the New England colonies.

headright (p. 54) A system of land distribution, adopted first in Virginia and later in Maryland, that granted colonists fifty acres for themselves and another fifty for each "head" (or person) they brought with them to the colony. This system was often used in conjunction with indentured servitude to build large plantations and supply them with labor.

Hepburn Act (p. 560) Federal legislation, passed in 1906, that gave the Interstate Commerce Commission sufficient power to inspect railroad companies' records, set maximum rates, and outlaw free passes.

Homestead Act (1862) (p. 396) Federal law granting 160 acres of public land in the West to any settler who would farm and improve it within five years of the grant; it encouraged migration into the Great Plains.

human immunodeficiency virus (HIV) (p. 821) A virus, usually spread through sexual contact, that attacks the immune system, sometimes fatally. HIV, which causes **acquired immunodeficiency syndrome (AIDS)**, first appeared in the United States in the 1980s.

impressment (p. 187) The policy whereby Britain forced people to serve in its navy. The impressment of sailors—even American citizens—on neutral vessels during the Napoleonic Wars outraged Americans and was a major cause of the **War of 1812**.

improvised explosive device (IED) (p. 851) Also known as "roadside bombs," IEDs are homemade bombs that usually consist of captured artillery shells that are wired to a detonator. Either they are exploded remotely or by suicide bombers. IEDs

accounted for over a third of the casualties sustained by American and United Nations forces in the Iraq and Afghanistan wars.

indentured servants (p. 55) Individuals working under a form of contract labor that provided them with free passage to America in return for a promise to work for a fixed period, usually seven years. Indentured servitude was the primary labor system in the Chesapeake colonies for most of the seventeenth century.

Industrial Workers of the World (IWW) (p. 546) A militant labor organization, founded in 1905 and inspired by European anarchists, that advocated "abolition of the wage system" and called for a single union of all workers, regardless of trade or skill level; it was repressed during and after World War I.

internment camps (p. 715) Detainment centers, mostly located in western states, that held approximately 110,000 Japanese aliens and American citizens of Japanese origin during World War II.

Interstate Commerce Act (p. 468) Federal law establishing the Interstate Commerce Commission in 1887, the nation's first regulatory agency.

Iran-Contra affair (p. 803) Scandal involving high officials in the Reagan administration accused of funding the Contra rebels in Nicaragua in violation of 1984 Congressional laws explicitly prohibiting such aid. The Contra funding came from the secret sale of arms to Iran.

Iranian hostage crisis (p. 794) Protracted crisis that began in 1979 when Islamic militants seized the American embassy in Tehran, Iran, and held scores of its employees hostage. The militants had been enraged by American support for the deposed Shah of Iran. The crisis, which lasted over a year, contributed to President Jimmy Carter's defeat in his reelection campaign in 1980.

isolationism (p. 575) A national policy that eschews foreign alliances, such as was propounded by George Washington in his "**Farewell Address**." Isolationism was also embraced by part of the **Monroe Doctrine** of 1823 and after the First World War, when the United States refused to join the **League of Nations** and sought to distance itself during the 1930s from the rumblings of another world war. Isolationism ended as national policy when Japan attacked Pearl Harbor on December 7, 1941.

Jacksonian democracy (p. 248) A political doctrine, chiefly associated with Andrew Jackson, that proclaimed the equality of all adult white males—the common man—and disapproved of anything that smacked of special privilege, such as chartered banks.

Jay's Treaty (p. 164) Named after John Jay, the American negotiator, and ratified in 1795, this treaty eased tensions with Great Britain. By its provisions Britain agreed to evacuate forts on the United States' side of the Great Lakes and submit questions of neutral rights to arbitrators.

joint-stock companies (p. 25) Businesses in which investors pooled capital for specific purposes, such as conducting trade and founding colonies. Examples include the English joint-stock companies that founded the Virginia, Plymouth, and Massachusetts Bay colonies.

judicial review (p. 150) A crucial concept that empowered the Supreme Court to invalidate acts of Congress. Although not explicitly propounded in the U.S. Constitution, Chief Justice John Marshall affirmed in *Marbury v. Madison* (1803) that the right of judicial review was implicit in the Constitution's status as "the supreme Law of the Land."

Kansas-Nebraska Act (p. 354) A compromise law in 1854 that superseded the **Missouri Compromise** and left it to voters in Kansas and Nebraska to determine whether they would be slave or free states. The law exacerbated sectional tensions when voters came to blows over the question of slavery in Kansas.

Kentucky and Virginia Resolves (p. 168) Political declarations in favor of states' rights, written by Thomas Jefferson and James Madison, in opposition to the federal **Alien and Sedition Acts**. These resolutions, passed by the Kentucky and Virginia legislatures in 1798, maintained that states could nullify federal legislation they regarded as unconstitutional.

Knights of Labor (p. 471) A national labor organization, formed in 1869 and headed by Uriah Stephens and Terence Powderly, that promoted union solidarity, political reform, and sociability among members. Its advocacy of the eight-hour day led to violent strikes in 1886 and the organization's subsequent decline.

Know-Nothing party (p. 355) A nativist, anti-immigrant and anti-Catholic party that emerged in response to the flood of Catholic immigrants from Ireland and Germany in the 1840s. The party achieved mostly local successes in the Northeast port cities; but in 1856 former President Millard Fillmore, whose Whig party had dissolved, accepted the nomination of southern Know-Nothings but carried only Maryland, a failure that contributed to the movement's decline.

Ku Klux Klan (p. 424) Founded as a social club in 1866 by a handful of former Confederate soldiers in Tennessee, it became a vigilante group that used violence and intimidation to drive African Americans out of politics. The movement declined in the late 1870s but resurfaced in the 1920s as a political organization that opposed all groups—immigrant, religious, and racial—that challenged Protestant white hegemony.

laissez-faire (p. 462) A French term—literally, "to let alone"—used in economic contexts to signify the absence of governmental interference in or regulation of economic matters.

League of Nations (p. 623) A worldwide assembly of nations, proposed by President Woodrow Wilson, that was included in the Treaty of Versailles ending World War I. The refusal of the United States to join the League limited its effectiveness.

Lecompton constitution (p. 362) A proslavery constitution, drafted in 1857 by delegates for Kansas territory, elected under questionable circumstances, seeking admission to the United States. It was rejected by two territorial governors, supported by President Buchanan, and decisively defeated by Congress.

Leisler's Rebellion (p. 73) An uprising in 1689, led by Jacob Leisler, that wrested control of New York's government following the abdication of King James II. The rebellion ended when Leisler was arrested and executed in 1690.

Lend-Lease Act (p. 703) A military aid measure, proposed by President Franklin D. Roosevelt in 1941 and adopted by Congress, empowering the president to sell, lend, lease, or transfer $7 billion of war material to any country whose defense he declared as vital to that of the United States.

Lewis and Clark expedition (p. 184) An exploration of the Louisiana Territory and the region stretching to the Pacific, commissioned by President Jefferson. Commanded by Meriwether Lewis and William Clark, the enterprise (1804–1806) brought back a wealth of information about the region.

Louisiana Purchase (p. 177) An 1803 agreement whereby the United States purchased France's North American Empire, the vast region drained by the Mississippi and Missouri Rivers, for $15 million; it doubled the size of the nation.

Loyalists (p. 120) Sometimes called Tories, the term for American colonists who refused to take up arms against England in the 1770s.

lyceums (p. 294) Locally sponsored public lectures, often featuring writers, that were popular in the nineteenth century.

Manhattan Project (p. 701) The code name for the extensive United States military project, established in 1942, to produce fissionable uranium and plutonium, and to design and build an atomic bomb. Costing nearly $2 billion, the effort culminated in the destruction of Hiroshima and Nagasaki in August 1945.

manifest destiny (p. 303) Originating in the 1840s, a term that referred to support of the expansion of the United States through the acquisition of Texas, Oregon, and parts of Mexico. The term was also used in the 1890s in reference to the conquest of foreign lands not meant to be incorporated into the United States.

Marbury v. Madison **(p. 176)** An 1803 Supreme Court ruling that declared the Judiciary Act of 1789 unconstitutional and established the precedent for judicial review of federal laws.

Marshall Plan (p. 737) A proposal, propounded in 1947 by Secretary of State George Marshall, to use American aid to rebuild the war-torn economies of European nations. Adopted by Congress in 1948 as the European Recovery Program, it pumped some $13 billion into Europe during the next five years.

massive retaliation (p. 747) The "New Look" military policy of the Dwight D. Eisenhower and Secretary of State John Foster Dulles relying on nuclear weapons to inhibit communist aggression during the 1950s.

Mayflower Compact (p. 31) An agreement, signed aboard the *Mayflower* among the Pilgrims en route to Plymouth Plantation (1620), to establish a body politic and to obey the rules of the governors they chose.

McCulloch v. Maryland **(p. 243)** An 1819 Supreme Court ruling that state governments could not tax a federal agency—in this case the second Bank of the United States—for "the power to tax involves the power to destroy." The decision affirmed the doctrine of the implied powers of the federal government.

Medicare (p. 769) A social welfare measure, enacted in 1965, providing hospitalization insurance for people over sixty-five and a voluntary plan to cover doctor bills paid in part by the federal government.

mercantilism (p. 81) A loose system of economic organization designed, through a favorable balance of trade, to guarantee the prosperity of the British empire. Mercantilists advocated possession of colonies as places where the mother country could acquire raw materials not available at home.

Mexican War (p. 308) Fought between the United States and Mexico from May 1846 to February 1848, the Mexican War greatly added to the national domain of the United States; see also **Treaty of Guadalupe Hidalgo**.

military-industrial complex (p. 757) A term, popularized by President Dwight D. Eisenhower in his 1961 farewell address, for the concert of interests among the U.S. military and its chief corporate contractors.

Missouri Compromise (p. 218) A legislative deal, brokered in 1820, that preserved the balance of slave and free states in the Union by admitting Missouri as a slave state and Maine as a free state; it also banned slavery from that part of the Louisiana Territory north of 36°30'.

Monroe Doctrine (p. 207) A foreign policy edict, propounded by President James Monroe in 1823, declaring that the American continents were no longer open to European colonization or exploitation and that the United States would not interfere in the internal affairs of European nations.

Moral Majority (p. 796) A term associated with the organization by that name, founded in 1979 by the Reverend Jerry Falwell to combat "amoral liberals," drug abuse, "coddling" of criminals, homosexuality, communism, and abortion.

muckraker (p. 545) A term for progressive investigative journalists who exposed the seamy side of American life at the turn of the twentieth century by "raking up the muck."

mugwumps (p. 524) A group of eastern Republicans, disgusted with corruption in the party, who campaigned for the Democrats in the 1884 elections. These anticorruption reformers were conservative on the money question and government regulation.

National American Woman Suffrage Association (NAWSA) (p. 554) An organization, founded in 1890, that united the National Woman Suffrage Association, headed by Elizabeth Cady Stanton and Susan B. Anthony, and the American Woman Suffrage Association, headed by Lucy Stone. After ratification of the Nineteenth Amendment granting women the vote in 1920, the NAWSA became the League of Women Voters.

National Association for the Advancement of Colored People (NAACP) (p. 571) A national interracial organization, founded in 1909, that promoted the rights of African Americans. Initially it fought against lynching, but from 1955 through 1977, under the leadership of Roy Wilkins, it launched the campaign that overturned legalized segregation and it backed civil rights legislation. The NAACP remains the nation's largest African American organization.

National Grange of the Patrons of Husbandry (p. 467) A farmers' organization, founded in 1867 by Oliver H. Kelley, that initially provided social and cultural benefits but then supported legislation, known as the Granger laws, providing for railroad regulation.

National Organization for Women (NOW) (p. 817) An organization, founded in 1966 by Betty Friedan and other feminists, to promote equal rights for women, changes in divorce laws, and legalization of abortion.

National Origins Act (p. 632) A federal law, passed in 1929 that curtailed immigration, especially from southern and eastern Europe and Asia.

National Recovery Administration (NRA) (p. 680) A New Deal agency, established in 1933, to promote economic recovery, that promulgated industry-wide codes to control production, prices, and wages.

nationalism (p. 135) An affinity for a particular nation; in particular, a sense of national consciousness and loyalty that promotes the interests and attributes of that nation over all others.

nativism (p. 486) A fear or hatred of immigrants, ethnic minorities, or alien political movements.

Navigation Acts (p. 82) Seventeenth-century Parliamentary statutes to control trade within the British empire so as to benefit Britain and promote its administration of the colonies.

Neolithic revolution (p. 4) The transition from a hunter-gather economy to one mostly based on the cultivation of crops.

neutrality acts (p. 698) Legislation affirming nonbelligerency in the event of war. In relation to American history, such legislation was passed in 1794 to preclude American entanglement in the Napoleonic Wars; similar laws were passed just before and after World War I, especially during the 1930s.

New Deal (p. 679) A broad program of legislation proposed by President Franklin D. Roosevelt to promote recovery from the Great Depression and provide relief for those in distress.

New Freedom (p. 564) Democratic candidate Woodrow Wilson's term in the 1912 presidential campaign for a proposed policy that would restore competition by breaking up the trusts and punishing corporations that violated rules of business conduct.

New Frontier (p. 755) President John F. Kennedy's term for a revitalized national agenda, particularly in relation to foreign policy and space exploration.

new immigration (p. 485) Reference to the influx of immigrants to the United States during the late nineteenth and early twentieth century predominantly from southern and eastern Europe.

New Jersey Plan (p. 148) The proposal to the Constitutional Convention of 1787 by New Jersey delegate William Paterson to create a federal legislature in which each state was represented equally. The concept became embodied in the United States Constitution through the Senate, in which each state has two representatives, though this was counterbalanced by the House of Representatives, in which each state's representation is proportional to its population.

New Nationalism (p. 563) Progressive candidate Theodore Roosevelt's term in the 1912 presidential election for an expansion of federal power to regulate big business and enact legislation to promote social justice.

Niagara movement (p. 570) A response by W. E. B. Du Bois and other blacks, following a meeting in Niagara Falls in 1905, in opposition to Booker T. Washington's advocacy of black accommodation to white prejudice; these leaders drafted a political program to achieve equal opportunity, equal justice, and an end to segregation that led to the founding of the **National Association for the Advancement of Colored People (NAACP)**.

North American Free Trade Agreement (NAFTA) (p. 839) A 1993 accord signed by Canada, Mexico, and the United States to reduce and eventually eliminate barriers to trade, including tariffs, among the signatories.

North Atlantic Treaty Organization (NATO) (p. 740) A military mutual-defense pact, formed in 1948, by the United States, Canada, and ten European nations, including Great Britain, France, and West Germany; the Soviet Union countered with the formation of the Warsaw Pact among communist regimes in Eastern Europe.

Northwest Ordinance (p. 137) A 1787 measure of the Continental Congress, passed according to the **Articles of Confederation**, to provide for governance of the region north of the Ohio River and the eventual admission of up to five territories—ultimately the states of Ohio, Indiana, Illinois, Michigan, and Wisconsin. The ordinance also prohibited slavery in the region and reserved lands for Indians.

NSC-68 (p. 741) A secret policy statement, proposed by the National Security Council in 1950, calling for a large, ongoing military commitment to contain Soviet communism; it was accepted by President Harry Truman after the North Korean invasion of South Korea.

nullification (p. 261) A doctrine, forcefully articulated by John C. Calhoun in 1828, asserting that a state could invalidate, within its own boundaries, federal legislation the state regarded as unconstitutional.

Open Door policy (p. 593) A policy, propounded by Secretary of State John Hay in 1899, affirming the territorial integrity of China and a policy of free trade.

Organization of Petroleum Exporting Countries (OPEC) (p. 788) A cartel of oil-producing nations in Asia, Africa, and Latin America that gained substantial power over the world economy in the mid- to late-1970s.

Ostend Manifesto (p. 351) A confidential 1854 dispatch to the U.S. State Department from American diplomats meeting in Ostend, Belgium, suggesting that the United States would be justified in seizing Cuba if Spain refused to sell it to the United States. When word of the document was leaked, Northerners seethed at this "slaveholders' plot" to extend slavery.

Paleolithic revolution (p. 1) Period 750,000 years ago when humans devised simple stone tools, inaugurating life based on hunting and gathering.

Pendleton Act (p. 523) An 1883 law bringing civil service reform to federal employment; it classified many government jobs and required competitive exams for these positions.

People's (Populist) party (p. 531) The People's party of America was an important "third party," founded in 1891, that sought to unite various disaffected groups, especially farmers. The party nominated James B. Weaver for president in 1892 and in 1896 joined with the Democratic party in support of William Jennings Bryan for president.

Persian Gulf War (p. 807) The 1991 war following Iraq's takeover of Kuwait; the United States and a coalition of allies defeated the army of Iraqi leader Saddam Hussein but failed to drive him from power.

Platt Amendment (p. 589) A law, passed in 1901 and superseding the **Teller Amendment**, which stipulated the conditions for the withdrawal of

American forces from Cuba; it also transferred ownership of the naval base at Guantanamo Bay to the United States.

***Plessy v. Ferguson* (p. 526)** Supreme Court ruling (1896) that held that racial segregation of public accommodations did not infringe on the "equal protection" clause of the Constitution; this "separate but equal" doctrine was overturned by *Brown v. Board of Education* in 1954.

popular sovereignty (p. 314) The principle of allowing people to make political decisions by majority vote. As applied to American history, the term generally refers to the 1848 proposal of Michigan Senator Lewis Cass to allow settlers to determine the status of slavery in the territories.

Potsdam Conference (p. 731) A wartime conference (April 1945) held in occupied Germany where Allied leaders divided Germany and Berlin into four occupation zones, agreed to try Nazi leaders as war criminals, and planned the exacting of reparations from Germany.

pragmatism (p. 513) A philosophical system, chiefly associated with William James, that deemphasized abstraction and assessed ideas and cultural practices based on their practical effects; it helped inspire political and social reform during the late nineteenth century.

predestination (p. 30) The Calvinist belief, accepted by New England puritans, that God had determined who would receive eternal grace at the dawn of time; nothing people did during their lifetime could alter their prospects of salvation.

Progressivism (p. 543) A cluster of movements for various forms of social change—some of them contradictory—during the early twentieth century; progressives generally opposed corruption and inefficiency in government, monopoly power among corporations, and wayward behavior among immigrants and others.

Protestant Reformation (p. 24) A religious movement of the sixteenth century initially focused on eliminating corruption in the Catholic Church; but under the influence of theologians Martin Luther and John Calvin, it indicted Catholic theology and gave rise to various denominations that advanced alternative interpretations.

puritans (p. 30) A term, initially derisive, referring to English religious dissenters who believed that the religious practices and administration of the Church of England too closely resembled those of the Catholic Church; many migrated to Massachusetts Bay after 1630 to establish a religious commonwealth based on the principles of John Calvin and others.

Quakers (p. 39) Adherents of a religious organization founded in England in the 1640s who believed that the Holy Spirit lived in all people; they embraced pacifism and religious tolerance, and rejected formal theology. In the decades after 1670, thousands of Quakers emigrated to New Jersey and Pennsylvania.

Radical Republicans (p. 382, 412) A faction within the Republican party, headed by Thaddeus Stevens and Benjamin Wade, that insisted on black suffrage and federal protection of the civil rights of blacks. After 1867, the Radical Republicans achieved a working majority in Congress and passed legislation promoting Reconstruction.

Reaganomics (p. 795) A label pinned on President Ronald Reagan's policies of tax cuts, social welfare cuts, and increased military spending; it generated huge federal deficits, but also promoted the reorganization of large corporations.

"reconcentration" camps (p. 580) A term that referred to the Spanish refugee camps into which Cuban farmers were herded in 1896 to prevent them from providing assistance to rebels fighting for Cuban independence from Spain.

"red scare" (p. 628) Public hysteria over Bolshevik influence in the United States after World War I; it led to the arrest or deportation of thousands of radicals, labor activists, and ethnic leaders.

Republican party (p. 356) One of the original two political parties, sometimes called "Democratic Republican," it was organized by James Madison and Thomas Jefferson and generally stood for states' rights, an agrarian economy and the interests of farmers and planters over those of financial and commercial groups, who generally supported the **Federalist** party; both of the original parties faded in the 1820s. A new Republican party emerged in the 1850s in opposition to the extension of slavery in the territories. It also adopted most of the old Whig party's economic program. The party nominated John C. Fremont for president in 1856 and Abraham Lincoln in 1860.

romanticism (p. 288) A loosely defined aesthetic movement originating in the late eighteenth century and flowering during the early nineteenth century; it encompassed literature, philosophy, arts, and music and enshrined feeling and intuition over reason.

Sanitary Commission (p. 398) A private and voluntary medical organization, founded in May 1861, that sought to improve the physical and mental well-being of Union soldiers during the Civil War.

scalawags (p. 419) White southern Republicans—mainly small landowning farmers and well-off merchants and planters—who cooperated with the congressionally imposed Reconstruction governments set up in the South following the Civil War.

Scopes trial (p. 643) Also called the "Monkey Trial," it was a celebrated 1924 contest that pitted Darwinian evolutionists against fundamentalist "Creationists." John T. Scopes, a teacher charged with defying Tennessee law by teaching evolution, was found guilty and fined $100.

Second Continental Congress (p. 114) A gathering of American Patriots in May 1775 that organized the **Continental army**, requisitioned soldiers and supplies, and commissioned George Washington to lead it.

Second Great Awakening (p. 275) A wave of religious enthusiasm, commencing in the 1790s and lasting for decades, that stressed the mercy, love, and benevolence of God and emphasized that all people could, through faith and effort, achieve salvation.

second party system (p. 263) A term for the political contention between the Democratic party, as rejuvenated by Andrew Jackson in 1828, and the **Whigs**, who emerged in response to Jackson.

Sedition Act (p. 614) Federal legislation, first passed in 1798 and expired in 1801, that placed limits on freedom of speech during wartime. Another such act was passed in 1918 and led to the imprisonment of Socialist Eugene V. Debs and others during World War I.

Seneca Falls Convention (p. 287) A meeting, held at Seneca Falls, New York in 1848, that affirmed that "all men and women are created equal" and sought the franchise (vote) for women.

settlement houses (p. 495) Community centers, founded by reformers such as Jane Addams and Lillian Wald beginning in the 1880s, that were located in poor urban districts of major cities; the centers sought to Americanize immigrant families and provide them with social services and a political voice.

Seven Years' War (p. 93) The global conflict, sometimes known as the **French and Indian War**, that lasted from 1756 to 1763 and pitted France and its allies against Britain and its allies. Britain ultimately prevailed, forcing France to surrender its claims to Canada and all territory east of the Mississippi River.

Shakers (p. 277) A religious commune founded by Ann Lee in England that came to America in 1774. Shakers practiced celibacy, believed that God was both Mother and Father, and held property in common.

sharecropping (p. 422) A type of agriculture, frequently practiced in the South during and after Reconstruction, in which landowners provided land, tools, housing, and seed to a farmer who provided his labor; the resulting crop was divided between them (i.e., shared).

Shays's rebellion (p. 145) An armed rebellion of western Massachusetts farmers in 1786 to prevent state courts from foreclosing on debtors. Nationalists saw such unrest as proof of the inadequacy of the federal government under the **Articles of Confederation**.

Sherman Antitrust Act (p. 469) A federal law, passed in 1890, that outlawed monopolistic organizations that functioned to restrain trade.

Sherman Silver Purchase Act (p. 534) An 1890 law that obliged the federal government to buy and coin silver, thereby counteracting the deflationary tendencies of the economy at the time; its repeal in 1894, following the Depression of 1893, caused a political uproar.

social Darwinism (p. 464) A belief that Charles Darwin's theory of the evolution of species also applied to social and economic institutions an practices: The "fittest" enterprises or individuals prevailed, while those that were defective naturally faded away; society thus progressed most surely when competition was unrestricted by government.

Social Gospel (p. 495) A doctrine preached by many urban Protestant ministers during the early

1900s that focused on improving living conditions for the city's poor rather than on saving souls; proponents advocated civil service reform, child labor laws, government regulation of big business, and a graduated income tax.

Social Security Act (p. 689) A component of Franklin Roosevelt's **New Deal**, it established in 1935 a system of old-age, unemployment, and survivors' insurance funded by wage and payroll taxes.

Southern Christian Leadership Conference (SCLC) (p. 755) A civil rights organization, founded in 1957 by Martin Luther King, Jr. and his followers, that espoused Christian nonviolence but organized mass protests to challenge segregation and discrimination; it played a major role in support of the **Civil Rights Act of 1964** and the **Voting Rights Act of 1965**.

Specie Circular (p. 262) An edict, issued by President Andrew Jackson in 1836, obliging purchasers of public land to do so with gold coins rather than the paper currency issued by state banks; it caused the speculative boom in real estate to collapse and exacerbated a financial panic the following year.

spoils system (p. 252) A term, usually derisive, whereby newly elected office-holders appoint loyal members of their own party to public office.

Square Deal (p. 559) The phrase, initially employed by President Theodore Roosevelt in 1904, to describe an arbitrated settlement between workers and an employer, but more generally employed as a goal to promote fair business practices and to punish "bad" corporations that used their economic clout unfairly.

stagflation (p. 791) A term coined in the 1970s to describe the period's economic downturn and simultaneous deflation in prices.

Stamp Act Congress (p. 101) A meeting in New York City of delegates of most of the colonial assemblies in America to protest the Stamp Act, a revenue measure passed by Parliament in 1765; it was a precursor to the Continental Congress.

Strategic Arms Limitation Treaty (SALT) (p. 778) A treaty, signed by the United States and the Soviet Union in 1972, restricting the testing and deployment of nuclear ballistic missiles, the first of several such treaties.

Strategic Defense Initiative (SDI) (p. 798) The concept of a space-based missile defense system—popularly known as "Star Wars," after the movie by that name—proposed by President Ronald Reagan in 1983. Controversial and costly, the concept was never fully realized.

Student Nonviolent Coordinating Committee (SNCC) (p. 764) A civil rights organization, founded in 1960, that drew heavily on younger activists and college students. After 1965, under the leadership of Stokely Carmichael and then H. Rap Brown, the group advocated "Black Power."

Students for a Democratic Society (SDS) (p. 771) An organization created by leftist college students in the early 1960s; it organized protests against racial bigotry, corporate exploitation of workers, and, especially after 1965, the Vietnam war.

"surge" (p. 852) The sudden increase in troop strength that appeared to have been used successfully against the Iraq insurgency in 2007. President Barack Obama similarly adopted a surge in 2009 to stabilize a deteriorating situation in Afghanistan.

Taft-Hartley Act (p. 735) A 1947 federal law that outlawed the closed shop and secondary boycotts and obliged union leaders to sign affidavits declaring that they were not communists.

Tariff of Abominations (p. 193) An exceptionally high tariff, passed in 1828, that provoked Vice President John C. Calhoun to write the "South Carolina Exposition and Protest"—a defense of the doctrine of **nullification**.

Teapot Dome scandal (p. 659) A scandal during the administration of Warren Harding in which the Secretary of the Interior, Albert Fall, accepted bribes from oil companies that then leased the Teapot Dome federal oil reserve in Wyoming.

Teller Amendment (p. 582) A rider to the 1898 war resolution with Spain whereby Congress pledged that it did not intend to annex Cuba and that it would recognize Cuban independence from Spain.

temperance movement (p. 281) A reform movement of the nineteenth and early twentieth centuries in which women and ministers played a major role and that advocated moderation in the use of alcoholic beverages, or, preferably, abstinence. The major organizations included the American Temperance Society, the Washingtonian movement, and the Women's Christian Temperance Union (WCTU).

Ten Percent Plan (p. 411) A measure drafted by President Abraham Lincoln in 1863 to readmit states that had seceded once 10 percent of their prewar voters swore allegiance to the Union and adopted state constitutions outlawing slavery.

tenement (p. 489) Four- to six-story residential apartment house, once common in New York and certain other cities, built on a tiny lot with little regard for adequate ventilation or light.

Tennessee Valley Authority (TVA) (p. 683) A New Deal agency that built and operated dams and power plants on the Tennessee River; it also promoted flood control, soil conservation, and reforestation.

Tet offensive (p. 774) A wide-ranging offensive, launched by North Vietnamese and Vietcong troops throughout South Vietnam in February 1968. It failed to cause the South Vietnamese government to collapse, but persuaded many Americans that the war was not winnable. President Lyndon B. Johnson announced his decision not to run for reelection several months later.

Thirteenth Amendment (p. 413) Passed in 1865, this amendment declared an end to slavery and negated the Three-fifths Clause in the Constitution, thereby increasing the representation of the southern states in Congress.

Three-Fifths Compromise (p. 149) The provision in the Constitution that defined slaves, for purposes of representation in the House of Representatives and state tax payments, not as full persons, but as constituting only three-fifths of a person.

Trail of Tears (p. 259) The name for the 1838 forced removal of Cherokee and other Indians from Georgia and the western Appalachians to Indian Territory in Oklahoma and nearby regions.

transcendentalism (p. 288) A diverse and loosely defined philosophy that promoted a mystical, intuitive way of looking at life that subordinated facts to feelings. Transcendentalists argued that humans could transcend reason and intellectual capacities by having faith in themselves and in the fundamental benevolence of the universe. They were complete individualists.

Transcontinental Treaty (p. 207) Also called the Adams-Onís Treaty. Ratified in 1821, it acquired Florida and stretched the western boundary of the Louisiana Territory to the Oregon coast.

Treaty of Guadalupe Hidalgo (p. 312) Signed in 1848, this treaty ended the **Mexican War**, forcing that nation to relinquish all of the land north of the Rio Grande and Gila Rivers, including what would eventually become California, in return for monetary compensations.

Treaty of Tordesillas (p. 17) Negotiated by the pope in 1494, this treaty resolved the territorial claims of Spain and Portugal; in the Western Hemisphere Portugal was granted Brazil, while Spain was granted nearly all of the remaining lands.

triangular trade (p. 69) An oversimplified term for the trade among England, its colonies in the Americas, and slave markets in Africa and the Caribbean.

Truman Doctrine (p. 736) A foreign policy, articulated by President Harry Truman in 1947, that provided financial aid to Greek and Turkish governments then under threat by communists rebels.

underground railroad (p. 348) A support system established by antislavery groups in the upper South and the North to help fugitive slaves who had escaped from the South to make their way to Canada.

Underwood Tariff (p. 566) A 1913 reform law that lowered tariff rates and levied the first regular federal income tax.

United Nations (UN) (p. 729) An international organization, founded in 1945, that sought to promote discussion and negotiation and thereby avoid war; it was joined by nearly all nations.

United States v. Richard M. Nixon (p. 784) A Supreme Court ruling (1974) that obliged President Richard Nixon to turn over to the Watergate special prosecutor sixty-four White House audiotapes; these helped prove that Nixon had known about the cover-up of the Watergate burglary.

utopian (p. 278) Any of countless schemes to create a perfect society.

Virginia Plan (p. 148) An initiative, proposed by James Madison of Virginia, calling on the

Constitutional Convention to declare that seats in the federal legislature would be proportionate to a state's population, a concept that caused smaller states to propose a New Jersey plan in which each state would have the same number of representatives. The controversy was resolved in the Great Compromise.

Voting Rights Act of 1965 (p. 769) Federal legislation that empowered federal registrars to intervene when southern states and municipalities refused to let African Americans register to vote.

Wade-Davis bill (p. 412) An 1864 alternative to Lincoln's "**Ten Percent Plan**," this measure required a majority of voters in a southern state to take a loyalty oath in order to begin the process of Reconstruction and guarantee black equality. It also required the repudiation of the Confederate debt. The president exercised a pocket veto, and it never became law.

Wagner Act (p. 688) Officially the National Labor Relations Act and sometimes called Labor's Magna Carta, it gave workers the right to organize and bargain collectively. It also created the National Labor Relations Board to supervise union elections and stop unfair labor practices by employers.

War Hawks (p. 196) Young congressional leaders who in 1811 and 1812 called for war against Great Britain as the only way to defend the national honor.

War Industries Board (WIB) (p. 612) A federal agency, established during World War I, that reorganized industry for maximum efficiency and productivity.

War of 1812 (p. 197) A war fought by the United States and Britain from 1812 to 1815 over British restrictions on American shipping.

war on terror (p. 843) Initially, a worldwide campaign to catch and prosecute those guilty of the September 11, 2001, attacks; as terrorist attacks spread throughout the world, the war became defined far more broadly.

Watergate scandal (p. 782) A complex scandal involving attempts to cover up illegal actions taken by administration officials and leading to the resignation of President Richard Nixon in 1974.

Webster-Ashburton Treaty (p. 301) A treaty between the United States and Britain, signed in 1842, that settled the controversy of the Maine-Canada boundary. The treaty allowed Canada to build a military road from Halifax to Quebec while the United States got most of the disputed territory.

Whigs (p. 264) Originally a reference to British politicians who sought to exclude the Catholic Duke of York from succession to the throne in the 1760s; in the United States after the 1830s, it referred to a political party that opposed the Jacksonian Democrats and favored a strong role for the national government, especially in promoting economic growth.

Whiskey Rebellion (p. 162) A violent protest by western Pennsylvania farmers who refused to pay the whiskey tax proposed by Alexander Hamilton. In 1794, the rebels threatened to destroy Pittsburgh; by the time the Union army had arrived, the rebels had dispersed.

Wilmot Proviso (p. 314) A proposed amendment to an 1846 appropriations bill that banned slavery from any territory the United States might acquire from Spain. It never passed Congress, but generated a great debate on the authority of the federal government to ban slavery from the territories.

woman suffrage (p. 553) The right of women to vote, ensured by the passage and ratification of the Nineteenth Amendment (1920).

Works Progress Administration (WPA) (p. 685) A **New Deal** agency, established in 1935 and run by Harry Hopkins, that spent $11 billion on federal works projects and provided employment for 8.5 million persons.

XYZ Affair (p. 167) A political furor caused by French diplomats who in 1797 demanded a bribe before they would enter into negotiations with their American counterparts; some **Federalists**, furious over this assault on national honor, called for war.

Yalta Conference (p. 730) A wartime conference (February 1945) held in the Russian Crimea, where the **Allies**—Franklin Roosevelt, Winston Churchill (Britain), and Josef Stalin (Soviet Union)—agreed to final plans for the defeat and joint occupation of Germany; it also provided for free elections in Poland, but such elections were never held.

Young America movement (p. 351) The confident enthusiasm, infused with a belief in the nation's "**manifest destiny**," that spread rapidly during the 1850s.

Credits

186 Werner Forman/Art Resource, N.Y. 188 Collection of The New-York Historical Society, [Neg. No. 7278]. 191 *Storming of the Bastille on 14th July 1789* (oil on panel), French School, (18th century)/Musee de la Ville de Paris, Musee Carnavalet, Paris, France/The Bridgeman Art Library International.

CHAPTER 7 195 (left and right) Public Domain. 198 Stephan Savoia/AP Wide World Photos. 199 The Mariners' Museum, Newport News, VA. 202 The Granger Collection, New York. 205 The Granger Collection, New York. 208 © CORBIS All Rights Reserved. 214 Samuel F.B. Morse, *The House of Representatives*. 1822–23. Oil on Canvas. 86 ⅞ × 130 ⅝. Corcoran Gallery of Art, Museum Purchase, Gallery Fund. 215 Hood Museum of Art, Dartmouth College, Hanover, New Hampshire, Gift of George C. Shattuck, Class of 1803. 221 Courtesy of the Pennsylvania Academy of Fine Arts, Philadelphia. Pennsylvania Academy purchase (from the estate of Paul Beck, Jr.).

CHAPTER 8 225 Paul Rocheleau. 228 N. Carter/North Wind Picture Archives. 233 © Bettmann/Corbis. 237 George Tattersall, English, 1817–1849 (active U.S. 1836), *Album of Western Sketches: Highways and Byeways of the Forest*, a Scene on "the Road", 1836. Pen and brown ink with brush and brown wash, heightened with white gouache, over graphite pencil, on gray paper. 21.0 × 29.8 cm (8-¼ × 11-¾ in.) Museum of Fine Arts, Boston. Gift of Maxim Karolik for the M. and M. Karolik Collection of American Watercolors and Drawings, 1800–1875, 56.400.11. Photograph © 2011 Museum of Fine Arts, Boston. 242 Museum of the City of New York.

CHAPTER 9 250 *Rachel Donelson* by Ralph Earl, 1826. The Hermitage. 251 © Bettmann/CORBIS All Rights Reserved. 254 Bob Krist/Bob Krist Photography. 258 George Catlin, *Osceola, the Black Drink, a warrior of Great Distinction*, 1838. Smithsonian American Art Museum/Art Resource, NY. 260 Samuel Barnard, *View along the East Battery, Charleston*, Yale University Art Gallery, Mabel Brady Garvan Collection. 266 Library of Congress, Washington D.C., USA/The Bridgeman Art Library.

CHAPTER 10 273 *Young Husband: First Marketing*, 1854 by Lilly Martin Spencer. The Metropolitan Museum of Art, New York, NY, U.S.A. Image copyright © The Metropolitan Museum of Art. 276 *Domestic Happiness*, 1849 (oil on canvas), Spencer, Lilly Martin (1827–1902)/Detroit Institute of Arts, USA/Gift of Dr and Mrs James Cleland Jr./The Bridgeman Art Library International. 278 From the Collection of the Oneida Community Mansion House, Oneida, NY. 280 Albert Vecerka, 2001. Courtesy of Eastern State Penitentiary Historic Site, Philadelphia, PA. 284 National Portrait Gallery, Smithsonian Institution/Art Resource, New York. 286 The Granger Collection, New York. 288 Frederic Edwin Church (American),

1826–1900). *Twilight in the Wilderness*, 1860. Oil on canvas; 101.6 × 162.6 cm. © The Cleveland Museum of Art. Mr. and Mrs. William H. Marlatt Fund 1965.233. 290 © Joseph Sohm; Chromosohm/ CORBIS All Rights Reserved. 291 Hulton Archive/ Getty Images. 293 The Granger Collection, New York.

CHAPTER 11 302 San Jacinto Museum of History, Houston. 304 Courtesy of the Library of Congress. 305 Kansas State Historical Society. 310 West Point Museum Art Collection, United States Military Academy, West Point, New York. 315 Getty Images Inc. - Hulton Archive Photos. 321 (left) Getty Images Inc. - Michael Ochs Archives. 321 (right) Touchstone Pictures/ Courtesy Everett Collection.

CHAPTER 12 325 Musee de l'Homme/ Paris/ RMN/Art Resource, NY. 328 The Historic New Orleans Collection, Museum/Research Center, Acc. No. 1960.46. 332 The Granger Collection, New York. 336 Accession no. 1959.46. Collection of The New-York Historical Society. 338 Niday Picture Library/Alamy Images.

CHAPTER 13 348 Courtesy of the Library of Congress. 350 Warsaw Collection of Business Americana - Theater, Archives Center, National Museum of American History, Behring Center, Smithsonian Institution. 353 The Granger Collection, New York. 358 J. L. Magee, "Southern Chivalry-Argument Versus Clubs", 1856. Lithograph. Weitenkampf Collection #745, Prints Collection: Miriam and Ira D. Wallach Division of Art, Prints and Photographs, The New York Public Library, Astor, Lenox, and Tilden Foundations. 361 MPI/Stringer/Hulton Archive/Getty Images. 364 Abraham Lincoln Presidential Library & Museum (ALPLM). 366 Kansas State Historical Society, Copy and Reuse Restrictions apply. 368 The Granger Collection, New York.

CHAPTER 14 377 Courtesy of the Library of Congress. 378 Cook Collection, Valentine Richmond History Center. 381 Courtesy of the Library of Congress. 389 The Granger Collection, New York. 391 The Granger Collection, New York. 398 (left) Lauren Cook Wike/Mr. Jackson K. Doane, Sr. 398 (right) Used with Permission of Documenting the American South, The University of North Carolina at Chapel Hill Libraries. 402 (left) ICHi-20265/Photo by Alexander Hesler/Chicago Historical Society. 402 (right) Courtesy of the Library of Congress. 405 (left) Photofest. 405 (right) Everett Collection.

CHAPTER 15 410 CORBIS-NY. 411 Arthur Stumpf, *Andrew Johnson*, 1808–1875. National Portrait Gallery, Smithsonian Institution/Art Resource, NY. 418 Private Collection/Photo © Christie's Images/The Bridgeman Art Library. 420 The Granger Collection, New York. 426 The Granger Collection, New York.

Index

Note: Italicized letters *f*, *m*, and *n* following page numbers indicate figures (photos, illustrations, and graphs), maps, and footnotes, respectively.

Abolitionism, 282–285, 286, 358–359, 368

Abortion, 7

Adams, Abigail, 134–135, 135*f*

Adams, Henry, 180

Adams, John, 77, 90, 135, 168, 214, 215; alcohol consumption by, 282; Alien and Sedition Acts and, 167; American Revolution and, 120; Boston Massacre and, 106; at Constitutional Convention, 147; death of, 221; Declaration of Independence and, 117–118; election of 1796 and, 166; on events leading to revolution, 102; at First Continental Congress, 109, 110; gentility and, 225; Jefferson and, 210; judiciary and, 176–177; Louisiana Purchase and, 181; as president, 166–168; as vice president, 153; XYZ Affair and, 166–167

Adams, John Quincy, 252; in 1824 election, 219; in 1828 election, 249–250; background of, 214–215; on Missouri controversy, 219; on Monroe, 210; presidency of, 220; as secretary of state, 207; sectional issues and, 212*f*; Texas question and, 301; Transcontinental Treaty and, 206–207; Treaty of Ghent and, 203

Adams, Samuel, 105, 106, 107, 112, 113, 152

Adena communities, 4, 6*m*

Administration of Justice Act, 108

Adult education, 249

Africa, 9–11; Barbary pirates from, 177; colonization movement and, 235–236; diseases in, 11; first humans in, 1; population in 1500, 10*m*; slaves from, 23

African Americans; abolitionism and, 284–285; in American Revolution, 133; in Civil War, 392–393; colonization movement and, 235–236; discrimination against, in colonies, 61; Industrial Revolution and, 227–228; Missouri constitution and, 219; mistreatment of, in South, 414; in North, in nineteenth century, 236; politicians, during Reconstruction, 419–421, 420*m*; sharecropping and, 422–424; voting intimidation and, 425; voting rights for, 414, 417–419; in War of 1812, 200, 204; white violence against, 424–425

African Methodist Church, 235

African slaves, 23, 55–56, 57*m*, 61, 62*f*, 69; *See also* Slaves

Age of Reason, 88–90
Agricultural colleges, 396
Agriculture; *See also*
   Farming; in 1860,
   343*m*; in colonies, 28,
   40, 41, 44, 54, 57–61,
   68–71, 73; Columbian
   Exchange and, 22–24,
   44; corn, 5–6, 68–69;
   cotton and, 232–234;
   crop-lien system,
   423–424; indigo, 60;
   Industrial Revolution
   and, 232–234; maize,
   4–5; in Middle
   Colonies, 70–71, 73;
   in New England,
   68–69; railroads and,
   342, 344; rice, 9, 60, 61;
   sharecropping,
   422–424; in South,
   324–326, 422–424;
   technological
   advances in, 342;
   tobacco, 28, 37,
   57–60; wheat, 9, 58,
   71, 324, 342, 344
Aix-la-Chapelle, Treaty
   of, 91
Alabama, cotton in, 233
Alamo, 301, 320–321
The Alamo (film),
   320–321
Alaska, 2, 96*m*; Russian
   interest in, 207
Albany Plan, 87, 96
Albany Regency, 216
Albemarle settlement, 38
Alcohol consumption,
   in mid-nineteenth
   century, 281–282
Alcott, Bronson, 274
Alexander, Francis, 215*f*
Alexander VI (pope),
   17, 18, 42

Algonquian Indians, 38,
   44, 90
Alien Act, 175
Alien and Sedition Acts,
   167, 168
Alien Enemies Act, 167
Allan, John, 290
Allen, Richard, 235
Alliance of 1778,
   159–160
Almshouses, 280
America (ship), 198
American Anti-Slavery
   Society, 419
American Colonization
   Society, 235
American Empire; *See
   also* Expansionism,
   U.S.; Imperialism
American flag, 136
American Indians. *See*
   Indian Americans
American party,
   355–356, 359
American Progress
   (Gast), 304*f*
American Revolution,
   112–142; battles of,
   113–116, 120–122,
   121*f*, 126; beginning
   of, 113–114;
   Continental army,
   119, 125, 131; debt
   from, 156–157;
   Declaration of
   Independence and,
   116–119; events
   leading to, 97–110;
   fighting of, 119–128;
   financing of, 131;
   French involvement
   in, 123–125, 128–129;
   growth of nationalism
   following, 135–136;
   Hessian soldiers in,

117, 122; impact of,
   on society, 134;
   Loyalists during, 120,
   125; national heroes
   of, 140–141; peace
   negotiations,
   128–129; Saratoga
   campaign, 123–125,
   124*m*; in South,
   125–128, 126*m*; war
   debts from, 144;
   women during,
   134–135; Yorktown
   campaign, 126–128,
   127*m*
Americans; becoming,
   77; character of, 48
American System, 216,
   345
American Temperance
   Union, 282
Americas; ancient
   peoples of, 1–9;
   Columbus's discovery
   of, 16–17; geographic
   isolation of, 2;
   Spanish empire in,
   17–20, 24
Ames, Fisher, 165
Amherst, Jeffrey, 94, 97*f*
Anaconda Plan, 381
Anasazi Indians, 4, 5,
   6*m*, 8
Ancient peoples, of
   Americas, 1–9
Anderson, Alexander,
   188*f*
Anderson, Robert, 376
André, John, 127
Andrew Jackson (ship),
   339
Andros, Edmund, 66
Anglican Church, 25,
   30–31, 33, 62, 71,
   133

Anglo-American relations; Burr conspiracy and, 184–185; Embargo Act and, 187–189; impressment controversy and, 187; Jay's Treaty and, 163–164; post-Revolutionary, 144–145; shipping industry and, 160–161; in War of 1812. *See* War of 1812; after War of 1812, 206; Webster-Ashburton Treaty, 300–301

Animals; brought to New World by Europeans, 21, 23; domestication of, 9; of Eurasia, 9–10; Paleolithic era, 2

Annapolis Convention, 146–147

Anthony, Susan B., 287

Antietam, 387–388, 393, 401*t*

Antifederalists, 150, 151, 152, 153

Anti-Leislerians, 76

Antinomianism, 35

Antislavery movement, 132–134; *See also* Abolitionism

Antrobus, John, 328*f*

Apache Indians, 49–50

Appeal to the Coloured Citizens of the World (1829), 284

Appomattox Court House, 403

Archaic Indians, 2–9

Argall, Samuel, 90

Arizona, statehood for, 299

Arkansas, readmission of, to Union, 416

Arkansas Territory, 217

Arminianism, 30, 88

Army nurses, during Civil War, 397–398

Arnold, Benedict, 123, 126–127

Articles of Confederation, 130–131, 130*m*, 143–146

Artisans, 334

Asia; *See also specific countries*; goods from, 14; population in 1500, 10*m*

Associations, 276–277

Astor, Jacob, 305

Asylums, 280

Atchison, David R., 354

Atheism, 278

Atlantic Ocean, navigation of, 12

Atlantic slave trade, 57*m*, 69

Auburn system, 281

Austin, Stephen F., 301

Austria, 93

Aztalan, 8

Aztecs, 4, 9, 17, 19*f*, 40–41

Back country, 52, 62–63

Bacon, Nathaniel, 59–60

Bacon's rebellion, 59–60

Balboa, Vasci Nuñez de, 17

Baltimore, Lord, 37, 62

Baltimore, Maryland, in War of 1812, 201

Baltimore and Ohio Railroad, 340

Bank of the United States, 157–158, 162, 211–212, 243–244, 262, 265; second, 212–213, 253–256, 254*f*

Banks and banking; Jackson and, 253–256, 262–263; Marshal Court and, 243–244; national bank, 157–158; state banks, 265, 268; during War of 1812, 211–213

Bank war, 253–256

Barbados, 38

Barbary pirates, 177

Barnard, Henry, 295

Barron, James, 188

Barrow, Benney, 328

Barton, Clara, 398, 413

Bartram, John, 89

The Battle of Cowpens (Ranney), 139*f*

The Battle of Princeton (Mercer), 122*f*

Bayard, James A., 203

Beaumont, Gustave de, 272

Beauregard, Pierre G. T., 380

Beavers, 2

Beecher, Catharine, 274

Beecher, Lyman, 275

Beer, 112

Bell, John, 369–370

Beloved (Morrison), 348*f*

Benin, 11

Bennett, James Gordon, 294

Benton, Thomas Hart, 253, 310

Beringia, 2

Berkeley, William, 59
Berlin Decree (1806), 185
Bernard, Samuel, 260f
Bible, King James Version, 31
Biddle, Nicholas, 253–256
Bifocals, 89
Big business. *See* Business
Bill of Rights, 155, A13–A14
Bills of rights, 132
Biological diversity, 2
Birch, William Russell, 146f, 156f
Birney, James G., 284
Black Americans. *See* African Americans
Black Ball Line, 241
Black Belt, 233
Black Codes, 409, 414
Black Hawk, 258
Black nationalism, 235
Black Robe (film), 42–43
Blackwell, Elizabeth, 397–398
Blaine, James G., 427
Bleeding Kansas, 356–357, 357m
Blind, schools for the, 280
Board of Customs Commissioners, 104
Board of Trade, 80–84, 99
The Bombardment of Fort McHenry, 202f
Bonaparte, Napoleon; America and, threat to, 197; defeat of, 201; Great Britain and, 185–186; Louisiana Purchase and,

178–181; shipping policy and, 194
Bonomi, Patricia, 70f
Book of Mormon, 277
Books; *See also* Literature; in mid-nineteenth century, 294; printing press and, 12
Booths, John Wilkes, 410
Boquet, Henry, 97f
Border; Canadian, 206, 300–301; U.S.-Mexican, 299
Borders, map of, 209m
Boston, Massachusetts, 33, 63, 66, 69
Boston and Worcester Railroad, 340
Boston Associates, 227, 229
Boston Daily Times, 294
Boston Manufacturing Company, 227
Boston Massacre, 105–106, 105f
Boston Port Act, 108
Boston Tea Party, 107–108, 113, 119
Bourbons, 91
Bower, John, 202f
Bowie, Jim, 301, 320
Boycotts, colonial, 103, 104, 109
Braddock Edward, 93
Bradford, William, 31–32, 34, 36, 112
Braille, Louis, 280
Brandywine, Battle of, 123
Brazil, 17
Breckenridge, John C., 368, 368f, 370
Breed's Hill, 115f, 116

Brewster, William, 31
Bridgman, Laura, 280
British navy, 160–161
British troops; in American Revolution, 119; Boston Massacre and, 105–106; quartering of, 103
Brock, Isaac, 198
Brooks, Preston S., 358f, 359, 382
Brown, John, 357, 366–367, 366f
Brown, Moses, 226
Brown University, 86, 296
Bubonic plague, 20
Buchanan, James, 352; election of 1856 and, 359–360; inaugural address by, 362; Lecompton constitution and, 362; secession crisis and, 372
Budbury, Jones, 403
Bull Run, battle of, 380–381, 388, 401t
Bulwer, Henry Lytton, 351
Bunker Hill, battle of, 115–116, 115f
Burgoyne, John, 123, 124
Burk, John Daly, 167
Burke, Edmund, 108, 113
Burning of the Merchant's Exchange (Calyo), 242f
Burns, Anthony, 355
Burnside, Ambrose E., 393
Burr, Aaron; in 1800 election, 172–173, 172m; conspiracy of, 184–185; duel with Hamilton, 182–183,

182*f*; Federalists' secession attempt and, 182–183

Burr, William Henry, 336*f*

Bushman, Richard, 225*f*

Bushnell, Horace, 275

Business; *See also* Corporations; Industry and industrialization; Marshal Court and, 243–245

Butler, Andrew P., 358–359

Cabot, John, 15*m*, 24

Cahokia, 7–9, 8*f*

Calhoun, John C.; in 1844 election, 307; annexation of Texas and, 303; background of, 216; Compromise of 1850 and, 317; Jackson and, 256–257; nullification crisis and, 260–261; as secretary of state, 303; sectionalism and, 212*f*, 253; slavery resolutions of, 314; *South Carolina Exposition and Protest*, 220; tariffs and, 219, 220

California; annexation of, 311, 312; gold rush in, 313, 316–317; settlement of, 304–307; slavery in, 316–317; Spanish settlement of, 52; statehood for, 299, 318

Calvert, Cecilius, 37

Calvert, George, 37

Calvin, John, 12, 25

Calvinism, 88, 274, 275

Calyo, Nicolino V., 242*f*

Camels, 2

Canada; American appetites toward, 196; border issues with, 206, 300–301; British takeover of, 95, 96*m*; colonization of, 38; European exploration in, 24; fur trade in, 90; Indian relations and, 195; in War of 1812, 198–199

Canals, 339–340; construction of, 240–243; Erie Canal, 240–241, 340, 343; Panama Canal, 351

Canary Islands, 16

Canning, George, 208

Cannon, 12

Cape Coast Castle, 56*f*

Cape Cod, 32, 69

Cape Verde Islands, 20–21

Capitol building, 156*f*

Carey, Mathew, 158

Caribbean, Spanish empire in, 17–18

Caribou, 2

Carillo, Adriana, 299

Carlyle, Thomas, 215*f*

Carolinas; *See also* North Carolina; South Carolina; colonies of, 60–61; colony of, 37–38, 52

Carousing in Surinam (Greenwood), 82*f*

Carpetbaggers, 419

Carter, Robert, 62

Carteret, Sir George, 39

Cartier, Jacques, 24, 38

Cass, Lewis, 314, 315, 352

Cassava, 22

Catherine of Aragon, 25

Catholic missionaries, 18–20, 42–43, 51

Catholics and Catholic Church; in England, 30; indulgences sold by, 24, 30; Irish Americans and, 231; Protestant Reformation and, 24–25

Catlin, George, 258*f*

Cattle, 21, 41, 44

Central America, 351; *See also* Latin America; *specific countries*; development of maize in, 4

Central government, 150

Cereal crops, 10

Chaco Canyon, 5, 8

Champlain Canal, 241

Chancellorsville, battle of, 393–394, 401*t*

Chapman, John Gadsby, 92*f*

Charles I (king), 37; execution of, 66; puritans and, 33

Charles II (king), 39, 40, 66

Charles River Bridge case, 244–245, 245*f*

Charleston colony, 38

Charles V (king), 24

Charter of Privileges of Patroons, 39

Chase, Salmon P., 376, 382

Checks and balances, 150

Cheetahs, 2
Cherokee Indians, 257, 258–260
Cherokee Nation v. Georgia, 258
Chesapeake (ship), 188
Chesapeake colonies, 52–55; agriculture in, 57–59; Bacon's rebellion in, 59–60; headright system in, 54–55; life expectancy in, 54; slavery in, 55–56
Cheves, Langdon, 213, 253
Chicago, Illinois, railroads and, 342–343
Child, Lydia Maria, 274, 287
Child labor, 228–229, 335–336
Child labor laws, 336
Children; of Indian slaves and Hispanic fathers, 51; in mid-nineteenth century, 274; puritan, 64, 64f; slave, 327; in Southern colonies, 61–62; in workforce, 228–229, 335–336
Childs, Lydia Maria, 425
China, 9; American traders in, 186f; cities, 11m; population in 1500, 10m, 11; sixteenth-century, 11; trade route to, 16
Chinook Indians, 183f
Chippendale, Thomas, 226

Choctaw Indians, 257, 258
Christendom, 11–12
Christianity; conversion of Indians to, 49, 52; French Revolution and, 190; Protestant Reformation, 24–25; slaves and, 329; spread of, in New World, 20
Chubbock, Emily, 228–229
Church, Frederic Edwin, 288f
Churches; disestablishment of, 249; Great Awakening and, 86; New England, 64–65; puritan, 34, 64–65; separation of church and state, 133; in Southern colonies, 62
Churchill, Ward, 43
Church of England. *See* Anglican Church
Church of Latter-Day Saints, 278
Circular Letter, 104, 105
Cities; *See also* Urbanization; Chinese, 11m; emergence of, 10; established by Spanish, 18–19; Eurasian, 10; Indian, 7, 8, 9; of New England, 66; poverty in, 335–337; railroads and, 342–343; Southern, 330
Citizenship, Fourteenth Amendment and, 415
"Civil Disobedience" (Thoreau), 290

Civil Rights Act (1866), 414
Civil War; African American soldiers in, 392–393; Antietam, 387–388, 393; Bull Run, battle of, 380–381; casualties in, 381f, 384, 386, 399, 403, 406f; civilian participation in, 397; Confederate strategy in, 383–384; conscription in, 390–391; draft riots in, 391; economic effects of, 378, 396–397; Emancipation Proclamation and, 388–391; events leading to, 347–374; financing of, 381–382; Fort Sumter, 376–377, 377f; generals in, 385–388, 395–396, 398–400; Gettysburg campaign, 393–394, 394m; Lincoln's leadership during, 379, 381, 393; losses of, 403, 406; Northern strategy for, 381; Peninsular Campaign, 386, 387m; politics during, 382–383; reasons for, 377; reconstruction following, 409–430; recruitment during, 379; results of, 406; Sherman's march in, 400–402, 400m; surrender by South in, 403; turning points in,

401*t*; Vicksburg campaign, 395–396, 395*m*; in West, 384, 385*m*; women in, 397–398

Civil wars, 375

Clark, William, 183–184, 183*f*

Clay, Henry; in 1824 election, 219; in 1844 election, 303, 307; American System of, 216, 345; background of, 216; Bank of the United States and, 255; Compromise of 1850 and, 317–319, 348; Missouri constitution and, 219; National Republican party, 263–264; nullification crisis and, 261; sectional issues and, 212*f*; spoils system and, 252; Treaty of Ghent and, 203; Tyler and, 300; War of 1812 and, 198

Clayton, John M., 351

Clement VII (pope), 25

Clergyman, in colonies, 34

Clermont (ship), 239

Clinton, DeWitt, 240–241

Clinton, George, 153, 184

Clinton, Sir Henry, 123, 124, 125, 127

Clipper ships, 338–339

Clothes, colonial, 62

Clovis blades, 2

Coal industry, 231

Cochrane, Alexander, 201

Cockburn, George, 201

Cod, 24

Coercive Acts, 108–109, 109*t*, 124

Cold Harbor, Battle of, 399, 401*t*

College of Philadelphia, 89

College of William and Mary, 62

Colleges and universities, 89; *See also* Higher education; agricultural, 396; curriculum in, 296; enrollment in, 193; established by Spanish, 19; Great Awakening and, 86; in mid-nineteenth century, 296–297; in South, 62

Colonial troops, 97

Colonies; agriculture in, 28, 40, 41, 44, 54, 57–61, 68–71, 73; boycotts in, 103, 104, 109; British, 25–38, 39–40, 52–55, 53*m*, 63–73, 80–81; Carolinas, 37–38, 52, 60–61; Chesapeake, 52–55; differences among, 52; diseases in, 54; Dutch, 38–39; Enlightenment in, 88–90; environmental impact of, 41, 44; ethnic composition of, 72*m*; events leading to revolution by, 97–110; French, 38–39, 49; Georgia,

62–63; government in, 31, 33–34, 39–40, 65–66, 73, 76, 80–81; indentured servants in, 55, 56; Jamestown colony, 54; Maryland, 37, 52, 54; Massachusetts Bay Colony, 32–34; Middle colonies, 39–40, 52, 70–71; New England, 31–36, 52, 63–70; Plymouth, 31–32, 32*f*, 36; population growth in, 97; protests and uprisings in, 101–103, 101*f*, 107–108; relations between Indians and, 28–29, 31–32, 40–41, 44–45, 98; religion in, 37, 85–87; Rhode Island, 34, 35; scientific achievements in, 89–90; slavery in, 55–56; society of, 49; Spanish, 18–20, 50–52, 51*m*; taxation in, 77, 98–105, 107, 110; trade between England and, 81–84, 84*f*; trade between Indians and, 38, 39, 44–45; Virginia, 27–29, 52, 53; wars between Indians and, 36, 38; wars in, 90–95

Colonization movement, 235–236

Columbian Centinel, 210

Columbian Exchange, 21–24, 22–23*m*, 44

Columbia University, 89

Columbus, Christopher, 12, 14–17, 15m, 42

Comanche Indians, 49–51

Commerce; See also Business; in colonies, 81–84; foreign, 338–339; interstate, 244; maritime, 69; in New England colonies, 69–70; transportation and, 339–340

Commerce clause, 244

Common school movement, 295

Common Sense (Paine), 117, 134

Commonwealth v. Hunt, 336

Communitarians, 277–279

Compromise of 1850, 317–319, 319f, 348, 352

Compromise of 1877, 429

Concessions and Agreements, 39–40

Concord, battle of, 113–114

Conestoga Indians, 76

Confederacy; army of, 378f, 379f, 380; financial issues in, 383–384; foreign policy of, 383–384; government of, 379–380; military advantages of, 378–379; readmission of, to Union, 411–413; secession by, 371–373; at start of Civil War, 378–380; strategy of, 383–384; women of, 397

Confiscation Act, 389, 390

Confucianism, 11

Congo, 11

Congregationalists, 30, 86, 275

Congress, U.S., 149; See also House of Representatives; Senate, U.S.; first achievements of, 155; impeachment power of, 150; Reconstruction and, 416–417; taxes levyed by, 155–156, 244

Congress Hall, 146f

Congressional elections, of 1866, 415

Connecticut, 131; colony of, 35–36; ratification of Constitution by, 152

Conquistadores, 17–18

Conscription Act, 390–391

Constitution (ship), 197–198, 198f

Constitutional Convention, 146–150, 213

Constitutional Union party, 369–370

Constitutions, 103; See also U.S. Constitution; state, 131–132

Consumer revolution, 225–226

Continental army, 115, 119, 125, 131, 136

Continental Association, 109

Continental Congress; Articles of Confederation and, 130–131; First, 109–110, 113; Second, 114–116, 119

Contracts, 243

Convention of 1800, 178–179

Convention of 1818, 206

Convicts, transported to Americas, 63

Cooper, William, 325f

Copperheads, 382–383

Copyright, 143

Corn, 5–6, 29, 40, 44, 68–69

Cornbury, Lord, 70f

Corn-growing civilizations, 4–7

Corning, Erastus, 340

Corn Mother symbolism, 5, 5f

Cornwallis, General, 122, 125–127, 128f

Corporations; See also Business; rise of, 231–232

Cortés, Hernán, 17, 19f

Cosby, William, 76

Cotton; Confederacy and, 383–384; mechanized production and, 226–227; prices, 265; slavery and, 232–234, 233f, 234f, 235–236, 326m; in South, 232–234, 324, 326m, 378, 424; in Texas, 301

Cotton gin, 233, 233f

Council for New England, 32, 37

Courts; *See also* Supreme Court; colonial, 80; federal, 150, 155; vice admiralty, 104

Cowpens, Battle of, 126, 139*f*

Cows, 10

Coxe, Tench, 158

Craft, William and Ellen, 348–349

Cragin, Mary, 278*f*

Crawford, William H., 216, 219

Credit card debt, 171

Creek Indians, in War of 1812, 204

Crèvecoeur, Hector St. John de, 71–72

Crime, in New England colonies, 69–70

Crimean War, 344, 345

Criminals, treatment of, 280

Crittenden, John J., 372–373

Crittenden Compromise, 372–373

Crockett, Davy, 266–267, 301, 320, 321

Croghan, George, 91

Cromwell, Oliver, 66

Crop-lien system, 423–424

The Crucible (film), 74–75

Cuba; attempts to purchase, 351; Columbus's discovery of, 17; Spanish control of, 95

Cuffe, Paul, 235

Cult of True Womanhood, 274

Culture; clash between Indian and colonists, 40–41, 44; dissemination of, 294; regional, 323–324

Cumming, Kate, 397

Curry, John Stewart, 366*f*

Custer, George A., 413

Cutler, Timothy, 86

Dallas, Alexander J., 212

Dartmouth (ship), 107–108

Dartmouth College, 86

Dartmouth College v. Woodward, 243, 245*f*

Datang, China, 224

Davidson, Julia, 397

Davis, David, 427–428

Davis, Jefferson, 354, 383; career of, 380; as president of Confederacy, 373, 380

Deaf, schools for the, 280

Deane, Silas, 124

Dearborn, Henry, 199

Death penalty, 65

Debt, federal, 171, 173, 191–192

Declaration of Independence, 116–119, 132, 133, 134, 209, A1–A3

Declaration of Neutrality, 209

Declaratory Act, 103–104, 105

Deep South; *See also* South; slavery in, 324

Deer, 2

Deere, John, 342

Deerfield, Massachusetts, 91

De Grasse, François, 127, 128

Deism, 89

De Large, Robert, 420*m*

Delaware; colony of, 40, 70–71, 73; ratification of Constitution by, 152

Delaware and Hudson Canal, 242

Delaware Indians, 93

Democracy; in colonies, 33–34; Jacksonian, 247–270; Jeffersonian, 190–192, 248

Democracy in America (Tocqueville), 258, 272–273

Democratic party; beginnings of, 247; during Civil War, 382–383; election of 1840 and, 268–269; election of 1844 and, 307; election of 1848 and, 314–316; election of 1852 and, 353; election of 1856 and, 359; election of 1860 and, 368; election of 1876 and, 427–429; Jackson and, 263; in Reconstruction era, 425

Denmark Vesey's Rebellion, 331*t*

Dental cavities, 6

Depression(s), economic; of 1819, 211, 213; of 1830s, 262–263; of 1837, 262–263, 265, 336; of 1857, 337, 345; War of 1812 and, 196

Descartes, René, 88

Deslondes, Charles, 329

Deslondes' Rebellion, 331*t*

Detroit, Michigan, 42–43, 199

Dickens, Charles, 280

Dickinson, John, 104, 130

Dinwiddie, Robert, 92

Diphtheria, 20

Diplomacy; *See also* Foreign policy

Discourse on Western Planting (Hakluyt), 26–27

Diseases; in Africa, 11; among colonists, 54; in Eurasia, 10; European, and Indians, 12, 20–21, 32, 52

District of Columbia, 318

Divorce, 134, 271

Dix, Dorothea, 281

Domestic animals, 9

Domestic Happiness (Martin), 276*f*

Dominion of New England, 66

Douglas, Stephen A., 319, 363; Compromise of 1850 and, 352; election of 1860 and, 368–371; Freeport Doctrine, 365, 366, 368; Kansas-Nebraska Act and, 354–355; Lecompton constitution and, 362; Lincoln-Douglas debates, 347, 364–366; politics of, 352–353

Douglass, Frederick, 284–285, 284*f*, 392

Dow, Neal, 282

Draco, 1

Draft, 390–391

Draft riots, 391, 391f

Drake, Sir Francis, 20–21, 25–26, 81

Dred Scott decision, 360–362, 365, 370*t*

Dutch colonies, 38–39, 90

Dutch merchants, 82

Dutch traders, 25

Dwight, Timothy, 275

Dysentery, 54

Earl, Ralph, 114*f*

Early, Jubal, 400

East, linking of West and, 344

East Asia, passage to, 25

Eastern State Penitentiary, 280f

East Florida, 206

East India Company, 25, 106–107

Eaton, Peggy, 257

Ecological imperialism, 21–24

Economic crises. *See* Financial crises

Economy; colonial, 82–84; cotton boom in South and, 232–234; effects of Civil War on, 396–397; factory system, 226–229; gentility and consumer revolution, 225–226; household system and, 231; immigration and, 230–231;

Industrial Revolution and, 232; Marshal Court and, 243–245; of Middle Colonies, 70–71, 73; of New England colonies, 69; New York City and, 241–243; nineteenth century, 224–246; panic of 1837, 262–263, 265; post-Revolutionary, 144–145; pre–Civil War, 345; railroads and, 341–344; revival of slavery and, 235–236; transportation and, 236–238, 237–239

Education; *See also* Higher education; in mid-nineteenth century, 294–295; reform of, 294–296; in Southern colonies, 61–62; spread of, 249; of women, 135, 296

Edwards, Jonathan, 87, 182

Eighty Years and More (Stanton), 287

Election; *See also* Presidential elections; of president, 149–150

Electoral College, 150, 249; Twelfth Amendment and, 172–173

Electricity, 89

Elementary schools, 295

Elizabeth I (queen), 25–27, 27*f*, 30

Elliott, Robert Brown, 420*m*

Emancipation Proclamation, 388–392

Embargo Act, 187–189, 188*f*, 194

Emerson, John, 360

Emerson, Ralph Waldo, 264, 289

Encomienda system, 18

England. *See* Great Britain

English Bill of Rights, 155

English Church. *See* Anglican Church

English colonies, 25–40, 52–56, 53*m*, 63–73, 80–81; *See also* Colonies

Enlightenment, 88–90

Enumerated articles, 82

Era of Good Feelings, 210–211

Erie Canal, 240–241, 275, 340, 343

Erie Railroad, 340

Eriksson, Leif, 12

Essex Junto, 182

Ethnic diversity, in Middle Colonies, 71–72, 72*m*

Etowah, Georgia, 8

Eurasia, 9–11

Eurasian hunters, 2

Europe; *See also specific countries*; colonial wars and, 91–95; diseases from, and Indian Americans, 12, 20–21; Enlightenment in, 88–89; increase in population of, 22–24; medieval, 11–12;

population in 1500, 10*m*, 11

European exploration, 15–16, 15*m*, 24

Evangelists, 275

Examination of a Witch (Matteson), 67*f*

Excise taxes, 159

Executive branch, 149

Expansionism, U.S.; *See also* Imperialism; in California and Oregon, 304–307; life on the trail and, 303–304; manifest destiny and, 303; Mexican War and, 308–313; Young America movement, 351–352

Exports, 338

Extinction, of big mammals, 2

Factories; *See also* Industry and industrialization; Manufacturing; birth of, 226–227; Waltham system, 229; workers in, 227–229

Fallen Timbers, Battle of, 162–163, 183

Families and family life; crisis in, 271; middle-class, 274; in Middle Colonies, 71; in mid-nineteenth century, 271, 273–274; size, 274; slaves, 324, 327–328; in Southern colonies, 61–62; traditional, 271; working-class, 225–227

Famine; among Mississippian Indians, 9; in medieval Europe, 12

Farewell Address, 165

Farming; *See also* Agriculture; in Africa, 9; in Eurasia, 9, 10; Indian Americans and, 6, 7; in Middle Colonies, 70–71, 73; in New England, 68–69; sharecropping, 422–424; yeoman farmers, 325

Farragut, David, 384

Far West, 304–307; *See also* West

Fathers, in mid-nineteenth century, 273

FDIC. *See* Federal Deposit Insurance Corporation (FDIC)

Federalist Papers, 153, 156

Federalists, 150–153; in 1800 election, 172–173; contributions of, 173; election of 1796 and, 166; formation of party, 161–162; Jefferson and, 190–191; Louisiana Purchase and, 181; secession attempt by, 181–183; War of 1812 and, 203–205

Female sexuality, 68

Fenno, John, 161

Ferdinand (king), 25

Fessenden, William P., 413

Feudalism, in Carolina colonies, 37–38

Fifteenth Amendment, 360, 417–419

Fifth Amendment, 283

Fillmore, Millard, 318, 352, 359

Financial crises; See also Depression(s), economic

Finney, Charles Grandison, 275, 282, 283

First Amendment, 168

First Continental Congress, 109–110, 113

First Reconstruction Act, 416

Fish, 24, 69

Fishing industry, 69

Fitch, John, 231, 239

Five Nations, 90

Flag, 136

Florida; acquisition of, 206–207; during American Revolution, 125; British takeover of, 95; Seminole Indians in, 259m; Spanish in, 19

Flying Cloud (ship), 339

Food, tropical, 14

Foot, Samuel A., 253

Foote, Roxanna, 228

Forbes, John, 94

Force Acts, 424

Force Bill, 261

Foreign-born population; See also Immigrants

Foreign commerce, 338–339

Foreign mercenaries, in American Revolution, 117, 122

Foreign policy; See also Expansionism, U.S.;

of Confederacy, 383–384; Monroe Doctrine, 207–210; Young America movement, 351–352

Fort Dearborn, 199

Fort de Chartres, 49

Fort Duquesne, 92, 93, 94

Fort Le Boeuf, 92

Fort McHenry, 202

Fort Michilimackinac, 199

Fort Necessity, 92

Fort Niagara, 93, 94, 199

Fort Orange, 39

Fort Oswego, 123

Fort Pickens, 376

Fort Pitt, 94

Fort Presue Island, 92

Fort Sumter, 125, 376–377, 377f, 401t

Fort Ticonderoga, 114, 123

Fort Vancouver, 306

Fort Venango, 92

Founding Fathers, 112, 171

Fourier, Charles, 278–279

Fourteenth Amendment, 415, 417–418

France; American Revolution and, 123–125, 128–129; colonial wars of, 90–95; colonization by, 38–39; Embargo Act and, 187–189; explorers to New World, 24; Louisiana Purchase and, 177–181; Napoleon and, 168;

Reign of Terror in, 162; wars between Britain and, 91–95, 124, 159–162; XYZ Affair and, 166–167

Franciscan missionaries, 20, 52

Franco-American treaties, 168

Franklin, Benjamin, 71, 124; Albany Plan, 87, 96; as colonial agent, 81; Declaration of Independence and, 117–118; Deism of, 89; on George Whitefield, 86; as national hero, 140; nationalism of, 136; Paxton Boys and, 76; peace negotiations by, 128–129; population predictions of, 97; scientific discoveries of, 89; Second Continental Congress and, 114; on taxation, 98

Franklin stove, 89

Fredericksburg, Virginia, 393

Free blacks, 160f, 227–228, 327, 330, 349f

Freedman's Bureau, 414, 421

Freeman, Thomas, 184

Freeport Doctrine, 365, 366, 368

Free-school movement, 249

Free Soil party, 315–316, 357, 363

Free speech, 168

Frelinghuysen, Theodore, 85

Frémont, John C., 311, 359

French and Indian War, 91–95, 94m, 96m, 97, 98

French Revolution, 159–162, 179, 190

Freneau, Philip, 161

Frobisher, Martin, 25

Frontier; See also West; land ordinances and, 136–137, 140; life on the trail, 303–304

Frontier missions, 50–51

Fugitive Slave Act, 318, 348–349, 388

Fuller, Margaret, 286

Fulton, Robert, 239, 244

Fundamental Constitutions, 37

Fundamental Orders, 36

Fur trade, 38, 39, 44–45, 90, 91, 98, 184

Gabriel's Rebellion, 331t

Gadsden, Christopher, 114

Gage, Thomas, 113, 114, 116

Galilei, Galileo, 88

Gallatin, Albert, 191, 194, 203, 238

Gallaudet, Thomas, 279

Galloway, Joseph, 109

Gálvez, José de, 125

Garfield, James A., 415; Fifteenth Amendment and, 419

Garner, Margaret, 348f

Garrison, William Lloyd, 283–285, 287, 312

Gaspee affair, 106, 108

Gast, John, 304f

Gates, Horatio, 123, 125

Gates, Louis Henry, Jr., 409–410

Gazette of the United States, 161

General Court, 33–34, 80

General Pike (steamboat), 240

Genet, Edmond Charles, 160, 162

Geneva, Switzerland, 25

Genizaros, 51

Genoa, Italy, 12

Gentility, 225–226

George II (king), 93

George III (king), 96, 100, 108, 243; American Revolution and, 113, 114, 116–117; Declaration of Independence and, 118; proclamation of 1763, 98m, 99

Georgia, 52; during American Revolution, 125; colony of, 62–63; cotton in, 232; Indian relations and, 258–260; ratification of Constitution by, 152; Sherman's march through, 402; slavery in, 133

Georgia Female College, 296

German Americans, immigration and, 230

German immigrants, 63

Gettysburg campaign, 393–394, 394m, 401t

Ghana, 56f

Ghent, Treaty of (1814), 203, 206

Gibbons, Thomas, 244

Gibbons v. Ogden, 244, 245f

Gilbert, Sir Humphrey, 26

Gladwell, Malcolm, 323

Global economy, 224

Glorieta Pass, Battle of, 384

Glorious Revolution, 66, 104

Glory (film), 404–405

Glyptodonts, 2

Goats, 10

Godoy, Manuel de, 164

Godwin, Parke, 279

Gold, 18; discovery of, in California, 268, 313; European desire for, 45f; from New World, 24, 81

Goldberg, Whoopi, 409

Gold rush, California, 313, 316–317

Good, Sarah, 67, 68

Gorges, Sir Ferdinando, 32

Gouge, William, 213

Government(s); under Articles of Confederation, 130–131, 130m, 143–145; branches of, 150; central, 150; colonial, 31, 33–34, 39–40, 65–66, 73, 76, 80–81; of Confederacy, 379–380; representative, 132, 249; state, 131–132

Governors; colonial, 80; state, 132

Grant, James, 113

Grant, Ulysses S., 426f; during Civil War, 384, 395–396, 398–400; election of 1868 and, 417–419; election of 1872 and, 426–427; as president, 426–427

Graves, Thomas, 127

Gray, Robert, 305

Great Awakening; First, 85–87; Second, 274–276

Great Britain; See also Anglo-American relations; American Revolution and, 113–130; Anglican Church, 25; during Civil War, 383–384; colonial administration of, 80–81, 97–110; colonial wars of, 90–95; colonization by, 25–40, 52–55, 53m, 63–73; colonization of Northwest by, 51–52; under Cromwell, 66; exploration by, 24–26; Glorious Revolution in, 66, 104; mercantilism and, 81–84; Napoleon and, 185–186; Oregon territory and, 308; Protestantism in, 30–31; strains of empire on, 95–97; tensions between

Spain and, 25–26; tensions between U.S. and, 144–145; trade between colonies and, 81–84, 84f; view of colonists in, 97; wars between France and, 91–95, 124, 159–161, 162; Webster-Ashburton Treaty, 300–301

Great Compromise, 149, 150t

Great Lakes, 343

Great Lakes fleet, 206

Great Migration, 33, 64

Great Plains, 3, 49–51; See also Plains Indians

Great Salt Lake, 278

Great Serpent Mound, 1

Great War for the Empire, 91–95, 94m, 96m, 97

Greeley, Horace, 279, 335, 377, 426–427

Greenbacks, 382

Greene, Nathanael, 125–126

Greenland, 12

Green Spring faction, 59

Greenville, Treaty of, 164

Greenwood, John, 82f

Gregg, William, 333

Grenville, George, 99, 101

Grimké, Angelina, 286–287

Grimké, Sarah, 286–287

Griswold, Roger, 167f

Guadalupe Hidalgo, Treaty of, 312

Guerrière (ship), 197

Gunpowder, 12

Guns, 38, 45, 49, 50

Haiti, 179–180

Hakluyt, Richard, 26–27

Hale, Sarah, 271

Half-Way Covenant, 65

Halifax (ship), 188

Hall, Basil, 328

Halleck, Henry W., 387, 388

Hamilton, Alexander, 146–147, 155f, 168; 1800 election and, 172–173; Bank of the United States and, 162; Constitutional Convention and, 148; on cotton, 232; duel with Burr, 182–183, 182f; election of 1796 and, 165–166; Federalist Papers, 153, 156; Federalists and, 161; financial reform by, 155–159; Great Britain and, 162; Jefferson and, 161–162, 172–173; Louisiana Purchase and, 181; as secretary of treasury, 155–159; tea service of, 225f; on Washington, 154; whiskey tax and, 159, 162; XYZ Affair and, 167

Hamilton, Andrew, 76

Hancock, John, 113, 115

Harmar, Josiah, 159

Harpers Ferry, 366–367, 370t

Harris, Townsend, 352

Harrison, William Henry; in 1836 election, 265; in 1840 election, 268–269; death of, 269; Indian relations and, 195–196; in War of 1812, 199

Hartford, Connecticut, 35

Hartford Convention, 203–204

Harvard University, 89, 296

Hat industry, 83

Hawley, Joseph, 87

Hawthorne, Nathaniel, 291–292

Hayes, Rutherford B., election of 1876 and, 427–429

Hayne, Robert H., 253, 261

Headright system, 54–55

Henry, Patrick, 101, 152, 153

Henry the Navigator, 15–16

Henry VII (king), 24

Henry VIII (king), 25, 30

Herding peoples, 10–11

Herndon, William, 363n

Hessians, 117, 122

Higher education; See also Colleges and universities; in mid-nineteenth century, 296–297

Hillsborough, Lord, 105

His First Vote (Wood), 418f

Hispaniola, 17, 179–180, 179f

Hobbes, Thomas, 53

Hohokam Indians, 4, 5, 6m

Holbrook, Josiah, 294

Holton, Woody, 135f

Homestead Act, 396

Hooker, Joseph, 393, 399

Hooker, Thomas, 35–36

Hopewell mound builders, 4, 6m

Horses, 2, 10, 21f, 23, 49–50

Household system, persistence of, 231

House of Burgesses, 101

House of Representatives, 149; See also Congress, U.S.; election of president and, 150

House of Representatives (Morse), 214f

The House of the Seven Gables (Hawthorne), 291

Houses, in Southern colonies, 61

Houston, Sam, 301–302, 302f, 320

Howard, Oliver O., 422

Howard, Simeon, 132

Howe, Richard, 119

Howe, Samuel Gridley, 280

Howe, William, 116, 119–123

Hudson, Henry, 15m, 38–39

Hudson Bay, 91

Hudson's Bay Company, 308

Hudson Valley, 38–39

Huguenots, 71

Hull, Isaac, 197

Hull, William, 198

Human beings, first, 1

Hume, David, 89

Hunter, Robert, 76

Hunters and gatherers; Archaic, 3–4; gender divisions among, 9; Paleolithic, 1–2

Huron Indians, 45, 90, 91

Husbands; in mid-nineteenth century, 273–274; Southern, 327, 333

Hutcheson, Francis, 89

Hutchinson, Anne, 35

Hutchinson, Thomas, 102, 106–108

Hutchinson, William, 35

Ice age, 2

Illegal downloads, 143

Illegal immigrants, 299

Illinois Central Railroad, 341, 343

Immigrants, 77; discrimination against, 335; German, 63; illegal, 299; Irish, 334, 335; in Middle Colonies, 71; in mid-nineteenth century, 335; Scots-Irish, 63, 71

Immigration; in nineteenth century, 230–231; Know-Nothing party and, 356; "push" and "pull" factors for, 230

Impeachment, of
Johnson, 417
Imperialism; *See also*
Expansionism, U.S.;
ecological, 21–24
Implied powers doc-
trine, 158
Imports, 338; of British
goods, 144; taxes on,
145, 155–156
Impressment, 187
Incas, 4*n*1, 17
Indentured servants,
55, 56
Independence, evolu-
tion of doctrine of,
209–210
Independent Treasury
Act, 268
India, 9
Indiana, 242
Indian Americans;
Archaic, 2–9, 12; in
California, 52; during
Civil War, 384;
colonial wars and, 91,
93; colonists and,
28–29, 31–32, 40–41,
44–45; Columbus's
discovery of, 17;
conflicts between
settlers and, 159;
conquistadores and,
18; conversion of, to
Christianity, 49, 52;
corn-cultivating, 4–7;
disease and, 20–21,
32, 52; farming by, 6,
7; forced migration
of, 257–260; on fron-
tier, 303–304, 306;
Great Plains, 3,
49–51; horses and, 23;
Jacksonian policy

toward, 257–260; land
tenure among, 44;
liberation movement
of, 194–196; major
cultures, AD 1–1500,
6*m*; missionaries and,
18, 20, 42–43, 49, 52;
Mississippian, 7–9;
Paleolithic, 2; popula-
tion growth among,
6–7; population losses
in, 20–22, 24; rela-
tions between
colonists and, 28–29,
31–32, 40–41, 44–45,
98; sachems, 41;
shamans, 20; as slaves,
51; society of, 41,
49–52; of Southwest,
4–5; trade with, 38,
39, 44–45, 90; treaties
with, 164; warfare
among, 44; in War of
1812, 199–201, 204;
wars between colonists
and, 36, 38; women, 51
Indian removal,
257–260
Indian Territory, white
settlers in, 164–165
Indigo, 60
Indulgences, 24, 30
Industrial Revolution,
231–232; corpora-
tions and, 231–232;
factories and,
226–227
Industry and
industrialization;
See also Business;
Manufacturing; *specific
industries*; Civil War
and, 397; colonial, 83;
immigrant and, 335;

in North, 334;
poverty and,
337–338; workers
and, 335–337
Infant damnation, 274,
276*f*
Infanticide, 7
Infectious diseases. *See*
Diseases
Inflation, 254; after
American Revolution,
131; during Civil War,
397
Influenza, 20
Ingersoll, Jared, 102
Inner Light doctrine, 39
Internal improvements,
265
Interstate commerce,
federal control of, 244
Intolerable Acts,
108–109
Inventing the Cotton Gin
(Lawete), 233*f*
Inventions; colonial, 89;
in mid-nineteenth
century, 342
Iraq, violence in, 375
Irish Americans, in
nineteenth century,
230–231
Irish immigrants, 334,
335
Iron Act, 83
Iron industry, 83, 231
Iroquois Indians, 9, 38,
49, 90
Isabella (queen), 16, 25
Islam, 11
Islamic world,
sixteenth-century,
10*m*, 11
Isthmus of Panama,
17

Jackson, Andrew, 251*f*; in 1818 election, 247; in 1824 election, 219; in 1828 election, 249–250; annexation of Texas and, 302–303; Bank war and, 253–256; cabinet of, 252; Calhoun and, 256–257; Florida campaign of, 206–207; inauguration of, 248; Indian removal and, 257–260; nullification crisis and, 260–262; personality of, 250–251; political parties and, 263; popularity of, 251; presidency of, 252–264; sectionalism and, 253; Specie Circular, 262–263; spoils system and, 251–252; in War of 1812, 204–205

Jackson, Rachel, 250f, 251

Jackson, Thomas J. "Stonewall," 380, 386

Jacksonian democracy, 247–270

Jacksonians, 263

Jamaica, in War of 1812, 201, 204

James, Duke of York, 39

James, Thomas, 102

James I (king), 27, 29–31; puritans and, 33; tobacco and, 57–58

James II (king), 66, 73

Jamestown colony, 27–29, 54

Japan, Perry's expedition to, 352

Java (ship), 198

Jay, John, 128, 150, 161; as chief justice, 155; *Federalist Papers*, 153; treaty negotiated by, 163–164

Jay's Treaty, 163–164, 163*m*, 210

Jefferson, Thomas, 89, 112, 128, 248; in 1800 election, 172*m*; in 1804 election, 175; Adams (John) and, 210–211; Alien and Sedition Acts and, 168; Bank of the United States and, 158, 162; Barbary pirates and, 177; Burr conspiracy and, 184–185; on copyright laws, 143; death of, 221; debt and, 171; Declaration of Independence and, 117–118; democratic principles of, 190–192; elected president, 172–173; election of 1796 and, 165–166; Embargo Act and, 187–189; federal debt and, 173, 175, 191–192; Hamilton and, 157, 161–162; on impressment, 187; judiciary and, 176–177; Lewis and Clark expedition and, 183–184; Louisiana Purchase and, 177–181; mannerisms

of, 175; on Missouri controversy, 219; on Monroe, 210–211; Monticello home of, 171; on Napoleon, 197; Northwest Ordinance and, 137; portrait of, 174*f*; presidency of, 174–175, 175–192; Republican party and, 161; Second Continental Congress and, 114; slavery and, 333; Statute of Religious Liberty, 133; on Washington, 154

Jeffersonians, 161–162

Jenkins, Frederick, 349

Jervis, John B., 241

Jesuits, 42–43, 49

Jews, expulsion of, from Spain, Portugal, and Italy, 12

John, Lord Berkeley, 39

John II (king), 16

Johnson, Andrew; Congress and, 416–417; Fourteenth Amendment and, 415; impeachment of, 417; as president, 411*f*; Reconstruction and, 412–413, 414

Johnson, Richard Mentor, 268

Johnson, Samuel, 133

Johnson, William, 99

Johnston, Albert Sidney, 384

Johnston, Joseph E., 386, 400

Joint-stock companies, 25, 27, 158

Jones, Absalom, 160*f*
Jones, William, 213
Journalism, in mid-
  nineteenth century,
  294
Judges, colonial, 80
Judicial review, 150
Judiciary, Jefferson's
  attack on, 176–177
Judiciary Act (1789),
  176
Judiciary Act (1801),
  176
Junto, 182
Jury trials, 155

Kalm, Peter, 71
Kansas; Lecompton
  constitution, 362;
  settlement of, 356;
  slavery issue and,
  356–357, 357*m*
Kansas-Nebraska Act,
  353–357, 370*t*
Kaskaskia, 49
Kelley, Abby, 286
Kentucky and Virginia
  Resolves, 168
Key, David M., 429
Key, Francis Scott, 202
King George's War, 91,
  93, 98
King James Bible, 31
King Philip's War, 36
King's College, 89
King's Mountain, 126
King William's War,
  90, 93
Kitchen Cabinet,
  Jackson and, 252
Know-Nothing party,
  355–356, 359
Kremer, George, 248
Krimmel, John Lewis,
  221*f*

Kruger, Brittany, 143
Ku Klux Klan, 424–425

Labor; *See also* Workers
Labor laws, 336
Labor movement, in
  mid-nineteenth
  century, 336–337
Labor unions, in mid-
  nineteenth century,
  336–337
Labrador, 12, 24
Lafayette, Marquis de,
  125, 128
Lake Erie, Battle of,
  199*f*
Lakwete, Angela, 233*f*
Land; in colonies,
  54–55; Indian, 99,
  257–258; sectional
  controversy over, 213;
  of Southern planters,
  421–422; War of 1812
  and, 196
Land Act (1800), 213
Land grants; during
  Civil War, 396; in
  colonies, 39, 63, 73;
  to English settlers, 37;
  to railroads, 341
Land Ordinance of
  1785, 137, 137*f*
Land ordinances,
  136–137, 140
Land speculation, 137,
  262–263
Land tenure, among
  Indians, 44
Las Casas, Bartolomé
  de, 18
Latin America; *See also*
  specific countries;
  Monroe Doctrine
  and, 207–210
Laud, William, 33

Laurens, Henry, 128
Lawrence (ship), 199*f*
Laws; child labor, 336;
  colonial, 65, 80–81;
  copyright, 143;
  labor, 336; unconsti-
  tutional, 103
Lawson, Hugh, 265
Lawyers, 89
Leaves of Grass
  (Whitman), 292–294
Leclerc, Charles,
  179–180
Lecompton constitu-
  tion, 362, 370*t*
Lee, Ann, 277
Lee, Arthur, 124
Lee, Henry, 114
Lee, Richard Henry,
  117, 153
Lee, Robert E.; as
  commander of
  Confederate army,
  386, 387–388, 393,
  394, 399–400;
  Harpers Ferry and,
  366; secession crisis
  and, 371–372; surren-
  der by, 403
Leeches, 88*f*
Legislatures; colonial,
  80; state, 131–132
Leisler, Jacob, 73
Leislerians, 76
Leisler's Rebellion, 73
Le Jeune, Paul, 42, 43
Leopard (ship), 188
Leutze, Emanuel, 122*f*
Levant Company, 25
Lewis, Meriwether,
  183–184
Lewis and Clark expedi-
  tion, 183–184, 183*f*
Lexington, battle of,
  113–114

Liberal Republicans, 426

The Liberator, 283

Liberia, Republic of, 235

Liberty party, 284

Liberty Tree, 107*f*

Life expectancy, in Chesapeake colonies, 54

Lightning rod, 89

Lincoln, Abraham, 364*f*, 368*f*, 402*f*; assassination of, 410–411; Cabinet of, 375–376; Civil War and, 379, 381, 393; election of 1860 and, 367–371; election of 1864 and, 400, 402; Emancipation Proclamation and, 388–391; emergence of, 363; inaugural address by, 376, 403; on Know-Nothings, 356; personality of, 363; racial prejudice of, 391; on Reconstruction, 411–412; secession crisis and, 371–373; on slavery, 363; on wage earners, 337

Lincoln-Douglas debates, 347, 364–366

Literacy, in North, 327

Literature; in mid-nineteenth century, 289–294; romanticism and, 288–289, 290

Little Turtle, 159

Livingston, Robert, 117, 244

Livingston, Robert R., 178–180, 239

Lock, John, 89

Locke, John, 37, 99, 147, 235

Locofoco, 263

London Company, 27, 28, 29, 31, 37, 54, 58, 59

Long, Jefferson, 420*m*

Long Island, battle of, 120–121

Looms, 227

Loudoun, Lord, 97

Louisbourg, 91

Louisiana; colony of, 49; exploration of, 183–184

Louisiana Purchase, 177–181, 181*m*, 210

Louis XVI (king), 124, 162

L'Ouverture, Toussaint, 179–180, 179*f*

Lovejoy, Elijah, 283

Lowell, Francis Cabot, 227

Lowell, Massachusetts, 333

Loyalists, 120, 125, 129, 134

Loyalty oaths, 412, 413

Loyola, Ignatius, 42

Lucas, Eliza, 60, 61

Lucayans, 17

Lunatic asylums, 280

Luther, Martin, 12, 24–25

Lyceums, 294

Lyell, Charles, 334

Lyon, Matthew, 167f

Macdonough, Thomas, 203

Macedonian (ship), 197–198

Macomb, Alexander, 202–203

Macon, Nathaniel, 194

Macon's Bill No. 2, 194

Madagascar rice, 60

Madison, James; on Alien and Sedition Acts, 167; Bill of Rights and, 155; Canada and, 196; colonization movement and, 235; Constitutional Convention and, 147; *Federalist Papers*, 153; Hamilton and, 157; on impressment, 187; *Marbury v. Madison* and, 176–177; ratification of Constitution and, 151; shipping policy and, 194; Virginia Plan of, 148; Virginia Resolves, 168; in War of 1812, 201

Magellan, Ferdinand, 17

Main, Jackson Turner, 151

Maine, 32; boundary dispute in, 300–301; statehood for, 217

Mainline Canal, 242

Maize, 5*f*, 22

Maize revolution, 4–5

Malaria, 11, 20, 54

Mali, 11

Malnutrition, among Indians, 21

Mammals, extinction of big, 2

Mammoths, 2

Manhattan Island, 39

Manifest destiny, 303

Manioc, 22

Mann, Horace, 295
Manufacturing; *See also* Industry and industrialization; colonial, 83; growth of, 231–232; in North, 334; post-Revolutionary, 158; in South, 333–334
Marbury, William, 176–177
Marbury v. Madison, 176–177
Marcy, William L., 354
Marion, Francis, 125
Maritime economy, of New England, 69
Market revolution, 226
Marriage; in mid-nineteenth century, 274; slave, 324, 329
Marshall, James W., 313
Marshall, John, 248; Burr conspiracy and, 185; business and, 243–245; as chief justice, 176–177; colonization movement and, 235; Indian removal and, 258; Louisiana Purchase and, 181
Martin, Lily Spenser, 276*f*
Martinique, 159
Mary (queen), 30, 66
Maryland; colony of, 37, 52, 54; headright system in, 54–55; in War of 1812, 201
Mason, George, 132
Mason, James M., 317
Mason, John, 32
Massachusetts; *See also* Boston, Massachusetts;

colony of, 66; ratification of Constitution by, 152; Shays's rebellion in, 145–146; slavery in, 133; textile industry in, 227
Massachusetts Bay Colony, 32–34, 39, 104
Massachusetts Bay Company, 32–33
Massachusetts General Court, 65, 101, 204
Massachusetts Government Act, 108
Massachusetts Patriots, 113
Mastodons, 2
Mather, Cotton, 68
Mather, Increase, 44, 68
Matteson, T. H., 67*f*
Mayans, 4
Mayflower (ship), 31
Mayflower Compact, 31
Mayhew, Jonathan, 101
McCain, John, 347
McClellan, George B., 381, 384–388
McColl, Ada, 305*f*
McCormick, Cyrus, 342
McCulloch v. Maryland, 243–244, 245*f*, 253, 255
McDowell, Irvin, 380
McKay, Donald, 339
Meade, George C., 394
Measles, 20
Mechanical reaper, 342
Medicine, colonial, 89*f*
Melville, Herman, 292
Mennonites, 71
Mental hospitals, 281
Mercantilism, 81–84
Mercer, William, 122*f*

Merchant marine, 160–161; Embargo Act and, 187–189; impressment by British and, 187; Napoleonic wars and, 185–186
Merrell, James, 41*f*
Merrimack Manufacturing Company, 229
Merry, Anthony, 184
Mesoamerica, 4
Metacom, 36
Metallurgy, 12
Metal tools, 45
Methodists, 275
Mexican War, 308–312, 309*m*
Mexico; annexation of Texas from, 301–303; Aztecs in, 4, 9, 17, 19*f*; independence of, from Spain, 301; maize cultivation in, 4–5; Spanish *conquistadores* in, 18; U.S. border with, 299
Miami Indians, 91, 159
Middle Ages, in Europe, 11–12
Middle class, in mid-nineteenth century, 271, 273, 274, 337–338
Middle colonies, 39–40, 52; agriculture in, 70–71, 73; diversity in, 71–72, 72*m*; economy of, 70–71, 73; government in, 73, 76; Great Awakening in, 85; prosperity in, 73; slavery in, 70; society of, 71

Migration; from England to colonies, 33; risk-taking gene and, 48

Milan Decree (1807), 185

Military technology, 12

Militias, 113, 131

Miller, Arthur, 74–75

Ming Dynasty, 10

Ministers, 89

Minuit, Peter, 39

Minute Men, 113

Missionaries; Catholic, in New World, 18–20, 42–43, 51; Franciscan, 20, 52; Indians and, 18, 20, 42–43, 49; Jesuit, 42–43, 49; in mid-nineteenth century, 276; Spanish, 52

Mission of San José de Laguna, 50f

Missions, 50–51, 52

Mississippian civilization, 6m, 7–9

Mississippi River, 49, 164, 236–238

Mississippi Territory, 163m, 165

Mississippi Valley, trade and, 236–238

Missouri, statehood for, 216–219

Missouri Compromise, 216–219, 218m, 283, 314, 319f, 354, 360–361

Missouri Enabling Act (1819), 217

Moby-Dick (Melville), 292

Mogollon Indians, 4, 5, 6m

Mohawk Indians, 36

Mohegan Indians, 36

Molasses Act, 84

Money, paper, 382, 383

Money supply, 262, 268

Monopolies, Bank of the United States as, 255

Monroe, James; colonization movement and, 235; Era of Good Feelings and, 210–211; Florida campaign and, 206–207; Louisiana Purchase and, 179–180; Monroe Doctrine and, 207–210

Monroe Doctrine, 207–210

Montcalm, Louis Joseph de, 94

Monterey, California, 52

Montesquieu, 89

Montezuma, 19f

Monticello, 171

Montreal, Canada, 24

Moravians, 71

Morgan, Daniel, 126

Mormons, 277–278

Mormon Trail, 306m

Morrill Land Grant Act, 396

Morris, Lewis, 76

Morris, Robert, 171

Morrison, Tony, 348f

Morse, Samuel, 214f

Mothers, in mid-nineteenth century, 273

The Mother's Book (Child), 274

Mott, Lucretia, 287

Mound builders, 3–4, 7–8

Moundville, Alabama, 8

Moussa, Amr, 375

Moveable type, 12

Muscovy Company, 25

Music downloads, 143

Napoleon, 168

Narragansett Indians, 36, 41

Narrative of the Life of Frederick Douglass (Douglass), 285

Natchez Indians, 49

National debt, from American Revolution, 156–157

National Gazette, 161

National heroes, of American Revolution, 140–141

Nationalism; black, 235; post-Revolutionary, 135–136, 140–141; railroads and, 344; after Reconstruction, 425

National Republican party, 263–264

National Road, 238

National Trades Union, 336

Nation-states, emergence of, 12

Native Americans. See Indian Americans

Nativism, 355

Nat Turner's Rebellion, 330, 331t

Naturalization Act, 175

Nauvoo, Illinois, 277–278

Navajo Indians, 23

Navigation, early, 15–16

Navigation Acts, 82–83, 84, 99, 100

Navy, U.S., Jeffersonian policy and, 177
Navy Department, creation of, 166–167
Nebraska, 50, 354–355
Nelson, Horatio, 185
Neolithic revolution, 4, 9
Nesmith, James, 306
Netherlands; colonization by, 38–39; merchant fleet of, 25, 39
New Amsterdam, 39, 71, 90
New England; agriculture in, 68–69; colonies, 31–36, 52, 63–70; commerce in, 69–70; diet of colonial, 69; Dominion of, 66; Monroe in, 210; towns of, 66; utopian communities in, 279m; War of 1812 and, 204
New England Anti-Slavery Society, 283
Newfoundland, 24, 26, 69, 91, 95, 129
New France, 38, 49, 96m, 98m
New Hampshire, 32, 152
New Harmony, Indiana, 278
New Haven, Connecticut, 36
New Jersey; battles of, during American Revolution, 121f; colony of, 39, 70–71; ratification of Constitution by, 152; slavery in, 133
New Jersey Plan, 148
New Lights, 86

New Mexico; annexation of, 311, 312; society in, 49–52; Spanish in, 19–20; statehood for, 299, 318
New Netherland, 35, 38–39, 55
New Orleans, Louisiana, 164; Battle of, 204–205, 392; colony of, 49; importance of, 178; painting of, 178f; Spanish control of, 95; steamboats in, 240; in War of 1812, 204
New Side Presbyterians, 86, 87
New Spain, 17–20, 24, 50–52, 51m
Newspapers, 249; in mid-nineteenth century, 294
New Sweden, 39
Newton, Sir Isaac, 88
New World; See also Colonies; British exploration in, 24–26; Columbus's discovery of, 16–17; Spanish empire in, 17–20
New York (state); colony of, 39, 70–71, 73, 76; Erie Canal and, 241; ratification of Constitution by, 153; Safety Fund System, 265; slavery in, 133
New York Central Railroad, 340
New York City, 71, 73; battles of, during American Revolution,

120–122, 121f; as commercial center, 241–243; draft riots in, 391, 391f; tenements in, 335
New York Herald, 294
New York Pike, 238–239
New York Slave Revolt, 331t
New York Sun, 294
New York Tribune, 335
New York Weekly Journal, 76
Niagara (ship), 199f
Nicaragua, 351
Niña (ship), 16
Noble, Thomas S., 348f
Non-Intercourse Act, 189, 194
North; abolishment of slavery in, 133; advantages of, in Civil War, 378; blacks in, in nineteenth century, 236; conditions of working class in, 225–227; effects of Civil War on economy of, 396–397; fugitive slaves in, 348–349; industry in, 334; leaders in, in nineteenth century, 214–216; literacy rate in, 327; secession crisis and, 371, 372
North, Lord, 108–109, 110, 124
North America; British explorers in, 24; European claims in, 95, 96m; Spanish explorers in, 19–20

North Carolina, 63; colony of, 38, 60; ratification of Constitution by, 153

North River Steam Boat (ship), 239

Northwest; British in, 161, 163; colonization of, 51–52

Northwest Ordinance, 137, 140, 217, 357, 360

Nova Scotia, 24, 90, 91, 129

Noyes, John Humphrey, 278*f*

Nullification crisis, 260–262

Obama, Barack, 56*f*, 299; election of 2008 and, 247, 347; Iraq war and, 375

Oberlin College, 296

Ogden, Aaron, 244

Oglethorpe, James, 63

Ohio; Battle of Fallen Timbers, 162–163; settlement of, 159, 163

Ohio and Erie Canal, 242

Ohio Company, 91, 92

Old Lights, 86

Old National Road, 238

Old Side Presbyterians, 86

Old Spanish Trail, 306*m*

Oñate, Don Juan de, 19

Oneida County Female Missionary Society, 276*f*

Oneota Indians, 8

Onís, Luis de, 207

Openchancanough (chief), 29

Orders in Council, 185, 194, 196–197

Oregon, 52; British in, 308; settlement of, 304–307, 308

Oregon Trail, 305–306, 306*m*

Original sin, 88

Orphanages, 280

Orphans, 280

Osborne, Sarah, 67, 68

Osceola, 258*f*, 259*m*

Ostend Manifesto, 351

O'Sullivan, John L., 303

Oswald, Richard, 129

Otis, James, 99

Overpopulation, in Europe, 12

Owen, Robert, 278

Oxbow Route, 306*m*

Oxen, 10

Pacific Fur Company, 305

Pacific Ocean, 17

Pacific Railway Act, 396

Paine, Thomas, 117, 120

Pakenham, Edward, 204–205

Pakenham, Richard, 308

Paleo-Indians, 2

Paleolithic hunters, 2

Paleolithic revolution, 1–2

Panama Canal, 351

Panic of 1837, 262–263, 265, 336

Panic of 1857, 337, 345

Paper money, 254, 255, 256, 382, 383

Paredes, Mariano, 309

Parents, in mid-nineteenth century, 274

Paris, Treaty of, 95, 164

Paris Peace Conference, 128–129

Parliament, 98, 99, 100, 103, 117

Parris, Abigail, 67

Parris, Betty, 67

Parris, Samuel, 67

Paterson, William, 148

The Patriot (film), 138–139

Patriotism, 221

Pawnee Indians, 50

Pawtucket, Rhode Island, 226, 228*f*

Paxton Boys, 76

Peace Democrats, 382–383

Peace of Paris, 95

Peace of Ryswick, 90

Peale, Charles Wilson, 174*f*

Peale, Raphaelle, 160*f*

Peale, Rembrandt, 174*f*

"Pell-mell" policy, 175

Pemberton, John C., 395

Penn, William, 40, 41*f*, 71

Pennsylvania; colony of, 40, 70–73, 76; internal improvements in, 242; ratification of Constitution by, 152

Pennsylvania Dutch, 40, 76

Penny newspapers, 294

Pequot Indians, 36

Pequot War, 36

Percy, George, 29

Perkins Institution, 280

Perry, Matthew C., 352
Perry, Oliver Hazard, 199–200, 199f
Peru, Incas in, 17
Petersburg, siege of, 401t
Philadelphia, 71, 73; Constitutional Convention in, 146–150; prison system, 281; yellow fever epidemic in, 160f
Philadelphia (ship), 177
Philadelphia Public Ledger, 294
Philip II (king), 24, 26
Philippines, Spanish control of, 95
Phips, Mary, 68
Phips, William, 68
Phrenology, 287–288
Physicians, 89
Pickawillany, 91, 92
Pickering, Timothy, 182
Pickett, George E., 394
Pierce, Franklin, 351, 353–355, 353f, 357
Pigs, 10, 21, 41
Pike, Zebulon, 184
Pilgrims, 31–32
Pinckney, Charles, 61, 175
Pinckney, Henry L., 260
Pinckney, Thomas, 164, 166
Pinckney's Treaty, 164
Pinta (ship), 16
Pioneers, 236–238, 303–306
Pitt, William, 93–94, 95
Pizarro, Francisco, 17
Plagues, 10, 11
Plains Indians, 49–51; horses and, 23

Plantations; conditions on, 62; life on, 327–328; profits from, 325–326; rice, 61; sugar, 38; tobacco, 59
Plattsburgh, Battle of, 202–203
Plymouth colony, 31–32, 32f, 36
Plymouth Company, 32
Of Plymouth Plantation (Bradford), 32f
Pocahontas, 29f
Poe, Edgar Allen, 290–291, 291f
Political campaigns, rise of, 249
Political parties; See also specific parties; in early nineteenth century, 247; power of, 249; rise of, 161–162; Second American Party System, 251m, 264f; second party system, 263, 264
Politics, during Civil War, 382–383
Polk, James K.; election of 1844 and, 307; Mexican War and, 308–312; presidency of, 307–308
Polo, Marco, 12, 15
Polygamy, 278
Pontiac, 97f, 99
Pontiac's Rebellion, 99
Popé, 20
Pope, John, 387
Popular sovereignty, 314, 352, 354, 356–357
Population; Old World, 10m; rural vs. urban, 272f

Population growth; nineteenth century, 211, 230–231, 230m; among corn-cultivating peoples, 6–7; among slaves, 328–329; in colonies, 97; Eurasia, 10; Europe, 22–24
Port Act, 108
Port Royal, Novia Scotia, 90, 91
Portugal, 17
Portuguese explorers, 15–16
Potato, 22
Poverty; in Jacksonian America, 272; in mid-nineteenth century, 337–338; urban, 335–337
Poverty Point, 3–4
Powhatan, 29f
Powhatan Indians, 29
Pownall, Thomas, 95
Preble, Edward, 177
Predestination, 30, 275
Presbyterians, 30, 71, 86, 87
Presidency; Constitutional provisions for, 172–173; creation of, 149
President; election of, 149–150; veto power of, 150
Presidential elections; of 1796, 165–166; of 1800, 172m; of 1804, 175, 181–182; of 1816, 210; of 1824, 219; of 1828, 247, 249, 249–250; of 1836, 265; of 1840, 268–269; of 1844, 303, 307;

of 1848, 314–316; of 1852, 352–353; of 1856, 359–360; of 1860, 367–371, 369*m*, 370*t*; of 1864, 400, 402; of 1868, 417–419; of 1872, 426–427; of 1876, 427–429, 428*m*; of 2008, 247, 347

Presidios, 50, 52

Press, freedom of, 168

Press gangs. *See* Impressment

Prevost, George, 202–203

Primogeniture, 132–133

Princeton, battle of, 122*f*

Princeton University, 86, 87

Printing press, 12

Prisons, 280, 281

Privy Council, 80, 81

Proclamation of 1763, 98*m*, 99, 109*t*

Professions, 89; in South, 62

Property rights, 89, 99–100, 147, 243, 422

Proprietary party, 76

Protestantism, in England, 30–31

Protestant Reformation, 12, 24–25

Protests, in colonies, 101–103, 101*f*, 107–108

Providence, Rhode Island, 34

Providence Plantations, 34

Prussia, 93

Public schools; *See also* Education; Schools;

in mid-nineteenth century, 294–295

Pueblo Bonito, 5

Pueblo Indians, 19–20, 51

Puget Sound, 307

Puritans; attitudes toward women, 68; children, 64, 64*f*; churches of, 34; dissenters, 34–35, 39; government of, 65–66; migration to America by, 33; in New England, 63–70; origins of, 30–31; religion of, 64–65; visible saints of, 34, 35, 64; wars between Indians and, 36

Putnam, Ann, 67

Quakers, 65, 71, 76; beliefs of, 39; colonies of, 39–40

Quartering Act, 103

Québec, Canada, 38

Queen Anne's War, 91, 93

Quitrents, 133

Racial discrimination, 335

Radical Republicans, 382, 389, 412–415, 430–431*t*

Railroads, 339–340; in 1860, 342*m*; agriculture and, 343, 344; cities and, 342–343; construction of, 340, 426; economy and, 341–344; financing of, 340–341; land grants to, 341; sectional conflict and, 344; in South, 424;

subsidies for, 396; transcontinental, 396

Rainey, Joseph, 420*m*

Raleigh, Sir Walter, 26

Randolph, Edmund, 148

Randolph, John, 185*n*, 189

Ranney, William, 139*f*

Rats, 21

Raw materials, 81, 82, 83

Raymond, Daniel, 231–232

Raynell, John, 104

Reading, in mid-nineteenth century, 294

Reaping machine, 342

Reason, 88

Rebellions; *See also* Riots and uprisings; Bacon's rebellion, 59–60; by Indian Americans, 20; Leisler's Rebellion, 73; Nat Turner's Rebellion, 330; Paxton Boys, 76; Pontiac's Rebellion, 99; Shays's rebellion, 145–146; slave, 61, 331*t*; Whiskey Rebellion, 162–163

Reconstruction, 409–430; Congress and, 416–417; corruption during, 419–421; end of, 429; Fifteenth Amendment, 417–419; Fourteenth Amendment, 415; phases of, 430–431*t*; politics of, 419–421;

Reconstruction
(continued)
presidential, 411–413,
430t; Radical
Republicans and, 412,
413–415, 430t;
Reconstruction Acts,
416; Ten Percent Plan,
411–412; white back-
lash against, 409,
424–425
Reconstruction Acts,
416
Redcoats. See British
troops
Red Jacket (ship),
338f
Reform movements;
abolitionism,
282–285; in educa-
tion, 294–296; in mid-
nineteenth century,
271, 279–288; tem-
perance movement,
281–282; women's
rights, 285–288
Regional cultures,
323–324
Regulators, 63
Reign of Terror, 162,
190
Religion; See also
Christianity; Churches;
in colonies, 85–87;
of corn-cultivating
societies, 4–5;
Enlightenment
and, 88–89; freedom
of, 133; freedom of,
in colonies, 37;
Islam, 11; in mid-
nineteenth century,
274–276; Protestant
Reformation, 12; of
Puritans, 64–65;

separation of church
and state, 133; slave,
329
Religious tolerance, 87
Rensselaerswyck, 39
Report on Manufactures
(Hamilton), 158, 232
Report on the Public
Credit (Hamilton), 156
Representative govern-
ment, 132, 249
Republican party; See
also Radical
Republicans; during
Civil War, 382; elec-
tion of 1856 and,
359–360; election of
1860 and, 369–369;
election of 1876 and,
427–429; formation
of, 356; Liberal
Republicans in, 426;
during
Reconstruction,
419–421, 420m, 425;
in South, 427
Republicans
(Democratic); in 1800
election, 172–173;
election of 1796 and,
166; formation of
party, 161–162
Republic of California,
311
Republic of Texas, 302
Revere, Paul, 113
Revolutionary War. See
American Revolution
Revolutions; See also
American Revolution;
French Revolution,
159–162, 179, 190;
in medieval Europe, 12
Rhode Island, 131;
colony of, 34, 35;

ratification of
Constitution by, 152,
153
Rice, 9, 60, 61
Richmond, Virginia,
410f
Riots and uprisings;
See also Rebellions;
in colonies, 101–103;
draft riots, 391;
Harpers Ferry,
366–367; slave, 260,
329–330, 331t
Risk-taking gene, 48
Roads; construction of,
237–239; government
and, 238–239
Roanoke colony, 26
Robards, Lewis, 250f
Robespierre, 190
Robinson, John, 31
Rochambeau, Comte de,
127
Rock, Chris, 409
Rodney, Sir George, 127
Rolfe, John, 28, 29f
Roman Catholic
Church. See Catholics
and Catholic Church
Romanticism, 288–289
Ross, Robert, 201
Royal African
Company, 56
Royal charters, 37, 65
Rural population, in
mid-nineteenth cen-
tury, 272f
Rush, Benjamin, 282
Russell, Jonathan, 203
Russia, 96m; coloniza-
tion of Northwest by,
51–52; territorial
claims of, 207
Rutgers University, 86
Rye, 40

Sachems, 41

Saint Augustine, Florida, 19, 21, 91

Saint Domingue (Hispaniola), 179–180, 179f

Saints, 35

Salem, Massachusetts, 32, 34

Salem witch trials, 66–68, 74–75

Sales tax, 159

Salt Lake City, 278

Samuel Adams beer company, 112

San Antonio, Texas, 50, 51

San Diego, California, 52, 307

San Francisco, California, 52, 307, 316

Sanitary Commission, 398

San José de Laguna, 50f

San Lorenzo, Treaty of, 164

San Salvador, 16

Santa Anna, Antonio López de, 301–302, 320

Santa Barbara, California, 52

Santa Fe, New Mexico, 50

Santa Fe Trail, 306m

Santa Maria (ship), 16

Saratoga campaign, 123–125, 124m

Savannah, Georgia, 125

Scalawags, 419

The Scarlet Letter (Hawthorne), 291

Schools; *See also* Education; public, 294–295; in Southern colonies, 61–62

Schuyler, Philip, 123

Science; advances in, 88; colonial achievements in, 89–90

Scots-Irish immigrants, 63, 71

Scott, Dred, 360–361, 361f

Scott, Sir Walter, 294

Scott, Winfield, 310, 311, 352

Secession, Hartford Convention and, 204

Second American Party System, 251m, 264f

Second Bank of the United States, 253–256, 254f

Second Continental Congress, 114–116, 119

Second Great Awakening, 274–276

Second party system, 263, 264

Second Treatise on Government (Locke), 99

Sectionalism; banking, 211–213; election of 1848 and, 314–316; Jackson and, 253; key issues of, 212f; land policy, 213; meaning of, 221; under Monroe, 211–214; railroads and, 344; slavery, 213–214

Sedition Act, 167, 175, 176

Seminole Indians, 207, 258, 258f, 259m

Semmes, Raphael, 386

Senate, U.S., 149

Seneca Falls Convention, 287

Separatists, 31, 33

Serrano, Pedro, 51

Seven Pines, Battle of, 386

Seven Years' War, 93, 123

Seward, William H., 366, 369, 376, 379, 411

Seymour, Horatio, 417

Shakers, 277

Shakespeare, William, 30

Shamans, 20

Sharecropping, 422–424, 423m

Shawnee Indians, 194–196

Shays, Daniel, 145

Shays's rebellion, 145–146

Sheep, 10, 23

Sherman, Roger, 117, 148–149

Sherman, William Tecumseh, 398–402

Sherman's march, 400–402, 400m, 401t

Shiloh, battle of, 384, 401t

Shipbuilding, 83, 185

Shipping industry, 160–161, 338–339

Sierra Leone, 235

Silver, 17, 18; from New World, 24, 81

Slater, Samuel, 226

Slater's Mill, 228f

Slave revolts, 260, 329–330, 331t

Slavery; abolishment of, in North, 133; abolitionism and, 282–285; in California, 316–317; in Carolinas, 61; in Chesapeake colonies, 55–56; Clay on, 216; Compromise of 1850 and, 317–319; cotton and, 232–234, 233f, 234f, 326m; criticism of, 133–134; depicted in *Uncle Tom's Cabin*, 350–351; *Dred Scott* decision and, 360–362, 365; economics of, 324–327; Emancipation Proclamation and, 388–392; Fugitive Slave Act, 318, 348–349; Indians and, 51; Kansas-Nebraska Act and, 354–355; in Middle Colonies, 70; Missouri Compromise and, 216–219, 218m, 354, 360–361; nullification crisis and, 260; psychological effects of, 330–333; question of, 313–314; revival of, 235–236; sectional controversy over, 213–214; sociology of, 328–330; in Southwest, 311; Three-Fifths Compromise, 149; in West Indies, 38

Slaves, 62f; African, 23, 55–56, 57m, 61, 62f, 69; during American Revolution, 133; families, 324, 327–328; freed, 133; fugitive, 348–349; Hispaniola revolt of, 179, 179f; life for, on plantations, 327–328; mistreatment of, 61; population increases among, 328–329; rebellions by, 61, 329–330; runaway, 330; treatment of, 328, 329; urban, 330

Slave trade, 324; Atlantic, 57m, 69; illegal, 236, 325f

Sleeping sickness, 11

Slidell, John, 308–309

Sloat, John D., 311

Sloths, 2

Slums, 335

Smallpox, 20, 32

Smith, John, 28, 32

Smith, Joseph, 277

Smith, Lamar, 299

Smith, Samuel, 201

Smuggling, 84; of slaves, 236

Snaketown, 5, 8

Social reform; *See also* Reform movements; in Revolutionary era, 132–134

Society; in Middle Colonies, 71; in mid-nineteenth century, 337–338; Post-Revolution, 134; of South, 61–62

Songhay, 11

"Song of Myself" (Whitman), 293–294

Sons of Liberty, 101–102

South; *See also* Confederacy; agriculture in, 324, 325–326, 422–424; alliance with West, 260; American Revolution in, 125–128, 126m; Black Codes in, 414; cities in, 330; cotton in, 232–234; education in, 61–62; effects of Civil War on economy of, 396–397; extremism in, 367–368; home and family in, 61–62; illiteracy in, 327; impact of Civil War on, 421–422; lack of industrialization in, 60; leaders in, in nineteenth century, 216; manufacturing in, 333–334; plantation life in, 327–328; pre–Civil War economy, 345; railroads in, 424; Reconstruction in, 409–430; region of, 52; Republican party in, 427; secession by, 371–373, 372m; sharecropping in, 422–424, 423m; slavery in, 61, 133, 313–314, 324–333; transportation in, 324, 326, 344; women in, 61, 397

South America, 17; *See also* Latin America

South Carolina; colony of, 38, 60–61, 85; cotton in, 232; nullification crisis and, 260–262; ratification of Constitution by, 152; during Reconstruction, 420; secession by, 371; slavery in, 61, 133
South Carolina Negro Act, 61
Southern Homestead Act, 409
Southwest; acquisition of, from Mexico, 299; Indians of, 4–5, 9; slavery issue in, 311
Sovereignty, 103–104
Spain; American empire of, 17–20, 24, 50–52, 51m, 90, 144; *conquistadores*, 17–18; decline of, 24, 90; Louisiana Purchase and, 177–181; surrender of Florida by, 207; tensions between England and, 25–26; Transcontinental Treaty and, 207; Treaty of San Lorenzo, 164
Spanish Armada, 26
Spanish Inquisition, 40
Spanish missionaries, 52
Specie Circular, 262–263
Specie payments, 265
Speculation, land, 137, 262–263
Spencer, Lilly Martin, 273*f*

Spices, 14
Spoils system, 251–252
Squatters, 55
Squatter sovereignty, 314
Squatter's rights, 55
Stamp Act, 100–104, 109*t*, 116
Stamp Act Congress, 101, 104
Standard of living, 337
Stanton, Edwin M., 392, 417
Stanton, Elizabeth Cady, 287, 419
"The Star Spangled Banner" (Key), 202
State banks, 265, 268
State governments, 131–132
State representation, 148
States' rights, 412; Jackson and, 257; southern secession and, 371
Statute of Religious Liberty, 133
St. Clair, Arthur, 159
Steamboats, 239–240
Steamships, 339
Steel plow, 342
St. Eustache Cathedral, 43*f*
Stevens, John, 239
Stevens, Thaddeus, 382, 411, 421
St. Lawrence River, 24
St. Leger, Barry, 123, 124
Stoddard, Solomon, 87, 88
Stowe, Harriet Beecher, 228, 295, 347, 350–351

Strikes, in nineteenth century, 229
Stuart monarchy, 66
Sub-Saharan Africa, 11
Sugar, trade of, during Napoleonic wars, 186
Sugar Act, 99–101, 104, 109*t*
Sugar plantations, 38
Sumner, Charles, 358–359, 382, 411, 413, 421
Sumter, Thomas, 125
Supreme Court, 149; first, 155; Jefferson and, 176–177; *Marbury v. Madison* and, 176–177; Marshall and, 243–245
Swedish settlers, 39
Switzerland, 25

Talleyrand, Charles Maurice de, 166, 168, 180
Tallmadge, James, 217
Taney, Roger B., 245, 256, 262, 360–361
Tappan, Arthur, 283
Tappan, Lewis, 283
Tariff Act, 155–156
Tariff of Abominations, 193, 220
Tariffs, 144, 155–156; federal income from, 193–194; Jackson and, 253; nullification crisis and, 260–262; after War of 1812, 211
Tarleton, Banastre, 126
Tarring and feathering, 107*f*
Taverns, 112

Taxes; in colonies, 77, 98, 99, 100–105, 107, 110; in Confederacy, 383; excise, 159; on imports, 145; levying, by Congress, 155–156, 244; payment of, 79; sales, 159; Shays's rebellion and, 145–146; taxation without representation, 100, 103, 109

Taylor, Zachary, 315*f*; election of 1848 and, 314–316; Mexican War and, 308, 309, 310–311; slavery issue and, 316–317, 318

Tea Act, 106–108, 109*t*, 116, 124

Teachers, 295

Tecumseh, 194–196, 195*f*, 199–201, 268

Temperance movement, 281–282

Tenement houses, 335

Tenenbaum, Joel, 143

Ten-hour laws, 336

Tennent, William, 85

Tennessee, during Reconstruction, 416

Tenochtitlán, 9

Ten Percent Plan, 411–412

Tenskwatawa ("The Prophet"), 195–196, 195*f*

Tenth Amendment, 155

Tenure of Office Act, 417

Teosinte, 5*f*

Teotihuacan, 4

Terrill, Thomas, 325*f*

Texas; Alamo and, 301, 320–321; annexation of, 301–303; election of 1844 and, 307; slavery in, 313–314; society in, 49–52; statehood for, 299

Textile industry, 343; imports and, 338; mechanization and, 226–227, 335; in South, 333; tariffs and, 211; Waltham system, 229

Thames, Battle of, 200–201

Thirteenth Amendment, 413, 414

Thomas, Jesse B., 218

Thoreau, Henry David, 289–290

Three-Fifths Compromise, 149, 217, 413

Tilden, Samuel J., 427, 428–429

Timbuktu, 11

Tingman, Julius Caesar, 409

The Tipping Point (Gladwell), 323

Tituba, 67, 68

Tobacco, 37, 58*f*, 324; colonial cultivation of, 57–59, 60; discovery of, 28; mercantilism and, 84

Tocqueville, Alexis de, 48, 258, 263, 272–273

Toleration Act, 37, 62

Tompkins, Sally, 397

Tories, 120, 125, 129, 134

Total war, 402

Townshend, Charles, 104

Townshend Duties, 104–105, 106, 109*t*

Trade, 189*f*; in nineteenth century, 232; by Archaic Indians, 9; with Britain, 144; colonial, 38, 81–84, 84*f*; Embargo Act and, 187–189, 189*f*; fur, 38, 39, 44–45, 90, 91, 98; international, 338–339; Napoleonic wars and, 185–186; in sixteenth century, 25; slave. *See* Slave trade; trans-Sahara, 10–11; triangular, 69; after War of 1812, 206; with West Indies, 161, 163–164

Trade routes, to East, 14, 16

Trafalgar, Battle of, 185

Trail of Tears, 259

Transatlantic journeys, 339

Transcendentalism, 288–289

Transcontinental railroad, 396

Transcontinental Treaty, 207, 210

Transportation; *See also* Railroads; canal boom, 240–243; canals, 339–340; cheap, 344; clipper ships, 338–339; railroads, 339–340; road building and, 237–239; in South, 324, 326, 344;

steamboats and, 239–240; steamships, 339; transatlantic, 339; water-based, 339–340; in West, 236–238

Trans-Sahara trade, 10–11

Travel, transatlantic, 339

Travis, William B., 301

A Treatise on Domestic Economy for the Use of Young Ladies (Beecher), 274

Treaty of Tordesillas, 17

Trenton, battle of, 121f

Triana, Roderigo de, 16

Triangular trade, 69

Tripoli, war with, 177

Trist, Nicholas P., 312

True-Blooded Yankee (ship), 198

Trumbull, John, 128f

Truth, Sojourner, 332

Tsetse fly, 11

Tucker, Elsa, 409

Tuner, Nat, 260

Turner, Benjamin, 420m

Turner, Nat, 330

Turnpikes, 238

Tweed Ring, 420, 427

Twelfth Amendment, 172–173

Twice-Told Tales (Hawthorne), 291

Twilight in the Wilderness (Church), 288f

Tyler, John, 268; annexation of Texas and, 301–303; Clay and, 300; election of 1844 and, 307; as president, 269, 299–300

Typhoid, 20

Typhoid fever, 54

Uncle Tom's Cabin (Stowe), 228, 347, 350–351, 350f, 370t

Union Army, 379f; African Americans in, 392–393; early defeats of, 379; strength of, 379; supplies for, 381–382

Union League of America, 424

Unitarians, 88–89

United States (ship), 197

Universities. *See* Colleges and universities

University of Pennsylvania, 89

Unskilled workers, 337

Upshur, Abel P., 303

Urbanization; *See also* Cities

Urban population, in mid-nineteenth century, 272f

Urban poverty, 335–337

U.S. Constitution, 143–144; amendments to, 155, A13–A20; compromises in, 148–150; drafting of, 147–150; ideas shaping, 147; implied powers and, 158; loose interpretation of, 244; Missouri controversy and, 219; necessary and proper clause, 158; ratification of, 151–153, 151m; text of, A4–A12

U.S.-Mexican border, 299

USS *Princeton*, 303

U.S. Supreme Court. *See* Supreme Court

Utah, statehood for, 318

Utah Territory, 278

Ute Indians, 50, 51

Utica, 275, 276f

Utopian communities, 277–279, 279m

Utrecht, Treaty of, 91

Vallandigham, Clement L., 383

Valley Forge, 125

Van Buren, Martin; in 1836 election, 265; in 1840 election, 268–269; in 1844 election, 303, 307; Bank of the United States and, 256; banks and, 268; description of, 215–216; presidency of, 265, 268; as secretary of state, 252

Vancouver, 308

Van Rensselaer, Kiliaen, 39

Vasco de Gama, 15m

Velasquez, Janeta, 398f

Vergennes, Comte de, 124, 128–129

Verona, Congress of, 207

Verrazano, Giovanni da, 15m, 24

Vesey, Denmark, 329–330, 331

Veterans, of American Revolution, 144

Vetoes, presidential, 252

Vice admiralty courts, 104

Vicksburg campaign, 394, 395–396, 395*m*, 401*t*

Villages, sub-Saharan Africa, 11

Violence, against African Americans, 424–425

Virginia, 26; colony of, 27–29, 52, 53; head-right system in, 54–55; ratification of Constitution by, 152–153; slavery in, 133; tobacco cultivation in, 57–59, 324

Virginia Company, 31

Virginia Plan, 148

Virginia Resolves, 168

Virtual representation, 100, 132

Visible saints, 34, 35, 64

Voltaire, 89

Voluntary association, 276–277

Voter turnout, 247, 249

Voting rights; for African Americans, 414, 417–419; Fifteenth Amendment and, 419; Fourteenth Amendment and, 415, 417–418; intimidation of black voters and, 425

Wabash and Erie Canal, 242

Wade, Benjamin, 382, 412

Wade-Davis bill, 412

Wage labor, 337

Wagon trail, 303–304, 305–306, 306*m*

Wakeman, Sarah Rosetta, 398*f*

Walden (Thoreau), 289

Walden Pond, 290*f*

Walker, David, 284

Walker, Robert J., 362

Walker, William, 351

Walpole, Sir Robert, 84, 98

Wampanoag Indians, 36

Wampum, 45*f*

War bonds, in American Revolution, 131

Warfare; among Mississippian Indians, 8, 9; Indian, 44; in medieval Europe, 12

War Hawks, 196, 216

War of 1812, 197–206; British offensive in, 201; events leading to, 196–197; independence and, 210; opponents of, 196–197; phases of, 200*m*

War of the Austrian Succession, 91

War of the League of Augsburg, 90

War of the Spanish Succession, 91

Warren, Mercy Otis, 135*n*2

Wars; *See also specific wars*; colonial, 90–95; between colonists and Indians, 36, 38

Washington, 52

Washington, D.C., 156*f*, 202

Washington, George, 92*f*; Bank of the United States and, 157–158; Bill of Rights and, 155; as commander of Continental army, 115, 119, 120–123, 122*f*, 125, 127–128; Farewell Address by, 165; in French and Indian War, 92, 93; Genet affair and, 160; inauguration of, 154*f*; Jay's Treaty and, 164; as national hero, 140–141; on outbreak of American Revolution, 114; places named after, 112; as president, 153–154; Second Continental Congress and, 114; on Shays's rebellion, 145; on slavery, 133; Whiskey Rebellion and, 162–163; XYZ Affair and, 167

Washington, Lewis, 366

Washington, William, 409

Washington Crossing the Delaware (Leutze), 122*f*

Water, transportation by, 239–240, 339–340

Wayland, Francis, 296

Wayne, Anthony, 162–163, 183

Wealth disparities; in Jacksonian America, 272; in mid-nineteenth century, 337–338

Webster, Daniel, 215, 215f, 250, 253, 255, 265, 268, 300–301, 303, 318

Webster, Grace Fletcher, 250

Webster, Noah, 273

Webster-Ashburton Treaty, 300–301

Weeds, 21

Weld, Theodore Dwight, 283, 284

Wellington, Duke of, 203, 204, 205

Wells, Josiah, 420m

West; alliance with South, 260; canals and, 242; Civil War in, 384, 385m; expansion into, 299–322; Jeffersonian policy and, 177–179; land ordinances and, 136–137, 140; leaders in, in nineteenth century, 216; linking of East and, 344; settlement of, 99, 159, 164–165, 236–238; slavery in, 313–314; transportation and, 236–238

West, Benjamin, 41f

West Africa, 10–11

West Florida; acquisition of, 207; purchase of, 178

West India Company, 39

West Indian tobacco, 28

West Indies, 16–17; Alliance of 1778 and, 159–160; French interest in, 178–179; slavery in, 38; sugar trade and, 186; trade with, 161, 163–164

West Virginia, 412n1

Wheat, 9, 40, 58, 71, 324, 342, 344, 345. 424

Whig party; in 1840 election, 268–269; in 1844 election, 307; decline of, 352–353, 356; election of 1848 and, 314–316; election of 1852 and, 352–353; Mexican War and, 310–311; rise of, 263–265

Whigs, 247

Whiskey Rebellion, 162–163

Whiskey tax, 159, 162, 175

White, Canvass, 241

Whitefield, George, 85–86, 85f

White House, destruction of in War of 1812, 202

White settlers, in Indian territory, 164–165

Whitman, Walt, 292–294

Whitney, Eli, 232–233

Wigglesworth, Michael, 65

Wilderness, Battle of, 399, 401t

Wilderness Road, 238

Wilkinson, James, 184–185

William of Orange, 66

William Penn's Treaty with the Indians (West), 41f

Williams, Roger, 34, 35

Wilmot, David, 314, 318, 390

Wilmot Proviso, 314

Winfrey, Constantine, 409

Winfrey, Oprah, 409, 422

Winthrop, John, 33, 34, 69, 85

Witches, of Salem, 66–68, 74–75

Wives; in mid-nineteenth century, 273; Southern, 327, 333

Wolfe, James, 94, 97

Women; abolitionism and, 283–284, 285–286; during American Revolution, 134–135; during Civil War, 397–398; education of, 135, 296; as factory workers, 228–229; Indian, 51; middle class, 271, 274; in mid-nineteenth century, 271, 275–276; puritan, 68; reformers, 271; Southern, 327; southern, 397; in Southern colonies, 61; teachers, 295

Women in the Nineteenth Century (Fuller), 286

Women's rights, in mid-nineteenth century, 285–288

Wood, Gordon, 107f

Wood, Thomas Waterman, 418f

Wool Act, 83

Woolly mammoths, 2, 3f

Worcester v. Georgia, 258

Workers; child, 228–229, 335–336; factory, 227–229; immigrants as, 228, 230–231; industrial, 335–337; unskilled, 337; women, 228–229

Working class, in mid-nineteenth century, 335–337

Working day, length of, 336

Workingmen's parties, 336

Working women, 228–229

World Anti-Slavery Convention, 287

Wormley, James, 429n1

Wright, Benjamin, 241

XYZ Affair, 166–167

Yale University, 86, 89, 296

Yams, 29

Yancey, William L., 368

Yellow fever, 20, 160f

Yeoman farmers, 325

Yorktown campaign, 126–128, 127m

Young, Brigham, 278

Young America movement, 351–352

Young Husband (Spencer), 273f

Zenger, John Peter, 76

Zurich, Switzerland, 25